Digenis Akritis is Byzantium's only epic; it survives in a puzzling manuscript tradition. Recent work has seen acceptance of Kyriakidis' and Trapp's arguments that, of the six surviving manuscript versions, four (TAPO) are descended from a text (now lost) that was created from an amalgamation of a version of the Grottaferrata text and the Escorial manuscript itself, and furthermore that the Grottaferrata (G) and Escorial (E) versions represent separate reworkings of a poem that was originally created in the mid-twelfth century. However, despite the close similarities of their plots and much shared wording, too little of that original poem can be perceived in G and E to allow its reconstruction. This edition aims at the next best thing: the presentation consecutively in the one volume of G and E, the two oldest versions of *Digenis Akritis*, with indications of the points at which wording is significantly similar. The manuscripts have been newly collated; the critical apparatus aims also at recording significant textual proposals made since Trapp's 1971 edition of G and Alexiou's 1985 edition of E. The English prose translation is intended to provide a readable narrative whilst not obscuring the difference in linguistic level between the two versions. The brief notes highlight the evidence for the nature of the poem underlying G and E as well as contrasting the different narrative techniques of the two versions. The introduction is intended to provide a succinct guide through the maze of secondary literature, dealing with the epic's literary environment and historical background.

Cambridge Medieval Classics 7

Digenis Akritis

Cambridge Medieval Classics

General editor
PETER DRONKE, FBA
Professor of Medieval Latin Literature, University of Cambridge

This series is designed to provide bilingual editions of medieval Latin and Greek works of prose, poetry, and drama dating from the period *c.* 350–*c.* 1350. The original texts are offered on left-hand pages, with facing-page versions in lively modern English, newly translated for the series. There are introductions, and explanatory and textual notes.

The Cambridge Medieval Classics series allows access, often for the first time, to outstanding writing of the Middle Ages, with an emphasis on texts that are representative of key literary traditions and which offer penetrating insights into the culture of medieval Europe. Medieval politics, society, humour, and religion are all represented in the range of editions produced here. Students and scholars of the literature, thought, and history of the Middle Ages, as well as more general readers (including those with no knowledge of Latin or Greek), will be attracted by this unique opportunity to read vivid texts of wide interest from the years between the decline of the Roman empire and the rise of vernacular writing.

Digenis Akritis
The Grottaferrata and Escorial versions

EDITED AND TRANSLATED BY
ELIZABETH JEFFREYS

PUBLISHED BY THE PRESS SYNDICATE OF THE UNIVERSITY OF CAMBRIDGE
The Pitt Building, Trumpington Street, Cambridge, United Kingdom

CAMBRIDGE UNIVERSITY PRESS
The Edinburgh Building, Cambridge CB2 2RU, UK
40 West 20th Street, New York NY 10011–4211, USA
477 Williamstown Road, Port Melbourne, VIC 3207, Australia
Ruiz de Alarcón 13, 28014 Madrid, Spain
Dock House, The Waterfront, Cape Town 8001, South Africa

http://www.cambridge.org

First published 1998
First paperback edition 2004

Typeset in Photina 10/12pt [C E]

A catalogue record for this book is available from the British Library

Library of Congress cataloguing in publication data

Digenis Akritis (Byzantine poem). English.
Digenis Akritis: the Grottaferrata and Escorial versions / edited and translated by
Elizabeth Jeffreys.
　　p.　　cm. – (Cambridge medieval classics: 7)
Includes bibliographical references and index.
ISBN 0 521 39472 4 (hardback)
1. Digenis Akritis (Legendary character) – Poetry.
2. Byzantine literature – Criticism, Textual.
3. Epic poetry, Byzantine – Criticism, Textual.
I. Jeffreys, Elizabeth. II. Title. III. Series.
PA5310.D5E5　1998
883′.02–dc21　97–11306 CIP

ISBN 0 521 39472 4 hardback
ISBN 0 521 39776 6 paperback

Contents

Acknowledgements

Preparation of this edition has been a challenge which I would not have undertaken but for Peter Dronke's invitation to contribute to the series in which it appears: I thank him warmly for his initiative and his patience.

I have inevitably incurred many debts whilst preparing the book. My thanks are due especially to Professor Stylianos Alexiou; Professor Giuseppe Spadaro; Professor Erich Trapp; Father Petta, from the monastery of Grottaferrata, for his careful response to my queries; to the staff of Dumbarton Oaks, Washington, DC, and the Warburg Institute, London, who benevolently allowed a visitor from the Antipodes to make an inordinate number of photocopies; and to the interlibrary loan facilities of Fisher Library in the University of Sydney. The Australian Research Council has been generous in its support over the years: without its aid my research would have been impossible.

My greatest debt, however, is as always to my family – to Katharine, for her tolerance; and Michael, for his support, advice and challenging comments, which have saved me from numerous errors. Those that remain are my responsibility alone.

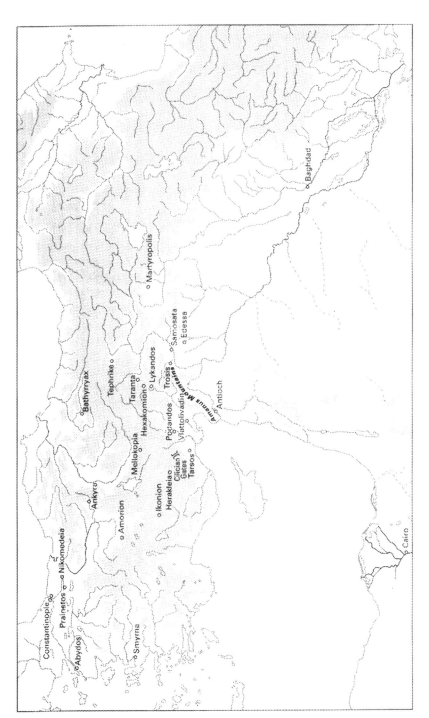

The world of Digenis

Introduction

Preamble

The edition with a critical apparatus seems one of the most transparent ways of expressing objective fact about a text. But the objective appearance can be illusory. Before text and apparatus are put together, a number of decisions has to be taken which may decisively influence the reader's impressions. Should one print a critical edition based on all or several manuscripts, or provide merely one or more of the manuscripts themselves? How should one choose the manuscripts to be printed? What references should be made to variations in manuscripts not given in full? Should any other poems be included? In the case of *Digenis Akritis* the manuscript variation is such that a critical reconstruction of the poem's original form will always be out of the question. The present volume contains editions and translations of the Grottaferrata and Escorial manuscripts only. But no previous edition has been content with exactly this choice of material. There are in all six manuscripts of the poem; how can one justify the omission of the other four? Each of the last two published editions (Alexiou, 1985; Ricks, 1990) has included only the Escorial manuscript, together with the *Lay of Armouris* as an adjunct to the text of *Digenis* itself; why include the Grottaferrata text and omit the *Lay?*

The other four manuscripts of *Digenis* (Trebizond, Andros, Paschalis [prose] and Oxford: details on pp. xxi–xxiii below) have been shown to be derived from a compilation, made in a text now lost, probably late in the fifteenth century. The materials used in the compilation were the surviving Escorial manuscript and another with some of the characteristics of Grottaferrata – though with different patterns of lacunas from the Grottaferrata text itself. An edition of the compiled version (as in Trapp, 1971a, where it is called Z) would be a useful addition to this volume, but its value would be disproportionately less than its bulk. It has seemed best to edit just the two surviving texts dating before the sixteenth century, which also provide nearly all the material used in the compilation. The few cases where the other manuscripts, in the form of Z, are of use in making a readable text of Grottaferrata and Escorial are included in the critical apparatus.

The history of textual study of *Digenis* is largely that of a struggle between partisans of the Grottaferrata and Escorial versions, arguing whether the original text was like the one or the other. Until the late seventies, the supporters of Grottaferrata seemed to be carrying the day. Since then, however, there has been a scholarly coup, led by the eminent Cretan professor Stylianos Alexiou, in favour of Escorial. In a series of papers followed by his impressive edition of the Escorial version, he has almost single-handedly turned the tide. The rhetoric of his work remains that of partisanship, praising Escorial and damning Grottaferrata in black and white terms. He has achieved almost total acceptance for the notion that the Escorial is the only text to be taken into consideration. His edition, and that of David Ricks which followed it, included the *Lay of Armouris*, almost implying that that is a more important text to be read in connection with *Digenis* than the Grottaferrata version of the poem itself. The *Lay of Armouris* is a two-hundred-line folk-song, surviving in manuscripts of which one is dated near the time when the Escorial text was written, and it provides a useful parallel to *Digenis*, especially in the episodic form in which Alexiou has edited it. But it is unclear why it ought to share the same volume.

The present writer has never accepted Alexiou's position, and has recently sensed the beginning of a negative reaction to it. This is not a swing of the pendulum back to support of Grottaferrata, but a determination to remove forever the rhetoric of manuscript partisanship from *Digenis* studies. This attitude had its roots in the Greek language question, with the supporters of the purist *katharevousa* seeking to appropriate this important national text for their side by claiming that the original was like the more purist Grottaferrata, while the demoticists who supported the language of the people favoured the more popular level of the Escorial. The destructive phase of the language question ended in 1975, and should no longer cast its shadow over *Digenis*: a century of partisanship has been unable to come up with persuasive evidence for the original status of either of the disputed manuscripts. It is time to attempt more subtle solutions.

The annotated texts and translations of the Grottaferrata and Escorial versions that make up this volume aim to provide readers with a balanced picture of the text of *Digenis* as it existed in the last centuries of Byzantium. These versions also include the bulk of the evidence for the original form of the poem and the pre-textual history of the tangle of material which it contains.

Scholarly history

The names 'Digenis' and 'Akritas' or 'Akritis' (rarely found together) have long been widely disseminated in Greek-speaking lands as heroes of folk-songs (Politis, N.G., 1909; Saunier, 1972). In the best known of these, Digenis as a kind of representative of mankind's struggles with Charos, death, at the marble threshing-floor, and is only finally defeated by a trick. Such songs are rather more common in Crete, Cyprus and the Asia Minor dialects than elsewhere, perhaps reflecting closeness to the Euphrates heartland of the epic.

In the last quarter of the nineteenth century, however, Greek scholarship became aware of another dimension of these names. No less than six manuscripts were announced of a medieval epic devoted to the story of Digenis Akritis, found in libraries from Northern Turkey to Greece, Italy and Spain. The first reaction was the assumption that this was to be the national epic of Modern Greece, performing a similar role to that of Homer in the ancient world and *Roland* and the *Cid* in France and Spain. Soon after, however, it was admitted that Digenis was no national hero: he was literally 'di-genis', that is, 'double-born' or 'twyborn' or 'of Double Descent'. His father was an Arab Emir, who is the major character of the first part of the story, part of which is told from an Arab point of view. The Emir, on a raid into Byzantine Cappadocia, seized a Greek girl, daughter of the provincial governor. Out of love for her, when defeated by her brother in single combat, he decided to be baptised, to marry her and to come over to the Byzantine side. When their son Digenis was born, he grew up very quickly, passed a *rite de passage* in hunting, and then followed family tradition by stealing a bride from another Byzantine castle. After a sumptuous wedding, he settled down to a solitary life as a kind of policeman of a large tract of the east of the Byzantine Empire, near the river Euphrates and the Arab border (see Map). But the criminals he defeated seem to be largely Christian Greek irregular troops. He did not take up the challenge of the national struggle against Islam: in fact, only special pleading can find any trace of such a struggle in the poem. He finally built a palace by the Euphrates and died young.

The existence of six manuscripts with wide and unconventional textual differences has been a chronic problem. The first issue to exercise Akritic scholarship this century was the establishment of chronological and textual priorities between them. As has been said above, this became involved in the language question, and was faced dogmatically and partially. Even so, the vital solution, the fact that four of the six derive from a compilation involving texts like the other two, was already worked out by Kyriakidis in 1946 (see also Kyriakidis, 1958), but it was not taken up. This solution was adopted as the basis for the edition of Trapp in 1971: but its importance was not stressed, nor fully defended (so plain did it seem to an editor who had studied the manuscripts in depth), and thus reviewers were not convinced. Only when a long and unreadable article was devoted to the repetition of the obvious was general acceptance of the compilation theory achieved (Jeffreys, M. J., 1975).

A second axis of scholarship was the question of priority between the epic and the folk-songs. Again there were political motivations behind the issues raised: on the one hand, the extent to which Greek folk-song, a potent demoticist symbol, gave rise to the beginnings of Modern Greek literature; on the other, how far one of its most powerful personalities may have derived from a semi-learned Byzantine text. One result of this struggle is the fact that the best histories of Modern Greek literature, written by demoticists, devote their first chapters to folk-songs which were largely collected in the nineteenth and twentieth centuries. Another element of confusion was the doctrine of continuity between Ancient and Modern Greek civilisations, in which continuity in folk-song plays a large part. In such a climate it was easy to avoid the obvious point that we have no real idea what the folk-songs of the late Byzantine centuries were like, since oral poetry in a live tradition changes: in better-documented parallel situations elsewhere, nobody would compare medieval epic and nineteenth-century folk-song, treating the two sides of the equation as contemporary and expecting the later songs to be more or less the same as their medieval predecessors. More recently, particularly in the work of Roderick Beaton (1980), this question has been defused by restricting the folk-song side of the equation to the limited medieval evidence.

But the largest category of scholarship which grew up around *Digenis* was that of historical and geographical identifications. The first systematic analysis of the proper names of the texts was made by Karolidis (1905/6), but the task was taken up by Henri Grégoire (1929/30, 1931a, 1931b etc.). Under his inspiration, the pages of the periodical *Byzantion* in the thirties and forties were full of claims that names, events and toponyms in the poem could be connected with particular places and historical circumstances. Reading these articles half a century later, one feels the lack of a theoretical framework to refine the blunt methods of identification being used. But the large number of sources covered and the numerous similarities found remain a most useful quarry for analysis which seeks to proceed with more justifiable methodologies.

More recent investigations have taken a wider variety of tracks. In the examination of a possible milieu for the decisive act of composition of the poem, the twelfth has become the most favoured century. On the one hand, this is the period of the rebirth of the romance, with the works of Prodromos, Manassis, Evgenianos and Makremvolitis, and the whole atmosphere of the court around the middle of the century (Magdalino, 1992 and 1993b). At the same time, the first experiments were being made in the writing of the Greek vernacular, particularly by the Ptochoprodromos poet. It is a moment of intense East–West contact, especially during the Crusades, when the Greeks might have been inspired by Westerners in the production of written versions of oral *chansons de geste* (Jeffreys, 1980). This would also be the time when the noble families driven out of Central and Eastern Anatolia by the results of the Battle of Manzikert in 1071 would need to come to terms with the loss of their homes and the way of life which *Digenis* portrays so graphically (Beaton, 1996).

The accuracy of that portrayal has been examined on two levels. With regard to administrative arrangements and terminology, both of the older versions of the poem have been shown to be unpredictable, with some surprisingly accurate references and other serious misunderstandings (Pertusi, 1970; Oikonomidès, 1979; Galatariotou, 1993). At a more general level, however, the picture is more convincing, especially in the Grottaferrata text. There are many parallels in other sources, especially in the *Strategikon* of Kekavmenos, for elements of the ideology used, particularly in the high value placed on the family and the concept of honour found in the story (Magdalino, 1989; Laiou, 1993; Galatariotou, 1996). Structural oppositions have been studied in both versions, particularly in connection with the position of women in the poem, where epic brutality in detail contrasts with the lofty position given to Digenis' wife (Galatariotou, 1987; Ekdawi *et al.*, 1993). Such issues have also been raised in discussions of the genre of *Digenis*, which seems to combine epic elements, clustering in the story of the hero's father, with a more romantic treatment of Digenis himself. The result of this research has been inconclusive: the poem is often described as an epic romance (Beck, 1971, 94–7; Trapp, 1972).

Another debate has concerned the way in which historical elements have entered the poem. There seems general agreement that oral sources have been very important, as one would expect in a poem of this kind with scattered historical references to a variety of periods (Beaton, 1980, 78–82; Fenik, 1991). However there have been many proposals of textual sources (as is discussed below, pp. xl–xlix). Direct textual contact has been suggested with chronicles, saints' lives, the Alexander-romance and even Homer. Certainly in G there is also strong romantic colouring from the romances of the Second Sophistic, especially Achilles Tatius and Heliodoros. It has been debated whether these elements are vestigially present also in E.

This wide range of investigations has largely been pursued in an open and independent spirit. However, many of them have at times been used in a partisan manner in favour of the Escorial text in the coup mentioned above. Readers should be warned in such cases to be specially aware of the influence of preconceived ideas.

Manuscripts

The two manuscripts used for the editions and translations in this book are G and E.

G: Grottaferrata, Z.α.XLIV (444), ff. 1r–73r

The manuscript, first identified as containing *Digenis* by Lambros in 1879 (1880, xc), is made up of 79 folios measuring 210 mm by 140 mm: see the brief catalogue entry by Rocchi (1884, 470). G contains *Digenis* on ff. 1r–73r and a version of *Spaneas* on ff. 73v–79v (Danezis, 1987, 163). The paper is of eastern manufacture and thus dated by current palaeographical criteria to the late thirteenth or early fourteenth centuries (Politis, 1970, 554). This makes it decisively the earliest surviving manuscript of the *Digenis* poem, and one of the earliest of any text connected with the Modern Greek vernacular. The manuscript was carefully restored and rebound in 1963 when the pages, many of whose edges had crumbled, were given a protective coating.

The manuscript, copied throughout by the same hand, is made up of 10 gatherings of 8 folios, with one folio missing after 62v. Gathering marks are visible on ff. 1r (A), 9r (B), 25r (Δ), 41r (ς), 49r (Ζ), 57r (H), 64r (Θ); from their position close by the text (with the margin crumbled away) these appear to be later additions, or reproductions of the original notation. Pages were left blank at 13v, 35v, 53v: the first two are now filled with prayers. A folio has been torn out between 62v and 63r, removing, perhaps in an act of censorship, Maximou's seduction of Digenis. Two or three lines are left blank in the body of the text, which is written as verse, on ff. 14v, 24v, 49v, 67v. The orthography is normally correct.

G was copied in South Italy, in the Terra d'Otranto. Its South Italian origins were noted by Legrand (1902, xvii) and by Kalonaros (1941: 1, vi), who commented that the epic had spread from one fringe region of the Greek world to another. The palaeographical basis for this localisation is now clear. G demonstrates the following characteristics of the Otrantine hand as defined by A. Jacob (1977; cf. Petta, 1972 and personal communication): grossly spread ω; o/ρ ligature in stirrup form; idiosyncratic α/φ ligature; ligatures of η, ι and κ which heighten the stem of the second letter; infilling of rounded letters with red blobs; intermittent enlarging of letters. While most of the intermittent large letters at line beginnings seem to have no textual implications, that at the beginning of G4.254 coincides with a major articulation of the text.

A number of the gnomic comments are signalled in the margins, at 7r (1.317 and 1.326), 10r (2.124), 11v (2.203, 2.207 and 2.128), 13r (2.285), 14v (3.34), 15v (3.81), 16r (3.124), 19r (3.271 and 3.284), 26r (4.276), 27r (4.342), 31r (4.549), 31v (4.565), 39r (4.945), 42r (4.1092), 43r (5.52), 53r (6.281), 56r (6.421) and 6.425), 59r (6.598). Sources for some of these comments (and others not so marked) can be traced: see Odorico, 1989 and pp. xliii–xliv below.

There is a neat head-piece in red ink with green and blue details on f. 1r, with an ornate and textually redundant capital 'e' to the first word. Book divisions (ff. 7v, 13v and 14r, 20v, 42r, 47r, 63r, 67v; 73v heading for *Spaneas*) are marked thereafter by a line of ornament in red, with blue details, and a capital for the first word of the book.

E: Escorial, Gr. 496 (Ψ.IV.22), ff. 139r–185v, 198r–201r

This manuscript, whose version of *Digenis* was first signalled by Krumbacher in 1904, is fully described in De Andrés' catalogue of the Greek manuscripts held in the Escorial (1967, 106–9); further information is given by Alexiou in his 1985 edition (1985, ιε´–κβ´), with especial attention to punctuation, orthography and copying errors.

In its present form E consists of three preliminary sheets and 228 folios, measuring 184 mm by 145 mm. Four hands are to be observed: ff. 1r–20v (a translation of a sermon of Thomas Aquinas and other religious texts); ff. 22r–213v (vernacular verse texts); ff. 214r–222v (hymns for Easter Saturday); and ff. 223r–228v (vernacular sermons on Christ's Passion). De Andrés notes different watermarks for ff. 1–4, 5–20, 22–213, 214–28, indicating that the sections were originally separate. However, on f. 1r is the ownership mark of Antonio Agostino (1517–86; archbishop of Tarragona, 1576–86); Agostino, a notable Spanish humanist and a collector of manuscripts, was in Italy from the 1540s to the 1560s and it is likely that it was then that he acquired this manuscript. The ownership mark suggests that the manuscript was already in its current form when in his possession. Agostino's books came to the Escorial in 1587, at his death and not long after the library's foundation (Sandys, 1908, vol. 2, 160–2).

In the section of interest here, ff. 22r–213v, there are normally 21 lines to the page, with many spaces left blank in the verse texts, presumably for illustrations. There are ornamental capitals to the first line after most of the spaces. There are no gathering marks and it is plain from the texts themselves that the order of the gatherings and folios has been disturbed. *Digenis* at present occupies ff. 139r–185v and 198r–201r (f.156 is now missing; De Andrés, 1967, 109), with perhaps 70–100 lines lost before 139r, after comparison with G (Alexiou, 1985, 77). The gathering sequence proposed by Chatziyia-koumis (1977, 74) suggests that *Digenis* began on the last sheets of the preceding gathering, with the implication that another short text might also be lost. The difference in the water stains on the lower sections of f. 138 and f. 139 onwards, as well as the confusion in folio sequence, suggests the book was unbound for some time; apart from the water-staining, however, it looks clean and relatively unused. The scribe has not been identified. The hand is neat and practised, the orthography is free, as is the case with most vernacular texts. The lines, written as prose, frequently extend beyond the metrical limits of a regular fifteen-syllable verse; line divisions are normally marked with a point at the line end and a comma at the mid-line break.

The watermarks for ff. 22–213 give approximate dates of 1485 (cf. Briquet 11194; Politis, 1970, 544, note 1) and 1493 (M. Sosower, personal communication), but watermarks are a notoriously imprecise guide and the manuscript can be dated no more firmly than to the late fifteenth century.

Other secular vernacular texts in this manuscript are *Livistros and Rhodamni* (ff. 22r–35v, 44r–51v, 36r–43v, 52r–88v, 186r–v, 188r–193v, 187r–v, 89r–137v), *Porikologos* (ff. 201v, 194v), *Opsarologos* (ff. 194v–195v) and *Poulologos* (ff. 196r–197v, 202r–213r, 186r–197v). Each of these displays orthographical and metrical usages (where relevant) not dissimilar to those found in

Digenis E and with a certain amount of interaction, though the orthography of *Digenis* E is markedly less consistent than that of *Poulologos* and the prose texts (Chatziyakoumis, 1977, 136–9).

That the scribe of *Digenis* was copying from an earlier exemplar, and not writing from dictation or composing as he wrote, is demonstrated by the lacuna that occurs in mid-line at E792.

This edition attempts to indicate something of the format of E by marking capitals and leaving notional spaces to indicate the manuscript's spaces.

There are other manuscripts of versions of *Digenis* which are cited occasionally in the apparatus to the text; their role in the transmission of the text is discussed in the next section.

Z

A hypothetical manuscript; its existence has to be postulated to account for the material common to the surviving manuscripts T(rebizond), A(thens), P(aschalis), O(xford). The version it contained was compiled from a manuscript in the G tradition and arguably from E itself since the structure of the prologue of Z indicates that the text from the E tradition began with the words with which E now begins, and the loss of previous lines is due to the loss of previous folios from E itself (Jeffreys, M. J., 1997). Since E was copied in the late fifteenth century and was in Spain by at least 1576, Z was written in the early part of the sixteenth century, possibly with a view to creating an omnibus version of the *Digenis* poem for printing, comparable perhaps to Loukanis' *Iliad* of 1526 and the *Theseid* of 1529. It is reconstructed as Z in Trapp's 1971 edition, largely on the basis of T and A, and is used occasionally in this edition to control aberrant readings, chiefly in G, and to fill the lacuna at G6.785–6.

T: Trebizond, Soumela Monastery (now lost), ff. 1–90

Discovered in 1868 by Savvas Ioannidis (1887, ζ´) in the Soumela monastery, the extracts published in Ioannidis' Ἱστορία καὶ στατιστικὴ Τραπεζοῦντος in 1870 alerted Sathas to this new text; it was then published in full by Sathas and Legrand in Paris in 1875, when they were sent the manuscript itself after a dramatic winter journey. The text was republished in Constantinople in 1887 by Ioannidis, who presented the manuscript to the library of the Phrontisterion of

Trebizond, where it was given a shelf mark (κατaλ. 17. Ἀριθ. αὔξ. 50;
Sathas-Legrand, 1875, facsimile). However, the manuscript has now
vanished. It does not appear in Papadopoulos–Kerameus' catalogue of
the Trebizond manuscripts, where no. 17 is an acephalic grammar and
no. 50 is simply not mentioned (1912, 225–49). In 1923 the
manuscripts from the Phrontisterion were dispersed; some were sold
while some came to the Philologikos Syllogos in Constantinople and
subsequently to Ankara. The *Digenis* manuscript is not among them
(Politis, 1970, 555; A. A. M. Bryer, personal communication). From
the facsimile in the Sathas-Legrand edition the manuscript would seem
to be of the late sixteenth or early seventeenth centuries. The version
found in T is closely related to that of A.

A: Athens, National Library 1074, ff. 1–189

Made up of 189 folios measuring 210 mm by 140 mm and
containing only *Digenis*, this version was discovered in Andros in 1878
and published by A. Miliarakis in 1881, the year in which he presented
it to the National Library in Athens. From the hand and the watermark
it is to be dated to the mid-seventeenth century (Politis, 1970, 555).
The version found in A is closely related to that of T.

P: Thessaloniki, University Library 27, ff. 1–101

Discovered in Andros, in 1898, by D. Paschalis and published by
him in 1926, this prose version (101 folios, measuring 205 mm by
145 mm) was written by Meletios Vlastos of Chios in 1632 (Paschalis,
1926; Politis, 1991, 27–8; Kechaioglou, 1993).

O: Oxford, Lincoln College 24, ff. 10r–107r

This rhymed version of *Digenis*, written by Ignatios Petritzis of Chios
in 1670 and published by Lambros in 1880, came to Lincoln College,
Oxford from a Fellow of the College, George Wheler, who had acquired
it during his travels in the East (1675–6) with Jacques Spon; the short
time that elapsed between the copying (and also the redaction?) and
the disposal of the manuscript presumably accounts for its pristine
condition. It consists of 104 folios, measuring 150 by 195 mm; ff. 1–8
are blank, 9r is a title page; *Digenis* appears on ff. 10–107; on
108r–112v, in a different hand, is an account of the miracles of
Nicholas Thaumatourgos; ff. 113r–127v are blank.

The existence of further manuscripts is attested but their where-abouts are not known: two, both apparently in the Z tradition and one illustrated, were seen in the Athonite monastery of Xeropotamou by Kaisarios Dapontis (1714–84) (Lambros, 1880, xcix); and a short prose version was sighted in Constantinople by Dr Mordtmann before 1887 (Ioannidis, 1887, i΄). Other manuscripts must be postulated, as is discussed in the next section. There are also Russian versions, but their interrelationships and their connections with the Greek texts remain problematic and so they are left out of account in this edition (on the Russian *Devgenij* see Syrkin, 1960; Kuz'mina, 1962; and the translation of Graham, 1968).

Textual tradition

The first point to be made about this, as about all other Early Modern Greek textual traditions, is that we must not assume that 'accurate copies' (in the modern sense) were the norm and 'rewriting' was the exception. Nearly all our evidence suggests the opposite assumption, which is supported by comparative evidence from other medieval situations. Evidence that word-for-word precision was regarded in the Byzantine or immediate post-Byzantine periods as a necessary precondition for successful copying of texts in the vernacular is hard to find. Though evidence is mounting that scribes of vernacular texts were not a separate group but included many professionals who also copied material at a more learned level (Agapitos/Smith, 1994), such professionalism does not seem to have excluded rewriting when copying in the vernacular.

In the case of *Digenis* we have six extant manuscripts, none of which is an accurate copy of another, and, as we shall see, the existence of several lost manuscripts has been proven. In examining these connections, we should expect each act of copying to involve some degree of rewriting, at least on the scale of variation of phrasing, and probably also in the inclusion and omission of episodes. It is easy to fall into the trap of assuming that the striking differences observable between extant manuscripts are exceptional, and that copyists behave more 'normally' when we cannot observe their work.

Let us begin the examination of the textual tradition from its later end. The TAPO group fall, in principle, outside the scope of this edition, and so have been described only briefly above. It has been shown that they all derive from one lost manuscript, baptised 'Z' by Trapp (1971a, 26–7; cf. Kyriakidis, 1946), and it is unlikely that any of TAPO had independent access to medieval texts beyond that provided by Z. The relation of TAPO to Z is complex, and also irrelevant to present concerns. The TAPO group remains an interesting object of study, both individually and as a whole, while P and O at least are in need of modern editions: but that work will belong to a different framework and will be published in a different series from this.

Though manuscript Z has not survived, a number of conclusions may be drawn about the activity of the redactor who was responsible for it. As is plain from its opening, it is an attempt to include in one text all that was known about Digenis Akritis. The raw material at the redactor's disposal turns out to be manuscript E itself (Grégoire, 1940/1, 98; Jeffreys, M. J., 1976, 394 and 1997) and another lost manuscript g with many of the characteristics of G. However g was not G: Z's source had not lost the folio now missing after G6.785, but it did have a lacuna (presumably a lost folio) after G2.278 (cf. Z868-9; Trapp, 1971a, 28). This lacuna arguably led to the difference in book numbers between G and Z (Trapp, 1971a, 28; Jeffreys, M. J., 1976, 386-8). The compilation was made with some care, jumping between the two sources frequently and abruptly, and thus leaving unmistakeable signs of what has happened (Jeffreys, M. J., 1975).

The group TAPO (via Z) is thus of significance for the establishment of the text of E and G, in rather different ways. In connection with E, Z may only be used to show the reaction to that text of an early reader, whose reception may be assumed to be more attuned to its problems, in some respects at least, than that of a modern critic. In the case of G, Z may be used to fill a lacuna after G6.785, though, granted the general fluidity of the tradition, the material from this source is printed in this edition in italics. It is also likely that at some points Z may be used to make G more readable, since Z used g, which must have had independent access to γ, a lost common source of G and g. In any cases where G has changed an acceptable reading in g and made it unintelligible, g may have preserved the acceptable form, it may have been taken up by Z, and it may be possible to reconstruct the reading of Z from TAPO. But the route to be followed in making such corrections is rather tortuous, again bearing in mind the general fluidity of the tradition, and one would not *a priori* expect many cases of successful correction of this kind. It should be stressed also that the text under edition here is G rather than γ. Even if we may somehow be confident of the reading of γ, it should only be used to correct G where G is manifestly inadequate.

E shows at E792 unmistakeable signs that it was copied from a manuscript with a lacuna, leaving a word split in two. That manuscript may be called e, but we know nothing further about it.

G and E (through their lost and rather unhelpful sources γ and e) share the same plot and a number of common lines, as we shall see – quite enough to suggest that they share an ultimate source in the same written archetype, which we may for convenience call *Digenis. The situation may be expressed diagrammatically as below (this should probably not be called a stemma codicum, since it is virtually useless for the Lachmannian reconstruction of any text). Extant manuscripts are represented by capitals, and the relation of TAPO to Z is indicated in a completely generalised way:

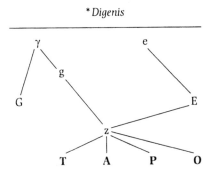

This diagram is printed with a bar between *Digenis and γ and *Digenis and e, because of the extreme nature of the differences between γ and e, as seen in G and E. This is a key point in the textual analysis of the poem. Supporters of the claims of G or E as close analogues of *Digenis have rarely been convincing in praising the features of the favoured text. But both sides have been much more successful in pointing out details which disqualify the other text from status as the original.

G, for example, has unexpected metrical characteristics, its language shows an unconvincing mixture of learned pretensions and inefficiency in using simple syntax, it has substantial references to other texts, especially the romance of Achilles Tatius, and it is full of moralising comments (all discussed below). In these respects it is different from E. But one could remove all these features from G and still leave a text some way from E and unlikely to have led to the production of E. The means of expression of E closely resemble those of modern folk-song, as has been well shown in a recent book (Fenik, 1991), and such features are absent from G.

E's unusual features begin from the state of the manuscript, whose neat appearance belies an almost incredible carelessness in writing at every level. Many lines are hypermetric, many words are unrecognisable, many passages have required drastic surgery to make any sense. Narrative consistency, not a strong point of G, becomes so poor in E that recent editors have found that the only way to save the narrator's blushes is to divide the text into separate 'songs' (as discussed in Ricks, 1989a). Yet it is almost impossible to imagine a reconstruction of E, even one where these faults had been corrected, which could have led in any direct way to G. G has impressed many historians with its grasp of the structure and ideology of eleventh-century frontier society (though it is not so good on details). E gives no such general picture, despite some verifiable details.

The conclusion seems inescapable that both of the older surviving manuscripts have inadequacies in themselves and bear poor witness to the nature of their common original. That original was not rather like G, leaving E rendered incoherent by some accident of transmission, nor rather like E, leaving G ruined by the obsessions of some half-learned monk. The authenticity of each of the older manuscripts is undermined by the other. *Digenis, their common source, was like neither of the preserved texts. There will be speculation later on what its characteristics might have been. But the above diagram, whatever its use in showing the bare bones of the manuscripts' relationships, is of only limited use in the role usually expected of a stemma – the reconstruction of the archetype.

Relationships between G and E

The narrative in G is presented in eight books of widely varying length, while in E there are no book divisions and the spaces in the text have little connection with stages in the narrative. The episodes in both can be summarised as in Table 1 on pp. xxvii–xxviii, where it can be seen that the poem falls into five sections.

Table 1 indicates that there is an overall correspondence in the sequence of episodes in G and E. There is perhaps greater correspondence in detail towards the beginning of the poem, though there are also many identical lines in the death scene at the end. There are episodes unique to each version; E621–701 (Digenis' encounter with the guerrillas) does not appear in G, and probably never did

Table 1

Episode	G	E
Lay of the emir		
The emir raids, carries off the girl; her brothers pursue and defeat the emir	1.1–197	[lacuna in E] 1–55
They cannot find their sister, emir produces her, converts, marries; birth of DA	1.198–337; 2.1–49	56–224
Emir's mother writes, he quarrels with the brothers, leaves his bride, returns to Syria, converts his mother and returns	2.50–300; 3.1–343	225–609
Romance of DA		
Education of DA	———	610–21
DA visits Philopappous and asks to join the guerrillas	———	622–701
Emir's exploits; education and first hunt of DA	4.1–47; 4.48–253	702–91
DA serenades the girl and carries her off	4.254–855	[lacuna in E's exemplar] 792–1065
The wedding of DA and the gifts	4.856–952	1066–88
DA on the borders with the girl	4.953–70	1089–94 1095–6 DA's parents die
Visit from the emperor	4.971–1093	———
DA's exploits (1st pers. narrative) DA's encounter with Aploravdis' daughter	5.1–289	———
Meadow in May, the encounter with the serpent, lion and guerrillas	6.1–175	1097–196
Defeat of the three guerrillas	6.176–310	1197–315
Guerrillas summon Maximou and Melimitzis	6.311–475	1316–420
DA defeats guerrillas and Maximou	6.476–713	1421–351
DA defeats Maximou again and commits adultery	6.714–805 [lacuna at 785/6] (6.795–8 kills Maximou)	1352–605
(end of exploits and 1st p. narrative)		

Table 1 *(contd)*

Episode	G	E
Palace and garden		
Garden and palace by Euphrates; DA keeps peace on borders	7.1–229 (7.106–55 death and burial of father; 7.189–98 death of mother)	1606–59 1660–94 tomb on bridge
Death		
DA falls ill, recalls his past life with the girl, advises her; they both die	8.1–141 8.142–98	1695–793 1794–867
Funeral and mourning	8.199–313 (8.238–44 tomb at Trusis)	———

(MacAlister, 1984); G4.971–1093 (the emperor's visit) and all of G5 (the encounter with Aploravdis' daughter) do not appear in E. Some details (the death of Digenis' parents, the reference to his tomb) occur at different points in the narrative, as if the redactors were indifferent to their position in the structure. Moreover, G and E each have their own style so that episodes may create very different impressions on the reader. Some of the most striking differences occur in the Maximou material and the laments on Digenis' death (Jeffreys, 1995 and 1996).

Alexiou perceives E as divided into six separate lays: 1. The Song of the Emir: E1–609 (= G1.134–3.343); 2. Digenis and the Guerrillas: E622–701 (not in G); 3. The Youth and Marriage of Digenis: E702–1088 (= G4.1–952); 4. The Serpent, the Lion, the Guerrillas and Maximou: E1089–605 (= G4.953–6.805); 5. The Palace, Garden and Tomb: E1606–59 (= G7.1–229); 6. The Death of Digenis: E1695–793 (= G8.1–141); relegated to appendices by Alexiou as extraneous are E610–621, a bridging passage on the hero's education (cf. G4.52–71; an awkward passage, placed after E738 by Kalonaros and Trapp though left *in situ* in this present edition) and E1794–867 (= G8.142–98, with several identical lines) which forms the last part of the lament on Digenis' death (rejected because, in Alexiou's view, the vocabulary and metre are not those of the rest of the poem; see Jeffreys, 1996, for counter-arguments). It should be noted that there is no indication of any of these divisions either in the text or in the layout of the manuscript.

The narrative sequence of E is awkward. E622–701 (Alexiou's 'Digenis and the Guerrillas'), the hero's first exploit, occurs before the passage common to both G and E in which Eros is invoked, the emir's deeds are recapitulated and the young hero is introduced in his own right. It is for this reason that Trapp repositioned this episode after E791, as had Z before him, placing material from this passage at a point equivalent to G4.253. E610–21 seem to be an attempt to smooth this awkwardness, anticipating the reference at E739–41 to Digenis' passage to adolescence.

Ricks (1989a, building on Alexiou) has suggested that E was never a unified whole but was made up of discrete episodes. His arguments are driven by the contention that E is a faithful representation of a twelfth-century poem, a position unlikely on linguistic and stylistic grounds and completely beyond proof (Fenik, 1991; Galatariotou, 1993; Mackridge, 1993b). However, the insight of Alexiou and Ricks into the episodic nature of E still has validity and may be applied to *Digenis, for G, despite its literary and moralising veneer, also shows narrative disjunctions; the arrival of the emir's mother in G3.329, for example, triggers a redundant wedding while the general and his daughter appear abruptly at G4.253. We should note too that there is some correlation between the book divisions of G and the sections perceived in E by Alexiou and Ricks (Kyriakidis, 1958, 29–30). It would seem very likely that *Digenis was itself episodic, perhaps a series of independent episodes loosely strung in chronological order around a legendary hero. If *Digenis had obvious weaknesses, this would provide an additional reason for the extensive changes which have to be postulated for the making of G and E, though both these attempts to solve the putative problems of the original have failed, as we have seen, in different ways. Suggestions will be made later as to when *Digenis might have been formed.

A significant proportion of the wording in G and E is common to both (Beaton, 1993a). This edition notes in each version lines from the other which have significant lexical similarities. Most of these can also be seen in Trapp's 1971 synoptic edition where the texts are set out in parallel. Fourteen lines are virtually identical (Trapp, 1971a, 46; Beaton, 1993a, 49–50): G1.164, E17; G2.196, E367; G2.234, E2; G4.127, E770; G4.158, E1326; G4.440, E857; G4.594, E918, E982; G4.758, E1058, E1290; G6.677, E1551; G8.1, E1695; G8.154, E1809; G8.163, E1829; G8.176, E1855; G8.179, E1858. The common lines and wording must be attributed to *Digenis. Nevertheless attempts to recreate *Digenis are unlikely to be successful in detail since the linguistic and stylistic differences between G and E are too great (see Beaton, 1993b and Jeffreys, 1996 on the opening and closing episodes respectively).

Historical references

Much has been written on the identification of persons and historical situations found in the different manuscripts of the poem, especially by Henri Grégoire. More recent discussions, however, sometimes seem to imply that the search for historical identifications was misguided and doomed in advance to failure (Lemerle, 1973, 110–13; Bryer, 1993). There have been few attempts to analyse what types of historical reference exist in the poem or what these might tell us about the history of the poem (but see Galatariotou, 1993).

On one level, from Karolidis (1905/6) onwards the poem has been linked to the Paulician heretics of Cappadocia in the second half of the ninth century, or similar frontier groups whose nature is disputed and whose voice is absent from the historical record (most recently Bartikian, 1993). However, little light has been shed by the poem on an otherwise dark period.

At another level, historical references are used in dating the poem. An unstated assumption was made that manuscripts G, E and the TAPO group represent 'versions' of the poem, fairly stable forms of the text, each with a copying history of its own, perhaps involving variation on the relatively minor scale observable between T and A. Historical references have then been used to compare the age and authority of these 'versions' (e.g. Grégoire, 1931a, 484–5). An 'original version' might be hypothesised as close as possible in form to whichever surviving manuscript is most favoured (on E, for example, see Alexiou, 1979, 77–8 and 1985, ϟα'–ρ'). But, as we have seen, the state of the surviving early texts of *Digenis* suggests constant change rather than conservative copying. Thus it is safer to date manuscripts rather than versions: the identification of a twelfth-century event only provides a *terminus post quem* for the manuscript where it is found, with no scope for the satisfactory definition of a 'version' to which the date may be extended. Ninth-century events found in one manuscript and not in others do not guarantee the greater antiquity of the first, since the possibility remains open of deliberate or haphazard omission in the others (cf. Grégoire on G: 1931a, 488–9). A particular case is the TA 'version' of *Digenis*, whose major characteristics demonstrably derive from a compilation probably made in the early sixteenth century. Grégoire dated this 'version' to the mid-eleventh century, with arguments similar to those still used to dispute the primacy of E and G (1932a, 299–302). The failure of such arguments to provide meaningful conclusions on T and A is not encouraging when attention is turned to E and G.

Historical identifications in the *Digenis* poems are usually based on the coincidence of more than one parallel: similarity of names and/or geographical references and other details of narrative or personal characteristics. The guerrilla chief Philopappous, for example, may be identified with the last member of the Commagene ruling house through his unusual name, the fact that Commagene is the scene for much of the poem, and a family penchant for hilltop burials. References to the Paulicians have been justified by a coincidence of two similar names, Chrysocheir and Karbeas, together with mention of their base in the North-East of Cappadocia and a history of raids into areas of Christian Asia Minor similar to those recorded for the family of the emir, Digenis' father. These points are discussed further below.

However, it is striking that the small nuggets of historical reference thus identified in the poem are usually not linked together in any accurate historical way. The two Paulicians are made brothers, when they were not so in reality. They are given close family connections with prominent Arabs, in a way which is also historically incorrect. The identifications often do not make for narrative consistency in the poem: Digenis' mother's family is said to be connected with the Kinnamades, a reference ignored when Digenis fights a guerrilla called Kinnamos, who must, on this information, have been a relative.

The question has been raised whether these references result from the poet's reading of historians and chroniclers, or whether they came to him via oral sources. Without excluding the first explanation if a good individual case may be made (on the use of Genesios and Theophanes Continuatus, discussed further below, see Grégoire, 1929/30, 335–9; cf. Markopoulos, 1989), I must express a strong preference for the second. The kinds of historical reference found and their haphazard connections point to a typical oral tradition, working in a homeostatic present with a dependent past (Goody/Watt, 1968, 31–4; Ong, 1982, 46–9; Jeffreys, forthcoming b). In such circumstances past names may well be remembered, but they are likely to be used in frameworks appropriate for present purposes, with little emphasis on their 'true' historical context. The consultation of a written historical source, even an imperfect chronicler, would probably have inspired in the poet more respect for historical accuracy than is shown in the surviving versions of the poem.

One may conclude that historical identifications made in a poem of this sort would show little more than a rough outline of the oral tradition on which it is based. For *Digenis*, they hint at a development of great length, with possible roots in the Alexander story and a substantial early stratum derived from ancient Commagene, followed by a long gap before ninth- and tenth-century events. Of the two ancient layers, the Alexander component has a demonstrable history in several oral and textual forms during Late Antiquity and the early Middle Ages, but the survival of the Commagene material is surprising. The hypothesis of its continuous preservation at an oral level for a millennium is a bold one, yet it cannot be dismissed out of hand, especially as there are massive archaeological remains which may have helped to keep this part of the story alive.

The ninth-century evidence is interesting in a different way, in that it seems to include stories from some of the Byzantine Empire's most implacable opponents, presented, in part at least, from their own hostile point of view. This suggests that at least one of the poem's sources was not of Byzantine origin, leading to the hypothesis of a separate 'Lay of the Emir'. Such a story could have been a completely Arab (or perhaps Paulician) text, made Orthodox at some point before its incorporation into *Digenis, so as to add sanitised heroic elements with an international pedigree to the hero's genealogy. Such a process worked in both directions, as may be seen in the presence of Akritis as a hero (on the Byzantine side) in some Moslem epic material (Grégoire, 1931b, 473–7).

Frontiersman (ἀκρίτης) and guerrilla (ἀπελάτης)

Not the least puzzling features of this poem are the two terms that are central to its structure: the opposition between Digenis the Frontiersman and the guerrillas.

The ἀκρίτης, a *miles limitaneus*, or soldier stationed on the border, was an element of the late Roman army whose role persisted as late as the eleventh century, by which time he had evolved into a frontier commander with a fortress and an army (e.g. Constantine Porphyrogenitus, *De caerimoniis*, 489.12; Kekavmenos, *Strategikon* 24.21; see Oikonomidès, 1979, 386; Haldon, 1990, 253; and for Arab parallels, Honigmann, 1935, 53). The application by G of the term to an Arab warrior (G1.155) suggests that need for responsible officers was felt on both sides of the border. 'Akritis' is also used in G of the emperor Basil

(G4.56). The word is, however, most usually used in both G and E as part of the hero's name; e.g. at G2.48 where it is applied to the infant Digenis. Kekavmenos (ca. 1020–ca. 1070) gives a vivid picture of life in the frontier castles which has many parallels to that of Digenis (Pertusi, 1971; Magdalino, 1989), though Digenis co-exists peaceably with his Arab neighbours rather than in a state of constant raiding.

Between the fourth and the tenth centuries the ἀπελάτης appears as a bandit (Synesius, *Epistulae* 132.16), a cattle-thief (Justinian, *Novellae* 22.15.1) or a member of a military squad with special duties (Constantine Porphyrogenitus, *De caerimoniis* 696.4; Oikonomidès, 1979, 387–9). The guerrillas encountered by Digenis seem to have hunting, especially of women, as their chief occupation (Ricks, 1989b; Mackridge, 1993a) with a vestigial suggestion of a more formal military role at E644. Further military elements are rebels (ἄτακτοι: G6.398), who are distinct from the guerrillas, and brigands (λσταί) who are occasionally equated with them (e.g. E1435).

Both Frontiersman and Guerrilla play what seem to be time-hallowed roles in the life of the Byzantine frontier communities, in a symbiotic existence with the Arabs.

Alexander

Alexander is referred to in three passages in G alone (G4.29: Digenis' deeds outdo those of Alexander; G4.397: Maximou is descended from the Amazons brought back by Alexander from India; G7.90–4: Alexander's deeds are amongst those depicted on Digenis' palace walls). Many parallels between the two heroes' careers have been pointed out: a parentage that transcends national boundaries, precocious childhood, horse-taming (G4.1054 ff.), premature death after bathing (G8.30 ff.) (Veloudis, 1968). Recent discussion, however, suggests that these resemblances are more apparent than real. Byzantine literary culture was more familiar with the imperial Alexander of the Old Testament and the chronicle tradition than with his legendary life. Connections with Pseudo-Callisthenes' *Life of Alexander* are limited to the imposition of a biographical structure onto the episodic Digenis material (Moennig, 1987 and 1993): this would have been present in *Digenis. The precise references to Alexander were added in the G tradition before, or at the same time as, the writing of γ.

Commagene

The buffer kingdom of Commagene in north Syria ceased to exist in AD 72. There are three reasons to connect it with the Digenis story: the unusual name Philopappous, hill-top monuments and geographical coincidence. The geographical setting around the Euphrates implied in G and E covers much of the former kingdom of Commagene. Philopappous appears in G and E as the leader of the guerrillas; this name is otherwise encountered as that of the last representative of the Commagene ruling house, C. Julius Antiochus Epiphanes Philopappos, consul in AD 109, in whose honour the Athenians built the monument still known as his on the hill opposite the Acropolis. Rulers of Commagene claimed double descent from the royal houses of Macedonia and Persia.

It has also been suggested that several surviving structures near the Euphrates, connected with the rulers of Commagene, prompted and sustained, over a period of a thousand years, stories of a hero who was both a frontiersman and of double descent (Grégoire, 1931a and 1932a; Jeffreys, M. J., 1978):

- the collection of sculptures and inscriptions on the Nimrud Dagh (reached from Kahta, site of the former Arsameia) which spectacularly, massively and relatively inaccessibly proclaim the double descent of Antiochos I of Commagene (Dörrie, 1964);
- the monument at Sesönk (now Diliktas), with columns and sculpted figures above them, near the village of Trush (now Kuyulu) identified as G's Trosis (Grégoire, 1931a);
- the remains of a once spectacular bridge over the Gök Su near Sesönk (photo: Hoepfner, 1983, pl. 39c, 40a), though there is no suggestion that it ever bore a tomb or any other superstructure.

Other structures that have been linked to the monuments associated with Digenis include the bridge over the Bolam Su (Cendere Su), erected by Septimus Severus in AD 199. This has columns at its approaches but no other additional structures (photo: Alexiou, 1985, pl. 6a, and discussion on E1661; Magie, 1950, 677, 1546). The description of Digenis' tomb is also reminiscent of a style of tomb with a free-standing domed ciborium over the sarcophagus which was developed in twelfth-century Constantinople (Bryer, 1993, with plates).

The references to Digenis' tomb and palace in both G and E suggest that these structures were persistent elements in the stories about the hero, which could well have been fuelled by visible monuments.

Paulician material

As mentioned earlier, a connection has long been suggested between Digenis' paternal ancestors and the leaders of the ninth-century Paulicians (Karolidis, 1905/6); on the Paulicians, their history and heretical dualist beliefs, see Lemerle, 1973.

Digenis' family tree is referred to at G1.266–88 and 4.37, 54–64 and at E135–46, 261, from which can be constructed the genealogies set out in Table 2.

There are obvious differences between these genealogies: the emir's father is Chrysovergis in G, Aaron in E; in G his maternal grandfather is Ambron while in E the emir is descended on his father's side from Mouselom and no details are given on his mother's family; Digenis' maternal grandfather is given as Antakinos Kinnamos in G while in E he belongs to the Doukas family; Digenis' maternal grandmother is from the family of Constantine Doukas in G and the Kirmagastroi in E. Nevertheless the similarities show that these must both hark back to the same underlying text: Digenis has five maternal uncles, of whom the youngest is named Constantine; there is a connection with the Doukas family; and there is a similarity of names for, e.g. the emir's paternal forbears (despite a change in generations) and his Arab uncles.

Of these Chrysovergis has been identified as Chrysocheir, leader of the Paulicians, who fought with Muslims against Basil I and raided throughout Asia Minor until his death in 878/9 (Theophanes Continuatus 5.43; Lemerle, 1973, 96–103); Karoïs/Karoïlis with Chrysocheir's uncle Karbeas, who died at the battle of Porson in 863 (Lemerle, 1973, 85–98); and Ambron with 'Umar, emir of Melitene and ally of the Paulicians, who also fell at the battle of Porson (Theophanes Continuatus 4.25). However, the relationships between these historical personages do not correspond to those between the characters in the Digenis text.

Other possible Paulician connections include references to Tephrike, their capital (G2.78 Aphrike, an alternative form attested in the sources); Taranta (G2.78), besieged by the Paulicians in 873 (Theophanes Continuatus 5.37); Soudalis (E928), known as a persecutor of the Paulicians (Polemis, 1968, 16) though in E he is simply an Arab. Further references for the identifications of these names with historical personages and places are given in the Name Index.

Arab material

Woven in with the putative Paulician references are names that have been similarly identified with Arab persons and places, notably G's Ambron/'Umar as mentioned above. The equivalent figure in E (E145: Aaron, the emir's father rather than grandfather) has been identified with Harun-al-Rashid (Alexiou, 1979, 25–7). Other Arab

1. G1.266–88, 4.37, 4.54–64

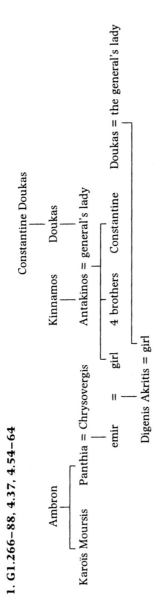

2. E135–46, 261

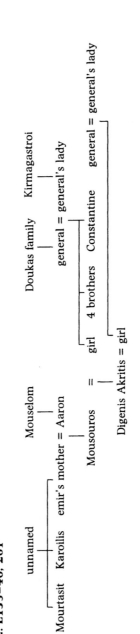

Table 2 Digenis' family tree

figures in Digenis' genealogy are his maternal uncles: Mourstasit (E261) has been tentatively identified with a twelfth-century caliph (Alexiou, 1979, 29) although this is removed from the historical context of other references and the equivalent figure in G has been identified, as noted above, with the Paulician and non-Arab Karbeas. The name Mouselom, from whom the emir's father descended, bears a superficial resemblance to Maslamah, the leader of the Arab siege of Constantinople in 717. Elsewhere there appear Apohalpis (E only), the Dilemites (G only), the emir Aploravdis (G only), Mouroufris (E only), Mousis (E only), Mousour (G only), Naaman (a holy man; G only): detailed references are in the Name Index. The proposed identifications are no more certain than for the Paulicians. Places with Arab connections include: Amorion, Baghdad, Basra (E only), Emek (= Homs; E only), Emet (= Amida; G only), Kufah (G only), Mecca (E only), Meferke (G only), Panormos (G only), Prainetos (E only), Rachab (G only) or Raqqa (E only); though identifications for many of these sites are disputed, several were prominent in the wars of the ninth century or returned to Byzantine control in the tenth (again, see the Name Index for details).

Other references may be to features of Arab customs or life-style: e.g. warrior-youths (G1.47 γουλαμίους; cf. Arabic 'ghulam') and the 'youngsters' who accompany the emir in both G and E (see *EI*, under 'Ghulam'); pilgrimage to Mecca via the port of Jeddah and worship at the holy sites (G1.101–4; E288, 537); miracles seen at the holy sites (G3.139–48); objurgations cast by 'Kasisi' (E244–9: priests or the sect of Assassins? Alexiou, 1979, 30; Galatariotou, 1993, 47–9); use of lions' teeth as a talisman (G3.105, E524); holding up of fingers as a sign of submission (G1.193, E53). These occur in E and G alike in the first part of the poem where the emir is the protagonist; there is an Arab element to G5 (not in E) in the names (Aploravdis, Mousour, Meferke), the desert environment of sand and palm-trees and the insights into the use of hostages in Arab-Byzantine diplomacy. Alexiou argues that E, as in the use of the Arab vocative μούλε 'lord', almost always preserves an Arab flavour more accurately than does G (1979, 33–5; 1985, 79): for counter-arguments see Galatariotou, 1993.

Ninth- and tenth-century historical references
These are both general and precise. General references to Arabs, their raids and their role in frontier society can only refer to the period after the invasions of the seventh century and before the Byzantine campaigns of the mid-tenth century, giving a context for the suggested

identifications with the Paulicians. Precise references are found in the use of place names that ceased to be of contemporary relevance after the Turkish incursions of the mid-eleventh century and the breakdown of the Byzantine civil and military administration: e.g. Bathyrryax (G only), Hexakomia (G only), Lykandos (E only), Podandos (G only), Vlattolivadin (G only); see Name Index for details. The majority of these appear only in G.

The battle described at G3.67 (cf. E503) and located at Mellokopia has been linked with the battle of Porson in 863 at which noted Paulicians and Arabs were slain (Grégoire, 1929/30, 333–9; Huxley, 1975), though other proposals have been made (Oikonomidès, 1979, 391, note 56). Grégoire (1931a, 486–90) identified, wrongly, the towel of the Arab holy man Naaman (G3.150) with the *mandylion* rescued from Edessa in 944; see now Cameron, 1980 on the history of the *mandylion*.

There is also a nexus of references to Armenian places and personalities largely from the tenth century, initially identified by Adontz (1929/30) but elaborated and summarised by Bartikian (1993). Of these the most significant are the identification of Maximou's henchman Melimitzis as the prince Mleh (d. 934), governor of Lykandos; the identification of the Charziane of G as the Armenian administrative district and not the Byzantine theme of Charsianon; and the identification of Maiakis (E507) as an Armenian duke of Edessa.

The emperor Basil who makes an appearance in G has been identified as both Basil I and Basil II (see Name Index): there is nothing in the poem to support one more than the other. The emperor is used as a foil to the youthful hero and as a recipient of advice: Basil is a suitably imperial name, shared with Digenis (cf. G4.1088) and borne by two of the emperors most associated with extensive Byzantine activity in Asia Minor. The tag from Genesios at G4.1072 comes from an episode in the life of Basil I.

Turks

Turks are conspicuous by their absence, appearing only as members of the emir's elite troops (G1.45, E728). At G4.1043 reference is made to tribute paid to Ikonion, capital of the Seljuk Turks from 1084.

Administrative terms

The major Byzantine provincial administrative unit for both fiscal and military purposes until the twelfth century was the 'theme', to which references are made in G (1.264, 2.63), though not in E. It was controlled by a military governor or general (στρατηγός); generals appear in both G and E as fathers of Digenis' mother and bride. Other ranks referred to include those of 'patrikios' (G2.68, 4.1049), a high-ranking dignity that fell into disuse in the early twelfth century and 'protostrator' (G2.69, 4.375; E522, 796, 797), literally 'first groom', a lowly office in the tenth century but one of the highest by the twelfth century. Apart from 'theme' and 'patrikios', these terms were in use until the time when E was copied. 'Kleisoura' (literally a 'pass' or 'defile'), used until the tenth century to refer to an administrative unit smaller than a theme, in G and E has only the sense of 'mountain pass' (Oikonomidès, 1979, 382). Technical terms for mustering troops appear in connection with the emir and his Arab forces and the guerrillas: these are a mixture of Byzantine (G1.48, E644, 655: ἀδνούμιν, ῥογεύομαι) and Arab (G1.47: γουλάμιοι).

Doukas and Kinnamos

Two Byzantine aristocratic names appear in Digenis' genealogy. One, Kinnamos and the Kinnamades (see Name Index), was not a particularly prominent family. The other, Doukas, represents one of the largest and most diffuse of the aristocratic groupings from the ninth century onwards. The Doukai were predominant in the manoeuvrings for power during the eleventh century and were then merged into the victorious Comnenian family by the marriage of Alexios Komnenos to Eirene Doukaina in 1078. Their place in the genealogies of Digenis is such that Kyriakidis (1932, 649) proposed two different Doukas redactions of the poem. Note that an unnamed 'son of Doux' was one of the three generals involved in a persecution of the Paulicians in ca. 855 (Theophanes Continuatus 4.16; Polemis, 1968, 16); and that in ca. 1080 Psellos was aware of oral information (assumed to be songs by Grégoire, 1933, 48–63) on Andronikos, Constantine and Pantherios, ancestors of Constantine X Doukas, emperor 1059–67 (Psellos, Chronographia 7.6; Polemis, 1968, 9).

Social structures

The society shown in G has been convincingly analysed by Magdalino (1989, cf. 1984) in terms of the structures of a twelfth-century aristocratic household: an 'oikos' with retainers and several generations of kin living within the same compound. In G there are several such establishments: that headed by the general, the father of the emir's bride, into which the emir is taken and subsequently his mother; that of Digenis's bride's family; and that of Digenis himself which, although housing initially only Digenis and his bride, is laid out on the same spacious scale as the others and eventually accommodates his mother as well as both his parents' tomb. The dowry (servants, estates and moveable goods) bestowed on Digenis is also part of a similar environment. Patriarchal attitudes (for example, the brothers' assumption at G1.328–9 that their sister can be given in marriage without her consent, though consistent with twelfth-century practice; Laiou, 1993, 210) contrast with the dominant role of the general's lady in her husband's absence on the frontier (G1.31 ff.) while the female warrior Maximou stretches male tolerance to its limits. The tensions inherent in the structures of G, both authorial and social, are well discussed in Galatariotou, 1987; for E, see Ekdawi et al., 1993. The society depicted in E is less historically convincing, despite the recurrent theme of the hunt (Ricks, 1989b).

Traditional equipment

Digenis operates with slightly unusual equipment. Thus he fights in a ποδέα, 'kilt', literally an ankle-length tunic (Constantine Porphyrogenitus, *De caerimoniis* 752.12, worn by 'runners' invited to participate in the Christmas Feast of the Nineteen Couches), perhaps to be envisaged as a kind of foustanella (cf. the Akritic plates: Notopoulos, 1964). At G4.116 and 1058 Digenis tucks his ποδέα up short to fight, while at E658 the garment is mocked by Philopappous as effeminate. Ποδέα is not a common term; it is used of curtaining over icons in the twelfth century or of a tunic worn by women in the fourteenth (DuCange, 1688, under ποδέα). The only other military contexts for this word known at present occur in Ptochoprodromos (Eideneier, 1991: 4.190), when a phrase identical to that in G refers to the emperor Manuel, and in Emmanouel Liminitis' version of *Belisarios* (ca. 1500) when a ποδέα is listed amongst the exotic clothing bestowed on Petraliphas by Justinian (Bakker/van Gemert, 1988, 174: L357). Was this traditional heroic costume?

Digenis' preferred weapon is the ῥαβδίν, perhaps originally an officer's symbolic staff of office and so translated in this version as 'stick' rather than 'club' or 'mace'; it is used by Digenis in both G and E as an offensive weapon. In G its use is confined to Digenis, in E it is also used by the guerrillas. Is this weapon too one of the original distinctive features of the hero?

Places

Many of the places mentioned in the text have been satisfactorily identified: see Map and Name Index. For a few (e.g. Orazabouron) no convincing identifications have been suggested. Some surely indicate local knowledge (e.g. Koukou Lithos, Lakkopetra, Chalkourgia, Mellokopia, Troglodytes as the cave-dwellers of Cappadocia). The significance of the conspicuous monuments of the late-Roman Euphrates frontier region has already been mentioned; the reference to the imperial Persian tombs at Pasargadai (E1671) may also have been prompted by visible remains, though this does not explain the presence in Digenis' bride's dowry in both G and E of the sword of Chosroes, a long-dead emperor of Persia.

Literary elements

Some of the literary sources discernible, especially in G, have been used to suggest the date of composition, either of the poem as a whole or of a particular recension. The texts most usually adduced in this context are the Life of Theoktiste of Lesbos and Melitiniotis' poem Εἰς τὴν Σωφροσύνην which are discussed below.

Conclusion

The world-view of both G and E, and thus of *Digenis, predates the arrival of the Turks in the mid-eleventh century, despite G's awareness of the Turkish occupation of Ikonion and demands for tribute, while the non-hostile interaction shown between Byzantines and Arabs has been taken as a mark of historical distance from the almost constant warfare of the ninth and tenth centuries. But the presence of antique details in one or other version may be due to late insertions in either, while their absence may result from later omissions. The Digenis poem as preserved in G and E covers a rag-bag of historical and geographical elements of much debated authenticity which cannot be used to give a firm date to any version, or even to *Digenis. The only sure chronological fact is that, of the manuscripts in which the G and the E versions are preserved, G can be dated ca. 1300 and E ca. 1485. Both versions reflect a text whose background is predominantly that of the Euphrates frontier region in the ninth to tenth centuries but each has acquired details from subsequent stages of transmission as well as, probably, losing elements of their original texts.

Literary affiliations and sources

While influences from other literary texts are to be found almost exclusively in G, there is sufficient common material with E to show that some were also in *Digenis. Thus Sophronios of Jerusalem's prayer for the Blessing of the Waters at Epiphany is reflected in both G8.153–4 and E1809–10 (as well as in Melitiniotis' Εἰς τὴν Σωφροσύνην); the elaborate garden description in Achilles Tatius' *Leukippe and Kleitophon* (1.15) is used extensively in G whether directly or indirectly and is reflected in E1633–59 (especially at E1657–8); the passages on the effects of love and the phrase from *Matthew* 19.6 on the indissolubility of marriage (G4.4–18, E702–11; G6.143, E1170) show an awareness of the conventions of the romantic novel as revived in the twelfth century. Thus a few of the elements of G that were undoubtedly elaborated at some stage between *Digenis* and γ would seem also to have been present to a certain extent in the former.

Religious and moralising texts

– The Nicene Creed. At G3.171–95, as part of the emir's attempt to convert his mother, there appears a paraphrase of the Creed which is very close to the original. There is substantial reflection of eleven of the twelve clauses, word-for-word in places, elsewhere differing to preserve the metre. Only the clause about the Holy and Apostolic Church is completely omitted, while there are gaps in three others. G3.188–9 are substantial additions. This passage does not appear in E, and so was probably added before γ was written.

– Vita Theoktistae (= VTh). Theoktiste from Lesbos, a female recluse, suffered under Arab raids, which may be the connection to the Digenis text. The novelistic saint's life by Niketas Magistros (d. after 946) refers to Arab raids and Byzantine rejoinders under Himerios (ca. 905–11), admiral of Leo VI. The Life was lightly reworked by Symeon Metaphrastes, ca. 1000 (both versions: Delehaye/Peeters, 1925, 221–33; English translation in Talbot, 1996, 95–116). It is reflected only in G (these passages are not marked in the edition): G2.112, cf. VTh §19; G4.974, cf. VTh §2; G5.62, cf. VTh §14; G5.137, cf. VTh §15; G6.621, cf. VTh §5; G7.163, cf. VTh §14; and note Z3822–4, cf. VTh §3 (see Grégoire, 1931a, 488–9; Trapp, 1976). VTh §4 (G4.974) refers to a recently deceased emperor and has been used to date the G recension; however, not only is it impossible to be sure to which emperor reference is made (Grégoire, 1931a, Kyriakidis, 1932, 652), but the words could have been borrowed at any time after the writing of VTh. The absence of these passages from E indicates that they were added between *Digenis* and γ.

– Lives of the Saints Theodore, who are mentioned several times in both G and E. Verbal reflections of their Lives appear only in G (Trapp,

1976, 279–85), and so were inserted after *Digenis and before γ. Originally there was only one saint, who developed two legends and cults, that of the General and the Recruit, both centred on Euchaita (see *ODB*). There are several versions of their lives (Delehaye/Peeters, 1925, 11–89), and one semi-independent episode of Miracles, attributed to both Theodores (Θαῦμα καὶ διήγησις; Delehaye/Peeters, 1925, 46–8), which is full of folk-tale elements involving the slaying of a serpent/dragon and the rescue of a maiden. The Life (Delehaye's versions III and IV) has a structural resemblance to the emperor's visit to Digenis in G4.971–1022 (Trapp, 1976, 282–4). The serpent/dragon-slaying of the Miracles has close verbal parallels at, e.g. G6.45–8, cf. Miracles 47a; G6.63–6, cf. Miracles 48cd; G6.74–6, cf. Miracles 48d (Trapp, 1976, 280–1); a similar passage is found in Melitiniotis' Εἰς τὴν Σωφροσύνην (433–48), but all this may simply be Anatolian monster lore (cf. ps-John of Damascus' *De draconibus* [PG 94, 1599–601], Kekavmenos, *Strategikon* 81–2 and E1089–111).

– Sophronios of Jerusalem. An interesting test case for learned influence in E and the nature of *Digenis. E1809 and G8.154 follow the wording of the prayer for the Blessing of the Water at Epiphany (Tiftixoglu, 1974, 8; Goar, 1730, 370 ff.) which is also found in Melitiniotis' Εἰς τὴν Σωφροσύνην 3036. E1808 is identical to G8.153, but does not appear in either Melitiniotis or Sophronios, while E1810 reflects Mel. 3038 and Sophr. 20, but does not appear in G. This shows E preserving more than G of the learned material which was present here in *Digenis: but the whole passage may be a familiar religious tag. Note that Alexiou (1985, λς') considers E1794–867 a later addition despite the lines shared with G (see Jeffreys, 1996, for counter-arguments).

– Gnomic comments and biblical quotations. Odorico, 1989 lists many moralising comments from G, some of which are marked in the manuscript itself (see p. xix above). A few also appear in E. Sources and analogues in the gnomological literature, the novels of the Second Sophistic and in the Bible are as follows (these passages are not marked in the edition):

G1.202 (Odorico 16: *Isaiah* 28.16, *Sirach* 2.10); G1.317–18 (Odorico 20; cf. Stobaios 4.47); G1.326–7 (Odorico 1; cf. Heliodoros 1.4); G2.16, E1860 (Odorico 15; *Job* 10.13); G2.35 (*Psalm* 112.9); G2.38–9 (Odorico 13; *Psalm* 21.5); G2.111 (Odorico 8; Hippocrates, *Aphorism* 2.46); G2.124 (Odorico 2; cf. *Melissa* in PG 136, 852a); G2.203 (Odorico 23; cf. Heliodoros 8.6); G2.218 (Odorico 25; cf. *Melissa* in PG 136, 852a); G2.274 (Odorico 3; *Psalms* 7.11, *Proverbs* 24.12); G3.55 (*Psalm* 54.7); G3.167 (*Titus* 3.5);

G3.183 (*Luke* 1.33); G3.198 (*Matthew* 13.42); G3.204 (*Matthew* 16.26); G3.208 (*Matthew* 25.41); G3.216–17 (*Matthew* 25.34); G3.284 (Odorico 9; Heliodoros 2.6.4); G4.276 (Odorico 10; Achilles Tatius 1.4.4); G4.549 (Odorico 39; cf. *Melissa* in *PG* 136, 857d); G4.661 (Odorico 54; cf. *Achilleis* N1369); G4.748 (Odorico 17; *1 Kings* 2.6–7); G4.838, cf. E1061 (*Psalm* 113.4); G4.1092 (Odorico 11; Gregory of Nazianzus, *Oratio* 40 in *PG* 36, 360b); G5.52 (Odorico 46; cf. *Melissa* in *PG* 136, 988a); G6.143, E1170, E1305 (Odorico 18; *Matthew* 19.6); G6.281 (Odorico 4; *Proverbs* 15.1); G6.421–2 (Odorico 5; cf. *Melissa* in *PG* 136, 852a); G6.499 (Odorico 49; cf. *Georgides* 17 [ed. Odorico, 1986]); G6.625 (*Psalms* 2.1, *Acts* 4.25); G6.642 (Odorico 7; Maurice, *Strategikon* [ed. Dennis, 1981] 7.b.12.4 and *Matthew* 5.44, *Luke* 6.27); G6.650 (Odorico 6; *Proverbs* 3.34); G6.669 (*Luke* 11.27); G7.65 (*Judges* 16.3); G7.76 (*2 Samuel* 21.19); G7.96 (*Exodus* 16.7–9); G8.1 (Odorico 55; cf. *Achilleis* N1573, Georgides 1213); G8.286 (Odorico 12; *Psalm* 88.49); E1846–7 (*Ezekiel* 33.1).

Others for which no precise source can be found are at:

G1.192 (Odorico 19); G2.44 (Odorico 21); G2.160–1 (Odorico 22); G2.207–8 (Odorico 24); G2.26–8 (Odorico 26); G3.1 ff. (Odorico 56); G3.18 (Odorico 27); G3.34–6 (Odorico 57); G3.59–60 (Odorico 28); G3.81 (Odorico 29); G3.124 (Odorico 30); G3.255 (Odorico 31); G3.271–2 (Odorico 32); G4.4 (Odorico 58); G4.10 (Odorico 33); G4.101 (Odorico 34); G4.342 (Odorico 35); G4.391 (Odorico 36); G4.473 (Odorico 37); G4.525 (Odorico 38); G4.565 (Odorico 40); 4.686–8 (Odorico 14); G4.945 (Odorico 41); G4.1024 (Odorico 42); G4.1030 (Odorico 43); G4.1040 (Odorico 44); G5.1 ff. (Odorico 45); G5.210–11 (Odorico 47); G6.425 (Odorico 48); G6.570 (Odorico 50); G6.598–9 (Odorico 51); G6.749–50 (Odorico 52); G8.244 (Odorico 53).

Most of these quotations appear only in G and would have been added between *Digenis* and γ. The few exceptions, like the quotation from *Job* (G2.14, E1860), would have been part of *Digenis*. The citation of *Matthew* 19.6 ('What therefore God hath joined together, let not man put asunder'), once in G and twice in E, both sums up a key element of the poem, which must have been part of *Digenis*, and also links *Digenis* with the twelfth-century revival of narrative fiction: this phrase was almost a leit-motif in the novel of Niketas Evgenianos (Kazhdan, 1967, 116).

Literary texts

Three texts in particular have wording in common with G, and probably a little with E. These are Achilles Tatius' prose novel *Leukippe and Kleitophon* (2nd cent. AD, probably), Melitiniotis' Εἰς τὴν

Σωφροσύνην (14th cent.) and Heliodoros' *Aithiopika* (4th cent.). There are also common passages with two twelfth-century texts – the Ptochoprodromic poems and Evstathios Makremvolitis' *Ysmini and Ysminias*. Most parallels are listed by Mavrogordato (1956, 265–6) and Trapp (1971a, *passim*).

– Achilles Tatius, *Leukippe and Kleitophon*. Reflections of this novel are obvious in G, and may exist in E. Several of these passages are also found in Melitiniotis' Εἰς τὴν Σωφροσύνην (see below). The portions of G which reflect Achilles Tatius' novel fall into three categories:

> *descriptions of people* (G1.35, G4.353–6, cf. Achilles Tatius 1.4.3: the emir and Digenis are described in phrases used of female characters, as also G1.39, cf. AT 5.11.5; G6.29–32, cf. AT 1.19.1 and G6.33–4 with Mel. 2841–3, cf. AT 1.4.3: on the girl's beauty), *seasons* (G6.4–11 and Mel. 33–40, cf. AT 2.1.2–3 where phrases used of the rose are applied to the month of May: see Dyck, 1987, 351–5), and *places* (G6.18–28, G7.14–41, E1657–8 and Mel. 2451, 2457 etc., cf. AT 1.15.1–8 and AT 1.1.3: the meadow where Digenis rested and the garden he constructed);
> *commonplaces* on the effects of love (G4.276–80, cf. AT 1.4.4–5: love enters through the eyes; G4.335, 546, cf. AT 1.9.7: the untried lover is ignorant of the paths of love);
> *striking phrases* from key points in the narrative (G4.398 and E827, cf. AT 1.5.4: strumming a kithara; G5.64, cf. AT 1.2.3: taking a seat on a low stool before beginning a narrative; G6.139–40, cf. AT 3.11.2: the heroine's voice died of fright before she did).

Some of these passages are also hinted at in E (e.g. the parrots in the garden: E1657–8, cf. G7.14–41; the May scene: E1087–8, cf. G6.18–28): these have been used to claim that a debt to Achilles Tatius was also owed by **Digenis*. Detailed analysis, however, might suggest that they need not derive directly from Achilles Tatius but from a collection of extracts (as is discussed below). A similar case is a passage on a young girl's breasts appearing through her tunic (G6.782), found in Melitiniotis (Mel. 359) and the novel of Makremvolitis (Conca, 1994: 2.4.3) as well as in Achilles Tatius (1.1.11); cf. the presence of roses on the girl's lips mentioned in Achilles Tatius (2.1.3) and Makremvolitis (3.6.4). Note that the two main descriptions taken from Achilles Tatius are each used twice in G (AT 1.4.3–5, cf. G1.35 and 4.276–80; AT 1.15.1–8, cf. G6.18–28 and 7.14–41). Achilles Tatius' novel was relatively widely read in the Byzantine Middle Ages (see Photios' *Biblioteca* and Psellos' comparison of Heliodoros and Achilles Tatius: Dyck, 1986, especially 80–7), while in the twelfth century it was possible for Manganeios Prodromos (writing ca. 1145) to make a casual reference to the novel's title (at Poem 52.67).

– Melitiniotis, Εἰς τὴν Σωφροσύνην is a difficult case, where dating evidence is partly contradicted by literary analysis. The passages common to G and Melitiniotis are of two varieties: single-line commonplaces (e.g. G1.42, cf. Mel. 520) or descriptions of gardens (e.g. G6.3–11, cf. Mel. 33–40), buildings (e.g. G7.17–25, cf. Mel. 2451–7; G7.65, cf. Mel. 1850 ff.) or people (e.g. G6.782–4, cf. Mel. 2841–3). Although authorship of Εἰς τὴν Σωφροσύνην is disputed between Demetrios and Theodore Melitiniotis (Trapp, 1976– nos. 17848, 18851; ODB, under 'Meliteniotes'), it must have been written some time after the mid-fourteenth century. Digenis G is preserved in a manuscript dated ca. 1300. This should prove that borrowing flows from G to Melitiniotis (Trapp, 1971a, 35), confirmed by apparently archaic 'anapaestic' elements in G's metre (see below), which are much rarer in Melitiniotis. There are also some passages in Trapp's reconstruction of Z that are closer to the wording of Melitiniotis than G (e.g. G5.37, Z2492, cf. Mel. 140) and others which are not present in G but which reflect Melitiniotis (Z3813, cf. Mel. 858; Z3840, cf. Mel. 972; Z 3845–6, cf. Mel. 824–6; Z3859, cf. Mel. 935; Z3872, cf. Mel. 1882). These passages must derive from γ, which would have had closer similarities to Melitiniotis' text than does G.

However, the direction of influence is not so easily settled. First there are passages in which the phrasing of Melitiniotis makes better sense than that of G, assuming that 'original' writing is more likely to be controlled than 'borrowing': G7.51, cf. Mel. 829–30; G7.73, cf. Mel. 839; G7.56, cf. Mel. 674 (Trapp, 1971a, 35–7; Jeffreys, 1993, 30). Equally, passages common to G and Melitiniotis which draw on Achilles Tatius (especially G6.3–11, Mel. 33–40 and AT 2.1.2.3) each include phrases from Achilles Tatius not found in the other (Tiftixoglu, 1974, 10–19; Dyck, 1987). While the reconstruction of the lost γ may be manipulated to cover all eventualities, it is probably easier to assume a common source, perhaps a model ekphrasis (set-piece description), rather than direct use of γ by Melitiniotis. The phrases mentioned above that are common to G, E, Melitiniotis and Sophronios of Jerusalem, as well as shared elements in the description of the serpent/dragon, may be similarly explained.

– Heliodoros, Aithiopika. Reflections from this novel too can be seen in G (Mavrogordato, 1956, 265, though most of those examples are unconvincing), and possibly also in E. Thus at G3.277–87 and E583–5 the revival of the fainting heroic couple with cold water, a scene that has much in common with Hel. 2.6.3, must have been in *Digenis. Similarly at G6.248–50 and E1264–72 Digenis' appeal to the girl and subsequent crippling of his antagonist's arm resembles Hel. 5.32.5–6. In both these cases G's wording is closer to Heliodoros than is that of E, either because G reflects the underlying text more accurately or because the relevant phrases were added before γ was written. In both these cases Alexiou (1979, 15–17, 61) has argued that E is more convincing than G as evidence for the original form of the poem. G4.394 (a comment that love is a disease and not the result of witchcraft) and G6.732 (reflecting the opening sentence of Heliodoros' novel) are not in E. This evidence suggests that *Digenis did contain reflections of Heliodoros which were preserved, and possibly enhanced, in the transmission of G, but were diluted before reaching E. Like Achilles Tatius, Heliodoros was quite widely read in the Byzantine Middle Ages (Gärtner, 1969).

– Ptochoprodromos (mid-twelfth century). G4.116 and 1058 are found in almost identical form in Ptochoprodomos (Eideneier, 1991: 4.190–1), referring to Manuel I Comnenos as a 'second Akritis'. This suggests that a version of the Digenis poem resembling G was in existence by that time. However, the absence of these lines from E makes it impossible to judge whether they were part of *Digenis, which current opinion would assign to the period in which Ptochoprodromos was writing.

– Chronicles. This is a much more shadowy connection. Grégoire (1929/30, 336–9) drew attention to general similarities between the account of the Battle of Porson in 863 given in Theophanes Continuatus (4.25) and the battle at Mellokopia described by the emir at G3.66–76, cf. E503–4; he also pointed out (1931a, 490–8) verbal analogies between Digenis' hunting and horse-taming before the emperor in G4.1054–76 and the deeds of Basil I in Theophanes Continuatus (5.13) and Genesios (4.40). As indicated earlier, analogies in the battle accounts have been doubted (Oikonomidès, 1979, 391, note 56). One should also remember both that not all historians of this period have survived (Markopoulos, 1989, 167–8) and that the historians we do know almost certainly drew on heroic songs about the leading figures of the heroic wars of the ninth and tenth centuries (Roueché, 1988, 127–8; cf. Galatariotou, 1993, 53, note 45), akin to the oral material on members of the Doukas family known to Psellos (mentioned above).

– Akritic ballads. From 1870, when Ioannidis published extracts from the Trebizond manuscript of Digenis Akritis, connections were

perceived with the folk-songs still being performed about the heroes
Digenis, Constantine and Porphyrios. These figures often had a castle,
garden, and wife, and were in conflict with brigands, most famously in
Digenis' struggle with Charos (for a convenient anthology of the most
significant texts, see Kalonaros, 1941: 2, 207–53, to which reference
is made in the following paragraphs). Debate has raged as to whether
the poem was the source of the ballads or the ballads were worn down
echoes of the poem (Beck, 1971, 48–63). Now that the difficulties of
using nineteenth-century ballads as evidence for the oral background
of a poem surviving in manuscripts of the fourteenth and fifteenth
centuries are better understood, this question is no longer put so
bluntly: some connection, however, is beyond dispute. Recent work
(e.g. Sifakis, 1989, and especially Fenik, 1991) has emphasised the
relationship between E and the ballad material, both metrically and in
line structure.

There are three categories of resemblance between the ballads and
Digenis, as seen in G and E:

1. Plot similarities to *Digenis* without particularly close wording: e.g.
G4.441, E858, cf. Kalonaros ιβ′ 143; G4.656–7, cf. ιε′ 70–1; G4.705,
E992, cf. ια′ 86; G4.745, ια′ 87; G7.8ff., E1633–59, cf. κδ′ 1–7 (garden and
birds); E1701, θ′ 1; E1708–28, cf. κϛ′ 2–12 (speech on death bed);
E1709–64, cf. κ′ (speech on death bed); G8.58, cf. κζ′ 2 (doctors); E1770–1,
cf. κζ′ 6 (angel); G8.137, κη′ 4. These resemblances are found in either G or
E or both.
2. A few formulaic phrases which are found throughout the tradition of
which both poem and ballads are part: e.g. the ubiquitous πηδᾶ καὶ
καβαλικεύει at E566, 567, 831, 927, 1009, 1274, 1281, 1357, 1440,
1555, cf. ια′ 62, ιβ′ 112; these formulas occur mainly in E. The action of
thrusting a spear into a tree root may come into this category: G5.59, cf. ε′
(*Lay of Armouris*) 50. For further discussion of repeated phrases, see the
section on Style below.
3. Some distinctive phrases which occur in both *Digenis* and the songs and
which link the poem closely to the songs: e.g. E674–5, cf. ε′ 36, 35; E828,
cf. ιβ′ 132, ιγ′ 8; E923–5, cf. ε′ 77–9 and *Achilleis* N 390; E930, cf. δ′ 23ff.
These phrases occur only in E and link E to a song tradition in a way that is
both suggested and supported by Fenik's metrical study (1991).

The *Lay of Armouris* (ed. Alexiou, 1985, 160–89 = Kalonaros ε′)
survives in a manuscript virtually contemporary with E and resembles
it closely in style and theme, though the name Digenis does not appear.
The earliest written folk-song which mentions Digenis is found in a
manuscript of ca. 1650 (Bouvier, 1960). Other ballads tell us nothing

about the material that may have been used in the composition of the poem and may, indeed, be worn-down versions of the epic. Songs are, nevertheless, envisaged as part of the structure of *Digenis* (e.g. at G4.427), as they are in other Byzantine romances whether from the twelfth or fourteenth centuries.

– Other medieval vernacular verse texts. The parallels between the *Achilleis* and both the G and E versions of *Digenis* need further examination (Mitsakis, 1963, 52–63). Some lines found in both G and E also occur elsewhere: e.g. G2.196, E367, cf. *Achilleis* N 877.

Language

The definitive linguistic analysis of early demotic Greek, to which the *Digenis* poems belong, has yet to be written, though Browning's general survey (1983) offers much useful information. Studies such as those of Joseph (1990) on syntactical developments in general, or Holton (1993) or Mackridge (1993b) on particular features, indicate lines for future progress. Some comments on the linguistic usages of E are found in Alexiou, 1985, οζ'-πα'. No attempt will be made here to place either G or E in the continuum of Greek linguistic development, though a few comments are made on particular usages, largely to eliminate repetitive notes on grammatical anomalies.

Participles

One of the most striking features of the language usage of *Digenis* G is the major role played by participles: some 1548 examples over 3709 lines. These cover a wide range of active and passive forms in the present, aorist and perfect tenses in a variety of syntactical situations. There are, however, some striking anomalies in the way in which they are used; these are listed here and not commented on in the notes to the translation:

> non-agreement of case or gender at: 1.12 (καθυποτάξας), 2.141 (διώκων), 4.458 (σκοπῶν), 4.775 (γενόμενοι), 4.831 (ἀδόμενα), 4.1062 (λακτίζων, στρηνιάζων, εἰκάζων), 5.205 (βλέπων), 5.209 (προσδοκῶσα), 6.307 (τερπόμενοι), 6.412 (ἔχων), 6.553 (ἔχων), 7.72 (κατέχων);
> hanging nominatives: 1.37 (ἔχων), 1.97 (γενόμενοι), 1.175 (δεξάμενος), 1.231 (θεασάμενοι), 3.158 (θέλουσα), 4.57 (ὧν: emendable), 4.253 (μεμυρισμένος), 4.369 (φθάσαντες), 4.483 (τεκμαιρομένη), 4.523 (θέλουσα), 4.569 (φθεγξαμένη), 4.584 (ἐμπεδώσαντες), 4.585 (προκύψασα), 4.670 (ὁρμήσαντες), 4.734 (εἰπών, κολακεύων), 4.800 (προσελθόντες), 4.856

(φθάσαντες), 4.873 (βουλόμενος), 4.879 (καταλαβόντες), 4.942 (ἐπισκέπτοντες), 4.949 (ποιήσαντες), 4.1054 (εἰπών), 4.1066 (βουλόμενος), 5.64 (καθίσαντες), 5.116 (καθεύδοντες), 5.177 (λέγουσα, δακρύουσα), 5.257 (παραγενόμενος), 6.2 (διεξιών), 6.15 (ἀπελθόντες), 6.63 (καταλαβών), 6.148 (θέλοντες), 6.223 (βουλόμενος, 6.308 (λαβών), 6.310 (διατρέχων), 6.330 (νομιζομένη), 6.331 (λέγοντες), 6.447 (προηγούμενος), 6.448 (γενόμενοι), 6.455 (πλησιάσαντες), 6.489 (ἐπαινῶν), 6.533 (ἀφέμενος), 6.629 (πατάξας), 6.777 (ἐλθόντες), 6.792 (εἰπών), 6.799 (ὑποστρέψας), 7.164 (ἐκτρέπων), 7.189 (ἐλθοῦσα), 7.193 (ζήσασα), 7.194 (ἐντρυφήσασα), 7.195 (φανεῖσα), 7.196 (τρέψασα), 7.197 (ἐλευθερώσασα), 7.198 (βραβεύσασα), 7.200 (καθελοῦσα), 7.201 (ἀντεισάξασα), 7.202 (τεκοῦσα), 8.20 (διατρίψας), 8.21 (δράσας), 8.22 (ἐξερχόμενος), 8.48 (ἀλγήσας), 8.58 (στενάξας, κλαύσας), 8.132 (εὐποροῦσα), 8.240 (ἱστάμενος), 8.241 (συντεθειμένος), 8.243 (δυνάμενος), 8.277 (συλλαβόντες);

inaccurate use of genitive absolutes: 1.177 (ἰσχύσαντος), 4.255 (πλησιάσαντος, 4.876 (προβάντων), 4.1063 (ἐλθόντος), 6.219 (δώσαντος), 6.497 (εἰπόντος), 8.15 (ἀφιγμένων), 8.55 (ἐλθόντος, ἁψαμένου);

accusative absolute where genitive required: 8.236 (δοθέντα);

strained usages: 1.49 (πνέων), 4.526–7 (τηροῦντα, κατέχοντα), 4.1037 (ἀποσοβῶν, κρατύνων).

These anomalies, which cannot easily be emended, affect 98 cases out of the 1548 participles found in G (at 4.762, 5.146, 8.24 emendation to a more regular form has been possible). They might be interpreted as an indication that the language of this poem is moving towards modern participial usages. The participial structures of Ermoniakos, writing ca. 1320 in Epiros, might well provide a parallel to those of G.

The majority of G's participles would seem to be due to the γ level of the G tradition rather than to *Digenis. They occur relatively infrequently in passages where connections with the wording of E are close (e.g. G4.35–44, cf. E720–33), though there are exceptions (e.g. G8.153–8, cf. E1808–23). They are also relatively rare in passages of speech (e.g. G1.155–65, 242–56) and seem to be a feature of the redactor's narrative style. They occur more frequently in areas affected by religious terminology (e.g. G3.160–98, 8.175–84).

In contrast, E makes relatively little use of participles, with only 168 examples from 1867 lines (that is, a participle is used on average every 11 lines, unlike G with a participle every 2 lines). There are few syntactical anomalies of the sort observed in G (but note masculines for feminines at E1806 and 1822), though the structures are much less adventurous; there are, for example, no genitive absolutes. Most participles are used adjectivally rather than with verbal force. The majority of the forms are passives in -μενος (present and perfect) or actives in -οντας, -ουσα. Note γεγονώς (E1817), δειχθεῖσαν (E989), κεκαλυμμένους (E1854), πεπτωκότι (E1822) but the masculine nominative singulars ὀνειδίζοντα (E353) and κλαίοντα (E393, though κλαίων E978). A notable exception to E's lack of participles occurs at E1853–66, a passage full of religious terminology (as noted above) and very close to the phrasing of G.

Future tense

G and E show marked contrasts in the formation of the future tense (on developments in this tense in early demotic Greek, see Joseph, 1990, 112–59 and Holton, 1993). The regular form in G is monolectic (123 examples); also observed are the subjunctive alone with a future sense (17), νά with the subjunctive (12), the present with a future meaning (12), θέλω and a form of the infinitive (7) and ἔχω with an infinitive (2); at G2.196–7 the future is expressed in three different ways: νά σύρω . . . σφάξω . . . κρίνειν ἔχει. In E the preferred usage is νά with the subjunctive (60 examples); also found are θέλω with an infinitive (9), a present with future meaning (8), ἔχω with an infinitive (4), θέλω with νά (2), the subjunctive alone (2) and the monolectic future (2: once by emendation [E71] and once in a line in which νά is already present [E689]); at E1420 it is tempting to emend ἀπέλθω ἔχω to ἀπέλθειν ἔχω.

Other features

Reflexive pronouns. G generally uses ἑαυτόν according to the classical system, though it is employed non-reflexively at G2.220, 3.251, 3.310, 4.62, 4.642, 4.871, 4.874, 6.722 and in place of ἐμαυτόν at G5.191, 6.728 and at 4.683 for σεαυτόν (which is not found); the modern form ἑαυτόν σου appears at G6.131. E uses only the modern reflexives, ἑαυτόν μου/σου/του, at E229, 367, 741, 955 and 1154. In G the language would appear to be in a transitional stage while E's usage is stable.

Object clitic pronouns. Mackridge (1993b) demonstrates that Digenis E shows a consistent system for positioning the pronoun: before the verb when the verb phrase is at the beginning of a clause or immediately after a co-ordinating conjunction or immediately after ὅτι, διότι, εἰ, οὐ; in all other cases the pronoun follows the verb.

At several points in both G and E ἄμφω and ἀμφότερος are used in the late sense of 'all' rather than the strict usage of 'both': e.g. ἄμφω G2.28, 6.177; ἀμφότερος 1.205, 2.244, 4.213, 6.634, E1752; cf. LSJ, *s.v.* ἀμφότερος II (note ἑκάτερος at G6.66).

G several times (e.g. G1.76, 1.243) uses διά for the second term in a comparison (Eideneier, 1970, 302).

Vocabulary. Attempts have been made to localise the versions of *Digenis*, with Crete being a favoured candidate (Xanthoudides, 1912). Recent work has pointed to a number of linguistic features which can be paralleled in the dialect of Pontus, the area in which many songs were collected in the late nineteenth and early twentieth centuries and where the first written version of the epic (T) was discovered (Trapp, 1971b; Prombonas, 1985, 8–32). The features are mainly discussed in connection with E: e.g. the puzzling forms ἐπαραβραδιάστης (E856), καυχάσεται (E51), the use of the negative οὐκ and the use of the double accusative after verbs of giving and speaking (Prombonas, 1989 and 1993). The number of such elements remains small and not all are confined exclusively to Pontus.

The language of *Digenis*

There are fourteen lines that are virtually identical in G and E (see p. xxix above and Trapp, 1971a, 46, Beaton, 1993a, 49–50) and that should thus be considered part of *Digenis*. Their evidence suggests that the language of *Digenis* was one of mixed registers. In these lines, for example, the future is expressed with νά at G2.196, G4.440 and E857, G6.677 and E1551 while elsewhere G regularly prefers the monolectic future; the ancient nominative aorist participle appears at G8.154 and E1809 while E's participle usage is normally low. Nevertheless, the redactors' different predilections can also be observed at work: thus at G2.234 = E2, G4.127 = E770 participles occur in G but not in E, conforming to the general pattern of archaising features in G and demoticising ones in E. However, the sample is too small to allow firm conclusions and in the present state of investigations into *Digenis* it would be rash to make proposals about the distribution of language registers within the poem.

Metre

Both G and E are written in the unrhymed fifteen-syllable line (the δεκαπεντασύλλαβος or πολιτικὸς στίχος) that is almost invariably used for literature in early demotic Greek. This verse, based on word

accent, demands a break after syllable 8, and stresses on syllables 14
and either 6 or 8:

1 2 3 4 5 6 7 8 || 9 10 11 12 13 14 15

$$(/ \;\smile\; \smile)$$
x   x   (˘) (/) (˘) (˘ \;\smile\; /) || x   x   (˘) (/) \;\smile\; / \;\smile
$$(/ \;\smile\; /)$$

[/ invariable stress; (/) frequent stress; x free in accentuation; (˘) rare
stress; ⌣ unstressed] (Jeffreys, M. J., 1974)

Both G and E show a number of unusual metrical features.

G's lines run for the most part smoothly, with few hiatuses and little
use of elision, but there is a remarkably high proportion of accents on
syllables 3 and 11, an 'anapaestic' rhythm (23 per cent: Tiftixoglu,
1974, 41). Such accents were not frequent at any stage of the history
of the fifteen-syllable line: 1–2 per cent in writers from the tenth,
eleventh and fourteenth centuries and avoided almost entirely in the
twelfth by the 'learned' practitioners of the metre such as Tzetzes and
Manasses, though with exceptions such as Kamateros whose work on
astrology shows 7.4 per cent of stresses in this position (Tiftixoglu,
1974, 43–61). G's figures suggest that *Digenis displayed some
unusual features and that G itself should be placed at an earlier,
twelfth-century, date rather than later (Tiftixoglu, 1974, 58; note,
however, that the fourteenth-century *War of Troy* shows approximately 16 per cent of syllable 3 stresses). Most of G's syllable 3 accents
were recast in Z into a smoother line (Politis, 1970, 561).

One striking feature of E is its metrical unevenness, with many
apparently unmetrical lines ranging from 12 to 17 syllables in length
and many independent half-lines of 7 or 8 syllables. The boundaries of
a metrical unit are, however, rarely in doubt, given the scribe's use of
commas and points to articulate the verses. Full lists of irregular lines
are given in Karayanni, 1976, 133–47. Though lines of non-standard
length may be found in other works in early demotic Greek
(Karayanni, 1976, 134–6) E is quite exceptional in the number that
it includes. Karayanni argues that E's metrical variations should be
respected with only minimal emendation, an argument that was first
denied but is now meeting with some support (Kambylis, 1995, 55–9,
64–7; but contrast Alexiou, S., 1995). Most editors, however, have
assumed that underlying E's irregularities are 15–syllable lines of a
conventional pattern, even if they have despaired of retrieving them all
(cf. Alexiou, 1985, πβ´–πϛ´). It was not until Alexiou's edition of 1985

(largely reproduced in Ricks, 1990) that the bold changes which these assumptions demand were made and many more regular 15–syllable lines were reconstructed, even if many of the half-lines were allowed to stand. This edition works on the assumption that E's line would normally contain 15 syllables, and has reconstructed 'regular' lines with the following exceptions:

independent half-lines of 7 syllables are found at: 101, 165, 198, 200a, 235, 272, 289, 377, 493, 500, 521, 533, 534, 540, 548, 673, 760, 764, 877, 1036, 1163, 1179, 1190, 1241, 1246, 1268, 1294, 1334, 1450, 1505, 1527, 1564, 1639, 1644, 1745, 1756, 1819;

independent half-lines of 8 syllables at: 25, 199, 210, 266, 284, 314, 410, 451, 563, 630, 795, 904, 978, 1003, 1011, 1034, 1118, 1336, 1676, 1828;

irregular full lines at: 283, 357, 397, 426, 1158, 1482.

Seriously hypermetric lines have been emended into 15 syllables at: e.g. 232/3, 279/80, 412, 443, 498, 567, 571/2, 587/8, 599/600, 604, 973a, 1820/1; redundant half-lines have been removed at: e.g. 568, 622/3, 1015, 1023/4. Stress on syllables 3 and 11, the 'anapaestic' rhythm, is part of E's style (as it is of G's) and, in spite of the practice of Alexiou, has not been used here as ground for emendation (Spadaro, 1989; Garandoudis, 1993, 198–213). The two halves of the line are taken to be self-contained units: partly as a result of this, hiatus occurs at the caesura, the mid-line break, in 10.4 per cent of the lines (Garandoudis, 1993, 210). Hence elision across the caesura has been regarded as irregular, with 'ς written for εἰς at syllable 9 at 178, 294, 339, 782, 1115, 1447, 1641, though 482, 530, 549, 1419, 1456 remain problematic. Much less should phrases be allowed to spill over the caesura: several cases have been removed but problems remain at, e.g., 137 and 549. There are frequent minor emendations to rectify the metre throughout the text

Fruitful comparisons have been made between the metrical structures of E and Modern Greek folk song (Prombonas, 1985; Sifakis, 1989; Fenik, 1991; cf. Mackridge, 1990).

Style

Repeated phrases are a prominent stylistic feature of verse texts in early Modern Greek, most notably the fourteenth-century romances and chronicles. The reasons for this are not fully understood (see Beaton, 1989, 160–84 for a survey of the debate). *Digenis* G and E also include a number of repeated lines.

These fall into two categories. There are those that appear in each version because they were part of *Digenis. The fourteen virtually identical lines that have been referred to already (pp. xxix and lii) are the prime instances of this. Further lists of lines that can be classed in this way are to be found in Beaton, 1993a. Beaton's lists, however, do not pretend to be exhaustive and, in particular, they under-report the internal parallels that exist within G and E. Some of these are not found in the other version (e.g. τὴν κονταρεὰν μὲ δώσει is found at E1283, 1445, 1540, 1557 but not in G) while others, after occurring once in one version, are then repeated in the other (e.g. τὰ ἔτη τῆς ζωῆς σου [μας/του etc] G4.758 but see E231, 784, 815, 820, 822, 1022, 1023, 1058, 1148, 1290). Lines of this sort make up the second category of repeated phrases and are the kind of repetition that is found in the fourteenth-century texts. However, in comparison with those texts the degree of repetition in either G or E is low, both in range of phrases repeated and in the number of repetitions (Jeffreys, M. J., 1993, 54, note 12). Contrast, for example (bearing in mind the difference in length of the texts concerned), the numbers of repetitions associated with proper names in the *Chronicle of the Morea* (e.g. 62 examples of ὁ πρίγκιπα Γυλιάμος: Jeffreys, M. J., 1973, 178) or the *War of Troy* (Αἴας ὁ Τελαμώνιος, 20 examples: Jeffreys, E. M. and M. J., 1979, 119) with those found in G and E: ὁ Διγενὴς Ἀκρίτης (nom., acc., and gen.) G3.339, 4.323, 7.1, 8.250, E219, 442, 465, 525, 610, 634, 639, 752, 1216, 1608, 1697, 1698; Ἀκρίτην τόν γενναῖον G3.106, 4.104; Βασίλειος Ἀκρίτης (nom. and acc.) G2.48, 4.66, 4.1088, 6.190, E1092; ὁ θαυμαστὸς Ἀκρίτης (nom., acc. and gen.) G4.1011, 8.5, 8.277, E722, 819, 1030, 1694, 1703; Κίνναμος καὶ Ἰωαννάκης (nom., acc. and gen.) G4.33, 6.396, 6.548, 6.620, 8.105, E1243, 1348, 1412, 1484, 1499; ὁ γέρων ὁ Φιλοπαππούς G6.332, E650, 656, 685, 1239, 1329, 1365, 1400, 1451, 1506; Φιλοπαππού τοῦ γέροντος G4.33, 6.548, 8.105, E1349. Further lists of repeated phrases, particularly from E, are given in Lord (1960, 213) and Alexiou (1985, πς΄–πθ΄). While consensus has not been reached on the reasons for the style of the fourteenth-century verse texts, it remains most likely that a high level of repetitions is an indication of contact with a process of oral composition, of the sort posited for the Homeric poems and medieval vernaculars elsewhere in Europe.

G and E are very different from the fourteenth-century texts, despite having a few phrases in common with them (as indicated *passim* in Trapp, 1971a), and cannot have passed through the same compositional processes. They are also different from each other since there are consistently more repeated phrases in E than in G. This is partly an index of the learned elements that have been layered on to G and partly an index of E's closer connections with ballads and folk-song. What is not clear, and probably never can be, is whether repeated phrases were a significant element in *Digenis* – and this despite the fact that there is every likelihood that much of the material concerning Digenis went through a prolonged period of oral transmission before being pulled together in written form some time in the twelfth century.

Conclusion

This edition is of G and E. The discussion to this point has focussed on them, while *Digenis*, the text that underlies them both, has remained in the background – inevitably since so little of it can be reconstructed. Let us now end by sketching the scenario that might have led to its creation.

Stories about the legendary past, almost certainly in verse, circulated in the frontier areas of Cappadocia and on the banks of the Euphrates, some prompted by the massive architectural remains of the memorials erected by the kings of Commagene, others by the skirmishes endemic to hostile frontier situations. They coalesced around a lone hero of Arab-Byzantine parentage. Our evidence that such stories existed comes from Psellos' comments made in about 1080 on tales told of the Doukas family. At some point these stories, perhaps in dialect, were brought to Constantinople, perhaps by refugees in the aftermath of the Byzantine defeat at Manzikert in 1071 (Magdalino, 1993b). The stories were limited in scope: they reflected the Arab-Byzantine society of the frontier and told of the hero's clashes with groups of bandits, how he hunted wild beasts, abducted a bride, built a palace and met an early death. When in the 1140s and 1150s it became briefly fashionable in Constantinopolitan literary circles to write narratives in the manner of the novelists of late antiquity, an attempt was made to string the material about the hero Digenis into a biographical sequence and trim it with appropriate romantic elements. It may well have been this material's non-literary background that attracted the cultured *littérateurs* who were then experimenting with varied genres and language levels. Interest in the stories on Digenis would have been given added relevance by the emperor Manuel's dealings in 1151–2 with the areas formerly associated with the hero (Jeffreys, E. M., 1993). The novel, or romance, on Digenis was never rounded out and it remained a sketch, a loosely linked sequence of episodes: it is this, *Digenis*, which lies behind G and E. It would have been in the fifteen-syllable line, with awkward metrical stresses, and its language would have moved between the standard Byzantine *koine* and the vernacular, possibly with an admixture of an Anatolian dialect. There would have been imitations of Achilles Tatius and Heliodoros at some key points while Digenis' death-scene would have had a strongly religious tone.

We do not know the subsequent history of *Digenis*, but some time in the fourteenth century, perhaps in Frankish Greece, it may have been available to the author of the *Achilleis*, who knew a version of *Digenis* with characteristics of both G and E (cf. Mitsakis, 1963, 52–63). At some stage, but before ca. 1300 (the date of G), gnomic passsages, more biblical quotations and more descriptive details were added to one copy of this text, giving rise to γ, the ancestor of g and G; a copy of this found its way to South Italy, where G was made. At some time between ca.1150 and ca.1485 (the date of E), another copy also underwent changes, now unrecoverable, to give rise to e and E. Given E's analogies with the *Song of Armouris* and more recent folk-songs, the final transformation probably took place toward the latter end of that period. Within perhaps fifty years of the copying of E, both this and a version of G were used, perhaps in Venice, to create Z, an omnibus version of the story of Digenis and the source of all other surviving written versions of *Digenis*. But *Digenis* itself had vanished almost without trace.

Principles of the edition

G and E present very different problems for an editor. In both cases, we must assume that the poets would originally have written lines that were grammatical and metrical. The text that survives in G has few metrical anomalies, its orthography generally conforms to historical conventions, and its syntax is close to the Byzantine *koine* with few irregularities.The text in E, however, bristles with hypermetric lines, the orthography is phonetic and the syntax is 'medieval', transitional between standard Byzantine and Modern Greek. Though it can be demonstrated, as was discussed earlier, that previous copies lie behind each version and that behind these lies a common original, it is impossible for earlier stages of the G and E traditions to be reached consistently, let alone *Digenis*. In effect, then, an editor is reduced to removing surface copying errors in the surviving manuscripts in order to produce a comprehensible text.

For G, the situation is relatively straightforward and most problems arise over irregular participial constructions. Since many of these cannot be regularised without major rewriting, they have usually been allowed to stand.

E is quite another matter. Here the many unmetrical lines are awkward, at times degenerate into prose and are full of redundant phrases. Yet the bulk of the text indicates that the poet intended to write regular fifteen-syllable lines. Thus drastic intervention is both inevitable and justified. It was Alexiou who first made these interventions and turned E into a readable poem. This edition, as can be seen from the apparatus, stands in Alexiou's shadow and is greatly in his debt.

The edition of E given here attempts to restrict intervention to the minimum that is necessary to restore fifteen-syllable lines that are metrically and syntactically viable. An 'anapaestic' rhythm is part of the poem's style and has not been taken as a reason for emendation; the mid-line caesura after syllable 8 has been observed (see pp. liii–liv above). Words such as ἦσαν or εἶχε appearing at the end of a hemistich have not been written as enclitics. The language used in E is one whose rules are not yet fully understood, and it is not easy to be certain at what point genuine linguistic choice merges into error: should, for example, one line include two forms of the infinitive (E1182) or both genitive and dative after δός (E1171)? This edition has been conservative and has attempted to allow the manuscript's readings to stand wherever it seemed justifiable. Repetitions that seem redundant to twentieth-century literary taste need to be treated tolerantly. Many of the half-lines (often relegated to a note by Ricks) are necessary for the sense, and must be kept whether or not they were originally written in this way. At the same time one should not neglect the layout of the manuscript, its capital letters and spaces, since there are a few signs that captions from an earlier stage of transmission may have entered the text (e.g. E637). These features would be most accurately shown by a facsimile or a diplomatic edition, but this would be of little help to a modern reader. So, as an uneasy compromise, they are indicated here by a few lines' gap to represent the spaces and a large letter where capitals appear; the paragraph divisions have no manuscript authority.

For neither G nor E are orthographic variants noted. The distinction between εὐφ-/ἐφ- has not been marked; in E τζ has been tacitly written as τσ. However, where either manuscript is cited in the apparatus the manuscript orthography is given (with abbreviations normally resolved). Elisions are not indicated even where several are required in the line, though 'ς τόν is written for εἰς τόν after a consonant where the metre demands it or across a caesura; καί is written out in full. Misreadings of the manuscripts by previous editors are corrected tacitly. Proposed but rejected emendations are sometimes cited if they are especially attractive.

Since the language of G and E differs so markedly, different accentuation and orthographical systems have been used for each: G is in a style appropriate to a text in the Byzantine *koine* while E is presented according to Triantaphyllidis' rules for modern demotic polytonic.

The references to G marked in the margins of E and vice versa are to lines where there is a lexical element in common. However, it is not claimed that all such parallels are noted, nor are parallels noted when the sense is clearly identical in both versions but not the vocabulary.

Principles of the translation

This translation is intended to provide an unvarnished prose version that follows the line-sequence of the Greek as far as is practicable and does little to soften the grammatical inconsequences of G or the frequent asyndeton of E. Especially in E the linking καί can have many significances, even adversative ones; thus many conjunctions other than 'and' have been used to translate it. Both G and E mix present and past tenses, often within the same line, with no apparent logic: this has not been followed in the English version.

Notes

The notes are not intended to be discursive. More detail on names and historical details can be found in the Introduction and Name Index. For reasons of space there are no discussions of emendations or linguistic points, while references to literary parallels are collected in the relevant sections of the Introduction.

Previous editions

Of G alone

E. Legrand, *Les exploits de Digenis Akritas d'après le manuscrit de Grotta-Ferrata*, Paris, 1892 (= Bibliothèque Grecque Vulgaire 6); 2nd edition, Paris, 1902

J. Mavrogordato, *Digenes Akrites*, Oxford, 1956
L. Politis, Ποιητικὴ Ἀνθολογία, vol. 1, Athens, 1967, 15–38. Extracts
  only: G1.86–197, 4.102–207, 360–408, 436–55, 6.170–269,
  544–95, 609–84, 712–85

Of E alone

K. Krumbacher, 'Eine neue Handschrift des Digenis Akritas', *Sitzungs-
  berichte der philos.-philol. und hist. Kl., Kgl. Bay. Akad. der Wiss.*,
  Munich, 1904, Hft. 2, 309–53. Extracts only: E1–70, 284–8,
  298–301, 646–8, 1071–3, 1120–2, 1365–9, 1449–52,
  1664–867
D. C. Hesseling, 'Le roman de Digénis Akritas d'après le manuscrit de
  Madrid', Λαογραφία 3, 1911: 537–604
S. Alexiou, Βασίλειος Διγενὴς Ἀκρίτης καὶ τὸ Ἄσμα τοῦ Ἀρμούρη,
  Athens, 1985 (full edition with notes)
S. Alexiou, Βασίλειος Διγενὴς Ἀκρίτης καὶ τὰ ἄσματα τοῦ Ἀρμούρη
  καὶ τοῦ Υἱοῦ τοῦ Ἀνδρονίκου, Athens, 1990
D. Ricks, *Byzantine Heroic Poetry*, Bristol and New Rochelle, 1990

Of G, E and Λ

P. P. Kalonaros, Βασίλειος Διγενὴς Ἀκρίτης, 2 vols., Athens, 1941
  (reprinted, 1970)

Of G, E and Z

E. Trapp, *Digenes Akrites, synoptische Ausgabe der ältesten Versionen*,
  Vienna, 1971

Previous English translations

Of G: J. Mavrogordato, *Digenes Akrites*, Oxford, 1956
  D. B. Hull, *Digenis Akritas: the two-blooded border lord*, Athens, Ohio,
  1972
Of E: D. Ricks, *Byzantine Heroic Poetry*, Bristol and New Rochelle, 1990

Bibliography

Much scholarly effort has been expended on these texts since their
rediscovery just over a hundred years ago, which has given rise to an

unwieldy mass of notes and comments. This edition does not aim at bibliographical completeness and refers only to those studies which have proved helpful in the course of preparing it. Useful bibliographical information is to be found in:

H.-G. Beck, *Geschichte der byzantinischen Volksliteratur*, Munich, 1971, 65–8

R. A. Fletcher, 'The epic of Digenis Akritas and the akritic songs: a short guide to bibliography', *Mantatoforos* 11, 1977: 8–12

R. Beaton and D. Ricks, *Digenes Akrites: new approaches to Byzantine heroic poetry*, London, 1993, 171–85.

There are useful textual notes on G in:

A. Tsopanakis, Ἑρμηνευτικὰ καὶ διορθωτικὰ στὸ κείμενο τοῦ Διγενῆ Ἀκρίτα, Ἑλληνικά 17, 1960, 75–94

N. Eideneier, Διορθωτικά στὸ κείμενο τοῦ Διγενῆ τῆς Κρυπτοφέρρης, Ἑλληνικά 23, 1970, 299–319

and on E in:

S. Xanthoudidis, Διγενὴς Ἀκρίτας κατὰ τὸ χειρόγραφον Ἐσκωριάλ, Χριστιανικὴ Κρήτη 1, 1912, 523–71

I. Karayianni, Ὁ Διγενὴς Ἀκρίτας τοῦ Ἐσκορίαλ: συμβολὴ στὴ μελέτη τοῦ κειμένου, Ioannina, 1976

S. Alexiou, Ἀκριτικά, Herakleion, 1979.

Sigla

E	Escorial, Ψ IV 22
G	Grottaferrata, Z α XLIV
Z	Compilation of the E and G versions, surviving in T (Trebizond, Soumela Monastery: now lost) and A (Athens, National Library, 1074); cited from Trapp, 1971

The following editions are cited in the textual apparatus by the editor's name alone:

Alexiou	S. Alexiou, *Βασίλειος Διγενὴς Ἀκρίτης καὶ τὸ Ἄσμα τοῦ Ἀρμούρη*, Athens, 1985
Hesseling	D. C. Hesseling, 'Le roman de Digénis Akritas d'après le manuscrit de Madrid', *Λαογραφία* 3, 1911: 537–604
Kalonaros	P. P. Kalonaros, *Βασίλειος Διγενὴς Ἀκρίτας*, 2 vols., Athens, 1941 (reprinted 1970)

Legrand   E. Legrand, *Les exploits de Digenis Akritas d'après le manuscrit de Grotta-Ferrata*, 2nd edn, Paris, 1902

Mavrogordato   J. Mavrogordato, *Digenes Akrites*, Oxford, 1956

Politis   L. Politis, Ποιητικὴ Ἀνθολογία, vol. 1, Athens, 1967, 15–38

Ricks   D. Ricks, *Byzantine Heroic Poetry*, Bristol and New Rochelle, 1990

Sathas-Legrand   C. Sathas and E. Legrand, *Les exploits de Digénis Akritas*, Paris, 1875

Trapp   E. Trapp, *Digenes Akrites, synoptische Ausgabe der ältesten Versionen*, Vienna, 1971

For all other references, see the Bibliography

G: Text and translation

2

\<Βασιλείου Διγενοῦς Ἀκρίτου· λόγος πρῶτος\>

Ἔπαινοι καὶ τρόπαια κατορθωμάτων 1r
τοῦ τρισμάκαρος Ἀκρίτου Βασιλείου,
τοῦ ἀνδρειοτάτου τε γενναιοτάτου,
ἰσχὺν ἔχοντος παρὰ Θεοῦ ὡς δῶρον
5 καὶ κατατροπώσαντος πᾶσαν Συρίαν,
τὴν Βαβυλῶνα, Χαρζιανήν τε ὅλην,
Ἀρμενίαν τε καὶ τὴν Καππαδοκίαν,
τὸ Ἀμόριν τε καὶ τὸ Ἰκόνιν ἅμα,
τὸ περίφημον καὶ μέγα κάστρον ἔτι,
10 τὸ δυνατόν τε καὶ κατωχυρωμένον,
τὴν Ἄγκυραν λέγω τε καὶ πᾶσαν Σμύρνην,
καὶ τὰ παρὰ θάλασσαν καθυποτάξας.
  Δηλώσω σοι γὰρ τὰς αὐτοῦ πράξεις ἄρτι
ἃς εἰργάσατο ἐν τῷ παρόντι βίῳ,
15 πῶς πολεμιστὰς δυνατοὺς καὶ ἀνδρείους
κατεπτόησε καὶ πάντα τὰ θηρία,
ἔχων συνεργοῦσαν τε Θεοῦ τὴν χάριν,
καὶ Θεοτόκου τῆς ἀκαταμαχήτου
καὶ τῶν ἀγγέλων ἅμα καὶ ἀρχαγγέλων,
20 τῶν ἀθλοφόρων καὶ μεγάλων μαρτύρων,

Title: not in G: added by Legrand on the basis of the headings in the remaining books.
1 κατορθωμάτων Papadimitriou, 1947, 124, note 6: ἐγκώμιόν κα . . . μ . τ G ἐγκώμιόν
τε Legrand
4 ἰσχὺν corr.: τοῦ τὴν ἰσχὺν G

The first book of Basil Digenis Akritis, the Frontiersman of Double Descent

Praises and trophies for the achievements
of the thrice-blessed Basil the Frontiersman,
the bravest and most noble,
who possessed his strength from God as a gift
5 and has overcome all Syria,
Babylon, and the whole of Charziane,
Armenia and Cappadocia,
and Amorion and Ikonion as well,
and that famed and still great fortress,
10 powerful and well-fortified,
Ankyra I mean, and all Smyrna,
and he subjugated the land by the sea.
    I shall now reveal to you the deeds
which he performed in this present life,
15 how powerful and brave warriors
he terrified and all beasts,
with aid of the grace of God
and of the unconquerable Mother of God,
together with the angels and archangels,
20 and the great victorious martyrs,

1–29 These lines form a prologue written in twelve-syllable verse, in contrast to the fifteen-syllable line used throughout the rest of the poem: their authenticity has been challenged. According to Grégoire (1931a, 483), the prologue's author had not read the whole poem, since he attributes to Digenis the achievements of his father's Moslem family (see G1.50–6, 290–5, 2.75–9, 4.39–42). Pertusi (1962, 37–40), shows that the prologue was in fact constructed carelessly out of the remainder of the text. The false information also appears in the compiled text Z (at Z4153–8, a point equivalent to G7.208–10) but must have been put together for this prologue since G itself was copied long before Z was made. However, although the prologue may sound like the attempt of a monk to defend the orthodoxy of a story he has hardly read, its composition need not be far removed in date from *Digenis, the written text that underlies both G and E (see Introduction, pp. xxiii–xxvi, lvi–lvii): the references to warrior saints are consonant with the ambience of the mid-twelfth century, when *Digenis was probably written. The prologue is included here because this edition is an attempt to provide a readable text of manuscripts G and E, rather than to correct cases of reworking.

4   Διγενὴς Ἀκρίτης

Θεοδώρων τε τῶν πανενδοξοτάτων,
τοῦ στρατηλάτου καὶ τοῦ τίρωνος ἅμα,
τοῦ πολυάθλου γενναίου Γεωργίου,
καὶ θαυματουργοῦ καὶ μάρτυρος μαρτύρων   1v
25 ἐνδοξοτάτου Δημητρίου, προστάτου
τοῦ Βασιλείου καὶ καύχημα καὶ κλέος
τοῦ νικοποιοῦ ἐν τοῖς ὑπεναντίοις
Ἀγαρηνοῖς τε καὶ τοῖς Ἰσμαηλίταις,
Σκύθοις βαρβάροις τοῖς λυσσῶσιν ὡς κύνες.

30 Ἦν ἀμιρᾶς τῶν εὐγενῶν πλουσιώτατος σφόδρα
φρονήσεώς τε μέτοχος καὶ ἀνδρείας εἰς ἄκρον,
οὐ μέλας ὡς Αἰθίοπες, ἀλλὰ ξανθός, ὡραῖος,
ἀνθῶν ἄρτι τὸ γένειον εὐπρεπέστατον, σγοῦρον.
Εἶχεν ὀφρύδιν πεπανὸν καθάπερ πεπλεγμένον·
35 βλέμμα γοργόν, ἐνήδονον, πλήρης ἔρωτος γέμον,
ὡς ῥόδον ἐξανέτειλεν ἐν μέσῳ τοῦ προσώπου·
ὡς κυπαρίσσιν ἔμνοστον τὴν ἡλικίαν ἔχων,
εἶπεν ἄν τις ἰδὼν αὐτὸν εἰκόνι ἐοικέναι·
σὺν τούτοις ἀκατάμαχον τὴν ἰσχὺν κεκτημένος
40 καθ' ἑκάστην ἐσχόλαζεν εἰς θηρίων πολέμους·
τόλμην πειράζων τὴν αὐτοῦ καὶ ἀνδρείαν θαυμάζων
ὡς θαῦμα πᾶσι προὔκειτο τοῖς αὐτὸν καθορῶσι.
Δεινὸν δὲ πρᾶγμα πέφηνεν εἰς τοὺς νέους ἡ δόξα.
Τῷ γὰρ πλουτεῖν διαπαρθεὶς καὶ ὄγκῳ τῆς ἀνδρείας
45 στρατολογεῖν ἀπήρξατο Τούρκους καὶ Διλεμίτας,
Ἀραβίτας τε ἐκλεκτοὺς καὶ πεζοὺς Τρωγλοδύτας·
εἶχε καὶ τοὺς ἀγούρους του χιλίους γουλαμίους,
ἀδνουμιάτας ἅπαντας ἐπαξίως ῥογεύσας.
†Ἐξέπνευσε† πνέων θυμοῦ κατὰ τῆς Ῥωμανίας·   2r
50 τὰ μέρη δὲ καταλαβὼν χώρας τοῦ Ἡρακλέος
πόλεις ἠρήμωσε πολλὰς ἐρήμους καταστήσας

---

31 ἄκρον Kalonaros, cf. G4.798, 6.795: ἄκρος G
38 εἶπεν Chatzis, 1932, 263: εἴπερ G
45 Διλεμίτας Karolidis, 1905/6, 218: Διλεβίτας G
47 γουλαμίους Grégoire, 1931b, 482: γουλαβίους G
49 †Ἐξέπνευσε† G, obelised by Trapp: ἐξέπλευσε Tsopanakis, 1960, 80 ἐξίππευσε Grégoire, 1942, 50

the all glorious Theodores,
both the general and the recruit,
the noble George of many labours,
and the wonder-working martyr of martyrs,
25 the most glorious Dimitrios, protector
of Basil and boast and fame
of him who achieved victory over the opposing
Agarenes and Ishmaelites,
Scythian barbarians ravening like dogs.

30 There was an emir, one of the high-born, exceedingly rich,
possessing good sense and bravery in the extreme,
not black like the Ethiopians but fair and handsome,
with a newly grown and most attractive curly beard.
35 He had well-developed eyebrows, knitted, as it were;
a swift, joyous gaze, fully brimming with passion,
radiated like a rose from the middle of his face.
In stature he was like a graceful cypress
and anyone who saw him would compare him to a picture.
As well as this he achieved unconquerable strength
40 and every day he found recreation in battles against wild beasts
and, testing his daring and displaying his bravery,
he became a wonder to all who observed him.
Fame has proved a serious matter for young men.
Exhilarated by his wealth and outstanding bravery,
45 he began to recruit Turks and Dilemites,
picked Arabs and Troglodyte infantry.
He also had his youngsters, a thousand warriors,
and he paid all the mustered forces fittingly.
He invaded Roman territory in wild fury;
50 reaching the district of the town of Herakles,
he laid waste many cities and made them desolate,

21–25 The cult of the four military saints was enhanced by their appearance on coins of the Comnenian emperors, especially John II (1118–43) and Manuel (1143–81) (Hendy, 1969).
30 ff. The phrases used in the description of the handsome young emir have parallels in the description of Digenis' future wife (G4.351, 353) and the novels of Heliodoros (7.10) and Achilles Tatius (1.4.3, 5.11.5). For elements of this introductory description common to fourteenth-century romances, see Beaton, 1989, 166–72.
48 A technical Roman/Byzantine term for mustering troops is used of an Arab warrior and his troop movements (cf. Alexiou, 1979, 115).

καὶ πλήθη ἠχμαλώτευσε λαοῦ ἀναριθμήτου,
ἀπροφυλάκτων τῶν μερῶν ἐκείνων τυγχανόντων
(οἱ γὰρ ἐκεῖ φυλάσσοντες ἔτυχον εἰς τὰς ἄκρας)
55 καὶ ὡς ἐκ τούτου ἄδειαν μεγάλην συναντήσας,
διαδραμὼν Χαρζιανὴν Καππαδοκίαν φθάνει
καὶ εἰς οἶκον τοῦ στρατηγοῦ ἀθρόως ἐπιπίπτει.
Τὰ δὲ πραχθέντα ἐν αὐτῷ τίς εἰπεῖν ἐξισχύσει;
Πάντας γὰρ ἐθανάτωσε τοὺς ἐκεῖ εὑρεθέντας,
60 πλοῦτον ἀφείλετο πολύν, ἐσκύλευσε τὸν οἶκον
καὶ κόρην ἠχμαλώτευσε πάνυ ὡραιοτάτην,
θυγατέρα τοῦ στρατηγοῦ, τυγχάνουσαν παρθένον.
Ὑπῆρχε δὲ ὁ στρατηγὸς ἐν ἐξορίᾳ τότε
καὶ οἱ τῆς κόρης ἀδελφοὶ ἔτυχον εἰς τὰς ἄκρας.
65 Ἡ μήτηρ δὲ τὰς τῶν ἐθνῶν ἀποφυγοῦσα χεῖρας
ἅπαντα γράφει παρευθὺς τοῖς υἱοῖς τὰ συμβάντα,
τὴν τῶν ἐθνῶν τὴν ἔλευσιν, τὴν ἁρπαγὴν τῆς κόρης,
τῆς φιλτάτης τὸν χωρισμόν, τῶν συμφορῶν τὸ πλῆθος.
Προσέθηκε δὲ τῇ γραφῇ καὶ τάδε μετὰ θρήνων·
70 «Ὦ τέκνα ποθεινότατα, οἰκτείρατε μητέρα
ψυχὴν ἀθλίαν ἔχουσαν καὶ μέλλουσαν τεθνάναι·
ἀγάπης μνημονεύσατε ἀδελφῆς τῆς ἰδίας,
ἐλευθερῶσαι σπεύσατε ἀδελφὴν καὶ μητέρα,
τὴν μὲν δουλείας τῆς πικρᾶς, κἀμὲ δὲ τοῦ θανάτου.
75 Δώσωμεν πᾶσαν ὕπαρξιν ἕνεκεν τῆς φιλτάτης·
ζωὴν μὴ προτιμήσητε διὰ τὴν ἀδελφήν σας, 2ν
ἀδελφὴν ἐλεήσατε, τέκνα μου, τὴν ἰδίαν,
ἀπέλθετε μετὰ σπουδῆς εἰς ἀνάρρυσιν ταύτης·
εἰ δ᾽ οὔ, θανοῦσαν ὄψεσθε μητέρα ὑπὲρ τέκνου
80 καὶ τὴν κατάραν τὴν ἐμὴν λήψεσθε καὶ πατρῴαν,
εἰ τοῦτο οὐ ποιήσητε καθὼς ὑμῖν ὑπέσχον.»
Οἱ δὲ ταῦτα ἀκούσαντες, στενάξαντες ἐκ βάθους
καὶ δακρύων κατάβροχοι οἱ πέντε γεγονότες,
ἀλλήλους προεπέμποντο τοῦ ἀπελθεῖν σπουδαίως,
85 «Ἂς ἀπέλθωμεν,» λέγοντες, «σφαγῶμεν ὑπὲρ ταύτης.»

---

53 ἀπροφυλάκτων Kalonaros: ἀπροσφυλάκτων G
75 Δώσωμεν corr.: δώσομεν G
79 εἰ δ᾽ οὔ Eideneier. 1970. 301. cf. Dangitsis. 1958/9. 228: εἰ δ᾽ οὖν G

and he took prisoner hosts of people beyond number
as these districts were unprotected
(for the troops on guard there were at the frontiers).
55 Since, as a result he enjoyed great license,
he overran Charziane, came to Cappadocia
and fell overwhelmingly upon the house of the general.
Who will have the strength to tell what happened in the house?
For he killed all those who were found there,
60 he took away much treasure, he plundered the house,
and took prisoner a very lovely girl,
daughter of the general, who was a virgin.
The general was at that time in exile,
and the girl's brothers were at the frontier.
65   Her mother escaped from the hands of the heathen
and immediately wrote to her sons all that had befallen,
the coming of the heathen, the abduction of the girl,
the separation from her dearest daughter, the host of disasters.
She added this sorrowfully to the letter:
70   "Most longed for children, pity your mother
whose soul is afflicted and who is about to die.
Remember the love of your own sister,
hasten to free your sister and your mother,
her from bitter slavery and me from death.
75 Let us surrender our very being for the sake of our dearest one;
do not prefer life to your sister;
pity your own sister, my children.
Go with speed to her rescue.
If not, you will see your mother dying for her child
80 and you will receive my curse and that of your father,
if you will not do as I have proposed for you."
    When they heard this, they sighed deeply
and the five were drenched with tears;
they urged each other on to set off eagerly.
85 "Let us go," they said, "let us be slaughtered on her behalf."

---

63 For the exile of the father of the Emir's bride, see also G1.270, 4.44, E140. This
element in the story has been connected with the historical Andronikos Doukas and with
the historical kernel of the *Song of Armouris* (Kalonaros, 1941: 2, 37).
65 ἔθνη, translated usually in this version as 'heathen', implies a group of outsiders,
whether the criteria are religious (as here), racial (e.g. Gentiles) or cultural (barbarians).
83 This abrupt reference is the first indication that there are five brothers.

Εὐθὺς ἵππων ἐπέβησαν καὶ ᾤχοντο τοῦ δρόμου
συνεπομένους ἔχοντες ὀλίγους στρατιώτας·
καὶ μηδὲν ἀμελήσαντες, ὕπνου μὴ κορεσθέντες,
διὰ βραχέων ἡμερῶν ἔφθασαν τὰ φουσσᾶτα
90 εἰς τὴν κλεισοῦραν τὴν δεινὴν ἣν Δύσκολον καλοῦσι·
καὶ μακρόθεν πεζεύσαντες ἔνθα τὰς βίγλας εὗρον,
δι' ὑπομνήσεως αὐτῶν δεήσεως ἐγγράφου
ἤχθησαν πρὸς τὸν ἀμιρᾶν τῇ ἐκείνου προστάξει.
Ὑπῆρχε δὲ καθήμενος ἐφ' ὑψηλοῦ του θρόνου,
95 χρυσοκολλήτου, φοβεροῦ, ἀπέξωθεν τῆς τένδας·
κύκλῳ αὐτοῦ παρίσταντο πλήθη ἀνδρῶν ἐνόπλων.
Καὶ πλησίον γενόμενοι, ἀκούει τούτων λόγους,
καὶ προσκυνήσαντες αὐτὸν μέχρι τρίτου ἐδάφους
μετὰ δακρύων ἔλεγον τῷ ἀμιρᾷ τοιάδε:
100 «Ἀμιρᾶ, δοῦλε τοῦ Θεοῦ καὶ πρῶτε τῆς Συρίας,   E59. 60. 129
νὰ φθάσῃς εἰς τὴν Πάνορμον, ἴδῃς τὸ μασγιδίον,
νὰ προσκυνήσῃς, ἀμιρᾶ, τὸν κρεμάμενον λίθον,   3r
καὶ ἀξιωθῇς ἀσπάσασθαι τὸ μνῆμα τοῦ Προφήτου,
νὰ ἀκούσῃς <καὶ> τῆς προσευχῆς τῆς καθιερωμένης.
105 Κόρην τερπνὴν ἀφήρπαξας, ἀδελφὴν ἡμετέραν·
πώλησον ταύτην πρὸς ἡμᾶς, δοῦλε Θεοῦ ὑψίστου,
καὶ ἀντ' αὐτῆς σοι δώσομεν πλοῦτον ὅσον κελεύεις.
Θρηνεῖ γὰρ δι' αὐτὴν ὁ πατὴρ ὡς μὴ ἔχων ἑτέραν,
θανεῖν ἡ μήτηρ βούλεται ταύτην μὴ καθορῶσα,
110 ἡμεῖς δὲ πόθον ἄπειρον πρὸς αὐτὴν κεκτημένοι
πάντες ἐπωμοσάμεθα ὅρκοις φρικωδεστάτοις,
ἂν τὴν οὐχ ὑποστρέψωμεν, καὶ οἱ πάντες νὰ σφαγῶμεν.»

---

86 Εὐθὺς Kalonaros: αὖθις G
94 του Papadimitriou, 1947, 125: τοῦ G
104 καὶ added by Politis, 1967, 15
108 γὰρ δι' αὐτὴν G: δι' αὐτὴν γὰρ Politis, 1967, 15

They mounted their horses immediately and went along the road,
with a few soldiers accompanying them.
Neglecting nothing and not taking their fill of sleep,
within a few days they came upon the camp,
90 in the dreadful pass they call Difficult.
Dismounting far off where they found the sentries,
through a written memorandum of their request
they were brought to the emir at his command.
He was seated on his lofty throne,
95 inlaid with gold, fearsome, outside the tent.
Around him were standing hosts of armed men.
When they were close by, he listened to their words,
and they made obeisance to him as far as the third degree
and spoke tearfully to the emir thus:
100   "Emir, servant of God and first man in Syria,
may you reach Panormos and see the mosque,
may you do obeisance, emir, to the hanging rock
and be deemed worthy to kiss the Prophet's tomb
and hear the sacred prayer.
105 You have abducted a delightful girl, our sister.
Ransom her to us, servant of the most high God,
and in return for her we will give you as much treasure as you ask.
For our father mourns for her since he has no other daughter,
our mother wishes to die since she cannot see her
110 and we who have a boundless desire for her
have all sworn with most terrible oaths
that if we do not recover her we shall all be slaughtered."

86 αὖθις, 'again', corrected perhaps unnecessarily to εὐθὺς, 'immediately' (Eideneier,
1970, 301), suggests that there may be a lacuna at some point between lines 64 and 83,
in which references have been lost to the number of brothers and a previous mounting on
horseback.
89–90 The φουσσᾶτα ('army' or 'camp') is at the κλεισοῦρα ('fort' or 'pass') called
Difficult. From the name it is a little easier to think of a camp at a pass rather than an
army at a fort.
92 The extremely bureaucratic vocabulary reinforces the impressive scene of the emir on
his throne, giving him an almost imperial dimension.
97–8 On the degrees of obeisance, see Vogt, 1935, 29–30 and Treitinger, 1938, 84–90;
here the brothers would seem to have prostrated themselves.
101–3 The list covers three places of significance to Islam: Panormos refers to Jeddah,
the port for Mecca and Medina; the mosque refers to the Ka'aba in Mecca; the 'hanging
rock' probably refers to the Temple Mount in Jerusalem with the Dome of the Rock, site of
Mohammed's Journey to Heaven; Mohammed's tomb is in Medina (Alexiou, 1979,
111–15; EI, under 'Kubbat-al-Sakhra'). The list is well-informed, unless it implies that all
the sites may be visited in one pilgrimage.

Ἀκούων ταῦτα ὁ ἀμιρᾶς καὶ τὴν τόλμην θαυμάσας
πρὸς τὸ μαθεῖν δῆτα στερεῶς εἰ τυγχάνουν ἀνδρεῖοι
115 (ἀκριβῶς γὰρ ἠπίστατο τὴν τῶν Ῥωμαίων γλῶτταν),
ἠρέμα ἀπεκρίνατο λέγων αὐτοῖς τοιάδε:
«Εἰ ποθεῖτε τὴν ἀδελφὴν ποιῆσαι ἐλευθέραν,
εἷς χωρισθήτω ἀφ' ὑμῶν ὃν ἔχετε γενναῖον,
καὶ ἂς καβαλλικεύσωμεν ἐγώ τε καὶ ἐκεῖνος,
120 καὶ ἂς μονομαχήσωμεν ἐγώ τε καὶ ἐκεῖνος.
Καὶ εἰ μὲν τρέψω τον ἐγώ, δούλους ὑμᾶς νὰ ἔχω·
εἰ δὲ κἀκεῖνος τρέψει με, χωρὶς λόγου παντοίου
νὰ λήψεσθε τὴν ἀδελφὴν μηδὲν ζημιωθέντες
καὶ ἕτερα αἰχμάλωτα παρ' ἐμοῦ εὑρεθέντα.
125 Ἄλλως γὰρ οὐ πεισθήσομαι τὴν ἀδελφὴν παρέξαι,
εἰ καὶ τὸν πλοῦτον δώσητε πάσης τῆς Ῥωμανίας.   3ν
Ἀπέλθετε, σκοπήσατε ὅπερ ὑμῖν συμφέρει.»
Εὐθὺς ἐξῆλθον ἅπαντες χαίροντες τῇ ἐλπίδι·
ἀλλ' ἵνα μὴ φιλονεικοῦν ποῖος νὰ πολεμήσῃ,
130 λαχνοὺς θεῖναι προέκριναν καὶ ἔλυσαν τὴν ἔριν·
ἔλαχε δὲ τὸν ὕστερον τὸν μικρὸν Κωνσταντῖνον,
ὃς δίδυμος ἐτύγχανε μετὰ τῆς αὐταδέλφης.
Ὁ πρῶτος νουθετῶν αὐτὸν ἤλειφε πρὸς ἀγῶνας,
«Μὴ ὅλως,» λέγων, «ἀδελφέ, φωναὶ καταπτοήσουν,   Ε1
135 μὴ κρότοι δειλιάσωσι, πληγαί σε ἐκφοβήσουν·   Ε1
κἂν γυμνὸν ἴδῃς τὸ σπαθίν, φυγεῖν οὕτω μὴ δώσῃς,
κἂν ἄλλο τι δεινότερον εἰς τροπὴν μὴ ἐκφύγῃς·
νεότητος μὴ φεῖσαι σῆς παρὰ μητρὸς κατάραν   Ε2
ἧς εὐχαῖς στηριζόμενος τὸν ἐχθρὸν καταβάλῃς·
140 οὐ γὰρ παρόψεται Θεὸς δούλους ἡμᾶς γενέσθαι.
Ἄπιθι, τέκνον, εὔθυμον, μὴ δειλιάσῃς ὅλως.»
Καὶ στάντες πρὸς ἀνατολὰς Θεὸν ἐπεκαλοῦντο:
«Μὴ συγχωρήσῃς, Δέσποτα, δούλους ἡμᾶς γενέσθαι.»
Καὶ ἀσπασάμενοι αὐτὸν προέπεμψαν εἰπόντες:
145 «Ἡ τῶν γονέων μας εὐχὴ γένηται βοηθός σου.»
Ὁ δὲ ἐφ' ἵππου ἐπιβὰς μαύρου, γενναιοτάτου,
σπαθὶν διαζωσάμενος λαμβάνει τὸ κοντάριν,
ἐβάσταξε καὶ τὸ ῥαβδὶν εἰς τὸ ῥαβδοβαστάκιν·

114 τυγχάνουν Legrand: τυγχάνον G
126 δώσῃｅτε G
135 μὴ κρότοι Tsopanakis, 1960, 80, cf. Ε1: μικρόν τι G
136 φυγεῖν G: perhaps φυγὴν
138 σῆς Eideneier, 1970, 302: σε G σὺ Legrand

When the emir heard this he admired their daring,
and in order to learn for certain whether they were brave
115 (for he knew the Roman language perfectly),
he replied calmly in the following words:
"If you desire to make your sister free,
let one of you whom you consider brave be chosen,
and let us mount our horses, he and I,
120 and let us fight in single combat, he and I.
And if I defeat him, I shall have you as slaves;
but if he defeats me, without any discussion
and suffering no punishment, you will take your sister
and other prisoners you find with me.
125 Otherwise I shall not be persuaded to hand over your sister,
even if you were to give me the wealth from all Roman territory.
Go and consider what is best for you."
    Immediately they all went out, pleased and hopeful,
but so that they should not wrangle over who should fight
130 they chose to cast lots and they resolved the dispute.
The lot fell to the last, the young Constantine,
who happened to be the twin of their sister.
The first brother gave him advice and encouraged him for the contest,
saying, "Do not, brother, let shouts shock you at all,
135 nor let noises alarm you nor wounds frighten you;
if you see the naked sword do not give way and flee,
if you see something yet more dreadful do not retreat and run away.
Do not spare yourself though you are young but think of your mother's
    curse;
may you be supported by her prayers and overthrow the enemy;
140 God will not permit our becoming slaves.
Go, child, be cheerful, do not be frightened at all."
And, facing towards the east, they addressed God,
"Do not allow us, Lord, to become slaves."
And, embracing him, they sent him out, saying,
145 "May our parents' prayer be your aid."
    Mounting his horse that was black and most noble,
he strapped on his sword, picked up his spear
and put his stick into its holder.

---

134 The version surviving in E begins at this point. G1.134–3.343 corresponds to
Alexiou's 'Song of the Emir' (see note on E1).

12   Διγενὴς Ἀκρίτης

τῷ δὲ σημείῳ τοῦ σταυροῦ φραξάμενος παντόθεν
150 τὸν ἵππον ἐπελάλησεν, εἰς τὸν κάμπον ἐξῆλθε. 4r
Ἔπαιζε πρῶτον τὸ σπαθίν, εἶθ᾽ οὕτως τὸ κοντάριν·
καί τινες τῶν Σαρακηνῶν ὠνείδιζον τὸν νέον:
«Ἴδε ποῖον ἐξέβαλον πρὸς τὸ μονομαχῆσαι
τὸν τρόπαια ποιήσαντα μεγάλα εἰς Συρίαν.»
155 Εἷς δέ τις τῶν Σαρακηνῶν ἀκρίτης Διλεμίτης
γαληνὰ πρὸς τὸν ἀμιρᾶν τοιόνδε λόγον ἔφη:
«Ὁρᾷς τὸ καταπτέρνισμα ἐπιδέξιον ὅπως,
σπαθίου τὴν ὑποδοχήν, γύρισμα κονταρίου;
Ταῦτα πάντα ἐμφαίνουσι πεῖράν τε καὶ ἀνδρείαν·
160 ὅρα λοιπὸν μὴ ἀμελῶς τὸ παιδίον προσκρούσῃς.»
Ἐξέβη καὶ ὁ ἀμιρᾶς εἰς φάραν καβαλλάρης·   E9
θρασύτατος ὑπάρχει γὰρ καὶ φοβερὸς τῇ θέᾳ,
τὰ ἄρματα ἀπέστιλβον ἡλιακὰς ἀκτῖνας·
κοντάριν ἐμαλάκιζε βένετον, χρυσωμένον·   E17
165 καὶ πάντες συνεξήλθασιν εἰς θέαν τοῦ πολέμου.
Ὁ φάρας ἔπαιζε τερπνῶς πάντας ὑπερεκπλήττων·
τοὺς γὰρ πόδας τοὺς τέσσαρας εἰς ἓν ἐπισυνάγων,
καθάπερ ὡς ἐν μηχανῇ, ἐκάθητο ἐκεῖσε·
ἄλλοτε δὲ ἐφαίνετο λεπτοπυκνοβαδίζων,
170 ὡς δοκεῖν μὴ περιπατεῖν ἀλλὰ χαμαὶ πετᾶσθαι.
Ὁ δ᾽ ἀμιρᾶς τερπόμενος, καθώσπερ ἐπηγγέλθη,
παρευθὺς ἐπελάλησεν, εἰς τὸν κάμπον ἐξῆλθε,   E32
κραυγάζων ὥσπερ ἀετὸς καὶ συρίζων ὡς δράκων,   E33-4
ὡς λέων ὠρυόμενος καταπιεῖν τὸν νέον.   E33
175 Ὁ δὲ τοῦτον δεξάμενος εὐθέως καὶ συντόμως,
καὶ κονταρέας δώσαντες, ἐκλάσθησαν τῶν δύο, 4v
ἑτέρου μὴ ἰσχύσαντος τὸν ἕτερον κρημνίσαι·
καὶ τὰ σπαθία σύραντες, ἔσωθεν χεῖρας δόντες
ἀλλήλους ἐσυνέκοπτον ἐπὶ πολλὰς τὰς ὥρας.
180 Τὰ ὄρη ἀντιδόνησαν, οἱ βουνοὶ βροντὰς εἶχον·   E38
τὸ αἷμα δὲ κατέρρεε τὴν γῆν ἐκείνην ὅλην.   E40
Οἱ ἵπποι ἠγανάκτησαν, πάντας ἔκπληξις εἶχεν·

149 τῷ δὲ σημείῳ Tsopanakis. 1960. 81: τὸ δὲ σημείον G φραξάμενος Legrand:
φραγξάμενος G
151 Ἔπαιζε G: ἔπαιξε Eideneier. 1970. 302
155 Διλεμίτης Mavrogordato: Διλεβίτης G
162 ὑπάρχει G: ὑπῆρχε Legrand
169 ἄλλοτε δὲ Legrand: ἄλλως τε G
171 ἐπηγγέλθη Eideneier. 1970. 302. cf. G3.189: ἐπηγγείλ^ω G ἐπεγέλα Legrand

Protecting himself on all sides with the sign of the cross,
150 he urged his horse on and went out onto the battle-field.
He brandished first his sword, then his spear,
and some of the Saracens jeered at the young man,
"See what sort of person they have sent to fight in single combat
against the man who has set up great trophies in Syria."
155 But one of the Saracens, a Dilemite frontiersman,
spoke gently as follows to the emir,
"Do you see the expert spurring,
the parrying with the sword, the wielding of the spear?
All these reveal experience and bravery.
160 See then that you are not careless in striking the youth."
    The emir went out mounted on his charger;
he was very audacious and fearsome to see,
his weapons reflected the sun's rays,
he wielded a blue gilded spear
165 and all gathered for the spectacle of war.
The charger frisked engagingly, astonishing everyone,
for it gathered its four hooves together
and stood there on one spot as if by some trick;
at other times it appeared to prance delicately
170 so that it seemed not to walk but to fly over the ground.
The emir, delighted, as the signal was given,
urged his horse on and went out on to the battle-field,
shrieking like an eagle, hissing like a serpent
and roaring like a lion, to devour the young man.
175 He faced the emir, swiftly and immediately,
and, exchanging spear-thrusts, both their weapons were broken,
neither being able to overthrow the other;
and drawing their swords and fighting hand to hand
they hacked at each other for many hours.
180 The mountains re-echoed, the hills shook with thunder
and blood flowed over all that ground.
The horses were enraged, everyone was astounded.

---

155 As with 'mustering' earlier (G1.48), a Byzantine military term, 'frontiersman', is
applied to an Arab not in Byzantine service.
168 The skills of dressage shown by the emir and his horse are such that the narrator is
forced to wonder whether he has used some mechanical trick.

14   Διγενὴς Ἀκρίτης

ὁλόπληγοι γεγόνασι, μηδεὶς τροπὴν ποιῶν τε.
  Ὡς δὲ καὶ τὸ παράδοξον Σαρακηνοὶ κατεῖδον,
185 καὶ τὸ πολὺ θαυμάσαντες τὸ πρόθυμον τοῦ νέου,
ἔνστασιν δὲ τὴν ἄπειρον καὶ τὴν γενναίαν τόλμην,
ἅπαντες πρὸς τὸν ἀμιρᾶν ὁμοφώνως ἐλάλουν·
«Ἀγάπην ἐπιζήτησον, τὸν δὲ πόλεμον ἄφες,
ὁ Ῥωμαῖος δεινός ἐστι, μή σε κακοδικήσῃ.»   E29
190 Καὶ πρὸς φυγὴν ὁ ἀμιρᾶς εὐθέως ἐξετράπη
καὶ ὁ πολλὰ καυχώμενος ἡττήθη κατὰ κράτος
(καὶ γὰρ καύχησις ἅπασα οὐκ ἀγαθὴ τυγχάνει).
Πόρρωθεν ῥίπτει τὸ σπαθίν, χεῖρας εἰς ὕψος ἄρας   E52
τοὺς δακτύλους ἐσταύρωσεν, ὡς ἦν αὐτοῖς τὸ ἔθος,   E53
195 καὶ ταύτην πρὸς τὸν ἄγουρον τὴν φωνὴν ἐπαφῆκεν·
«Παῦσαι, καλὲ νεώτερε· σὸν γάρ ἐστι τὸ νῖκος·   E55
δεῦρο λάβε τὴν ἀδελφὴν καὶ τὴν αἰχμαλωσίαν.»
  Καὶ λύσαντες τὸ θέατρον, ἀπῆλθον εἰς τὴν τένδαν·
καὶ ἦν ἰδεῖν τοὺς ἀδελφοὺς χαρμονῆς ἐμπλησθέντας.
200 Χεῖρας εἰς ὕψος ἄραντες Θεὸν δοξολογοῦσι,
«Ἡ δόξα,» πάντες λέγοντες, «σοὶ μόνῳ Θεῷ πρέπει·
ὁ γὰρ ἐλπίζων ἐπὶ σὲ οὐ μὴ καταισχυνθείη.» 5r
Τὸν ἀδελφὸν ἠσπάζοντο μετὰ περιχαρείας·
οἱ μὲν φιλοῦσι χεῖρας του, ἄλλοι τὴν κεφαλήν του.   E195
205 Τὸν δ' ἀμιρᾶν ἀμφότεροι θερμῶς παρακαλοῦσι·
«Δός, ἀμιρᾶ, τὴν ἀδελφήν, καθὼς ἡμῖν ὑπέσχου,   E61
καρδίαν παραμύθησον τὴν λύπη βαρυνθεῖσαν.»
  Ὁ ἀμιρᾶς δὲ πρὸς αὐτοὺς οὐκ ἀληθεύων ἔφη·
«Σφραγίδα λάβετε ἐμήν, γυρεύσατε τὰς τένδας,   E63
210 πανταχοῦ ἐρευνήσατε, ἴδετε τὰ φουσσᾶτα·
τὴν ἀδελφὴν γνωρίσαντες, λαβόντες πορευθῆτε.»
  Οἱ δὲ μετὰ πολλῆς χαρᾶς τὴν σφραγίδα λαβόντες,
τὸν δόλον ἀγνοήσαντες, ἐπιμελῶς ἠρεύνουν.
  Καὶ πανταχοῦ γυρεύσαντες, μηδὲν δὲ εὑρηκότες,   E66
215 λυπούμενοι ὑπέστρεφον πρὸς ἀμιρᾶν εὐθέως.
  Καὶ καθ' ὁδὸν Σαρακηνῷ ἀγροίκῳ συναντῶσιν·   E67

186 ἔνστασιν Mavrogordato: ἔκστασιν G

They were covered with wounds but no one was giving way.
When the Saracens saw this unexpected sight,
185 they were surprised by the young man's great eagerness,
his boundless energy and noble boldness,
and all said with one voice to the emir,
"Ask for a truce, abandon the battle;
the Roman is dangerous, don't let him harm you."
190 And the emir immediately turned to flight
and, though he had boasted exceedingly, he was completely defeated
(for no boasting ever achieves anything good).
He threw his sword far away and raising his hands up
he crossed his fingers, as was their custom,
195 and shouted this speech to the youngster,
"Stop, my fine young friend; victory is yours.
Here, take your sister and the prisoners."
They abandoned the spectacle and went to the tent,
and then you could see the brothers filled with joy.
200 They raised their hands up and praised God.
"Glory", they all said, "is due to you the only God;
for may he who sets his hope in you never be put to shame."
They embraced their brother with great delight,
some kissed his hands, others his head.
205 All begged the emir warmly,
"Give us our sister, emir, as you promised;
console our hearts which are weighed down with grief."
The emir said to them, not speaking the truth,
"Take my seal, go round the tents,
210 search everywhere, inspect the encampment.
When you recognize your sister, take her and be on your way."
They took his seal with great joy,
being unaware of the trick, and searched carefully.
They went round everywhere but found nothing,
215 and returned immediately in distress to the emir.
On the way they met a Saracen peasant;

---

194 At the equivalent point in E (E53) the emir shows the brother one finger, interpreted by Alexiou (1979, 35 and 1985, note) as recalling an Arab gesture of submission by the defeated, invoking the aid of the one God; G's version could either be a distortion of this or could reflect a tradition like that used in childhood games in most of Europe. Without medieval parallels it is hard to adjudicate between alternatives.

16   Διγενὴς Ἀκρίτης

ἐκεῖνος ἔφη πρὸς αὐτοὺς διὰ τοῦ δραγουμάνου:
«Τίνα ζητεῖτε, ἄγουροι, τίνος χάριν θρηνεῖτε;»
Οἱ δὲ ἀνταπεκρίθησαν λέγοντες μετὰ θρήνων:
220 «Κόρην ἠχμαλωτεύσατε ἀδελφὴν ἡμετέραν
καὶ ταύτην μὴ εὑρίσκοντες οὐ ζῆν θέλομεν ἔτι.»
Στενάξας δ᾽ ὁ Σαρακηνὸς τοιόνδε λόγον ἔφη:
«Διέλθετε εἰς τὸ ὑπαύχενον· εὑρήσετε ῥυάκιν·   E71
χθὲς ἐν αὐτῷ ἐσφάξαμεν εὐγενικὰς ὡραίας,   E72
225 διότι οὐκ ἐπείθοντο εἰς ἃ ταῖς ἐλαλοῦμεν.»   E73
Ἐλάλησαν τοὺς ἵππους των, ἀπῆλθον ᾽ς τὸ ῥυάκιν·
πολλὰς σφαμμένας εὕρηκαν εἰς τὸ αἷμα βαπτισμένας, 5v E79. 81. 87
ὧν μὲν αἱ χεῖρες ἔλειπον, κρανία τε καὶ πόδες,   E80
ὧν δὲ τὰ μέλη ἅπαντα, καὶ τὰ ἔγκατα ἔξω,
230 γνωρισθῆναι ὑπό τινος μὴ δυνάμενα ὅλως.   E85
Καὶ ταῦτα θεασάμενοι, ἔκπληξις τούτους εἶχεν
καὶ χοῦν λαβόντες ἀπὸ γῆς ταῖς κεφαλαῖς προσραίνουν, E86
ὀδυρμούς τε ἐκίνησαν καὶ θρήνους ἐκ καρδίας:
«Ποίαν χεῖρα συγκόψομεν, ποίαν κλαύσομεν κάραν;
235 Ποῖον μέλος γνωρίσαντες τῇ μητρὶ κομιοῦμεν;
Ὦ ἀδελφὴ παγκάλλιστε, πῶς ἀδίκως ἐσφάγης;
Ὦ γλυκυτάτη μας ψυχή, πῶς σοι τοῦτο συνέβη;
Πῶς δὲ παρ᾽ ὥραν ἔδυνας καὶ ἔσβεσας τὸ φῶς μας;
Πῶς κατεκόπης μεληδὸν ὑπὸ χειρὸς βαρβάρων;
240 Πῶς οὐκ ἐνάρκησεν ἡ χεὶρ τοῦ ἀσπλάγχνου φονέως,
τοῦ μὴ κατελεήσαντος σοῦ τερπνὴν ἡλικίαν,
τοῦ μὴ κατοικτειρήσαντος φωνήν σου τὴν ὡραίαν;
Ὄντως εὐγενικὴ ψυχή, διὰ τὴν ἀχρειοσύνην
ᾑρετίσω τὸν θάνατον καὶ σφαγὴν ὀλεθρίαν·
245 ἀλλ᾽, ὦ ἀδελφὴ παγκάλλιστε, ὦ ψυχὴ καὶ καρδία,
πῶς σε διαχωρίσομεν ἐκ τῶν λοιπῶν σωμάτων;
Ἕξομεν τοῦτο κἂν μικρὰν τινὰ παραμυθίαν;
Ὦ ὥρα πανδεινότατε καὶ δολία ἡμέρα,
μὴ ἴδοις ἥλιόν ποτε, μὴ φῶς σοι ἀνατείλοι·

217 δραγουμάνου Kalonaros: δρουγουμάνου G
226 ᾽ς Trapp: εἰς G
233 ὀδυρμοὺς Legrand: ὀδυρδοὺς G
243 διὰ G: παρὰ Legrand

he said to them through their interpreter,
"For whom are you looking, youngsters, for whom are you
    mourning?"
They replied, speaking with lamentations,
220 "You have taken prisoner a girl, our sister;
we have not found her, and so we no longer wish to live."
The Saracen sighed and spoke as follows,
"Go through to the lower ravine; you will find a ditch.
Yesterday we slaughtered some lovely high-born girls in it
225 because they refused to do what we told them."
    They urged their horses on, and went off to the ditch;
they found many girls slaughtered, soaked in blood;
some lacked hands, heads and feet,
others all their limbs and their entrails were on the ground;
230 no one at all could recognize them.
As the brothers gazed at them, they were overcome with shock;
they took dust from the ground and sprinkled it on their heads,
and uttered wails and lamentations from their hearts.
    "What hand shall we mourn? What head shall we weep over?
235 What limb shall we identify and bring to our mother?
Most beautiful sister, how have you been slaughtered unjustly?
Our sweetest soul, how did this happen to you?
How did your sun set before its time and extinguish our light?
How were you cut up limb from limb by barbarians' hands?
240 How was the hand of the heartless murderer not paralysed,
the murderer who did not have mercy on your delightful figure,
who did not take pity on your lovely voice?
Truly high-born soul, in place of worthlessness
you have chosen death and deadly slaughter
245 but, most beautiful sister, our heart and soul,
how shall we separate you from the other bodies?
Shall we have this as even a small comfort?
O most dreadful hour and deceitful day,
may you never see the sun, may light never dawn for you;

217 The emir speaks good Greek (G1.115; contrast E21), but the brothers, from the
Byzantine military aristocracy, have little or no Arabic and here use a translator to
address an Arabic-speaking peasant.
225 This line probably has sexual connotations (cf. the emir's protestations at G1.309),
though the brothers fear for their sister's death rather more than her potential dishonour
(cf. G1.324 and contrast E123).
234 The active of συγκόπτομαι ('beat oneself in lamentation') is unexpected and has
unfortunate connotations at this moment, but the sense is clear.

250 σκότους ἐμπλήσοι σε Θεός, ὅταν τὴν ἀδελφήν μας
  ἀνηλεῶς κατέκοπτον οἱ ἄνομοι ἀδίκως.   E171
  Ποῖον μητρὶ ἐλεεινῇ μήνυμα κομιοῦμεν;
  Ἥλιε, τί ἐφθόνησας τὸ ὡραῖον μας ἀδέλφιν, 6r
  ἀδίκως ἐθανάτωσας δι' οὗ ἀντέλαμπέ σου;»
255 Ἀλλ' ὅμως ὡς οὐκ ἴσχυσαν εὑρεῖν τὴν ἀδελφήν των,   E124
  τάφον ἕνα ποιήσαντες κατέθαψαν ἀπάσας   E125
  καὶ θρηνοῦντες ὑπέστρεφον πρὸς ἀμιρᾶν εὐθέως,   E126
  θερμὰ κινοῦντες δάκρυα ἐκ μέσης τῆς καρδίας·
  «Δός, ἀμιρᾶ, τὴν ἀδελφήν, εἰ δ' οὔ, θανάτωσόν μας·
260 οὐδεὶς ἡμῶν ἄνευ αὐτῆς ὑποστρέφει ἐν οἴκῳ
  ἀλλὰ σφαγῶμεν ἅπαντες διὰ τὴν ἀδελφήν μας.»
  Ἀκούων ταῦτα ὁ ἀμιρᾶς, ὁρῶν δὲ καὶ τοὺς θρήνους,
  ἤρξατο τούτους ἐρωτᾶν· «Τίνες ἐστὲ καὶ πόθεν;   E133
  Γένους ποίου τυγχάνετε; Ποῖον θέμα οἰκεῖτε;»   E134
265 «Ἡμεῖς ἐκ τὸ Ἀνατολικόν, ἐξ εὐγενῶν Ῥωμαίων·
  ὁ πατήρ μας κατάγεται ἀπὸ τῶν Κινναμάδων,   E137
  ἡ δὲ μήτηρ μας Δούκισσα, γένους τῶν Κωνσταντίνου·   E138
  στρατηγοὶ μὲν οὖν δώδεκα ἐξάδελφοι καὶ θεῖοι,   E139
  ἐξ οὖν ὅλοι τυγχάνομεν μετὰ τῆς αὐταδέλφης.   E139
270 Ὁ πατήρ μας ἐξόριστος διὰ τὴν τιμωρίαν,   E140
  ἣν αὐτῷ προεξένησαν τινὲς τῶν συκοφάντων.
  Οὐδεὶς ἀφ' ἡμῶν ἔτυχεν εἰς τὴν ἐπέλευσίν σου,
  καὶ γὰρ ἡμεῖς ὑπήρχομεν στρατηγοὶ εἰς τὰς ἄκρας·
  εἰ γὰρ ἐκεῖ ἐτύχομεν, οὐκ ἂν τοῦτο συνέβη,
275 οὐκ ἂν εἰς οἶκον μάς ποτε εἴχετε πορευθῆναι·
  ἀφ' οὗ δὲ οὐκ ἐτύχομεν, καλῶς νὰ τὸ καυχᾶσαι.
  Ἀλλ', ὦ ἀμιράδων μέγιστε καὶ πρῶτε τῆς Συρίας,
  νὰ προσκυνήσῃς τὸν Βαγδᾶ· εἰπὲ καὶ σὺ τίς εἶ γε. 6v
  Καὶ εἰ στραφοῦν οἱ συγγενεῖς ἀπὸ τοῦ ταξιδίου,

259 Δός Legrand: δὸς ἡμῖν G
263 Τίνες Dangitzis. 1958/9. 228: τίνος G
269 ἐξ οὖν Eideneier. 1970. 302: ἐξ ὧν G
270 τὴν τιμωρίαν Eideneier. 1970. 302: τινα μωρίαν G. cf. διὰ μούρτη E140
272 ἐπέλευσίν Legrand: ἔλευσιν G

250 may God fill you with darkness since our sister
has been unjustly and pitilessly butchered by lawless men.
What message shall we convey to our pitiable mother?
Sun, why did you envy our lovely sister
and kill her unjustly because she outshone you?"
255   But, nonetheless, as they could not find their sister,
they made one tomb and buried all the girls
and, lamenting, they returned immediately to the emir,
shedding hot tears from the depths of their hearts.
"Give us, emir, our sister, or if not, kill us:
260 not one of us returns to our house without her,
but let us all be slaughtered instead of our sister."
    On hearing this and seeing their lamentations,
the emir began to ask them, "Who are you and where do you come from?
What family do you belong to? Which theme do you live in?"
265   "We are from the Anatolikon theme, of high-born Roman stock:
our father is descended from the Kinnamades,
our mother is a Doukas, of the family of Constantine.
And so there are twelve generals, our cousins and uncles,
and we are six in all, including our sister.
270 Our father is in exile as a punishment
which some informers have contrived for him.
None of us were present at your attack,
for we were serving as generals on the frontier.
If we had been there, this would not have occurred,
275 you would never have invaded our house.
Since we were not there, you can well boast of it.
But, greatest of the emirs and first man of Syria
– may you worship in Baghdad – you must say who you are.
And if our kinsmen return from their campaign

---

259 The illogicality of this request, immediately after burying the bodies which they
believe to include their sister's, struck Lord as typical of oral narrative inconsistency
(Lord, 1960, 217).
264 The emir asks about their theme, an administrative unit in dissolution from the
eleventh century onwards, rather than, say, their city or family (as in E134).
266–7 On the background to these Anatolian clan names in the ninth to twelfth
centuries, see the Introduction, p. xxxix and the Name Index.
271 The mention of informers is consistent with the atmosphere of court politics in the
mid-twelfth century where intrigue was rife; see Magdalino, 1993a, 217–27.
278 Baghdad, capital of the Abbasid caliphate, was an administrative rather than
religious centre, unlike the places listed at G1.101–3.

280 φέρουν καὶ τὸν πατέρα μας ἀπὸ τὴν ἐξορίαν,
νά σε καταζητήσωμεν ὅπου δ᾽ ἂν καὶ τυγχάνῃς·
οὐ γὰρ ἂν ἀνεκδίκητον ἐάσομεν τὴν τόλμην.»
«Ἐγώ, καλοὶ νεώτεροι,» ὁ ἀμιρᾶς ἀντέφη,
«Χρυσοβέργου υἱός εἰμι, μητρὸς δὲ τῆς Πανθίας,
285 Ἄμβρων ὑπῆρχε μου παπποῦς, θεῖος μου ὁ Καρόης.   E145
Τέθνηκε γάρ μου ὁ πατὴρ ἔτι νηπίου ὄντος,
παρὰ μητρὸς ἐδόθην δὲ εἰς συγγενεῖς Ἀράβους,
οἵτινές με ἀνέθρεψαν εἰς Μωάμετ τὸν πόθον·
ὁρῶντες δέ με εὐτυχῆ εἰς πάντας τοὺς πολέμους
290 ἐξουσιαστὴν ἐποίησαν εἰς ὅλην τὴν Συρίαν
291 καὶ ἐκλεκτούς μοι ἔδωκαν τρισχιλίους κονταράτους.
293 Καὶ μικρόν τι καυχήσομαι πρὸς ὑμᾶς ἀληθεύων·
292 πᾶσαν Συρίαν ὑπέταξα καὶ ἐπίασα τὸ Κοῦφερ,
294 τὴν Ἡράκλειαν ὕστερον ἐξήλειψα ταχέως·
295 τὸ Ἀμόριν δὲ καταλαβὼν ἄχρι τοῦ Ἰκονίου
πλήθη λῃστῶν ὑπέταξα καὶ πάντα τὰ θηρία.
Ἐμοὶ οὐκ ἀντεστάθησαν στρατηγοί, οὐ φουσσᾶτα,   E149
γυνὴ δέ με ἐνίκησε πάνυ ὡραιοτάτη·
ταύτης τὰ κάλλη φλέγουν με, τὰ δάκρυα μαραίνουν,
300 οἱ στεναγμοὶ φλογίζουν με, τί ποιῆσαι οὐκ ἔχω.
Δι᾽ αὐτὴν ὑμᾶς ἐπείραζον ἵνα τὸ βέβαιον μάθω·
οὐδέποτε γὰρ παύεται ὑπὲρ ὑμῶν θρηνοῦσα.
Πάντως ἐξαγορεύω σας, τὴν ἀλήθειαν λέγω, 7r
εἰ οὐκ ἀπαξιώνετε τοῦ ἔχειν με γαμβρόν σας,   E162
305 διὰ τὰ κάλλη τὰ τερπνὰ τῆς ὑμῶν αὐταδέλφης   E175
νὰ γένωμαι Χριστιανὸς στραφεὶς εἰς Ῥωμανίαν.   E177
Καὶ μάθετε τὸ βέβαιον, μὰ τὸν μέγαν Προφήτην,
οὔτε φίλημά μ᾽ ἔδωκεν οὔτε τινὰ λαλίαν.   E166
Δεῦτε οὖν εἰς τὴν τένδαν μου· ἴδετε ἣν ζητεῖτε.»   E169
310 Ἐκεῖνοι ταῦτα ὡς ἤκουσαν, ἀπὸ περιχαρείας
τὴν τένδαν ἀνεσήκωσαν καὶ ἔσωθεν εἰσῆλθον·
εὗρον κλίνην χρυσόστρωτον, χαμαὶ δὲ τὸ κορίτζιν.   E179-80

288 εἰς Μωάμετ τὸν πόθον Trapp (cf. Z483 εἰς Μωάμετ τὸν πόθον Sathas-Legrand
from εἰς ἀμετμὲ τοῦ πόθου): εἰς τὸ εὖ μετὰ πόθου G
291, 293, 292 rearranged thus by Eideneier, 1970, 303
292 Κοῦφερ Legrand: Κοῦφε G
299 ταύτης Legrand: ταύτην G
304 εἰ Legrand: ἢ G

280 and bring our father back from exile,
     we shall seek you out wherever you are.
     We shall not let your boldness pass unavenged."
        "I, my fine young friends," the emir replied,
     "I am the son of Chrysovergis, and Panthia was my mother,
285 Ambron was my grandfather, Karoïs my uncle.
     My father died while I was still a little child
     and I was given by my mother to Arab kinsmen,
     who brought me up in the love of Mohammed.
     When they saw that I was fortunate in all wars,
290 they set me in authority over the whole of Syria,
     and they gave me three thousand picked spearsmen.
     I shall boast a little to you in speaking the truth:
     I subdued all Syria and I captured Kufah,
     then I swiftly wiped out Herakleia.
295 Coming past Amorion as far as Ikonion,
     I subdued hosts of brigands and all wild beasts.
     The generals could not withstand me, nor the armies,
     but a most lovely woman has completely conquered me.
     Her beauty enflames me, her tears are wasting me away,
300 her sighs torture me; I don't know what to do.
     Because of her I was testing you, to know for certain,
     for she never stops lamenting for you.
     However, I declare to you and I tell you the truth,
     if you do not reject having me as a brother-in-law,
305 because of the delightful beauty of your sister
     I shall come over to Roman territory and become a Christian.
     And know this for certain, by the great Prophet,
     she has given me neither a kiss nor a word.
     Come, then, to my tent and see the girl you are looking for."
310   When they heard this, with great joy
     they lifted up the tent-flap and went inside.
     They found a couch draped with gold, and on it the girl.

284–5 These lines refer to the Paulicians, one of several Arab leaders and the novels of late antiquity; see the Introduction, pp. xxxiv–xxxviii and Name Index.

295 This sequence of cities is geographically illogical: E's list of Herakleia, Ikonion and Amorion (E732) gives the south-north thrust of Arab incursions.

296 The emir's military raid surprisingly reflects Digenis' later heroic activities – hunting and putting down brigands.

Ὡς ἔκειτο, Χριστέ, ἐκεῖ, ἔλαμπεν ὡς ἀκτῖνες·   *E183–4*
οἱ ὀφθαλμοὶ κατάβροχοι ἦσαν ἐκ τῶν δακρύων.
315 Ἢν ἰδόντες οἱ ἀδελφοὶ ἀνέστησαν σπουδαίως
καὶ ταύτην μετ᾽ ἐκπλήξεως ἕκαστος κατεφίλει·
ἀπροσδοκήτου γὰρ χαρᾶς ἐλθούσης παρ᾽ ἐλπίδα,
χαίρονται πάντες οἱ αὐτῆς τυχόντες ἀνελπίστως.
Ὁμοῦ θλῖψιν ὑπέφερον, τὰ δάκρυα καὶ πόνους
320 καὶ χαρὰν τὴν πανθαύμαστον τὴν τότε γεναμένην.
Ὡς δὲ ταύτην ἠσπάζοντο μετὰ περιχαρείας,
καὶ δάκρυα προσέβαλλον ποιοῦντες μέγα θρῆνον
καὶ «Ζῆς,» ἔλεγον, «ἀδελφή, ζῆς, ψυχὴ καὶ καρδία.
Ἡμεῖς θανοῦσαν σε εἴχομεν καὶ σπαθοκοπημένην,   *E190*
325 ἀλλ᾽ οὖν τὰ κάλλη ζῶσαν σε ἐτήρησαν, φιλτάτη·
τὰ κάλλη γὰρ καὶ τοὺς ληστὰς ἡμέρους ἐκποιοῦσι
καὶ πολεμίους φείδεσθαι νεότητος καὶ κάλλους.»
Εἶθ᾽ οὕτως βεβαιώσαντες τὸν ἀμιρᾶν μεθ᾽ ὅρκου
γαμβρὸν ἵνα τὸν λάβωσιν, ἂν ἔλθῃ εἰς Ῥωμανίαν, 7v   *E197–8*
330 τὰ βούκινα ἐδώκασιν, ὑπέστρεφον εὐθέως.
Καὶ πάντες ἐξεπλήσσοντο λέγοντες πρὸς ἀλλήλους:
«Ὢ θαῦμα ὅπερ βλέπομεν, δύναμις τῶν Ῥωμαίων,
αἰχμάλωτα ἀναρρύουσι, φουσσᾶτα καταλύουν,
πίστιν ἀρνεῖσθαι πείθουσι, θάνατον μὴ φοβεῖσθαι.»
335 Καὶ ἀκουστὸν ἐγένετο εἰς τὸν σύμπαντα κόσμον   *E213*
ὅτι κόρη πανεύγενος μὲ τὰ τερπνά της κάλλη   *E214*
φουσσᾶτα ἐκατέλυσε περίφημα Συρίας.   *E214*

322 μέγα θρῆνον Eideneier, 1970, 303, cf. Z515: μετὰ θρήνων G
332 Ῥωμαίων G: ἐρώτων Mavrogordato (cf. Z527)
333 ἀναρρύουσι Tsopanakis, 1960, 81, cf. Z528, G 1.78, 2.18 etc: ἀναλύουσι G

As she lay there, o Christ, she gleamed like beams of light.
Her eyes were drenched with tears.
315 When they saw her, her brothers came up eagerly
and each kissed her with astonishment,
for when unexpected joy comes contrary to hope
all who share in it rejoice at their unforeseen happiness.
At the same time they experienced grief, tears and anguish
320 and the quite marvellous joy which had then arisen.
As they embraced her with great joy
they shed tears with a great lament
and said, "You are alive, sister, you are alive, our soul and heart.
We thought you were dead and hacked by a sword
325 but your beauty, dearest, has kept you alive;
for beauty makes even brigands gentle
and makes enemies spare youth and beauty."
    Then, assuring the emir with an oath
that they would accept him as a brother-in-law if he came to
    Roman territory,
330 they sounded the trumpets, and immediately set off home.
And everyone was amazed, saying to each other,
"We see a miracle! the power of the Romans!
They rescue prisoners, they break up armies,
they persuade people to renounce their faith, and to have no fear of
    death."
335   And it became well known throughout the whole world
that an exceedingly high-born girl, with her delightful beauty,
had broken up the famed armies of Syria.

---

313 The narrator is so moved by the sight he describes that he calls on Christ's name.
328–9 Their sister's consent is apparently not asked but her family can use marriage to
remove the taint of her abduction since it took place by force in time of war (Laiou, 1993,
210).

Περὶ τῆς γεννήσεως τοῦ Ἀκρίτου· λόγος δεύτερος

Ἐπειδὴ ὅρκους προύβάλλοντο γαμβρὸν νὰ τὸν ἐπάρουν,
ἐπῆρε τοὺς ἀγούρους του ὁ ἀμιρᾶς εὐθέως·
εἰς Ῥωμανίαν ὑπέστρεφε διὰ τὴν ποθητήν του.
Ὅταν δὲ κατελάμβανε μέρη τῆς Ῥωμανίας, ·
5 ἠλευθέρωνεν ἅπαντας οὓς εἶχεν αἰχμαλώτους,
ἑκάστῳ δοὺς ἐφόδια εἰς τὴν ὁδὸν ἀρκοῦντα.
Οἱ δὲ τῆς κόρης ἀδελφοὶ τῇ μητρὶ πάντα γράφουν,
τῆς ἀδελφῆς τὴν εὕρεσιν, τοῦ ἀμιρᾶ τὸν πόθον,
τὸ πῶς πίστιν ἠρνήσατο, συγγενεῖς καὶ πατρίδα·   E363
10 καὶ «Ὦ μῆτερ παμπόθητε, μή τινα θλῖψιν ἔχῃς·
γαμβρὸν <γὰρ> ἔχειν θέλομεν πάγκαλον καὶ ὡραῖον·
τὴν χρείαν δὲ ἑτοίμασον ἅπασαν τὴν τοῦ γάμου.»
Ἡ δὲ ταῦτα ἀκούσασα τῷ Θεῷ ηὐχαρίστει,
«Δόξα, Χριστέ μου,» λέγουσα, «τῇ σῇ φιλανθρωπίᾳ,
15 δόξα τῇ δυναστείᾳ σου, ἐλπὶς τῶν ἀνελπίστων·
ὅσα γὰρ θέλεις δύνασαι, οὐδὲν ἀδυνατεῖ σοι. 8r   E1860
Αὐτὸν γὰρ τὸν πολέμιον ἥμερον κατειργάσω
καὶ θυγατέρα τὴν ἐμὴν ἐρρύσω ἐκ θανάτου.
Ἀλλ', ὦ θύγατερ ποθεινή, φῶς τῶν ἐμῶν ὀμμάτων,
20 πότε σε ζῶσαν ὄψομαι, φωνῆς τῆς σῆς ἀκούσω;
Ἰδοὺ καὶ γάμον γὰρ τὸν σὸν ηὐτρέπισα καὶ χρείαν.
Ἆρα νυμφίος ἔσται σοι παρόμοιος τοῦ κάλλους;
Ἆρα τὴν γνώμην θέλει σχεῖν τῶν εὐγενῶν Ῥωμαίων;
Φοβοῦμαι, τέκνον μου καλόν, μὴ ἄστοργος ὑπάρχῃ,
25 μὴ θυμώδης ὡς ἐθνικός, καὶ ζῆν με οὐ συμφέρῃ.»

10 ἔχῃς G in margin and ἐξ εἰς in text
11 γὰρ added by Legrand
25 με G: σε Trapp

The second book, concerning the birth of the Frontiersman

Since they gave oaths that they would accept him as a brother-in-law,
the emir immediately took his youngsters
and returned to Roman territory, for the sake of his beloved.
When he reached the area of Roman territory,
5 he set free all those whom he had taken prisoner,
giving each sufficient provisions for the journey.
    The girl's brothers wrote everything to their mother,
the finding of the girl, the emir's desire,
how he had renounced his faith, his kinsmen and his country,
10 saying, "Much beloved mother, do not be distressed,
for we shall have a very good-looking and handsome brother-in-law.
Prepare all that is required for the wedding."
    When she heard this, she gave thanks to God,
saying, "Thanks be to your benevolence, Christ,
15 thanks be to your might, hope of the hopeless;
you can accomplish whatever you wish, nothing is impossible for you.
For you have made this enemy gentle,
and you have rescued my daughter from death.
But, my longed-for daughter, light of my eyes,
20 when shall I see you alive, when shall I hear your voice?
See, I have prepared your wedding and what is required.
Will the bridegroom be your equal in beauty?
Will he share the views of high-born Romans?
I fear, my lovely child, that he may be lacking in affection,
25 being a heathen, he may have a fierce temper, and there may be no
    point in my living."

The title does not accurately represent the contents of the book, which is concerned more
with the emir's journey to his mother. The equivalent material in E appears at
E218–483.
11 The insistence on good looks reflects racial prejudice (cf. G1.32, 2.22 and 2.36;
Magdalino, 1989, 193) and the twelfth-century aristocracy's concern that physical
beauty was necessary for an appropriate marriage (cf. G4.940; Laiou, 1992, 94–6).
25 This comment is perhaps an indication of the realities of life in an extended family on
a Cappadocian estate; on such households see Magdalino, 1984, 98–9.

Ταῦτα μὲν ἡ στρατήγισσα χαίρουσα ἐμελῴδει.
Ὁ δ᾽ ἀμιρᾶς καὶ μετ᾽ αὐτοῦ οἱ ἀδελφοὶ τῆς κόρης
χαίροντες ἄμφω τῆς ὁδοῦ ἤρχοντο μετὰ μόχθου·
ἡνίκα δ᾽ ἐπλησίασαν εἰς τὸν ἴδιον οἶκον,
30 λαὸς πολὺς καὶ συγγενεῖς εἰς ἀπαντὴν ἐξῆλθον,
εἶθ᾽ οὕτως ἡ στρατήγισσα μετὰ δόξης μεγάλης.
Τὴν δὲ χαρὰν τὴν ἄπειρον τὴν τότε γιναμένην
τίς φράσαι ὅλως δυνηθῇ ἢ ὅλως παρεικάσαι;
Τὰ τέκνα γὰρ ἠσπάζοντο μητέρα μετὰ πόθου
35 καὶ ἡ μήτηρ εὐφραίνετο ἀληθῶς ἐπὶ τέκνοις·
ἰδοῦσα δὲ καὶ τὸν γαμβρὸν περικαλλῆ τῷ ὄντι
χάριν Θεῷ ἀνέπεμψεν ἐξ ὅλης τῆς καρδίας,
«Κύριε,» λέγουσα, «Χριστέ, πᾶς ὁ εἰς σὲ ἐλπίζων
οὐκ ἀπέτυχε πώποτε τῶν ἐπιθυμουμένων.»
40 Εἰς δὲ τὸν οἶκον φθάσαντες ἐποίησαν τοὺς γάμους
καὶ τῷ θείῳ βαπτίσματι τὸν γαμβρὸν τελειοῦσι. 8v
Ἡ δὲ χαρὰ ἐπηύξανε ἡ πάνδημος ἐκείνη·
ἔχαιρε γὰρ ὁ ἀμιρᾶς τυχὼν τῆς ἐρωμένης·
οὐ γάρ ἐστιν ἐρωτικῆς ἀγάπης χαρὰ κρείττων
45 (ὅσον φλέγεται ὁ ἐρῶν ἐπὶ ἀποτυχίᾳ
τοσοῦτον χαίρει ὁ ἐρῶν τυχὼν τῆς ἐρωμένης).
Μετὰ δὲ τὴν συνάφειαν συνέλαβεν ἡ κόρη
καὶ ἔτεκε τὸν Διγενῆ Βασίλειον Ἀκρίτην·   E219
ἔτι δὲ μᾶλλον ηὔξανε τοῦ ἀμιρᾶ ὁ πόθος.
50 Ἡ δὲ μήτηρ τοῦ ἀμιρᾶ γραφὴν ἀπὸ Συρίας   E226
θρήνου μεστὴν ἐξέπεμψεν, ὀνειδισμοῦ καὶ ψόγου: E227
53 «Ὦ τέκνον ποθεινότατον, πῶς μητρὸς ἐπελάθου,   E228

---

28 ἄμφω G: ἅμα Legrand, cf. Z560
36 περικαλλῆ Legrand: περιχαρῆ G περιχαρῆς Mavrogordato
44 οὐ γάρ ἐστιν Legrand: οὐδὲ γὰρ ἐστὶν G
53, 52 reversed by Trapp, cf. Z596–8

This is what the general's lady sang as she rejoiced.
  The emir and with him the girl's brothers,
all rejoicing, set off on their way wearily.
When they came near their own house
30 a great retinue and their kinsmen came out to greet them,
then so did the general's lady with great magnificence.
The boundless joy that arose then,
who can describe it completely or picture it completely?
For the children embraced their mother with fervour,
35 and the mother rejoiced truly in her children;
and seeing that her son-in-law was exceedingly handsome,
she gave thanks to God with all her heart,
saying, "Lord Christ, no one whose hope is in you
has ever failed to achieve what they desire."
40   When they reached the house, they celebrated the wedding
and administered holy baptism to the son-in-law.
The universal joy grew and grew,
for the emir rejoiced since he had won his beloved;
for there is no joy greater than passionate love
45 (and the more the lover is enflamed by lack of success,
the more he rejoices when he wins his beloved).
    After the union the girl conceived
and bore Basil Digenis Akritis, the Frontiersman of Double Descent,
and the emir's desire increased yet more.
50   But the emir's mother sent a letter from Syria,
full of lamentation, reproach and blame:
53 "Most beloved child, how could you have forgotten your mother,

---

26 The words of the general's lady just given contain more doubts than rejoicing, and hardly seem appropriate for song. Is this a clue to some stage in the performance history of the poem, or does it perhaps result from awkwardly juxtaposed material from oral sources?

30 The retinue and the throng of supporting kinsmen are elements in an aristocratic house necessary to maintain prestige: cf. Magdalino, 1989, 195.

40, 42 These verses are repeated in subsequent marriages in the poem (G3.25, 3.334, 4.932). The general's wife makes the arrangements since the general remains absent, presumably still in exile or on campaign (cf. G1.63, 1.270 above). This could be derived from a surviving oral story, or an indication that mixed-race marriage is easier to imagine in the absence of senior males from the previous generation. The emir's father too is dead.

48 As at E219, the poem's hero is introduced with all his mature heroic names, without explanation and with an apparent assumption that they are familiar to the audience. Since it is not clear whether 'Digenis Akritis' is a name or a title it has been translated here (and elsewhere).

52 τὰ ὀμμάτια μου ἐτύφλωσας καὶ ἔσβεσας τὸ φῶς μου;   E229
   Πῶς ἀπηρνήσω συγγενεῖς καὶ πίστιν καὶ πατρίδα
55 καὶ ἐγενήθης ὄνειδος εἰς πᾶσαν τὴν Συρίαν;   E230
   Βδελυκτοὶ δὲ γεγόναμεν ἀπὸ παντὸς ἀνθρώπου
   ὡς ἀρνηταὶ τῆς πίστεως, ὡς παραβάται νόμου,
   ὡς μὴ τηρήσαντες καλῶς τοὺς λόγους τοῦ Προφήτου.
   Τί συνέβη σοι, τέκνον μου, πῶς αὐτῶν ἐπελάθου;
60 Πῶς γὰρ οὐκ ἐμνημόνευσας τὰς πράξεις τοῦ πατρός σου,   E254
   ὅσους Ῥωμαίους ἔσφαξε, πόσους ἔφερε δούλους;   E255
   Οὐκ ἐγέμισε φυλακὰς στρατηγῶν καὶ τοπάρχων;   E256
   Οὐκ ἐκούρσευσε θέματα πολλὰ τῆς Ῥωμανίας
   καὶ αἰχμαλώτους ἔφερεν εὐγενικὰς ὡραίας;
65 Μὴ ἐπλανήθη ὥσπερ σὺ γενέσθαι παραβάτης;
   Ὅταν γὰρ τὸν ἐκύκλωσαν φουσσᾶτα τῶν Ῥωμαίων,
   οἱ στρατηγοί τον ὤμνυον ὅρκους φρικωδεστάτους 9r
   πατρίκιος νὰ τιμηθῇ παρὰ τοῦ βασιλέως,
   νὰ γένῃ πρωτοστράτορας, ἂν ῥίψῃ τὸ σπαθίν του.
70 Ἀλλ᾽ ἐκεῖνος προστάγματα φυλάττων τοῦ Προφήτου
   δόξης μὲν κατεφρόνησε, πλοῦτον δὲ οὐ προσέσχε·
   καὶ μελῃδόν τον ἔκοψαν καὶ ἀπῆραν τὸ σπαθίν του.
   Σὺ δὲ ἀνάγκην μὴ εἰδὼς πάντα ὁμοῦ παρεῖδες,
   τὴν πίστιν μέν, τοὺς συγγενεῖς κἀμὲ τὴν σὴν μητέρα.
75 Ὁ ἀδελφός μου, ὁ θεῖος σου, ὁ Μουρσῆς ὁ Καρόης   E261
   εἰς Σμύρνην ἐταξίδευσεν εἰς τὸ παραθαλάσσιν,
   τὴν Ἄγκυραν ἐκούρσευσε, τὴν Ἄβυδον τὴν πόλιν,
   τὴν Ἀφρικήν, τὴν Τάρανταν, καὶ τὴν Ἑξακωμίαν
   καὶ ταῦτα τροπωσάμενος ἐστράφη εἰς Συρίαν.
80 Σὺ δὲ ὁ δυστυχέστατος ἐποίησας ταξίδιν·
   ὅταν ἤθελες δοξασθῆν παρ᾽ ὅλην τὴν Συρίαν,   E252
   τὰ πάντα προσαπώλεσας δι᾽ ἀγάπην χανζυρίσσης   E269
   καὶ κατάρατος γέγονας εἰς πάντα μασγιδίον.

---

62 τοπάρχων G: τρομάρχων Oikonomidès. 1979. 384
69 πρωτοστράτορας Legrand: πρωτοστάτωρας G
72 τὸ Legrand: τὸν G
76 εἰς Σμύρνην Legrand: εἰς μύρνην G
78 Ἀφρικήν G: Τεφρικήν Karolidis. 1905/6. 227   Τάρανταν Mavrogordato: Τέρενταν G

52 blinded my eyes and extinguished my light?
How could you renounce your kinsmen and faith and country
55 and become a reproach to all Syria?
We are abominated by all men
as deniers of the faith, as law-breakers
and for not having observed well the Prophet's words.
What has happened to you, my child? How have you forgotten these
    things?
60 How could you not remember your father's deeds,
how many Romans he slew, how many he carried off as slaves?
Did he not fill prisons with generals and toparchs?
Did he not plunder many of the themes in Roman territory
and carry off beautiful high-born girls as prisoners?
65 Was he not pressured, like you, to become a renegade?
For when the Roman armies encircled him,
the generals swore him most terrible oaths
that he would be honoured as a patrikios by the emperor
and become a protostrator, if he were to throw down his sword.
70 But he kept the Prophet's commandments,
spurned renown and paid no attention to wealth,
and they hewed him limb from limb and took away his sword.
But you, not even under compulsion, have abandoned everything at
    once,
your faith, your kinsmen and me, your mother.
75 My brother, your uncle, Moursis Karoïs,
made an expedition to Smyrna, to the sea-board;
he plundered Ankyra, the city of Abydos,
Aphrike, Taranta and Hexakomia,
and when he had won these victories he returned to Syria.
80 You too, most miserable man, have made a campaign.
When you were about to be honoured by all Syria,
you destroyed everything for the love of a pig-eater
and have become accursed in every mosque.

52–98 Cf. E228–91. Here the emir's mother's letter gives the Arab point of view with an aristocratic dignity equal to the Christian: the emir's betrayal of faith and family is firmly censured.
69 On these titles see the Introduction, pp. xxxviii–xxxix.
75–9 The reference appears to be to the expeditions of the Paulicians Chrysocheir and Karbeas, as listed in, e.g., Genesios 4.35–7 or Theophanes Continuatus 4.16, 5.37–45; see the Introduction, pp. xxxiv–xxxvii.
78 The emir's uncle, like his father and uncle at E258, is envisaged as having made a broad sweep across Asia Minor.

30   Διγενὴς Ἀκρίτης

Εἰ μὴ παρέλθῃς γὰρ ταχὺ καὶ ἔλθῃς εἰς Συρίαν,
85 οἱ ἀμιρᾶδες βούλονται ἐμὲ ν' ἀποταμήσουν,   E286
τὰ τέκνα σου νὰ σφάξωσιν ὡς πατρὸς ἀποστάτου,   E286
τὰ τερπνά σου κοράσια νὰ παραδώσουν ἄλλοις,   E287
ἃ καὶ στενάζουν διὰ σέ, ὑπομονὴν οὐκ ἔχουν.
Ὦ τέκνον μου γλυκύτατον, οἰκτείρησον μητέρα·
90 μὴ καταγάγῃς γῆρας μου εἰς Ἅδου μετὰ λύπης
καὶ μὴ θελήσῃς τέκνα σου τοῦ σφαγῆναι ἀδίκως,
μηδὲ παρίδῃς δάκρυα τερπνῶν σου κορασίων 9v
καὶ ἐκδαφίσῃ σε Θεὸς ὁ μέγας ἐκ τοῦ κόσμου.
Ἰδοὺ ἔστειλά σοι, ὡς ὁρᾷς, ἐπίλεκτα φαρία·   E275
95 τὴν βάδεαν καβαλλίκευε, παράσυρε τὴν μαύρην,   E279–80
ἡ δαγάλ' ἃς ἀκολουθῇ, καὶ οὐδεὶς οὐ μή σε φθάσῃ.
Λάβε καὶ τὴν Ῥωμάϊσσαν, εἰ δι' αὐτὴν λυπεῖσαι·
εἰ δὲ καὶ παρακούσῃς μου, ἔσῃ κατηραμένος.»   E291
Λαβόντες δὲ τὰ γράμματα ἐκλεκτοὶ Ἀραβῖται
100 διὰ πολλῆς ταχύτητος ἦλθον εἰς Ῥωμανίαν.   E292
Ἦν δέ τις οἴκου μήκοθεν τόπος ἡ Λακκοπέτρα·
ἐκεῖσε ἡμπλικεύσασι τοῦ μὴ φανερωθῆναι,   E293
οἳ καὶ τούτῳ ἐδήλωσαν διὰ γραμματηφόρου:
«Τὸ φέγγος λάμπει ὁλονυκτί, ὁδεύσωμεν, εἰ βούλει.»   E297
105   Ὡς δὲ εἶδεν ὁ ἀμιρᾶς τὴν γραφὴν τῆς μητρός του,
ἐσπλαγχνίσθη κατὰ πολὺ ὡς υἱὸς τὴν μητέρα,
τὰ τέκνα κατηλέησε καὶ τὰς αὐτῶν μητέρας.
Ζῆλος ἀνήφθη εἰς αὐτὸν εἰ περιλάβουν ἄλλους·   E287
οὐ γάρ ποτε λανθάνεται ἀρχαιότερος πόθος·
110 τοῦτον δὲ κατημαύρωσεν ἡ ἀγάπη τῆς κόρης·
πόνος γὰρ ὁ σφοδρότερος ἀμαυροῖ τὸν ἐλάσσω.
Καὶ ἵστατο διαπορῶν τί θέλων διαπρᾶξαι.
Εἰς τὸ κουβοῦκλιν δ' εἰσελθὼν λέγει τὴν ποθητήν του:
«Λόγον τινὰ ἀπόκρυφον βούλομαί σοι θαρρῆσαι
115 ἀλλὰ φοβοῦμαι, πάντερπνε, μὴ οὐκ ἔνι εἰς ἀρεστόν σου·
ἰδοὺ καιρὸς ἐφέστηκε τὸ βέβαιον νὰ μάθω,
ἐὰν ἀγάπην εἰς ἐμὲ ἔχῃς καθαρωτάτην.»
Ἡ δὲ ταῦτα ἀκούσασα ἐδήχθη τὴν καρδίαν 10r

85 ν' ἀποταμήσουν Tsopanakis, 1960, 82: νὰ ποταμίσουν G, Prombonas, 1985, 215
νὰ ποταμήσουν Legrand ν' ἀποτομήσουν Kalonaros ν' ἀποτομίσουν Trapp
101 οἴκου Mavrogordato: οἶκος G
109 ἀρχαιότερος πόθος Trapp, cf. Z659: ἀρχὴ ἑτέρου πόθου G
111 σφοδρότερος Trapp, cf. Z661: σφοδρότατος G
112 τί θέλων Eideneier, 1970, 304, cf. Z662: θέλων τι G

If you do not leave quickly and come to Syria,
85 the emirs intend to behead me,
and kill your children since their father is a rebel,
and to give to others your delightful girls,
who are lamenting for you and are losing patience.
My sweetest child, pity your mother:
90 do not send me in my old age to Hades in sorrow,
do not allow your children to be slain unjustly,
do not ignore the tears of your delightful girls
and let God in his greatness remove you from the world.
Look, I have sent you, as you see, choice horses.
95 Mount the chestnut, lead the black,
let the bay follow and no one will catch you.
Bring the Roman girl too, if you are upset because of her,
but if you disobey me, may you be accursed."
    Picked Arabs took the letter
100 and came with great speed to Roman territory.
There was a place, Lakkopetra, far from the house.
They encamped there, so as not to be seen,
and told the emir by means of the letter-carrier:
"There is moonlight shining all night, let us make our journey if you
    wish."
105   When the emir saw his mother's letter,
he was filled greatly with the compassion a son feels for his mother,
he pitied his children and their mothers.
Jealousy seized him, should they embrace others,
for a former passion is never forgotten
110 though love of the girl had quite blotted it out,
for the more intense pain blots out the lesser.
And he was left wondering what he was to do.
    Going into their chamber, he said to his beloved,
"I wish to entrust some secret information to you,
115 but I am afraid, my dearest, that it may not be to your liking.
See, the time has come for me to know for certain
if the love you have for me is quite pure."
    When she heard this, she was pierced to the heart

88 Mention of wives and children (cf. E240) is at variance with the picture of the emir's
devotion to Digenis' mother at the beginning of Book I, implying an idealised first love.

32   Διγενὴς Ἀκρίτης

καὶ στενάξασα βύθιον τοιόνδε λόγον λέγει:
120 «Ἴω ἄνερ μου γλυκύτατε, αὐθέντα καὶ προστάτα,
πότε λόγον σου ἤκουσα μὴ οὐκ ἔνι εἰς ἀρεστόν μου;
Ποία δέ γε περίστασις χωρίσει με σοῦ πόθου;
Πάντως κἂν δέῃ με θανεῖν, οὐκ ἀπαρνήσομαί σε·
οἶδε γὰρ ἡ περίστασις φιλίαν δοκιμάζειν.»
125 «Οὐ πρὸς θάνατον, φίλτατε,» ὁ ἀμιρᾶς ἀντέφη,
«τὸ δοκεῖς καὶ βουλεύεσαι μὴ γένοιτο, ψυχή μου.
Ἀλλὰ μητρὸς ἀπέλαβον γραφὴν ἀπὸ Συρίας   E307
καὶ κινδυνεύει δι' ἐμέ, βούλομαι δὲ ὑπάγειν.
Ἐὰν καὶ σύ, ψυχίτζα μου, ἔρχεσαι μετ' ἐμέναν
130 (οὐ θέλω χωρισθῆναι σοι οὐδὲ πρὸς ὥραν μίαν),
καὶ πάλιν ὑποστρέψομεν διὰ πολλοῦ τοῦ τάχους.»   E449
«Μετὰ χαρᾶς, ὦ κύρκα μου,» ἡ κόρη ἀπεκρίθη,
«τούτου χάριν μὴ θλίβεσαι· ὅπου κελεύεις ἔλθω.»   E1101
Θεὸς δέ τι θαυματουργῶν παράδοξον ἐνταῦθα
135 καὶ τὸ κρύφιον βούλευμα κατ' ὄναρ εἰς φῶς ἄγει.
Ὁ γὰρ ὕστερος ἀδελφὸς τῆς κόρης ὄναρ εἶδεν   E318
καὶ ἐκ τοῦ ὕπνου ἀναστάς, τοὺς ἀδελφοὺς καλέσας,
τὸ ὄναρ διηγήσατο τῆς νυκτὸς ὅπερ εἶδεν.
«Ἤμην καθήμενος,» φησίν, «ἐπάνω ἐν τῷ οἴκῳ,
140 καὶ ἱέρακας ἔβλεπον ἐπὶ τὴν Λακκοπέτραν   E321
καὶ φάλκωνα πολεμικὸν διώκων περιστέραν·   E323
ὡς δὲ ταύτην ἐδίωκε καὶ τελείωσιν εἶχεν,
ἀμφότεροι εἰσήλθοσαν ἔνδον τοῦ κουβουκλίου,   E322
ἔνθα διάγει ὁ γαμβρὸς μετὰ τῆς αὐταδέλφης.
145 Συντόμως ἐξεπήδησα, ἔδραμον νὰ τὴν πιάσω· 10v   E324
συνεταράχθη μου ἡ ψυχή, ἔξυπνος ἐγενόμην.»   E325
Τότε ὁ πρῶτος ἀδελφὸς τὸ ὅραμα συγκρίνει: E326
«Ἱέρακες, ὡς λέγουσιν, ἄνδρες ἅρπαγες εἶναι,   E327
φάλκωνα δὲ ὃν ἔβλεπες, φοβοῦμαι τὸν γαμβρόν μας   E328
150 περιστερὰν τὴν ἀδελφὴν μήπως την ἀδικήσῃ·   E329
ἀλλ' ἂς ἀπέλθωμεν ἐκεῖ ἔνθα τὸ ὄναρ εἶδες,   E331
ἔνθα καὶ τοὺς ἱέρακας ἔβλεπες πετωμένους.»   E321
Καβαλλικεύουν παρευθύς, ἀπῆγον εἰς τὴν πέτραν,   E332
τοὺς Ἀραβίτας ηὗρηκαν μετὰ καὶ τῶν φαρίων·   E333

121 πότε λόγον σου Kalonaros, cf. Z673: ποτὲ λόγον οὐκ G μου Legrand: σου G

and, sighing deeply, spoke as follows:
120 "My most sweet husband, my lord and defender,
when have I heard any word from you that is not to my liking?
What circumstances will separate me from your desire?
Indeed, even if I have to die, I shall not renounce you,
for circumstances are a test of affection."
125   "No question of death, dearest," the emir replied,
"may what you expect and decide never happen, my soul.
But I have received a letter from my mother in Syria,
and she is in danger because of me, so I wish to go.
If you, my dear soul, come with me
130 (I do not wish to be separated from you even for one hour),
we shall also return once more with great speed."
    "With pleasure, my sweetheart," the girl replied,
"do not grieve because of this, I will go wherever you command."
    But God performed an unexpected wonder
135 and brought the secret plan to light through a dream.
For the girl's youngest brother had a dream,
and on rising from sleep called his brothers
and told them the dream he had had in the night.
    "I was seated," he said, "up in the house,
140 and I was watching hawks at Lakkopetra,
and a fierce falcon pursuing a dove.
As he pursued it and neared success,
both came into the chamber
where our brother-in-law lives with our sister.
145 Suddenly I leapt up and ran to seize her;
my soul was troubled and I woke from sleep."
    Then the eldest brother interpreted the vision:
"Hawks, so they say, stand for abductors,
and as for the falcon whom you saw, I fear that our brother-in-law
150 might do some harm to the dove, our sister.
But let us go to where you had your dream,
where you saw the hawks flying."
    They mounted immediately and went to the rock,
and found the Arabs with the horses.

---

149 The very loose syntax in the transition from falcon to brother-in-law suggests that a line may have fallen out (cf. Z724–5).
151–2 The brothers visit the place seen in the dream, not the site of the dream.

34   Διγενής Ἀκρίτης

155 ἰδόντες δ' ἐξεπλάγησαν, τὸ ὅραμα θαυμάζουν,
«Καλῶς ἤλθετε,» λέγοντες, «ἄγουροι τοῦ γαμβροῦ μας,   E335
πῶς ὧδε ἠμπλικεύσατε τὸν οἶκον μας ἀφέντες;»
Οἱ δέ γε μὴ δυνάμενοι ἀντειπεῖν ὡμολόγουν
τὸ βέβαιον ἐκφαίνοντες, οὐδὲν δὲ ἀπεκρύβη·
160 φόβος γὰρ ἀπροσδόκητος ἀληθείας ἐκφέρει,
ὁ δέ γε προσδοκώμενος γεννᾷ ἀπολογίας.
Οὓς παρευθὺς λαβόμενοι εἰς τὸν γαμβρὸν ἀπῆλθον,
κατονειδίζοντες αὐτὸν ὡς κακόβουλον ὄντα·
μᾶλλον δὲ καὶ ὁ ὕστερος θρασύτατος ὑπάρχων
165 «Τὸ ἐνεθυμήθης,» ἔλεγε, «μὴ τὸ ἀποδοκιμάσῃς,
καὶ γίνωσκε, Σαρακηνέ, οὐ μὴ ἴδῃς τὴν Συρίαν·   E349
ἀλλ' ἐπειδὴ παράνομος καὶ ἐχθρὸς ἀπεφάνθης,
τὴν ἀδελφήν μας ἔασον, τὸ τέκνον σου ἀρνήσου,   E346
καὶ λαβὼν ἅπερ ἔφερες, πορεύου ὅθεν ἦλθες.»   E345
170 Ἀκούων ταῦτα ὁ ἀμιρᾶς καὶ τοὺς ἐλέγχους βλέπων,   E350
μὴ δυνάμενος ἀντειπεῖν παντελῶς ἐσιώπα, 11r
αἰσχύνης, φόβου, θλίψεως ἀνάμεστος ὑπάρχων·
ᾐσχύνετο γὰρ φωραθείς, ὡς ξένος ἐφοβεῖτο,
ἐλυπεῖτο μὴ χωρισμὸν ὑποστῇ τῆς φιλτάτης.
175 Μὴ ἔχων τί ποιήσειεν, εἰς τὴν κόρην εἰσῆλθε·
ταύτην γὰρ μόνην ἤλπιζεν εὑρεῖν παρηγορίαν,
μὴ γινώσκων ὅ,τι Θεὸς ἐδήλωσε κατ' ὄναρ.
Καὶ «Τί τοῦτο ἐποίησας;» ἐπεφώνει δακρύων,
«Αὕτη ἔνι ἡ ἀγάπη σου καὶ οὕτως μοι ὑπέσχου;
180 Οὐχί μου πᾶσαν τὴν βουλὴν εἰς σὲ προσανεθέμην;
Οὐχὶ συνέθου τοῦ ἐλθεῖν μετὰ περιχαρείας;
Μὴ γάρ σε κατηνάγκασα ἢ παρεβίασά σε;
Μᾶλλον σύ με ἠνάγκασας μετ' ἐμοῦ πορευθῆναι,
καὶ καθ' ὁδοῦ συγχαίρεσθαι καὶ πάλιν ὑποστρέψαι.
185 Σὺ δὲ φόβον μὴ ἔχουσα Θεοῦ πρὸ ὀφθαλμῶν σου,
σοὺς ἀδελφοὺς ἠνάγκασας ἵνα με θανατώσουν.
Οὐ μνημονεύεις ἐξ ἀρχῆς τί μετὰ σοῦ ἐποίουν;

162 Οὓς Mavrogordato, cf. Z739: οἳ G
184 καθ' ὁδοῦ G: καθ' ὁδὸν Legrand
186 ἠνάγκασας G: ἀνήγγειλας Tsopanakis, 1960, 82

155 On seeing them they were amazed and astonished at the vision,
saying, "Welcome, our brother-in-law's youngsters.
Why are you encamped here, avoiding our house?"
   They could make no denial and confessed,
revealing what was certain; nothing was hidden.
160 For unexpected fear brings out the truth,
but when it is expected it leads to excuses.
Gathering them up immediately, they came to their brother-in-law
and reproached him for being malicious.
Indeed the youngest, who was very hot-headed,
165 said, "Don't reject what you had in mind,
though you must understand, Saracen, that you will not see Syria.
But since you have proved to be a law-breaker and an enemy,
leave our sister, renounce your child,
take what you brought and go back where you came from."
170   On hearing this and seeing the evidence,
the emir could make no denial and remained utterly silent,
full of shame, fear and distress.
For he was ashamed to be caught as a thief, he was afraid since he
   was a foreigner,
and he grieved because he could not endure separation from his
   dearest.
175 Not knowing what to do, he came to the girl,
for from her alone he had hoped to find consolation,
not realising what God had revealed in a dream.
And "Why did you do this?" he cried out in tears,
"Is this your love and is this what you promised?
180 Did I not entrust my whole plan to you?
Did you not agree joyfully to accompany me?
Surely I didn't insist or compel you?
On the contrary, you insisted that you should accompany me,
that we should enjoy the journey together and then return.
185 But you, having no fear of God before your eyes,
have insisted that your brothers kill me.
Do you not remember what I did with you at the beginning?

---

155 It is not clear whether they are surprised at seeing the Arabs, or at the effect of the
dream.
166–9 It is hard to see how the threat of G2.166 may be reconciled with the dismissal of
G2.169.
179 The emir here, as elsewhere (cf. G3.179), demonstrates respect for his new faith; at
E354 the emir's comments on oath-breakers are anti-Christian.

Αἰχμάλωτόν σε ἥρπαξα, ἐτίμουν ὡς κυρίαν·   E359
δούλην σε ἔχειν ἤθελον, μᾶλλον εἶχες με δοῦλον·   E357
190 τοὺς γονεῖς καὶ τὴν πίστιν μου διὰ σὲ ἠρνησάμην,
καὶ διὰ τὴν ἀγάπην σου ἦλθον εἰς Ῥωμανίαν·   E362
σὺ δὲ θάνατον ἀντ᾽ αὐτῶν ἐμνημόνευσας, κόρη.
Βλέπε, καλή, μὴ παραβῇς τοὺς ἐν τῷ μέσῳ ὅρκους,
μὴ ἀρνηθῇς τὸν ἔρωτα ὃν εἴχομεν ἐκ πόθου·
195 εἰ γὰρ καταναγκάσουν με θλίβοντες οἱ ἀδελφοί σου,
πάντως νὰ σύρω τὸ σπαθὶν καὶ σφάξω ἐμαυτόν μου   E367
καὶ κρίνειν ἔχει ὁ Θεὸς μέσον τῶν ἀμφοτέρων. 11v
Σὲ δὲ τὰ εὐγενικόπουλα πάντα νά σε ὀνειδίζουν,   E368
ὅτι ἀνδρὸς μυστήριον οὐκ ἴσχυσας φυλάξαι,
200 ὡς Δαλιδὰ δὲ τὸν Σαμψὼν παρέδωκας σφαγῆναι.»
Πάντα θρηνῶν ὁ ἀμιρᾶς ἔλεγε πρὸς τὴν κόρην,
ταύτην γὰρ ὑπελάμβανε τὴν βουλὴν φανερῶσαι·
ὁ ἔρως γὰρ ἀτιμασθεὶς φέρει κακολογίας.
Καὶ ἡ κόρη, ὡς ἤκουσεν, ἐνεὸς ἐγεγόνει
205 μήτε λόγον προπέμψασθαι μηδόλως δυναμένη,
ἔμεινε δὲ στυγνάζουσα ἐπὶ πολλὰς τὰς ὥρας.
Πᾶς γὰρ ὁ πταίων ἕτοιμος φέρειν ἀπολογίας,
ὁ δὲ μὴ πταίων σιωπᾷ, μὴ ἔχων τί λαλῆσαι.
Μόλις ποτὲ δὲ ἑαυτὴν ὡς ἑσπέραν λαβοῦσα,
210 «Τί μάτην ὀνειδίζεις με;» ἐπεφώνει δακρύοις.
«Τί, ἄνερ μου, κατηγορεῖς τὴν σὲ πολλὰ ποθοῦσαν;
Οὐκ ἔστι μοι, μὴ γένοιτο, τὴν βουλὴν φανερῶσαι·
εἰ γὰρ τοῦτο ἐποίησα, ζῶσαν ἡ γῆ με πίοι,
νὰ γένωμαι παράδειγμα πᾶσι τοῖς ἐν τῷ κόσμῳ
215 ὡς τοῦ ἀνδρὸς μυστήρια κατάδηλα ποιοῦσα.»
Καὶ βλέπουσα τὸν ἀμιρᾶν αὐξήσαντα τὸν θρῆνον,
παρὰ μικρὸν δὲ γέγονε παράφρων ἐκ τὴν θλῖψιν
(τὸ γὰρ πολὺ τῆς θλίψεως γεννᾷ παραφροσύνην,
ἐντεῦθεν καὶ παράνομον πολλοὶ κατατολμῶσι),
220 ἐφοβήθη μὴ ἑαυτὸν ἀναιρέσῃ τῷ ξίφει.
Ἐξῆλθε πρὸς τοὺς ἀδελφοὺς τὰς τρίχας ἀνασπῶσα·
«Ὦ γλυκύτατοι ἀδελφοί, τί μάτην ἐνοχλεῖτε
τὸν μηδὲν ἀδικήσαντα; Ἰδοὺ γὰρ ἀποθνήσκει, 12r
ἰδοὺ ἀναιρέσει ἑαυτὸν ἀπὸ παραπληξίας.

---

197 ἔχει ὁ Θεὸς Legrand: ὁ Θεὸς ἔχει G
209 ὡς ἑσπέραν Mavrogordato: ὡς εἰς πέρας G ὡς ἑσπέρας Tsopanakis, 1960, 82

I seized you as my prisoner, but I honoured you as my lady.
I had intended to keep you as a slave, but instead you made me the
    slave.
190 I renounced my parents and my faith for your sake,
and for love of you I came to Roman territory,
but you have thought of death in return for this, girl.
See, my beauty, that you do not break the oaths between us,
do not renounce the love which was ours through passion.
195 If your brothers use force and overpower me,
without fail I shall draw my sword and kill myself,
and God will judge between the two of us.
May all scions of noble families reproach you
because you could not keep your husband's secret,
200 but delivered him to his death, as Delilah did with Samson."
    The emir said all this sorrowfully to the girl,
for he supposed that she had revealed his plan;
for love that is dishonoured brings harsh words.
When the girl heard it she became dumb,
205 completely unable to utter a word;
she remained despondent for many hours.
For every wrong-doer is capable of finding excuses,
but the one who has done no wrong is silent, not knowing what to say.
Scarcely coming to herself by evening,
210 "Why do you reproach me without reason?" she cried out in tears.
"Why, my husband, do you accuse the one who longs for you so
    much?
It is unthinkable for me – may this never happen – to reveal your plan.
If I did that, may the earth swallow me up alive,
so that I may become an example to all the world
215 of one who makes public her husband's secrets."
    And seeing the emir increasing his lament
she went almost out of her mind with grief
(for excess of grief brings delirium,
in which state many people attempt unlawful deeds),
220 she feared he might kill himself with his sword.
She went out to her brothers, tearing her hair:
"Sweetest brothers, why do you harass without reason
a man who has done no wrong? See, he is about to die;
see, he will kill himself out of madness.

225 Μή, πρὸς Θεόν, ἀδέλφια μου, μὴ ἀδικηθῇ ὁ ξένος,
    ὃς δι' ἐμὲ ἠρνήσατο συγγενεῖς καὶ τὴν πίστιν,
    οὐ γὰρ ἐνάντιόν ποτε καθ' ὑμῶν ἐβουλήθη·
    ἀρτίως δὲ φοβούμενος κατάραν τῆς μητρός του   E403
    εἰς Συρίαν ἀπέρχεται, σὺν αὐτῇ ἐπανήκει·
230 ἐξεῖπε γάρ μου τὴν βουλήν, ἔδειξε καὶ τὸ γράμμα.
    Καὶ πῶς ὑμεῖς φειδόμενοι κατάρας τῆς μητρός μας   E404
    μόνοι κατετολμήσατε ἐλθεῖν εἰς χιλιάδας
    καὶ πόλεμον συνάψασθαι δι' ἐμοῦ εἰς κλεισοῦραν   E405
    μὴ φοβηθέντες θάνατον, ἀλλὰ μητρὸς κατάραν;   E2, 406
235 Δέδοικε ταύτην καὶ αὐτός, βούλεται πορευθῆναι.»
    Καὶ ταῦτα πρὸς τοὺς ἀδελφοὺς ἡ κόρη πάντα λέγει
    θερμὰ κινοῦσα δάκρυα, τίλλουσα καὶ τὴν κόμην.
    Οἱ δὲ μὴ φέροντες ὁρᾶν τὴν ἀδελφὴν θρηνοῦσαν
    ὁμοφώνως ἀνέκραζον, ταύτην καταφιλοῦντες:
240 «Σὲ γὰρ οἱ πάντες ἔχομεν ψυχὴν καὶ θυμηδίαν·   E408
    ἐπεὶ δὲ βούλει καὶ αὐτὴ τὸν γαμβρόν μας ἐκπέμψαι,
    Θεὸν παράσχοι μάρτυρα τάχιον ὑποστρέψαι,
    ἡμεῖς δὲ νὰ εὐχώμεθα καλῶς εὐοδωθῆναι.»
    Καὶ ἀμφότεροι παρευθὺς εἰς τὸν γαμβρὸν εἰσῆλθον,
245 συγχώρησιν αἰτούμενοι τῶν πρώην λαληθέντων:
    «Καὶ μὴ μνησθῇς ἡμῶν, γαμβρέ, ἀγνωσίας ῥημάτων·
    οὐ γὰρ ἡμῶν τὸ αἴτιον, πάντως γὰρ σὸν τὸ κρῖμα,
    τοῦ μὴ γνωρίσαντος ἡμῖν ἅπερ ἐβούλου πράξειν.»
    Ὁ δὲ καὶ συνεχώρησε πάντας καταφιλήσας·
250 σταθεὶς δὲ πρὸς ἀνατολάς, χεῖρας εἰς ὕψος ἄρας,   12v   E1806
    «Χριστέ μου,» ἐξεφώνησεν, «Υἱὲ Θεοῦ καὶ Λόγε,
    ὁ ὁδηγήσας με πρὸς φῶς τῆς σῆς θεογνωσίας,
    τοῦ σκότους λυτρωσάμενος καὶ τῆς ματαίας πλάνης,
    ὁ γινώσκων τὰ κρύφια καὶ λογισμοὺς καρδίας,
255 εἰ ἐπιλάθωμαι ποτὲ γαμετῆς τῆς φιλτάτης
    ἢ τοῦ τερπνοῦ ἀνθήματος τέκνου τοῦ παμποθήτου
    καὶ οὐχ ὑποστρέψω τάχιον ἐκ τὴν ἐμὴν μητέρα,
    θηρίοις γένωμαι βορὰ καὶ πετεινοῖς ἐν ὄρει,
    μὴ καταλογιζόμενος Χριστιανοῖς ἐν μέρει.»

227 ὑμῶν G: ἡμῶν Tsopanakis. 1960. 83. cf. Z816
235 ταύτην Legrand: ταῦτα G

225 My brothers, before God, do not let your guest be wronged:
he has renounced kinsmen and his faith for my sake,
he has never wished to act against you.
Now, out of fear of his mother's curse,
he is going off to Syria and is returning with her.
230 He told me of his plan, he also showed me the letter.
And how did you, out of respect for our mother's curse,
dare to go alone against thousands
and to join battle for my sake in the pass,
not fearing death but your mother's curse?
235 He fears this too, he wants to make the journey."
     The girl said all this to her brothers,
shedding hot tears and tearing at her hair.
They could not bear to see their sister lamenting
and cried out together, kissing her,
240 "We all think of you as our soul and delight.
Since you too want to send our brother-in-law off,
may he take God as his witness that he will return quickly,
and let us wish him all success on his journey."
     And they all went in immediately to their brother-in-law
245 and asked pardon for what had been said earlier.
"And do not, brother-in-law, hold against us words spoken in
     ignorance,
for we were not the cause but the fault is surely yours,
as you did not inform us of what you planned to do."
     And he forgave them and embraced them all.
250 Facing towards the east and raising his hands on high,
"Christ," he declared, "Son of God and Word,
who has guided me to the light of your knowledge of God,
who has freed me from darkness and futile error,
who knows the secrets and reckonings of my heart,
255 if ever I forget my dearest spouse
or our delightful offspring, our beloved child,
and do not return swiftly from my mother,
may I become food for wild beasts and birds on the mountain,
and be no longer reckoned on the side of the Christians."

---

225 The word ξένος is double-edged: as a 'foreigner' (G2.173), it showed why the emir
has to fear, but here, as 'guest', it marks a reason why he should be safe. The emir is a
ξένος in both senses of the word: a foreigner who fears that he lacks the protection
afforded to its citizens by the Roman state and also a guest who is protected by the
customary laws of hospitality.

260 Καὶ ἀπὸ τότε ἥρξατο τῆς ὁδοῦ εὐτρεπίζειν
καὶ συσκευάσας ἅπαντα ἡμερῶν δεκαπέντε,
γνωστὴ πᾶσιν ἐγένετο ἡ ἐξέλευσις τούτου
καὶ πᾶν πλῆθος συνήρχετο συγγενῶν τε καὶ φίλων.
Καὶ ἦν ἰδεῖν τὸν ἔρωτα ὄνπερ εἶχον οἱ δύο·
265 κρατήσας γὰρ ὁ ἀμιρᾶς ἐκ τῆς χειρὸς τὴν κόρην
εἰσῆλθε μόνος μετ' αὐτῆς ἔνδον εἰς τὸ κουβοῦκλιν   E467. 583
καὶ δάκρυα ἐκίνησαν ὡς ὄμβρος ἐκ καρδίας·   E420. 468
οἱ στεναγμοὶ ἀνέπεμπον ἦχον παρηλλαγμένον.   E469
«Δός μοι λόγον, αὐθέντρια, δός μοι σὸν δακτυλίδιν,   E472–3
270 ἃς τὸ φορῶ, καλόγνωμε, ἕως οὗ ὑποστρέψω.»
Ἡ δὲ κόρη στενάζουσα τὸν ἀμιρᾶν ἐλάλει:
«Βλέπε, χρυσὲ αὐθέντα μου, μὴ παραβῇς τοὺς ὅρκους,
καὶ Θεὸς ἀποδώσει σοι, εἰ περιλάβῃς ἄλλην·   E479
Θεὸς γὰρ δίκαιος κριτὴς ἀξίως ἀποδίδων.»
275 «Εἰ τοῦτο πράξω, φίλτατε,» ὁ ἀμιρᾶς ἀντέφη,
«ἢ ἀθετήσω ἔρωτα ὃν ἔχομεν ἐκ πόθου
ἢ θλίψω τὴν καρδίαν σου, ὦ πανευγενεστάτη, 13r
χανοῦσα γῆ με λήψεται, Ἅδης με καταπίοι,
καὶ μὴ ἐχάρην εἰς ἐσέ, τὴν μοσχομυρισμένην.»
280 Περιλαβόντες δὲ στερπνά, ἀπλήστως κατεφίλουν   E481
ὡς καὶ τὴν ὥραν εἰς πολὺ παρακατεκταθῆναι·
καὶ γέγοναν κατάβροχοι ἐκ τῶν πολλῶν δακρύων,
μόλις δὲ ἠδυνήθησαν ἀλλήλοις ἀποστῆναι
τὸ πλῆθος μὴ αἰδούμενοι τῶν ἐκεῖ ἀθροισθέντων·
285 ἡ γὰρ ἀγάπη ἡ φυσικὴ φέρει ἀναισχυντίαν
καὶ τοῦτο πάντες οἴδασιν οἱ τὸ φιλεῖν μαθόντες.
Εἶτα καὶ τέκνον τὸ αὐτοῦ λαβὼν εἰς τὰς ἀγκάλας,
θρηνῶν ταῦτα ἐφθέγγετο εἰς ἐπήκοον πάντων:
«Ἆρα ποιήσει με Θεὸς ἄξιον τοῦ ἰδεῖν σε,
290 ὦ παιδίον γλυκύτατον, καβαλλάρην ἐμπρός μου;
Ἆρα, υἱέ μου Διγενές, διδάξω σε κοντάριν,
ὡς ἂν καυχήσωνται ἐν σοὶ πάντες οἱ συγγενεῖς σου;»
Καὶ ἐδάκρυσαν ἅπαντες τὸν ἀμιρᾶν ὁρῶντες.
Εἶθ' οὕτως ἵππον εὔθειον καὶ κομιδῇ γενναῖον
295 ἐπιβάντες οἱ ἄγουροι ἐξῆλθασι τοῦ οἴκου,

260 τῆς ὁδοῦ G: Trapp suggests τὰ τῆς ὁδοῦ
268 στεναγμοὶ Legrand: στεναγμὸν G
278 καταπίοι Legrand: καταπίῃⁱ G
280 στερπνά G, cf. στρεφνά E481, 915, 1594: τερπνά Legrand
281 παρακατεκταθῆναι Legrand: παρακατακταθῆναι G

260   And from that moment he began to prepare for the journey
        and made everything ready within fifteen days;
        his departure became known to everyone,
        and the whole host of kinsmen and friends gathered together.
        And then the love between the two could be seen,
265 for the emir took the girl by the hand
        and went alone with her inside the chamber,
        and heartfelt tears fell like showers;
        their sighs re-echoed each other's.
        "Give me your word, my lady, give me your ring;
270 let me wear it, my noble wife, until I return."
        The girl sighed and said to the emir,
        "Take care, my golden lord, that you do not break your oaths,
        and God will repay you, if you embrace another woman;
        for God is a just judge who settles accounts appropriately."
275 "If I do that, my dearest," the emir replied,
        "or nullify the love which is ours through passion
        or grieve your heart, my most high-born wife,
        the earth will gape and receive me, may Hades swallow me up,
        and may I not have rejoiced in you, my sweet-perfumed darling."
280   Embracing closely, they kissed insatiably,
        so that the moment was drawn out;
        they became soaked with their many tears
        and were scarcely able to part from each other,
        and had no modesty before the host of those gathered there.
285 For physical love brings shamelessness,
        and all who have learned of love know this.
        Then, taking his child in his arms
        and lamenting, he said this in the hearing of all,
        "Surely God will make me worthy of seeing you,
290 my sweetest child, on horseback in my presence?
        Surely, my son of double descent, I shall teach you to use the spear,
        so that all your kinsmen may boast of you?"
        And all wept as they saw the emir.
            Then, each mounting a swift and altogether noble horse,
295 the youngsters left the house

καὶ ὕστερον ὁ ἀμιρᾶς εἰς φάραν καβαλλάρης.

Ἦτον τὸ πλῆθος δὲ πολὺ συγγενῶν τε καὶ φίλων,
καὶ συνεξέβαλον αὐτὸν μέχρι τριῶν μιλίων·
καὶ πάντας ἀσπασάμενος ἐποίει ὑποστρέψαι,
300   αὐτὸς τῆς ὁδοῦ ἥπτετο ἅμα σὺν τοῖς ἀγούροις.

and after them the emir, riding his charger.
The host of kinsmen and friends was large
and they accompanied him for three miles.
And embracing them all, he made them return,
300 while he himself set off on the journey, together with his youngsters.

44

Ἡ ἀπὸ Συρίας ὑπόστρεψις μετὰ καὶ τῆς μητρὸς αὐτοῦ: λόγος τρίτος

Οὕτως δοῦλος πᾶς ὁ ἐρῶν τοῦ ἔρωτος ὑπάρχει·   14r
ἔστι γὰρ οὗτος δικαστὴς βασανίζων καρδίας
τῶν μὴ τηρούντων ἀκριβῶς τὰς ὁδοὺς τῆς ἀγάπης·
εὐστόχως πέμπει τὰς βολὰς καὶ τοξεύει καρδίας
5 καὶ ἵπταται μετὰ πυρὸς τὸν λογισμὸν φλογίζων·
πᾶς δὲ ὃς τοῦτον κέκτηται οὐ δύναται ἐκφεῦξαι,
κἂν τῶν ἐνδόξων τίς ἐστι, κἂν τῶν πλουσιωτάτων·
ἐπαιρόμενος γὰρ αὐτοῦ ταχέως τοῦτον φθάνει.
    Οὕτω τυχὼν ὁ ἀμιρᾶς ὁ θαυμαστὸς ἐκεῖνος
10 δόξης μὲν κατεφρόνησε καὶ ἀρχῆς τῆς μεγίστης,
ἐπελάθετο συγγενῶν, γονέων καὶ πατρίδος·
πίστιν δὲ ἀπηρνήσατο διὰ κόρης ἀγάπην
τερπνῆς τῷ ὄντι ἀληθῶς καὶ πανευγενεστάτης
καὶ ὅ ποτε πολέμιος δοῦλος ἔρωτος ὤφθη·
15 εἰς Ῥωμανίαν ᾤκησε διὰ τὴν ποθητήν του.
Γραφὴν ἀπολαβὼν αὐτὸς μητρὸς ἀπὸ Συρίας
ἐτύπωσε τοῦ ἀπελθεῖν δεδιὼς τὴν κατάραν·
πάντως γὰρ δίκαιόν ἐστι γονεῖς μὴ παροργίζειν.
    Καὶ γενομένης συμβουλῆς καὶ ὅρκου ἐν τῷ μέσῳ
20 πάντες προέπεμψαν αὐτὸν μετὰ περιχαρείας
καὶ τραγῳδεῖν ἀπήρξατο παραμυθῶν τὴν κόρην:
«Ἄγουροι, δυναμώνεσθε· φαρία, μὴ κατοκνεῖτε·   E487
τὰς ἡμέρας σπουδάζετε, τὰς νύκτας ἀγρυπνεῖτε,

Title: λόγος τρίτος appears twice, at the foot of 13r and at the head of 14r (13v was
originally blank)
5 ἵπταται Trapp, cf. Ach.Tat. 2.5.2: ἵσταται G
6 ἐκφεῦξαι Legrand: ἐφεῦξαι G
8 ἐπαιρόμενος γὰρ αὐτοῦ G: ἐπαιρόμενον γὰρ αὐτὸς Chatzis, 1951, 213
20 πάντες G, Kalonaros: πάντων G, after correction

The third book, the return from Syria with his mother

Thus every lover is a slave of Eros,
for Eros is a judge who tortures the hearts
of those who do not follow correctly the paths of love;
he aims his darts accurately and shoots hearts,
5 and flies around enflaming reason with fire.
No one who possesses him can escape,
not even if he is renowned, not even if he is very rich,
for when Eros rises against him he quickly reaches him.
Being in this state that marvellous emir
10 spurned renown and the highest authority
and forgot his kinsmen, parents and country;
he renounced his faith for the love of a girl,
who was in reality truly delightful and very high-born.
And he who was once the enemy proved to be a slave of love,
15 he settled in Roman territory for the sake of his beloved.
Receiving a letter from his mother in Syria,
he decided to leave, fearing her curse,
for it is certainly right not to provoke one's parents.
So when a discussion had taken place and an oath made before
everyone,
20 they all escorted him with great rejoicing
and he began to sing, comforting the girl:
"Youngsters, let us be strong; horses, do not be lazy.
Make haste by day, be wakeful by night,

F.13v now contains a prayer against impure thoughts, in another hand. Some common phrasing with the folio torn out from the Maximou episode (after G6.785 and now found only in Z3699–738) makes one wonder if this prayer is connected with the censorship shown in the removal of that folio. The equivalent material in E is found at E484–581, after which point a folio is missing.
1–18 After introducing an Eros personified with the attributes of the Hellenistic God of Love, the passage gives a misleading, idealised summary of Books 1–2 – perhaps a sign of careless redaction in the G version?
21 Again words of consolation are sung (cf. G2.26 above), though here consolation for his wife consists of the encouragement of his companions on the journey.

βροχάς, χιόνας, παγετοὺς ἀντ' οὐδενὸς ἡγεῖσθε,   E490
25 μὴ βραδύνω τὸ σύνολον κατὰ τὴν ὡρισμένην
καὶ ὀνειδισθῶ εἰς ὑποστροφὴν καὶ ζῆν με οὐ συμφέρῃ.»
Εἶτα «Χαίρεσθε,» προσειπών, «ὦ συγγενεῖς καὶ φίλοι,»
καὶ πάντας ἀσπασάμενος εὔχεσθαι παρεκάλει. 14v
Ὃ δὴ καὶ πεποιήκασι παρευθὺς ὁμοφώνως:
30 «Ὁ Θεὸς ὁ φιλάνθρωπος ἵνα σε εὐοδώσῃ
καὶ καταξιωθείημεν διὰ τάχους ἰδεῖν σε.»
    Κἀκεῖθεν μὲν ὑπέστρεφον πάντες ἐπὶ τὸν οἶκον,
στυγνοὶ ὄντες καὶ σκυθρωποὶ ὡς δεινὸν πεπονθότες·
τοιοῦτος γὰρ ὁ χωρισμὸς πάντων τῶν ἀγαπώντων,
35 διότι καίει τὰς ψυχάς, δαμάζει τὰς καρδίας,
ταράσσει καὶ τοὺς λογισμοὺς παντελὴς χωρισία.
    Ἥπτετο δὲ ὁ ἀμιρᾶς μετὰ σπουδῆς τοῦ δρόμου,
καθ' ἑκάστην ἐξέπεμπε γραφὰς τῇ ποθητῇ του:
«Μὴ λυπηθῇς, παρακαλῶ· τοῦτο δ' εὔχεσθε μᾶλλον.»
40 Ἀγούρους δὲ τοὺς ἑαυτοῦ ἱκέτευεν ἐκ πόθου,
«Ἄρχοντες,» λέγων, «ἄγουροι, φίλοι καὶ ἀδελφοί μου,
ἀγρυπνήσατε δι' ἐμὲ καὶ κόπον ὑποστῆτε,
συνταγὰς γὰρ ποιήσατε καὶ πολλὰς ὑποσχέσεις,
ἃς ὑπέσχεσθε λέγοντες δι' ἐμοῦ ἀποθνήσκειν·
45 τοῦτο δὲ οὐ πρὸς θάνατον, ἐρωτικὸς ὁ μόχθος·
φλέγεται γάρ μου ἡ ψυχή, καίεται ἡ καρδία,
κατανοῶν τὸ ἄπειρον διάστημα τοῦ δρόμου.
Πότε κάμπους τοὺς φοβεροὺς διέλθωμεν, ἀγοῦροι,
καὶ τοὺς βουνοὺς τοὺς φοβεροὺς καὶ τὰς δεινὰς κλεισούρας,
50 καὶ τὴν Ῥαχὰβ θεάσωμαι, ἴδω μου τὴν μητέρα;
Καὶ πότε πάλιν ἅπαντα ταῦτα διαπεράσω, 15r
ἐν τοῖς μέρεσιν ἔλθωμεν τῆς καλῆς Ῥωμανίας
καὶ τὴν ἐμὴν θεάσωμαι πέρδικαν τὴν ὡραίαν
καὶ ἄνθος τὸ πανεύγενον, τὸν πάγκαλον υἱόν μου;   E458
55 Τίς μοι παράσχοι πτέρυγας καὶ πετάσαι, φιλτάτη,
καὶ εἰς ἀγκάλας δὲ τὰς σὰς πρὸς ὥραν καταπαῦσαι;
Πόσα στενάζει καὶ αὐτὴ δι' ἐμὲ ἀγρυπνοῦσα

24 ἡγεῖσθε Legrand: μιμεῖσθε G
29 ὁμοφώνως G (probably) after correction. Legrand: ὁμοφρόνως G
39 εὔχεσθε corr.: εὔχεσθαι G
40 ἱκέτευεν G after correction. Legrand: ἱκέτευων G before correction
48 κάμπους τοὺς φοβεροὺς G: γὰρ κάμπους τοὺς πολλοὺς Trapp (cf. Z900) γὰρ
κάμπους τοὺς ξηροὺς Tsopanakis, 1960, 83
50 θεάσωμαι Tsopanakis, 1960, 83: θεάσομαι G

consider rain, snow and frost as nothing,
25 so that I should not be even a minute later than the appointed time,
and be reproached on my return and life be not worth living."
Then, "Farewell," he said, "kinsmen and friends",
and embracing them all he asked for their good wishes,
Which they gave immediately with one voice:
30 "May God in his benevolence grant you a safe journey,
and may we be allowed to see you swiftly."
    And from that point they all returned to the house,
downcast and gloomy, as if they had suffered a dreadful blow,
For such is separation for all who love,
35 because souls are seared, hearts subdued
and reason confused by complete separation.
    The emir started his journey with haste,
he sent letters to his beloved every day:
"Do not be grieved, I beg you; rather all of you make this prayer."
40 He pleaded with his youngsters in his desire,
"Lords," he said, "youngsters, my friends and brothers,
be wakeful for me and endure toil,
for you have made vows and many promises
which you promised when you said you would die for me;
45 but this is not to the death, for the labour is to do with Eros.
For my soul is on fire, my heart is burning,
when I contemplate the boundless length of my journey.
When shall we cross the fearful plains, youngsters,
and the fearful mountains and dreadful passes,
50 and when shall I gaze on Rachab and see my mother?
And when shall I cross all this once more
and come to the districts of the fair Roman territory,
and gaze on my lovely partridge, my wife,
and my high-born offspring, my very lovely son?
55 Who will provide me with wings to fly, my dearest,
and to rest for a while in your arms?
How much does she too sigh as she is vigilant for me

28–9 Between these lines G leaves a three-line space: there is no sign of erasure, nor of
parallel material preserved in Z.
38 There is an inherent difficulty in the logistics of the daily transmission of letters.
55–6 The wish to fly to the distant beloved (often expressed in terms of Ps. 54.7) is a
motif common in late antique epistolography (Thraede, 1970, 174–9).

καὶ σκοπεύουσα τὰς ὁδοὺς καθ' ἑκάστην ἡμέραν;
Πεφύκασι γὰρ μέριμναι πολλαὶ τοῖς ποθουμένοις
60 καὶ φροντίδες διηνεκῶς, κίνδυνοί τε καὶ φόβοι.
Ἀλλ', ὦ καλοὶ νεώτεροι, εὐγενικοί μου ἀγοῦροι,
ὕπνον ἀποτινάξατε καὶ πᾶσαν ῥαθυμίαν,
ὡσὰν ταχέως φθάσωμεν εἰς τὸ Ῥαχὰβ τὸ κάστρον,   E527
εἶτ' οὖν ἐντεῦθεν ἔλθωμεν πάλιν εἰς Ῥωμανίαν,
65 οὗ πολλάκις ἐρρύσθητε δι' ἐμὲ ἐκ κινδύνων.
Καὶ παρεάσας τὰ πολλὰ ἐν ὑμῖν ὑπομνήσω,
ὃ καὶ πρὸς ὥραν γέγονεν εἰς τὰ Μελλοκοπία,   E503
ὁπότε μας ἐκύκλωσαν οἱ στρατηγοὶ ἀθρόως
καὶ ὥσπερ τεῖχος γύρωθεν ἔστησαν τὰ φουσσᾶτα,
70 ὑμεῖς δὲ εἰς ἀπόγνωσιν κατήχθητε θανάτου,
ἀποκλεισθέντες ἔνδοθεν πάντες ὥσπερ ἐν τάφῳ,
μὴ ἐλπίζοντές τις ὑμῶν ἐξελθεῖν τῶν ἐκεῖσε·
ἐγὼ δὲ ἐπελάλησα, μέσον αὐτῶν εἰσῆλθον,
ὅσους εἰς Ἅδην ἔπεμψα οὐδ' ὑμεῖς ἀγνοεῖτε,
75 μόνος δὲ τρέψας ἅπαντας καὶ φυγάδας ποιήσας,
ἀβλαβεῖς διεσώθημεν μὲ τὴν αἰχμαλωσίαν.
Ἄρτι δ' οὐκ ἔστι πόλεμος, ἐρωτικὸς δ' ὁ μόχθος 15v
καὶ ἐν τούτῳ παρακαλῶ συνεργοί μου γενέσθαι.»
Ταῦτα καὶ ἄλλα πλείονα τοῖς σὺν αὐτῷ ἐλάλει
80 ὁ ἀμιρᾶς ἐν τῇ ὁδῷ μετὰ πόνου καρδίας·
οὕτως γὰρ φλέγει τοὺς αὐτῷ ὑπηκόους ὁ ἔρως,
ὡς πάντων μὲν καταφρονεῖν, αὐτὸν δὲ προσαγγέλλειν.
Καὶ ἀκούσαντες ἔλεγον οἱ ἄγουροι εὐθέως:
«Ὅπου θέλεις, αὐθέντα μου, ἂς γίνουν τ' ἄππληκτά σου,
85 οὐ γὰρ εὑρίσκεις ἐφ' ἡμῖν ἀφορμὴν ῥαθυμίας.»
Καὶ ἦν ἰδεῖν θαῦμα φρικτόν, ἀλλ' οὐκ ἄπιστον πᾶσι
(ἔρως γὰρ ἦν ὁ ὑπουργῶν καὶ συνεργῶν εἰς πάντα),
τρεῖς γὰρ μονὰς διήρχοντο καθ' ἑκάστην ἡμέραν.
Ὅτε δὲ κατελάμβανεν εἰς ἀοίκους κλεισούρας,
90 διήρχετο γὰρ γύρωθεν φυλάττων τοὺς ἀγούρους.
Ἐν μιᾷ οὖν ὁδεύοντες εἰς πάνδεινον κλεισοῦραν,
λέοντα εὗρον φοβερὸν κρατοῦντα ἐλαφῖναν·   E514

---

64 εἶτ' οὖν ἐντεῦθεν Grégoire, 1929/30, 332: εἶθ' οὕτως θέντες G
65 οὗ G: οὐ Grégoire, 1929/30, 332
67 πρὸς ὥραν G: πρὸ ὥρας Trapp
75 μόνος Legrand: μόνοις G

and watches the roads each day?
For those who are desired have many cares,
60   and incessant concerns and dangers and fears.
But, my good young men, my high-born youngsters,
shake off sleep and all lethargy,
so that we reach the fortress of Rachab swiftly,
and then return from there to Roman territory,
65   where you have often been rescued by me from danger.
And, passing over many others, I shall remind you of one event
which happened recently at Mellokopia,
when the generals had surrounded us in a group
and the armies stood round about like a wall,
70   and you were reduced to contemplating death,
all of you enclosed as if in a tomb
and none of you expecting to get out of there.
But I urged you on, I made an attack in the midst of them,
and you are not unaware how many I sent to Hades,
75   I who, single-handed, routed them and put them to flight,
and we survived unharmed with our prisoners.
But now it is not war, but the labour has to do with Eros,
and in this I beg you to be my comrades."
    These and many other thoughts the emir addressed to those with
    him
80   as he was on the road with pain in his heart,
for Eros enflames in this way those who are subject to him,
so that they spurn all else and proclaim him.
And listening, the youngsters said immediately,
"Let your camps be set up, my lord, wherever you wish,
85   for you find no pretext for lethargy in us."
And then could be seen a terrible wonder, but one that not all would
    find incredible
(for it was Eros who helped and assisted in everything),
for they completed three stages each day.
    When he reached the uninhabited passes,
90   as he journeyed he guarded the youngsters on all sides.
And so, one day as they were travelling in a very terrible pass,
they found a fearsome lion carrying a hind.

---

67 For the identifications of the places and battles possibly referred to here, see the
Introduction, pp. xxxiv–xxxv, and the Name Index.
73 This verb is more usually used with horses as its object.
88 The stages are between hostels on the public highway – a regular day's journey.

ὡς δὲ τοῦτον ἐσκέψαντο οἱ ἄγουροι, εὐθέως E515
θροηθέντες ἀνέδραμον πάντες ἐπὶ τὸ ὄρος.
95 Καὶ λυπηθεὶς ὁ ἀμιρᾶς πρὸς τὸν λέοντα ἔφη:
«Πῶς τοῦτο κατετόλμησας, δεινότατον θηρίον,
καὶ παρεμπόδισας ὁδὸν ἐρωτικῆς φιλίας;
Ἀλλ᾽ ἐγὼ τὴν ἀνταμοιβὴν ἀξίαν σοι παράσχω.»
Μὲ τὸ ῥαβδὶν τὸν ἔδωκε πλήρης εἰς τὴν μεσίαν,
100 καὶ εὐθὺς ἔμεινε στυγνὸς εἰς γῆν ἐξηπλωμένος.
Καὶ εὐθέως προσέταξε τοὺς ἰδίους ἀγούρους:
«Τοὺς ὀδόντας ἐκσπάσατε πάντας τοὺς τοῦ θηρίου, E524
ὡσαύτως καὶ τοὺς ὄνυχας τῆς δεξιᾶς χειρός του, E524
ἵνα, ὁπότε σὺν Θεῷ στραφῶ εἰς Ῥωμανίαν, 16r
105 φορέσωμεν αὐτούς, φημί, τὸν πάγκαλον υἱόν μου,
τὸν Διγενῆ Καππάδοκα Ἀκρίτην τὸν γενναῖον.» E525
Καὶ αὖθις πάλιν ἥπτετο τῆς ὁδοῦ μετὰ πόθου
ἀλλήλοις προτρεπόμενος τοῦ προθύμως βαδίζειν.
Οὐδεὶς ἐν τούτῳ ῥάθυμος, οὐδεὶς ὕπνου μετέσχεν·
110 ἔρως γὰρ ἦν μέσον αὐτῶν τίς νικήσει τὸν ἄλλον.
Ὅτε δὲ ἐπλησίασαν εἰς τὸ Ῥαχὰβ τὸ κάστρον, E527
προσέταξεν ὁ ἀμιρᾶς ἔξω στῆσαι τὰς τένδας
καὶ δύο τῶν ἀγούρων του εἰσελθεῖν εἰς τὸ κάστρον,
ὡσὰν εἴπωσι τῇ μητρὶ τὴν ἐπέλευσιν τούτου·
115 καὶ πορευθέντες τάχιον πεποιήκασι τοῦτο.
Ἡ δὲ μήτηρ ὡς ἤκουσε τοιαύτην ἀγγελίαν,
μικρόν περ καὶ ὠρχήσατο ἀπὸ περιχαρείας.
Ὁμοίως καὶ οἱ συγγενεῖς ἐν γνώσει γεγονότες
συνεξήλθασιν ἅπαντες εἰς ἀπάντησιν τούτου
120 καὶ πλησίον γενόμενοι ἔνθα ἦσαν αἱ τένδαι,
προϋπήντα ὁ ἀμιρᾶς πεζὸς μετὰ τζαγγίων·
ὃν ἐπιγνόντες καὶ αὐτοὶ ἐπέζευον εὐθέως
ἐμπεπλησμένοι ἡδονῆς, δακρύων γεμισμένοι

100 στυγνὸς G: νεκρὸς Trapp. cf. Z949
102 τοὺς Legrand: τὰς G
109 ἐν τούτῳ G: ἦν τούτων Tsopanakis. 1960. 83. cf. Z958

When the youngsters saw it, immediately
they grew frightened and all ran up the mountain.
95 And the emir said sorrowfully to the lion,
"How have you dared to do this, most terrifying beast,
and block the path of passionate affection?
But I will provide you with a fitting recompense."
With his stick he struck it full in the middle,
100 and immediately the hated animal fell, stretched out on the ground.
And immediately he ordered his youngsters,
"Pull out all the beast's teeth,
and also the claws of its right paw,
so that, when with God's help I return to Roman territory,
105 we may give them to wear, I say, to my very handsome son,
Digenis Akritis, the Cappadocian of double descent, the noble
    Frontiersman."
And he once more started his journey again with desire,
each encouraging one another to push ahead eagerly.
No one was lethargic at this time, no one partook of sleep,
110 for Eros was amongst them, to see who would defeat the other.
    When they approached the fortress of Rachab,
the emir gave orders to pitch the tents outside,
and two of his youngsters were to enter the fort,
to tell his mother of his arrival.
115 And going forward swiftly, they did this.
When his mother heard this news,
she gave a little dance for joy.
Likewise their kinsmen, when they were informed,
all gathered to receive him
120 and when they came near to where the tents were,
the emir went out to meet them on foot, wearing his boots.
When they recognised him, they immediately dismounted,
filled with pleasure and brimming with tears

102–5 The version of this scene at E523–6 makes it plain that the lion's teeth and claws
are intended to function as amulets (Alexiou, 1979, 35).
110 Presumably rivalry amongst the travelling companions, rather than between Eros
and sleep.
119–21 The insistence on both parties being on foot is plainly a question of etiquette,
perhaps indicating some tension to be resolved in the meeting. The significance of the
boots is not certain: τζάγγια once referred exclusively to imperial buskins, a sign of very
high rank, but by the twelfth century have become a regular term for boots; this phrase
also appears in the Ptochoprodromic poems (4.76). It is likely that some idea of rank is
implied here; cf. the emir's throne at G1.94–6.

(φέρει γὰρ δάκρυα χαρά, ἀθρόως ὅταν ἔλθῃ),
125 καὶ κατησπάζοντο αὐτὸν μοιράζοντες τὸν πόθον,
ἐντεῦθεν μὲν οἱ συγγενεῖς, ἐκεῖθεν δὲ ἡ μήτηρ·
καὶ τὰ αὐτοῦ κοράσια ἀληθῶς μετὰ τέκνων
περιεπλέκοντο αὐτόν, ἀπλήστως κατεφίλουν
καὶ χωρισθῆναι ἀπ᾽ αὐτοῦ οὐκ ἤθελον οὐδ᾽ ὅλως.
130 Εἰς δὲ τὴν τένδαν φθάσαντες ἐκάθισαν εὐθέως 16v
καὶ λέγειν οὕτως ἤρξατο τοῦ ἀμιρᾶ ἡ μήτηρ:
«῏Ω τέκνον μου γλυκύτατον, φῶς τῶν ἐμῶν ὀμμάτων,
καὶ παραμύθιον ψυχῆς τῆς ἐμῆς ἐν τῷ γήρει
καὶ τερπνὸν ἀγαλλίαμα, ἡ ἐμὴ θυμηδία,
135 εἰπέ μοι τί ἐβράδυνας, τέκνον, εἰς Ῥωμανίαν;
Ἐγὼ γὰρ μὴ ὁρῶσα σε οὐκ ἤθελον φῶς βλέπειν
οὔθ᾽ ἥλιον τὸν λάμποντα οὔτε ζῆν ἐν τῷ κόσμῳ.   E463
Μὴ θαύματα παράδοξα γίνονται εἰς Ῥωμανίαν
οἷα τελοῦνται, τέκνον μου, εἰς τὸ μνῆμα τοῦ Προφήτου,   E541
140 εἰς ὃ κατῆλθες μετ᾽ ἐμοῦ εἰς εὐχὴν ἀγομένης;
Εἶδες θαῦμα παράδοξον πῶς, τῆς νυκτὸς παρούσης
καὶ φωτὸς μὴ ὑπάρχοντος, φέγγος ἦλθεν ἐξ ὕψους
καὶ ἀπορρήτως ἔπλησε φωτὸς τὸν ὅλον οἶκον.
Εἶδες ἄρκτους καὶ λέοντας, λύκους μετὰ προβάτων
145 καὶ ζώων γένη πάμπολλα ὁμοῦ συμβοσκομένων
μὴ βλάπτοντα τὸ ἕτερον τὸ ἕτερον οὐδ᾽ ὅλως,
ἀλλὰ πάντα προσμένοντα μέχρις εὐχῆς καὶ τέλους,
εἶθ᾽ οὕτως γόνυ κλίναντα εὐθὺς ὑποχωροῦσι.
Μὴ τούτων θαυμαστότερον εἶδες εἰς Ῥωμανίαν;
150 Οὐ παρ᾽ ἡμῖν τοῦ Νεεμὰν ὑπάρχει τὸ μανδίλιν
ὃς βασιλεὺς ἐγένετο μετὰ τῶν Ἀσσυρίων
καὶ διὰ πλῆθος ἀρετῶν θαυμάτων ἠξιώθη;
Πῶς τούτων πάντων, τέκνον μου, γέγονας παραβάτης,
ἀρχῆς δὲ κατεφρόνησας καὶ τῆς μεγίστης δόξης;
155 Οἱ πάντες σε ἐφρόντιζον τῆς Αἰγύπτου κρατῆσαι,
σὺ δὲ τύχης τῆς ἑαυτοῦ ἐμποδιστὴς ἐγένου,

---

138 θαύματα Legrand: θαυμαστὰ G
150 τοῦ Νεεμὰν Legrand: τὸ Νέευμα G
151 ὃς Legrand: ὡς G

(for joy brings tears when it comes suddenly),
125 and they embraced him, sharing their longing,
with the kinsmen on the one side and his mother on the other.
And truly his girls with their children
embraced him and kissed him insatiably
and did not wish at all to be parted from him.
130   When they came to the tent, they immediately sat down
and the emir's mother began to speak as follows:
"My sweetest child, light of my eyes
and comfort of my soul in my old age,
my charming delight, my consolation,
135 tell me why you have lingered, child, in Roman territory?
For when I did not see you I no longer wished to see the light
or the gleaming sun or to live in the world.
Do wonderful miracles happen in Roman territory,
such as are performed, my child, at the Prophet's tomb,
140 to which you came with me when I went to pray?
You saw a wonderful miracle, how when night fell
and there was no light a radiance came from on high
and mystically filled the whole house with light.
You saw bears and lions, wolves with sheep,
145 and very many species of animals feeding together,
the one not hurting the other at all
but all waiting until the final blessing,
then bending the knee thus and immediately leaving.
Have you seen anything more marvellous than this in Roman
     territory?
150 Do we not have the towel of Naaman,
who was emperor over the Assyrians
and because of the number of his virtues was able to perform miracles?
How have you, my child, become a renegade from all this
and spurned power and great renown?
155 All expected you to conquer Egypt,
but you have thwarted your own fortune,

144–8 The animals' role may reflect Byzantine awareness of the status of the Ka'aba
and its precinct in Mecca (not Medina, site of Mohammed's tomb) as a place of refuge,
even for animals (*El* under 'Ka'ba'); or it may be inspired by Isaiah 11.6–7, with the
curious addition of the blessing at the end. The passage is not reflected in E. and has not
been taken up by Z.
150 On this relic, not mentioned in E, see the Introduction, p. xxxviii and Name Index.
155 The reference is probably to one of the many moments at which the Moslem
dynasties of Syria and Egypt were at loggerheads.

διὰ μίαν Ῥωμάϊσσαν τὰ πάντα ἀπολέσας.» 17r
Ἔτι δὲ λέγειν θέλουσα καὶ ἕτερα τοιαῦτα,
ἐκκόψας ὁ νεώτερος τῇ μητρὶ οὕτως λέγει:
160 «Τούτων πάντων, ὦ μῆτερ μου, καθέστηκα ἐν γνώσει·
μήπω φωτός τε μετασχὼν ὡς ἀληθῶς ἐτίμων
τὰ σκότους ὄντως ἄξια καὶ πάσης ἀπωλείας.
Ἡνίκα δὲ ηὐδόκησε Θεὸς ὁ ἐν ὑψίστοις,
ὁ δι' ἐμὲ ἑκούσιον πτωχείαν ὑπομείνας
165 καὶ τὴν ἐμὴν ἀσθένειαν βουληθεὶς τοῦ φορέσαι,
ἀφαρπάσαι τοῦ φάρυγγος τοῦ νοητοῦ θηρίου
καὶ τοῦ λουτροῦ ἠξίωσε τῆς παλιγγενεσίας,
ταῦτα πάντα κατήργησα λήρους ὄντα καὶ μύθους
καὶ πρόξενα ὑπάρχοντα πυρὸς τοῦ αἰωνίου·
170 οἱ γὰρ σεβόμενοι αὐτὰ πάντοτε τιμωροῦνται.
Ἐγὼ πιστεύω εἰς Θεὸν, Πατέρα τῶν ἀπάντων,
ποιητὴν οὐρανοῦ καὶ γῆς καὶ ἀοράτων πάντων·
καὶ εἰς Χριστὸν τὸν Κύριον, Υἱὸν Θεοῦ καὶ Λόγον,
τὸν γεννηθέντα ἐκ Πατρὸς πρὸ πάντων τῶν αἰώνων,
175 φῶς ἐκ φωτὸς ὑπάρχοντα, Θεὸν ἀληθῆ, μέγαν,
τὸν κατελθόντα ἐπὶ γῆς δι' ἡμᾶς τοὺς ἀνθρώπους
καὶ γεννηθέντα ἐκ μητρὸς Μαρίας τῆς παρθένου,
τὸν ὑπομείναντα σταυρὸν δι' ἡμῶν σωτηρίαν
καὶ ταφέντα ἐν μνήματι ὃ καὶ αὐτὴ θαυμάζεις,
180 καὶ ἀναστάντα ἐκ νεκρῶν ἐν τῇ τρίτῃ ἡμέρᾳ,
καθὼς ἡμᾶς διδάσκουσιν αἱ γραφαὶ αἱ ἅγιαι,
τὸν ἀεὶ καθεζόμενον τοῦ Πατρὸς δεξιόθεν,
οὗ βασιλείας τῆς αὐτοῦ οὐκ ἔσται ποτὲ τέλος·
καὶ εἰς Πνεῦμα τὸ ἅγιον ζωοποιοῦν τὰ πάντα, 17v
185 ὃ προσκυνῶ σὺν τῷ Πατρὶ καὶ τῷ Υἱῷ καὶ Λόγῳ·
ἐν βάπτισμα ὁμολογῶν εἰς ἄφεσιν πταισμάτων,
καὶ προσδοκῶ ἀνάστασιν πάντων τῶν τεθνεώτων,
ἑκάστου ἀνταπόδοσιν καὶ τῶν πλημμελημένων,
τῶν δὲ δικαίων ἄφεσιν, καθώσπερ ἐπηγγέλθη,
190 ζωὴν τὴν ἀτελεύτητον τοῦ μέλλοντος αἰῶνος.
Πᾶς ὁ πιστεύων ἐν αὐτῇ τῇ ἁγίᾳ Τριάδι
καὶ βαπτισθεὶς εἰς ὄνομα τοῦ Πατρὸς τοῦ ἀνάρχου

171 Ἐγὼ πιστεύω Trapp, cf. Z1064: ὁ δὲ πιστεύων G
184 ζωοποιοῦν τὰ Legrand: ζωοποιοῦντα G

you have destroyed everything for the sake of one Roman girl."
  While she was still wishing to say other such things,
  the young man cut his mother off and spoke thus:
160 "I used to be well-informed on all these things, mother,
  And before I had a share in the light, I honoured, as if true,
  things which in reality were worthy of darkness and complete
     destruction.
  But when God in the highest,
  who for my sake willingly endured poverty
165 and decided to clothe himself in my weakness,
  was pleased to snatch me from the jaws of the wily beast
  and thought me worthy of the washing of regeneration,
  all these things I abandoned as nonsense and fables
  and leading to eternal fire;
170 those who revere these things are always punished.
  I believe in God, Father of all,
  maker of heaven and earth and all things invisible;
  and in Christ the Lord, Son of God and Word,
  born of the Father before all ages,
175 being light of light, true God, great,
  who came down to earth for us men,
  and was born of his mother Mary the virgin,
  who endured the cross for our salvation
  and was buried in the tomb which you too revere
180 and rose from the dead on the third day,
  as the holy Scriptures teach us,
  who is always seated on the Father's right hand,
  whose kingdom shall have no end;
  and in the Holy Spirit who gives life to all,
185 whom I worship with the Father and the Son and Word,
  confessing one baptism for the forgiveness of sins;
  and I look for the resurrection of all the dead,
  retribution for each man's wrong-doing,
  the forgiveness of the just, as has been proclaimed,
190 and the unending life of the world to come.
  Everyone who believes in this holy Trinity
  and is baptised in the name of the Father who has no beginning

171 On this paraphrase of the Nicene Creed, see Introduction, p. xlii.
179 See the *Koran*, Sura 19 for Islamic reverence for Christ. However, according to
Islamic tradition Christ did not die but ascended to God (*EI* under 'Isa'): there is thus no
tomb to revere.

καὶ τοῦ Υἱοῦ τοῦ ἐξ αὐτοῦ ἀχρόνως γεννηθέντος
καὶ τοῦ ἁγίου Πνεύματος τοῦ ζωοῦντος τὰ πάντα
195 οὐκ ἀπόλλυται πώποτε, ἀλλὰ ζῇ εἰς αἰῶνας.
Ὁ δὲ μὴ ταῦτα ἐγνωκώς, ὦ γλυκυτάτη μῆτερ,
εἰς τὴν γέενναν τοῦ πυρὸς ἐσαεὶ τιμωρεῖται·
κλαυθμὸς πολὺς ἐκεῖ ἐστι καὶ βρυγμὸς τῶν ὀδόντων.»
Ταῦτα εἰπὼν ὁ ἀμιρᾶς καὶ ὁδὸν ὑπανοίξας
200 τῆς ἀμωμήτου πίστεως τῇ μητρὶ οὕτως λέγει·
«Ἐγώ, μῆτερ, ἀπέρχομαι πάλιν εἰς Ῥωμανίαν
τὴν πίστιν ἐπιβεβαιῶν τῆς ἁγίας Τριάδος·
οὐ γὰρ ἀντάξιός ἐστι μιᾶς ψυχῆς ὁ κόσμος.
Εἰ γὰρ πάντα κερδήσωμεν, ψυχὴν ζημιωθῶμεν,
205 πάντως οὐδὲν τὸ ὄφελος ἐν ἐκείνῃ τῇ ὥρᾳ,
ὅταν Θεὸς ἐξ οὐρανοῦ ἔλθῃ κρῖναι τὸν κόσμον
καὶ παραστήσῃ ἅπαντας ἀποδώσοντας λόγον,
ὅταν φωνῆς ἀκούσωμεν πορευθῆναι λεγούσης
εἰς τὸ πῦρ τὸ ἐξώτερον τὸ κεκατηραμένον,
210 εἰς αἰῶνα ἐσόμενοι μετὰ τοῦ διαβόλου 18r
ὡς προσταγμάτων τῶν αὐτοῦ ἀπειθεῖς γεγονότες.
Οἱ δέ γε ἐν Χριστῷ . . . πιστεύοντες, ὡς θέμις,
καὶ ἐντολὰς τηρήσαντες αὐτοῦ τὰς σεβασμίας
ὡς ἥλιος ἐκλάμψουσιν ἐν ἐκείνῃ τῇ ὥρᾳ
215 καὶ τῆς φωνῆς ἀκούσουσι τοῦ ἀγαθοῦ Δεσπότου·
Δεῦτε κληρονομήσατε, Πατρὸς εὐλογημένοι,
ἣν ὑμῖν προητοίμασα οὐρανῶν βασιλείαν.
Καὶ οὗτοι μὲν πορεύσονται εἰς ζωὴν αἰωνίαν·
κριτὴς γὰρ δίκαιός ἐστιν ἀξίως ἀποδίδων.
220 Καὶ εἴπερ βούλει, μῆτερ μου, ζωῆς ἀξιωθῆναι,
λυτρωθῆναι τε τοῦ πυρὸς καὶ σκότους αἰωνίου,
πλάνης ματαίας ἔκφυγε καὶ πεπλασμένων μύθων
καὶ τὸν Θεὸν ἐπίγνωθι τὸν ἐν τρισὶ προσώποις
ἀσυγχύτως ἑνούμενον ἐν μιᾷ ὑποστάσει.
225 Πείσθητι δὲ τῷ σῷ υἱῷ καὶ ἐλθὲ μετ' ἐμέναν·
πατὴρ δέ σου γενήσομαι ἐν Πνεύματι ἁγίῳ
καὶ βαπτισθεῖσαν δέξομαι ἐν τῇ ἀναγεννήσει.»
Τοιαῦτα μὲν ὁ ἀμιρᾶς, τῆς δὲ μητρὸς ὁποῖα;
Οὐ παρῃτήσατο παιδὸς συμβουλὴν τὴν καλλίστην

212 γε ἐν Χριστῷ G: εἰς Χριστὸν τὸν κύριον Mavrogordato: perhaps ἀληθῶς might be added
215 ἀκούσουσι Trapp: ἀκούσωσι G
224 μιᾷ Legrand: μία G

and of the Son who was begotten by him out of time
and of the Holy Spirit who gives life to all,
195 will never die but will live throughout the ages.
He who does not know this, sweetest mother,
will be punished for ever in the Gehenna of fire.
And in that place there is much wailing and gnashing of teeth."
     The emir said these things, opening the way
200 of blameless faith to his mother, and spoke thus:
"I, mother, am leaving once more for Roman territory,
affirming my faith in the holy Trinity,
for the world is not worth as much as one soul.
For if we gain everything but forfeit our soul,
205 there is no benefit at all in that hour
when God comes from heaven to judge the world
and summons all men to give an account,
when we shall hear his voice telling us
to go to the accursed outer fire,
210 to be for eternity with the devil,
having been disobedient to God's commands.
But those who believe in Christ, as is right,
and observe his revered commands
will shine like the sun in that hour
215 and will hear the voice of the good Lord,
'Come and receive your inheritance, blessed of the Father,
the kingdom of heaven which I have made ready for you.'
And these will go forward to life eternal,
for he is a just judge who distributes recompense fittingly.
220 If you wish, my mother, to become worthy of life
and to be freed from the fire and eternal darkness,
escape from vain error and invented fables,
and recognise the God in three persons,
united yet distinct in one hypostasis.
225 Listen to your son and come with me;
I shall become your father in the Holy Spirit
and I shall receive you in your rebirth when you are baptised."
     Such were the emir's words, but what were his mother's?
She did not reject her child's excellent counsel

---

224 'Hypostasis' is a theological term used of the separate yet united persons of the
Trinity.

230 ἀλλ', ὥσπερ γῆ τις ἀγαθὴ δεξαμένη τὸν σπόρον,
εὐθὺς προσήγαγε καρπὸν φθεγξαμένη τοιαῦτα:
«Πιστεύω, τέκνον, διὰ σοῦ Θεῷ τῷ ἐν Τριάδι
καὶ μετὰ σοῦ πορεύσομαι καλῶς εἰς Ῥωμανίαν,
βαπτισθεῖσα εἰς ἄφεσιν τῶν πολλῶν μου σφαλμάτων,
235 χάριν ὁμολογοῦσά τε διὰ σοῦ φωτισθῆναι.» 18v
Ὡσαύτως καὶ οἱ συγγενεῖς οἱ ἐκεῖσε τυχόντες
καὶ οἱ λοιποὶ οἱ μετ' αὐτῆς ἐλθόντες πολὺ πλῆθος
μίαν φωνὴν ἀνέκραξαν Χριστὸν ὁμολογοῦντες:
«Μεθ' ὑμῶν γὰρ ἐρχόμεθα πάντες εἰς Ῥωμανίαν
240 καὶ βαπτισθέντες τύχοιμεν ζωῆς τῆς αἰωνίου.»
Καὶ θαυμάσας ὁ ἀμιρᾶς τὴν τούτων προθυμίαν,
«Δόξα σοι,» ἔφη, «τῷ Θεῷ τῷ μόνῳ φιλανθρώπῳ,
τῷ μὴ θέλοντι θάνατον ἁμαρτωλοῦ μηδ' ὅλως,
ἀλλ' ἀναμένων τὴν εἰς σὲ ἐπιστροφὴν οἰκτίρμων,
245 ὡσὰν ποιήσῃς κοινωνοὺς πάντας σῆς βασιλείας.»
Εἶτα πλοῦτον τὸν ἄπειρον μεθ' ἑαυτῶν λαβόντες,
ὁμοῦ πάντες ἐξήλθασι πρὸς τὰ τῆς Ῥωμανίας.
Ὅτε δὲ καὶ κατέλαβον Καππαδοκίας μέρη,
βουλεύεται ὁ ἀμιρᾶς τοὺς ἑαυτοῦ ἀγούρους:
250 «Ἔννοιά τις εἰσῆλθέ μοι, ὦ καλοὶ στρατιῶται,
τοῦ προλαβεῖν με ἑαυτὸν καὶ συγχαρίκια δοῦναι·
εἰ γὰρ προλάβῃ ἕτερος, πάντως κατηγοροῦμαι
ὡς ὀκνηρὸς καὶ ῥάθυμος παρὰ τῆς ποθητῆς μου.»
Οἱ δὲ ἀνταπεκρίθησαν καλὸν τοῦτο ποιῆσαι,
255 ἄξιον γὰρ ἐρωτικὴν ἐκπληρῶσαι ἀγάπην.
Ἐκεῖνος δὲ τὸ βούλευμα καλῶς ἐπινοήσας,
ἤμειψε τὴν στολὴν εὐθύς, περιβαλὼν ῥωμαίαν,
θαυμαστὸν ἐπιλούρικον, χρυσὸν ῥεραντισμένον,
ὀξέον λευκοτρίβλαττον, γρύψους ὡραϊσμένους,
260 φακεώλιν χρυσόγραμμον, πολυτίμητον, ἄσπρον· 19ρ
μοῦλαν ἐκαβαλλίκευσε βάδεαν, ἀστεράτην.
Καὶ τρεῖς λαβὼν μεθ' ἑαυτοῦ τῶν ἰδίων ἀγούρων   E10

230 but, like fertile soil that has accepted the seed,
    she immediately brought forth fruit and pronounced these words:
    "I believe, my child, through you in the Triune God
    and with you I will travel happily to Roman territory,
    being baptised for the remission of my many faults
235 and acknowledging thanks that through you I have been enlightened."
    Likewise the kinsmen too who were there
    and the rest of those who had come with her, a great host,
    cried out with one voice, acknowledging Christ:
    "We are all coming with you to Roman territory,
240 and when we are baptised may we win life eternal."
    And the emir was amazed at their eagerness:
    "Glory to you," he said, "the only benevolent God,
    who has no desire at all for a sinner's death,
    but mercifully waits for his return to you,
245 so that you may make all share in your kingdom."
    Then, taking their boundless wealth with them,
    they all set off together for Roman territory.
    When they came to the district of Cappadocia,
    the emir called a meeting of his youngsters:
250 "A thought has come to me, good soldiers,
    that I should go ahead and deliver the good news;
    for if someone else were to arrive before me, I should be utterly
       condemned
    by my beloved as feeble and lethargic."
    They replied that it was good to do this,
255 for it is right to fulfil the demands of passionate love.
    He thought out his plan well;
    he immediately changed his clothes, putting on Roman dress,
    a marvellous surcoat sprinkled with gold,
    of purple silk with a white triple border and ornamental griffins,
260 a very costly white turban with gold letters;
    he rode a chestnut mule with a star.
    Taking three of his own youngsters with him

258–60 Again the emir's dress may have semi-imperial connotations. The ἐπιλούρικιν
(breast-plate tunic) was normally padded and worn over chainmail, but was also often, as
here, a silk ceremonial costume; τρίβλαττον (with triple border) implies three silk stripes
or patches are attached (Haldon, 1990, 205–7, 277). Note that the turban is classed as
particularly 'Roman' Byzantine dress (Mango, 1981, 51). One might emend
χρυσόγραμμον to χρυσόγαμμον, 'with golden gammas', symbols of the Trinity, used
on imperial regalia in the sixth century (Lydus, De magistratibus 2.4) and later (Kazhdan
in ODB, under Gammata); cf. G4.922.

καί, τὸ τοῦ λόγου, πετασθεὶς ἔφθασεν εἰς τὸν οἶκον
καὶ ἔβαλεν εὐθὺς φωνὴν χαρᾶς ἐμπεπλησμένην·
265 «Περιστερά μου πάντερπνε, δέξαι τὸ σὸν γεράκιν
καὶ παραμύθησον αὐτὸ ἀπὸ τῆς ξενιτείας.»
    Καὶ διὰ ταύτην τὴν φωνὴν αἱ βάγιαι παρακύπτουν
καὶ ὡς τοῦτον ἐσκέψαντο, τὴν κυρὰν οὕτω λέγουν·
«Χαίροις, χαίροις, αὐθέντρια, ὁ αὐθέντης μας ἦλθεν.»
270 Ἐκείνη δὲ ὡς ἄπιστον ἐλογίζετο τοῦτο
(ὁ γὰρ τυχὸν αἰφνίδιον τοῦ ἐπιθυμουμένου
ὄναρ δοκεῖ φαντάζεσθαι ἀπὸ περιχαρείας)
καὶ πρὸς τὰς βάγιας ἔλεγε· «Φαντάσματα ὁρᾶτε;»
Ἔτι δὲ λέγειν θέλουσα καὶ πλείονα τοιαῦτα,
275 ὡς εἶδε τὸν νεώτερον ἐξαίφνης ἀνελθόντα,
λίαν ὠλιγοψύχησεν εἰς ἔκπληξιν ἐλθοῦσα
καὶ χεῖρας περιπλέξασα τὰς αὐτῆς τῷ τραχήλῳ
ἀπεκρεμάσθη ἄφωνος, δάκρυα μὴ κινοῦσα.
Ὡσαύτως καὶ ὁ ἀμιρᾶς γέγονεν ὥσπερ ἔνθους
280 καὶ τὴν κόρην περιλαβὼν καὶ βαλὼν εἰς τὸ στῆθος,
συμπεπλεγμένοι ἔμειναν ἐπὶ πολλὰς τὰς ὥρας.
Καὶ εἰ μὴ ἡ στρατήγισσα ἔβρεχε τούτους ὕδωρ,
εἰς γῆν ἂν ἔπεσον εὐθὺς ἀπ' ὀλιγοθυμίας.
Ἀγάπη γὰρ ὑπέρμετρος γεννᾷ πολλὰ τοιαῦτα
285 καὶ χαρὰ ὑπερβάλλουσα εἰς θάνατον ἀπάγει,
ὡς καὶ αὐτοὶ παρὰ μικρὸν ἔμελλον ὑποστῆναι, 19ν
μόλις δὲ ἠδυνήθησαν αὐτοὺς ἀποχωρίσαι.
Ἐφίλει γὰρ ὁ ἀμιρᾶς τοὺς ὀφθαλμοὺς τῆς κόρης,
περιεπλέκετο αὐτήν, μεθ' ἡδονῆς ἠρώτα·
290 «Πῶς ἔχεις, φῶς μου τὸ γλυκύ, πάντερπνόν μου δαμάλιν;
Πῶς ἔχεις, φίλτατε ψυχή, ἐμὴ παραμυθία,
περιστερά μου πάντερπνε, πανώραιόν μου δένδρον,
μετὰ τοῦ σοῦ ἀνθήματος, τέκνου τοῦ παμποθήτου;»
    Ἡ κόρη δ' ἀνανεοῦσα τὸν ἔρωτα ἐκ πόθου,
295 τοιαῦτα πρὸς τὸν ἀμιρᾶν ἐφθέγγετο γλυκέως·
«Καλῶς ἦλθες, ἐλπὶς ἐμή, ἀναψυχὴ τοῦ βίου,

---

294 ἀνανεοῦα G. cf. Kriaras. 1969– under ἀνανεῶ: ἀνανέουσα Kalonaros: Legrand
suggests δὲ τὸν ἔρωτα ἀνανεοῦσ' ἐκ πόθου

and, as the saying goes, flying, he reached the house,
and immediately let out a cry full of joy:
265 "My delightful dove, receive your hawk
and comfort him after his exile."
     At this cry the serving girls looked out
and, as they saw him, they spoke thus to their mistress:
"Rejoice, rejoice, my lady, our lord has come to us."
270 But she considered this incredible
(for he who unexpectedly achieves what he yearns for
is likely, in his great joy, to imagine it a dream)
and said to the serving girls, "Are you seeing visions?"
She was still wanting to make more such remarks
275 when she saw the young man suddenly coming up
and she fainted right away in her astonishment,
and clasping her arms around his neck
she hung in a trance, speechless, not shedding a tear.
The emir too became as if possessed
280 and embraced the girl and clasped her to his breast;
they remained entwined for many hours.
And if the general's lady had not splashed them with water,
they would have immediately fallen down in a faint.
For excessive love causes many such effects
285 and overwhelming joy leads to death,
a fate to which they were on the point of succumbing,
and with difficulty could the bystanders separate them.
The emir was kissing the girl's eyes,
clasping her and asking her with passion:
290 "How are you, my sweet light, my adorable heifer?
How are you, my dearest soul, my consolation,
my very delightful dove, my most beautiful tree,
with your offspring, our much loved child?"
     The girl, lovingly renewing passion,
295 uttered this sweetly to the emir:
"You are welcome, my hope, my life's refreshment,

266 The emotive word ξενιτεία reinforces the strength of the emir's allegiance to his new home in Roman territory.
275 Fainting is a frequent reaction to pleasant surprises in the ancient novels, as well as in the later popular Byzantine romances.
282–3 Splashing the lovers with water is somewhat bizarre (Alexiou, 1979, 61). This scene echoes Heliodoros: see Introduction, pp. xlvi–xlvii.
290 δαμάλι, 'heifer', praise for a pretty young woman in a society dominated by agriculture. The speech continues with bird and vegetable metaphors.

μεγίστη μου ἀντίληψις, ψυχῆς μου θυμηδία,
τὰ γὰρ ἡμέτερα καλῶς τῇ τοῦ Θεοῦ δυνάμει
τοῦ ἡμᾶς ἀξιώσαντος θεάσασθαι ἀλλήλους·
300 εἰπὲ καὶ σύ, αὐθέντα μου, τὰ περὶ σοῦ πῶς ἔχουν.»
«Πάντα καλῶς,» ἀντέφησε, «χάριτι τοῦ Χριστοῦ μου
τοῦ καρδίας φωτίσαντος μητρὸς καὶ συγγενῶν μου
καὶ ὁδηγήσαντος αὐτοὺς πρὸς φῶς θεογνωσίας,
οὓς μετ' ὀλίγον ὄψεσθε ἐρχομένους ἐνταῦθα.»
305 Εἶτα καὶ τέκνον τὸ αὐτοῦ λαβὼν εἰς τὰς ἀγκάλας,
τοιαῦτα ἀπεφθέγγετο ἐκ βάθους τῆς καρδίας:
«Πότε, γεράκιν μου καλόν, τὰς πτέρυγας ἀπλώσεις
καὶ κυνηγήσεις πέρδικα, ληστάδας ὑποτάξεις;»
Καὶ ταῦτα μὲν ὁ ἀμιρᾶς τὸ παιδίον ἐλάλει.
310 Ἔλευσιν δὲ τὴν ἑαυτοῦ πάντες ἀναμαθόντες
εἰς τοὺς οἴκους ἀπέτρεχον εἰπεῖν τὰ συγχαρίκια·
καὶ γέγονε πολλὴ χαρά, ἀμήχανον τὸ λέγειν· 20r
καὶ χοροὺς συστησάμενοι χορείας ἐποιοῦντο.
Ἐν τῇ χαρᾷ πάλιν χαρὰ ἐπέρχεται ἑτέρα·
315 ἦλθε γάρ τις <τὴν> τῆς μητρὸς ἄφιξιν ἐπαγγέλλων.
Καὶ ἦν ἰδεῖν πάντας ὁμοῦ, ἄνδρας τε καὶ γυναῖκας,
ἐξελθόντας εἰς ἀπαντὴν μετὰ τῆς στρατηγίσσης,
ὥστε μὴ σώζειν εὐχερῶς τούτους ἀπαριθμῆσαι.
Ὄντως θαῦμα παράδοξον ἔργον ὀρθῆς ἀγάπης·
320 τίς τοῦτο μὴ καταπλαγῇ, τίς μὴ θαυμάσῃ μᾶλλον
καὶ καταμάθῃ ἀκριβῶς ἔρωτος τὰς δυνάμεις,
πῶς ἀλλοφύλους ἥνωσεν, εἰς μίαν φέρων πίστιν;
Καὶ πλησίον γενόμενοι ἐπέζευον εὐθέως
καταμανθάνοντες αὐτούς, ἀκριβῶς ἐρωτῶντες·
325 ἡ νύμφη μὲν τὴν πενθερὰν καὶ τοὺς λοιποὺς ἰδίους,
ἡ δὲ τοὺς συγγενεῖς αὐτῆς χαίρουσα κατεφίλει.
Αἱ φάραι χρεμετίζουσαι ἔχαιρον σὺν ἀλλήλαις
καὶ χαρὰ πᾶσι γέγονε μείζω τῆς προλαβούσης.
Εἰς δὲ τὸν οἶκον φθάσαντες, γάμους εὐθὺς ποιοῦσι·

315 τὴν added by Legrand
327 χρεμετίζουσαι Legrand: σχηματίζουσαι G

my greatest defence, my soul's consolation,
for our affairs prosper through the might of God,
who has found us worthy to see each other again.
300 Now you too tell me, my lord, how are your concerns?"
"All go well," he replied, "by the grace of my Lord Christ,
who has enlightened the hearts of my mother and my kinsmen
and brought them to the light of knowledge of God.
You will see them soon, for they are coming here."
305   Then he took his child in his arms
and pronounced these words from the depths of his heart:
"When will you spread your wings, my fine hawk,
and hunt partridges and lay brigands low?"
This is what the emir said to the little boy.
310   Everyone learnt of his arrival
and ran to the houses to bring the good news.
And there was great joy, impossible to describe;
they began to dance and they held a celebration.
Amidst this joy, yet another joy was added,
315 for someone came announcing his mother's arrival.
And everyone could be seen together, both men and women,
going out with the general's lady to meet her,
so that it was not easy to count them accurately.
The results of sanctioned love are truly a strange wonder.
320 Who would not be astounded at this, who indeed would not be
         surprised
to learn precisely the power of Eros,
how he united those of different race, bringing them into one faith?
     So when they came near they immediately dismounted,
finding out about them, asking detailed questions,
325 the bride questioning her mother-in-law and the rest of those with her,
while the mother-in-law kissed the bride's kinsmen joyfully.
The horses neighed and rejoiced among themselves,
and joy came to all, greater than that which they had felt before.
     When they reached the house, they immediately held the wedding.

308 The emir's words provide a statement of frontier life consistent with Digenis' actual later activities.
316 It seems to be implied that men and women rarely acted together in this way.
321 It is unclear whether this moralising envisages a personified Eros or an abstract passion.
329 The wedding has, of course, already taken place and there already exists a son from it. This episode (not in E or Z) must be due to the redactor's assumption that the only reason for a woman to make a ceremonial arrival with attendant kinsmen is as a bride

330 καὶ τὴν μητέρα τὴν αὐτοῦ ὁ ἀμιρᾶς βαπτίσας   *E608*
    αὐτὸς ταύτην ἐδέξατο ἐν τῇ ἀναγεννήσει,
    ὡσαύτως καὶ τοὺς συγγενεῖς τοὺς σὺν αὐτῷ ἐλθόντας·
    καὶ πατὴρ πάντων γέγονεν ἐν Πνεύματι ἁγίῳ.
    Ἡ χαρὰ δὲ ἐπηύξανεν ἡ πάνδημος ἐκείνη·
335 ἔχαιρε γὰρ ἐπὶ μητρὶ υἱὸς τῇ πιστευσάσῃ,
    ἡ δὲ μήτηρ εὐφραίνετο ἐπὶ υἱῷ φιλτάτῳ.
    Μέρος δέ τι ὁ ἀμιρᾶς τοῦ οἴκου ἀφορίσας
    συγγενεῦσιν ἀπένειμεν ἐνδιαίτημα ἔχειν.   20v
    Τὸ δὲ παιδίον ηὔξανεν ὁ Διγενὴς Ἀκρίτης,   *E610*
340 χάρισμα ἔχων ἐκ Θεοῦ παράδοξον ἀνδρείας,
    ὥστε πάντας ἐκπλήττεσθαι τοὺς αὐτὸν καθορῶντας
    καὶ θαυμάζειν τὴν σύνεσιν καὶ τὴν γενναίαν τόλμην·
    φήμη δὲ ἦν περὶ αὐτοῦ εἰς ἅπαντα τὸν κόσμον.

330 And the emir stood sponsor for his mother in baptism,
     and himself received her on her rebirth,
     and likewise the kinsmen who had come with him.
     He became in the Holy Spirit the father of them all.
          That universal joy grew and grew.
335 The son rejoiced in his mother who had come to the faith,
     the mother took delight in her dearest son.
     The emir separated off an area of the house
     and set it apart for his kinsmen to have as a dwelling.
     The little boy, Digenis Akritis, the Frontiersman of Double Descent,
          grew,
340 having from God an extraordinary gift of bravery,
     so that all who saw him were astounded,
     and amazed at his understanding and noble daring.
     Stories about him spread throughout the whole world.

and as the prelude to a wedding, despite the fact that on this occasion it is the mother-in-law who makes a belated entrance. The omission of this passage in Z is presumably due to the compiler's common sense; absence in E could be because it was never present in *Digenis or dropped out in transmission. Either way it is a compositional roughness in G, though note (G4.930 ff.) that Digenis himself has a double wedding.

337 The establishment envisaged is such that a part of the house could be set aside for a group which probably included several nuclear families.

339–43 Here, as at his birth (G2.47–9), news of Digenis comes as a brief interpolation in the story of the conversion of the emir and his kinsmen, suggesting that this was once a separate poem. Elsewhere (G2.287–92, 3.105–6, 305–9) the integration is better, but the focus of the story remains the emir's need to leave and return to his family rather than the early career of Digenis himself.

Λόγος τέταρτος

Ἀνδραγαθίαι ἄρχονται ἐντεῦθεν τοῦ Ἀκρίτου,
καὶ πῶς τὴν κόρην ἥρπαξε τὴν πάγκαλον ἐκείνην
καὶ περὶ γάμου τοῦ αὐτοῦ λόγος τέταρτος ἔστιν.

Καὶ εὐθὺς περὶ ἔρωτος ὑμᾶς ἀναμιμνήσκω·
5 ῥίζα γὰρ οὗτος καὶ ἀρχὴ καθέστηκεν ἀγάπης,
ἐξ ἧς φιλία τίκτεται, εἶτα γεννᾶται πόθος,   E702
ὃς αὐξηθεὶς κατὰ μικρὸν φέρει καρπὸν τοιοῦτον,
μερίμνας μὲν διηνεκεῖς, ἐννοίας καὶ φροντίδας,   E703
εὐθὺς κινδύνους παμπληθεῖς καὶ χωρισμὸν γονέων.   E704
10 Νεότης γὰρ ἀκμάζουσα καρδίας ἀνασπάει,
εἶτα πάντα κατατολμᾷ τῶν ἀνεπιχειρήτων,   E704
θαλάττης μὲν ἐφίκεσθαι, πῦρ μηδόλως πτοεῖσθαι·   E705
δράκοντας δὲ καὶ λέοντας καὶ τὰ λοιπὰ θηρία
οὐδοτιοῦν λογίζεται στερεωθεὶς ὁ πόθος   E706
15 καὶ τοὺς λῃστὰς τοὺς τολμηροὺς ἀντ' οὐδενὸς ἡγεῖται,
νύκτας ἡμέρας προσδοκᾷ καὶ τὰς κλεισούρας κάμπους,   E708
ἀγρυπνίαν ἀνάπαυσιν καὶ τὰ μακρὰν πλησίον·   E708
πολλοὶ καὶ πίστιν τὴν αὐτῶν ἀρνοῦνται διὰ πόθον.
Καὶ τοῦτο μηδεὶς ἄπιστον ἐξ ὑμῶν λογισθήτω, 21r

---

4 εὐθὺς G: αὖθις Kalonaros, cf. Z1253   ἀναμιμνήσκω Legrand: ἀναμιμνήκω G
16 προσδοκᾷ Legrand: προσδοκᾶν G

Fourth book

From this point begin the brave deeds of Akritis the Frontiersman,
and how he abducted that very lovely girl,
and the fourth book is about his marriage.

    And immediately I remind you about passion,
5 for this is established as the root and beginning of love,
from which affection is begotten, then desire is born,
which as it increases gradually bears such fruit
as constant anxieties, worries and concerns,
and immediately brings abundant dangers and separation from
    parents.
10 For youth in its prime breaks hearts,
then dares every deed that has never been ventured,
to reach the sea and have no fear at all of fire;
ogres and lions and other wild beasts
desire, once established, considers as trifles,
15 and it regards bold brigands as worth nothing;
it reckons night as day and mountain passes as plains,
sleeplessness as rest and what is far off as near.
And many renounce their faith because of desire.
    And let none of you consider this incredible,

Book 4, the longest of G's eight books, deals with the hero's transition to manhood
through hunting exploits, culminating in his wooing of the girl who is abruptly
introduced at G4.254. At G4.971 ff. the emperor's visit is loosely linked to the main
narrative as the ultimate demonstration of Digenis' fame. The equivalent material in E
(without the emperor episode) is found at E702-1094.
1-64 The first part of Book 4 provides the point of articulation between the two parts of
the poem and is reflected, though more briefly, in E. This confirms that *Digenis* included
both the emir's story and that of Digenis, linked by similar narratives of the latter's
childhood and by their common exemplification of the power of love.
4-18 This passage, reflected in E702-8, begins with details (separation from parents
and the sea) of dubious relevance to Digenis, though the emir is separated from his
mother and his father has raided the sea (probably not for love). These are more general
characteristics of the ancient romance and its twelfth-century revival. Later items on the
list are specific to Digenis and especially the emir.

20 μάρτυρα γὰρ ἐπαινετὸν εἰς μέσον παραστήσω
ἀμιρᾶν τὸν πανεύγενον καὶ πρῶτον τῆς Συρίας,
ὃς εἶχε κάλλη πάντερπνα καὶ τόλμην θηριώδη
καὶ μέγεθος πανθαύμαστον, ἰσχὺν γενναιοτάτην,
καὶ μᾶλλον δεύτερος Σαμψὼν αὐτὸς ἐπενοήθη·
25 ἐκεῖνος γὰρ ἠρίστευσε χερσὶ λέοντα σχίσας,
οὗτος δὲ πλῆθος ἄπειρον ἀπέκτεινε λεόντων.
Παύσασθε γράφειν Ὅμηρον καὶ μύθους Ἀχιλλέως   E718
ὡσαύτως καὶ τοῦ Ἕκτορος, ἅπερ εἰσὶ ψευδέα.
Ἀλέξανδρος ὁ Μακεδὼν δυνατὸς ἐν φρονήσει,
30 Θεόν τε ἔχων συνεργὸν γέγονε κοσμοκράτωρ.
Αὐτὸς δὲ φρόνημα στερρὸν ἔχων Θεὸν ἔπεγνω,
ἐκέκτητο καὶ μετ' αὐτοῦ ἀνδρείαν τε καὶ τόλμην.
Φιλοπαπποῦ τοῦ γέροντος, Κιννάμου καὶ Ἰωαννάκη
οὐδ' ὅλως ἔστιν ἄξιον τὰ αὐτῶν καταλέγειν·
35 οὗτοι γὰρ ἐκαυχήσαντο μηδὲν πεποιηκότες,
τούτου δὲ πάντα ἀληθῆ καὶ μεμαρτυρημένα.   E721
Ἄμβρων ὑπῆρχεν ὁ παπποῦς, θεῖος του ὁ Καρόης·   E145
διαλεκτοὺς τὸν ἔδωκαν τρισχιλίους κονταράτους,   E728
πᾶσαν Συρίαν ὑπέταξεν, ἐπίασε τὸ Κοῦφερ·
40 εἶθ' οὕτως ἐν τοῖς μέρεσιν ἦλθε τῆς Ῥωμανίας,   E731
κάστρα πολλὰ ἐκούρσευσε χώρας τοῦ Ἡρακλέος,   E732
Χαρζιανὴν ἐπραίδευσε καὶ τὴν Καππαδοκίαν·
κόρην τερπνὴν ἀφήρπαξεν εὐγενῆ τῶν Δουκάδων   E733
διὰ κάλλος τὸ θαυμαστὸν καὶ τερπνὴν ἡλικίαν, 21v   E734
45 τὰ πάντα ἀρνησάμενος, πίστιν ὁμοῦ καὶ δόξαν,
καὶ γέγονε Χριστιανὸς ὀρθόδοξος διὰ ταύτην·   E735

20 for I shall set before you a renowned witness,
the most high-born emir and first man of Syria,
who possessed the most handsome grace and savage daring,
and quite amazing stature, most noble strength,
and indeed was thought to be a second Samson.
25 For Samson achieved distinction by rending a lion with his bare hands,
but the emir killed a boundless host of lions.
Cease writing of Homer and the legends of Achilles
and likewise of Hektor; these are false.
Alexander of Macedon, mighty in his judgement,
30 with God to work with him became ruler of the world.
But the emir with steadfast good sense recognised God,
and with him achieved bravery and daring.
As for old Philopappous, Kinnamos and Ioannakis,
it is not at all worth recounting stories about them:
35 for they have boasted but achieved nothing
while all stories about the emir are true and have witnesses.
Ambron was his grandfather, his uncle Karoïs;
they gave him three thousand picked spearsmen,
he subdued all Syria, he captured Kufah.
40 So then he came into the districts of Roman territory;
he plundered many fortresses of the land of Herakles,
he pillaged Charziane and Cappadocia.
He abducted a delightful high-born girl from the Doukas family,
because of her marvellous beauty and pleasing appearance,
45 renouncing everything including his faith and his reputation,
and he became an Orthodox Christian because of her;

25–36 This passage seems to move away from the power of love (though each of the heroes listed has a romantic attachment: Achilles with Briseis, Hektor with Andromache, even Alexander with e.g. Kandake and Roxane). Alexander was a potent symbol in Byzantine political mythology (Gleixner, 1961; Moennig, 1993). That the focus changes to general heroic renown is confirmed by mention of Philopappous and his friends who are not obviously motivated by love. It has been said that 'the tale of Digenis is unmistakably here claiming its place in the prestigious literary tradition of which Homer stands at the head' (Beaton, 1989, 44). But that claim is made in a most unpretentious way, using the convention of the 'lying Homer' prominent in the twelfth century in, e.g., the writings of John Tzetzes (Jeffreys, 1978, 126–31). The main point is to stress the veracity of stories about the emir: the other names are examples from different sources chosen to mark that point by contrast. This is the first mention in G before Book 6 of Philopappous, the leader of the guerrillas, Digenis' later opponents; they are not identified as such here (cf. G4.965, 6.120 ff.). Philopappous is not found in E at this point, but will soon appear in the controversial 'First meeting with the guerrillas' (beginning at E624 and Z1044); see G4.253 below.
38–42 For this expedition, cf. G1.49–56, 291–6.

καὶ ὅ ποτε πολέμιος δοῦλος ὤφθη Ῥωμαίων.
Ἐξ ὧν παιδίον τίκτεται περικαλλὲς τῷ ὄντι
καὶ ἐξ αὐτῆς γεννήσεως Βασίλειος ἐκλήθη·
50 λέγεται δὲ καὶ Διγενὴς ὡς ἀπὸ τῶν γονέων,
ἐθνικὸς μὲν ἀπὸ πατρός, ἐκ δὲ μητρὸς Ῥωμαῖος·
φοβερὸς δὲ γενόμενος, ὡς ὁ λόγος δηλώσει,
Ἀκρίτης ὀνομάζεται τὰς ἄκρας ὑποτάξας.
Τούτου πάππος Ἀντάκινος ἀπὸ τῶν Κινναμάδων,
55 ὃς τέθνηκεν ἐξόριστος προστάξει βασιλέως
Βασιλείου τοῦ εὐτυχοῦς, ἀκρίτου τοῦ μεγάλου·
πολὺς ὢν κλῆρος ἐν αὐτῷ καὶ ἀνείκαστος δόξα,
μέγας μὲν ἐφημίζετο στρατηγὸς παρὰ πάντων.
Μάμμη δὲ ἡ στρατήγισσα εὐγενὴς τῶν Δουκάδων·
60 θείους εἶχε τοὺς θαυμαστούς, ἀδελφοὺς τῆς μητρός του,
οἵ καὶ ἐμονομάχησαν διὰ τὴν ἀδελφήν των
τὸν ἀμιρᾶν τὸν θαυμαστὸν τὸν ἑαυτοῦ πατέρα.
Οὗτος ἐβλάστησε φυλῆς ἐξ εὐγενῶν Ῥωμαίων
καὶ γέγονε περίβλεπτος εἰς τὰς ἀνδραγαθίας.
65 Ἤδη λοιπὸν ἀρξώμεθα τὰ αὐτοῦ καταλέγειν.
Οὗτος τοίνυν ὁ θαυμαστὸς Βασίλειος Ἀκρίτης
παιδόθεν εἰς καθηγητὴν παρὰ πατρὸς ἐδόθη
καὶ τρεῖς ὅλους ἐνιαυτοὺς μαθήμασι σχολάσας
τῇ τοῦ νοὸς ὀξύτητι πλῆθος ἔσχε γραμμάτων. 22r
70 Ἐντεῦθεν ἱππηλάσια, καὶ κυνηγεῖν ποθήσας
μετὰ πατρὸς ἐσχόλαζε καθ' ἑκάστην ἐν τούτοις.
Μιᾷ τοίνυν τῶν ἡμερῶν τὸν πατέρα του λέγει:
«Πόθος, αὐθέντα καὶ πατήρ, ἐσέβη εἰς τὴν ψυχήν μου
τοῦ δοκιμάσαι ἐμαυτὸν εἰς θηρίων πολέμους·
75 καὶ εἴπερ ὅλως ἀγαπᾷς Βασίλειον υἱόν σου,
εἰς τόπον ἂς ἐξέλθωμεν ἔνθα εἰσὶ θηρία,
καὶ πάντως βλέψεις λογισμὸν ἀεί με ἐνοχλοῦντα.»

47 ὅ ποτε Legrand: ὁ ποτὲ G
51 Ῥωμαῖος Legrand: ῥωμαίας G
57 ὢν G: ἦν Z1320, perhaps correctly
77 βλέψεις G: σβέσεις Grégoire, 1942, 274, cf. Z1357

and he who had once been an enemy proved to be a slave of the
  Romans.
    From these was born a little boy, really very beautiful,
    and at his birth he was named Basil:
50 and he is called Digenis, Of Double Descent, because of his parents,
    for he was a heathen on his father's side and a Roman on his mother's:
    and since he became feared, as the story will reveal,
    he is called Akritis, the Frontiersman, because he subjugated the
      frontiers.
    His grandfather was Antakinos from the Kinnamos family,
55 who died whilst an exile on the orders of the emperor,
    Basil the fortunate, the great frontiersman:
    a great inheritance falling to him and unimaginable glory,
    he was famed among all as a great general.
    The hero's grandmother was a high-born general's lady, from the
      Doukas family.
60 He had marvellous uncles, brothers of his mother,
    who fought in single combat for the sake of their sister
    the marvellous emir, his father.
    He was an offspring of the race of high-born Romans,
    and became celebrated for his brave deeds.
65 Now then, let us begin to recount his achievements.
    And so this marvellous Basil the Frontiersman
    from childhood was given by his father to a teacher:
    and after he had devoted three whole years to his lessons,
    through the sharpness of his mind he had acquired a mass of learning.
70 Then on to horsemanship, and as he wanted to hunt
    he devoted himself with his father every day to these matters.
    And so, one day, he said to his father:
    "A desire, my lord and father, has entered my soul,
    to test myself by fighting wild beasts:
75 and, if you love Basil your son at all,
    let us go out to a place where there are wild beasts,
    and you will certainly see the thought that is always troubling me."

56 On the possible identities of an emperor named Basil, see the Name Index. There may
also be reference to the common root with the word βασιλεύς itself, or an explanation for
the baptismal name of Digenis, or a reference to the emperor's visit later in this book (not
in E).
68 Not to be taken as information on contemporary educational practice but as a
conventional sign of heroic achievement in this sphere comparable to other, later,
romance heroes.

Λόγους τοιούτους ὁ πατὴρ ἀκούων τοῦ φιλτάτου
ἠγάλλετο τῷ πνεύματι, ἔχαιρε τῇ καρδίᾳ,
80 μετὰ πολλῆς τῆς ἡδονῆς τοῦτον ἐκατεφίλει:
«Ὢ τέκνον ποθεινότατον, ὦ ψυχὴ καὶ καρδία,   E228
θαυμαστοὶ μὲν οἱ λόγοι σου, γλυκεῖα καὶ ἡ γνώμη,
πλὴν οὐ παρέστηκε καιρὸς τῆς θηριομαχίας·
θηρίων γὰρ ὁ πόλεμος δεινότατος ὑπάρχει,
85 καὶ σὺ παῖς δωδεκάχρονος ἥβης ἐκτὸς ὑπάρχεις   E742
ἀνάξιος παντάπασι πολεμεῖν τὰ θηρία.
Μή, γλυκύτατον τέκνον μου, τοῦτο εἰς νοῦν ἐμβάλῃς,
μηδὲ ῥόδα σου τὰ καλὰ πρὸ καιροῦ ἐκτρυγήσῃς·
ὅταν δὲ θέλοντος Θεοῦ ἀνὴρ τέλειος φθάσῃς,
90 τότε λοιπὸν λόγου ἐκτὸς πολεμεῖν τὰ θηρία.»
Καὶ ὡς ταῦτα ἀκήκοε τὸ εὐγενὲς παιδίον,
ἐλυπήθη κατὰ πολύ, ἐτρώθη τὴν καρδίαν·
καὶ δακρύσας τοῖς ὀφθαλμοῖς λέγει πρὸς τὸν πατέρα:
«Εἰ μετὰ τὴν τελείωσιν ἀνδραγαθήσω, πάτερ,
95 τί μοι ἐκ τούτου ὄφελος; Τοῦτο πάντες ποιοῦσιν.   22v
Ἄρτι ποθῶ δοξάσασθαι καὶ τὸ γένος λαμπρῦναι·
πληροφορῶ δὲ καὶ ἐσὲ τὸν ἐμὸν εὐεργέτην
ὅτι δοῦλον θέλεις ἔχειν με ἀνδρειότατον, μέγαν,
καὶ συνεργὸν καὶ βοηθὸν εἰς πάντας τοὺς πολέμους.»
100 Καὶ κατένευσεν ὁ πατὴρ τῇ προθυμίᾳ τοῦ νέου·
φύσεως γὰρ τὸ εὐγενὲς ἐκ παιδόθεν προφαίνει.
Τῇ δὲ ἐπαύριον λαβὼν τὸν γυναικάδελφόν του
τὸν γεννηθέντα ὕστερον, τὸν χρυσὸν Κωνσταντῖνον,   E753
καὶ τὸν υἱὸν μεθ᾽ ἑαυτοῦ Ἀκρίτην τὸν γενναῖον
105 καὶ ἀπὸ τῶν ἀγούρων του τινὰς καβαλλαρίους
ἀπὸ τὴν ἕλην παρευθὺς ἐξῆλθον εἰς τὰ ἄλση.
Καὶ μακρόθεν ἐσκέψαντο ἄρκτους φοβερωτάτους·
ἄρσεν καὶ θῆλυ ὑπήρχασιν, ἀρκοπούλια δύο.   E757
Βάλλει φωνὴν ὁ θεῖός του: «Βασίλειε, ἄρτι ἂς ἴδω·
110 πλὴν τὸ ῥαβδίν σου ἔπαρον, ξίφος μηδὲν βαστάσῃς·
ἄρκτους οὐκ ἔνι ἐπαινετὸν πολεμεῖν μετὰ ξίφους.»
Καὶ ἦν θαῦμα φρικτὸν ἰδεῖν καὶ ξένον τοῖς ὁρῶσι·
καὶ γὰρ φωνῆς ὡς ἤκουσε τοῦ θείου τὸ παιδίον,

---

85 ἥβης ἐκτὸς Chasiotis (Eideneier, 1970, 306): ἡβήσεκστος G
86 ἀνάξιος Legrand: ἀνάξιον G
90 πολεμεῖν G: perhaps πολεμεῖς
106 ἀπὸ Mavrogordato: εἰς G
108 ἀρκοπούλια G: καὶ ἀρκοπούλια Mavrogordato

Hearing such words from his very dear son, the father
was glad in spirit, he rejoiced in his heart
80 and with much pleasure he kissed him:
"Most beloved child, my heart and soul,
your words are marvellous and your opinion sweet,
except that the time for battling with wild beasts has not come.
For fighting wild beasts is very terrible,
85 and you are a boy of twelve, not yet in your prime,
in every way unfit to fight wild beasts.
Do not, my sweetest child, set your heart on this,
do not pluck your fair roses before their time;
when, by God's will, you have come to full manhood,
90 then indeed without argument you may fight wild beasts."
When the high-born youth heard this,
he was much grieved, he was cut to the heart
and with tears in his eyes he said to his father:
"If I do valiant deeds after I have reached manhood, father,
95 what benefit do I gain from that? This is what everyone does.
It is now that I want to achieve renown and to shed lustre on my
family,
and I tell you, my benefactor,
that you will have in me a great servant, your bravest,
and an associate and assistant in all your wars."
100 And the father consented to the young man's eagerness,
for nobility of nature is apparent from childhood.
On the next day, taking his wife's brother,
the last-born, the golden Constantine,
and with him his son Akritis, the noble Frontiersman,
105 and some horsemen from among his youngsters,
they immediately went out from the thicket to the woods.
From a distance they caught sight of some very fierce bears.
There were a male and female and their two cubs.
His uncle let out a shout: "Basil, now let me see.
110 Just take your stick, don't carry your sword.
There is no glory in fighting bears with a sword."
And it was a terrifying and strange sight for the onlookers to see,
for when the boy heard his uncle's shout,

111 A rationalisation of Digenis' bare-handed encounter with the bears although he was
on a well-armed hunting expedition?

παραυτίκα ἐπέζευσε καὶ λύει τὸ ζωνάριν,
115 ἐκδύει τὸ ὑπολούρικον (ἦτον πολὺς ὁ καύσων)
καὶ τὰς ποδέας ὀχυρῶς πήξας εἰς τὸ ζωνάριν,
καμηλαυκίτζιν χαμηλὸν βαλὼν εἰς τὸ κεφάλιν,
ὡς ἀστραπὴ ἐξεπήδησεν ἀπὸ περιστηθίου·
μηδὲν ἐπιφερόμενος εἰ μὴ λιτὸν ῥαβδίτζιν,
120 εἶχε δὲ δύναμιν πολλήν, ἀκόλουθον τὸ τάχος. 23r
Καὶ πλησίον γενόμενος ἔνθα ἦσαν οἱ ἄρκτοι,
προϋπαντᾷ τὸ θηλυκὸν φθονοῦν διὰ τὰ παιδία   E766
καὶ σφόδρα μυκησάμενον πρὸς ἐκεῖνον ἐξῆλθεν.
Ἐκεῖνος ὢν ἀπείραστος εἰς θηριομαχίαν
125 οὐκ ἐγυρίσθη ὄπισθεν νὰ τοῦ δώσῃ ῥαβδέαν   E768
ἀλλ᾽ ἐπεσέβη σύντομα, ἐκ τὴν μέσην τὸ πιάνει
καὶ σφίγξας τοὺς βραχίονας εὐθὺς ἀπέπνιξέ τον   E770
καὶ τὰ ἐντὸς ἐξήρχετο ἐκ τοῦ στόματος τούτου·
ἔφυγε δὲ τὸ ἀρσενικὸν εἰς τὴν ἕλην ἀπέσω.
130   Ὁ θεῖος του τὸν ἐφώνησε: «Βλέπε, τέκνον, μὴ φύγῃ.»
Κἀκεῖνος ἀπὸ τῆς σπουδῆς ἀφῆκε τὸ ῥαβδίν του
καὶ πετάσας ὡς ἀετὸς ἔφθασε τὸ θηρίον·
ἡ ἄρκτος ἐστράφη πρὸς αὐτὸν στόμα χανοῦσα μέγα
καὶ ὥρμησε τὴν κεφαλὴν τοῦ παιδὸς ἐκλαφῦξαι.
135 Τὸ δὲ παιδίον σύντομα τὸ μάγουλόν του πιάνει   E776
καὶ τινάξας ἀπέκτεινε χαμαὶ βαλὼν τὸ θηρίον,
στρέψας τὸν τράχηλον αὐτοῦ ἐξεσφονδύλισέ το
καὶ παρευθὺς ἀπέψυξεν εἰς τὰς χεῖρας τοῦ νέου.
Ἐκ δὲ τῶν ἄρκτων τοὺς βρυγμοὺς καὶ τῶν ποδῶν τοὺς κτύπους,
140 ἔλαφος ἐξεπήδησε μέσον τῆς παγαναίας·
ὁ ἀμιρᾶς ἐλάλησε: «Δέχου, τέκνον, ἐμπρός σου.»
Καὶ τοῦ πατρὸς ὡς ἤκουσεν, ὥσπερ πάρδος ἐξέβη,
καὶ εἰς ὀλίγα πηδήματα φθάνει τὴν ἐλαφῖναν
καὶ τῶν ποδῶν δραξάμενος αὐτῆς τῶν ὀπισθίων,
145 ἀποτινάξας ἔσχισε ταύτην εἰς δύο μέρη.
Τίς μὴ θαυμάσῃ μέγεθος Θεοῦ τῶν χαρισμάτων 23v
καὶ τὴν αὐτοῦ ἀσύγκριτον δύναμιν μεγαλύνῃ;

---

115 ἐκδύει Trapp: ἐκδύεται G
120 ἀκόλουθον Eideneier, 1970, 306: ἀκολουθὸν G ἀκολουθοῦν Kalonaros ἀκολουθῶν
Politis
121 γενόμενος Politis, 1967, 19: γενόμενοι G
133 ἄρκτος Legrand: ἄκτος G
135 σύντομα Legrand: συντόμως G   136 Trapp corrects to θήριον
137 ἐξεσφονδύλισέ Legrand: ἀπε^ἐξε^σφονδήλισέ G

he immediately dismounted and undid his belt.
115 He took off his surcoat (the heat was intense)
and tucking his kilts firmly into his belt,
putting a low cap on his head,
lightning seemed to flash from his breast-plate.
Although he carried nothing except a simple stick,
120 yet he possessed great strength and the speed that goes with it.
As he drew near where the bears were,
the female came out to meet him, protective of her cubs,
and made for him, growling loudly.
He, lacking experience in fighting wild beasts,
125 did not turn around to strike it with his stick
but rushed up quickly and seized it round the waist
and, tightening his grasp, immediately throttled it,
and its innards came out through its mouth.
The male fled back to the thicket.
130   His uncle shouted to him: "Child, see it doesn't get away."
And in his haste he abandoned his stick
and flew like an eagle and overtook the wild beast.
The bear turned towards him with its huge mouth agape
and charged up to swallow the boy's head.
135 The boy suddenly seized its jaw
and shook and killed the beast, throwing it to the ground;
he twisted its neck and snapped its spine
and immediately it expired in the young man's hands.
After the roars from the bears and the drumming of feet,
140 a deer sprang up from the middle of the covert.
The emir cried: "Take it, my child, in front of you."
As soon as he heard his father, he rushed out like a leopard
and with a few strides reached the deer
and, grasping it by its rear legs,
145 shook it and tore it in two.
Who would not marvel at the greatness of God's blessings
and who would not praise his incomparable might?

---

115 The ὑπολούρικον must be the same external ἐπιλώρικον which Maximou removes
in the heat at G6.781 (Kolias, 1988, 59, note 161).
116 Cf. G4.1058 and Ptochoprodromos 4.190–1, the earliest external evidence for the
existence of a version of *Digenis*; see Introduction, p. xlvii.
140–5 The emperor Basil I was also said to have caught a deer by the back legs and torn
it apart (Genesios 4.40); cf. G4.1072.

Ὄντως ἔργον παράδοξον τὰς ἐννοίας ἐκπλῆττον,
πῶς τὴν ἔλαφον ἔφθασε παιδίον χωρὶς ἵππου,
150 πῶς τοὺς ἄρκτους ἐφόνευσε μηδὲν ἐν χερσὶν ἔχον,
ὄντως Θεοῦ τὸ δώρημα καὶ δεξιᾶς ὑψίστου.
Ὦ πόδες ὡραιότατοι, ἐφάμιλλοι πτερύγων,
οἱ δορκάδος νικήσαντες τὸ τάχος παραδόξως
καὶ συντρίψαντες δύναμιν τῶν φοβερῶν θηρίων.
155 Ἅπερ ὁρῶντες οἱ ἐκεῖ τότε παρατυχόντες,
τὸ θαῦμα ἐκπληττόμενοι ἔλεγον πρὸς ἀλλήλους: E780
«Θεοτόκε, τὸ θέαμα ὃ βλέπομεν 'ς τὸν νέον.   E781–2
Οὐκ ἔστιν τοῦτος ἄνθρωπος ὥσπερ οἱ ἐκ τοῦ κόσμου· E1326
ὁ Θεὸς τοῦτον ἀπέστειλε διὰ τοὺς ἀνδρειωμένους   E783
160 νὰ τὸν βλέπουν, νὰ χαίρωνται, πῶς πολεμεῖ, πῶς τρέχει.»
Ὡς δὲ ταῦτα ἐλέγασιν ὁ πατὴρ καὶ ὁ θεῖος,   E785
λέων ἐξέβη μέγιστος ἀπὸ τοῦ καλαμιῶνος   E786, 1123
καὶ εὐθὺς περιεστράφησαν ἰδεῖν τὸν ἀγουρίτζην·
εἰς ἔλην τὸν ἐσκέψαντο σύρνοντα τὰ θηρία.
165 Μὲ τὴν δεξιὰν ἔσυρνε γὰρ οὓς ἐφόνευσεν ἄρκτους,
καὶ μετὰ τὴν ἀριστερὰν σύρει τὴν ἐλαφῖναν.
Ὁ θεῖος του τὸν ἐλάλησεν: «Ἐλθέ, τέκνον, ἐνθάδε·
καὶ τὰ νεκρὰ κατάλειψον, ἔχομεν ἄλλα ζῶντα,
ἐν οἷς καὶ δοκιμάζονται τῶν εὐγενῶν οἱ παῖδες.»
170 Ὁ παῖς ἀνταπεκρίνατο λέγων αὐτῷ τοιάδε:
«Εἰ θέλημα Θεοῦ ἐστι τοῦ εὐδοκοῦντος πάντα,
εἰ ἔχω τοῦ πατρὸς εὐχὴν καὶ τῆς καλῆς μητρός μου, 24r
νεκρὸν θεάσῃ καὶ αὐτὸν ὥσπερ τοὺς δύο ἄρκτους.»
Καὶ ὥρμησε ξίφους χωρὶς εἰς τὸν λέοντα ὑπάγειν
175 καὶ λέγει τον ὁ θεῖος του: «Ἔπαρον τὸ σπαθίν σου·
οὗτος οὐκ ἔστιν ἔλαφος ἵνα τὸν σχίσῃς μέσον.»
Εὐθὺς δὲ ὁ νεώτερος τοιόνδε λόγον ἔφη:
«Ὁ Θεὸς οὐκ ἀδυνατεῖ, θεῖέ μου καὶ αὐθέντα,
παραδοῦναι εἰς χεῖράς μου καθάπερ καὶ ἐκεῖνον.»
180 Καὶ τὸ σπαθὶν δραξάμενος κινᾷ πρὸς τὸ θηρίον·
ὅταν δὲ ἐπλησίασεν, ἀποπηδᾷ ὁ λέων
καὶ χαρζανίσας τὴν οὐρὰν ἔδερε τὰς πλευράς του
καὶ μέγα βρυχησάμενος εἰς τὸν νέον ἐξῆλθε.

157 τὸ θέαμα ὃ G: τί θέαμα Politis   'ς Trapp: εἰς G
160 νὰ χαίρωνται Politis: πῶς χαίρεται G
161 ὁ θεῖος Eideneier, 1970, 307, cf. G4.190, E785: οἱ θεῖοι G
171 written twice in G (23v/24r)
183 μέγα Legrand, cf. Z1469: μεγάλα G

Truly it was an extraordinary deed that confounds the understanding,
how the boy caught up with the deer without a horse,
150 how he slew the bears with nothing in his hands,
truly a gift from God and from the right hand of the Highest.
Most beautiful feet, the equal of wings,
which against all expectation defeated the deer's speed,
and crushed the might of fearsome wild beasts!
155   When the bystanders who were there at that time saw this,
they were astonished at the miracle and said to each other:
"Mother of God, the spectacle that we see in this young man!
This is not a man like those of this world.
God has sent him so that men of bravery
160 can see and rejoice at how he fights and how he runs."
While his father and uncle were saying this,
a huge lion came out of the reed-bed
and immediately they turned around to see the young lad;
they caught sight of him in the thicket dragging the wild animals.
165 For with his right hand he was dragging the bears he had killed
and with his left he was dragging the deer.
His uncle cried out to him: "Come here, my child,
and abandon the dead bodies, we have other living creatures
against which the sons of the high-born may test themselves."
170   The boy said this in reply to him:
"If it is the wish of God who looks kindly on all things,
and if I have the blessing of my father and my lovely mother,
you will see it dead too, like the two bears."
And he rushed to go against the lion without a sword
175 and his uncle said to him: "Take your sword,
this is not a deer for you to tear apart."
Immediately the young man spoke these words:
"God is not unable, my uncle and lord,
to deliver it into my hands like the deer."
180 And grasping his sword, he made for the beast.
When he came near, the lion leaped up
and swished its tail and lashed its flanks
and, roaring loudly, attacked the young man.

Τὸ δὲ παιδίον τὸ σπαθὶν εἰς ὕψος ἀνατείνας
185 κρούει τον κατὰ κεφαλῆς πλήρης εἰς τὴν μεσίαν,
καὶ διεσχίσθη ἡ κεφαλὴ ἄχρι τῶν ὤμων κάτω.
Καὶ πρὸς τὸν θεῖον του ὁ Διγενὴς τοιόνδε λόγον ἔφη:
«Ὁρᾷς, χρυσὲ αὐθέντα μου, Θεοῦ τὰ μεγαλεῖα;
Οὐ κεῖται ἄφωνος, νεκρός, ὥσπερ οἱ δύο ἄρκτοι;»
190 Καὶ κατεφίλησαν αὐτὸν ὁ πατὴρ καὶ ὁ θεῖος,
χεῖρας τε καὶ βραχίονας, ὀμμάτια καὶ στῆθος.
Καὶ ἀμφότεροι χαίροντες εἶπον αὐτῷ τοιάδε:
«Πᾶς ὁ βλέπων τὴν ἔμνοστον ἡλικίαν καὶ κάλλος
τὸ σόν, ὦ περιπόθητε, ὄντως οὐ μὴ ἀμφιβάλῃ,
195 ἀλλὰ βεβαίως δέξεται τὰς σὰς ἀνδραγαθίας.»
Εἶχε γὰρ ὁ νεώτερος εὔνοστον ἡλικίαν,
κόμην ξανθήν, ἐπίσγουρον, ὀμμάτια μεγάλα, 24v
πρόσωπον ἄσπρον, ῥοδινόν, κατάμαυρον ὀφρύδιν,
καὶ στῆθος ὥσπερ κρύσταλλον, ὀργυιὰν εἶχε τὸ πλάτος.
200 Τοῦτον ὁρῶν ἠγάλλετο ὁ πατὴρ αὐτοῦ λίαν
καὶ χαίρων ἔλεγεν αὐτῷ μεθ' ἡδονῆς μεγάλης,
ὅτι «Τὸ καῦμα ἔστι πολύ, ἔνι καὶ μεσημέριν
καὶ τὰ θηρία κρύβονται ἀπάρτι εἰς τὴν ἕλην·
καὶ δεῦρο ἂς ἀπέλθωμεν εἰς τὸ ψυχρὸν τὸ ὕδωρ
205 καὶ νίψον σου τὸ πρόσωπον ἐκ τῶν πολλῶν ἱδρώτων·
ἀλλάξεις δὲ καὶ τὰ φορεῖς, εἰσὶ γὰρ μεμιαμμένα
ἐκ τῶν θηρίων τοὺς ἀφροὺς καὶ λέοντος τὸ αἷμα.
Καὶ τρισμακάριστος ἐγὼ ἔχων τοιοῦτον παῖδα,
πλύνω δὲ καὶ τοὺς πόδας σου μὲ τὰς ἰδίας χεῖρας·
210 ἀπάρτι πᾶσαν μέριμναν ῥίψω ἐκ τὴν ψυχήν μου,
νὰ εἰμὶ καὶ ἀφρόντιστος ἔνθα σε ἀποστείλω,
εἴς τε τὰ κούρση τὰ πολλὰ καὶ πολεμίων βίγλας.»
Καὶ παρευθὺς ἀμφότεροι εἰς τὴν πηγὴν ἀπῆλθον
(ἦν δὲ τὸ ὕδωρ θαυμαστόν, ψυχρὸν ὡς τὸ χιόνιν)
215 καὶ καθεσθέντες γύρωθεν, οἱ μὲν ἔνιπτον χεῖρας,
οἱ δὲ τὸ πρόσωπον αὐτοῦ, ὁμοίως καὶ τοὺς πόδας.
Ἔρρεεν ἔξω τῆς πηγῆς καὶ ἔπινον ἀπλήστως,
ὡς ἂν ἐκ τούτου γένωνται κἀκεῖνοι ἀνδρειωμένοι.

193 τὴν G, corrected from σὴν
208–9 Trapp transposes these two lines, cf. Z1493–4
218 τούτου Legrand: τού (sic) G

The boy, raising his sword up high,

185 struck down on its head, full in the middle,
and its head was split as far down as the shoulders.
And Digenis spoke these words to his uncle:
"You see, my golden lord, God's mighty work.
Does it not lie silent, dead like the two bears?"

190   And his father and his uncle kissed him,
his hands and his arms, his eyes and his chest.
And both said this to him joyfully:
"Everyone who sees your graceful appearance and your beauty,
our beloved child, will certainly have no doubts

195 but will surely accept your valiant deeds."
For the young man had a graceful appearance,
with fair curly hair, large eyes,
a white and rosy face, deep black eyebrows,
and he had a chest like crystal, a fathom broad.

200   Looking at him, his father was absolutely delighted
and joyfully said to him with great pleasure
that "The heat is great, it is also mid-day
and the wild beasts are now lying low in the thicket.
Come, let us go off to the cold water

205 and you can bathe your face after your copious sweating.
You will change what you are wearing, for it is stained
with foam from the wild beasts and the lion's blood.
And I, who am thrice-blessed in possessing such a boy,
will also wash your feet with my own hands;

210 from now on I shall abandon all the concern I felt in my soul
and have no anxiety about where I send you,
both on many raids and against enemy guard-posts."
    And immediately they all went off to the spring
(the water was marvellous, cold as snow)

215 and as they sat round him, some bathed his hands,
others his face and likewise his feet.
Water flowed out from the spring and they drank insatiably,
so that they too would become valiant by doing this.

---

197 This brief portrait (cf. G1.356) with its string of adjectives relates to a tradition of
physiognomic literature represented in the twelfth century by the descriptions of Homeric
heroes by Isaac Porphyrogennetos and John Tzetzes.
216 Two lines are here left blank in G for no apparent reason (there is no extra material
in Z).
218 No parallels have been found for this action.

Ήλλαξε δὲ καὶ τὸ παιδὶν τὴν ἑαυτοῦ ἐσθῆτα·
220 βάλλει πτενὰ μαχλάμια διὰ τὸ καταψυχῆσαι,
τὸ μὲν ἐπάνω κόκκινον μὲ τὰς χρυσὰς τὰς ῥίζας, 25r
αἱ δὲ ῥίζαι του χυμευταὶ μετὰ μαργαριτάρων,   E1465
τὸν τράχηλόν του γεμιστὸν ἄμβαρ ὁμοῦ καὶ μόσχον·
τρανὰ μαργαριτάρια εἶχεν ἀντὶ κομβίων,
225 τὰ δὲ θηλύκια στρεπτὰ ἐκ καθαροῦ χρυσίου.
Τουβία ἐφόρει ἐξάκουστα, γρύψους ὡραϊσμένους,   E1494
τὰ πτερνιστήρια πλεκτὰ μετὰ λίθων τιμίων·
ἐπὶ τῶν ἔργων τῶν χρυσῶν εἶχε λυχνίτας λίθους.
Πάμπολλα δὲ ἐσπούδαζε τὸ εὐγενὲς παιδίον
230 εἰς τὴν μητέρα ἀπελθεῖν μὴ δι' αὐτὸν λυπῆται,
καὶ ἠνάγκαζεν ἅπαντας εἰς τὸ καβαλλικεῦσαι.
Ἵππον ἐμετεσέλλισεν ἄσπρον ὡς περιστέριν,
ἦτον ὁ σγόρδος του πλεκτὸς μετὰ λίθων τιμίων
καὶ κωδωνίτζια χρυσὰ μέσον τῶν λιθαρίων,
235 πάμπολλα κωδωνίτζια, καὶ ἦχος ἐτελεῖτο
ἐνήδονος καὶ θαυμαστός, πάντας ὑπερεκπλήττων·
πρασινορρόδινον βλαττὶν εἶχεν εἰς τὸ καποῦλιν
καὶ τὴν σέλλαν ἐσκέπαζε νὰ μὴ κονιορτοῦται·
τὸ σελλοχάλινον πλεκτὸν μετὰ χρυσῶν σβερνίδων,   E1489
240 τὰ ὅλα ἔργα χυμευτὰ μετὰ μαργαριτάρων.   E1465
Ἦτον ὁ ἵππος τολμηρὸς καὶ θρασὺς εἰς τὸ παίζειν,
τὸ δὲ παιδίον εὔθειον εἰς τὸ καβαλλικεύειν·
πᾶς ὁ βλέπων ἐθαύμαζε τὸν ἄγουρον ἐκεῖνον,
πῶς μὲν ὁ ἵππος ἔπαιζε κατὰ γνώμην τοῦ νέου,
245 πῶς δὲ αὐτὸς ἐκάθητο ὥσπερ μῆλον εἰς δένδρον.
Καὶ ὥρμησαν τοῦ ἀπελθεῖν εἰς τὸν ἴδιον οἶκον·
οἱ μὲν ἄγουροι ἔμπροσθεν κατὰ τάξιν ὑπάγουν, 25v
ἀπ' αὐτοῦ δὲ ὁ θεῖος του καὶ ὁ πατὴρ ὀπίσω
καὶ μέσον ὁ νεώτερος ὡς ἥλιος ἀστράπτων
250 κοντάριν ἐμαλάκιζε μετὰ τὴν δεξιάν του
πρασινοαραβίτικον μετὰ χρυσοῦ διβέλλου·
ὡραῖος ἦν εἰς ὅρασιν, τερπνὸς εἰς συντυχίαν,

---

220 πτενὰ μαχλάμια Kalonaros, cf. G6.715, Z3615: στενὰ μοχλόβια G
223 τὸν Legrand: τὸ G ἄμβαρ Trapp: ἀβὰρ G
226 ἐξάκουστα G: ὀξυκάστορα Alexiou, 1979, 61, cf. E1494
233 ἦτον ὁ σγόρδος του πλεκτὸς Trapp, cf. Z1519: πλεκτὸς ἦτον ὁ σγόρδος του
Legrand ὁ σγόρδος του πλεκτὸς ἦτον G
237 πρασινορρόδινον Legrand, cf. Z1523: πράσινον ρόδινον G

And the young boy changed his garments.
220 He put on thin robes to cool himself;
the upper one was red, with golden hems,
and its hems were embroidered with pearls,
its neck was full of ambergris together with musk;
it had large pearls in place of buttons
225 and its buttonholes were twisted from pure gold.
He wore resplendent leggings, ornamental griffins,
spurs which were plaited with precious stones;
on the gold work he had glowing red stones.
The high-born boy made great haste
230 to return to his mother, so that she should not be upset about him,
and he urged everyone to ride back.
He put his saddle on another horse as white as a dove;
its forelock was plaited with precious stones
and there were little golden bells amongst the gems,
235 very many little bells, and the sound they made
was pleasant and marvellous, astonishing everyone.
It had a green and rosy silk on its rump
and this covered the saddle so that it should not get dusty;
the saddle and bridle were plaited with golden points,
240 the whole work was set with pearls.
The horse was bold and lively in its exercises,
the boy was quick in his horsemanship.
Everyone who saw him was amazed at that youngster,
how the horse pranced in response to the young man's wishes,
245 how he himself sat like an apple on a tree.
And they hastened to return to their own home.
The youngsters went in front in line,
then his uncle, and his father in the rear,
and in the middle the young man, glittering like the sun,
250 brandished in his right hand his spear of Arab green, with a gold
pennon.
He was handsome to look on, delightful in conversation,

μόσχος εἰς τὸ ἀνάβλεμμα ὅλος μεμυρισμένος.
Οἶκος ὑπῆρχε καθ' ὁδὸν στρατηγοῦ τοῦ μεγάλου,
255 καὶ πλησιάσαντος αὐτοῦ ἀναφώνημα εἶπε:
«Ἄγουρος ὅταν ἀγαπᾷ κόρην ὡραιοτάτην,
ὅταν ἐκεῖ ἀπέρχεται καὶ βλέπει της τὰ κάλλη,
δαμάζεται ἡ καρδίτζα του, οὐ θέλει ζῆν εἰς κόσμον.»
Τῆς ἡδονῆς ὡς ἤκουσαν τῷ οἴκῳ οἱ παρόντες,
260 ἐξέστησαν ὥσπερ ποτὲ ὁ Ὀδυσσεὺς ἐκεῖνος,
ὅτε τὸ μέλος ἤκουε Σειρήνων ἐν τῷ πλοίῳ.
Ἀλλ' οὐδ' ἡ κόρη ἔμεινεν ἀνήκοος τοῦ νέου,
πάγκαλος ἡ διάφημος ἡ ἀκουστὴ ἐκείνη,
ἧς τὸ κάλλος ἀμήχανον, παράδοξον τὸ γένος,
265 οὐσίαν τε καὶ κτήματα καὶ ἑτέραν πλουσίαν
ἀδύνατον ἀπαριθμεῖν ἢ ἀπεικάζειν ὅλως.
Μόνον γὰρ οἶκον τὸν αὐτῆς οὐδεὶς ἐγκωμιάσει·
ἅπας γὰρ χρυσομάρμαρος, ὅλος μεμουσιωμένος,
τὸ μοναχὸν κουβούκλιον ἔνθα ἦτον ἡ κόρη
270 ἀπέξωθεν ὁλόχρυσον, ὅλον μεμουσιωμένον,
ὃ καὶ ἐπωνομάζετο τῆς κόρης τὸ κουβοῦκλιν.
Αὕτη τοίνυν ἡ πάμπλουτος καὶ πανωραία κόρη,
ὡς εἶδε τὸν νεώτερον, καθὼς ἐκδιηγούμαι, 26r
ἐφλέχθη ἡ καρδίτζα της, οὐ θέλει ζῆν εἰς κόσμον.
275 Πόνος ἀνήφθη εἰς αὐτήν, ὡς τὸ δίκαιον ἔχει·
τὸ γὰρ κάλλος ὀξύτερον καὶ τοῦ βέλους τιτρώσκει

253 μεμυρισμένος G: μεμερισμένος Tsopanakis, 1960, 83–4
276 τὸ Trapp: οὐ G ὀξύτερον καὶ τοῦ βέλους Kalonaros, cf. Z1665, Ach. Tat. 1.4.4:
ὀξύτατον καὶ τὸ βέλος G

all redolent of musk in his gaze.
The house of the great general was on their road
255 and as he came close, Digenis uttered this cry,
"When a boy loves a very beautiful girl,
when he comes there and sees her beauty,
his poor heart is tamed, he does not wish to live in the world."
When those present in the house heard this sound,
260 they were amazed as the famous Odysseus once was
when he heard the Sirens' song on his ship.
But the girl too did not remain deaf to the young man,
that very lovely maiden, famed and renowned,
whose beauty was incredible, whose family was remarkable
265 and whose possessions and goods and other wealth
it was impossible to count or conjecture at all.
Even her house no one will be able to praise,
for it was all of gold and marble, entirely covered with mosaics.
The solitary chamber where the girl dwelt
270 was all of gold on the outside, entirely covered with mosaics,
and it was called the Girl's Chamber.
    And so when the very rich and very beautiful girl
saw the young man, as I am relating,
her heart was enflamed, she did not wish to live in the world.
275 Pain was lit within her, as is right,
for beauty wounds deeper than an arrow

253 After this line the compiler of Z draws from E624–701 the episode where Digenis first met the guerrillas. Little in G here suggests that a section has fallen out at this point, except a sense that the transition from the *rite de passage* of hunting to courtship is sudden (a reaction which may say less about the poem than about our reception of it). When Digenis does meet the guerrillas in G6, there is no sign of a previous meeting (but G4.33–4 refers to independent circulation of material on the guerrilla chiefs). It is almost certain that the episode was never included in the G version (Eideneier, 1970, 307–8; MacAlister, 1984, 551–74), in spite of Mavrogordato's assumption of a lacuna and his attempt to fill it.

254 Οἶκος is marked in G with a large capital O, though not the ornamental form used for book-divisions. Such capitals occur elsewhere (e.g., a T at the beginning of the hunt scene at G4.102), perhaps marking an informal (and unsystematic) division into episodes.

258 Several songs such as this exist in *Digenis* (e.g., G4.401–4, 432–5) and also in contemporary and subsequent romances. Their relationship to songs then circulating orally can only be guessed at on the basis of linguistic prejudice since we have no idea of the scope of twelfth-century song.

261 A more substantial Homeric reference than G4.27, but still no proof of direct knowledge.

273 The first trace of an authorial presence, which – interestingly – appears shortly after the introduction of a new, and easily separable, topic.

καὶ δι' αὐτῶν τῶν ὀφθαλμῶν εἰς ψυχὴν ἐπανήκει.
Ἤθελε μὲν τοὺς ὀφθαλμοὺς ἐκ τοῦ νέου ἐπᾶραι,
ἀλλὰ πάλιν οὐκ ἤθελε τοῦ κάλλους χωρισθῆναι,
280 ἀλλὰ εἷλκεν αὐτοὺς ἐκεῖ προδήλως ἡττηθέντας·
καὶ πρὸς τὴν βάγιαν ἔλεγε γαληνὰ εἰς τὸ ὠτίον:
«Παράκυψαι, βαγίτζα μου, ἴδε ἔμνοστον νέον,
ἴδε κάλλος πανθαύμαστον καὶ ξένην ἡλικίαν·
ἂν ἤθελεν ὁ κύρης μου γαμβρὸν νὰ τὸν ἐπῆρε,
285 νὰ εἶχε, πίστευσον, γαμβρὸν οἷον ἄλλος οὐκ ἔχει.»
Ἀπέμεινε δὲ βλέπουσα ἐκ τῆς ὀπῆς τὸν παῖδα·
ὁ δὲ νέος ἠρώτησεν ἀληθῶς μὴ γινώσκων:
«Ὁ οἶκος οὗτος τίνος ἐστὶν ὁ φοβερὸς καὶ μέγας;
Μὴ οὗτος ἔνι τοῦ στρατηγοῦ τοῦ ἀκουστοῦ ὃν λέγουν
290 καὶ ἡ κόρη ἡ πανεύφημος ἐνταῦθα καταμένει;»
«Ναί, τέκνον μου γλυκύτατον,» ὁ πατὴρ ἀπεκρίθη,
«δι' ἧς πολλοὶ ἀπώλοντο τῶν εὐγενῶν Ῥωμαίων.»
«Καὶ πῶς, πάτερ, ἀπώλοντο;» αὖθις ὁ παῖς ἠρώτα.
«Ἐβουλήθησαν, τέκνον μου, τὴν κόρην ἀφαρπάσαι
295 διὰ τὰ κάλλη τὰ τερπνὰ ἅπερ ἔχει, ὡς λέγουν·
καὶ τούτους γνοὺς ὁ στρατηγός, τῆς κόρης ὁ γεννήτωρ,
ἐγκρύμματα ἐποίησε καὶ ἐκράτησε πάντας,
τοὺς μὲν ἀπεκεφάλισεν, τοὺς δὲ τυφλοὺς ἐποίησεν·
ἔχει γὰρ δύναμιν πολλὴν καὶ δόξαν εἰς τὴν χώραν.» 26v
300   Στενάξας δὲ ὁ Διγενὴς ἔφη πρὸς τὸν πατέρα:
«Εὔχου, πάτερ, μὴ δόξῃ με ἵνα την ἀφαρπάσω,
ὅτι ἐμὲ ἐγκρύμματα ποτὲ οὐ θορυβοῦσι·
τοῦτο δὲ μόνον εὔχομαι, εἴπερ ἀποδεκτόν σοι,
νὰ μηνύσῃς τὸν στρατηγὸν διὰ συμπενθερίαν·
305 καὶ εἰ μὲν ἴσως ἀρεσθῇ γαμβρὸν νά με ἐπάρῃ,
ἵνα τὸν ἔχω πενθερὸν τῇ ἰδίᾳ του γνώμῃ·
εἰ δὲ μή, γνώσῃ, πάτερ μου, μετὰ ταῦτα τὸ τέλος.»
«Πολλάκις τον ἐμήνυσα, γλυκύτατε υἱέ μου,
ἀλλ' οὐδὲ ὅλως πείθεται εἰς τοῦτο κατανεῦσαι.»
310 Ὡς δὲ τοιαῦτα ὁ πατὴρ ἔλεγε πρὸς τὸν παῖδα,
ἐσκέφθη ὁ νεώτερος ἐκ τῆς ὀπῆς τὴν κόρην·
καὶ ταύτην θεασάμενος ἐμπρὸς οὐ βηματίζει,

---

280 ἀλλὰ Legrand: ἀλλ' G
288 ἐστὶν Legrand: ἔνι G

and penetrates the soul through the eyes themselves.
She wanted to take her eyes away from the young man,
but then again she did not wish to be parted from his beauty,
280 but dragged her eyes there, clearly defeated,
and she said softly to her serving-girl, in her ear:
"Peer out, my maid-servant, see the graceful young man,
see his quite marvellous beauty and wondrous appearance;
if my father wished to take him as a son-in-law,
285 he would have – believe me – a son-in-law like no one else's."
     She stayed looking out of the peep-hole at the boy;
but the young man asked, truly in ignorance,
"This fearsome and great house – whose is it?
Might this belong to the renowned general of whom they speak?
290 And does that most estimable girl live here?"
"Yes, my sweetest child," his father replied,
"she for whom many high-born Romans have perished."
"And how, father, did they perish?" asked the boy again.
"They wanted, my child, to abduct the girl
295 because of the delightful beauty which she has, so they say.
And when the general, the girl's father, heard of them,
he set ambushes and caught them all;
some he beheaded, others he blinded,
for he has great might and reputation in the land."
300   Sighing, Digenis said to his father:
"Pray, father, that I do not decide to abduct her,
because ambushes never frighten me.
I make this prayer only that, if it is acceptable to you,
you send messages to the general about becoming fellow
     parents-in-law,
305 so that if perhaps it pleases him to take me as a son-in-law,
I may have him as my father-in-law of his own volition;
but if not, my father, you will discover the consequences later."
     "I have often sent messages to him, my sweetest son,
but in no way does he agree to consent to this."
310   As the father was saying this to the boy,
the young man caught sight of the girl through the peep-hole.
And having seen her he took no further step forward.

---

299 The traditional motif of the well-guarded daughter and punished suitors (e.g. Thompson, 1946, 100, 482: Type 310). Note that these major new characters are presented as known to the emir (see G4.308–9) and even Digenis, though without any previous mention in the text – a sign of unsophisticated narrative technique.

ἀλλ' εἶχεν ἔκπληξις αὐτὸν καὶ τρόμος τὴν καρδίαν.
Τὸν βοῦλχαν ἐπελάλησε, πλησιάζει τῇ κόρῃ
315 καὶ πρὸς αὐτὴν ἠρέμα τε λόγον εἶπε τοιόνδε:
«Γνώρισόν μοι, κοράσιον, εἰ ἔχεις με εἰς νοῦν σου
καὶ εἰ ποθεῖς κατὰ πολὺ τοῦ λαβεῖν σε γυναῖκα·
εἰ δ' ἀλλαχοῦ ἔχεις τὸν νοῦν, πολλὰ οὐ παρακαλῶ σε.»
Τὴν βάγιαν δὲ παρακαλεῖ τὴν ἑαυτῆς ἡ κόρη:
320 «Κατάβα, βάγια μου καλή, εἰπὲ τὸν ἀγουρίτζην:
Τὸν Θεόν, σε πληροφορῶ, εἰς τὴν ψυχήν μου ἐσέβης·
ἀλλ' οὐκ οἶδα, νεώτερε, ποίου γένους τυγχάνεις.
Εἰ μὲν εἶ σὺ Βασίλειος ὁ Διγενῆς Ἀκρίτης,
ὑπάρχεις μὲν τῶν εὐγενῶν καὶ τῶν πλουσιωτάτων
325 καὶ συγγενὴς ἡμέτερος ὡς ἀπὸ τῶν Δουκάδων. 27r
Ἀλλ' ὁ πατήρ μου ὁ στρατηγὸς διὰ σὲ βίγλας ἔχει,
ἤκουσε γὰρ κατὰ πολὺ τὰς σὰς ἀνδραγαθίας·
καὶ φυλάττου, νεώτερε, δι' ἐμοῦ <μὴ> κινδυνεύσῃς
καὶ στερηθῇς νεότητος τῆς πανωραιοτάτης·
330 οὐδ' ὅλως γάρ σου φείσεται ὁ ἄσπλαγχνος πατήρ μου'.»
Καὶ αὖθις ὁ νεώτερος πρὸς τὴν κόρην ἀντέφη:
«Παράκυψον, ὀμμάτια μου, ἃς ἴδω σου τὸ κάλλος,
ἃς ἔμβῃ εἰς τὴν καρδίτζαν μου ἡ ἄπειρός σου ἀγάπη·
εἰμὶ γὰρ νέος, ὡς ὁρᾷς· οὐκ οἶδα τί ἔνι ὁ πόθος,
335 οὔτε γινώσκω κἂν ποσῶς τὰς ὁδοὺς τῆς ἀγάπης,
καὶ εἰ μὲν εἰσέλθῃ ὁ πόθος σου εἰς τὴν ψυχήν μου ἀπέσω,
ὁ πατήρ σου ὁ στρατηγὸς καὶ τὸ συγγενικόν του
καὶ ἄπαντες οἱ μετ' αὐτοῦ, ἐὰν γένωνται βέλη
καὶ ξίφη ἀπαστράπτοντα, οὐ δύνανταί με βλάψαι.»
340 Καὶ ἦν ἰδεῖν οὐδέποτε τέλος ἐκείνων λόγοις·
ἔρως τότε παρώξυνεν ἄσεμνον διαπρᾶξαι,
δουλοῖ γὰρ τὰ φρονήματα ἔρως ὡς ὢν δεσπότης,
ὑποτάσσει τὸν λογισμὸν ὡς ἡνίοχος ἵππον·
καὶ διὰ τοῦτο ὁ ποθῶν εὐταξίαν οὐκ ἔχει,
345 οὐ συγγενεῖς αἰσχύνεται, οὐ γείτονας πτοεῖται,
ἀλλ' ἔστιν ὅλως ἀναιδὴς δοῦλος ὢν τῆς φιλίας,

---

316 εἰ Legrand: εἰς G
318 ἔχεις τὸν νοῦν Trapp: τὸν νοῦν ἔχεις G
328 μὴ added by Tsopanakis, 1960, 84

but astonishment came over him and his heart began to tremble.
He urged his horse on, he approached the girl
315 and spoke these words to her calmly:
"Let me know, girl, if you have me in your mind,
and if you desire very much that I should take you as my wife;
if you have your mind elsewhere, I shall not importune you."
    The girl requested her serving-girl:
320 "Go down, my lovely maid, tell the lad:
'By God, I inform you that you have found your way into my soul,
but I do not know, young man, from what family you are.
If you are Basil Digenis Akritis, the Frontiersman of Double Descent,
you are from a noble and very wealthy background
325 and are our kinsman through the Doukas family.
But my father the general has set guards because of you,
for he has heard a great deal about your brave deeds.
Take care, young man, lest you run into danger because of me
and are deprived of your very beautiful youthfulness,
330 for my pitiless father will in no way spare you.'"
    And once more the young man replied to the girl:
"Peer out, my darling, let me see your beauty,
let boundless love for you enter my heart.
For I am young, as you see, I do not know what desire is,
335 nor do I have the least knowledge of the paths of love,
and if desire for you enters my soul,
your father the general and his kinsmen
and all those with him, even if they turn into weapons
and flashing swords, are not able to harm me."
340   No end could ever be seen to their words.
Then passion urged them to an immodest act,
for when passion is the master it enslaves good sense
and subjugates reasoning, as a charioteer subjugates a horse.
And because of this, he who desires has no sense of propriety,
345 he is not ashamed before his kinsmen, he has no fear of his neighbours
but is completely shameless and a slave to affection,

---

325 See the genealogy in Table 2 (Introduction, p. xxxvi). From the twelfth century onwards, the preference of aristocratic clans for marriage between kin frequently flouted church rulings (Laiou, 1992, 21–58).
331 The maid, carefully established as a go-between, vanishes and the principals speak directly to each other.
341–2 Once again it is hard to be sure whether this is an abstract passion or the personalised Eros of G3.1–8; G4.345–7 are repeated at 4.528–30.

ὥσπερ καὶ ἡ πανεύγενος κόρη πέπονθε τότε,
καὶ παρέκυψε μερικῶς ἐκ τὴν χρυσῆν θυρίδα.
Τὰ κάλλη τοῦ προσώπου της κωλύουν τοὺς ὀφθαλμούς του
350 καὶ οὐ δύναται καλῶς ἰδεῖν τὴν ἡλιογεννημένην·
ὡς γὰρ ἀκτὶς ἀνέτειλεν ἐν μέσῳ τοῦ προσώπου. 27v
Ἦν γὰρ ἡ κόρη ἀληθῶς ὥσπερ ἱστορισμένη·
ὄμμα γοργὸν ἐνήδονον, κόμην ξανθὴν καὶ σγοῦρον,
ὀφρὺν εἶχε κατάμαυρον, ἄκρατον δὲ τὸ μέλαν,
355 ὡς χιόνα τὸ πρόσωπον, μέσον δὲ βεβαμμένον,
οἷα πορφύρα ἐκλεκτὴ ἦν βασιλεῖς τιμῶσι.
Οὕτως ἰδὼν ὁ θαυμαστὸς ἐκεῖνος νεανίας
εὐθὺς ἐτρώθη τὴν ψυχήν, ἐπλήγη τὴν καρδίαν
καὶ πόνον εἶχεν ἄπειρον, ἀδημονῶν εἱστήκει.
360 Κόρη δὲ ἡ πανεύγενος οὕτως αὐτὸν ἰδοῦσα
οὐ παρεῖδε κατὰ πολὺ τῷ ἄλγει ἐπιμένειν,
ἀλλὰ ταχέως ἔστειλε πρὸς αὐτὸν τὴν ἀγάπην
πολλῆς χαρᾶς ἀνάπλεων, ἡδονῆς μεμιγμένην·
τὸ δακτυλίδιν ἔδωκεν εἰποῦσα πρὸς ἐκεῖνον:
365 «Ἄπιθι χαίρων, ἄγουρε, κἀμοῦ μὴ ἐπιλάθῃς.»
Ὁ δὲ δεξάμενος αὐτὸ εἰς τὸν ἴδιον κόλπον
εὐθὺς ἀνταπεκρίνατο: «Αὔριόν με ἐκδέχου.»
Καὶ χαρᾶς ὅλως ἐμπλησθεὶς ὥδευε μετὰ πάντων.
Εἰς δὲ τὸν οἶκον φθάσαντες, εὐθὺς φροντίδας εἶχε
370 καὶ τὸν Θεὸν ἱκέτευεν ἐξ ὅλης τῆς καρδίας,   E1839
«Δέσποτα,» λέγων, «ὁ Θεός, ἐπάκουσον εὐχῆς μου
καὶ δῦνον μου τὸν ἥλιον, ἀνάτειλον τὸ φέγγος,
ὡσάν μοι γένῃ συνεργὸς ἐν τῇ δουλείᾳ ταύτῃ·
ἐπειδὴ γὰρ μονώτατος βούλομαι πορευθῆναι.»
375 Καὶ κατ' ἰδίαν ἔλεγε τὸν πρωτοστράτορά του: E796
«Ἀπόστρωσε τὸν βοῦλχαν μου, στρῶσον μου δὲ τὸν μαῦρον,   E798
δύο κίγκλας τον κίγκλωσον καὶ δύο ἐμπροσθελίνας, 28r   E800
καὶ κρέμασε εἰς τὴν σέλλαν μου τὸ ὡραῖον μου σπαθορράβδιν, E802
καὶ θὲς βαρὺ τὸ μάσσημα ἵνα γοργὸν γυρίζῃ.»   E801
380   Καὶ εἰς τὸν δεῖπνον προσκληθεὶς οὐ μετέσχε βρωμάτων,
οὐ πόσεως τὸ σύνολον θέλοντα τοῦ γευθῆναι,

363 ἀνάπλεων G: ἀνάπλεον Politis, 1967, 24
375 πρωτοστράτορά Legrand: πρωτοστάτορά G
380 προσκληθεὶς G: προσκλιθεὶς Politis, 1966, 351

just as the very high-born girl was then
when she peered a little way out of the golden window.
   The beauty of her face inhibited his eyes
350 and he could not see the sun-born girl clearly,
for a ray seemed to shine out from the middle of her face.
The girl was truly as if painted in a picture,
with a swift, joyful eye and fair curly hair;
she had deep black eyebrows, the black undiluted;
355 her face was like snow, with a tint at the centre
like the choice purple which emperors honour.
     Seeing her thus that marvellous youth
was immediately wounded in his soul, he was struck to the heart
and felt boundless pain, he stood in anguish.
360 When the very high-born girl saw him in this state,
she could not allow him to remain for long in pain
but quickly conveyed to him her love,
which was full of great joy and mixed with pleasure;
she gave him her ring, saying to him:
365 "Go on your way joyfully, youngster, and do not forget me."
He put it into his pouch
and immediately replied: "Expect me tomorrow."
And completely full of joy he went on his way with all his companions.
   When they reached the house, he immediately began to be
   concerned
370 and prayed to God with all his heart:
"Lord God," he said, "hear my prayer
and make the sun set for me and the moon rise,
so that it can help me in this task,
since I plan to set out entirely alone."
375 And he said privately to his protostrator,
"Unsaddle my horse for me and saddle the black;
gird on for me two saddle-girths and two martingales,
and hang my handsome sword-stick from my saddle,
and put on the heavy bit so that he turns quickly."
380   And when he was summoned to the evening meal,
he took no food, not wishing to taste drink at all,

356 Another portrait within the physiognomic tradition. The range of colours covered
by imperial purple included the red of healthy cheeks.
375–9 The secret instructions must mean that the double harness is unusual and
connected with Digenis' plans, though whether for fighting or for carrying the girl, or
both, is hard to say.

τὴν κόρην στρέφων κατὰ νοῦν, τὸ κάλλος εἰκονίζων.
Καὶ ποτὲ μὲν οὐκ ἔχρῃζε ταύτην ἀπογινώσκων·
ἄλλοτε δ' ἐφαντάζετο ἔχων χρηστὰς ἐλπίδας,
385 καὶ τοῖς πᾶσιν ἐφαίνετο ἐν ὀνείρῳ θεᾶσθαι.
Ὃν καὶ ἡ μήτηρ ἡ αὐτοῦ ἵστατο ἀποροῦσα·
«Τί συνέβη σοι, τέκνον μου, καὶ λυπεῖς τὴν ψυχήν μου;
Μὴ θηρίον προσέκρουσε καὶ ἐτάραξε φόβος;
Μὴ δαίμων σε ἐβάσκανε, βλέπων σου τὴν ἀνδρείαν;
390 Ἀνάγγειλόν μοι τάχιον, μὴ θλίβῃς τὴν ψυχήν μου·
ὁ γὰρ κρύπτων τὸ νόσημα ὑπ' αὐτοῦ δαπανᾶται.»
«Οὔτε θηρίον προσέκρουσεν,» ὁ νέος ἀπεκρίθη,
«ἀλλ' οὔτε πάλιν θόρυβος ἐτάραξε ψυχήν μου.
Εἴπερ δέ τις μ' ἐβάσκανε, μή με τὴν καταρᾶσαι,
395 τὴν μηδὲν ἀδικήσασαν· ἐγὼ γὰρ ὑγιαίνω.»
Εἶτα κἀκεῖθεν ἀναστὰς ἀνέβη εἰς τὸ κουβοῦκλιν   E826
καὶ βαλὼν ὑποδήματα λαμβάνει καὶ κιθάραν,
ψιλαῖς δὲ πρῶτον ταῖς χερσὶ τὰς χορδὰς ἐκτινάξας
(κάλλιστα δ' ἐπεπαίδευτο ἐν μουσικοῖς ὀργάνοις)
400 καὶ ταύτην ἁρμοσάμενος ἔκρουε ψιθυρίζων·
«Ὅστις φιλήσειεν ἐγγύς, τοῦ ὕπνου οὐχ ὑστερεῖται,   E839–40
ὁ δὲ φιλῶν ἀπόμακρα μὴ ἀμελῇ τὰς νύκτας·   E839–40
ἐγὼ μακρόθεν ἀγαπῶ καὶ γοργὸν ἃς ὑπάγω, 28v   E842
ἵνα μὴ θλίβω τὴν ψυχὴν τὴν δι' ἐμὲ ἀγρυπνοῦσαν.»
405   Ὅταν ἔδυνε ὁ ἥλιος, κατέλαβε τὸ φέγγος,
μόνος ἐκαβαλλίκευσε κρατῶν καὶ τὴν κιθάραν.
Ἦτον δάος ὁ μαῦρος του, τὸ φέγγος ὡς ἡμέρα,   E844
σύναυγα δὲ κατέλαβε τῆς κόρης τὸ κουβοῦκλιν.
Ἐκείνη δὲ ὡς ἐκδέχετο ὁλονυκτὶ ἀγρυπνοῦσα,
410 τὴν αὐγὴν ἐρραθύμησε καὶ εἰς ὕπνον ἐτράπη.
Ὡς δὲ ταύτην οὐκ ἔβλεπε τὸ εὐγενὲς παιδίον,
ἠνιᾶτο κατὰ πολύ, ἐταράττετο σφόδρα,
λογισμοὶ ἔκοπτον αὐτοῦ πονηροὶ τὴν καρδίαν,
θλῖψιν εἶχεν ἀφόρητον καὶ ὀδύνην μεγίστην·
415 ἔλεγε γὰρ ἐν ἑαυτῷ· «Ἆρα μετεμελήθη;
Ἆρα πτοεῖται τοὺς γονεῖς μήπως αὐτὴν νοήσουν;
Τί πρὸς ταῦτα βουλεύσομαι; Πῶς τὸ βέβαιον μάθω;

384 ἄλλοτε Legrand: ἄλλωστε G
394 Εἴπερ δέ τις Legrand: ὑπὲρ δὲ τὴν G
397 βαλὼν Tsopanakis, 1960, 84: λαβὼν G
405 ἔδυνε ὁ ἥλιος Legrand: ἔδυνεν ὁ ἥλιος καὶ G

turning the girl over in his mind, picturing her beauty.
And at one moment in despair he wanted nothing to do with her,
at another he imagined he had good expectations,
385 while to everyone he seemed to be staring as if in a dream.
    His mother in great bewilderment stood and asked him:
"What has happened to you, my child, for you to grieve my soul?
Did a wild beast strike you and has fear shaken you?
Has some evil spirit bewitched you, seeing your bravery?
390 Tell me quickly, do not distress my soul,
for he who conceals the disease is consumed by it."
    "No wild beast has struck me," the young man replied,
"nor, again, has panic shaken my soul.
If some one has bewitched me, do not curse her,
395 since she has done no wrong, for I am in good health."
    Then rising from there he went up to his chamber,
and taking off his sandals, he picked up his kithara too,
first strumming the strings with his slender hands
(for he had been well instructed in musical instruments),
400 and tuned it and played, murmuring:
"Anyone who has his love close by loses no sleep,
but he who loves at a distance should not neglect nights.
I love from far away, and let me set off quickly,
so that I do not distress the soul that is lying awake for me."
405   When the sun had set and the moon had risen,
he rode off alone, holding his kithara.
His black horse was swift, the moonlight like day
and at dawn he reached the girl's chamber.
Since she had stayed awake and waited for him all night,
410 at dawn she was tired and turned to sleep.
When the high-born boy did not see her,
he was very upset, he was extremely disturbed,
dreadful thoughts cut him to the heart,
he felt unbearable grief and the greatest pain.
415 For he said to himself: "Has she changed her mind?
Is she afraid that her parents might find her out?
What plan shall I make about this? How can I find out for certain?

Ἐξαπορεῖ γάρ μου ὁ νοῦς, οὐκ ἔχω τι διαπρᾶξαι·
εἰ γὰρ λαλήσω, κράζοντος ἕτεροί μου ἀκούσουν,
420 δώσουν, ὑπονοήσουν με οἱ φυλάττοντες ὧδε
καὶ πρὸ τῆς πράξεως γνωσθῶ μὴ τυχὼν τῆς φιλτάτης,
ὡς ἂν μὴ ἔχων εὐχερῶς ἰδεῖν τὴν ποθουμένην·
καὶ τί μοι ἔστιν ὄφελος ζῆν ἐν τῷδε τῷ βίῳ;»
Ταῦτα λέγων ἐν ἑαυτῷ ἐκπληττόμενος σφόδρα
425 δέον εἶναι προέκρινε τοῦ κροῦσαι τὴν κιθάραν,
ὅπως λάβῃ ἀπόπειραν περὶ ὧν ἠδημόνει,
«Φείσασθαι,» λέγων, «ἐμαυτῷ δοκιμάζων τὴν κόρην
κιθάραν ταύτην συνεργὸν παραστήσω ἐν μέσῳ
καὶ τοῦ Θεοῦ τὸ θέλημα πάντως ἔχει γενέσθαι.» 29r
430 Καὶ ταύτην ἁρμοσάμενος τῷ πλήκτρῳ τε πατάσσων
μέλος γὰρ πάνυ ἥδιστον ἐτέλει ψιθυρίζων·
«Πῶς ἐπελάθου, πάντερπνε, νέας ἡμῶν ἀγάπης
καὶ ἡδέως καθύπνωσας ἀμερίμνως, εὐκόλως;
Ἀνάστα, ῥόδον πάντερπνον, μῆλον μεμυρισμένον·
435 ὁ αὐγερινὸς ἀνέτειλεν, δεῦρο ἃς περιπατῶμεν.»
Ὡς δὲ κιθάρας ἤκουσε τῆς ἡδονῆς ἡ κόρη,
τῆς κλίνης ἐξεπήδησε, σφίγγει της τὸ ζωνάριν
καὶ χαμηλὰ προκύψασα λέγει τὸν ἀγουρίτζην:
«Ἐγώ, κύρκα, σε ὠνείδισα, δι' οὗ πολλὰ ἐβράδυνας·   E856
440 ὡς ὀκνηρὸν καὶ ῥάθυμον πάντα νά σε ὀνειδίζω;   E857
Τὴν δὲ κιθάραν ἣν κρούεις, δοκεῖς τὸ ποῦ εἶσαι οὐκ οἶδας·   E858
καλέ, ἄν σε νοήσῃ ὁ κύρης μου νά σε κακοδικήσῃ   E860. 863
καὶ νὰ ἀποθάνῃς δι' ἐμέ, ὦ τῆς παρανομίας.
Ὁ Θεὸς γὰρ ἐπίσταται ὁ τῶν κρυφίων γνώστης,
445 ὅτι ἐρριζώθη ὁ πόθος σου εἰς τὴν ἐμὴν καρδίαν
καὶ συμφορὰν λογίζομαι τὴν σὴν ἀποτυχίαν.
Σώζου λοιπόν, ψυχὴ ἐμή, πρὶν τὸ φῶς καταλάβῃ,
καὶ μνήσκου μου διὰ παντὸς τῆς σὲ πολλὰ ποθούσης·
καὶ γάρ, καλὲ νεώτερε, οὐ θέλω ἐλθεῖν μετά σου·
450 οἶδα ὅτι ὁ πόθος φλέγει σε καὶ ἡ ἀγάπη ἡ ξένη,   E866
ὁ λογισμὸς εἰσπείθει σε δι' ἐμοῦ ἀποθνήσκειν·   E867-8
ἀλλ' ἂν παροδηγήσῃς με καὶ ἔλθω μετὰ σένα

---

418 Ἐξαπορεῖ Legrand: ἀπορεῖ G
434 Ἀνάστα Legrand: ἀλλ' ἀνάστα G
439 ἐβράδυνας corr.: ᾿βραδύνας Trapp βραδύνας G

My mind is bewildered, I don't know what to do.
If I call out, others will hear me shouting,
420 those who are keeping watch here will attack, they will notice me,
and I shall be discovered before my deed, not winning my dearest,
not even having a chance to see the one I desire.
What is the use of my living in this life?"
   Saying these things to himself in his great puzzlement,
425 he decided it was right to play his kithara,
to try out the things about which he was mystified.
"To spare myself as I test the girl," he said,
"I shall make this kithara my helpful go-between,
and God's wish will certainly take its course."
430   And tuning it and plucking it with the plectrum,
he performed this very sweet tune, murmuring:
"How, my most delightful girl, could you forget our new love
and sleep sweetly without a care and contentedly?
Rise up, my most delightful rose and perfumed apple.
435 The morning star has risen, come, let us stroll a while."
   When the girl heard the sound of the kithara,
she jumped out of bed, did up her belt,
and leaning out low she said to the lad:
"I blamed you, sweetheart, because you were very late;
440 am I always to be blaming you for being hesitant and lethargic?
As for the kithara you are playing, you seem not to know where
      you are.
My fine one, if my lord father catches sight of you,
he will punish you and you will die for me – alas for the lawlessness!
For God who is aware of secrets knows
445 that desire for you is rooted in my heart
and that I consider it a disaster if you fail.
Make your escape then, my soul, before the light comes,
and forever remember me, one who desires you greatly.
For, my fine young man, I do not wish to come with you.
450 I know that desire and an extraordinary love enflame you,
that reason is persuading you to die for me.
But if you lead me astray and I come with you,

427–9 It is unclear why a musical approach is preferable to conventional speech. Does it
expose Digenis less if the girl has changed her mind, or is it more likely to be missed by the
guards?
435 On the many manifestations of the genre of lovers' songs at dawn, see Hatto, 1965,
and Pring, *ibid.*, 264–70 on Greek versions.

καὶ γνώσουν το τὰ ἀδέλφια μου καὶ τὸ συγγενικόν μου   E871
καὶ καταφθάση σε ὁ πατὴρ ὁ ἐμὸς μετὰ πλήθους, 29v
455   πῶς ἔχεις ἐξηβάλειν με καὶ σῶσαι τὴν ψυχήν σου;»
Καὶ λυπηθεὶς ὁ θαυμαστὸς πρὸς τὴν κόρην ἀντέφη:
«Ἐπαινῶ σου τὴν ἔνστασιν, ὦ πανευγενεστάτη·
τὸ γὰρ ἐνάντιον σκοπῶν τῶν μελλόντων συμβαίνειν,
προκρίνεις γὰρ τὰ βέλτιστα σαφῶς λογιζομένη,
460   σὺ δὲ μηδὲν γινώσκουσα τὰ κατ' ἐμὲ οὐδ' ὅλως·
εἰ γὰρ ἐν γνώσει γέγονας ἐμῶν ἀνδραγαθίων,
οὐκ ἂν ἔλεγες ἀδελφοὺς καὶ τὸ συγγενικόν σου
φθάσουν καὶ ἐγκρημνίσουν με καὶ σὺ δι' ἐμὲ λυπῆσαι.
Ἀλλ' ἔστω σοι τοῦτο γνωστὸν καὶ βέβαιον, ψυχή μου,
465   ὅτι φοσσᾶτα προσδοκῶ μόνος καταπονέσαι,   E876
νικῆσαι τε παραταγὰς καὶ κράτη ὑποτάξαι·
τὸν δὲ πατέρα τε τὸν σὸν καὶ τοὺς αὐτοῦ ἀγούρους
ὡσαύτως καὶ τοὺς ἀδελφοὺς μετὰ τῶν συγγενῶν σου
πάντως βρέφη λογίζομαι καὶ μηδὲν ὅλως ὄντα.
470   Τοῦτο μόνον ζητῶ μαθεῖν παρὰ τῶν σῶν χειλέων,
εἰ προθυμεῖς κατὰ πολὺ ἐμοὶ ἀκολουθῆσαι,
ὡς ἂν ὁδοὺς ἐξέλθωμεν τοὺς στενωποὺς πρὶν φέξη·
ῥύμαι γὰρ καὶ στενώματα ἀποκτείνουν ἀνδρείους,
εἰς δὲ τοὺς κάμπους ἄνανδροι τολμηροὶ ἐκποιοῦνται.
475   Εἰ δ' ἴσως ἐμετέγνωσας, ἑτέρου ἡρετίσω   E881
καὶ διὰ τοῦτο ἀφορμὰς προβάλλεσαι τοιαύτας,
μὰ τοὺς ἁγίους μάρτυρας τοῦ Χριστοῦ Θεοδώρους,   E891
οὐκ ἂν ἄλλος ζῶντος ἐμοῦ εἰσακουσθῆ ἀνήρ σου.»
Αὖθις ἡ ἡλιόκαλος πρὸς τὸν ἄγουρον ἔφη: 30r
480   «Σὺ μὲν οὖν, ὦ παμπόθητε, ἀπείραστος ὡς πρῶτον
πάσης ἀγάπης πέφυκας καὶ φιλίας, ὡς ἔφης·
νυνὶ δὲ πάσχεις δι' ἐμὲ καὶ ἴσως ἀληθεύεις,
ἐκ τῶν ὁμοίων καὶ αὐτὴ τοῦτο τεκμαιρομένη.
Εἰ γὰρ καὶ λίαν ἀπρεπὲς τὰ κατ' ἐμὲ εἰπεῖν σοι,
485   ὅμως ἐρῶ σοι ἅπαντα τῷ πόθῳ δουλωθεῖσα.
Πολλοὶ ἐμὲ τῶν εὐγενῶν ἄρχοντες, μεγιστᾶνες
καὶ βασιλέων συγγενεῖς ἐζήτησαν καὶ τέκνα
βασιλικὴν παράταξιν ἔχοντες καὶ ἐσθῆτα,
καὶ ποθοῦντες θεάσασθαι τὸν ἐμὸν χαρακτῆρα

457 ἔνστασιν Tsopanakis, 1960, 84, cf. Z1867: ἔκστασιν G
464 ἔστω Legrand, cf. Z1874: ἔστι G
469 λογίζομαι Legrand: λογίζονται G
473 ἀποκτείνουν Legrand: ἀποκτέ^{αι}νουν G

and my brothers and my kinsmen learn of this,
and my father with his troops catches you,
455 how can you extricate me and save your life?"
　　And the marvellous youth replied in grief to the girl:
"I praise your opposition, my most high-born girl.
For you consider the opposite of what is going to happen
and choose the best solution by making clear calculations,
460 but you do not know anything at all about me.
For if you had any knowledge of my brave deeds,
you would not say that your brothers and your kinsmen
will catch me and hurl me down and that you will grieve because of
　　me.
But let this be understood and certain to you, my soul,
465 that I expect to crush armies on my own
and to defeat divisions and subdue states.
Your father and his youngsters
and likewise your brothers with your kinsmen
I reckon as complete babes-in-arms and as nothing at all.
470 This only I seek to learn from your lips,
whether you are very eager to follow me,
so that we might be through the narrow passes before daybreak.
For alleyways and passes are death to brave men
while on the plains cowards become bold.
475 If perhaps you have changed your mind and have chosen another
and because of this are putting forward excuses such as these,
by the Saints Theodore, the holy martyrs of Christ,
no one else while I am alive shall be called your husband."
　　Again the sun-lovely girl said to the youngster:
480 "And so you, my beloved, are untried in this your first
experience of all love and affection, as you said.
Now you are suffering because of me, and perhaps you are telling
　　the truth,
to judge this myself from similar feelings.
For even if it is most unseemly for me to talk to you about myself,
485 nevertheless I, enslaved as I am to desire, will tell you everything.
Many from among the high-born, lords and magnates,
have wooed me, and also kinsmen and children of emperors
with imperial retinues and robes,
and in their desire to gaze on my features

490 πυκνότερον διήρχοντο τοῦ οἴκου μου πλησίον,
ἀλλ᾽ οὐδενὶ τὸ σύνολον ἠρκέσθη ὁ πατήρ μου·
οὐ τὴν σκιὰν δὲ τὴν ἐμὴν τὶς ἰδεῖν ἠξιώθη,
φωνῆς οὐδείς μου ἤκουσεν ἢ συντυχίας ὅλως,
οὐ γέλωτος μειδίασμα, οὐ βαδίσματος ψόφον·
495 τῆς θυρίδος οὐδέποτε τὴν κεφαλήν μου ἦγον,
ἀλλοτρίοις ἀθέατον ἐμαυτὴν διετήρουν·
ἐκτὸς γάρ μου τῶν συγγενῶν καὶ τῶν γνωστῶν ἰδίων
οὐδείς μου εἶδε πώποτε προσώπου χαρακτῆρα,
τάξιν τηροῦσα ἀκριβῆ τὴν πρέπουσαν παρθένοις.
500 Τούτων δὲ γέγονα ἐκτὸς καὶ τοὺς ὅρους παρῆλθον
καὶ ἐγενόμην ἀναιδὴς διὰ τὴν σὴν ἀγάπην·
καὶ ἡ μηδέποτε ἀνδρὶ ἀλλοτρίῳ ὀφθεῖσα
λόγους νῦν μεταδίδωμι ὅλως μὴ αἰδουμένη
καὶ τὸ ὄντως ἐλεύθερον φρόνημα παρθενίας
505 δοῦλον ὁρῶ γινόμενον καὶ ἀναιδὲς ἀθρόως.   30ν
Ἀφ᾽ ἧς γὰρ ὥρας πρόσωπον τὸ σὸν εἶδον, ὦ νέε,
ὡς πῦρ κατέφλεξεν εὐθὺς τὴν σώφρονα ψυχήν μου,
μετήλλαξε τὸν λογισμὸν ὁμοίως καὶ τὴν γνώμην,
τὸ φρόνημα ἐδούλωσεν, ἀναίσχυντόν μ᾽ ἐποίησε.
510 Εἰς σὲ καὶ μόνον, ποθητέ, καὶ πρὸς τὴν σὴν ἀγάπην
πείθομαι νῦν καὶ βούλομαι μετὰ σοῦ πορευθῆναι,
δι᾽ οὗ ἀρνοῦμαι συγγενεῖς, γονέας ὑστεροῦμαι,   E897
ἀλλοτριοῦμαι ἀδελφῶν καὶ τοῦ ἀπείρου πλούτου   E898
καὶ μετὰ σοῦ πορεύομαι ὅπου δ᾽ ἂν καὶ κελεύῃς,
515 Θεὸν ἔχουσα μάρτυρα τὸν πᾶσι βοηθοῦντα   E900
ἐκδικητὴν παγκάλλιστον, μή με παροδηγήσῃς·   E900
σὲ μὲν ἡ ἀγάπη φλέγει σε, ἡ ἀγάπη παροξύνει
καὶ πείθει σε ὁ λογισμὸς δι᾽ ἐμὲ τοῦ θανεῖν σε,   E316
ὅπερ ἀπεύχομαι ἰδεῖν ἢ τοῖς ὠσὶν ἀκοῦσαι.»
520   Ὡς δὲ ταῦτα ἐφθέγγετο ἡ πανώραιος κόρη,
ἐδάκρυσε τοῖς ὀφθαλμοῖς, ἐστέναξε μεγάλως
καὶ ἑαυτὴν ἐμέμφετο τῆς πολλῆς ἀναιδείας,

517 σὲ Legrand: καὶ σὲ G
521 ὀφθαλμοῖς Legrand: ἀδελφοῖς G

490 they used quite frequently to pass close by my house,
      but my father was not completely satisfied with anyone;
      no one was deemed worthy to see my shadow,
      no one heard my voice or conversation at all,
      no hint of laughter, no sound of footsteps.
495 I never put my head out of the window,
      I kept myself unseen by others.
      Apart from my kinsmen and close friends,
      no one ever saw the features of my face
      as I observed carefully the role that is appropriate to unmarried girls.
500 I have gone beyond these bounds and I have broken the rules
      and I have become shameless for love of you.
      And I who have never been seen by a strange man
      am now engaging in conversation without the least shame,
      and the truly free mind of the unwedded state
505 I see becoming a slave and totally shameless.
      From the moment I saw your face, young man,
      a kind of fire immediately enflamed my chaste soul,
      it transformed my reasoning and likewise my nature,
      it enslaved my mind and made me shameless.
510 To you alone, beloved, and to my love for you
      I am now obedient, and I want to journey with you,
      for whom I renounce my kinsmen, I deprive myself of parents,
      I make myself a stranger to my brothers and our boundless wealth
      and with you I journey wherever you command,
515 taking as my witness God, who helps all
      and is the fairest avenger, that you will not lead me astray.
      As for you, love enflames you, love drives you on
      and reason persuades you to die for me,
      which I pray never to see nor to hear with my ears."
520   As the most beautiful girl uttered this,
      tears fell from her eyes, she sighed deeply
      and reproached herself for her great immodesty,

492–9 No doubt an exaggerated picture of ideal behaviour for a Byzantine girl, since stress here is on pressures which are making her break the rules, but the general sentiment is correct; cf. Kekavmenos' advice (*Strategikon* 102, 121) on the care to be taken of wives and daughters.

505–11 A passage contrasting the official Byzantine view of sex as a probably necessary evil with a recognition of its force; this is more often expressed in Byzantine texts from the male point of view (Galatariotou, 1989). Such issues are more canvassed in twelfth-century Byzantium, in the courtly romances as well as *Digenis*, than in previous or subsequent centuries (Beck, 1984, 112–28).

καὶ θέλουσα κατὰ πολὺ μεταβαλεῖν τὴν γνώμην,
ὁ ταύτης ἔνδον ἄπειρος οὐ συνεχώρει πόθος.
525 Δύναμις γὰρ τοῦ ἔρωτος πόθος καὶ ἡ φιλία,
εἴπερ τὴν τάξιν ἀκριβῶς τηροῦντα τὴν ἰδίαν,
σώφρονα νοῦν κατέχοντα, ὁ πόθος πολεμεῖ τον·
καὶ διὰ τοῦτο ὁ ποθῶν εὐταξίαν οὐκ ἔχει,
οὐ συγγενεῖς αἰσχύνεται, οὐ γείτονας πτοεῖται,
530 ἀλλ᾽ ἔστιν ὅλως ἀναιδὴς καὶ δοῦλος τῆς φιλίας·
ὡς καὶ οὕτως πεπόνθασιν οἱ παγκάλλιστοι νέοι. 31r
Εἶτα ὁ θαυμαστὸς <ἰδὼν> δακρύσασαν τὴν κόρην
μετὰ δακρύων καὶ αὐτὸς ἀντέλεγε τοιαῦτα:
«Ἐγώ, κόρη παγκάλλιστε, τὰ περὶ σοῦ γινώσκω·
535 τὸν πλοῦτον γὰρ τὸν ἄπειρον ὂν κέκτηται ὁ πατήρ σου,
δι᾽ οὗ πολλοὶ τῶν εὐγενῶν ἐπόθουν τοῦ λαβεῖν σε,
ἐν γνώσει πάντων γέγονα ἀκριβῶς ἐρευνήσας.
Ἐγὼ γάρ, φιλτάτη ψυχή, οὐκ ἐφίεμαι πλούτου,
οὐ κτήματα ἐπιθυμῶ, οὐκ ὀρέγομαι δόξης,
540 πάντα χόρτον λογίζομαι ἐντρυφῶν τοῦ σοῦ κάλλους.
Ἀφ᾽ ἧς ὥρας, μαυρόμματε, ὠψόμεθα ἀλλήλους,
οὐκ ἀπέστης ἐκ τὴν ἐμὴν ψυχὴν ὡρίτζαν μίαν·
ἐρριζώθης γὰρ ἔσωθεν καὶ συνεπλέχθης ταύτη
καὶ σὲ πάντα φαντάζομαι καὶ βλέπω σε μὴ οὖσαν.
545 Οὐ γὰρ ἠράσθην πώποτε οἱουδήποτε κάλλους,
οὐ τὰς ὁδοὺς ἐγνώρισα κἂν ποσῶς τῆς ἀγάπης·
δεῦρο, τὸ φῶς μου τὸ γλυκύ, ἔπου τῷ ἐραστῇ σου·
ἤνπερ ἔχεις ἀπέσωθεν ἐμφάνισον ἀγάπην·
ἀκριβὴς γὰρ ἀπόδειξις συνίσταται ἐξ ἔργων,
550 καὶ συμβιώσομεν Θεοῦ νεύσει χαίροντες ἄμφω.
Ἐπὶ τοῦτο γεννήτορες καὶ οἱ σοὶ εὐφρανθῶσιν,
γαμβροῦ οἵου τετύχηκαν ἐν γνώσει γεγονότες·
καὶ οὐδεὶς ὀνειδίσει σε, μᾶλλον δὲ μακαρίσει.»
Ταῦτα καὶ ἕτερα πολλὰ φθεγξάμενος ὁ νέος,
555 «Ἐν σοί μου πᾶσα ἡ ἀρχή,» ἔφησε, «καὶ τὸ τέλος·
σὺν Θεῷ ἐναρχόμενον μέχρι τῆς τελευτῆς μου·

---

526 εἴπερ Trapp: ἄπερ G
527 κατέχοντα corr.: κατέχων τις G
529 συγγενεῖς Legrand: συνεγγεῖς G
530 ὅλως Eideneier, 1970, 309, cf. G4.346: ὅλος G
532 ἰδὼν added by Legrand
542 ὡρίτζαν Legrand: κἂν ὡρίτζαν G
550 Θεοῦ νεύσει Legrand: νεύσει Θεοῦ G

and although she wished very much to change her mind,
the boundless desire within her would not permit this.
525 For the power of passion is desire and affection,
and anyone who attempts to keep strictly to his proper role
desire overcomes him, though his mind be chaste.
And because of this, he who desires has no sense of propriety,
he is not ashamed before his kinsmen, he has no fear of his neighbours
530 but is completely shameless and a slave to affection.
And this is what happened to these beautiful young people.
  Then the marvellous young man, seeing the girl weeping,
responded thus to her, also with tears:
"I, most beautiful girl, know about you.
535 The boundless wealth which your father has acquired
and because of which many of the high-born desire to marry you,
I know all about after detailed enquiries.
But I, dearest soul, do not yearn for wealth,
I do not crave for possessions, I do not aspire to fame,
540 I count all things grass as I delight in your beauty.
From the moment, dark-eyed one, that we saw each other,
you have not been absent from my soul for one moment.
For you are rooted within me and entwined there
and I imagine you all the time and I can see you even when you
    are not present.
545 For I have never been in love with any kind of beauty,
nor do I have the least knowledge of the paths of love.
Come, my sweet light, follow your lover.
Reveal the love which you have within,
for a sure demonstration comes from actions,
550 and we will both live together joyfully with God's consent.
And may your parents be delighted at this
when they become aware what sort of son-in-law they have acquired.
And no one will reproach you, but rather will congratulate you."
  Saying this and many other things, the young man
555 went on: "In you is my every beginning and my end
that had its beginning with God, until my death;

528–30 These sentiments are also found at G4.345–7.

καὶ εἰ πώποτε βουληθῶ λυπῆσαι σε, ψυχή μου,   31v
καὶ οὐ φυλάξω ἀθόλωτον τὴν πρὸς ἐμέ σου ἀγάπην
πόθον τε καθαρώτατον ἄχρι τῆς τελευτῆς μου,
560 νὰ μὴ ἀποθάνω Χριστιανός, νὰ μὴ κατευοδοῦμαι,   E906
νὰ μὴ κερδίσω τὰς εὐχὰς τῶν ἐμῶν γεννητόρων·   E907
καὶ αὐτὴ δέ, πανεύγενε, τὰ ὅμοια φυλάξῃς.»
    Ταῦτα ἡ κόρη τοῖς ὠσὶν ἐνηχηθεῖσα εἶπεν·
«Εἰ καὶ λίαν παράνομον τοῦ ἐμαυτὴν προδοῦναι
565 (ἡ τάξις γὰρ ἡ ἀληθὴς εὐγένεια καλεῖται,
ἥνπερ κἀγὼ ἠθέτησα, οὐκ οἶδα τι παθοῦσα),
πόθος γὰρ ὅμως ἀκραιφνής, ἀγάπη σου ἡ βεβαία
προτιμοτέραν ἔποισε σὴν καλλίστην ἀγάπην.»
    Εἶθ' οὕτως ὅρκον ἔρωτος ἡ κόρη φθεγξαμένη·
570 «Καταλιμπάνουσα γονεῖς, ἀδελφοὺς καὶ οἰκίαν
ἀπὸ τὸν Θεόν, ὦ ἄγουρε, σοὶ ἐμαυτὴν πιστεύω,
αὐτόν μοι δίδου μάρτυρα ὅλως μή με λυπῆσαι,
ἀλλὰ γυναῖκαν ἔννομον ἄχρι τέλους ποιῆσαι·
καὶ γὰρ πολλοὶ τῶν ἐραστῶν ἠθετήκασι λόγους,
575 ταῖς ποθουμέναις πρώην γὰρ ἐρωτικῶς δειχθέντες.»
    Καὶ ὡς τὸ ἤκουσεν ὁ παῖς ἐξεπλάγη θαυμάζων
τῆς παρθένου τὴν σύνεσιν· ἐπώμοσε δὲ ὅμως·
«Μὰ τὸν Πατέρα καὶ Υἱὸν καὶ τὸ ἅγιον Πνεῦμα,
οὐ λυπήσω σε πώποτε, ὦ πανευγενεστάτη,
580 ἀλλὰ κυρίαν τῶν ἐμῶν καὶ δέσποιναν ποιήσω,
γαμετήν τε καὶ σύνοικον μέχρι τέλους ζωῆς μου,
εἰ καθαρὸν τὸν πρὸς ἐμὲ διατηρήσεις πόθον,
καθώσπερ καὶ προέφην σοι, ὦ ποθεινὴ ψυχή μου.»   32r
    Καὶ ἐμπεδώσαντες καλῶς ἀλλήλους ἐκ τῶν ὅρκων,
585 ἡ παρθένος προκύψασα ἐκ τὴν χρυσῆν θυρίδα,   E912
ὁ παῖς τὴν ὑπεδέξατο ὀρθωθεὶς ἐν τῷ ἵππῳ·   E914
ἡ πέρδικα ἐξεπέτασεν, ὁ ἱέραξ τὴν ἐδέχθη.
    Καὶ κατεφίλησαν τερπνῶς, ὡς ἔπρεπεν, ἀλλήλους   E915
ἀνεκλαλήτως χαίροντες καὶ δακρύοντες ἄμφω·
590 πεφύκασι γὰρ ἀκαρῆ ἐν χαρμονῇ μεγίστῃ

---

560 μὴ G: μὴν Trapp
562 φυλάξῃς G: φυλάξοις Legrand
568 προτιμοτέραν G: προθυμοτέραν Tsopanakis, 1960, 85 ἔποισε Tsopanakis, ibid.:
ἔπεισε G σὴν καλλίστην ἀγάπην Mavrogordato: σὴ καλλίστη ἀγάπη G
569 ἔρωτος Mavrogordato: μ' ἔρωτος G

and if ever I should wish to grieve you, my soul,
and if I do not preserve untroubled your love for me
and your most pure desire until my death,
560 may I not die a Christian, may I not prosper,
may I not win my parents' blessings;
and may you, high-born girl, preserve the same feelings."
    The girl, with these words resounding in her ears, said:
"Even if it was quite against the law to betray myself
565 (for true propriety is called high birth,
which I have set aside, experiencing I know not what),
nevertheless your innocent desire and your true love
have made your fairest love preferable."
    Then the girl pronounced this oath of passion:
"Leaving parents, brothers and household,
I entrust myself to you, youngster, with God:
grant me him as a witness that you will not grieve me
but make me your lawful wife till the end.
For many lovers have set aside their words,
575 despite having previously shown themselves passionate to the girls
      they desire."
    When he heard this, the boy was amazed and admired
the girl's good sense; nevertheless he swore:
"By the Father and the Son and the Holy Spirit,
I will never grieve you, highest-born of girls,
580 but I will make you mistress of my possessions and my lady,
my wife and spouse until the end of my life,
if you keep your desire for me pure,
as I said to you before, my dearest soul."
    And when they had bound each other well through their oaths,
585 the girl leaned out of the golden window,
the boy raised himself upright on his horse and took her:
the partridge had flown away, the hawk had taken her.
And they embraced each other delectably, as was fitting,
rejoicing inexpressibly and both weeping,
590 for they immediately achieved the greatest happiness,

557–60 Digenis' vows almost suggest that he is promising the girl's faithfulness, not his
own.
574–5 Cynicism owing more to hard-headed negotiation than to romantic or Christian
idealism.
582–3 If the reference is back to 557–62, there is a significant change of expression
here.

καὶ δάκρυα μεθ᾽ ἡδονῆς θερμότατα ἐκίνουν.
Ὁ δέ γε παῖς ὑπὸ χαρᾶς κινηθεὶς καὶ ἀνδρείας,
σταθεὶς τοῦ οἴκου ἄντικρυς ἐξεφώνησε λέγων·
«Εὖξαι μου, κύρη πενθερέ, μετὰ τῆς θυγατρός σου,   E918. 982
595 εὐχαρίστει δὲ τῷ Θεῷ ἔχων γαμβρὸν τοιοῦτον.»
Τῆς δὲ φωνῆς ὡς ἤκουσαν τοῦ στρατηγοῦ αἱ βίγλαι,
διελάλησαν ἅπασιν εἰς τὸ καβαλλικεῦσαι.
Καὶ ὁ στρατηγὸς παρευθὺς ἐξάπινα ἀκούσας
ἄλλος ἐξ ἄλλου γέγονεν οὐκ ἔχων ὅ,τι δρᾶσαι·
600 καὶ ἐκ βάθους ἀνέκραξεν· «Ἀπώλεσα τὸ φῶς μου,
θυγάτηρ ἡ μονογενὴς ἐξ ὀφθαλμῶν μου ἤρθη.»
Στρατήγισσα δ᾽ ὡς ἤκουσεν ἠλάλαζε βοῶσα·
«Οἴχεται ἡ μονογενής, ἡρπάγη ἡ θυγάτηρ.»
Οἱ ἀδελφοὶ ἑτέρωθεν θρηνοῦντες ἀνεβόων·
605 «Τίς τοῦτο κατετόλμησε τὸ ἀνόμημα πρᾶξαι;
Τίς ἀφ᾽ ἡμῶν τὴν ἀδελφὴν ἀπέσπασεν ἀθρόως;»
Ἔκλαιον αἱ οἰκέτιδες, οἰμωγὰς ἀνεβόων,
ὀδυρμὸς ἀκατάσχετος διὰ παντὸς ἐχώρει·
στρατός τε πολὺς ἔνοπλος εἰς δίωξιν τοῦ νέου
610 καὶ ὀπίσω ὁ στρατηγὸς μετὰ τῶν δύο τέκνων· 32v
ἀλλ᾽ οὐδὲ ἡ στρατήγισσα κατελείφθη ἐν οἴκῳ
τῆς θυγατρὸς τὸν χωρισμὸν μὴ φέρουσα οὐδ᾽ ὅλως·
πλῆθος γὰρ οἰκετίδων τε μεθ᾽ ἑαυτῆς λαβοῦσα,
πεζῇ ὡς εἶχεν εἵπετο, λυσίκομος, θρηνοῦσα·
615 «Φιλτάτη ψυχή,» κράζουσα, «ποῦ πορεύῃ οὐκ οἶδα.»
Οὐδεὶς δὲ ἐναπέμεινε γηραιὸς οὔτε νέος
ὃς οὐκ ἐκαβαλλίκευσεν εἰς δίωξιν τοῦ νέου,
πάντες ὑπεραλγήσαντες τὴν ἁρπαγὴν τῆς κόρης,
ὡς μὴ ἰσχύειν ἀκριβῶς ἀριθμῆσαι τὸ πλῆθος.
620 Καὶ τοῦ φωτὸς αὐγάζοντος ἀπάρτι τῆς ἡμέρας,
ἐκεῖ τοὺς ἐκατέλαβον εἰς τοὺς ἀδήλους κάμπους.
Οὕσπερ ἰδοῦσα μήκοθεν ἡ πανώραιος κόρη
(καὶ γὰρ ἔβλεπεν ὄπισθεν σκοπεύουσα ὀξέως,
ἐν ταῖς ἀγκάλαις οὖσα τε τοῦ πανηγαπημένου)
625 πρὸς αὐτὸν ταῦτα ἔλεγε σφικτὰ τοῦτον κρατοῦσα·
«Ἀγωνίζου, ψυχίτζα μου, μή μας ἀποχωρίσουν,
καὶ ἴσχυε κατὰ πολὺ τὸν μαῦρον ἀποπλήττων·

598 παρευθὺς Legrand: εὐθὺς G

and they shed hot tears in their pleasure.
Then the boy, moved by joy and bravery,
stood in front of the house and shouted out, saying:
"Give me your blessing, my lord father-in-law, and your daughter too,
595 and give thanks to God for having such a son-in-law."
    When the general's watch-men heard the shout,
they cried out for all to mount their horses.
Immediately, when the general heard this sudden cry,
he was beside himself, not knowing what to do,
600 and he shouted in despair: "I have lost my light,
my only daughter has been snatched from my sight."
When the general's lady heard this, she wailed and cried out:
"My only daughter has gone, my darling has been abducted."
Her brothers for their part lamented and shouted:
605 "Who has dared to do this lawless deed?
Who has torn our sister away from us so suddenly?"
    The women of the household wept, they wailed loudly.
Uncontrollable lamentation spread everywhere.
A great armed force set off in pursuit of the young man
610 and behind them came the general with his two sons.
But not even the general's lady was left behind in the house,
being quite unable to bear separation from her daughter,
for, collecting a host of household women with her,
she followed on foot, with her hair loose, mourning:
615 "Dearest soul," she cried out, "where you are going I do not know."
There remained no one, old or young,
who did not ride out in pursuit of the young man,
all grieving excessively over the girl's abduction,
so that it was not possible to count the host precisely.
620   And just as the light of day was dawning,
they caught up with them there on the shadowy plains.
The most beautiful girl saw them from a distance
(for she was looking behind, keeping a sharp watch
from the arms of her best beloved)
625 and she said to him, holding him tightly:
"Strive, my dear soul, not to let them part us;
be very strong and urge on your black horse,

605 See Laiou, 1993, 200–11 on the ecclesiastical and legal implications of Digenis'
pursuit of the girl; it should be classed as consensual elopement, which can be rectified by
marriage, rather than abduction, which incurs severe penalties.

ἰδοὺ γὰρ μέλλουσιν ἡμᾶς οἱ διώκοντες φθάνειν.»
    Ὡς ταῦτα δὲ ὁ θαυμαστὸς ἤκουσε νεανίας,
630 θάρσους εὐθέως ἐμπλησθεὶς καὶ τῆς ὁδοῦ ἐκκλίνας
δένδρον εὑρίσκει διφυὲς κλάδους φέρον τε δύο
καὶ τὴν κόρην ἀποβαλὼν μέσον τῶν δύο κλάδων:
«Αὐτοῦ κάθου, παγκάλλιστε, καὶ σὸν φίλτατον βλέπε.»
Καὶ πρὸς πόλεμον ἑαυτὸν καθοπλίζει εὐθέως·
635 καὶ τότε τὸ ἡλιογέννημα τὸν ἄγουρον ἐλάλει:
«Τοὺς ἀδελφούς μου πρόσεχε μὴ τοὺς κακοδικήσῃς.»   33r
    Ξένον πρᾶγμα ἐδείκνυτο τοῖς ἐκεῖσε παροῦσι
πῶς μόνος κατετόλμησε συμβαλεῖν χιλιάσιν·
καὶ ἐν βραχεῖ ἀπέκτεινε στρατιώτας ἀπείρους
640 καθωπλισμένους, ἱππικούς, πολέμου γυμνασμένους,
οἷς συμβουλεύειν ἤρξατο στραφῆναι εἰς τὰ ὀπίσω
καὶ μὴ πεῖραν τῆς ἑαυτοῦ μεταλαβεῖν ἀνδρείας.
Ἐκεῖνοι δὲ τὴν τοῦ ἑνὸς αἰσχυνόμενοι ἧτταν
τὸ θανεῖν ᾑρετίσαντο ἢ φυγεῖν ὑπ' ἐκείνου.
645 Κἀκεῖνος ἐπελάλησε, σύρνει τὸ σπαθορράβδιν,
καὶ πρὶν ἐλθεῖν τὸν στρατηγὸν οὐδὲ εἷς ὑπελείφθη.
Καὶ τοῦ πολέμου πέρας τε ὁ παῖς ἀποπληρώσας
ὡς νικητὴς ὑπέστρεφε πρὸς τὴν παρθένον χαίρων
καὶ ἐκ τοῦ ἵππου καταβὰς καὶ μυρία φιλήσας:
650 «Ἔχεις με, κόρη πάντερπνε, ἀπόδειξιν τῶν ἔργων.»
    Ἡ δὲ κόρη τὸν ἄγουρον ὡραΐζουσα πλέον
ἡδέως ὑπεδέχετο φιλημάτων τοὺς ψόφους,
ἠρέμα πρὸς τὸν ἄγουρον οὕτωσὶ φθεγξαμένη:
«Μὴ ἀδικήσῃς, ὦ ψυχή, τοὺς ἐμοὺς αὐταδέλφους·
655 ἐκείνους γὰρ οὕσπερ ὁρᾷς πρὸς ἡμᾶς ἐρχομένους
ἐκ τῶν ἵππων τεκμαίρομαι ἀδελφοὺς ἐμοὺς εἶναι
καὶ ὁ τρίτος ὁ μετ' αὐτῶν ὁ πατήρ μου τυγχάνει·
τούτους μοι σώους χάρισον, ἀβλαβεῖς συντηρήσας.»
    «Γενήσεται ὅπερ αἰτεῖς,» ὁ παῖς τῇ κόρῃ ἔφη,
660 «εἰ μή τι ἕτερον συμβῇ ἐκ τῶν ἀπροσδοκήτων·
ὁ γὰρ ἐχθρῶν φειδόμενος ἐν ὥρα τοῦ πολέμου
ὑπ' ἐκείνων ἀσυμπαθῶς κατεβλήθη πολλάκις.»   33v
    Ταῦτα <εἰπὼν> εἰσπήδησεν ἐν τῷ ἰδίῳ ἵππῳ
καὶ τοῖς περὶ τὸν στρατηγὸν σπουδαίως ὑποπίπτει.

---

629 θαυμαστὸς Legrand: θαύμαστος G
644 φυγεῖν Trapp: θανεῖν G
663 εἰπὼν added by Legrand

for look – the pursuers are about to catch up with us."
      As the marvellous young man heard this,
630 he was immediately filled with courage, and swerving off the road,
    he found a forked tree with two branches
    and put the girl between these two branches:
    "Sit there, my loveliest, and watch your dearest."
    And he immediately armed himself for war,
635 and then the sun-born girl cried out to the youngster:
    "Take care that you do not harm my brothers."
      An extraordinary deed was seen by those present there,
    how he on his own dared to clash with thousands.
    And in a short time he killed countless soldiers
640 in full armour, on horseback, trained for war,
    and he began to counsel them to turn back
    and not to test his bravery.
    But they were ashamed to be defeated by one man
    and chose death rather than to be put to flight by him.
645 So he urged on his horse, he drew his sword-stick
    and before the general arrived not one remained.
    And when the boy had come to the end of the battle
    he returned joyfully to the girl as victor
    and dismounting from his horse he kissed her a thousand times:
650 "You have me, my delightful girl, as proof of my deeds."
      The girl, honouring the youngster further,
    sweetly accepted his resounding kisses
    and addressed the youngster calmly thus:
    "Do not, my soul, harm my brothers,
655 for the men whom you see coming towards us
    I can guess from their horses are my brothers,
    and the third man with them is my father.
    Grant these to me in safety, preserve them unharmed."
      "What you ask shall be done," the boy said to the girl,
660 "unless something unexpected happens,
    for he who spares enemies in time of battle
    is often attacked by them mercilessly."
      Saying this he leaped onto his own horse
    and swiftly attacked the general's companions.

665 Οἱ δὲ τῆς κόρης ἀδελφοὶ ζήλου πολλοῦ πλησθέντες
ἀνελεῖν τοῦτον ἔλεγον τοῖς ἰδίοις ἀγούροις,
τὸν φόνον προσδοκώμενοι ὑφ' ἑτέρων γενέσθαι·
ὁ δὲ παῖς τὸ παράγγελμα φυλάττων τῆς φιλτάτης
εὐτέχνως τούτους ὑπελθὼν σοφῶς ἀνεῖλε πάντας.
670 Οἱ δ' ἀδελφοὶ ὁρμήσαντες μανικῶς ἐπ' ἐκεῖνον,
οὕτως αὐτοὺς ἐκύκλευσεν ἐκ τῶν ἵππων εἰσρίψας
ὡς ἂν μὴ βλάψαι ἀκριβῶς ἢ ὅλως τραυματίσαι.
Καὶ στραφεὶς πρὸς τὸν στρατηγὸν μακρόθεν καὶ πεζεύσας,
σφικτὰ δήσας τὰς χεῖρας του, χαμηλὰ προσκυνήσας,   E649. 979-80
675 ἤρξατο λέγειν πρὸς αὐτὸν θαρσαλέᾳ τῇ ὄψει:
«Συγχώρησόν μοι, αὐθέντα μου, μηδέν με καταμέμφου·
ὁ στρατός σου ἦτον χωρικὸς τοῦ κρούειν καὶ μὴ λαμβάνειν
καὶ διὰ τοῦτο οἱ πλείονες εἰς τὸν Ἅδην ἀπῆλθον.
Οὐ γὰρ εἰμὶ τῶν ἀγενῶν οὐδὲ τῶν ἀνανδρείων,
680 καὶ εἰ ποτὲ προστάξῃς με ποιῆσαί σοι δουλείαν,
τότε λοιπὸν βεβαιωθῇς οἷον γαμβρὸν ἐπῆρες·   E986
εἰ δὲ καὶ πεῖραν λάβῃς μου ἀκριβῆ ἐκ τῶν ἔργων,
τῆς εὐτυχίας ἑαυτὸν μακαρίσεις πολλάκις.»
Αὐτίκα δὲ ὁ στρατηγὸς χεῖρας εἰς ὕψος ἄρας
685 καὶ ὄμμα πρὸς ἀνατολὰς τῷ Θεῷ ηὐχαρίστει,
«Δόξα σοι,» λέγων, «ὁ Θεὸς ὁ συμφερόντως πάντα
οἰκονομῶν τὰ καθ' ἡμᾶς σοφίᾳ τῇ ἀρρήτῳ·
ὡς γὰρ αὐτὸς ἠθέλησα γαμβροῦ κατηξιώθην 34r
ὡραίου τε καὶ εὐγενοῦς, σώφρονος καὶ ἀνδρείου,
690 οἵου οὐδεὶς ἐπέτυχε πώποτε εἰς τὸν κόσμον.»   E990
Ταῦτα ἐξ ὅλης τῆς ψυχῆς Θεῷ εὐχαριστήσας,
πρὸς τὸν παῖδα ἐφθέγξατο ἐπιεικῶς τοιάδε:
«Χάρις μέν, ὦ χρυσόγαμβρε, τῷ Θεῷ ἐπὶ πᾶσι,
τῷ τὰ συμφέροντα ἡμῖν καλῶς οἰκονομοῦντι·
695 ἔπαρον δέ, παγκάλλιστε, ἣν ἔλαβες ἐκ πόθου·
εἰ μὴ γὰρ πόθον ἄπειρον πρὸς αὐτὴν πάντως εἶχες,   E1210
οὐκ ἂν μόνος ἐτόλμησας ἐμβῆναι εἰς χιλιάδας.
Δεῦρο οὖν ἃς ἀπέλθωμεν εἰς τὸν ἐμὸν τὸν οἶκον
καὶ μὴ λογίζου παρ' ἡμῶν λυπηρὸν ὑποστῆναι,
700 ἀλλ' ἵνα καὶ τὰ σύμφωνα ποιήσωμεν τοῦ γάμου
συμβόλαια ἐν γράμμασι τοῦ πατρός σου παρόντος·
τάχιστα γὰρ ὡς μηνυθεὶς πρὸς ἡμᾶς ἐπανήξει

670 ἐπ' Kalonaros: ὑπ' G
674 σφικτὰ Legrand: σφικτὰς G

665 The girl's brothers were full of energy
and told their own youngsters to destroy him,
expecting the killing to be done by others.
The boy, following his dearest's instructions,
set about these skilfully and cleverly destroyed them all.
670 Then the brothers rushed on him in a frenzy
but he circled them and threw them off their horses,
in such a way that they were not seriously hurt or wounded at all.
And turning towards the general, he dismounted at a distance
and, clasping his hands tightly and making a deep obeisance,
675 he began to address him with a confident air:
    "Forgive me, my lord, do not blame me;
your army was uncouth in giving and receiving blows,
and because of that most of them have gone to Hades.
For I am not one of those of low birth or cowardly disposition,
680 and if ever you command me to do you service,
then indeed you will be certain what kind of son-in-law you have
    acquired.
And if you test me strictly by my deeds,
you will frequently congratulate yourself on your good fortune."
    The general straight away raised his hands on high
685 and turned his eyes to the east and gave thanks to God.
"Thanks be to you," he said, "God, who arranges all our affairs
in his ineffable wisdom to our advantage,
for I have been granted a son-in-law such as I wished,
handsome and high-born, sensible and brave,
690 of a kind that no one has ever found in the world."
    Giving thanks to God for this with all his soul,
he pronounced these mild words to the boy:
    "Thanks be to God, my golden son-in-law, for all things,
for he arranges well what is to our advantage.
695 Take, handsome youth, the girl whom you seized out of desire.
For if you were not certain in feeling boundless desire for her,
you would not have dared single-handed to set upon thousands.
Come, therefore, let us go into my house
and do not think of experiencing anything distressing at our hands,
700 but it is so that we can draw up the agreed marriage contract
in writing with your father present;
for as soon as he has been informed, he will come to us

καὶ τὴν προῖκα τῆς θυγατρὸς τῆς ἐμῆς ἀπολήψεις.
Ποιήσω καὶ τοὺς γάμους σου ἀκουστοὺς εἰς τὸν κόσμον,
705 νὰ λάβῃς καὶ τὴν προῖκα σου ἀπ' αὐτῆς τῆς ἡμέρας,   E992
κεντηνάρια εἴκοσι, νομίσματα παλαῖα,   E992
ἃ πρὸ καιροῦ ἐχώρισα καὶ ἐθέμην ἰδίως
τῆς φιλτάτης εἰς ὄνομα, καὶ ἀργυραῖα σκεύη,
βιστιάριον χρῇζον τε πεντακοσίας λίτρας,   E995
710 κτήματα πολλὰ ἀκίνητα τριανταὲξ εἰσόδων,
716 καὶ μετὰ τούτων πάντων <τε> εὑρισκόμενα ζῷα,
πρωτεῖα τετρακόσια, στράτορας ὀγδοήντα,
μαγείρους δεκατέσσαρας καὶ μάγκιπας ὡσαύτως
719 καὶ ἕτερα ψυχάρια ἑκατὸν καὶ πενήντα,
711 βάγιας ἑβδομήκοντα σὺν τῷ μητρῴῳ οἴκῳ
περιφανεῖ τυγχάνοντι καὶ πολυτίμῳ ὄντως·
ὡσαύτως καὶ ἐξαίσια κόσμια τῆς μητρός της,   E996
στέφανον τὸν παγκόσμιον, ἀξιέπαινον ἔργον 34v
715 συντεθειμένον ἐκ χρυσοῦ, λίθων τιμιωτάτων·
720 δώσω σοι καὶ προτίμησιν τῶν λοιπῶν μου παιδίων,
πλοῦτον πολὺν καὶ ἄπειρον, κτήματα οὐκ ὀλίγα·
σὺν τούτοις ἄλλα πλείονα παράσχω τῶν ῥηθέντων
πρὸ τοῦ γενέσθαι, τέκνον μου, τὴν ἱερολογίαν.
Ποιήσω καὶ τοὺς γάμους σου ἀκουστοὺς εἰς τὸν κόσμον
725 τοῦ μὴ κράζειν σε πώποτε κλεψίγαμον οἱ νέοι,
καὶ ὅτι κόρην ἥρπασας πραγμάτων ἀμοιρούσαν,
ὅπερ αἰσχύνη πέφυκε πᾶσι τοῖς εὖ φρονοῦσιν·

710 τριανταὲξ εἰσόδων Legrand: εἰσόδων τριανταὲξ G: perhaps one could read
εἰσόδων τριανταέξι
716–19, 711–15 are transposed thus by Trapp (cf. Z2081–4)
716 τε corr., Mavrogordato suggests τὰ

and you will receive my daughter's dowry.
I will make your wedding renowned throughout the world:
705 you will receive for your dowry from this day
     twenty *centenaria* in old *nomismata*,
     which some time ago I set aside and kept especially
     in my dearest's name, and silver vessels,
     a wardrobe worth five hundred *litrai*,
710 much landed property providing thirty-six revenues,
716 and with all the livestock they contain,
     four hundred beasts of the first quality, eighty grooms,
     fourteen cooks and as many bakers,
719 and another one hundred and fifty slaves,
711 seventy female servants together with the bride's mother's house,
     which is famous and truly rich,
     likewise exceptional jewelry from her mother,
     her world-famous crown, a work of art worthy of praise,
715 crafted from gold and very costly stones.
720 And I shall give you preference over the rest of my children,
     great wealth beyond counting, possessions not few in number.
     In addition I shall provide other things, more than have been
        mentioned,
     my child, before the wedding service is held.
     And I shall make your wedding renowned throughout the world,
725 so that young men can never call you a match-stealer,
     saying that you abducted a girl who lacked possessions,
     which is a reproach to all men of good sense.

704–33 This proposed dowry resembles historical examples, especially in its general terms for the expression of wealth (see Hendy, 1985, 201–20, especially 217–18). A likely picture of the power games involved is given by Angold, 1989; this rich dowry is offered in an attempt to make Digenis part of his wife's father's household. Digenis' refusal is not generosity but the maintenance of independence.

706 References to old *nomismata* in the eleventh century are positive, in the context of the gradual debasement of the currency from around 1034 till Alexios I's reform of 1092 (Hendy, 1969, 3–6; Tiftixoglou, 1974, 60–1, note 322). This seems to be the case here (cf. also the 1083 Typikon of Pakourianos; Lemerle, 1977, 137). In the twelfth century such references imply the discounting of old coins as worn (Hendy, 1969, 37–8).

709 The imperial *vestiarion* was a public warehouse or the imperial wardrobe (Haldon, 1990, 159–60, 191–2); presumably the reference here is to a private version of the latter.

720 The legal implications are explored by Angold, 1989, 212; if Digenis were to accept the dowry, his loyalty would in future be to his wife's family. Note however that this marriage is between kin groups.

723 This is the only indication that the Church has a role to play in this marriage.

724–7 As pointed out by Laiou (1993, 207; cf. Angold, 1989, 211) the bride's father has as much to lose as Digenis here. Match-stealing demeaned both sides of the marriage, and was worthy only of slaves and paupers.

καὶ ταῦτα πῶς οὖν ἐκφυγεῖν ῥᾳδίως ἐξισχύσεις,
εἰ μὴ τανῦν <σὺ> μεθ᾽ ἡμῶν ὑποστραφῇς ἐν οἴκῳ,
730 ὅπως καὶ ἡ στρατήγισσα παρηγορίαν λάβῃ   E997
(οὐδαμῶς γὰρ ἐπίσταται ποῖος ἄρα τυγχάνεις)
καὶ χαίρουσα τῶν ἀγαθῶν μεγαλύνῃ δοτῆρα;
Πείσθητι οὖν, καλὲ γαμβρέ, καὶ ἐλθὲ μετ᾽ ἐμένα.»
    Ταῦτα εἰπὼν ὁ στρατηγὸς κολακεύων τὸν νέον,
735 παρευθὺς ὁ νεώτερος τῷ στρατηγῷ ἀντέφη·
«Πεισθῆναι σου τῆς συμβουλῆς ἀρίστης ὑπαρχούσης,
αὐθέντα μου καὶ πενθερέ, δίκαιόν με τυγχάνει·
καὶ δέδοικα μὴ κίνδυνος ἐκ τούτου μοι ἐπέλθῃ
καὶ μετ᾽ αἰσχύνης θάνατον οἰκτρότατον ὀφλήσω,
740 ὡς ἐχθρὸς καὶ ἐπίβουλος καὶ ἐχθρὸς γεγονώς σου· 35r
πείθει με γὰρ τὸ συνειδὸς τηρεῖν τὰ ἐναντία
καὶ τὴν ὄψιν ἐρυθριῶ ἰδεῖν τῆς στρατηγίσσης.
Ἐγώ, κύριέ μου πενθερέ, ἐπιθυμίαν εἶχον
τὴν θυγατέρα σου λαβεῖν διὰ τὸ ταύτης κάλλος,
745 οὐχὶ δὲ πλούτου εἵνεκα ἢ διὰ τῶν κτημάτων·
ταῦτα πάντα χαρίζομαι τοῖς γυναικαδελφοῖς μου.   E1007
Ἀρκοῦν ἐμοὶ τὰ κάλλη της ἀντὶ πολλῶν προικίων·
πλοῦτον παρέχει ὁ Θεὸς καὶ πενίαν ὡσαύτως
καὶ ταπεινοῖ καὶ ἀνυψοῖ, κατάγει καὶ ἀνάγει.
750 Ὑπὲρ δὲ τοῦ ὑποστραφῆν, οὐ μή σε παρακούσω,
ἀλλ᾽ ἂς ἀπέλθω πρότερον εἰς τὴν ἐμὴν μητέρα,
ἵν᾽ ἴδῃ ὁ ἐμὸς πατὴρ νύμφην ἣν θέλει ἔχειν
καὶ <νὰ> δοξάσῃ τὸν Θεόν, καὶ ταχὺ ὑποστρέφω·
ἀλλὰ μὴ τοῦτο λυπηθῇς, ὑπερεύχου δὲ μᾶλλον,
755 τέκνα σου γὰρ τυγχάνομεν καὶ δοῦλοι τῆς ψυχῆς σου.»
    Καὶ θαυμάσας ὁ στρατηγὸς τὴν σύνεσιν τοῦ νέου,
«Ὁ Θεός,» ἔφη, «τέκνον μου, ἵνα σε εὐλογήσῃ
καὶ ἀξιώσῃ χαίρεσθαι τὰ ἔτη τῆς ζωῆς σου.»   E1058, 1290
Καὶ ἀσπασάμενος αὐτὸν ἐπέβηκε τοῦ ἵππου
760 καὶ εἰς τὴν κόρην μὲν αὐτός, στρατηγὸς δὲ ἐν οἴκῳ,
συνοδοιπόρους τοὺς υἱοὺς ἐκ τοῦ πτώματος ἔχων,
σφόδρα ὑπερθαυμάζοντας τὴν τοῦ παιδὸς ἀνδρείαν.

728 οὖν Tsopanakis. 1960. 85–6: οὐκ G
729 σὺ added by Legrand   ὑποστραφῇς Legrand: ὑποραφῇς G
739 καὶ ... οἰκτρότατον repeated in G
753 νὰ added by Legrand
762 ὑπερθαυμάζοντας corr. : ὑπερθαυμάζοντες G

And how will you be able easily to escape this,
unless you now return with us to the house,
730 so that the general's lady can be reassured
(for she has no idea at all who you might be)
and in her joy praise the Giver of all good things?
Therefore be persuaded, my fine son-in-law, and come with me."
    The general said this, flattering the young man,
735 and immediately the young man replied to the general:
"To obey your counsel, which is excellent,
my lord and father-in-law, is right for me;
yet I am afraid that danger might come to me from this
and I may incur a most pitiful death in disgrace
740 for becoming your enemy and plotting against you and being an
    enemy of yours.
For conscience persuades me to do the reverse,
and I blush to look on the face of the general's lady.
I had the desire, my lord father-in-law,
to carry off your daughter for the sake of her beauty,
745 not because of her wealth or possessions.
All these I bestow on my wife's brothers.
Her beauty is sufficient for me in place of many dowries;
God provides wealth and likewise poverty,
he humbles and raises up, he brings low and makes high.
750 As for returning, I shall not disobey you,
but let me first go to my mother,
so that my father may see the daughter-in-law he will have
and may praise God; and I shall return quickly.
But do not be grieved over this – instead give your blessing,
755 for we are your children and servants of your soul."
    The general was amazed at the young man's understanding.
"May God bless you, my child," he said,
"and grant you happiness all the years of your life."
And embracing him, he mounted his horse,
760 and the young man returned to the girl while the general went home
with his sons as his companions after their fall,
marvelling exceedingly at the boy's bravery.

---

738 It is not clear whether the enmity whose consequences Digenis fears is connected
with the abduction and battle which have just occurred, or with his refusal (about to be
announced) to accept the generous dowry and its likely attendant obligations.
742 Is this embarrassment really because he has abducted the girl for love and not for
her money?

Ὁ δέ γε ὄντως θαυμαστὸς ἐκεῖνος νεανίας
ἐν τῷ τόπῳ καταλαβὼν ἔνθα ἦτον ἡ κόρη,
765 «Δεῦρο, γλυκύτατόν μου φῶς,» ἐξεφώνησε λέγων,
«δεῦρο, ἄνθος γλυκύτατον, ῥόδον μεμυρισμένον,
δεῦρο, δάμαλις ἡ ἐμὴ ἣν ἔζευξεν ὁ ἔρως, 36r
τὴν ὁδὸν διανύσωμεν, οὐδεὶς γὰρ ὁ κωλύων,
δρόμον οὐδείς, πανεύμορφε, ἐστὶν ὁ ἐμποδίζων,
770 μόνον πατρὸς καὶ ἀδελφῶν τῶν σῶν περισωθέντων·
οὐ γὰρ τὸ πρόσταγμα τὸ σὸν ἠθέλησ᾽ ἀθετῆσαι.»
Καὶ ἐκ τοῦ δένδρου παρευθὺς κατελθοῦσα ἡ κόρη,
χαρᾶς καὶ ἡδονῆς πολλῆς ὑποπλησθεῖσα λίαν,
περιπατοῦσα γαληνὰ τὸν ἄγουρον ὑπήντα
775 καί, πλησίον γενόμενοι, μετὰ πόθου ἠρώτα:
«Πάντως οὐδὲν ἐνάντιον συνέβη σοι, ψυχή μου;
Ἀνάγγειλόν μοι τάχιον περὶ τῶν ἀδελφῶν μου.»
«Μὴ θλίβεσαι, ψυχίτζα μου,» ὁ ἄγουρος ἀντέφη,
«ἐκτὸς γὰρ τῶν ἐπαινετῶν ἀγούρων τοῦ πατρός σου,
780 οὐδεὶς ὑπέστη μερικῶς οὔτε καθόλου βλάβην.»
Καὶ κύψας εἵλκυσεν αὐτὴν ἐπάνω ἐν τῷ ἵππῳ
καὶ ὑποδέχεται αὐτὴν ἐν τῷ ἰδίῳ ἵππῳ·
φιλήματός τε καθαροῦ ἡδέως κορεσθέντες
καὶ χαίροντες διώδευον μεθ᾽ ἡδονῆς μεγάλης.
785 Καὶ ὡς ἐσκέψαντο αὐτὸν αἱ βίγλαι τοῦ πατρός του
ἐν ταῖς ἀγκάλαις φέροντα τὴν ῥοδόμορφον κόρην,
μετὰ σπουδῆς ἀπέτρεχον εἰπεῖν τὰ συγχαρίκια.
Ὡς δὲ ἤκουσεν ὁ πατὴρ τὴν τούτου ἔλευσιν ὅλως,
πλήρης γενόμενος χαρᾶς εὐθὺς καβαλλικεύει,
790 οἱ πέντε γυναικάδελφοι, τρισχίλιοι ἀγοῦροι,
δώδεκα σελλοχάλινα ἔστρωσαν γυναικεῖα,
δύο ὑπῆρχον χυμευτὰ μετὰ μαργαριτάρων   E1465
καὶ τὰ λοιπὰ ὁλόχρυσα μάλιστα μετὰ ζώων·
πέπλα δὲ εἶχον ἅπασαι αἱ σέλλαι παγκαλλίστως· 36v
795 βλαττία ἦσαν σκεπαστοὶ οἱ ἵπποι πάντες μάλα
ὑπ᾽ αὐτῶν καλυπτόμενοι καὶ τοῦ πολλοῦ χρυσίου·
ὄπισθεν τούτων σάλπιγγες καὶ βούκινα βαρέα,
τύμπανά τε καὶ ὄργανα ἐκρούοντο εἰς ἄκρον
καὶ ἦν ἦχος ἐξάκουστος ἐν ἐκείνῃ τῇ ὥρᾳ,

---

766 Fol. 35v, originally left blank, now has prayers added in a later, inexpert hand
787 ἀπέτρεχον Legrand: ἀπέτρεχεν G

That truly marvellous young man,
reaching the place where the girl was,
765   shouted out and said: "Come here, my sweetest light,
come here, my sweetest flower, perfumed rose,
come here, my heifer whom Eros has yoked,
let us complete our journey, for there is no one to stop us,
there is no one, my lovely girl, to block our way,
770   since only your father and your brothers have survived,
for I did not wish to disobey your command."
      And the girl immediately came down from the tree,
overflowing with joy and great pleasure;
walking calmly she went to meet the young man,
775   and as they came close she asked lovingly,
"Has nothing unpleasant happened to you at all, my soul?
Tell me quickly about my brothers."
      "Do not be distressed, my dear soul," the youngster replied,
"apart from your father's famous youngsters
780   no one has suffered any harm either in part or in any way."
And bending down he pulled her up on to the horse
and sat her on his own horse.
Sweetly taking their fill of a pure embrace,
they continued on their journey joyfully with great pleasure.
785   And when his father's guards caught sight of him
holding in his arms the rose-lovely girl,
they ran off swiftly to deliver the good news.
When his father heard fully of his arrival,
he was filled with joy and immediately mounted his horse,
790   as did his wife's five brothers, and three thousand youngsters.
They prepared twelve women's saddles and bridles,
two were set with pearls
and the rest were all of gold with animal decoration.
The saddles all had coverings, very beautifully made;
795   all the horses too were draped with silks
and were covered with these and much gold.
Behind them cornets and heavy trumpets
and drums and organs were played at full pitch,
and there was a splendid sound to be heard at that time

800 ὡς ἄχρι τρία μίλια τοῦ οἴκου προσελθόντες·
οὖσπερ ἰδοῦσα μήκοθεν ἡ πανώραιος κόρη
σύντρομος ὅλη γέγονε τοὺς ὄντας ἀγνοοῦσα
καὶ πρὸς τὸν παῖδα ἔφησε λίαν συντετριμμένη:
«Ἐὰν ξένοι τυγχάνωσιν, ἡμᾶς ἀποχωρίσουν.»　　　　　E1038
805 «Μὴ φοβοῦ, φῶς μου τὸ γλυκύ,» ὁ νέος ἀπεκρίθη,
«ὁ πενθερός σου ἔνι αὐτός, διὰ σὲ ἐκοπώθη.»　　　　　E1040
Πάλιν τὸ ἡλιογέννημα τὸν ἄγουρον ἀντέφη:
«Ἐντρέπομαι, ψυχίτζα μου, δι᾿ οὗ μόνη τυγχάνω·
εἰ τοῦ πατρός μου ἤκουσας καὶ μετ᾿ ἐμοῦ ἐστράφης,　　E1043
810 ἄρτι νὰ εἶχον τὰς βάγιας μου καὶ τὴν ἐξόπλισίν μου,　E1044
νὰ ἐγίνωσκε καὶ ὁ σὸς πατὴρ τίνος παιδὶν ἀπῆρες·　　E1046
ἀλλ᾿ ὅμως ὡς τὸ ἐδίκησας, ἀπολογίας ἔχε.»
«Μὴ λυπεῖσαι, πανεύγενε, διὰ τὴν μοναξίαν,　　　　　E1049
σὲ γὰρ πάντες γινώσκουσι κἂν καὶ μόνη τυγχάνεις,
815 καὶ τούτου μέμψις ἕνεκα ὑπάρχει οὐδεμία.»
Ὅτε δὲ ἐπλησίασαν, χαιρετίζουν ἀλλήλους·
ἐπέζευσεν ὁ νεώτερος μετὰ τῆς ποθητῆς του,
ἐπέζευσε καὶ ὁ ἀμιρᾶς, ἠσπάσατο τοὺς δύο·　　　　　E1052
«Ὁ Θεός,» ἔφη, «τέκνον μου, ἵνα σας εὐλογήσῃ,　　　E1055
820 αὐξήσῃ καὶ τὰ ἔτη σου ἐν εἰρήνῃ καὶ πλούτῳ 37r
καὶ βασιλείας τῆς αὐτοῦ ἐπιδείξῃ μετόχους.»
Εἰς δὲ σέλλαν τὴν χυμευτὴν καθίσαντες τὴν κόρην　　E1059
καὶ πολύτιμον στέφανον αὐτῇ περιβαλόντες,
καὶ ἕκαστος τῶν συγγενῶν τῶν ἐκεῖ εὑρεθέντων
825 δῶρα αὐτῇ προσήνεγκαν ὑπέρτιμα τῷ ὄντι·
καὶ τὸν παῖδα κοσμήσαντες ὡς ἔπρεπε τῷ νέῳ
τὰ βούκινα ἐδώκασιν, ὑπέστρεφον εὐθέως·
ἠλάλαζον αἱ σάλπιγγες, τὰ τύμπανα ἐφώνουν,
ἐκρούοντο τὰ ὄργανα, ἐμελῴδουν τὰ πάντα,
830 κιθάραι ἦχον ἔπεμπον καὶ πᾶν μουσικὸν εἶδος·
ᾀδόμενα ὑπέστρεφον ἐν τῷ οἴκῳ συντόμως.
Χαρὰν τὴν ὑπερβάλλουσαν τὴν γιναμένην τότε
τίς ἑρμηνεῦσαι δυνηθῇ ἢ εἰπεῖν ἐξισχύσει;
Ἐδόκουν γὰρ ὡς καὶ ἡ γῆ ἐν ᾗ περιεπάτουν
835 καὶ αὐτὴ συνετέρπετο περιπατούντων πάντων·

800 προσελθόντες G: προελθόντες Trapp
806 ὁ πενθερός σου ἔνι αὐτός Legrand: αὐτός ὁ πενθερός σου ἔνι G
810 ἐξόπλισίν Kalonaros: ἐξόμπλισίν G
827 βούκινα Legrand: βύκινα G
829 ἐκρούοντο Legrand: ἐκρόουντο G

800 and they came out from the house as far as the third mile-stone.
When the most beautiful girl saw them from afar
she was completely overcome with fear since she did not know who
they were
and she said to the boy, quite cast down,
"If they are strangers, they will separate us."
805   "Do not be afraid, my sweet light," the young man replied,
"that is your father-in-law, it is for you that he has gone to this
trouble."
Again the sun-born girl replied to the youngster,
"I am embarrassed, my dear soul, because I am on my own.
If you had listened to my father and gone back with me,
810 I would now have my serving girls and my retinue,
so that your father could be aware whose child you have taken.
But all the same, since you thought this right, make your excuses."
    "Do not be grieved, my high-born girl, that you are unescorted,
for everyone knows who you are, even if you are alone,
815 and there is no blame attached to this."
When they came near, each greeted the other.
The young man with his beloved dismounted,
and the emir also dismounted and embraced them both.
"May God bless you," he said, "my child,
820 may he make your years long in peace and wealth,
and may he show you to be heirs of his kingdom."
    They sat the girl on the decorated saddle
and placed the precious crown upon her,
and each of the kinsmen who was there
825 offered her gifts truly of great value;
and adorning the boy as befitted him,
they sounded the trumpets and immediately made their way back.
The cornets shrilled, the drums rolled,
the organs played, everything made music,
830 the kitharas sent out their sound, as did every musical instrument.
Singing the company returned promptly to the house.
    The overwhelming joy that then arose
who can interpret or who has the power to describe?
For it seemed as though even the earth on which they walked
835 itself rejoiced with them as they all walked over it.

καὶ πᾶς ὅστις ἐτύγχανεν εἰς τὴν χαρὰν ἐκείνην
ἄλλος ἐξ ἄλλου γέγονεν ἀπὸ τῆς θυμηδίας·
τὰ βουνία ἐσκίρτιζον, ἐχόρευον αἱ πέτραι,   E1061
ἀνέβλυζον οἱ ποταμοί, ἠγάλλοντο τὰ δένδρα,
840 ὁ ἀὴρ ἐφαιδρύνετο ἐν τῇ χαρᾷ ἐκείνῃ.   E1062
   Ὡς δὲ τοῦ οἴκου ἔμελλον ἀπάρτι πλησιάσαι,
πλῆθος ἄπειρον γυναικῶν αὐτοῖς συναπαντῶσιν·
ἦν γὰρ καὶ ἡ στρατήγισσα πρὸς ἀπαντὴν τῶν νέων
καὶ σὺν αὐτῇ ἡ πάντερπνος μήτηρ ἡ τοῦ Ἀκρίτου,
845 οἰκέτιδές τε εὐπρεπεῖς λαμπρῶς ἠγλαϊσμέναι,
αἱ μὲν ἄνθη κατέχουσαι ῥόδα τε καὶ μυρσίνας, 37v
τὸν ἀέρα μυρίζουσαι ὀσμαῖς θυμιαμάτων·
ἕτεραι χειροκύμβαλα ἔκρουον μελῳδοῦσαι
μέλος λίαν ἡδύτατον, ἐπαινοῦσαι τὸν παῖδα
850 καὶ τὴν παρθένον μετ' αὐτοῦ καὶ γονεῖς ἀμφοτέρων·
ἔδαφος ἐπανέστρωτο μυρσίνας τε καὶ δάφνας,
ῥόδα, ναρκίσσους καὶ πολλὰ εὐωδέστατα ἄνθη.
   Ἡ πενθερὰ τὴν ἑαυτῆς κατησπάζετο νύμφην,
ἔργα αὐτῆς ἐξαίρετα φιλοτίμως παρέχει,
855 καὶ ἦν ἄπληστος ἡδονὴ καὶ μεγίστη τερπνότης.
   Εἰς δὲ τὸν οἶκον φθάσαντες, ὁ ἀμιρᾶς εὐθέως
γυναικαδελφοὺς τοὺς ἑαυτοῦ καὶ στρατὸν οὐκ ὀλίγον
συναριθμήσας ἔστειλε τρισχιλίους ἀγούρους
νὰ εἴπωσι τὸν στρατηγὸν ἵν' ἔλθῃ εἰς τοὺς γάμους·
860 «Κέλευσον, ὦ συμπενθερέ, τοῦ ἐλθεῖν εἰς τοὺς γάμους,
οὒς ὁ Θεὸς ἡτοίμασεν, ἡμῶν μὴ βουλομένων.»
   Ὡς δὲ καὶ τούτων ἤκουσεν μὴ ἀμελήσας ὅλως
ἅπαντα ἅπερ εἰς τιμὴν τῶν φιλτάτων <προσῆκον>,
μεθ' ἑαυτοῦ παραλαβὼν ἀνείκαστόν τε πλῆθος
865 τῇ ἑξῆς ἐπορεύετο μετὰ τῆς στρατηγίσσης·
οὐδὲν γὰρ εἶχον λέγειν τι ἢ ποσῶς ἀμφιβάλλειν,
οἵου γαμβροῦ τετύχηκαν γεγονότες ἐν γνώσει·
σὺν προθυμίᾳ τὸ λοιπὸν καὶ χαρμονῇ μεγίστῃ
τὴν ὁδὸν μᾶλλον ἤνυον ᾄδοντες τὰ τοῦ γάμου
870 καὶ οἱ τῆς κόρης ἀδελφοὶ μετὰ τῶν συμπαρόντων.

---

847 ὀσμαῖς Dangitsis. 1958/9. 228: ὀσμαὶ G
863 προσῆκον added by Legrand: προσῆκε Trapp
866 λέγειν τι Trapp: τί λέγειν G

and all who chanced to be present at that celebration
became quite beside themselves with delight.
The hills skipped, the rocks danced,
the rivers bubbled up, the trees were glad,
840 the air brightened at that celebration.
     As they were just about to approach the house,
a countless host of women came to meet them.
The general's lady was there to greet the young people,
and with her the most delightful mother of Akritis, the Frontiersman,
845 and good-looking serving-women of the household, brightly adorned:
some held flowers, roses and myrtle,
others perfumed the air with the scent of incense,
others struck hand-cymbals as they sang
a very sweet song, praising the boy
850 and the unwed girl with him and the parents of both.
The ground was strewn with myrtle and bay,
roses, narcissus and many of the sweetest smelling flowers.
Her mother-in-law embraced the bride,
she generously offered her outstanding pieces of craftsmanship,
855 and there was abundant pleasure and the greatest delight.
     When they reached the house, the emir immediately
collected up his wife's brothers and an army not small in size
and sent three thousand youngsters
to tell the general to come to the wedding:
860 "Be pleased, fellow father-in-law, to come to this wedding
which God has made, though we had not wished it."
     When the general heard this, not neglecting anything at all
that was appropriate to honour his dearest ones
and taking with him an incomparable host,
865 on the next day he set off with his lady,
for they could make no objection or have the slightest hesitation
once they had become aware what sort of son-in-law they had
     acquired.
And so, with eagerness and the greatest happiness
they pressed on along the road, singing wedding songs,
870 and the girl's brothers were in the company.

843–5 The women of the house, led by Digenis' grandmother ('the general's lady') and mother, have their role in greeting the couple. For all its warrior ethos, the poem, especially in the G version, does not ignore female social structures.
854 Presumably, as Mavrogordato points out, these would be women's handicrafts, to fit the occasion.

Ἄφιξιν δὲ τὴν ἑαυτῶν ὁ τοῦ παιδὸς ἀκούσας
πατὴρ πρὸς ὑπαντὴν καλὴν μετὰ λαοῦ ἐξῆλθε·
βουλόμενος δ' ὁ θαυμαστὸς κατελθεῖν ἐκ τοῦ ἵππου, 38r
ὁ στρατηγὸς ἐκώλυσεν ἑαυτὸν ἐξορκίσας·
875 ἀλλήλους τε, ὡς ἔπρεπεν, ἀσπασάμενοι μάλα
ἐπὶ τὸν οἶκον ἔσπευδον καὶ ὀλίγον προβάντων
πεζοπόροι ἡπήντησαν ἀναρίθμητον πλῆθος,
καὶ μετ' ἐκείνους ἕτεροι, σύστημα οἰκετίδων·
τοῦ οἴκου δὲ τὰ σύνορα καταλαβόντες ἤδη
880 μετὰ κόσμου τοῦ πρέποντος πλήθους θυμιαμάτων
ῥοδόσταμμα καὶ τῶν λοιπῶν παντοίων μυρισμάτων.
Ταῦτα ἡ μήτηρ τοῦ παιδὸς ἤγαγεν ἡ ὡραία·
τὰ δὲ ἐντεῦθεν ποῖος νοῦς φράσαι ὅλως ἰσχύσει –
τὴν θαυμαστὴν ὑποδοχὴν τοῦ ἀμιρᾶ ἐκείνην,
885 τὴν καλὴν συναναστροφὴν τῆς ἑαυτοῦ συζύγου,
εὐωχίαν τὴν εὔτακτον καὶ ἁρμόδιον τάξιν,
ἐδεσμάτων τὴν ἄπειρον πολυποίκιλον θέαν
τὴν ἐκ πάντων παράθεσιν ζῴων ἀναριθμήτων,
τῶν μίμων τὰς μεταβολάς, αὐλητῶν μελῳδίας,
890 χορευτρίων λυγίσματα, ποδῶν τὰς μεταβάσεις,
τῶν χορῶν τὸ ἐνήδονον καὶ ξένην μελῳδίαν;
Κάλλος γὰρ εἶχον ἅπαντα τέρψιν ἄλλο πρὸς ἄλλο.
Προικὸς δὲ τὰ συμβόλαια τῇ ἑξῆς πληρωθέντα,
τὰ ἐν αὐτοῖς ἀδύνατον κατ' ἔπος ἐξιέναι·
895 ἅπερ δὲ οὖν συνέθεντο ἀμφότεροι τοῖς τέκνοις
καλῶς τε καὶ τὰ κτήματα εὐαρίθμητα ὄντα
μὴ λέξαι ἐξ ὀνόματος ἀπρεπέστατον ἔστιν
τῶν τε ζῴων τὸν ἀριθμὸν καὶ τῶν λοιπῶν πραγμάτων.
Δέδωκε μὲν ὁ στρατηγὸς ἵππους δώδεκα μαύρους,
900 τερπνὰ φαρία δώδεκα εὐμορφότατα λίαν, 38v
δώδεκα μούλας ἐκλεκτὰς μετὰ σελλοχαλίνων   E1074
ἀργυρῶν τε καὶ χυμευτῶν, ἔργων ἀξιεπαίνων,
οἰκέτας νέους δώδεκα, στράτορας χρυσοζώνους,   E1076
δώδεκα παρδοκυνηγοὺς λίαν δοκιμωτάτους,   E1073

875 ἀσπασάμενοι Legrand: ἀσπασάμενος G
881 ῥοδόσταμμα Legrand: ῥοδοστάμματα G
895 οὖν Eideneier, 1971, 310: οὐ G

When the boy's father heard of their arrival,
he went out with his people to greet them well.
When the marvellous man wished to dismount from his horse,
the general stopped him with an oath.
875 Having embraced each other fittingly,
they hastened to the house and, going forward a little,
they were met by a host beyond number,
and with them others, a group of household women;
they reached the boundaries of the house, already
880 with an appropriate escort, and a host of incense-bearers
with rose-water and all other such perfumes.
These things the boy's beautiful mother brought out.
But what mind has the power to describe completely what followed –
the marvellous reception by the emir,
885 the pleasing hospitality from his wife,
the well-arranged feasting and harmonious propriety,
the abundant and highly varied display of meats,
the dishes prepared from every kind of beast, beyond number,
the mimes' tricks, the flute-players' tunes,
890 the dancers' gyrations, the feet's movements,
the joy of the dances and the wonderful singing?
For each display had more beauty and enchantment than the next.
The dowry contracts were completed on the next day,
but it is impossible to go through in detail what was in them.
895 Yet what both families agreed on for their children,
especially the numerous possessions,
it is most unseemly not to mention by name,
both the number of beasts and of the remaining goods.
The general gave twelve black horses,
900 twelve delightful and very handsome chargers,
twelve choice mules with their saddles and bridles
of silver and metal-work, praiseworthy craftsmanship,
twelve young menservants, gold-belted grooms,
twelve well-proven hunting leopards,

873 Epithets like θαυμαστός usually refer to the current hero of the poem, i.e. to the emir in G1–3 and Digenis later. This is an unusual later reference to the emir.
874 Note the frequent use of conventions on dismounting: presumably here the emir offers acknowledgement of his lower status, which the general rejects, accepting equality and annulling his previous refusal of Digenis as a son-in-law.
879 The house envisaged appears to consist of an estate with a surrounding wall: see Magdalino, 1984, 96–7 on the buildings likely to be included within an aristocratic establishment.

905 χιονίδας ἱέρακας δώδεκα Ἀβασγίτας,
φαλκωναρίους δώδεκα καὶ φάλκωνας ὡσαύτως,
εἰκόνας δύο χυμευτὰς ἁγίων Θεοδώρων   E1078
καὶ τένδαν χρυσοκέντητον, ὡραίαν, παμμεγέθη,
ζώων ἔχουσαν συγκοπάς, πολυμόρφους ἰδέας,
910 τὰ σχοινία μεταξωτά, ἀργυροῖ δὲ οἱ πάλοι,
κοντάρια κυπρίζοντα ἀραβίτικα δύο,
καὶ τοῦ Χοσρόου τὸ σπαθὶν τὸ διαφημισμένον.   E1080
      Καὶ ταῦτα μὲν ὁ στρατηγὸς χαρίσματα παρέσχε
γαμβρὸν αὐτοῦ τὸν Διγενῆ· ὁ δ᾽ ἀμιρᾶς ὡσαύτως
915 θεώρετρον πολύτιμον παρέδωκε τῇ κόρῃ,
ὁμοίως καὶ ἡ στρατήγισσα ἡ μάμμη τοῦ Ἀκρίτου,
οἱ πέντε γυναικάδελφοι καὶ συγγενεῖς οἱ ἄλλοι
μαργαριτάριν ἄπειρον, χρυσίον καὶ λιθάριν
καὶ βλαττία πολύτιμα ἄπειρα καὶ ὀξέα·
920 ἡ δέ γε τούτου πενθερὰ παρέδωκεν ὡσαύτως
πράσινον λευκοτρίβλαττον καὶ ζώνας πολυτίμους,
τέσσαρα χρυσογράμματα φακεώλια ἄσπρα,
καβάδην τε χρυσοϋφῆ ὄπισθεν γρύψους ἔχον·
ὁ πρῶτος γυναικαδελφὸς δέδωκε δέκα νέους
925 ἀσκευάστους καὶ εὐειδεῖς καὶ τῇ κόμῃ ὡραίους,
ἠμφιεσμένους περσικὴν στολὴν ἀπὸ βλαττίου 39r
καὶ χρυσομανιάκια εἰς τοὺς αὐτῶν τραχήλους·
θάτερος γυναικαδελφὸς σκουτάριν καὶ κοντάριν·
ἄλλοι δὲ τούτου συγγενεῖς ἔδωκαν ἄλλα πλεῖστα,
930 ὧν οὐκ ἐξὸν ἀπαριθμεῖν τὸ εἶδος τῶν πραγμάτων.
      Καὶ τρεῖς μῆνας ἐποίησε τελούμενος ὁ γάμος,   E1083
ἡ δὲ χαρὰ οὐκ ἔληγεν ἡ πάνδημος ἐκείνη.
      Μετὰ δὲ τὸ συντελεσθῆν τὸν τριμηναῖον γάμον   E1084
παραλαβὼν ὁ στρατηγὸς πάντας τοὺς συμπενθέρους
935 καὶ τὸν γαμβρὸν τὸν ἴδιον ἦλθεν εἰς τὴν οἰκίαν
καὶ γάμος ἄλλος γέγονεν φαιδρότερος τοῦ πρώτου.
      Ἠγάλλετο ὁ στρατηγὸς τοῦ παιδὸς ὡς ἑώρα

---

906 φαλκωναρίους Mavrogordato: φαλκωνάρια G
907 χυμευτὰς Legrand: χυτὰς G
923 καβάδην τε χρυσοϋφῆ Trapp: καββάδδην τε χρυσοφυῆ G ἔχον G: ἔχων
Eideneier, 1971, 310
927 χρυσομανιάκια corr.: χρυσομάνικα καλὰ G

905 twelve snowy hawks from Abasgia,
twelve falconers and the same number of falcons,
two enamelled icons of the saints Theodore,
and a beautiful tent, very large, embroidered with gold
and decorated with multiform shapes of animals,
910 – the ropes were of silk and the poles of silver – ,
two Arab spears of young wood,
and the famed sword of Chosroes.
      These gifts the general provided
for his son-in-law, Digenis. The emir likewise
915 handed over to the girl a precious morning gift,
as did the general's lady, the grandmother of Akritis the Frontiersman;
the five brothers of the emir's wife and the other kinsmen
gave countless pearls, gold and precious stones,
and countless valuable purple silks.
920 His mother-in-law handed over likewise
green material with a border of three white stripes, and precious belts,
four white turbans with gold letters,
a caftan interwoven with gold with griffins on the back.
His wife's eldest brother gave ten young men,
925 eunuchs, all good-looking and with beautiful hair,
dressed in Persian garments of silk
and with golden torques around their necks.
His wife's other brother gave a shield and a spear.
His remaining kinsmen gave very many other gifts,
930 whose kinds it is impossible to count.
      For three months the wedding continued to be celebrated
and that universal joy did not cease.
After the completion of the three-month-long wedding,
the general gathered up all his in-laws
935 and his son-in-law himself, and went to his house,
and another wedding was held, more brilliant than the first.
      The general was glad when he observed the boy's

909 There seems to be a reference here to appliqué work. For a discussion of figural decoration of tents, see Anderson-Jeffreys, 1994, referring particularly to Manganeios Prodromos, Poems 145–6.
912 The significance of this unexpected item is unknown; both G and E retain hints of Byzantium's wars with Persia.
915 Angold, 1989, 212–13, finds it surprising that there is no mention of the ὑπόβολον, the regular nuptial gift, but only of the θεώρητον, the gift made to reward the bride's virginity.
922 As at G3.260 perhaps this should be 'with gold gammata', symbols of the Trinity.

τὴν εὔτακτον κατάστασιν, τὴν νουνεχῆ ἀνδρείαν,
τῶν ἠθῶν τὴν πραότητα καὶ λοιπὴν εὐκοσμίαν·
940 ἡ στρατήγισσα ἔχαιρε καθορῶσα τὸ κάλλος
καὶ τὴν αὐτοῦ πανευπρεπῆ καὶ ξένην ἡλικίαν·
οἱ τούτου γυναικαδελφοὶ ἐπισκέπτοντες σφόδρα
οἱ ταῖς αὐτοῦ καυχώμενοι ἀεὶ ἀνδραγαθίαις.
Καὶ δόξα τῷ μόνῳ ἀγαθῷ ἐπιτελοῦντι ἔργον·
945 ἐν γὰρ ταῖς διοικήσεσι τῶν μεγίστων πραγμάτων
ὁ Θεὸς συνεισέρχεται, καὶ μηδεὶς ἀπιστείτω·
εὐλόγως τοίνυν πρὸς Θεὸν ἀναπέμψωμεν χάριν,
αὐτὸς γὰρ πάντων ὁ δοτὴρ τῶν ἀγαθῶν ὑπάρχει.
Ἐκεῖσε τοίνυν ἱκανὰς ποιήσαντες ἡμέρας,
950 ὁ ἀμιρᾶς ὑπέστρεψεν ἐν τῷ ἰδίῳ οἴκῳ
καὶ μετ' αὐτοῦ ὁ Διγενὴς καὶ ἡ τούτου φιλτάτη
μεγίστης προσελεύσεως γεναμένης καὶ αὖθις.
Εἴθ' οὕτως λίαν δόκιμος ἀποφανθεὶς ὁ νέος 39ν
γέγονε δὲ περίφημος ἐν ταῖς ἀνδραγαθίαις
955 ὥστε σχεδὸν εἰς ἅπαντα βεβαιωθεὶς τὸν κόσμον·
καὶ μόνος ᾑρετίσατο διάγειν εἰς τὰς ἄκρας,
τὴν κόρην φέρων σὺν αὐτῷ καὶ ἰδίους οἰκέτας.
Πόθον γὰρ εἶχεν ἄπειρον τοῦ μόνος συνδιάγειν
καὶ τοῦ μόνος περιπατεῖν δίχα τινὸς ἑταίρου.
960   Ἔνθα γὰρ ἐπορεύετο τένδαν εἶχεν ἰδίαν,
εἰς ἣν ἡ κόρη καὶ αὐτὸς συνεδίαγον μόνοι·
καὶ τένδαν ἄλλην εἴχασιν αἱ βάγιαι αἱ δύο,
ἑτέραν δὲ οἱ θαυμαστοὶ ἀγοῦροι τοῦ Ἀκρίτου
ἐκ διαστήματος πολλοῦ ἀπέχοντες ἀλλήλοις.
965 Πολλοὶ δὲ τῶν ἀπελατῶν τοῦτο ἀναμαθόντες,

---

942 ἐπισκέπτοντες G: ἐπισκώπτοντες Tsopanakis, 1960, 86
943 αὐτοῦ corr.: αὐτῶν G
959 ἑταίρου Kalonaros: ἑτέρου G

well-disciplined propriety, his prudent bravery,
the gentleness of his manners and the rest of his good demeanour.
940 The general's lady rejoiced as she saw his beauty
and his great good looks and his wondrous appearance,
as did his wife's brothers, watching him closely,
for ever boasting of his brave deeds.
Thanks be to Him, the one good being who brings things to their end;
945 for into the disposition of the greatest matters,
God enters; and let no one disbelieve this.
Therefore let us offer up eloquent gratitude to God,
for He is the giver of all good things.
And so, when they had spent several days there,
950 the emir returned to his own house,
and with him Digenis and his beloved,
a great procession taking place once again.
   Then the young man, who had shown himself to be really
   outstanding,
became famous because of his valiant deeds,
955 so that his status was established throughout almost the whole world.
And he chose to spend his time in solitude on the frontiers,
taking the girl with him and his own servants.
For he had a boundless desire to spend his time alone
and to walk alone with no companion.
960   In the area where he journeyed he had his own tent
in which he and the girl lived together in solitude.
The two serving-girls had another tent,
and Akritis the Frontiersman's marvellous youngsters yet another,
and they were at a considerable distance from each other.
965 Many of the guerrillas learnt of this

940 As at G2.11 and 21 physical beauty is a necessary element in an aristocratic
marriage (Laiou, 1992, 94–6).
953–70 A bridging passage which, like the emperor's visit of G4.1071 ff., is not found in
E.
958–9 Digenis' desire to be alone (albeit with wife, servants and 'youngsters') is a
leitmotif throughout the second half of G. One may speculate that this shows influence
from popular saints' lives, or marks the inappropriateness of the heroic figure of Digenis
to the social and administrative structures of the Middle Byzantine period.
965–7 This reads like a brief summary of G6; perhaps the whole passage is an attempt to
indicate and fill a gap in the story. Narrative in G is continuous from the hunt, in which
the immature hero first showed his mettle, to the end of the marriages at G4.953.
G4.953–5 on their own are hardly enough to explain the renown which brings the
emperor to visit him. On the guerrillas, of whom this is the first mention since G4.34, see
the Introduction, pp. xxxii–xxxiii.

συμβούλιον ἐποίησαν τὴν κόρην ἀφαρπάσαι·
καὶ πάντας συναπέκτεινε καθυποτάσσων τούτους,
ὅπως τε κατεπτόησε πᾶσαν τὴν Βαβυλῶνα,
Ταρσὸν ὁμοῦ καὶ τὸν Βαγδᾶ, τοὺς Μαυροχιονίτας
970 καὶ ἄλλα μέρη ἱκανὰ τῶν δεινῶν Αἰθιόπων.
Ταῦτα τὰ κατορθώματα ὁ βασιλεὺς ἀκούσας
ὁ τηνικαῦτα τὴν ἀρχὴν τοῖς Ῥωμαίοις διέπων,
Βασίλειος ὁ εὐτυχὴς καὶ μέγας τροπαιοῦχος,
ὁ καὶ συνθάψας μεθ' ἑαυτοῦ τὴν βασίλειον δόξαν
975 (ἔτυχε γὰρ κατὰ Περσῶν ποιῶν τὴν ἐκστρατείαν
ἐν ἐκείνοις τοῖς μέρεσιν ἐν οἷς ὁ παῖς διῆγεν),
καὶ μαθὼν τὰ περὶ αὐτοῦ ἐξεπλήττετο σφόδρα.
Ποθήσας οὖν κατὰ πολὺ θεάσασθαι τὸν νέον,
γραφὴν πρὸς αὐτὸν ἔστειλε περιέχουσαν τάδε: 40r
980 «Τὰ περὶ σοῦ, ὦ τέκνον μου, ἡ ἐμὴ βασιλεία
μαθοῦσα κατορθώματα ηὐφράνθημεν ἐν τούτοις
τῷ συνεργοῦντί σοι Θεῷ ἀναπέμποντες χάριν·
ἐν ἐφέσει γεγόναμεν αὐτοψεὶ τοῦ ἰδεῖν σε
καὶ παρασχεῖν σοι ἀμοιβὰς τῶν σῶν ἔργων ἀξίας·
985 ἐλθὲ τοίνυν ὡς πρὸς ἡμᾶς χαίρων ἀνενδοιάστως,
μὴ ὑποπτεύων λυπηρὸν παρ' ἡμῶν ὑποστῆναι.»
Ὁ δὲ ταύτην δεξάμενος ἀντιγραφὴν ἐκπέμπει:
«Ἐγὼ μὲν δοῦλος ἔσχατος τοῦ σοῦ κράτους τυγχάνω,
εἰ καὶ πάντων τῶν ἀγαθῶν ἀμέτοχος ὑπάρχω.
990 Ποῖον δέ, δέσποτα, ἐμὸν κατόρθωμα θαυμάζεις
τοῦ ταπεινοῦ καὶ εὐτελοῦς καὶ παντελῶς ἀτόλμου;
Ἀλλ' ὅμως πάντα δυνατὰ τῷ πρὸς Θεὸν θαρροῦντι·

971 Ταῦτα Legrand: ταῦτα τοινῦν G
975 κατὰ Legrand: μετὰ G   ἐκστρατείαν Legrand: εὐστρατείαν G
983 ἐφέσει Trapp: ἐφέσει δὲ G

and made a plan to abduct the girl.
And he killed them all and subdued them,
just as he terrified all Babylon,
together with Tarsos and Baghdad, the men of the Black Snow
970 and several other territories belonging to the terrible Ethiopians.
    When the emperor heard of these achievements,
the emperor who at that time exercised authority over the Romans,
Basil the fortunate and the great winner of victories,
who interred the imperial glory with himself,
975 (for he happened to be on campaign against the Persians
in the regions where the boy was living)
– when he learnt about him, he was absolutely astounded.
Desiring very much, therefore, to see the young man,
he sent him a letter, whose contents were as follows:
980   "Learning of your achievements, my child,
my Majesty took great pleasure in them,
offering up gratitude to God who is your helper.
We are desirous of seeing you with our own eyes
and providing you with fit recompense for your deeds.
985 Come then to us with unhesitating joy
and have no suspicion of any unpleasant experience at our hands."
    When he received this Digenis sent a reply:
"I am the most abject servant of your state,
even if I have no share in all its good things.
990 Which deed of mine, emperor, do you admire,
achieved by my humble and worthless and altogether timid self?
Nevertheless all things are possible for him who trusts in God.

968 On the basis of the redundant τε, Mavrogordato suggests a line has fallen out here
(cf. Z2296)
968–70 An apparently haphazard group of places, suggesting greater interest in filling
the narrative gap than in geography.
971–1086 On the identification of the emperor, see G4.56 and the Name Index. This
narrative of the visit of the emperor to Digenis is completely absent from E, and has been
widely used in attempts to date the different versions. Alexiou, 1979, 70 comments that
this episode could easily have been added to increase the hero's glory, and was unlikely to
fall out once included in the text. Note, however, that this passage includes a line
(G4.1058, cf. G4.116) also used by the twelfth-century Ptochoprodromos.
980–1000 This exchange of letters is couched in a caricature of official phraseology,
with the third person use of 'Majesty' and the first person plural imperial 'we' in the
emperor's letter, ending in a reassurance which implies a cynical attitude in relationships
between emperor and subjects (cf. Kekavmenos, *Strategikon* 12 and the exchange
between Digenis and his future father-in-law at G4.738). Digenis' reply makes totally
insincere use of the humility-topos, and shows why it is easier for the narrative to keep
the hero on his own and not to make him a soldier or imperial official.

καὶ ἐπειδήπερ βούλεσαι ἰδεῖν τὸν σὸν οἰκέτην,
μετ' ὀλίγων παραγενοῦ πρὸς ποταμὸν Εὐφράτην
995 κἀκεῖ με ὄψει, δέσποτα ἅγιε, ὅταν βούλει.
Καὶ μὴ νομίσῃς ἀπειθῶ πρὸς σὲ παραγενέσθαι,
ἀλλ' ὅτι κέκτησαι τινὰς ἀπείρους στρατιώτας,
καὶ εἰ μὲν ἴσως εἴπωσι τινὲς ὅπερ οὐ δέον,
ποιήσω σε εἰς τὸ βέβαιον ἄμοιρον τῶν τοιούτων·
1000 τοῖς γὰρ νέοις, ὦ δέσποτα, συμβαίνουσι τοιαῦτα.»
    Καὶ τὴν γραφὴν ὁ βασιλεὺς διεξιὼν κατ' ἔπος
ἐθαύμαζε τὴν τοῦ παιδὸς ταπείνωσιν τοῦ λόγου
καὶ ἔχαιρε κατανοῶν τὸ ὕψος τῆς ἀνδρείας.
Σφόδρα δὲ ὀρεγόμενος ἰδεῖν τὸν νεανίαν,
1005 παραλαβὼν μεθ' ἑαυτοῦ ἑκατὸν στρατιώτας 40ν
καὶ δορυφόρους ἱκανοὺς ἦλθεν εἰς τὸν Εὐφράτην
πᾶσιν ἐπαγγειλάμενος τοῦ φθέγξασθαι μηδ' ὅλως
λόγον τινὰ ἐπίμωμον ἔμπροσθεν τοῦ Ἀκρίτου.
    Οἱ δέ γε τούτου ἕνεκα φυλάττειν συνταχθέντες
1010 παρὰ μικρὸν ἀπήγγειλαν τὴν ἄφιξιν συντόμως
βασιλέως πρὸς Διγενῆ τὸν θαυμαστὸν Ἀκρίτην.
Καὶ πρὸς αὐτὸν ὁ Διγενὴς μονώτατος ἐξῆλθεν,
ὃς μέχρι γῆς τὴν ἑαυτοῦ κεφαλὴν ὑποκλίνας,
«Χαίροις,» ἔφη, «ὁ ἐκ Θεοῦ λαβὼν τὴν βασιλείαν
1015 καὶ δι' ἀσέβειαν ἐθνῶν ἅπασι κυριεύσας,
πόθεν μοι τοῦτο γέγονεν ὁ γῆς πάσης δεσπόζων
παραγενέσθαι πρὸς ἐμὲ τὸν ἐξουθενημένον;»
    Τοῦτον ἰδὼν ὁ βασιλεὺς καὶ ἐκπλαγεὶς τὴν θέαν,
παντὸς ἐπιλαθόμενος ὄγκου τῆς βασιλείας,
1020 μικρὸν τοῦ θρόνου προελθὼν κατησπάζετο χαίρων,
κατεφίλει περιχαρῶς ἡλικίαν θαυμάζων
καὶ τὴν πολλὴν κατάθεσιν τοῦ εὐμεγέθους κάλλους,
«Ἔχεις,» λέγων, «ὦ τέκνον μου, ἀπόδειξιν τῶν ἔργων,
τοῦ γὰρ κάλλους ἡ σύνθεσις ἀνδρείαν εἰκονίζει·
1025 εἴθε τοιούτους τέσσαρας εἶχεν ἡ Ῥωμανία.
Λέγε λοιπόν, ὦ τέκνον μου, πεπαρρησιασμένως
καὶ ὅπερ βούλει λάμβανε τῆς ἐμῆς βασιλείας.»

1002 λόγου Legrand: λ . . G
1020 προελθὼν Trapp: προσελθὼν G

Since you wish to see your servant,
come with a few followers to the river Euphrates,
995 and there you will see me, holy emperor, whenever you wish.
And do not think that I am disobedient in not coming to you,
but you have acquired some inexperienced soldiers
and if perhaps some of them make an inappropriate remark,
I will undoubtedly deprive you of such men;
1000 for, emperor, such things happen to young men."
The emperor went through the letter word by word,
admired the humility of the boy's language
and rejoiced as he perceived the extent of his bravery.
Being extremely eager to see the young man
1005 and taking with him a hundred soldiers
and a number of bodyguards, he came to the Euphrates,
ordering them all not to utter
even one blameworthy word before the Frontiersman.
Those who had been set to keep watch for this purpose
1010 shortly announced the imminent arrival
of the emperor before Digenis Akritis, the marvellous Frontiersman of
Double Descent.
And Digenis went out towards him, entirely alone,
and bowed his head to the ground.
"Welcome," he said, "you who have received imperial power from
God,
1015 and are lord over all because of the impiety of the heathen,
how has it come about that he who is master of the whole earth
is visiting me in my total insignificance?"
On seeing him the emperor was astonished at the sight
and, forgetting all the weight of empire,
1020 he came forward a little from the throne and embraced him joyfully;
he kissed him with great joy, admiring his appearance
and his great endowment of imposing beauty.
"You have," he said, "my child, proof of your deeds,
for your beautiful physique is a picture of bravery.
1025 Would that the Roman territories possessed four such men!
Speak now, my child, in all freedom
and receive whatever you wish from my Majesty."

«Τὰ πάντα ἔχε, δέσποτα,» ὁ παῖς ἀνταπεκρίθη,
«ἐμοὶ γὰρ ἔστιν ἱκανὴ μόνον ἡ σὴ ἀγάπη·
1030 οὐ δίκαιον δὲ τοῦ λαβεῖν ἀλλὰ διδόναι μᾶλλον,
ἔχεις καὶ γὰρ ἐν τῷ στρατῷ ἐξόδους ἀνεικάστους.
Ἀξιῶ καὶ ἀντιβολῶ τῆς σῆς δόξης τὸ κράτος 41r
ἀγαπᾶν τὸ ὑπήκοον, ἐλεεῖν πενομένους,
ἐξ ἀδικούντων ῥύεσθαι τοὺς καταπονουμένους,
1035 τοῖς παρὰ γνώμην πταίουσι συγχώρησιν παρέχειν,
μὴ προσέχειν διαβολαῖς, ἄδικον μὴ λαμβάνειν,
αἱρετικοὺς ἀποσοβῶν, ὀρθοδόξους κρατύνων.
Ταῦτα γάρ, δέσποτα, εἰσὶν ὅπλα δικαιοσύνης,
μεθ' ὧν δυνήσῃ τῶν ἐχθρῶν πάντων περιγενέσθαι·
1040 οὐ γὰρ ἔστι δυνάμεως κρατεῖν καὶ βασιλεύειν,
Θεοῦ μόνον τὸ δώρημα καὶ δεξιᾶς ὑψίστου.
Ἐγὼ δὲ ὁ πανευτελὴς τῷ σῷ κράτει δωροῦμαι
ὃ ἐδίδου κατὰ καιρὸν τέλος τῷ Ἰκονίῳ
ἄλλο τοσοῦτον σε λαβεῖν παρ' ἐκείνων ἀκόντων,
1045 καὶ ποιήσω σε, δέσποτα, ἀμέριμνον ἐκ τούτου,
ἄχρις ἂν ἡ ἐμὴ ψυχὴ ἐκ τοῦ σκήνους ἐξέλθῃ.»
Καὶ ἐχάρη ὁ βασιλεὺς ἐπὶ τούτοις τοῖς λόγοις,
καὶ φησίν: «Ὢ θαυμάσιε, κάλλιστε νεανία,
ἡ βασιλεία ἡ ἐμὴ πατρίκιόν σε ἔχει
1050 δωρουμένη σοι ἅπαντα κτήματα τοῦ σοῦ πάππου
καὶ ἐξουσίαν νέμω σοι τοῦ διοικεῖν τὰς ἄκρας·
ταῦτα δὲ εἰς χρυσόβουλον σῶα ἐπικυρώσω
καὶ ἐσθῆτας βασιλικὰς παρέχω πολυτίμους.»

1034 ἐξ ἀδικούντων ῥύεσθαι τοὺς Kalonaros. cf. Z2352: τοὺς ἀδικοῦντας ῥύεσθαι καὶ G
1035 πταίουσι Kalonaros, cf. Z2353: παίουσι G
1036 διαβολαῖς Legrand: διαβου°λαῖς G
1037 ἀποσοβῶν G: ἀποσοβεῖν Legrand κρατύνων G: κρατύνειν Legrand

"Keep everything, emperor," the boy replied.
"For me your love alone is sufficient.
1030 It is not right to receive but rather to give,
for you have unimaginable expenses for the army.
I ask and entreat your glorious Majesty
to love his subjects, to pity the needy,
to rescue the oppressed from wrong-doers,
1035 to give pardon to those who err unintentionally,
to pay no heed to slanders, not to accept what is unjust,
frightening off heretics and strengthening the orthodox.
These, emperor, are the weapons of justice
with which you will be able to get the better of your enemies;
1040 for to govern and rule as emperor is not the result of strength
but is a gift from God alone and the right hand of the Most High.
I, quite worthless as I am, grant to your Highness
that the tribute you once paid Ikonion
will, against their will, come to you in equivalent amounts;
1045 and I shall free you from this care, emperor,
until my soul departs its habitation."
    The emperor rejoiced at these words,
and said: "Marvellous and loveliest of youths,
my Majesty ranks you as a patrikios,
1050 bestowing on you all your grandfather's possessions
and I grant you authority to administer the frontiers.
I shall ratify this securely in a chrysobull,
and I shall provide you with precious imperial robes."

1028 This speech may be seen as a statement of the self-confidence of the magnates of
Asia Minor, expressing a feeling of both material and ethical superiority over
Constantinople and the emperor; compare the advice, in the tradition of a 'Mirror of
Princes', attached to Kekavmenos' tract (Wassiliewsky-Jernstedt, 1896, 93–4). At
another level, the speech shows the heroic dominance of the epic hero over even the most
powerful figure in the 'historical' world.
1043 Mention of tribute paid to Ikonion reflects a time after 1084 when Ikonion was a
Turkish capital, with particular signs of large subsidies in the first decade of this period.
This fact, once used to date the G 'version' (Kyriakidis, 1932, 651 and 1958, 6; Alexiou,
1979, 55), provides a *terminus post quem* only for G itself, already known on codicological
evidence to be later.
1050 Digenis' grandfather had been exiled before the emir's capture of Digenis' mother
(G1.63).
1053 The imperial favours are authentic: the high-ranking title of patrikios (conferred
on governors and generals in the eight to tenth centuries), a chrysobull (document with
imperial gold seal) for estates and appropriate robes.

Ταῦτα εἰπὼν ὁ βασιλεύς, εὐθὺς ὁ νέος προστάξας
1055 ἕνα τῶν ἵππων τῶν αὐτοῦ ἀγροικῶν, ἀδαμάστων,
κομίσαι ἔμπροσθεν αὐτῶν σιδήροις δεδεμένον,
ὃν λῦσαι ἔφη τοῖς παισὶν καὶ «Ἄφετέ τον τρέχειν.»
Καὶ τὰς ποδέας ὀχυρῶς πήξας εἰς τὸ ζωνάριν 41v
ἤρξατο τρέχειν ὄπισθεν τοῦ καταλαβεῖν τοῦτον·
1060 καὶ εἰς ὀλίγον διάστημα τῆς χαίτης τε κρατήσας
ὄπισθέν τον ἐγύρισε τὸν ἀγροικὸν καὶ μέγαν,
λακτίζων στρηνιάζων <τε>, φυγεῖν ὅλως εἰκάζων·
καὶ ἔμπροσθεν τοῦ βασιλέως ἐλθόντος τοῦ γεννάδα
κάτω τον ἐκατέρραξεν εἰς γῆν ἐφηπλωμένον
1065 καὶ πάντες ἐξεπλάγησαν τῇ παραδόξῳ θέᾳ.
Ὑποχωρεῖν βουλόμενος, λέων τις ἐκ τοῦ ἄλσους
ἐξελθὼν διεπτόησε τοὺς μετ' αὐτοῦ παρόντας
(πολλοὶ γὰρ λέοντες εἰσὶν ἐν ἐκείνῳ τῷ τόπῳ)
καὶ πρὸς φυγὴν δὲ καὶ αὐτὸς ὁ βασιλεὺς ἐτράπη.
1070 Ὁ δὲ παῖς πρὸς τὸν λέοντα ὑποδραμὼν εὐθέως,
ποδὸς αὐτοῦ δραξάμενος ἑνὸς τῶν ὀπισθίων,
ἀποτινάξας ἰσχυρῶς καὶ τῇ γῇ καταρράξας
νεκρὸν αὐτὸν ἀπέδειξε πάντων ὁμοῦ βλεπόντων.
Τοῦτον κρατῶν ἐν τῇ χειρί, καθάπερ τις τὸν πτῶκα,
1075 πρὸς βασιλέα ἤνεγκε «Δέξαι,» λέγων, «κυνῆγιν
τοῦ σοῦ οἰκέτου, δέσποτα, διὰ σοῦ θηρευθέντα.»
Καὶ πάντες ἐξεπλάγησαν ἔντρομοι γεγονότες,
τὴν ὑπεράνθρωπον αὐτοῦ ἰσχὺν κατανοοῦντες.
Καὶ τὰς χεῖρας ὁ βασιλεὺς πρὸς οὐρανὸν ἐκτείνας,
1080 «Δόξα σοι,» ἔφη, «δέσποτα, ποιητὰ τῶν ἁπάντων,
ὅτι με κατηξίωσας τοιοῦτον ἄνδρα βλέψαι
ἐν τῇ παρούσῃ γενεᾷ ἰσχυρὸν παρὰ πάντας.»
Καὶ τὴν δορὰν τοῦ λέοντος ἐπαρθῆναι κελεύσας
καὶ πλείστας πρὸς τὸν θαυμαστὸν ἐποίει ὑποσχέσεις· 42r
1085 ἀλλήλους ἀσπαζόμενοι, ὑπεχώρουν εὐθέως
πρὸς τὸν στρατὸν ὁ βασιλεύς, ὁ δὲ παῖς πρὸς τὴν κόρην.

1062 τε added by Legrand
1066 Ὑποχωρεῖν Legrand: ὑποχωρεῖν δὲ G
1084 πλείστας Legrand: πλείστα G

As the emperor said this, the young man immediately gave orders
1055   that one of his wild, unbroken horses,
should be brought before them, bound with iron.
He told his lads to set him loose, saying "Let him run."
And tucking his kilts firmly into his belt,
he began to run behind him so as to catch him.
1060   And within a short distance he grasped its mane
and brought the great wild beast back,
kicking and struggling, altogether looking like getting away.
And when the young noble came before the emperor,
he flung the horse down so that it sprawled over the ground
1065   and everyone was astonished at the extraordinary sight.
While he was wanting to withdraw, a lion came out of the grove
and terrified those who were present with him
(for there are many lions in that place),
and even the emperor himself turned in flight.
1070   But the boy immediately ran up to the lion
and seized one of its back legs;
he shook it vigorously, dashed it to the ground
and showed that it was dead as everyone watched.
Holding it in his hand as you would a hare,
1075   he took it to the emperor. "Accept," he said,
"your servant's prey, lord, hunted for you."
And all were amazed and terrified
as they became aware of his superhuman strength.
The emperor lifted his hands to heaven,
1080   "Thanks be to you," he said, "Lord, Maker of all things,
because you have found me worthy of seeing
in this present generation a man of this sort, whose strength surpasses
    all others."
And ordering the skin to be stripped from the lion,
he made very many promises to the marvellous youth.
1085   They embraced each other and immediately withdrew,
the emperor to the army and the boy to the girl.

1054–78 The hunting scene is a doublet of the earlier hunt of G4.102–212, suggesting
limitations to the material in circulation on Digenis. The catching of the unbroken horse
may derive ultimately from the story of Alexander the Great and Boukephalos.
1058 Cf. Ptochoprodromos 4.190–1 (and G4.116): evidence that a text like G existed in
the mid-twelfth century (Introduction, p. xlvii).
1072 A similar hunting exploit was attributed to Basil I before Michael III (Genesios
4.40); cf. G4.140–5.

Ἔκτοτε κῦρος ἔλαβε παρὰ πάντων ὁ λόγος
καὶ τὸν παῖδα ὠνόμαζον Βασίλειον Ἀκρίτην,
τοῦ χρυσοβούλλου εἵνεκα τοῦ ἄρχειν εἰς τὰς ἄκρας.
1090 Ἡμεῖς δὲ καταπαύσωμεν τὸν λόγον μέχρις ὧδε,
τῶν ἐφεξῆς ἐχόμενοι συντάξεως ἑτέρας·
κόρος γὰρ λόγου, ὡς φησὶν ὁ ἐμὸς θεολόγος,
ταῖς ἀκοαῖς πολέμιος διὰ παντὸς ὑπάρχει.

Thereafter the story gained credence from everyone,
and they called the boy Basil the Frontiersman,
because of the chrysobull that he should rule over the frontiers.
1090   But let us break our story off at this point,
reserving what comes next for another composition.
For excess of speech, as my Theologian says,
is ever an enemy to hearing.

1090 A rare self-conscious authorial intervention, implying a section-break. It is interesting that this comes just before the introduction of first-person narrative (found also in E) – indirect in G5 and direct in G6.
1092–3 The Theologian is Gregory of Nazianzus (*Oratio* 40; PG 36, 360b).

134

Λόγος πέμπτος

Νεότης πᾶσα ἀληθῶς ματαιότης ὑπάρχει, E1606
ὁπηνίκα πρὸς ἡδονὰς ἐκτείνει τὰς ἀτάκτους· E1606
ὁ δέ γε ταύτης ἀσφαλῶς τὰς ἡνίας ἰθύνων
ἀχείρωτος τοῖς πάθεσιν ἐσαεὶ διαμένει
5 καὶ κληρονόμος δείκνυται ζωῆς τῆς αἰωνίου
ἀντὶ προσκαίρου ἡδονῆς τῆς αἰσχρᾶς καὶ βεβήλου.
Ὃς γὰρ τρυφᾷ, ἀδύνατον τυχεῖν τῆς αἰωνίου·
ὡς γὰρ οὐκ ἔστιν ἐμπρησμὸν μετὰ ἐλαίου σβέσαι,
οὐδὲ τρυφῶν τις δυνατὸν φυγεῖν τὴν ἁμαρτίαν
10 δι' ἧς τὸ πῦρ ἐκτρέφεται πᾶσι τοῖς ἀκολάστοις.
   Καὶ γὰρ οὗτος ὁ θαυμαστὸς καὶ γενναῖος Ἀκρίτης,
ὁ τοῖς χαρίσμασι Θεοῦ πᾶσι πεπλουτισμένος,
πρὸς ὀλίγον τὴν ἑαυτοῦ νεότητα χαυνώσας
ἀμελῶς περιπέπτωκεν ἐγκλήματι μοιχείας·
15 ὕστερον δὲ μετάμελος γεγονὼς ὑπὲρ τούτου 42v
τοῖς ἐντυγχάνουσιν αὐτῷ ἀνήγγειλε τὸ σφάλμα,
οὐ καυχήσεως ἕνεκεν, ἀλλὰ μεταμελείας.
   Καὶ γὰρ μιᾷ τῶν ἡμερῶν ἐντυχὼν Καππαδόκι,
τὴν ἑαυτοῦ βουλόμενος ἁμαρτίαν φαυλῆσαι
20 πρὸς αὐτὸν διηγήσατο τάδε μετρίως λέγων:

19 φαυλῆσαι G: φαυλίσαι Trapp

Book five

All youthfulness truly is vanity
when it reaches out for unruly pleasures;
but he who controls its reins securely
remains forever unconquered by the passions,
5 and is proven to be the heir of life eternal
rather than fleeting pleasure that is shameful and impure.
Those who indulge themselves cannot win eternal life;
for just as it is impossible to quench fire with oil,
10 so those who lead indulgent lives cannot escape sin
by which fire is nurtured for all the licentious.
    And Akritis, this marvellous and noble Frontiersman,
who had been enriched by gifts from God,
for a while indulged his own youthfulness
and fell carelessly into the crime of adultery.
15 Afterwards he repented of this
and proclaimed his fault to those to whom he spoke,
not to boast but for the sake of repentance.
    For one day, speaking with a Cappadocian
and wishing to show the foulness of his sin,
20 he told him about it, speaking moderately thus:

G5 is not found in E, except perhaps for E1606-7; it is thus hard to be certain of the
episode's relation to *Digenis. The awkwardness with which this book fits into G as a
whole (e.g. first person narrative to an unnamed Cappadocian interlocutor, the
psychological crudity of Digenis' treatment of the rescued girl largely duplicated in the
scene with Maximou in G6, the abrupt temporal markings at G5.281 ff.) is a further
indication that the material available on Digenis was episodic (cf. Dyck, 1983), and also
limited in extent. Digenis' adultery and repentance contrasts with the chastity advocated
by the twelfth-century novelists (Beck, 1984, 112-28).
1-10 The two parts of this maxim (Odorico, 1989, 157) clearly show an attempt to
sanitise a morally reprehensible story. While it is tempting to see the ethical sentiments as
late additions, these thoughts, partially present in E, may be part of *Digenis.
18-20 The introduction of the first-person narrative is not convincing, as is confirmed
by the redactor of Z, who has improved the passage (Z2424-31). Again, a natural
assumption is that this is a late insertion in G, to conceal a blunt change in narrative. The
silent interlocutor is probably made a Cappadocian so that Digenis may speak frankly to
someone from his own area.

«Ὁπηνίκα ἐθελοντὶ τοῦ πατρὸς ἐχωρίσθην
καὶ ἐν ταῖς ἄκραις κατοικεῖν μόνος ἡρετισάμην,
ταξιδεῦσαι ἠθέλησα εἰς τὴν ἔνδον Συρίαν,
ἔτος πεντεκαιδέκατον ἄγων τῆς ἡλικίας·
25 ἀνύδρους τε καταλαβὼν κάμπους τῆς Ἀραβίας,
τὴν ὁδόν, ὥσπερ εἴωθα, μόνος μου διοδεύων,
φάραν ἐπικαθήμενος, βαστάζων καὶ κοντάριν,
ἔνδιψος ὅλος γέγονα (πολὺς γὰρ ἦν ὁ καύσων)
καὶ πανταχοῦ ἐσκόπευα ποῦ τὸ ὕδωρ ὑπάρχει.
30 Δένδρον ὁρῶ ἀπόμηκα πρὸς τὴν δασέαν βάλτον
καὶ τὴν φάραν ἐπιλαλῶ νομίσας ὕδωρ ἔχειν
καὶ οὐδαμῶς ἀπέτυχον· φοῖνιξ δὲ ἦν τὸ δένδρον
καὶ ἐκ τῆς ῥίζης θαυμαστὴ ἀνεπέμπετο βρύσις.
Ταύτῃ δ᾽ ὡς ἐπλησίαζον ὀλολυγμοὺς ἀκούω
35 καὶ κλαυσώδεις ὀλοφυρμοὺς μετὰ πλείστων δακρύων·
ἡ δὲ θρηνοῦσα κόρη ἦν πάνυ ὡραιοτάτη.
Κἀγὼ νομίσας φάντασμα τὸ ὁρώμενον εἶναι
ἔκδειλος ὅλος γέγονα, τριχῶν μου ὀξυνθέντων,
καὶ τὸ φρουροῦν με δὴ ἀεὶ διεχάραττον ὅπλον·
40 ἦν γὰρ ὁ τόπος ἔρημος, ἄβατος καὶ ἀλσώδης.
Ἐκείνη δὲ ὡς εἶδε με, ἀνέθορεν εὐθέως,
ἑαυτὴν περιστείλασα ἐν τῷ πρέποντι κόσμῳ   43r
τάς τε βροχὰς τῶν ὀφθαλμῶν ἄρασα τῇ ὀθόνῃ,
πρός με λέγειν ἀπήρξατο περιχαρῶς τοιάδε:
45 Πόθεν, καλὲ νεώτερε, καὶ ποῦ μόνος ὁδεύεις;
Μὴ διὰ πόθον καὶ αὐτὸς ἐπλανήθης ἐνταῦθα;
Ἀλλ᾽ ἐπειδή, ὡς ἔοικεν, ἐκ Θεοῦ ὡδηγήθης
τῆς ἐρημίας ὅπως με τὴν ἀθλίαν ἑλκύσῃς,
πρὸς μικρὸν ἀναπαύθητι, κύριέ μου, ἐνταῦθα,
50 ἵν᾽ ὅπως ἀκριβέστερον τὰ κατ᾽ ἐμοῦ ἀκούσῃς
καί τινα <γε> τῶν ὀδυνῶν παρηγορίαν λάβω·
λόγοις γὰρ συνεπαίρεται ἐκ τῆς ψυχῆς ἡ λύπη.᾽
Ταῦτα κἀγὼ ὡς ἤκουσα, εἰς χαρὰν μετεβλήθην

---

24 τῆς ἡλικίας Legrand: τὴν ἡλικίαν G
28 ἔνδιψος Legrand: ἔδιψος G
51 γε added by Legrand

"When I willingly separated from my father
and chose to live alone on the frontier,
I wished to journey to inner Syria,
being fifteen years of age.
25 Reaching the waterless plains of Arabia
and making my way along the road alone, as was my custom,
seated on my charger and carrying my spear,
I became incredibly thirsty (for the heat was intense)
and I looked all round for where water might be found.
30 I saw a tree some way off, by the dense swamp,
and I urged my charger on, expecting there to be water,
and I was not out of luck. It was a palm-tree,
and at its root rose a marvellous spring.
As I drew near to it, I heard laments
35 and loud sobs of distress accompanied by copious tears.
The wailing came from a girl who was very beautiful.
I thought that what I saw was an apparition
and I was absolutely terrified; my hair stood on end
and I drew out the weapon that always protects me,
40 for the place was deserted, pathless and marshy.
As soon as she saw me, she immediately jumped up
and covered herself in the proper manner,
and wiping the rain of tears from her eyes with a handkerchief,
she began to speak to me most joyfully, like this:
45 'Where are you from, fine young man, and where are you travelling
        on your own?
Surely you too are not lost here because of passion?
But since it looks as though you have been guided by God
to rescue me in my misery from the desert,
rest here for a while, my lord,
50 so that you can hear more exactly what has happened to me
and I can find some consolation for my sorrow.
For grief can be removed from the soul with words.'
    When I heard this, my mood changed to joy,

26 Digenis is now literally alone. There are problems over his identity as a lonely hero;
perhaps the servants and youngsters who share his solitude at G4.960–4 were added by
a redactor unable to accept a hero without a retinue, or maybe the retinue (and especially
his wife) is now temporarily absent because of the needs of this episode.
37 Finding a girl on her own in a deserted spot is unthinkable, so Digenis suspects a
supernatural trick.
42 Propriety of female dress is foregrounded in G, when flouted by this woman
(G5.121–2) and by Maximou (G6.736, 766).

ἀληθὲς τὸ φαινόμενον ἀκριβῶς ἐννοήσας·
55 μετὰ πολλῆς τῆς ἡδονῆς ἐπέζευον εὐθέως
(ἥψατο γάρ μου τῆς ψυχῆς τὸ ἀπόρρητον κάλλος
ὥστε δευτέραν τῆς ἐμῆς ταύτην εἶναι νομίσας)
καὶ τὴν μὲν φάραν ἔδησα εἰς τοῦ δένδρου τὸν κλῶνα,
τὸ δὲ κοντάριν ἔστησα μέσον αὐτοῦ τῆς ῥίζης·
60 καὶ ὕδατος μεταλαβὼν πρὸς αὐτὴν τάδε ἔφην:
'Λέγε μοι, κόρη, πρότερον πῶς ἐνταῦθα διάγεις
καὶ τίνος χάριν ᾤκησας ἐν τῇ ἐρήμῳ ταύτῃ.
Εἶθ' οὕτως γνώσῃ καὶ αὐτὴ ποῖος κἀγὼ ὑπάρχω.'
Εἶτα καθίσαντες ὁμοῦ ἐν θώκῳ χαμαιζήλῳ,
65 τάδε λέγειν ἀπήρξατο στενάξασα ἐκ βάθους:
''Ἐμὴ πατρίς, νεώτερε, τὸ Μεφερκὲ τυγχάνει·
τὸν Ἀπολορράβδην ἤκουσας, τὸν ἀμιρᾶν τῶν πάντων,
οὗτος πατὴρ ἐμὸς ἐστί, μήτηρ ἡ Μελανθία.
Ῥωμαιογενῆν ἠγάπησα ἐπὶ κακῷ ἰδίῳ, 43v
70 ὄντινα εἶχε δέσμιον τρεῖς χρόνους ὁ πατήρ μου
(καὶ γὰρ ἐνδόξου στρατηγοῦ υἱὸς ἔλεγεν εἶναι),
τῶν δεσμῶν ἠλευθέρωσα, φυλακῆς ἐρρυσάμην,
φαρία τον ἐχάρισα, πρωτεῖα τοῦ πατρός μου,
ἄρχοντα τοῦτον ἔδειξα περιφανῆ Συρίας
75 μετὰ βουλῆς καὶ τῆς μητρός, τοῦ πατρός μου ἀπόντος
(ἐν τοῖς πολέμοις γὰρ ἀεὶ εἴωθεν ἀσχολεῖσθαι).
Ἐφαίνετο δὲ εἰς ἐμὲ πολλὴν ἔχων ἀγάπην
καὶ θνήσκειν εἰ συμβέβηκε πρὸς ὥραν μὴ ἰδεῖν με·
ὑπῆρχε δὲ ἐπίπλαστος, ὡς ἔδειξε τὸ τέλος.
80 Καὶ γὰρ μιᾷ τῶν ἡμερῶν δρασμὸν ὑπονοήσας,
βουλόμενος τοῦ ἐξελθεῖν ἐπὶ τὴν Ῥωμανίαν
καὶ τὴν βουλὴν ἐξεῖπέ μοι, καὶ ὅνπερ εἶχε φόβον
διὰ πατέρα τὸν ἐμὸν μήποτε ἐπανήξῃ·
καὶ ἐμὲ κατηνάγκαζε σὺν αὐτῷ πορευθῆναι
85 ὅρκοις ἐπαγγειλάμενος λίαν φρικωδεστάτοις
μὴ ἀρνηθῆναί με ποτέ, ἀλλὰ σύμβιον ἔχειν·
οἷσπερ κἀγὼ πιστεύσασα συμφυγεῖν κατεθέμην.

---

57 νομίσας G, cf. G4.142, 955, Eideneier, 1070, 311: νομίσαι Legrand
67 τῶν πάντων Legrand: που πάντως G

for I clearly understood that what I saw was real.
55 I immediately dismounted with great pleasure
(for her ineffable beauty touched my soul
so that I thought her equal to mine)
and I tied my charger to the branch of the tree
and stood my spear between its roots;
60 I took some water and said this to her:
    'Tell me, girl, first, how you come to be living here
and why you settled in this desert.
And then you will find out yourself what sort of person I am.'
Then as we sat down together on a low seat,
65 she began to speak, sighing deeply:
    'My city, young man, is Meferke.
You have heard of Aploravdis, who is emir over all –
he is my father; my mother is Melanthia.
To my own misfortune I fell in love with a man of Roman birth,
70 whom my father held captive for three years
(for he said he was the son of a famous general).
I set him free from his chains, I saved him from prison,
I gave him horses, my father's best,
I set him up as a proud ruler in Syria,
75 with my mother's advice, for my father was away
(as he was always busy in the wars).
He seemed very much in love with me
and ready to die if he happened not to see me for a while;
but he was a deceiver, as what followed showed.
80 For one day, when he was thinking of flight
and wanting to escape into Roman territory,
he described his plan to me and also his fear
of my father, should he return.
And he insisted I set off with him,
85 declaring with the most terrifying and solemn oaths
that he would never disown me but keep me as his wife;
I believed this and agreed to run away with him.

56 An ambiguous phrase: Digenis could be comparing the girl to his wife or to his own soul.
68 Both the mother's name and the romantic story seem inspired by the ancient novels.
69 Another mixed race liaison, an unsuccessful and unheroic counterpart to that of Digenis' parents.
75–6 The absence of the girl's father again parallels the circumstances of Digenis' parents, perhaps stressing that no question of a spouse of different race will arise if the patriarchal family is intact.

Ἄδειαν εἶτα ἐφευρεῖν ἄμφω διεσκοποῦμεν
τὸν πλοῦτον ὅπως ἄρωμεν τῶν ἐμῶν γεννητόρων.
90 Καὶ δὴ κατά τινα πικρὰν καὶ δαιμονίαν τύχην,
νόσος ἐπῆλθε τῇ μητρὶ θανάτῳ γειτνιῶσα·
καὶ οἱ μὲν ἄλλοι ἅπαντες πρὸς θρήνους οἱ ἐν οἴκοις
ἔτρεχον ἀνοιμώζοντες ἔνθα θάνατος ἦγεν·
ἐγὼ δέ, ἡ παντάλαινα, ἀδείας ἐντυχοῦσα,
95 πλοῦτον πολὺν διάρασα τῷ πλάνῳ συνεξῆλθον,
ὑπουργησάσης τῆς νυκτὸς εὐχερῶς πρὸς τὸ ἔργον·   44r
ἀσέληνος γὰρ ἔτυχε καὶ ἀφώτιστος πάντῃ.
    Ἐφ' ἵπποις δὲ ἀμφότεροι τοῖς προητοιμασμένοις
ἐποχηθέντες τῆς ὁδοῦ ἠρχόμεθα σπουδαίως
100 καὶ φόβον μέγαν εἴχομεν ἄχρι τοῦ τριμιλίου·
ὡς δὲ παρήλθομεν αὐτὸ ὑπ' οὐδενὸς γνωσθέντες
τὰ λοιπὰ διηνύομεν ἀδεῶς μετὰ μόχθου
τροφῆς μεταλαμβάνοντες ὅτε καιρὸς ἐκάλει,
ὕπνου τε κορεννύμενοι καὶ τρυφῆς μετασχόντες.
105 Ἐρώτων δὲ μυστήρια ἐρυθριῶ τοῦ λέγειν
ἀγάπην τε τὴν πρὸς ἐμὲ παρ' αὐτοῦ δεικνυμένην·
ψυχὴν γάρ με ὠνόμαζε, φῶς ὀφθαλμῶν ἐκάλει
καὶ μετ' ὀλίγον γαμετὴν ἔλεγε καὶ φιλτάτην
ἀκορέστως καταφιλῶν, κρατῶν με ταῖς ἀγκάλαις.
110   Οὕτως ἐν πάσῃ τῇ ὁδῷ συγχαίροντες ἀλλήλοις
ἐν ταύτῃ κατελάβομεν τῇ ὁρωμένῃ βρύσει
καὶ τρεῖς ἀναπαυσάμενοι ἡμέρας τε καὶ νύκτας
ἐρωτικὰς μεταβολὰς τελοῦντες ἀκορέστως,
γνώμην αὐτοῦ τὴν ἔνδοθεν δολίως κεκρυμμένην
115 ἀνακαλύπτειν ἄρχεται ὁ δεινὸς παραβάτης.
Καὶ γὰρ ὁμοῦ καθεύδοντες ἐν τῇ νυκτὶ τῇ τρίτῃ,
λάθρα τῆς κοίτης ἀναστὰς ἐπέστρωσε τοὺς ἵππους,
τόν τε χρυσὸν ἀφείλετο καὶ τὰ κρείττονα σκεύη.
Ὡς δὲ τοῦτο ἐπέγνωκα τοῦ ὕπνου ἀναστᾶσα,
120 ἐμαυτὴν ὡς πρὸς τὴν ὁδὸν ηὐτρέπιζον εὐθέως
εἰς νεανίσκου τὴν στολὴν μεταβαλοῦσα εἶδος·
τοιούτῳ γὰρ τῷ σχήματι τῆς πατρίδος ἐξῆλθον.
Ἐφ' ἵππου τοίνυν ἐπιβὰς τοῦ ἰδίου ἐκεῖνος   44v
εἷλκε χερσὶ τὸν ἕτερον καὶ ᾤχετο τοῦ δρόμου.
125   Τοῦτο γοῦν τὸ παράλογον ἀνέλπιστον ὡς εἶδον,

104 τρυφῆς Eideneier, 1970, 311–12: τροφῆς G

Then we both kept a look-out for an opportunity
to make off with my parents' wealth.
90 And, by some bitter and devilish chance,
sickness bordering on death attacked my mother,
and while all the others in the house
rushed to lament, wailing at the death-bed,
I, in my utter wretchedness, found my opportunity,
95 seized much wealth and made off with the seducer;
night helped to make the deed easy,
for it was moonless and quite without light.
   We both set off on horses that had been prepared beforehand
and we began our journey hurriedly.
100 We were very frightened up until the third milestone;
but when we had passed that without being recognised by anyone,
we completed the rest of our journey without fear but with difficulty,
partaking of food when the moment called,
having our fill of sleep and sharing our delight.
105 I blush to speak of our rites of passion
and the love shown me by him.
For he named me his soul, he called me the light of his eyes,
and after a while he said I was his wife and his dearest,
kissing me insatiably, holding me in his arms.
110   While we were thus taking pleasure in each other all along the road,
we came to this spring that you see.
We rested there for three days and nights,
indulging in insatiable and passionate lovemaking,
and then the purpose that had been deceitfully hidden within
115 began to be revealed by that dreadful renegade.
For while we were sleeping together on the third night,
he secretly got out of bed, saddled the horses
and took the gold and most of our baggage.
As soon as I woke up and realized what had happened,
120 I immediately got myself ready for the road,
changing my appearance by dressing as a young lad,
for it was in that disguise that I had left my country.
But when that man had mounted his own horse,
he had led the other with his hand and gone off along the road.
125   When I saw this unexpected disaster,

121–2 It was against canon law and Scripture for a woman to wear men's clothing; cf. Galatariotou, 1987, 59, note 128.

πεζῇ ὡς εἶχον ἔτρεχον κατόπισθε βοῶσα:
«Ἀπέρχεσαι, ὦ φίλτατε, ἐμὲ λιπὼν ποῦ μόνην;
Ἐπελάθου τῶν ἀγαθῶν ὧν σοι ἐνεδειξάμην;
Οὐ μνημονεύεις ἐξ ἀρχῆς τοὺς ἐξαιρέτους ὅρκους;»
130 Ὡς δὲ οὐχ ὑπεστρέφετο, ἔτι μᾶλλον ἐφώνουν:
«Ἐλέησον, οἰκτείρησον, σῶσον με τὴν ἀθλίαν,
μὴ ἐνταῦθα ἐάσῃς με ὑπὸ θηρῶν βρωθῆναι.»
Καὶ ἄλλα πλείονα αὐτῷ ἔλεγον θρηνῳδοῦσα,
ὁ δὲ γέγονεν ἀφανὴς μὴ φθεγξάμενος ὅλως·
135 ἐμοῦ δὲ ἤδη τῶν ποδῶν ἀπάρτι ἀποκαμόντων
τοῖς τῶν πετρῶν προσκρούσμασι πάντοθεν αἱμαχθέντων,
ἐκεῖσε που κατέπεσον νεκρὰ ἐφηπλωμένη·
καὶ μεθ᾽ ἡμέρας ἑαυτὴν μόλις ἀναλαβοῦσα,
ἐν τῇ πηγῇ ὑπέστρεψα ἀνάγκῃ βαδιοῦσα.
140   Καὶ εἰμὶ πάντων ἔρημος μὴ ἔχουσα ἐλπίδας·
οὐ γὰρ τολμῶ εἰς τοὺς γονεῖς τοὺς ἐμοὺς ὑποστρέψαι,
αἰσχύνομαι τοὺς γείτονας, τὰς συνομήλικάς μου·
ποῦ εὑρεῖν τὸν πλανήσαντα παντελῶς οὐ γινώσκω
καὶ δέομαί σου μάχαιραν τοῦ δοῦναί μοι εἰς χεῖρας
145 καὶ κατασφάξω ἐμαυτὴν ὡς πράξασαν ἀφρόνως·
οὐ γὰρ συμφέρει μοι τοῦ ζῆν πάντων ἀποτυχούσῃ.
Ὢ τῶν ἐμῶν ἀτυχιῶν, ὦ συμφορῶν μεγίστων,
ἠλλοτριώθην συγγενῶν, γονέων ἐχωρίσθην
πρὸς τὸ κερδῆσαι φίλτατον καὶ αὐτοῦ ὑστερήθην.᾽
150   Ὡς δὲ ταῦτα ἐφθέγγετο ἡ κόρη θρηνῳδοῦσα, 45r
τοὺς βοστρύχους συντέμνουσα, τύπτουσα καὶ τὴν ὄψιν,
ἐγὼ ταύτην, ὡς δυνατόν, ἀνέστειλα τοῦ θρήνου,
τὰς χεῖρας τε τῶν πλοκάμων ἀπέσπασα ἐν μέτρῳ
ἔχειν παραμυθούμενος ἐλπίδας χρηστοτέρας
155 καὶ ἐπηρώτησα μαθεῖν, ᾽Πόσαι εἰσὶν ἡμέραι
ἀφ᾽ ἧς ὁ πλάνος μόνην σε κατέλιπεν ἐνταῦθα;᾽
Ἡ δὲ αὖθις στενάξασα, ᾽Δέκα ἡμέρας,᾽ ἔφη,
᾽μέχρι τοῦ νῦν ἐπλήρωσα ἐν ταύτῃ τῇ ἐρήμῳ,
μὴ ἰδοῦσα ἐκτός σου ἕτερον ἀνθρώπου χαρακτῆρα
160 καί τινος ἄλλου γηραιοῦ κατὰ τὴν χθὲς ἡμέραν
ὃς ἔλεγε καὶ τὸν υἱὸν αὐτοῦ παρὰ Ἀράβων
ἀφαιρεθῆναι πρὸ μικροῦ καὶ αἰχμάλωτον εἶναι

146 ἀποτυχούσῃ Trapp: ἀποτυχοῦσα G
159 ἕτερον Legrand: ἄλλον G
161 αὐτοῦ Legrand: αὐτοῦ ποτὲ G

I ran behind, on foot as I was, shouting,
"Are you going off, my dearest? Where are you leaving me on my
   own?
Have you forgotten the kindnesses which I showed you?
Do you not remember your exceptional oaths at the beginning?"
130 When he did not turn around, I cried out all the more,
"Have mercy, take pity, save me in my misery,
do not leave me here to be eaten by wild beasts."
And I made further pleas like this to him as I lamented,
but he just vanished without saying a word.
135 With my feet now already worn out
and bloody all over from pounding on the rocks,
I fell down somewhere over there, collapsed in a dead faint.
Coming to with difficulty as day broke,
I returned to the spring, walking painfully.
140   And I am bereft of everything, without hope;
for I dare not return to my parents,
I am ashamed in front of my neighbours and my girl friends.
I have no idea at all where I can find the deceiver,
and I beg you to put a dagger into my hands –
145 and I will kill myself because I have acted so stupidly.
There is no point in my living, now that I have lost everything.
Alas for my misfortunes, alas for my great disasters,
I estranged myself from my kinsmen, I parted from my parents
to win my beloved, and I have been deprived of him.'
150   As the girl was saying this in her lamentations,
tearing at her curls, striking her face,
I, so far as I could, stopped her lament
and pulled her hands gently from her braids,
encouraging her to hope for something better,
155 and I enquired and asked, 'How many days
is it since the deceiver left you alone here?'
She sighed again, 'Ten days,' she said,
'up till now I have spent in this desert,
not seeing another person's face apart from yours,
160 and one other's, an old man's, yesterday morning,
who said his son had just been abducted
by Arabs and was a prisoner.

καὶ σπεύδειν εἰς ἀνάρρυσιν αὐτοῦ εἰς Ἀραβίαν.
Οὗτος μοι διηγήσατο, τὰ κατ᾽ ἐμὲ ἀκούσας,
165 ὅτι πρὸ πέντε ἡμερῶν εἰς τὸ Βλαττολιβάδιν
παιδὶν ξανθόν, ἀρτιγενές, μακρὸν τῇ ἡλικίᾳ,
εἰς φάραν ἐποχούμενον καὶ συρτὸν ἄλλον φέρον,
ὁ Μουσοὺρ ἐστασίασε καὶ σπαθέαν τον ἐδῶκε·
καὶ εἰ μὴ ὁ νεώτερος ὁ Ἀκρίτης εὑρέθη,
170 ἐφόνευε τὸν ἄγουρον ἐν τῇ ὥρᾳ ἐκείνῃ·
λέγω δὲ τοῦτον ἐκ παντὸς τὸν παραβάτην εἶναι,
ταῦτα γὰρ τὰ γνωρίσματα ἐκεῖνον βεβαιοῦσι.
Οἴμοι, οἴμοι, παντάλαινα καὶ παναθλία τύχη,
ἡ ἀδοκήτως ἀγαθοῦ τοιούτου στερηθεῖσα,
175 ἡ τὸ γλυκὺ πρὸ τοῦ πιεῖν ἀπολέσασα κάλλος,
καὶ ὡς δένδρον νεόφυτον πρὸ καιροῦ ξηρανθεῖσα.᾽ 45v
Ταῦτα ἡ κόρη λέγουσα, δακρύουσα ἀσχέτως,
καὶ Ἄραβοι ἐξῆεσαν ἄφνω ἀπὸ τῆς ἕλης
ὑπέρτεροι τῶν ἑκατόν, πάντες δὲ κονταρᾶτοι,
180 οὕτως δέ μοι ὑπέπεσαν ὡς γῦπες εἰς τὸ βρῶμα·
καὶ ὁ φάρας πολλὰ φθαρεὶς ἀπέσπασε τὸν κλῶνον,
ἐγὼ δὲ τοῦτον κατασχὼν ἐχόμενον τοῦ δρόμου
μετὰ σπουδῆς ἐπέβαινον κατέχων τὸ κοντάριν
καὶ πρὸς αὐτοὺς ἐπιδραμὼν πολλοὺς τούτων ἀνεῖλον.
185 Τινὲς δέ με γνωρίσαντες ἔλεγον πρὸς ἀλλήλους:
'Αὕτη ἡ τόλμη ἀληθῶς καὶ ἡ πολλὴ ἀνδρεία
τὸν Ἀκρίτην ἐμφαίνουσιν· ἀπωλόμεθα πάντες.'
Οἱ δὲ τοῦτο ἀκούσαντες ἔφυγον εἰς τὴν ἕλην,
τὰ κοντάρια ῥίψαντες ἔνιοι καὶ ἀσπίδας
190 μήτε μίαν προσμείναντες κἂν στιγμὴν τὸ παράπαν.
Ὡς δὲ καὶ μόνον ἑαυτὸν εἶδον περιλειφθέντα,
πρὸς τὴν πηγὴν ὑπέστρεφον ἔνθα ἦτον ἡ κόρη·
ἐκείνη δὲ εἰς εὐχερὲς δένδρον ἐπανελθοῦσα
ἑώρα τὰ λεγόμενα καὶ γεγονότα πάντα·
195 ἰδοῦσα δέ με πρὸς αὐτὴν ἀπερχόμενον μόνον

---

170 ἄγουρον Legrand: ἐκ παντὸς G
176 G writes νεώτατον with νεόφυτον above
184 τούτων Legrand: τούτους G
194 λεγόμενα G: γενόμενα Legrand

and he was hurrying to Arabia to rescue him.
He told me, when he heard my story,
165 that five days previously, at Vlattolivadin,
a fair-haired boy, with a new beard, tall in height,
riding one charger and leading another,
had a disagreement with Mousour who had struck him with his sword;
and if Akritis, the young Frontiersman, had not been there,
170 Mousour would have killed the youngster at that moment.
I say that this is unquestionably the renegade,
for the points of his description prove it was he.
Alas, alas, most wretched and most miserable fate,
to be deprived unexpectedly of such a benefit,
175 to have lost sweet beauty before drinking it,
and to have withered before time like a newly planted tree.'
        As the girl was saying this and weeping copiously,
Arabs suddenly burst out of the marsh,
more than a hundred, all armed with spears.
180 They fell on me like vultures on a carcase,
and my charger in great panic broke the branch away,
but I caught him as he started down the road
and mounted hastily, grasping my spear;
I made an onslaught on them and killed many of them.
185 Some recognised me and said to each other,
'This boldness and great bravery truly
reveal that this is the Frontiersman; we are all done for.'
Those who heard this fled back to the marsh,
throwing down their spears and some even their shields,
190 not waiting even a second longer.
        When I saw that I was left on my own,
I returned to the spring where the girl was.
She had climbed a nearby tree
and watched all that was said and done.
195 Seeing me returning to her on my own,

166–8 The seducer's whereabouts are discovered through a coincidence – a useful motif, poorly handled. The reader has been told nothing of Mousour. Digenis, the narrator here, conceals his own previous killing of Mousour and rescue of the seducer (revealed at G5.214), with considerable loss of clarity in the narrative. Why does he not reassure her at G5.169–70? At Z2431–57 and 2465–76, at the equivalent of G5.20 and 27, the Mousour story is filled out; the vocabulary is very close to that in the girl's narrative at G5.66 ff., suggesting that the text in the G tradition used by the redactor of Z was not more complete here than the extant G version and the redactor was working with what he could extrapolate.

ἐκ τοῦ δένδρου κατήρχετο καὶ σπουδαίως ὑπήντα,
παρεκάλει τε λέγουσα μετὰ δακρύων τάδε·
'Κύριέ μου καὶ τῆς ἐμῆς πρόξενε σωτηρίας,
εἰ ὁ Ἀκρίτης ἀληθῶς σὺ ὑπάρχεις ἐκεῖνος
200 ὁ τὸν ἐμὸν ῥυσάμενος φίλτατον ἐκ θανάτου,
οὗ τὸ ὄνομα ἔφριξαν καὶ νῦν οἱ Ἀραβῖται,
ἀπάγγειλόν μοι, δέομαι, μὴ ἀποκρύψῃς ὅλως, 46r
καὶ τὴν σπαθέαν τοῦ Μουσούρ, εἰ μετεῖχε θανάτου.'
        Ἐμὲ δὲ εἶχεν ἔκπληξις καὶ θαυμάζειν ἐποίει
205 τῆς κόρης βλέπων τὴν πολλὴν ἀγάπην πρὸς τὸν παῖδα
τὸν ταύτῃ προξενήσαντα συμφορὰς ἀνεικάστους,
τῶν γεννητόρων χωρισμόν, ἀφαίρεσιν τοῦ πλούτου
καὶ φρικώδη κατάλειψιν ἐν ἐρήμῳ ἀβάτῳ
μὴ προσδοκῶσα ἄλλο τι ἢ τὸ θανεῖν ἀδίκως.
210 Καὶ τότε πρῶτον ἔμαθον ἀγάπην γυναικείαν
θερμοτέραν κατὰ πολὺ ὑπάρχειν τῶν ἀρρένων·
φθείρει δὲ μᾶλλον ἄθεσμος καὶ παράνομος μίξις.
        Ἐγὼ δὲ ἔφην πρὸς αὐτήν· 'Παῦσαι, κόρη, τοῦ κλαίειν
καὶ τοῦ θρηνεῖν ὑπὲρ αὐτοῦ τοῦ δι' ἐμοῦ σωθέντος·
215 ἐγὼ εἰμὶ ὁ τὸν Μουσοὺρ δικαίως θανατώσας
τὸν ὁδοστάτην καὶ λῃστήν, τὸν τὰς ὁδοὺς κρατοῦντα,
ὡς μηδένα κατατολμᾶν διελθεῖν τοῖς ἐκεῖσε·
ἐγὼ εἰμὶ <ὁ> ἐξ αὐτοῦ ἑλκύσας καὶ θανάτου
ὃν οὐκ οἶδα πῶς ἀγαπᾷς καὶ ἐπὶ μνήμην φέρεις
220 φίλτατον τὸν ἀβέβαιον ὀνομάζουσα παῖδα.
Ἀλλὰ δεῦρο καὶ πρὸς αὐτὸν ἐγώ σε ἀπαγάγω,
παρασκευάσω τε αὐτὸν τοῦ γαμετήν σε ἔχειν,
εἰ καὶ τὸ σέβας ἀρνηθῇς τῶν αἰσχρῶν Αἰθιόπων.'
        Ἡ δὲ τοῦτο ἀκούσασα, χαρᾶς ἐμφορηθεῖσα,
225 'Κύριέ μου,' ἀντέφησε, 'μέγιστε ἀντιλῆπτορ,
καὶ τοῦ θείου βαπτίσματος γέγονα ἐν μεθέξει
πρὶν συναφθῆναι τῷ ἀνδρὶ παρ' αὐτοῦ κελευσθεῖσα·
οὐδὲν γὰρ εἶχον δυνατὸν τῷ πόθῳ δουλωθεῖσα 46v

218 ὁ added by Legrand
223 ἀρνηθῇς Legrand: ἀρνήσῃ G

she came down from the tree and rushed to meet me,
and said to me pleadingly, with tears:
'My lord, you who are responsible for my safety,
if you are truly the famous Frontiersman
200 who saved my dearest from death
and whose name just now made the Arabs tremble,
tell me, I beg you, do not conceal anything –
the thrust of Mousour's sword, did it bring death?'
      Astonishment seized me and made me wonder
205 as I saw the girl's great love for the boy
who was responsible for her unimaginable disasters –
separation from her parents, deprivation of her wealth,
and horrifying desertion in a trackless desert
where she could expect nothing except an unjust death.
210 And then for the first time I discovered that a woman's love
is much more intense than that of men,
and wrongful and illegal intercourse corrupts it more.
      I said to her: 'Stop crying, girl,
and weeping over him, for he was saved by me.
215 It was I who justly put to death Mousour,
the highwayman and brigand who controlled the roads
so that no one dared to travel to these parts.
It was I who rescued from Mousour and death
the one whom you love – I can't think why – and whose memory
      you cherish,
220 calling the fickle boy your dearest.
But come, I will bring you to him,
and I will arrange for him to take you as his wife,
if you renounce the faith of the shameful Ethiopians.'
      When she heard this she was carried away with joy.
225 'My lord,' she replied, 'greatest protector,
I had received holy baptism
before my union with the man, on his instructions;
for, enslaved as I was by desire, I could do nothing other

207 Once again the loss of parents is considered a major disaster; cf. G4.9.
210–12 The moralising is startlingly insulated from any thought of the rape which
Digenis is about to commit. The masculine code cannot conceive of loyalty towards a
person who has behaved as badly as the man in this case: in looking for reasons for her
continuing love, Digenis is unable to think beyond her womanly weakness in
surrendering to illicit sexual urges. On how the patriarchal code has been breached,
see Galatariotou, 1987, 57–8 and Laiou, 1993, 213–14.
223 This contempt for Islam belies earlier positive references in the emir's story.

148   Διγενὴς Ἀκρίτης

τὰ παρ' αὐτοῦ λεγόμενα μὴ ἀγαγεῖν εἰς ἔργον,
230 δι' ὃν γονεῖς καὶ ἀγχιστὰς εἰς οὐδὲν ἐλογίσθην.'
    Ταῦτα, φίλε, ὡς ἤκουσα ἐκ στόματος τῆς κόρης,
καθάπερ φλὸξ εἰς τὴν ἐμὴν καρδίαν ἐπεισῆλθεν
καὶ προσέφερεν ἔρωτα καὶ παράνομον μίξιν·
καὶ πρῶτα μὲν ἀνέστελλον τὴν ἀκάθεκτον γνώμην
235 καὶ ἤθελον, εἰ δυνατόν, φυγεῖν τὴν ἁμαρτίαν·
ἀλλὰ πάντως ἀδύνατον πῦρ παραμεῖναι χόρτῳ.
    Ὡς γὰρ ταύτην ἀνήγαγον ἐν τῷ ἰδίῳ ἵππῳ
καὶ τῆς ὁδοῦ ἡπτόμεθα ὡς πρὸς τὴν Χαλκουργίαν
(τόπος γὰρ οὗτος πέφυκε πλησίον τῆς Συρίας),
240 οὐκ εἶχον ὅ,τι γένωμαι, πῦρ ὅλος ἐγενόμην
τοῦ ἔρωτος ὁλοσχερῶς ἐν ἐμοὶ αὐξηθέντος·
καταβαλόντες τὸ λοιπὸν χρείαν τάχα ποιῆσαι,
ἐν τῷ κάλλει τοὺς ὀφθαλμούς, ἐν τῇ ἁφῇ τὰς χεῖρας,
τὸ στόμα τοῖς φιλήμασι καὶ ἀκοὴν τοῖς λόγοις,
245 ἠρξάμην ἅπαντα ποιεῖν πράξεως παρανόμου·
καὶ γεγόνασιν ἅπαντα ὅσα ἤθελον ἔργα,
καὶ ἐμιάνθη ἡ ὁδὸς ἀπὸ τῆς ἀνομίας
συνεργείᾳ σατανικῇ καὶ ψυχῆς ἀμελείᾳ,
εἰ καὶ πολλὰ ἀνθίστατο ἡ κόρη πρὸς τὸ ἔργον,
250 εἰς Θεὸν καθορκίζουσα καὶ εἰς ψυχὰς γονέων.
    Ἀλλὰ ὁ ἀντικείμενος, τοῦ σκότους ὁ προστάτης,
ὁ ἐχθρὸς καὶ πολέμιος τοῦ ἡμετέρου γένους,
καὶ αὐτοῦ παρεσκεύασε Θεοῦ ἐπιλαθέσθαι
καὶ τῆς ἀνταποδόσεως τῆς φοβερᾶς ἡμέρας, 47r
255 ἐν ᾗ πάντα τὰ κρύφια πταίσματα φανεροῦνται
τῶν ἀγγέλων ἐνώπιον καὶ τῶν ἀνθρώπων πάντων.
    Εἶτα παραγενόμενος ἐπὶ τὴν Χαλκουργίαν,
ἐκεῖσε τὸν πλανήσαντα ταύτην εὕρομεν παῖδα.
    Ἦν δὲ ἄρα τοῦ στρατηγοῦ υἱὸς τοῦ Ἀντιόχου,

244 τὸ στόμα τοῖς φιλήμασι Legrand: τῷ στόματι φιλήματα G
259 τοῦ στρατηγοῦ υἱὸς Legrand: υἱὸς στρατηγοῦ G

than carry out what I was told by him,
230 the man for whom I reckoned my parents and relations as nothing.'
    When, my friend, I heard this from the girl's mouth
it was as if a flame entered my heart
and aroused passion and illegal intercourse.
At first I tried to subdue this ungovernable intention
235 and I wanted, if possible, to escape the sin,
but it is altogether impossible for fire to stay in grass.
For as I took her off on my horse
and we began the journey to Chalkourgia
(this was a place near Syria),
240 I could not control what came over me, I was all on fire,
with passion growing overwhelmingly within me.
Dismounting then to perform our natural functions
– my eyes in beauty, my hands in touch,
my mouth with kisses and my hearing with words –
245 I began to do everything that was unlawful.
And all that I wanted to do was done,
and our journey was besmirched by the lawlessness,
with the complicity of the devil and my soul's heedlessness,
even if the girl resisted the act vigorously,
250 calling to witness God and her parents' souls.
But the adversary, the prince of darkness,
the enemy and antagonist of our race,
led me to forget God himself
and the retribution of that dreadful day
255 on which all hidden faults will be revealed
before the angels and all mankind.
    Then, arriving at Chalkourgia,
we found there the boy who had seduced her.
He was indeed the son of the general Antiochos

---

231 Reference to Digenis' interlocutor reinforces the framework of the first-person narrative.
242–4 The earthiness of G5.242 has struck commentators as extreme bad taste (Trapp obelised the line). The next two have lyricism and balance (after Legrand's correction), spoiled by a lack of integration into the passage by sense or syntax. Probably the text has been distorted by a prurient reaction to its sexual content (cf. G5.247–56 below), though it is unclear when in the poem's textual history this happened.
256 The prior life of Aploravdis' daughter and her being alone on the open highway meant Digenis' actions were almost inevitable, though legally there was no question of rape since this was applicable only to virgins (Laiou, 1993, 213–15).

260 τοῦ πρὸ χρόνων ἐν τῷ Ζυγῷ ὑπὸ Περσῶν σφαγέντος.
    Ὡς γὰρ αὐτὸν ἀπὸ χειρῶν τοῦ Μουσοὺρ ἐρρυσάμην,
    ἔμπροσθέν μου οὐκ εἴασα τοῦ πορευθῆναι τοῦτον,
    γνωστὸν δὲ πᾶσιν ἔφηνα καὶ παράνομον μάλα
    καὶ τοῦτον παραδέδωκα πρὸς τοὺς ἐκεῖ μου φίλους,
265 ὡς ἂν διάγῃ μετ' αὐτῆς ἄχρις οὗ ὑποστρέψω –
    Ἐἰ δ' οὖν καὶ ταύτην ἐκβαλεῖν τὴν κόρην βουληθείης,
    μὰ τὸν σωτῆρα μου Χριστόν, πλεῖον ζωὴν οὐχ ἕξεις.'
    Φήσας αὐτῷ μὴ ἀδικεῖν τὴν κόρην μήτε βλάπτειν,
    τοῦτον ἐκεῖ καταλιπὼν πλεῖστά τε νουθετήσας,
270 δεύτερον ἐντειλάμενος μὴ ταύτην ἀθετῆσαι
    ἀλλ' ἔχειν, ὡς ὑπέσχετο, γαμετὴν διὰ νόμου,
    διηγησάμην ἅπασι πῶς τε εὗρον τὴν κόρην
    καὶ πῶς ταύτην ἀφήρπασα ἀπὸ τῶν Ἀραβίτων·
    τὰ δὲ μὴ δέον ἐξειπεῖν παρέτρεχον τῷ λόγῳ,
275 ἵνα μὴ σκάνδαλον ὁ παῖς εἰς διάνοιαν λάβῃ.
    Εἶτα τὸν πλοῦτον ἅπαντα παραδοὺς ἀμφοτέροις
    ὃν ἡ κόρη ἀφείλετο ἐξ οἰκείων γονέων
    καὶ ἵππους δύο τοὺς αὐτῶν ἀπέπεμπον ἐκεῖθεν,
    αὖθις ἐπαγγειλάμενος τῷ νέῳ δημοσίως
280 τοῦ μηδέποτε ἄδικον ἔτι τῇ κόρῃ πρᾶξαι. 47v
    Καὶ μετ' ὀλίγον καὶ αὐτὸς ἦλθον εἰς τὴν καλήν μου
    τοῦ Ἀπριλίου τρέχοντος πρὸς μεσότητα ἤδη,
    τὸ συνειδὸς κατήγορον φέρων τῆς ἁμαρτίας
    καὶ ταλανίζων ἐμαυτὸν ἐν τῇ ἀθέσμῳ πράξει·
285 ὁπηνίκα τὸν ἥλιον, τὴν ἐμὴν ψυχὴν εἶδον,
    ὡς αἰσχυνόμενος αὐτὴν μεγάλως ἀδικήσας,
    μετ' ὀλίγον γὰρ ἔδοξα μετοίκησιν ποιῆσαι
    (διὰ τὸ γνῶναι καὶ αὐτὴ τὴν παράνομον μίξιν),
    ἣν δὴ καὶ πεποιήκαμεν ἀπάραντες ἐκεῖθεν.»

265 Legrand suggests αὐτῶν
270 δεύτερον Trapp: καὶ δεύτερον G

260 who years before had been killed by the Persians in the Zygos
       mountains.
   When I rescued him from Mousour's hands,
   I did not allow him to travel on ahead of me
   but told everyone about him and especially that he was a law-breaker;
   and I handed him over to my friends there,
265 so that he should live with her until my return –
   'If ever you plan to turn this girl out,
   by my saviour Christ, you will cease to live.'
   I told him not to wrong the girl or to harm her,
   left him there with much advice,
270 and instructed him for a second time not to reject her
   but to take her, as he had promised, as his lawful wife.
   I told everyone how I found the girl
   and how I saved her from the Arabs,
   but I passed over in my story what should not be told,
275 so that the boy should not take offence.
   Then, handing over to both of them all the wealth,
   which the girl had taken from her own parents,
   and their two horses, I sent them away from there,
   once more instructing the young man publicly
280 never again to do any wrong to the girl.
       And after a while I myself returned to my lovely girl,
   as April was already hastening towards its mid-point,
   having a guilty consciousness of my sin
   and castigating myself for my illicit deed.
285 When I saw my sun, my soul,
   since I was ashamed of having greatly wronged her,
   after a while I decided to move our home
   (because she too knew of my unlawful intercourse),
   which we did, removing ourselves from there."

260 If Ζυγός is a proper name, it will refer to the Anti-Tauros range; if not, it could mean
a mountain ridge in general, or a line of troops, or, more likely, the yoke of slavery and
captivity. 'Persians' here are unlikely to refer to pre-Islamic times and may be a twelfth-
century linguistically conservative reference to Turks.
288 Digenis' wife, here as later in the case of Maximou, acts as a kind of extension of his
conscience. The change of residence, as well as underlining the disjointed nature of this
book, also has a psychological basis, since there is no sign of wide local knowledge of
Digenis' rape, and its victim has been sent off with her man.

Λόγος ἕκτος

<Ὁ> ἕκτος λόγος ὁ παρὼν πλείστων ἀνδραγαθίων
διεξιὼν τὰ θαύματα τοῦ Διγενοῦς Ἀκρίτου,
ὡς αὐτὸς διηγήσατο πρὸς τοὺς ἰδίους φίλους.
«Εἰ βασιλέα τῶν μηνῶν θεῖναι τις ἐβουλήθη,
5 Μάϊος ἐβασίλευσεν εἰς ἅπαντας τοὺς μῆνας·
κόσμος οὗτος τερπνότατος γῆς ἁπάσης τυγχάνει,
ὀφθαλμὸς πάντων τῶν φυτῶν καὶ τῶν ἀνθῶν λαμπρότης,
τῶν λειμώνων ἐρύθημα καὶ κάλλος ἀπαστράπτων,
ἔρωτας πνέει θαυμαστῶς, Ἀφροδίτην ἐπάγει·
10 γῆν τοῦ μιμεῖσθαι οὐρανὸν αὐτὸς παρασκευάζει
ἀγλαΐζων τοῖς ἄνθεσι ῥόδοις τε καὶ ναρκίσσοις.
Ἐν τούτῳ δὴ τῷ θαυμαστῷ μηνὶ τῷ γλυκυτάτῳ
ἠθέλησα μεταβαλεῖν μόνος μὲ τῆς καλῆς μου,
τοῦ στρατηγοῦ τῆς θυγατρὸς τοῦ Δουκὸς τῆς ὡραίας.
15 Καὶ δὴ πρός τινα θαυμαστὸν λειμῶνα ἀπελθόντες,
ἐκεῖ τὴν τένδαν ἔστησα καὶ τὴν ἰδίαν κλίνην
κύκλωθεν ταύτης τεθεικὼς πάντων φυτῶν τὰ εἴδη. 48r
Κάλαμοι ἐπεφύοντο εἰς ὕψος ἐπηρμένοι,
ὕδωρ ψυχρὸν ἀνέβλυζεν ἐν μέσῳ τοῦ λειμῶνος
20 καὶ πανταχοῦ διέτρεχεν τῆς γῆς ἐκείνης πάσης.
Ὀρνέων γένη ἱκανὰ ἐνέμετο τῷ ἄλσει,

---

1 Ὁ added by Legrand
6 τερπνότατος Legrand: τερπνότητος G
10 αὐτὸς Mavrogordato: αὐτὴν G
16 ἔστησα Legrand: ἔστησαν G

Book six

The present sixth book of many valiant deeds
will narrate the marvellous actions of Digenis Akritis, the Frontiersman
   of Double Descent,
as he himself related them to his own friends.
"If any one should wish to choose an emperor of the months,
5 May would reign over them all.
He is the whole earth's most delightful adornment,
the budding eye of all plants and the brightness of flowers,
flashing forth the blushing and the beauty of the meadows;
he breathes out passions marvellously and brings on Aphrodite,
10 he makes the earth ready to mimic heaven,
decorating it with flowers, both roses and narcissus.
   In this marvellous, most sweet month
I wished to move away on my own with my lovely girl,
the beautiful daughter of the general Doukas.
15 And after we had arrived at a marvellous meadow,
I put up the tent there and my own couch,
setting all sorts of plants around it.
Reeds grew there, reaching upwards,
cold water bubbled up in the middle of the meadow
20 and flowed out all over the ground there.
Several kinds of birds lived in the grove –

Like G4, this book is markedly longer than the average and is made up of awkwardly
juxtaposed episodes (the serpent's assault on the girl, the guerrillas' attack, the duel with
Maximou) with many doublets (the attempted abduction, the duels), evidence that
Digenis, which will have included all these episodes, was constructed from originally
discrete material (see Tiftixoglu, 1974, 10–14; Dyck, 1987). The corresponding material
in E appears at E1097–605.
1–3 This introduction serves as a justification for the first-person narrative of G6 (cf.
G5.15–20), again giving the impression of a perfunctory late addition.
4–11, 18–28 The encomium of the month of May and the garden description (cf.
G7.11–41) are based on Achilles Tatius and connected with Melitiniotis' Εἰς τὴν
Σωφροσύνην (see Introduction, p. xlvi and Dyck, 1987, 352–5). Similar literary praise,
including that of the *locus amoenus* or May meadow which follows, was widely
disseminated through European literature (Curtius, 1953, 194–200).

ταῶνες χειροήθεις τε ψιττακοὶ καὶ οἱ κύκνοι·
οἱ ψιττακοὶ κρεμώμενοι ἐπὶ τοῖς κλώνοις ᾖδον,
οἱ κύκνοι ἐν τοῖς ὕδασι τὴν νομὴν ἐποιοῦντο,
25 οἱ ταῶνες τὰς πτέρυγας κυκλοῦντες εἰς τὰ ἄνθη
ἀντέλαμπον τῇ τῶν ἀνθῶν ἐν ταῖς πτέρυξι χρόᾳ,
αἱ δὲ λοιπαὶ ἐλεύθερα τὰ πτερὰ κεκτημέναι
ἔπαιζον ἐποχούμεναι εἰς τῶν δένδρων τοὺς κλώνους.   E1657
Καὶ τὸ κάλλος τῆς εὐγενοῦς κόρης ὑπεραστράπτον
30 κρεῖττον ταῶνος ἔλαμπε καὶ τῶν φυτῶν ἁπάντων·
ναρκίσσου γὰρ τὸ πρόσωπον τὴν χροίαν ἐμιμεῖτο,
αἱ παρειαὶ ὡς εὔθαλον ἐξανέτελλον ῥόδον,
ἄνθος ῥόδων ἀρτιφυὲς ὑπέφηνε τὰ χείλη,
ὁπηνίκα ταῖς κάλυξιν ἄρχεται ἀνατέλλειν·
35 βόστρυχοι ἐποχούμενοι τῶν ὀφρυδίων λίαν
χρυσοτερπεῖς ἀνέπεμπον ἀκτινοβόλους μάλα
καὶ διὰ πάντων ἄρρητος ὑπῆρχεν εὐφροσύνη.
Περὶ τῆς κλίνης πέμματα ἐκάπνιζον παντοῖα,
μόσχοι, νίται καὶ ἄμβαρα, καμφοραὶ καὶ κασσίαι,
40 καὶ ἦν πλείστη <ἡ> ἡδονὴ καὶ ὀσμὴ εὐφροσύνης·
τοσαύτην ὁ παράδεισος τὴν τερπνότητα εἶχεν.
    Ἐν ὥρᾳ τῇ μεσημβρινῇ πρὸς ὕπνον ἀνετράπην
ῥοδόσταμμα τῆς εὐγενοῦς ῥαντιζούσης με κόρης,
ἀδονίδων καὶ τῶν λοιπῶν ὀρνίθων μελῳδούντων.   48v
45 Ἡ δὲ κόρη διψήσασα πρὸς τὴν πηγὴν ἀπῆλθε·
καὶ ὡς ἐκεῖσε ἔβρεχε τοὺς πόδας τερπομένη,
δράκων μορφώσας ἑαυτὸν εἰς εὐειδὲς παιδίον
πρὸς αὐτὴν παρεγένετο βουλόμενος πλανῆσαι·
ἡ δὲ τὸν ὄντα οὐδαμῶς ἀγνοήσασα ἔφη:
50 Ἄφες, δράκον, ὃ βούλεσαι· ἐγὼ οὐκ ἀπατοῦμαι,
ὁ φιλῶν με ἠγρύπνησε καὶ ἀρτίως καθεύδει
(ἔλεγε γὰρ ἐν ἑαυτῇ: Δράκων οὗτος ὑπάρχει,
πώποτε οὐ τεθέαμαι ὧδε τοιαύτην ὄψιν)·
εἰ ἐγερθῇ καὶ εὕρη σε, νὰ σὲ κακοδικήσῃ.'
55   Ὁ δὲ πηδήσας ἀναιδῶς βιάζειν ἐπεχείρει

23 κλώνοις Legrand: κλώνοι G
29 ὑπεραστράπτον Legrand: ὑπεραστράπτων G
32 ἐξανέτελλον Legrand: ἐξανέτελλε G
33 ῥόδων Trapp: ῥόδον G
34 ἀνατέλλειν G: ἀναθάλλειν Tsopanakis. 1960. 87
38 πέμματα Legrand: πέγματα G
40 ἡ added by Legrand

tame peacocks, parrots and swans;
the parrots hung on the branches and sang,
the swans browsed for food in the water,
25 the peacocks paraded their wings among the flowers
and reflected the flowers' colours in their wings;
the rest, having won freedom for their wings,
played as they perched on the branches of the trees.
And the brightly flashing beauty of the high-born girl
30 outshone the peacocks and all the plants.
For her face mimicked the narcissus' colour,
her cheeks burgeoned like a blooming rose,
her lips resembled a newly opened rose
when it begins to burst out of its bud.
35 Curls floating just above her brows
sent out rays of golden delight,
and over all there was an ineffable joy.
Around the bed were burning spices of all kinds,
musk, nard and ambergris, camphor and cassia,
40 and great was the pleasure and the scent of joys.
Such were the delights this garden offered.
     At the hour of noon I turned to sleep,
while the high-born girl sprinkled rose-water over me
and the nightingales and other birds sang.
45 The girl was thirsty and went to the spring,
and as she was enjoying herself there, wetting her feet,
a serpent, who had transformed himself into a good-looking boy,
came up to her, wishing to seduce her.
She, not at all unaware who he was, said:
50 'Serpent, abandon your scheme, I am not taken in.
He who loves me has been keeping watch and has just gone to sleep
(for she said to herself: 'This is a serpent,
I have never before seen a sight like this');
if he wakes up and finds you, he will do you harm.'
55   But he jumped up and shamelessly tried to violate her,

29–36 On the combined ekphrasis of the girl and a beautiful garden which adds power
to both descriptions, see Littlewood, 1979.
47 The translation of δράκων as 'serpent' and not 'ogre' derives from a degree of
parallelism in this scene to the temptation of Eve, and the fact that the character of the
beast seems more reptilian than anthropomorphic, as in the description preserved by
Kekavmenos or in the tale of St Theodore's encounter with a δράκων; see Introduction,
pp. xlii–xliii. However, this is clearly an early foreshadowing of the δράκος or ogre of
Modern Greek folklore (see Kriaras, 1969 – under δράκος and δράκων).

καὶ φωνὴν ἔπεμπεν εὐθὺς καλοῦσά με ἡ κόρη:
"Ἐξύπνησον, αὐθέντα μου, καὶ λάβε τὴν φιλτάτην."
Τῆς δὲ φωνῆς εἰς τὴν ἐμὴν καρδίαν ἠχησάσης
τάχιον ἀνεκάθισα καὶ τὸν ὀχλοῦντα εἶδον
60 (ἄντικρυς γάρ μου ἡ πηγὴ ἦν ἐξεπιτηδείως)
καὶ ἐξελκύσας τὸ σπαθὶν εἰς τὴν πηγὴν εὑρέθην·
οἱ γὰρ πόδες μου ἔτρεχον ὡς πτέρυγες ὀξέως.
   Καὶ τοῦτόν τε καταλαβών, φάντασμά μοι ἐδείκνυ
φρικῶδές τε καὶ φοβερὸν ἐν ἀνθρώποις καὶ μέγα,
65 τρεῖς εὐμεγέθεις κεφαλὰς πυρφλογιζούσας ὅλως·   E1109
ἐξ ἑκατέρων ἔπεμπεν ἐξαστράπτουσαν φλόγα·
ἐκ τόπου δὲ κινούμενος βροντῆς ἦχον ἐτέλει,
ὥστε δοκεῖν σαλεύεσθαι γῆν τε καὶ πάντα δένδρα.
Σῶμα παχύνων, κεφαλὰς εἰς ἓν ἐπισυνάγων,
70 ὄπισθεν λεπτυνόμενος καὶ οὐρὰν ἀποξύνων,   49r
ποτὲ μὲν συστελλόμενος, ἐξαπλούμενος δ' αὖθις
καὶ ἐπάνω μου ἅπασαν τὴν ὁρμὴν ἐποιεῖτο.
Ἐγὼ δὲ τὰ ὁρώμενα ἀντ' οὐδενὸς νομίσας,
εἰς ὕψος ὅλῳ τῷ θυμῷ τὸ σπαθὶν ἀνατείνας
75 εἰς κεφαλὰς κατήγαγον θηρὸς τοῦ δεινοτάτου
καὶ ἁπάσας αἴρω ὁμοῦ· ὃς καὶ πρὸς γῆν ἡπλώθη
ἄνω καὶ κάτω τὴν οὐρὰν κινῶν τὰ τελευταῖα.
Καὶ ἀπομάξας τὸ σπαθὶν καὶ βαλὼν εἰς τὴν θήκην
πόρρωθεν ὄντας τοὺς ἐμοὺς προσεκαλούμην παῖδας
80 καὶ ἀρθῆναι προσέταττον τὸν δράκοντα εὐθέως.
Ὡς δὲ τοῦτο ἐγένετο ταχέως ὑπὲρ λόγον,
οἱ παῖδες μὲν ἀπέτρεχον εἰς τὰς ἰδίας τένδας,
ἐπὶ τὴν κλίνην δὲ κἀγὼ ὑπνωσόμενος αὖθις,
ἡδὺς γὰρ ὂν ἐκάθευδον εἷλκέ με πάλιν ὕπνος·
85 οὔπω γὰρ τούτου κορεσθεὶς ἀφύπνωσα τὸ πρῶτον.
   Ἡ δὲ κόρη πρὸς γέλωτα ἄμετρον κινηθεῖσα,   E1120
φαντάσματα τοῦ δράκοντος φέρουσα ἐπὶ μνήμης
καὶ τὸν σύντομον θάνατον ἐκείνου τοῦ μεγέθους,
πρὸς τὸ μὴ ἐξυπνῆσαί με ἐξῆλθε πρός τι δένδρον
90 παρηγορίαν τε λαβεῖν μικρὰν ἀπὸ τοῦ φόβου.
Καὶ ἰδού, λέων φοβερὸς ἐξῆλθεν ἐκ τοῦ ἄλσους,   E1123
ὃς πρὸς τὴν κόρην καὶ αὐτὸς τὴν ὁρμὴν ἐποιεῖτο·

65 εὐμεγέθεις κεφαλὰς Legrand: κεφαλὰς εὐμεγέθεις G
66 ἔπεμπεν Legrand: ἔπεμπον G
84 ὂν Legrand: ὢν G

and the girl immediately let out a shriek, calling for me:
'Wake up, my lord, and rescue your dearest.'
The shriek rang in my heart,
and I promptly sat up and saw the intruder
60 (for the spring was straight in front of me on purpose);
I drew my sword and found myself at the spring,
for my feet ran swiftly like wings.
      As I reached him he revealed a hideous apparition to me,
huge and terrifying to human eyes –
65 three gigantic heads, completely engulfed in fire;
from each it gushed out flame like lightning flashes;
as it changed its position it let out a thunderclap,
so that the earth and all the trees seemed to shake.
Thickening its body and drawing its heads into one,
70 growing thin behind and making a sharp tail,
at one moment coiling itself and then unfolding again,
it launched its whole attack against me.
But I, reckoning this spectacle as nothing,
stretched my sword up high with all my might
75 and brought it down on the ferocious beast's heads,
and cut them all off at once. It collapsed on the ground,
twitching its tail up and down in its last spasms.
I wiped my sword and replaced it in its scabbard,
summoned my boys who were some way off
80 and ordered that the serpent be removed at once.
When this had been done at indescribable speed,
the boys ran back to their own tents,
while I went back to my couch to sleep once more,
for the sweet sleep I had been enjoying drew me back again
85 as I had not yet had my fill of it when I was first woken.
      The girl was moved to unbounded laughter
as she remembered the serpent's apparitions
and the huge monster's sudden death,
and she went towards a tree so as not to wake me
90 and to pull herself together a little after her fright.
And, look, a fearsome lion came out of the wood
and also began to attack the girl.

---

79 Again Digenis' lonely life includes (as well as his wife) servants, but their help needs
to be summoned even in emergencies.
89 The daughter of Aploravdis took refuge up a tree (G5.193–6), and Digenis' wife was
placed for safety in a tree at her abduction (G4.631–2): there seems to be a pattern here.

ἡ δὲ φωνὴν ἐξέπεμψε βοηθόν με καλοῦσα.
Καὶ ἐπακούσας τάχιστα ἐπανέστην τῆς κλίνης
95 καὶ ὡς εἶδον τὸν λέοντα συντόμως εἰσπηδήσας,
φέρων ῥάβδον ἐν τῇ χειρὶ τοῦτον εὐθὺς ἐμπίπτω,
πατάξας δὲ εἰς κεφαλήν· ἔθανε παραχρῆμα. 49v
Ὡς δὲ καὶ οὗτος μήκοθεν ἐρρίφη τε ὁ δράκων,
ἡ κόρη <μου> εἰς ἑαυτὴν καθώρκισεν εἰποῦσα:
100 ''Ἄκουσόν μου, αὐθέντα μου, νά με ἐπιχαρείης,
ἔπαρον τὴν κιθάραν σου, κροῦσον αὐτὴν ὀλίγον, E1142
μετάβαλόν μου τὴν ψυχὴν ἐκ τοῦ θηρὸς τοῦ φόβου.' E1143
Καὶ ὡς οὐκ ἦν μοι δυνατὸν παρακοῦσαι τῆς κόρης,
ταύτην ἀνέκρουον εὐθύς, ἡ δὲ ἐνετραγῴδει:
105 Εὐχαριστῶ τῷ ἔρωτι γλυκὺν δόντι μοι κύρκαν E1147
καὶ χαίρω βασιλεύουσα, μηδένα φοβουμένη·
κρίνον ὑπάρχει εὐθαλές, μῆλον μεμυρισμένον,
καὶ ὡς ῥόδον πανεύοσμον θέλγει μου τὴν καρδίαν.'
Ὡς δὲ τὸ ῥόδον ἔλεγεν ἡ κόρη μελῳδοῦσα,
110 ἐνόμιζον ὅτι κρατεῖ ῥόδον ἐπὶ τὰ χείλη,
ἐοίκασι γὰρ ἀληθῶς ἄρτι ἀνθοῦντι ῥόδῳ.
Τῆς δὲ κιθάρας ἡ ᾠδὴ καὶ ἡ φωνὴ τῆς κόρης
ἦχον τερπνὸν ἀνέπεμπον, ὀρέων ἀντηχούντων,
ὡς καὶ τοὺς ὄντας μήκοθεν αἰσθάνεσθαι τοῦ μέλους·
115 Καὶ τοῦτο ἐπεγνώκαμεν ἐκ τούτου τοῦ σημείου·
κατὰ τύχην διήρχοντο ἐν ἐκείνῃ τῇ ὥρᾳ
στρατιῶται ἐν τῇ ὁδῷ τῇ καλουμένῃ Τρώσει,
ἐν ᾗ πολλοὺς συμβέβηκε πολλὰ τραυματισθῆναι,
καὶ δῆλον ἐκ τὸ ὄνομα ὃ εἴληφεν ὁ τόπος.
120 Ὑπῆρχον δέ, ὡς ὕστερον παρ' αὐτῶν τοῦτο ἔγνων,
Ἰωαννάκης θαυμαστὸς καὶ νέος ἀπελάτης, 50r
Φιλοπαπποῦς ὁ γέρων τε καὶ ὁ Κίνναμος τρίτος·
καὶ ὡς ᾤχοντο τῆς ὁδοῦ, ἤκουσαν τῶν ἀσμάτων
μίλιον ἓν ἀπέχοντες ἀφ' ἡμῶν, ὡς εἰκάζω,

---

96 ἐμπίπτω Mavrogordato: ἐκπίπτω G
99 μου added by Legrand   ἑαυτὴν Kalonaros: ἐμαυτὴν G
102 μετάβαλόν Tsopanakis, 1960, 87: μεταβαλών G

She let out a shriek, calling me to help.
I heard her and got up from my bed with all speed;
95 when I saw the lion I promptly leaped forward,
brandishing my stick in my hand, and charged at it immediately,
striking it on the head. It died on the spot.
When the lion, and the serpent too, had been flung far away,
my girl swore upon her life, saying,
100 'Listen to me, my lord, if you would give me pleasure,
take your kithara, play it for a while
and distract my soul from fear of the wild beast.'
    As I could not disobey the girl,
I immediately began to play it, and she began to sing:
105 'I offer thanks to Eros who gives me my delectable sweetheart,
and I rejoice as an empress, fearing nobody;
he is a flourishing lily, a perfumed apple,
and like a fragrant rose he enchants my heart.'
    As the girl spoke of the rose while she sang,
110 I thought she held a rose between her lips,
for they truly seemed like a freshly opened bloom.
The notes of the kithara and the voice of the girl
gave out a delightful sound as the hills re-echoed,
so that even people far distant heard the melody.
115   And we realised it from this sign.
By chance, at that hour, soldiers were
passing along the road called Trosis,
where it had happened that many had been badly wounded,
as is clear from the name that the place had acquired.
120 They were – as I learnt from them later –
Ioannikis, the marvellous young guerrilla,
old Philopappous and Kinnamos, the third.
And, as they were travelling along the road, they heard the songs
whilst they were a mile distant from us, as far as I can tell;

110–11 Roses on a girl's lips are perhaps a twelfth-century cliché; Dyck, 1987, 355, note 26.
117–19 Punning etymologies similar to that here on Trosis (see the Name Index) are found in Theophanes Continuatus 4.25 in connection with the battle of Porson in 863.
121–2 Digenis, as narrator, says that he learned the guerrillas' names later (see G6.154–5, 6.210–11) while at 133 they seem similarly ignorant: this text shows no sign of any previous meeting; it is also unclear how the leaders of the guerrillas mentioned here avoided the slaughter of G6.145–56, and survived to go looking for their troops at G6.176–92. All this points to the incoherent nature of the poem's raw material.

125 καὶ ταύτης ἐκστρατήσαντες ἦλθον ἡμῶν πλησίον.
Καὶ ὡς μόνην ἐσκέψαντο τὴν περίβλεπτον κόρην,
ὡς ὑπὸ βέλους τὰς ψυχὰς ἐτρώθησαν τῷ κάλλει
καὶ εἰς ἔρωτα ἄπειρον ἐκινήθησαν πάντες,
σώζοντες τεσσαρακοστὸν ἀριθμὸν πρὸς τοῖς πέντε.
130 Ἐμὲ δὲ μόνον βλέποντες λόγοις ἤλπιζον τρῶσαι,
'Ἄφες τὴν κόρην,' λέγοντες, 'καὶ σῶσον ἑαυτόν σου·   E1154
εἰ δ᾽ οὔ, κερδίσῃς θάνατον, ἀπείθειαν ὡς ἔχων.'
Ἀκμὴν γὰρ οὐκ ἠπίσταντο ποῖος ἄρα τυγχάνω·
ἡ δὲ ἡλιογέννητος ἄφνω τούτους ἰδοῦσα
135 ἁρματωμένους ἅπαντας ἐφ᾽ ἵππους καθημένους,
λόγοις αὐτῶν πιστεύσασα ἐδειλίασε σφόδρα
καὶ τῇ ὀθόνῃ τὰς αὐτῆς καλυψαμένη ὄψεις
ἐπὶ τὴν τένδαν ἔδραμε, παντελῶς φοβηθεῖσα.
Ἐγὼ δὲ ἔφην πρὸς αὐτήν: 'Τί οὐ λαλεῖς, φιλτάτη;'
140 '"Οτι,' φησί, 'πρὸ τῆς ψυχῆς τέθνηκεν ἡ φωνή μου·
ἰδοὺ γὰρ χωριζόμεθα καὶ ζῆν οὐ θέλω φέρειν.'
'Παῦσαι,' ἔφην, 'ψυχὴ ἐμή, λογίζεσθαι τοιαῦτα·
οὓς ὁ Θεὸς συνέζευξεν, ἄνθρωποι οὐ χωρίσουν.'   E1170. 1305
Εὐθὺς τὴν ῥάβδον εἴληφα καὶ τὸ χειροσκουτάριν,
145 ὡς ἀετὸς πρὸς πέρδικας ἀφ᾽ ὕψους ἐκπετάσας·
ὅσους ἡ ῥάβδος ἡ ἐμὴ ἔφθασε τοῦ προσψαῦσαι,
ζωῆς ἐν τούτοις λείψανον οὐδαμῶς ὑπελείφθη.
Πολλοὶ δὲ θέλοντες φυγεῖν, κατελάμβανον τούτους 50v
(οὐ γὰρ ἐνίκησεν ἐμὲ ἵππος ποτὲ εἰς δρόμον
150 καὶ οὐ σεμνύνων ἐμαυτὸν ταῦτα διαγορεύω
ἀλλ᾽ ἵνα καταμάθητε τὰς δωρεὰς τοῦ πλάστου)·
τινὲς δέ με ἐλάνθανον εἰς βάλτα κρυβηθέντες
καὶ πρὶν ὀλίγον ἅπαντας θανάτῳ παραδώσας,
ἕνα ζωγρήσας μοναχὸν παρ᾽ οὗ ἔμαθον τίνες
155 ὑπῆρχον οἱ ἀσύνετοι καὶ παράφρονες οὗτοι·
καὶ ὑπερζέσας τῷ θυμῷ οὐδενὸς ἐφεισάμην.
Εἶθ᾽ οὕτως ῥίπτω τὸ σπαθὶν καὶ τὸ χειροσκουτάριν
καὶ τὸ μανίκιν ἔσειον καὶ πρὸς τὴν κόρην ἦλθον.   E1185
Ἡ δὲ κόρη ὡς εἶδε με μόνον περιλειφθέντα,
160 ἐξῆλθεν εἰς ἀπάντησιν χαρᾶς ἐμπεπλησμένη

129 τεσσαρακοστὸν Kalonaros: τὸν τεσσαρακοστὸν G   πρὸς τοῖς Legrand: πρὸ τῶν
G
153 παραδώσας G: παραδῶσαι Legrand
155 ὑπῆρχον Legrand: ὑπῆχον G

125 they left the road and came near us.
When they saw that the renowned girl was on her own,
they were wounded in their souls by her beauty, as if by an arrow,
and they were all moved to boundless passion,
all forty-five of them.
130 Seeing that I was on my own, they hoped to wound me with words.
'Leave the girl,' they said, 'and save yourself.
If you do not, you will win death for your disobedience.'
    They still had no idea who I was.
The sun-born girl, suddenly glimpsing
135 all these armed men astride their horses,
believed their words and was utterly terrified;
she covered her face with her veil
and ran to the tent, overwhelmed by fear.
I said to her, 'Why do you not speak, dearest?'
140 'Because,' she said, 'my voice has died before my soul.
For look, we are being separated and I don't want to go on living.'
'My soul,' I said, 'stop thinking such things.
Those whom God has joined, men shall not separate.'
    Immediately I picked up my stick and my hand-shield,
145 attacking them like an eagle swooping on partridges from above,
and in those my stick managed to touch
no remnant of life whatever was left.
Many wanted to get away, but I caught up with them
(for no horse has ever got the better of me in running,
150 and I am stating this not to glorify myself
but so that you can appreciate the gifts of the Creator).
Some got away from me by hiding in the marshes,
and just before I had put all to death,
I captured one on his own alive, from whom I learnt who
155 these senseless and witless people were.
And boiling over with fury, I spared none.
Then I threw down my sword and my hand-shield,
shook off my sleeve-guard and went to the girl.
    When she saw that I alone was left,
160 she came out to meet me, filled with joy,

---

130 The phrase 'on my own' is again used of both the hero and his wife, as if it is their
characteristic epithet, although each has at least the other's company.
143 A key phrase for placing *Digenis in a twelfth-century literary context: see
Introduction, p. xliv.

καὶ ῥοδόσταμμα ἔρριπτε μὲ τὰς ἰδίας χεῖρας,
φιλοῦσα μου τὴν δεξιὰν καὶ ζῆν ἐπευχομένη.
Κἀγὼ ταύτης βουλόμενος τὸ δέος ὀνειδίσαι
λόγους μεθ᾽ ὑποκρίσεως ἐρωτικοὺς ἐκίρνων·
165 'Μὴ γὰρ ἐγὼ πρὸ τοῦ παθεῖν ὥσπερ σὺ ἀποθνήσκω;'
Ἡ δὲ συνιεῖσα ἃ λαλῶ γλυκερῶς ἐμειδία,
'Τὸ πλῆθος εἶδον,' λέγουσα, 'τῶν ἱππέων ἐξαίφνης
ἁρματωμένους ἅπαντας, σὲ δὲ πεζὸν καὶ μόνον·
ἐπὶ τούτῳ, αὐθέντα μου, ὁ φόβος μοι ἐπῆλθε.'
170 Καὶ μυρία φιλήσαντες ἤλθομεν εἰς τὴν τένδαν
καὶ τῇ ἑξῆς πρὸς ποταμὸν λουθῆναι ἀπηρχόμην,
ὅπως ἀλλάξω τὴν στολὴν τὴν αἵματι χρανθεῖσαν,
καὶ τῇ κόρῃ παρήγγειλα ἑτέραν ἀγαγεῖν μοι·
καὶ δὴ παραγενόμενος τοῦ ὕδατος πλησίον,
175 ἐπί τι δένδρον καθεσθεὶς τὴν κόρην ἐκδεχόμην. 51r
Καὶ ἰδοὺ τρεῖς ἀνέφανον ὡραῖοι καβαλλάροι,   E1199
στολάς τε ἀνεφέροντο ἄμφω παρηλλαγμένας
καὶ πρὸς ἐμὲ ἀνήρχοντο τὸν ποταμὸν κρατοῦντες·
εἶδον γάρ με καθήμενον εἰς τοῦ δένδρου τὴν ῥίζαν.
180 Καὶ πλησίον γενόμενοι ἐχαιρέτισαν πάντες·
ἐγὼ δὲ οὐκ ἠγέρθην τους, ἀλλ᾽ ἐκαθούμην μᾶλλον.
'Μὴ στρατιώτας, ἀδελφέ, οἵους ἐνταῦθα εἶδες;'
Κἀγὼ ἀντέφην πρὸς αὐτοὺς μὴ δειλιάσας ὅλως·
'Ναί, εἶδον,' ἔφην, 'ἀδελφοί, κατὰ τὴν χθὲς ἡμέραν,
185 ἤθελον γὰρ καὶ τὴν ἐμὴν γαμετὴν ἀφαρπάσαι,
καί, μὰ τὸν λόγον τοῦ Θεοῦ, οὐδὲ ἵππου ἐπέβην·
τί δὲ αὐτοῖς συμβέβηκε γνώσεσθε μετὰ ταῦτα.'
Οἱ δὲ ταῦτα ἀκούσαντες ἐθεώρουν ἀλλήλους,
πρὸς αὐτοὺς ψιθυρίζοντες, χείλη κινοῦντες μόνα·
190 'Μὴ οὗτος ἔνι ὃν λέγουσι Βασίλειος Ἀκρίτης;   E1216
Ἀλλὰ πάντως γνωσόμεθα δοκιμάσαντες τοῦτον.'
Καὶ λέγει μοι ὁ πρόκριτος· 'Πῶς ἔχομεν πιστεῦσαι

---

163 ἔρριπτε G: ἔνιπτε or ἔρρανε Trapp
170 φιλήσαντες Legrand: φιλήσαντας G
184 Ναί G in margin: ἀλλ᾽ G in text
187 τί Legrand: τίς G

and scattered rose-water with her own hands,
kissing my right hand and praying for my long life.
And I, wishing to reproach her for her timidity,
mixed words of love with this careful comment:
165 'Do I, like you, die before being hurt?'
She understood what I meant and smiled sweetly,
saying: 'I saw the host of horsemen suddenly,
all armed, while you were on foot and on your own.
It was because of that, my lord, that fear came over me.'
170   And after kissing a thousand times, we came to the tent,
and on the next day I was going off to the river to bathe
so that I could change my clothes, which were foul with blood,
and I told the girl to bring me others;
and when I was near the water
175 I sat down by a tree and waited for the girl.
And look, three handsome horsemen appeared
who were all wearing magnificent garments,
and they were coming towards me, keeping to the river,
for they saw me sitting at the root of the tree.
180 When they had come close they all greeted me,
yet I did not bestir myself for them – but on the contrary, I remained
     seated.
'Have you perhaps, brother, seen soldiers of this sort?'
And I replied to them, with absolutely no fear:
'Yes,' I said, 'I saw them, brothers, yesterday,
185 for they wanted to abduct my wife
and, by God's Word, I didn't even mount my horse.
What happened to them you will find out after this.'
     When they heard this they looked at each other,
whispering to themselves, moving their lips only:
190 'Isn't he the one they call Basil Akritis, the Frontiersman?
But we'll know for sure by testing him.'
     And their spokesman said to me: 'How can we believe

163 As Galatariotou, 1987, 66 points out, a tragic element in this poem is the fact that
Digenis is able to convince everyone of his superhuman strength apart from his wife; the
tension is made plain for the first time by his criticism of her here.
171 The scene of the action in this book is not clear. Although Trosis was probably on
the Euphrates, we have only so far been told about a spring. Now we are presumably
moving to the Euphrates itself.
176–82 See G6.121–2 above.
173–307 and E1199–315 agree over the main features of Digenis' encounter with the
guerrillas, though with variations attributable to the different narrative styles.

ὅτι μόνος καὶ ἄοπλος, πεζός, καθάπερ λέγεις,
μετ' αὐτῶν κατετόλμησας μάχην ἐπισυνάψαι;
195 Ἅπαντας γὰρ δοκιμαστοὺς εἴχομεν ἐν ἀνδρείᾳ·
ἀλλ' εἴπερ λέγεις ἀληθῆ, φάνηθι ἐκ τῶν ἔργων,
ἕνα ἔκλεξον ἀφ' ἡμῶν τῶν τριῶν ὅνπερ βούλει,   E1225
καὶ μονομάχησον αὐτῷ καὶ γνωσόμεθα πάντες.'
Καὶ μειδιάσας πρὸς αὐτοὺς ἐγὼ ἀνταπεκρίθην:
200 'Εἰ βούλεσθε, πεζεύσατε καὶ δεῦτε οἱ τρεῖς εἰς ἕνα·   E1236
εἰ δ' ἴσως οὐκ αἰσχύνεσθε, δεῦτε καὶ καβαλλάροι,   E1237
καὶ ἐκ τῶν ἔργων μάθετε ποῖος ἄρα τυγχάνω· 51v
καί, εἰ δοκεῖ, ἀρξώμεθα τῆς μάχης ἀπεντεῦθεν.'
'Ραβδὶν λαμβάνω σύντομα, ὄρθιος ἐγενόμην
205 καὶ τὸ χειροσκουτάριν μου (καὶ γὰρ ἐκράτουν ταῦτα)
καὶ πρὸς ὀλίγον προσελθών, 'Εἰ κελεύετε,' ἔφην.
Καὶ ὁ πρῶτος ἐφώνησεν: 'Οὐ ποιοῦμεν ὡς λέγεις·
ἡμεῖς ἔθος οὐκ ἔχομεν ἐλθεῖν οἱ τρεῖς εἰς ἕνα,
οἱ θαρροῦντες μετακινεῖν ὁ καθεὶς χιλιάδας.
210 Ἐγὼ γὰρ ὁ Φιλοπαπποῦς εἰμὶ ὅνπερ ἀκούεις,   E1243
Ἰωαννάκης οὗτος δὲ καὶ Κίνναμος ὁ τρίτος   E1243, 1499
καὶ αἰσχυνόμεθα οἱ τρεῖς πολεμῆσαι εἰς ἕνα·
ἀλλ' ἐπίλεξον ἀφ' ἡμῶν ἕνα οἷον κελεύεις.'   E1225
<Κἀγώ,> 'Ναί,' ἔφην πρὸς αὐτούς, 'δεῦρο λοιπὸν ὁ πρῶτος.'
215 Καὶ εὐθὺς ὁ Φιλοπαπποῦς κατῆλθεν ἐκ τοῦ ἵππου
σπαθὶν ἀράμενος αὐτοῦ ἅμα καὶ τὴν ἀσπίδα,
τρανῶς εἰσῆλθε πρὸς ἐμὲ πτοῆσαί με ἐλπίζων·
εἶχε καὶ γὰρ ὡς ἀληθῶς ὁρμὴν ἀνδρειοτάτην
καὶ σπαθέαν μου δώσαντος τρανὰ εἰς τὸ σκουτάριν   E1248
220 ἐν τῇ χειρὶ τὸ κράτημα μόνον μοι ἀπελείφθη.   E1250
Οἱ δύο ἀντεφώνησαν ἄντικρυς καθορῶντες:
'Ἄλλην μίαν, Φιλοπαπποῦ γέρον μου, τὸν ἐπίθες.'   E1252
Ὁ δὲ αὖθις βουλόμενος τὴν σπάθην ἀνατεῖναι,
τῇ ῥάβδῳ κατὰ κεφαλῆς τοῦτον ἐγὼ πατάσσω,
225 καὶ εἰ μὴ ταύτην ἐφύλαττε καθόλου τὸ σκουτάριν,
σῶον οὐκ ἔμενεν ὀστοῦν ἐν αὐτῇ τὸ παράπαν.
Ὅμως ὁ γέρων τραλισθείς, κατὰ πολὺ τρομάξας,
βοῦς ὥσπερ μυκησάμενος ἐπὶ τὴν γῆν ἡπλώθη.
Καὶ τοῦτο θεασάμενοι οἱ ἕτεροι ὡς εἶχον 52r
230 καβαλλάροι ἐπάνω μου ἤρχοντο παραχρῆμα

211 Ἰωαννάκης Legrand: Ἰωαννάκην G
214 Κἀγώ added by Legrand

that you, on your own, unarmed, on foot as you say,
dared to join battle with them?
195 For the men we had were all experienced in bravery.
But if you are telling the truth, make it plain from your deeds.
Choose whichever of the three of us you want,
and fight him in single combat, and we shall all know.'
    And smiling at them I replied:
200 'If you want, dismount and come here three against one,
or if you are not ashamed, attack me on horseback,
and learn from the results who I am.
If you like, let us begin the battle from this instant.'
    I promptly picked up my stick and stood upright,
205 and took my hand-shield (for I had these with me);
advancing a little, I said, 'If this is your command.'
And the first one shouted: 'We won't do as you say;
it's not our custom to come three against one,
we who take pride, each of us, in repelling thousands.
210 For I, whom you are listening to, am Philopappous,
this is Ioannakis and the third is Kinnamos,
and the three of us are ashamed to fight against one man.
But choose one of us, whichever you decide on.'
    And, 'Yes,' I said to them, 'let the first come forward then.'
215 And immediately Philopappous dismounted from his horse,
taking his sword and shield as well,
and rushed at me vigorously, hoping to terrify me,
for truly he attacked extremely bravely.
And when he gave me a sturdy sword-thrust on the shield,
220 only the handle was left in my hand.
The two others shouted out as they watched from the other side:
'Hit him again, old Philopappous!'
He wanted to lift up his sword once more
but I struck him on the head with my stick,
225 and if the shield had not offered his head some protection,
not a single bone would have remained unbroken in it.
As it was, the old man was stunned, he trembled violently
and he sprawled over the ground bellowing like a bull.
Seeing this, the others charged at me
230 without hesitation, just as they were, on horseback,

210 The narrator now provides the names of the guerrillas, as foreshadowed at
G6.121–2 above.

μηδαμῶς αἰσχυνόμενοι, ὡς πρώην ἐκαυχῶντο.
Τούτων ὡς εἶδον τὴν ὁρμήν, ἁρπάζω τὸ σκουτάριν
ἀπὸ χειρῶν τοῦ γέροντος καὶ πρὸς αὐτοὺς ἐκτρέχω.
Γεναμένης δὲ συμπλοκῆς καὶ ἐνστάτου πολέμου
235 ὁ μὲν Κίνναμος ὄπισθεν ἔσπευδε τοῦ λαθεῖν με·
Ἰωαννάκης ἔκρουεν εὐθέως καὶ συντόμως
καὶ τότ᾽ εἶδον πολεμιστὰς ὡς ἀληθῶς δοκίμους.
Ἀλλ᾽ οὐδεὶς τούτων ἴσχυσεν ἐμοὶ περιγενέσθαι·
καὶ γὰρ ἡνίκα τὴν ἐμὴν ἀπετίνασσον ῥάβδον,
240 ὅλοι ὡς ἀπὸ λέοντος ἔφευγον ἐναντίον
ὡσεὶ πρόβατα μήκοθεν ἐμὲ περισκοποῦντες
καὶ αὖθις πάλιν ἤρχοντο ὡς κύνες ὑλακτοῦντες.
Ὡς δὲ οὕτως ἐγένετο ἐφ᾽ ὥραν οὐκ ὀλίγην,
καὶ ἡ κόρη κατέλαβε, πλὴν ἵστατο μακρόθεν,
245 ἀντικρὺς ἐξεπίτηδες τοῦ παρ᾽ ἐμοῦ ὁρᾶσθαι.
Καὶ ὡς εἶδε κυκλοῦντας <με> τοὺς δύο ὡσεὶ κύνας,
λόγον μοι ἐνετόξευσεν ἐπίκουρον εἰποῦσα·
"Ἀνδρίζου, ὦ παμφίλτατε.᾽ Καὶ εὐθὺς σὺν τῷ λόγῳ
ἰσχὺν ἀναλαβόμενος πλήττω τὸν Ἰωαννάκην
250 ἐν τῇ χειρὶ τῇ δεξιᾷ ἄνωθεν τοῦ ἀγκῶνος·
τὰ ὀστᾶ συνετρίβησαν, ἡ χεὶρ ὅλη ἡπλώθη   E1271
καὶ τὸ σπαθὶν ἐπὶ τὴν γῆν πέπτωκε παραχρῆμα·   E1272
ὀλίγον δέ μου παρελθὼν πέπτωκεν ἐκ τοῦ ἵππου
καὶ εἰς πέτραν ἀκούμπησεν ἐχόμενος τοῦ πόνου.
255   Βουληθεὶς δὲ ὁ Κίνναμος μόνος ἀνδραγαθῆσαι, 52v
ἄνω καὶ κάτω τὸν αὐτοῦ ἵππον ἐπιλαλήσας,
τεθαρρηκὼς ὁ δείλαιος τὸν λέοντα πτοῆσαι
ὡς πρὸς ἐμὲ κατήρχετο σὺν τῷ ἰδίῳ ἵππῳ.
Ῥαβδέαν τοῦτον ἔπληξα μέσον τῶν δύο ὤμων,
260 ἀφ᾽ ὧν αἷμα ποταμηδὸν ἔρρεε παραχρῆμα
ἔκ τε κροτάφων καὶ αὐτοῦ τοῦ στόματος τοῦ φάρα
καὶ αὐτίκα συμποδισθεὶς πίπτει σὺν τῷ Κιννάμῳ·
τὸν δὲ φόβος ἐλάμβανε καὶ δειλία συνεῖχε,
νομίζων ὅτι κείμενον θέλω αὐτὸν πατάξαι.
265 Λέγω δ᾽ ἐγώ τε πρὸς αὐτόν· Ὦ Κίνναμε, τί τρέμεις;
Τὸν πεσόντα οὐδέποτε ἔθος ἔχω τοῦ κρούειν·   E1279. 1287
ἀλλ᾽ εἰ βούλει, ἀνάστηθι καὶ λάβε σου τὰ ὅπλα
καὶ δώσομεν εἰς πρόσωπον, ὡς δοκεῖ τοῖς ἀνδρείοις·

246 με added by Legrand
249 πλήττω Legrand: πλήττει G

not in the least ashamed despite their earlier boasts.
When I saw their onslaught, I seized the shield
from the old man's hands and ran towards them.
   As the clash began and the fighting became intense,
235 Kinnamos hurried behind me, to catch me unprepared,
while Ioannakis struck swiftly and directly,
and then I saw that they were truly experienced warriors.
But neither of them was able to get the better of me,
for when I brandished my stick
240 they fled before me as if from a lion,
like sheep who caught sight of me from a long way off;
then they came back again like howling dogs.
When this had been going on for some time,
the girl came up – though she kept her distance –
245 and deliberately stood in front, to be seen by me.
And when she saw the two of them circling me like dogs,
she darted a supportive word to me, saying:
'Be brave, my dearest.' And at her word immediately
I regained strength and struck Ioannakis
250 on his right arm, above the elbow.
The bones were crushed, the whole arm hung down
and his sword promptly fell to the ground.
Going just past me, he fell from his horse
and leaned on a rock, overwhelmed by pain.
255   Kinnamos, wishing to perform valiant deeds on his own,
urged his horse on, up and down,
confident – the wretch – that he would terrify the lion,
and charged at me with his own horse.
I struck it a blow from my stick between its two withers,
260 from which blood immediately flowed in a stream
as well as from the charger's temples and mouth,
and it promptly fell, entangled with Kinnamos.
Fear seized him, terror possessed him,
thinking that I would strike him as he lay there.
265 But I said to him: 'Kinnamos, why are you trembling?
It is never my custom to hit a man when he is down.
But, if you wish, stand up and take your weapons,
and we shall fight face to face, as befits brave men.

---

244 The girl's intervention at this point is more clearly motivated in E1262–6, where
she has been asked to bring a tunic (Alexiou, 1979, 64).

τὸ δὲ πατάσσειν πτώματα τοῖς ἀδρανέσι πέλει.'
270 Ἐκεῖνος δὲ τοῖς νεύμασιν ὑποταγὴν ἐδείκνυ·
οὐκ ἴσχυε γὰρ τοῦ λαλεῖν ἐχόμενος τοῦ τρόμου.
Ἐκεῖ τοῦτον ἀφέμενος ὄπισθεν ἐστρεφόμην
καὶ ὁρῶ τὸν Φιλοπαππούν εἰς ἑαυτὸν ἐλθόντα,
κινοῦντα τε τὴν κεφαλὴν καὶ λέγοντα τοιαῦτα:
275 Τὸν Θεὸν τὸν ποιήσαντα οὐρανὸν καὶ γῆν πᾶσαν,
τὸν σὲ κατακοσμήσαντα τοῖς χαρίσμασι πᾶσι,
κατάλειπε τὸν πόλεμον καὶ ποίησον ἀγάπην
καὶ δοῦλοι σου ἐσόμεθα, εἴπερ αὐτὸς κελεύεις,
παρὰ σοῦ προστασσόμενοι καὶ ποιοῦντες ἀόκνως.'
280 Ὡς ταῦτα φίλα ἤκουσα κατηλέησα τούτους 53r
(πραΰνουσι γὰρ τὸν θυμὸν ὑποπίπτοντες λόγοι)
καὶ μειδιάσας πρὸς αὐτὸν μετ' εἰρωνείας ἔφην:
Φιλοπαππού, ἐξύπνησας καὶ ὁράματα βλέπεις·   E1298
ἀλλ' ἐπεὶ εἰς κατάνυξιν μετέστρεψας τὸ γῆρας,
285 ἀνάστα, λάβε τοὺς σὺν σοί, ἄπελθε ὅπου βούλει,
οἰκείους ἔχων ὀφθαλμοὺς μάρτυρας τοῦ πραχθέντος,
καὶ οὓς ζητεῖτε πίστευσον νὰ λείψουν ἐκ τὸ ἀδνούμιν.
Ἄρχειν δὲ οὐκ ἐφίεμαι ἀλλὰ μόνος διάγειν,   E1299
ἐπειδὴ καὶ μονογενὴς πέφυκα τοῖς γονεῦσιν·   E1299
290 ὑμῖν δὲ ἄρχειν ἔξεστι καὶ συνεργεῖν ἀλλήλοις
ἐφ' οἷς ἔχετε δυνατόν, ποιεῖσθαι καὶ τὰ κούρση·
καὶ εἰ πολλάκις θέλετε πάλιν με πολεμῆσαι,
ἄλλους ἀνθολογήσατε ἐκ νέου ἀπελάτας
τοὺς μὴ εἰδότας πεῖραν μου μηδὲ γινώσκοντάς με·   E1310
295 ὅσοι γὰρ οἶδαν πεῖραν μου, ὑμῖν οὐ συνεργήσουν.'
Καὶ ἐχάρη ὁ Φιλοπαππούς δεξάμενος τὴν λῦσιν
καὶ ἐφώνει τοῖς μετ' αὐτοῦ λύτρωσιν ἐκμηνύων·
οὐδεὶς γὰρ τούτων ἤλπιζε ζωῆς ἀξιωθῆναι
ἀλλ' εἶχον ἤδη τὰς ψυχὰς πρὸς πύλας τοῦ θανάτου
300 καὶ ὡς ἤκουσαν τῆς φωνῆς, ἀνελάμβανον ταύτας.
Καὶ τὸ στόμα διήνοιγον πλεῖστα εὐχαριστοῦντες,
Ὄντως εἴδομεν,' <λέγοντες,> ἔργα νικῶντα φήμην

---

275 Τὸν Θεὸν G: Μὰ τὸν Θεὸν Legrand
283 βλέπεις G in text: λέγεις G in margin
295 ὅσοι γὰρ οἶδαν Trapp: εἶδον γὰρ ὅσοι G
302 λέγοντες added by Legrand

Striking corpses is for the feeble.'
270   He indicated his submission by gestures,
for he was incapable of speaking, overwhelmed by fear.
Leaving him there, I turned back
and saw Philopappous coming to himself,
shaking his head and saying this:
275 'By God who made the heaven and the whole earth,
who adorned you with every grace,
abandon the battle and make peace,
and we shall be your servants, if you give the command,
following your orders and working without respite.'
280   When I heard these friendly offers,
I took pity on them (for submissive words diminish anger),
and smiling at him I said with irony:
'Philopappous, you have woken up and you are still seeing visions.
But since you have brought your old age to contrition,
285 stand up, take your companions, go where you wish,
with your own eyes as witnesses of what has been done,
and be certain that those you are looking for will be absent from the
        muster.
I do not aspire to rule but to spend my time on my own,
since I am the only child born to my parents.
290 It is for you to rule and to work with each other
where you can, and to make raids.
And if you should ever wish to fight me again,
collect up a fresh group of guerrillas
who have had no experience of me and do not know me;
295 for those who do will not work with you.'
       Philopappous was happy to accept his release
and shouted to his companions to announce their deliverance,
for none of them had hoped to be allowed to live:
they had already left their souls at the portals of death
300 but as soon as they heard the shout, they summoned their souls back.
They opened their mouths to give hearty thanks,
saying: 'Truly we have seen deeds which are beyond praise

289–91 Key lines for the poem's view of the different roles of Digenis and the guerrillas.
His lonely heroic position outside society is again stressed, in some way confirmed by his
status as an only child. More surprising is the institutionalised role given to his
opponents, who have similar powers and responsibilities to the Roman *miles limitaneus*
and the Byzantine ἀκρίτης (see Introduction, pp. xxxii–xxxiii). Digenis' chrysobull from
the emperor seems to have been forgotten.

καὶ τὴν σὴν ὑπεράνθρωπον μεγίστην εὐσπλαγχνίαν,
ἣν οὐδεὶς ὑπεδείξατο ἐν τῷ παρόντι βίῳ·
305 καὶ ἀντιδῴη σοι Θεὸς ἀντάξια τῆς γνώμης 54r
μείζονα τὰ χαρίσματα καὶ ζῆν μετὰ συμβίου
εἰς ἀπεράντους χρόνους τε τερπόμενοι ἀλλήλοις.'
    Εἶτα τὴν πολυώραιαν λαβὼν ἐν ταῖς ἀγκάλαις,
πόρρωθεν ἐκαθέσθημεν ὑποκάτω εἰς δένδρον,
310 οὐρανοῦ μέσον ἥλιος ἀπάρτι διατρέχων.
    Ἐκεῖνοι δὲ συνήχθησαν οἱ τρεῖς εἰς ἕνα τόπον   E1317
καὶ θαυμάζοντες ἔλεγον οἱ δύο πρὸς ἀλληλους
νεωτέρας οἱ ἄγοντες ἡλικίας καὶ φρένας:
'Ὄντως λίαν τὸ ὁραθὲν παράδοξον καὶ ξένον,
315 ἄνθρωπος ἄοπλος, πεζός, ῥάβδον κατέχων μόνην
ἡμᾶς τοὺς ἐν τοῖς ἄρμασι καλῶς καθωπλισμένους,
τοὺς μυριάδας τρέψαντας καὶ πόλεις κατασχόντας,
καθολικῶς ἐνίκησεν ὥσπερ τινὰς ἀπείρους
καὶ αἰσχύνης ἐνέπλησε καὶ δειλίας καὶ φόβου.
320 Βέβαιον γόης πέφυκεν ἢ στοιχεῖον τοῦ τόπου,
ἐπεὶ αὐτὸς ἀντ' οὐδενὸς ἡγεῖτο τὰς σπαθέας
καὶ ἀνυπόστατον θυμὸν εἶχεν ἐπὶ τὴν ῥάβδον.
Εἰ γὰρ ὑπῆρχεν ἄνθρωπος ὥσπερ οἱ ἐκ τοῦ κόσμου,
εἶχεν ἂν σῶμα καὶ ψυχήν, θάνατον ἐδεδοίκει
325 καὶ οὐ μὴ ὥσπερ ἄσαρκος ξίφεσι κατετόλμα·
ἀλλὰ στοιχεῖον ἐκ παντὸς ἐτύγχανε τοῦ τόπου
καὶ φαντασία μεθ' ἡμῶν τὸν πόλεμον συνῆψε.
Ἴδετε καὶ τὸ ἄπειρον κάλλος τῆς φαινομένης
τηλαυγέστερον πέμπον τι ἡλιακῶν ἀκτίνων,
330 καὶ ὥσπερ στήλη ἔμψυχος ἡμῖν νομιζομένη.'
    Ταῦτα καὶ τούτοις ὅμοια λέγοντες ἀσυνέτως,
ὁ γέρων ὁ Φιλοπαππούς γηραιὸν ἔφη λόγον·
'Ταῦτα πάντα, ὦ τέκνα μου, εἰσὶ παραμυθίαι,
περιγραφαὶ ἀτυχιῶν, ψυχῶν παρηγορίαι·
335 ἐγὼ δὲ εἶδον ἀληθῶς δοκιμώτατον ἄνδρα
τοῖς τοῦ Χριστοῦ χαρίσμασι πᾶσι πεπλουτισμένον·

---

308 πολυώραιαν Legrand: πολυωραίαν G
314 παράδοξον καὶ Trapp: καὶ παράδοξον G
324 θάνατον Legrand: θανάτου G
327 φαντασία G (Politis, 1973, 349): φαντασίᾳ Legrand
329 πέμπον τι G: λάμπον τε Trapp

and your great and superhuman compassion,
which no one has demonstrated in this present life.
305 And may God grant you in return greater favours
worthy of your reputation and that you may live with your spouse
for endless years, delighting in each other.'
    Then, taking the very beautiful girl in my arms,
we sat beneath a tree some distance away,
310 the sun now just reaching the middle of the sky.
    The three of them gathered in one spot
and in amazement the two said to each other
who were younger in age and sense:
'That sight really was completely strange and unexpected:
315 an unarmed man, on foot, using only a stick,
has overcome us, though we were properly armed with our weapons,
we who have routed thousands and captured cities.
He soundly defeated us as if we were novices
and he has filled us with shame and cowardice and fear.
320 Surely he must be a magician or else the spirit of this place,
since he thought nothing of our sword-thrusts
and put irresistible force into his stick.
For if he were a man like those of this world,
he would have a body and soul; he would fear death
325 and would not dare fight against swords as though he had no flesh to
    wound.
It is certain he was the spirit of this place,
and it was a vision that fought with us.
Look at the boundless beauty of the woman who appeared,
who sends out rays brighter than the sun's
330 and seems to us like a statue brought to life.'
    While they were making these and other such senseless excuses,
old Philopappous made an old man's comment:
'All that, my children, is mere consolation,
a story of bad luck, comfort for your souls.
335 I have truly seen a most experienced man,
endowed with every grace from Christ;

---

330 'statue brought to life': the phrases 'living statue' or 'living picture' (cf. G6.413)
were terms of artistic criticism particularly in vogue in eleventh- and twelfth-century
Byzantium (*Alexiad* 3.4, Manganeios Prodromos, 20.350; cf. Belting, 1990, 292–303).
Digenis' responses also reflect the Byzantine assumption that unexplained phenomena,
particularly antique statuary, are emanations of the spirit world (Cameron/Herrin, 1984,
31–4).

κάλλος, ἀνδρείαν, φρόνησιν καὶ πολλὴν εὐτολμίαν
ἔχει καὶ δρόμον ἄπειρον τῶν ἀγαθῶν προσθήκην.
Ἡμῖν δὲ τοῦτο γέγονε μόνον παρηγορία
340 ὅτι οὐκ εὑρέθησάν τινες εἰς θέαν τοῦ πολέμου·
ὄνομα δὲ ὃ εἴχομεν τὸ τῆς ἀνδρείας μέγα,   E1338
τοῦτο νῦν ἀπωλέσαμεν ὑφ' ἑνὸς ἡττηθέντες.
Ἀλλ' εἴπερ θέλετε βουλήν, ὦ ἡμέτερα τέκνα,
μηδαμῶς ἀμελήσωμεν τὴν ὕβριν ἐκδικῆσαι,
345 ἀλλὰ παντοίους σπεύσωμεν ἐφευρεῖν τοὺς οἰκείους·
εἰ γὰρ καὶ ἐκαυχήσατο, ἀλλ' οὐ πάντας ἀνεῖλε   E1345
καὶ εἰ θελήσει ὁ Θεὸς καὶ περισυσταθοῦμεν
ἵνα του ἐπιπέσωμεν ἐν νυκτὶ ἀδοκήτως,
καὶ εἰ κατάσχωμεν αὐτόν, ἀφαιρεθῇ ὁ πόνος,
350 ὃν εἰς ψυχὰς κατέσπειρε τὰς ἡμῶν ὁ γεννάδας.
Καὶ ἡ κόρη εἰς ὄνομα σόν, Ἰωαννάκη, ἔσται·
ῥηθῆναι δὲ ἀμήχανον τὸ κάλλος της εἰκάζω
καὶ ἀληθῶς οὐδέποτε τοιοῦτον ἐν ἀνθρώποις
κάλλος τις ἐθεάσατο, ὥσπερ ὑπολαμβάνω.
355 Καὶ γὰρ πεντηκοστὸν <ἐγὼ> δεύτερον ἔτος ἄγω,
πλείστας πόλεις διέδραμον χώρας τε οὐκ ὀλίγας,
ἀλλ' ἡττήθησαν ἅπασαι, οἷα χορὸς ἀστέρων,
ὁπηνίκα ὁ ἥλιος τὰς ἀκτῖνας ἐκτείνει. 55r
Ἀλλὰ θάρσει, παγκάλλιστε, σοῦ τοῦ λοιποῦ ὑπάρχει.'
360   Ταῦτα ὁ γέρων εἰρηκὼς καλῶς ἔδοξε λέγειν·
καὶ ἀνῆλθον εἰς τὸν φανὸν τὴν σύναξιν ποιοῦντες,
τῇ δὲ νυκτὶ ἐπὶ πολὺ τὸν πυρσὸν δᾳδουχοῦντες,
καὶ τὸ παράπαν οὐδὲ εἷς παρῆν τῶν δοκουμένων.
Οἱ δὲ περὶ Φιλοπαπποῦν λέγειν ἄρχονται τάδε·
365 'Τί, γέρον ἀνδρικώτατε, κόπους ἡμῖν παρέχεις;
Οὐχὶ πιστεύων εἴληφας τὰς ἡμῶν εὐτολμίας,
ἐξ ὧν οἶδας ἀριστειῶν καὶ μεγίστων ἐπάθλων
τῶν τελεσθέντων παρ' ἡμῶν ἐν κραταιοῖς πολέμοις;
Οὐ πολλάκις ἐθαύμασας ἡμᾶς ὡς ἀηττήτους,

---

345 παντοίους σπεύσωμεν G: φανοὺς ποιήσωμεν Tsopanakis, 1960, 87, cf. Z3208
355 ἐγὼ added by Legrand
359 ὑπάρχει G as corrected: ὑπάρξει G before correction
363 δοκουμένων G in margin: φαινομένων G in text

he has beauty, bravery, good sense and great daring,
and also boundless speed, an addition to his virtues.
Our only comfort is
340 that no one was around to see the battle.
The great reputation that we had for bravery
we have now lost after being defeated by one man.
But if you want advice, my children,
let us certainly not neglect avenging this insult:
345 let us hurry to find all our supporters of every kind.
For even if he was boasting, he still has not killed everyone,
and, if God is willing and we get ourselves together
to attack him by night unexpectedly,
and if we capture him, then the pain will be removed
350 which the noble youth has sown in our souls.
And the girl will be designated yours, Ioannakis;
it is impossible, I consider, to describe her beauty,
and truly no one has ever seen
such beauty among mankind, as I judge.
355 For I am now in my fifty-second year,
I have visited very many cities and not a few countries,
but all the women I have seen are surpassed by her, like a group of
      stars
when the sun sends out its rays.
But cheer up, handsome Ioannakis, she is yours from now on.'
360   What the old man said seemed very good,
and they went off to the beacon to hold a rally;
they kept flares blazing for most of the night
but not even one of those they expected turned up.
      Philopappous' companions began to speak thus:
365 'Why, bravest of old men, are you making work for us?
Have you not had faith in our bravery,
from your knowledge of the mighty deeds and very great achievements
we have performed in hard-fought battles?
Have you not often admired us because we were undefeated,

356–57 The comparisons in beauty are not explicit in the Greek: syntactically it seems
that the comparison is made between the girl and the cities and countries Philopappous
has seen.
361 At E1343–8 the guerrillas' beacons burn day and night, though only smoke is
mentioned; on beacon technology, see Pattenden, 1983, especially 270.
364–798 and E1350–605 Digenis' encounter with the warrior-maiden Maximou would
have been part of *Digenis.

370 τὰς παραδόξους καθορῶν ἀεὶ ἀνδραγαθίας;
Καὶ παρ' αὐτοῦ ἡττήθημεν ὡς ἄπειροι πολέμου·
περὶ ἐκείνων ἀπιστεῖς μὴ παρ' αὐτοῦ κτανθῆναι;
'Αλλ' εἰ κελεύεις, πείσθητι τῇ βουλῇ τῶν σῶν τέκνων,
καταλείψωμεν τοὺς πολλοὺς καὶ ἀνονήτους μόχθους
375 καὶ ἄπελθε πρὸς Μαξιμοῦν τὴν ἡμῶν συγγενίδα,
καὶ παρακάλεσον αὐτὴν ἡμῖν τοῦ συνεργῆσαι,
λαὸν γὰρ ἔχει ἐκλεκτὸν ὡς καὶ αὐτὸς γινώσκεις·   E1354
πλὴν τὰ συμβάντα πρὸς αὐτὴν μηδαμῶς ἀναγγείλῃς,
εἰ γὰρ ἐν γνώσει γένηται, οὐ πεισθῇ συνελθεῖν σοι·
380 ἀλλ' ὡς ἐχέφρων, νουνεχεῖς ποίησον ἀποκρίσεις
ὅπως ἑλκύσῃς εἰς βουλὴν τὴν ἡμετέραν ταύτην·
καὶ ἐὰν τοῦτο γένηται ἐξόμεθα τὸ νῖκος,
ἡμεῖς δὲ ἐνωθοῦμεν σοι, τὸν πυρσὸν ὅταν δείξῃς.'
Καὶ ἤρεσεν ἡ συμβουλὴ τῷ γέροντι ἀσμένως· 55v
385 εὐθὺς ἐφ' ἵππου ἐπιβὰς πρὸς Μαξιμοῦν ἀπῆλθε.   E1357
Αὕτη δὲ ἦν ἀπόγονος γυναικῶν Ἀμαζόνων,
ἃς βασιλεὺς Ἀλέξανδρος ἤγαγεν ἐκ Βραχμάνων·
εἶχε δὲ τὴν ἐνέργειαν μεγίστην ἐκ προγόνων
βίον ἀεὶ τὸν πόλεμον καὶ τέρψιν ἡγουμένη.
390 Πρὸς ταύτην ὁ Φιλοπαππποῦς γεγονώς, ὡς ἐρρέθη,
προσηνῶς κατησπάζετο· 'Πῶς ἔχεις,' ἐπερώτα,
τῆς δὲ εἰπούσης: 'Ζῶ καλῶς, τῇ τοῦ Θεοῦ προνοίᾳ·
ἀλλὰ σύ, ὦ πανάριστε, πῶς μετὰ τέκνων ἔχεις;
Χάριν δὲ τίνος πρὸς ἡμᾶς τούτων χωρὶς ἐπῆλθες;'
395 Αὖθις ὁ γέρων ἔφησε τάδε, οὐκ ἀληθεύων:
'Οἱ μὲν παῖδες, κυρία μου, Κίνναμος καὶ Ἰωαννάκης,
καλῶς ἔχοντες σὺν Θεῷ ἀπῆλθον εἰς τὰς βίγλας
τοὺς ἀτάκτους ὁλοσχερῶς σπεύδοντες ἀφανίσαι.
Τῶνδε κἀγὼ ἀπολυθεὶς ἀναπαύσεως χάριν
400 ἢ μᾶλλον οἰκονομικῶς Θεοῦ τῇ εὐδοκίᾳ

377 αὐτὸς Legrand: αὐτὴ G
380 νουνεχεῖς Eideneier, 1970, 314: νουνεχής G
387 ἃς Legrand: ἦν G Βραχμάνων Legrand: Βραγμάνων G
389 βίον Mavrogordato: βίου G

370 seeing our constant and unexpected brave deeds?
And yet we have been defeated by him, as if we were novices.
Do you have any doubt that those others were killed by him?
But, if you so please, follow your children's advice:
let us abandon all these useless efforts.
375 You should go off to Maximou, our kinswoman,
and ask her to join with us,
for she has a picked troop, as you yourself know.
Only be certain not to tell her what has happened,
for if she does find out, she won't agree to come with you.
380 But, sensible as you are, make your approaches reasonable,
so that you win her over to this plan of ours.
And if this happens, victory will be ours
and we shall join you when you show the beacon.'
     This advice pleased the old man greatly.
385 Mounting his horse at once, he went off to Maximou.
She was a descendant of the Amazon women
whom the emperor Alexander had brought from among the
     Brahmans.
She had inherited the greatest vigour from her ancestors
and always considered battle to be her life and delight.
390 When Philopappous reached her, as had been agreed,
he embraced her warmly and asked: 'How are you?'
and she replied: 'I am well, through God's providence.
But, best of men, how are you and your children?
For what reason have you come to see me without them?'
395   The old man said this in reply, not telling the truth:
'The boys, my lady, Kinnamos and Ioannakis,
are well, with God's help, and they have gone to the guard-posts,
since they are keen to get rid of the rebels completely.
I took leave of them to take a rest,
400 or rather, by God's benevolent dispensation,

378–80 Philopappous is asked to hide the truth diplomatically, not so much the shame of their recent defeat but also the fact that Digenis fights alone, a fact which will discourage Maximou from coming or at least from bringing her full forces.
385 On Maximou as an Amazon, see Grégoire, 1936; Moennig, 1993; (= Penthesileia) Trapp, 1972, 640; Dyck, 1987, 361.
393 Alexiou (1979, 64–5) considers that G's πανάριστε conceals an earthy phrase such as E's γεράκιν μου μουτάτον (E1361: 'moulting hawk'), implying that Philopappous is balding.
397–8 As at G6.288–91 above, the guerrillas seem to have a peacekeeping role against an even less established group, the rebels (Pertusi, 1971, 53).

εἰς τοῦ καλοῦ ἀνεύρεσιν καὶ ἀτιμήτου δώρου,
ὡς γὰρ οὐκ ἦν μοι πώποτε τέλεον ἠρεμῆσαι,
μετὰ τὴν ὑποχώρησιν τῶν ἐμῶν παμφιλτάτων
μόνος τοῦ ἵππου ἐπιβὰς ἀνέτρεχον τὰς ὄχθας
405 καὶ τοὺς πόρους ἐσκόπευον ἰδεῖν τοὺς ἐναντίους·
ὡς δὲ ἦλθον ἐν τῇ ὁδῷ τῇ καλουμένῃ Τρώσει,
πρὸς μέρος τὸ εὐώνυμον ἐν τῷ δασεῖ λειμῶνι
θηράματι ἐνέτυχον χρυσοῦ τιμιωτέρῳ,
κόρῃ, οἵαν οὐδέποτε οἱ ὀφθαλμοί μου εἶδον.
410 Ἐν τῷ κάλλει ἀμήχανον τὴν φαιδρότητα εἶχεν,
ἐξ ὀφθαλμῶν ἀπόρρητον ἀνέπεμπε τὴν χάριν, 56r
ἔρνος ὥσπερ εὐθέατον τὴν ἡλικίαν ἔχων
καὶ θέλγει πάντων τὰς ψυχάς, εἰκὼν καθάπερ ἔμπνους.
Ἔστι δέ, ὡς ἀνέμαθον, τοῦ Δουκὸς ἡ θυγάτηρ,
415 ἦν λόγῳ οἰκειούμεθα τοῦ Χρυσοϊωαννάκη·   E1373
ἕτερος δὲ προέλαβεν, ἀγνοῶ ποίῳ τρόπῳ,
καὶ μετ' αὐτῆς εὐφραίνετο νυνὶ ἐν τῷ λειμῶνι.
Καὶ εἴπερ ὅλως συγγενοῦς κήδεσαι τοῦ φιλτάτου,
ὑπὲρ αὐτοῦ κοπίασον, δέξαι καὶ ἀγρυπνίαν,
420 τὴν ἀγάπην βεβαίωσον, κυρία μου, ἐξ ἔργων·
ὁ γὰρ προθύμως κοινωνῶν θλίψεσι τῶν φιλτάτων,
ἐκεῖνος φίλος ἀληθὴς καὶ συγγενὴς ὑπάρχει.'
Γέρων δὲ ὁ Φιλοπαπποῦς τοιαῦτά τε λαλήσας
κατὰ πάντα πειθήνιον τὴν Μαξιμοῦν ποιεῖται·
425 καὶ γὰρ εὐεξαπάτητον φρόνημα γυναικεῖον.
Οὐδαμῶς γὰρ ἠρεύνησε τίς ὁ τὴν κόρην ἔχων,
ἀλλ' αὐτίκα περιχαρῶς καλεῖ τὸν Μελιμίτζην,
ὃν εἶχε πρῶτον ἄγουρον ἐξάρχοντα τῶν ἄλλων.
Καὶ μειδιῶσα πρὸς αὐτὸν περιχαρῶς ἐξεῖπεν:
430 '«Ἔμαθες ὡς ὁ θαυμαστὸς Φιλοπαπποῦς ὁ γέρων   E1400
κυνῆγιν εὗρε κάλλιστον ἀρτίως εἰς τὰς ἄκρας   E1400
καὶ ἀξιοῖ μεθ' ἑαυτοῦ καὶ ἡμᾶς πορευθῆναι
τῆς τε χαρᾶς μεταλαβεῖν καὶ τρυφῆς τῆς ἐντεῦθεν;
Ἀλλὰ τάχιον ἄπελθε, εὑρὲ τοὺς ἀπελάτας
435 καὶ ἀπὸ πάντων <ἑκατὸν> ἔκλεξαι τοὺς δοκίμους,   E1403
ἵππους τε ἔχοντας καλούς, ὀχυρώτατα ὅπλα,   E1404
ἵνα ᾧπερ ἐντύχωμεν, κατάσχωμεν ῥᾳδίως.' 56v

416 ἀγνοῶ Legrand: ἀγνοῶν G
417 εὐφραίνετο Kalonaros, cf. Z3292: ἐφαίνετο G
435 ἑκατὸν added by Legrand

to seek out a fair and priceless gift,
since it has never been possible for me to be completely still.
After the departure of my beloved boys,
I mounted my horse and travelled on my own along the river banks
405 and kept watch on the fords to see our opponents.
When I was going along the road called Trosis,
on the left-hand part in the lush meadow
I chanced upon a prey more precious than gold,
a girl such as my eyes had never seen before.
410 In her beauty she had an inconceivable brilliance,
she radiated ineffable grace from her eyes,
her appearance was that of a lovely young plant
and she enchants the souls of all, like a breathing picture.
She is, as I have learnt, the daughter of Doukas,
415 and we claim her for our own golden Ioannakis.
But some one else had got in first, I don't know how,
and was enjoying himself with her at that time in the meadow.
And if you have any concern at all for your dearest kinsman,
take pains on his behalf, accept sleepless nights,
420 demonstrate your love, my lady, in your actions.
For he who willingly makes his dearest ones' woes his own
is a true friend and kinsman.'
      As old Philopappous talked on in this way,
he won Maximou over completely,
425 for a woman's mind is very liable to be deceived.
She never asked who it was who had the girl,
but immediately sent a cheerful summons to Melimitzis,
whom she had as her chief youngster in charge of the others.
And she smiled at him and said cheerfully:
430 'Have you learnt that marvellous old Philopappous
has just now found the loveliest prey on the frontiers,
and is asking us to go off with him
to share in the pleasure and delight there?
But come quickly, find the guerrillas
435 and choose from among them all a hundred experienced men
with fine horses and the sturdiest weapons,
so that we can easily capture anyone we come across.'

---

408 The girl is the ultimate hunting prize, as is even more explicitly expressed in E. at
E809 and 1383 (Ricks, 1989b).

Ὁ δὲ πρόσταγμα μὴ τολμῶν δεσποίνης ἀθετῆσαι,
ἐν τῇ βίγλᾳ γενόμενος ἐν ταύτῃ τῇ ἑσπέρᾳ
440 καὶ ἐπιδείξας τὸν πυρσὸν καὶ πλείστους συναθροίσας
πρὸς χιλίων ἐπέκεινα δοκίμους στρατιώτας
ἐκ τούτων ἀπεχώρισεν ἑκατὸν τοὺς γενναίους
καὶ τούτους συμπαραλαβὼν πρὸς τὴν κυρίαν ἦλθεν.
Ἡ δὲ τὰς χρείας ἅπασας εἰκότως ἐπιδοῦσα
445 ἐνετείλατο τῇ ἑξῆς γενέσθαι ἐν τοῖς ὅπλοις·
μεθ᾽ ὧν ὥρμησε κατ᾽ ἐμοῦ ζήλῳ πολλῷ πλησθεῖσα,
τοῦ στρατοῦ προηγούμενος Φιλοπαπποῦς ἐν πόθῳ.
Ἐν δὲ τῷ ἀναστήματι γενόμενοι τοῦ λόφου,
ὁ γηραιὸς τὸ σύνθημα τοῖς φίλοις προσμηνύει,
450 πυρσὸν ἐξῆπτε τῇ νυκτὶ τοῖς περὶ Ἰωαννάκην
καὶ μεθ᾽ ἡμέρας καὶ αὐτοὶ ἐν τῷ στρατῷ παρῆσαν
ἀσμένως πρὸς τῆς Μαξιμοῦς λίαν ἀποδεχθέντες·
ἑτοίμως γὰρ ὡς ἀγχιστὰς τούτους καὶ ὡς συμμάχους
ἐδέξατο ἡ Μαξιμοῦ ὁλοσχερῶς τερφθεῖσα.
455   Πρὸς δὲ ὄχθας τοῦ ποταμοῦ πλησιάσαντες ἤδη,
ἄρχεται τοῦ δημηγορεῖν Φιλοπαπποῦς τοιάδε·
"Ὁ μὲν τόπος, κυρία μου καὶ ὑμεῖς στρατιῶται,
ὑπάρχει δυσκολώτατος ἐν ᾧ τὴν κόρην εὗρον·
καὶ μὴ πάντες ἀπέλθωμεν ὡς κρότον ἐμποιοῦντες,
460 διάγνωσιν παρέχοντες τῷ φυλάττοντι ταύτην,
καὶ πρὶν ἢ πλησιάσωμεν, δύνωσιν ἐν τῷ ἄλσει
καὶ οὐδ᾽ ὅλως ἰσχύσωμεν τὸ θήραμα κρατῆσαι
καὶ γένηται διακενῆς πάντων ἡμῶν ὁ κόπος.
Ἀλλ᾽ εἰ δοκεῖ, προλάβωμεν δύο ἢ καὶ τρεῖς μόνοι
465 λάθρα ἐπισκοπεύοντες ποῦ ἡ κόρη ὑπάρχει 57r
καὶ οἱ μὲν δύο μείνωμεν ταύτην ἐπιτηροῦντες,
ὁ δέ γε τρίτος πρὸς ὑμᾶς ἐπανελθὼν δηλώσει
καὶ σὺν αὐτῷ ἐλεύσεσθε μηδαμῶς πλανηθέντες.᾽
Πρὸς δὲ ταῦτα ἡ Μαξιμοῦ τῷ γέροντι ἀντέφη·
470 "Ὦ γέρον τε καὶ νουνεχές, σοὶ τὴν ἀρχὴν πιστεύω·
πράττε λοιπὸν ὡς βούλεσαι, πάντων σοι πειθομένων.᾽
Καὶ εὐθὺς ὁ Φιλοπαπποῦς λαβὼν τὸν Μελιμίτζην
καὶ τὸν Κίνναμον σὺν αὐτῷ τὸν ποταμὸν διῆλθε
τοῖς ἄλλοις ἐντειλάμενος προσκαρτερεῖν ἐκεῖσε,

444 ἅπασας Legrand: ἀπάσας G
453 ἑτοίμως Trapp: ἑτοίμους G ἐντίμως Tsopanakis, 1960, 88

Melimitzis, not daring to countermand his lady's order,
went to the guard-post that evening,
440 and when he had displayed the beacon and collected very many
experienced soldiers, more than a thousand,
he selected out from them one hundred noble men
and, bringing them along with him, returned to the lady.
She distributed all the necessary supplies as was appropriate
445 and instructed them to be under arms the next day.
With these she set off against me, filled with great vigour,
while Philopappous enthusiastically led the expedition.
When they were at the crest of the hill,
the old man told his friends of the agreed signal
450 and lit a beacon at night for Ioannakis and his men.
And at day-break they too joined the expedition
and were accepted gladly by Maximou,
for Maximou welcomed them readily as relatives and as allies,
and was completely delighted.
455 When they had already drawn near the banks of the river,
Philopappous began to harangue them thus:
'The place, my lady and you soldiers,
in which I found the girl is very difficult,
and we must not all go forward, since we will make a noise
460 and give the man who is guarding her warning,
so that they can slip off into the wood before we get near
and we shall have no chance of catching our prey
and all our effort will become useless.
But, if you like, let two or three of us go ahead alone
465 to spy out secretly where the girl is,
then let two stay observing her
while the third returns to you and reports,
and you will come with him quickly without losing your way.'
Maximou said to the old man in reply to this,
470 'You who are old and shrewd, I entrust the command to you;
do what you want then and all of us will obey you.'
Philopappous immediately took Melimitzis
and Kinnamos with him and crossed the river,
instructing the others to wait on the other side

438–45 While this may be an exotic pattern created for the Amazon warrior, the
process of selecting the best men bears some resemblance to tenth-century advice on
managing muster rolls (Dennis, 1985, 320–2).

475 ἄχρις ἂν μήνυμα αὐτοῖς ἐκ τούτων ἐπανέλθῃ.
     Ἐμοὶ δὲ τότε ἔτυχε διάγειν ἐν τῇ βίγλᾳ,
     ἵππον κρατῶν τοῦ χαλινοῦ καθέζεσθαι ἐν πέτρᾳ
     καὶ τούτων <τε> διὰ παντὸς τὴν ἔλευσιν ἐτήρουν.
     Ἰδών με ὁ Φιλοπαπποῦς λέγει τὸν Μελιμίτζην: E1430
480 "Ὁρᾷς ἐκεῖνον' (τῇ χειρὶ ἐμὲ ὑποδεικνύων)
     'τὸν ἐν πέτρᾳ καθήμενον ἐπὶ τὴν ἀκρωρείαν;
     Αὐτὸς ὑπάρχει, γίνωσκε, ὁ τὴν κόρην κατέχων·
     μὴ τοίνυν ἐλευσώμεθα κατὰ πρόσωπον τούτου,
     ἀλλὰ ἃς ἐρευνήσωμεν ὅπου τὴν κόρην ἔχει   E1432
485 καὶ εἶθ' οὕτως γνωρίσομεν τῷ λαῷ, ὡς ἐρρέθη.
     Εἰ γὰρ καὶ μόνος πέφυκεν, πλὴν καλὸς εἶναι πάντως·
     οἶδα γὰρ οἷος καὶ αὐτὸς ὑπάρχει ἐν ἀνδρείᾳ,
     καὶ παραινῶ μηδὲ ποσῶς μόνοι αὐτῷ φανῆναι.'
     Ὡσαύτως καὶ ὁ Κίνναμος ἐπαινῶν τὰ λεχθέντα,
490 ἀλλ' οὐδαμῶς συνέθετο τούτοις ὁ Μελιμίτζης,
     εἰρηκὼς ὡς: 'Οὐ δύναμαι νῦν ὑμᾶς ἐπιγνῶναι·
     εἰς χιλίους οὐδέποτε συνεργοῦ ἐδεήθην, 57v
     καὶ εἰς τὸν ἕνα λέγετε τὸν λαὸν περιμένειν;   E1437
     Πάντως εἰ τοῦτο ἀκουσθῇ πρὸς τῆς ἐμῆς κυρίας
495 καταμεμφθῶ ὡς ἄνανδρος τὸν ἕνα δειλιάσας·
     καὶ ζῆν οὐκέτι βούλομαι, εἰ ἄτολμος ἀκούσω.'
     Οὕτως εἰπόντος κατ' ἐμοῦ ὅλῳ θυμῷ ἐκινήθη
     τὰς τοῦ γέροντος παρ' οὐδὲν θέμενος παραινέσεις·
     ἔστι γὰρ καὶ τὸ βάρβαρον δύσπιστον ἔθνος ἅπαν.
500 Τούτου ὡς εἶδον τὴν ὁρμήν, τοὺς δὲ ἐφεπομένους
     (καὶ αὐτοὶ γὰρ παρείποντο σκοπεύοντες τὸ μέλλον),
     τοῦ ἵππου μου ἐπέβαινον καὶ αὐτοῖς προσυπήντων.
     Ὡς δὲ ἔμπροσθεν ἤρχετο πάντων ὁ Μελιμίτζης,
     τὸ μὲν κοντάριν ἴθυνε δοῦναι μοι κονταρέαν·   E1445
505 τοῦτο δὲ τέχνῃ παρελθὼν ἐν τῷ με παρατρέχειν
     τῇ ῥάβδῳ τοῦτον ἔπληξα καὶ πρὸς γῆν κατηνέχθη·
     ἱστάμην δὲ ἐγὼ τηρῶν εἰ ἐγερθῆναι ἔχει.
     Καὶ ὡς ἐν τούτῳ μου τὸν νοῦν εἰς ὥραν ἠσχολούμην,
     λαθών με ὁ Φιλοπαπποῦς καὶ ἐλθὼν ἐκ πλαγίου   E1451
510 κονταρέαν ἐν τῷ μηρῷ τιτρώσκει μου τὸν ἵππον   E1452

475 αὐτοῖς Legrand: αὐτῆς G
478 τε added by Legrand
486 καλὸς εἶναι πάντως Legrand: καλὸν εἶναι πάντας G
489 ἐπαινῶν G: ἐπήνει Kalonaros
494 πρὸς Trapp: πρὸ G

475 until a message got back to them from the scouts.
    I happened at that time to be on guard,
    holding my horse by the rein and sitting on a rock,
    and I was all the time watching out for their coming.
    Catching sight of me, Philopappous said to Melimitzis:
480 'Do you see him' (pointing to me with his hand),
    'that man sitting on the rock on the ridge?
    That's the one, you must understand, who has the girl.
    Let us not advance to meet him face to face,
    but let us find out where he keeps the girl,
485 and then we shall pass the information to the troops, as was agreed.
    Although he is on his own, he is extremely tough,
    for I know the quality of this man's bravery,
    and my advice is not to appear before him on our own.'
    Kinnamos likewise praised what was said,
490 but Melimitzis in no way agreed with the proposal,
    saying: 'Now I can't support you.
    I've never needed an assistant against thousands,
    and you are telling me to wait for the army to fight against one man?
    If anything of this were reported to my lady,
495 I would be reproved for cowardice, for being afraid of one man;
    and I have no wish to carry on living if I am going to be called timid.'
    Having said this, he rushed against me with all his might,
    putting no weight at all on the old man's advice,
    for all barbarians are disbelieving heathen.
500 When I saw him attacking, and the others following
    (for they were accompanying him, watching what was going to
        happen),
    I mounted my horse and went out to meet them.
    As Melimitzis came up in front of all the rest,
    he aimed his spear to strike me with it.
505 Avoiding this skilfully as he ran past me,
    I struck him with my stick and he was knocked to the ground;
    I stood there to see if he would get up.
    While my mind was preoccupied with him for a moment,
    Philopappous slipped past me and came up beside me
510 and wounded my horse with a spear-thrust in the haunch

---

499 The moral comment makes Melimitzis a barbarian heathen: the implication may be
that Philopappous is not.

(ὑπῆρχον δὲ συνηρεφῆ καὶ θαμινὰ τὰ δένδρα),
τοῦ ἵππου δὲ πονέσαντος καὶ ταραχθέντος λίαν
ἐπιστραφεὶς τὸν γέροντα φευγόμενον κατεῖδον
καὶ ἐπεφώνησα αὐτῷ· 'Τί με ἀποδιδράσκεις;
515 Ἔκδεξαί με δὲ εἰς πρόσωπον, ἐὰν ᾖς στρατιώτης,
καὶ μὴ ὥσπερ κυνάριον λυσσῶν λάθρα με δάκης.'   E1460
Ὁ δὲ μᾶλλον σφοδρότερον τὸν δρασμὸν ἐποιεῖτο
καὶ διῆλθε τὸν ποταμὸν ἅμα σὺν τῷ Κιννάμῳ·
κἀγὼ ἄχρι τοῦ ὕδατος αὐτοῖς ἀκολουθήσας, 58r
520 ὡς εἶδον πέρα τὸν λαόν, πάντας καθωπλισμένους,
οὐκ ἔκρινα τοῦ ἀπελθεῖν πρὸς αὐτοὺς χωρὶς ὅπλων,
μάλιστα δ' ὅτι ὤκλαζεν ὁ ἵππος ἐν τῇ τρώσει.
Καὶ αὐτίκα ὑπέστρεψα πρὸς τὴν κόρην εὐθέως,
εἶτα λαβὼν τὰ ἄρματα, ἀλλάξας καὶ τὸν ἵππον
525 πρὸς τὴν ὡραίαν εἴρηκα· 'Δεῦρο, φῶς μου, ἐν τάχει,
ἵν' ὅπως σε ἐν τῇ κρυπτῇ τοῦ λόφου ἐπαγάγω·
κἀκεῖθεν βλέπε τοὺς ἐχθροὺς ἡμῶν ἀπολλυμένους
καὶ μάθε τίνα σοι ὁ Θεὸς ἐκδικητὴν παρέσχε,
καὶ τὸ πανάγιον αὐτοῦ κράτος καὶ νῦν δοξάσεις.'
530   Ἡ δὲ εὐθὺς ἐπέβηκεν ἐφ' ἵππῳ τῷ ἰδίῳ,
καὶ γὰρ τὴν ἔφοδον αὐτῆς προηυτρέπισα μάλα·
ὡς δὲ καὶ κατελάβομεν ἐν τῷ ῥηθέντι τόπῳ,
τὴν μὲν ἐν τῇ περιωπῇ ἀφέμενος τοῦ ὄρους,
ἐν ᾧ ἄντρον αὐτοφυὲς ὡς οἴκημα ὑπῆρχεν
535 ὑπὸ δένδρων κρυπτόμενον καὶ δυσεύρετον λίαν·
τοῦ ὁρᾶν μὲν τὰ πόρρωθεν πραττόμενα παρεῖχε
καὶ μηδὲ τὸ κρυπτόμενον παρά τινος ὁρᾶσθαι.
Ἐκεῖσε, ὡς δεδήλωται, τὴν κόρην κατακρύψας
καὶ παραγγείλας μηδαμῶς δειλιᾶν τὰ συμβάντα
540 μηδὲ μὴν ἐν ταῖς συμπλοκαῖς φωνῆσαι τὸ παράπαν –
'Ἵνα μὴ τούτοις γένηται ὁδηγὸς ἡ φωνή σου
καὶ ἐπανέλθωσι πρὸς σὲ ἐμοῦ ἀσχολουμένου
καὶ προφανὴς ὁ κίνδυνος ἐκ τούτου μοι ἐπέλθῃ' –
καὶ ὥρμησα πρὸς ποταμὸν τὸν λαὸν ἔνθα εἶδον,
545 καὶ τὰς ὄχθας ἀνέτρεχον ἵνα τὸν πόρον εὕρω.
    Καὶ θεωρῶ τὴν Μαξιμοῦν τῶν λοιπῶν χωρισθεῖσαν 58v
καὶ σὺν αὐτῇ τοὺς τέσσαρας μεγίστους ἀπελάτας,

520 εἶδον Legrand: εἶδε G
524 λαβὼν Kalonaros: βαλὼν G
526 κρυπτῇ Legrand: κρηπῇ G
537 τὸ G: perhaps τὸν

(the trees were shady and dense),
so that my horse was in pain and great distress;
I turned and I saw the old man fleeing,
and I shouted out to him: 'Why are you running away from me?
515 Confront me face to face, if you are a soldier,
and don't snap at me behind my back like a rabid puppy.'
     But he continued his flight more vigorously still
and crossed the river together with Kinnamos.
I followed them as far as the water;
520 when I saw the host on the other side, all in armour,
I resolved not to venture out against them without weapons,
especially as my horse was hobbling from its wound.
And at once I came straight back to the girl;
then, picking up my weapons and changing my horse,
525 I said to the beautiful one: 'Come quickly, my light,
so that I can take you to the hiding place in the hill;
from there watch our enemies being destroyed
and learn what avenger God has provided for you,
and from now on you will glorify His all-holy might.'
530   She immediately mounted her own horse,
for I had already prepared provisions for her;
when we came to the place I spoke about,
I left her at the vantage point on the mountain,
where there was a natural cave as a shelter,
535 hidden by trees and very hard to find,
which allowed a view of what was going on a long way off
and where what was concealed could not be seen by anyone.
Hiding the girl there as has been described,
and ordering her not to be in the least alarmed at what might happen
540 nor to make the slightest sound during the fighting –
'so that your voice should not guide them,
and they attack you while I am preoccupied
and clear danger come my way because of this' –
I rushed to the river where I had seen the army,
545 and I was running along the banks to find the ford.
     I saw Maximou separated from the rest
and with her the four greatest guerrillas,

541–3 Slippage into second-person direct speech within first-person narrative suggests
that the text, despite its learned features, is not fully controlled by conventions of written
discourse.
543 An example of androcentric heroic selfishness.

Φιλοπαπποῦν τὸν γέροντα, Κίνναμον καὶ Ἰωαννάκην,   E1243, 1499
καὶ τὸν δόκιμον Λέανδρον τὸν μέγαν ἐν ἀνδρείᾳ·   E1500
550 χαρζανιστοὶ κατήρχοντο τοῦ ποταμοῦ τὸ χεῖλος,   E1501
δύο ἔνθεν κἀκεῖθεν τε, ἡ Μαξιμοὺ δὲ μέσον,
ἐποχουμένη εἰς λευκὸν βοῦλχαν καθάπερ γάλα,
χαίτην ἔχων καὶ τὴν οὐράν, τὸν σγοῦρδον καὶ τὰ ὦτα,   E1487
ὄνυχάς τε τοὺς τέσσαρας κοκκίνους βεβαμμένους,   E1488
555 ἅπαν τὸ σελλοχάλινον χρυσῷ πεποικιλμένον·
τὸ λουρίκιν ἀπέστραπτε χρυσέας ῥίζας ἔχον.   E1491
Στραφεῖσα πρὸς τὸν γέροντα ἐπιμελῶς ἠρώτα: E1502
'Λέγε μοι, ὦ Φιλοπαπποῦ, τίς ὁ τὴν κόρην ἔχων;'
Ὁ δὲ φησίν: 'Οὗτός ἐστι,' κἀμὲ τῇ χειρὶ δείξας.
560 Ἡ δέ, 'Καὶ ποῦ οἱ σὺν αὐτῷ', ἤρετο, 'στρατιῶται;'
'Οὗτος,' φησί, 'κυρία <μου>, τῶν συνεργῶν οὐ δεῖται,
ἀλλ' εἰς τὴν ἄπειρον αὐτοῦ ἐπιθαρρῶν ἀνδρείαν
μόνος ὁδεύει πάντοτε, καύχημα τοῦτο ἔχων.'
Ἡ δέ, 'Ὦ τρισκατάρατε γέρον,' ἀνταπεκρίθη,
565 'καὶ διὰ ἕνα κόπους μοι καὶ τῷ λαῷ παρεῖχες,
πρὸς ὃν μόνη περάσασα, σὺν Θεῷ καυχωμένη,
ἀρῶ αὐτοῦ τὴν κεφαλὴν ὑμῶν μὴ δεηθεῖσα;'   E1524
Ταῦτα εἰποῦσα ἐν θυμῷ ὥρμησε τοῦ περάσαι.   E1528
Ἐγὼ δὲ λέγω πρὸς αὐτήν: 'Μαξιμοῦ, μὴ περάσῃς·   E1529–30
570 ἀνδράσι καὶ γὰρ πέφυκεν ἔρχεσθαι πρὸς γυναῖκας·   E1531
ἔλθω λοιπὸν ἐγὼ πρὸς σέ, ὡς τὸ δίκαιον ἔχει.'   E1533
Καὶ αὐτίκα τὸν ἵππον μου κεντήσας ταῖς περόναις
πρὸς τὸ ὕδωρ ἐξώρμησα ἀποτυχὼν τοῦ πόρου· 59r
ἦν δὲ πολὺς ὁ ποταμὸς καὶ ἔπλευσεν ὁ ἵππος·
575 ὕδατος τούτου ἔκχυσις ἄποθεν δὲ ὑπῆρχεν
βραχυτάτην ἐμφαίνουσα λίμνην συχνήν τε πόαν·
ἐν ᾗπερ στᾶσα ἀσφαλῶς λίαν εὐτρεπισμένη
ἡ Μαξιμοὺ τὴν προσβολὴν τὴν ἐμὴν ἐπετήρει·
οἱ δὲ συνόντες ἄλλοι μὲν ἔτρεχον πρὸς τὸν πόρον,
580 ἕτεροι δὲ ἐνήδρευον ἐγκρύμματα ποιοῦντες.
Ἐγὼ δὲ ὅταν ἔγνωκα εἰς γῆν πατεῖν τὸν ἵππον,
τρανὰ αὐτὸν ἠρέθιζον καὶ τὸ σπαθὶν ἑλκύσας
ὁλοψύχως πρὸς Μαξιμοῦν εὐτέχνως ἀπηρχόμην.
Ἡ δέ, ὡς προηυτρέπιστο, προσαπαντᾶν δραμοῦσα

550 χαρζανιστοὶ Politis, 1967, 31: χαρζανιστὶ G
552 λευκὸν βοῦλχαν Politis, 1967, 31: βουλχᾶν λευκὸν G
557 Στραφεῖσα Legrand: στραφεῖσα καὶ G
561 μου added by Legrand

old Philopappous, Kinnamos and Ioannakis
and the trusty Leandros, outstanding in bravery.
550 They were coming along the edge of the river lashing their horses,
two on each side and Maximou in the middle,
riding a horse white as milk,
with mane, tail, forelock and ears
and all four hoofs dyed red,
555 and all the saddle and reins decorated with gold;
her breastplate glittered with golden edging.
    She turned to the old man and asked him anxiously:
'Tell me, Philopappous, who is it who has the girl?'
And he said: 'That's the one,' and pointed to me with his hand.
560 But she asked: 'Where are the soldiers with him?'
'That man,' he said, 'my lady, needs no assistants
but, relying on his boundless courage,
he always journeys on his own and boasts of this.'
'You thrice-accursed old man,' she replied,
565 'was it because of one man that you have put me and my people to
    such trouble?
I shall cross over to get to him on my own, making my boast with
    God's help,
and shall remove his head, without need of you.'
    Saying this in her anger she hurried to make the crossing.
But I said to her: 'Maximou, don't cross over.
570 It is natural for men to come to women.
So let me come over to you, as is right.'
    And immediately, spurring on my horse,
I rushed to the water, missing the ford.
The river was high and the horse swam.
575 There was an overflow from this water some way up,
creating a very small lake and luxuriant grass;
there, standing safely and very well equipped,
Maximou observed my attack.
Of those with her, some ran to the ford,
580 others lay in wait, setting ambushes.
    But when I realised that my horse had touched bottom,
I roused him vigorously, and drawing my sword
I made for Maximou with all my heart and skill.
Since she was already well-prepared, she ran to meet me

549 Leandros' promotion to this group remains unexplained.

585 κονταρέαν μοι δέδωκεν ξυστὴν εἰς τὸ λουρίκιν·
καὶ μηδαμῶς ἀδικηθεὶς ἔκοψα τὸ κοντάριν.
Τινάξας δ' αὖθις τὸ σπαθὶν ταύτης μὲν ἐφεισάμην,
τοῦ δὲ βοῦλχα ἀποτεμὼν τὴν κεφαλὴν εὐθέως
<καὶ> τὸ μὲν πτῶμα χαλεπῶς ἐπὶ γῆν κατηνέχθη·
590 ἡ δὲ ἀναποδίσασα, τρόμῳ συνεχομένη,
προσπίπτουσα ἐφθέγγετο: '᾽Ω νέε, μὴ ἀποθάνω·
πεπλάνημαι γὰρ ὡς γυνὴ Φιλοπαππoῦ πεισθεῖσα.'
Καὶ ταύτης <μὲν> εὐλαβηθείς, εἰσακούων τοῖς λόγοις
κάλλος τε τὸ θαυμάσιον ὃ εἶχεν ἐλεήσας,
595 ἐκεῖ ταύτην ἀφέμενος πρὸς τοὺς λοιποὺς ἐξῆλθον.
῞Οπως τε πάντας ἴσχυσα αἰσχύνομαι τοῦ λέγειν,
ἵνα μὴ ὡς καυχώμενον λογίσησθέ με, φίλοι·
ὁ γὰρ ἐκδιηγούμενος ἰδίας ἀριστείας
κενόδοξος λογίζεται ὑπὸ τῶν ἀκουόντων.
600 Ἐγὼ δὲ οὐ καυχώμενος ταῦτα ὑμῖν ἐκφαίνω, 59v
οὔ, μὰ τὸν διδόντα ἰσχὺν καὶ γνῶσιν τοῖς ἀνθρώποις
(αὐτὸς γὰρ μόνος πάροχος τῶν ἀγαθῶν ὑπάρχει)·
διὰ τοῦτο ῥηθήσονται ὡς γεγόνασι πάντα,
συγγνώμην ὅπως παρ' ὑμῶν ἔξω τῶν ἀκουόντων.
605 Αὖθις καὶ γὰρ ὠλίσθησα εἰς βόθυνον μοιχείας
δι' ἐλαφρότητα φρενῶν καὶ ψυχῆς ἀμελείαν·
ὑπὲρ τούτου κατὰ πολὺ ὁ λόγος μὲν δηλώσει,
ἔχει δὲ οὕτω καθεξῆς ὥσπερ ὑμῖν ἐξεῖπω.
Ἡ Μαξιμοὺ τὸν ἴδιον ἀπολέσασα ἵππον
610 ἀπελείφθη ἐν τῇ ποᾷ, ὡς ἄνωθεν ἐρρέθη,
καὶ πρὸς τοὺς ἄλλους ἐκδραμὼν τὸν πόλεμον συνῆψα.
Καὶ πρὶν λάβωσι πεῖραν μου, εἰσήγοντο μὲν πρός με·
ὡς δὲ πάντας τοὺς μετ' ἐμοῦ συμβεβληκότας εἶδον
κατερραγμένους ἐπὶ γῆν, ἀφ' ἵππων ἀπωσμένους,
615 καὶ ἐξ αὐτῶν ἐγνώρισαν τῶν ἔργων ὅστις ἤμην,
φυγῇ μόνῃ ἐπίστευον ἰδεῖν τὴν σωτηρίαν
καὶ ἐκ πάντων ὀλιγοστοὶ ἴσχυσαν ἀποδρᾶσαι.
Καὶ τοῦ πολέμου παύσαντος ὄπισθεν ἐστρεφόμην
καὶ ἐξαίφνης τοὺς τέσσαρας καθορῶ ἀπελάτας

---

587 μὲν ἐφεισάμην Trapp, cf. Z3486: ἐνεφεισάμην G
589 καὶ added by Legrand
590 ἡ δὲ ἀναποδίσασα ... συνεχομένη Legrand: τὴν δὲ ἀναποδίσασαν ...
συνεχομένην G
593 μὲν added by Legrand
614 ἵππων Trapp: ἵππον G

585 and struck me a glancing blow on the breast-plate with her spear.
I was not hurt at all, but I broke her spear.
Brandishing my sword again I spared her,
but promptly cut off her horse's head,
and the carcase collapsed awkwardly to the ground.
590 She leapt off, overwhelmed with terror,
and falling down before me cried out: 'Young man, let me not die.
I have been led astray by listening to Philopappous, like a woman.'
And I felt respect for her, listening to her words
and pitying her marvellous beauty,
595 and left her there as I went after the remaining men.
I am ashamed to relate how I got the better of them all,
in case you think me boastful, friends;
for he who narrates his own feats at length
is thought a braggart by his hearers.
600 But I do not tell you of this as a braggart,
no, by Him who gives strength and knowledge to men
(for it is He alone who provides good things).
For this reason everything will be told as it happened,
so that I may be pardoned by you, my audience.
605 For once again I slipped into the pit of adultery,
through weakness of mind and spiritual neglect.
The story will reveal many details about this,
and it happened thus, as I am about to tell you.
    When Maximou lost her horse
610 she was left on the grass, as was said earlier,
and I ran off after the others and engaged them in battle.
And before they had any experience of me, they made for me.
But when they saw that all those who had fought with me
were scattered over the ground and forced off their horses,
615 and they realised from these deeds who I was,
they believed that in flight alone would they see their salvation;
and of them all very few managed to escape.
    And when the battle ended and I turned around,
I suddenly saw the four guerrillas,

597–608 The interlocutors are the friends of G6.3, a justification for the use of first-person narrative. It is interesting that they reappear here in a moralising framework, suggesting a connection between the moralising of the text and attempts to tidy its narrative.
608 Digenis' acts of wrong-doing in both G and E involve adultery. Is this a reflection of literary and moral preoccupations at the time when *Digenis* was constructed?

620 Φιλοπαπποῦν καὶ Λέανδρον, Κίνναμον καὶ Ἰωαννάκην,
τοῦ ἄλσους ἀνακύψαντας καὶ πρός με ἐρχομένους·
Λέανδρος δὲ καὶ Κίνναμος ἤρχοντο ἐκ προσώπου,
ὁ γέρων δὲ καὶ οἱ λοιποὶ ἤλαυνον ἐξοπίσω
ἐλπίζοντές με ἀνελεῖν μέσον αὐτῶν βαλόντες·
625 ἀλλ' ἠνέχθησαν μάταια καὶ κενὰ μελετῶντες.
Ὡς γὰρ εἶδον τοὺς ἔμπροσθεν σφόδρα ἐπιλαλοῦντας, 60r
πρὸς αὐτοὺς ὥρμησα εὐθὺς τῶν ἄλλων μὴ φροντίσας.
Ὁ Λέανδρος ἐπέδραμεν, οὐ γὰρ εἶχέ μου πεῖραν·
ὃν καὶ πατάξας, ἐπὶ γῆν πέπτωκε σὺν τῷ ἵππῳ.
630 Τοῦτον ἰδὼν ὁ Κίνναμος ἐτράπη τῆς εὐθείας,
οἱ δὲ λοιποὶ συνάψαντες τοὺς ὤμους καὶ τὰ ξίφη
ἐκ πλαγίου προέβαλον δοῦναί μοι κονταρέας·
πρὸς οὓς συντόμως τὴν ἐμὴν ἀνθυποστρέψας σπάθην
τὰ κοντάρια ἔτεμον παρευθὺς ἀμφοτέρων
635 καὶ πρὸς φυγὴν ἐτράπησαν τοὺς ἵππους ἐκκεντοῦντες,
μηδαμῶς αὐτῶν ὄπισθεν θεάσασθαι τολμῶντες.
Οὕτως ὡς εἶδον ἔχοντας, μετὰ γέλωτος εἶπον·
'Στράφητε, οὐκ αἰσχύνεσθε τὸν ἕνα δειλιῶντες;'
Οἱ δὲ μᾶλλον σφοδρότερον τὸν δρασμὸν ἐπετέλουν·
640 καὶ οὐκ ἐδίωξα αὐτοὺς τῆς συμφορᾶς οἰκτείρας
(ἔλεος καὶ γὰρ πάντοτε πρὸς τοὺς φεύγοντας εἶχον,
νικᾶν καὶ μὴ ὑπερνικᾶν, φιλεῖν τοὺς ἐναντίους)
ἀπέστρεφόν τε ὄπισθεν κατὰ σχολὴν βαδίζων.
Πλησίον δὲ τῆς Μαξιμοῦς ἐλθὼν τοιάδε ἔφην·
645 ''Η καυχωμένη ἄμετρα καὶ ἰσχύϊ θαρροῦσα,
ἄπελθε, ἐπισύναξον τοὺς φυγεῖν σωζομένους
καὶ ἀνδραγάθει σὺν αὐτοῖς δυνατῶς ἔνθα ἔχεις
ἔθος, ὡς οἶσθα καὶ αὐτὴ καλῶς πεῖραν λαβοῦσα.
Ἐξ ὧν ἔπαθες μάνθανε καὶ μὴ ἀλαζονεύου·
650 Θεὸς γὰρ ἀντιτάσσεται πᾶσιν ὑπερηφάνοις.'
Ἐκείνη δὲ πρὸς ὑπαντὴν ἐλθοῦσα ἡμετέραν,
τὰς χεῖρας αὐτῆς δήσασα πρεπόντως τὰς ἰδίας 60v
καὶ μέχρι γῆς τὴν κεφαλὴν κλίνασα εὐκοσμίως,
''Απάντων γενναιότατε,' ἔφησε, 'νῦν ἐπέγνων
655 τὴν σὴν ἀνείκαστον ἰσχὺν καὶ τὴν φιλανθρωπίαν,
ἣν οὐδεὶς ἔσχε πώποτε τῶν πάλαι ἐν ἀνδρείᾳ·

621 τοῦ Legrand: τοὺς G
625 ἠνέχθησαν G: ἠλέγχθησαν Tsopanakis. 1960, 88
655 ἰσχὺν Legrand, cf. Z3591: εὐχὴν G

620 Philopappous and Leandros, Kinnamos and Ioannakis,
     emerging from the wood and coming towards me.
     Leandros and Kinnamos were approaching in front,
     the old man and the rest were attacking from the rear,
     hoping to destroy me between them as they attacked.
625 But they were carried away by vain and empty aspirations.
     For when I saw those in front energetically urging on their horses,
     I rushed straight towards them, paying no attention to the others.
     Leandros attacked, for he had no experience of me;
     I struck him, and he fell to the ground with his horse.
630 On seeing him Kinnamos turned aside from his direct attack.
     The rest joined shoulders and swords
     and tried pushing forward from the side to deliver spear-thrusts at me.
     I at once turned my sword back on them
     and promptly broke both their spears.
635 They turned to flight, spurring on their horses,
     never daring to cast one glance behind them.
     When I saw them in this state, I laughed and said:
     'Turn back! Aren't you ashamed to be afraid of one man?'
     But they carried on running even more vigorously.
640 I did not pursue them, pitying their defeat
     (for I always had mercy on those who fled,
     being victorious but not over-victorious, and loving my enemies),
     and I came back, walking calmly.
        When I came up to Maximou, I said this:
645 'You who boast excessively and rely on your strength,
     go, collect up those who are running away and escaping,
     and continue your powerful feats of arms with them where you are
     used to fighting, as you yourself have full knowledge from your
        experience.
     Learn from what you have undergone and do not be arrogant,
650 for God sets himself against all those who are presumptuous.'
        She came to meet me,
     clasping her hands fittingly,
     and decorously bowed her head to the ground,
     'Most noble of all men,' she said, 'now I have recognised
655 your incomparable strength and benevolence,
     which none of the brave men of old ever possessed.

623 'The rest' implies that there were more than the four named guerrillas involved in
this attack.

ἀφ' οὗ γάρ με ἐκρήμνισας, εἶχες καὶ τοῦ φονεῦσαι,
ἀλλ' ἐφείσω ὡς θαυμαστὸς καὶ μέγας ἐν ἀνδρείᾳ.
Ὁ Κύριος φυλάξοι σε, γενναῖε στρατιῶτα,
660 αὐθέντα μου πανθαύμαστε, μετὰ τῆς ποθητῆς σου,
εἰς χρόνους πλείονας καλοὺς ἐν δόξῃ καὶ ὑγείᾳ·
ὅτι πολλοὺς τεθέαμαι γενναίους στρατιώτας,
πολεμιστὰς περιφανεῖς καὶ στερροὺς ἐν τῇ μάχῃ,
ἀλλ' οὔτε κραταιότερον ἐν ταῖς ἀνδραγαθίαις
665 οὐκ εἶδον ἄλλον πώποτε παρ' ὅλον μου τὸν βίον.'
Εἶτα περιλαβοῦσά μου τοὺς πόδας, κατεφίλει
τὴν χεῖρά μου τὴν δεξιάν, ἠρέμα φθεγγομένη:
'Εὐλογημένος ὁ πατὴρ καὶ μήτηρ ἡ τεκοῦσα
καὶ οἱ μαστοὶ οἱ θρέψαντες μητρὸς εὐλογημένης·
670 τοιοῦτον γὰρ οὐδέποτε ἄλλον ἄνδρα κατεῖδον.
Πληρῶσαι οὖν παρακαλῶ σὲ τὸν ἐμὸν δεσπότην
καὶ ἑτέραν μου αἴτησιν, ἐκ ταύτης ὅπως γνώσῃς
ἀκριβέστερον τὴν ἐμὴν ἐν τῷ πολέμῳ πεῖραν.
Κέλευσόν με τοῦ ἀπελθεῖν καὶ ἐπιβῆναι ἵππου,
675 καὶ τὸ πρωῒ ἐλεύσομαι ἐν τῷ παρόντι τόπῳ,
ὅπως μονομαχήσωμεν μηδενὸς συμπαρόντος
καὶ νὰ νοήσῃς, πάγκαλε, καὶ τὴν ἐμὴν ἀνδρείαν.'
'Μετὰ χαρᾶς, ὦ Μαξιμοῦ,' πρὸς αὐτὴν ἐγὼ ἔφην,   E1551
'ἄπελθε ἔνθα βούλεσαι, κἀμὲ ὧδε εὑρήσεις· 61r
680 μᾶλλον δὲ φέρε καὶ τοὺς σοὺς ἑτέρους ἀπελάτας
καὶ δοκίμασον ἅπαντας καὶ τοὺς κρείττονας μάθε.'
Καὶ τότε ἕνα συλλαβὼν τῶν πλανωμένων ἵππων
τῶν πεπτωκότων σὺν αὐτῇ ἐν ὥρᾳ τοῦ πολέμου
ἤγαγον τοῦτον πρὸς αὐτὴν ἐπιβῆναι προστάξας.
685 Ὡς γὰρ εἶδέ με <ὁ> λαὸς κρημνίσαντα τὴν κόρην,
κύκλῳ περιεχύθησαν ὡς ἀετοὶ σπουδαίως·
οἱ μὲν σπαθέας ἔκρουον ἔσω χειρὶ συντόμως,
ἄλλοι δὲ κονταρέας μοι ἐδίδων κατὰ κράτος,
ἕτεροι δὲ τοῖς βέλεσιν αὐτῶν ἐξένυττόν με.
690 Καὶ τότε τίς ὁ βοηθῶν, τίς ὁ φρουρῶν καὶ σκέπων;
Οὐκ ἄλλος πάντως ἢ Θεὸς δικαιοκρίτης μέγας·
αὐτὸς γὰρ ἐξαπέστειλε βοήθειαν ἐξ ὕψους
καὶ ἐμὲ διεφύλαξεν ἀβλαβῆ παρ' ἐλπίδα,

672 γνώσῃς Legrand. cf. Z3600: γνώσω G
673 ἐμὴν Legrand. cf. Z3601: σὴν G
678 αὐτὴν Legrand: αὐτὸν G
685 ὁ added by Legrand κρημνίσαντα Legrand: κνημνίσαντα G

From the moment you overthrew me you could also have slain me,
but you spared me, since you are admirable and of great bravery.
May the Lord protect you, most noble soldier,
660 and your beloved girl, my most wonderful lord,
for many more fair years in honour and health.
For I have seen many noble soldiers,
noted warriors and men redoubtable in battle,
665 but I have never in my whole life seen anyone mightier in brave deeds.'
     Then she clasped my feet and kissed
my right hand, saying gently,
'Blessed is your father, and the mother who bore you,
and the breasts of your blessed mother which nourished you:
670 for I have never seen any other man like you.
I beg you, my master, to fulfil
another request of mine, so that you may gain from it
more accurate knowledge of my experience in battle.
Tell me to go and mount a horse,
675 and in the morning I shall come to this present place
so that we can fight in single combat with no one else present
and you will understand, handsome lord, my bravery also.'
     'With pleasure, Maximou,' I said to her,
'go where you wish and you will find me here.
680 But rather bring the rest of your guerrillas
and test them all and find out who are the strongest.'
And then I caught one of the stray horses
that had belonged to the men who had fallen with her at the time of
     battle,
and I brought it to her, telling her to mount it.
685 For when the army had seen that I had overthrown the girl,
they had flooded all round me swiftly like eagles.
Some promptly struck with their swords in hand to hand fighting,
others thrust their spears at me with all their might,
yet others tried to strike me with their arrows.
690 And who was there then to help, who was my guardian and protector?
No one else at all but God, the great just judge.
For he sent down aid from on high
and unexpectedly preserved me unharmed,

685–709 This battle with Maximou's men took place earlier (G6.595–7), with Digenis
modestly refusing to narrate it. Justification for the narrative here is slim, and Z3518–28
has transposed it to a more appropriate place.

ὡς δὲ εἰς μέσον κέκλεισμαι τοσούτων πολεμίων,
695 καὶ πάντοθεν πληττόμενος τὴν φυγὴν ἠσχυνόμην·
εἶχον γὰρ ἅρματα καλὰ καὶ κατωχυρωμένα
καὶ σὺν Θεῷ πεφύλαγμαι ἄτρωτος ἐν τῇ μάχῃ.
Εἰς πολὺ δὲ οὐ γέγονεν ἡ ἐκείνων θρασύτης
ἀλλὰ ταχέως ἔσβεσται τοῦ Θεοῦ βοηθοῦντος·
700 ἔχων τε καὶ τοὺς μάρτυρας ἁγίους Θεοδώρους,
Γεώργιον, Δημήτριον, τούτους ἔτρεψα πάντας.
Κοντάριν γὰρ οὐκ ἔλαβον ἐν αὐτοῖς οὐδὲ τόξον,
τὴν ἐμὴν σπάθην ἔσυρα καὶ ἦλθον ἔσω χεῖρας·
καὶ ὅσους μὲν ἐλάγχανον, ἔκοπτον τούτους μάλα
705 καὶ γῇ αὐτοὺς ἐλάμβανε ψυχὴν μὴ κεκτημένους· 61v
ἄλλοι δὲ φεύγειν θέλοντες, κατελάμβανον τούτους
καὶ μὴ δυνάμενοι ποσῶς ἐμοὶ προσαντιστῆναι
ἐπέζευον τοὺς ἵππους των, ἔρριπτον τὰ ἅρματά των
καὶ προσελθόντες ἔφευγον, ἐχόμενοι τοῦ τρόμου.
710 Καὶ οὕτω τε ἀπέμενον ἵπποι πολλοὶ ἐκ τούτων,
ἐξ ὧν, ὡς ἔφην, δέδωκα τῇ Μαξιμοῦ τῷ τότε
καὶ διῆλθον τὸν ποταμόν, ἡ δὲ πρὸς τὰ οἰκεῖα,
χάριν μοι, ὡς ἐφαίνετο, πολλὴν ὁμολογοῦσα.
Καὶ εἰς τὴν τένδαν μου ἐλθὼν ἀπέβαλον τὰ ὅπλα
715 καὶ ἐδυσάμην θαυμαστὸν λεπτότατον μαχλάμιν
βαλών τε καὶ σγουρούτζικον κόκκινον καμηλαύκιν
καὶ ἵππον μετεσέλλισα δαγάλην, ἀστερᾶτον,
ὃς εἶχε γνώμην κάλλιστον ἐν ταῖς ἀνδραγαθίαις·
σπαθίν, σκουτάριν εἰληφὼς καὶ βένετον κοντάριν
720 τὸν ποταμὸν ἐπέρασα ἑσπέρας ἤδη οὔσης·
ἐπὶ τούτῳ καὶ ὤκνησα ἀνελθεῖν ἐν τῇ κόρῃ
ἀλλ᾽ ἔστειλα τὰς ἑαυτῆς δύο θαλαμηπόλους.
Εἴχομεν καὶ γὰρ ἱκανοὺς τοὺς ἡμῖν ὑπουργοῦντας,
τὴν οἴκησίν των ἔχοντας ἀπόμακρα τῆς τένδας,
725 οὐχὶ δὲ ἅπαντες ὁμοῦ, ἀλλ᾽ ἄνδρες μὲν ἰδίως
καὶ αἱ γυναῖκες ἄποθεν εἶχον αὐτῶν τὰς τένδας.
Περάσας οὖν, ὡς εἴρηκα, τὸν ποταμὸν Εὐφράτην,

701 πάντας G in margin: μάλλον G in text
705 γῇ αὐτοὺς ἐλάμβανε Mavrogordato, cf. Z3528: γὰρ αὐτοὺς ἐλάμβανον G
711 δέδωκα Legrand: δώδεκα G
715 μαχλάμιν Grégoire, 1931b, 482: μαχλάβιν G
716 καμηλαύκιν Legrand: καμαλαύκην G
717 δαγάλην, ἀστερᾶτον Legrand, cf. Z3617: γαδάλην, ἀστεράταᵒν G
726 ἄποθεν Legrand, cf. Z3626: ὡσαύτως G

when I was surrounded in the midst of so many enemies
695 and struck at from all sides, but was ashamed to flee.
For I had good sturdy weapons
and through God's aid I was preserved unwounded in the battle.
Their boldness did not last for long
but was quickly quenched, with God's help.
700 With the holy martyrs the Theodores,
George and Dimitrios, I routed them all.
I did not use a spear or a bow against them,
but I drew my sword and fought them hand to hand.
All those I encountered I killed,
705 and the earth received them without their souls.
Others I caught as they were seeking to flee
and they were quite unable to stand against me;
they jumped off their horses, threw away their weapons
and, giving themselves up, they fled, overwhelmed by terror.
710 And so there were many horses left which had belonged to them,
one of which, as I said, I bestowed then upon Maximou.
And I crossed the river and she returned to her own quarters,
giving me many thanks, it seemed.
       And going into my tent, I cast aside my weapons
715 and dressed myself in a marvellous very light robe,
putting on a red cap of curly fur,
and I saddled my starred chestnut horse
which had an excellent spirit for brave deeds.
Taking my sword, my shield and a sea-blue spear,
720 I crossed the river, it being already evening;
for that reason I was reluctant to go up to the girl,
but I sent her two chamber-maids.
We had several servants to attend us,
who had their quarters far from the tent,
725 though they were not all together, for the men were separate
and the women had their own tents at a distance.
       So having crossed the river Euphrates, as I said,

723–6 Again Digenis' solitude is mitigated by the servants and it is carefully shown that the servants keep to the proprieties. Should one sense that this is an unusual, fictional ménage?

ἐν τῷ λειμῶνι τῷ τερπνῷ ἑαυτὸν ἀνακλίνας
τόν τε ἵππον ἀνέπαυσα διαγαγὼν τὴν νύκτα.
730 Πρὸς ὄρθρον δὲ ἐξαναστὰς καὶ ἐπιβὰς τοῦ ἵππου,
εἰς τὸ πεδίον ἀνελθών, ἱστάμην ἀναμένων.
Τῆς δὲ ἡμέρας τῷ φωτὶ ἄρτι διαυγαζούσης 62r
καὶ τοῦ ἡλίου λάμποντος ἐπὶ τὰς ἀκρωρείας,
ἰδοὺ μόνη ἡ Μαξιμοὺ ἐφάνη ἐν τῷ κάμπῳ.
735 Εἰς φάραν ἐπεκάθητο μαύρην, γενναιοτάτην,
ἐφόρει ἐπιλώρικον ὁλόβηρον, καστόριν,
φακεολίτζιν πράσινον, χρυσὸν ῥεραντισμένον,
σκουτάριν ἔχον ἀετοῦ πτέρυγας γεγραμμένας,
κοντάριν ἀραβίτικον καὶ σπαθὶν ἐζωσμένη.
740   Ταύτης ἐγὼ πρὸς ἀπαντὴν ἐκίνησα εὐθέως
καὶ πλησίον γενόμενοι ἠσπασάμεθα ἄμφω,
χαιρετίσαντες, ὡς εἰκός, ἀλλήλους παμφιλτάτως,
τῆς μάχης τε ἠρξάμεθα λαλήσαντες τοὺς ἵππους,
ἄνω καὶ κάτω πρὸς μικρὰν διαδραμόντες ὥραν·
745 κονταρέας δεδώκαμεν, μηδενὸς κρημνισθέντος.
Χωρισθέντες οὖν παρευθὺς εἱλκύσαμεν τὰς σπάθας
καὶ κρούοντες ἐνστατικῶς, ἐμπεσόντες ἀλλήλοις.
Ἐφειδόμην γάρ, βέλτιστε, τοῦ ἀδικῆσαι ταύτην·
ἀνδρῶν γὰρ ἔστι μωμητὸν οὐ μόνον τοῦ φονεῦσαι,
750 ἀλλ' οὐδὲ ὅλως πόλεμον στῆσαι μετὰ γυναῖκας.
Αὕτη δὲ ἦν ὀνομαστὴ τῶν τότε ἐν ἀνδρείᾳ·
τούτου χάριν τὸν πόλεμον οὐδαμῶς ἐπησχύνθην,
χεῖρα αὐτῆς τὴν δεξιὰν πλήξας τε πρὸ δακτύλων·
ἡ μὲν σπάθη ἐπὶ τὴν γῆν πέπτωκεν ἣν κατεῖχεν,
755 τρόμος δὲ ταύτην εἴληφε καὶ δειλία μεγίστη.
Ἐγὼ δὲ ἐξεφώνησα· 'Μαξιμοῦ, μὴ φοβεῖσαι,
οἰκτείρω γάρ σε ὡς γυνὴν καὶ κάλλους πεπλησμένην·   E1543
ἵνα δὲ γνώσῃ τίς εἰμι ἀκριβῶς ἐκ τῶν ἔργων,
τὴν ἰσχὺν ἐπιδείξω σοι τὴν ἐμὴν ἐν τῷ ἵππῳ.'   62v
760 Καὶ σπαθέαν καταβατὴν εἰς τοὺς νεφροὺς εὐθέως
τοῦ φαρίου κατήγαγον καὶ διῃρέθη μέσον,
πεσόντος τοῦ ἡμίσεος εἰς μέρος μετ' ἐκείνης,
τοῦ δὲ λοιποῦ ἑτέρωθεν εἰς γῆν κατενεχθέντος.
Ἡ δὲ ἀναποδίσασα λίαν τεταραγμένη
765 συγκεκομμένη τῇ φωνῇ ''Ελέησον,' ἐβόα,

---

742 χαιρετίσαντες Legrand: χαιρετήσαντος G
750 γυναῖκας Tsopanakis. 1960. 89: γυναικός G

I lay down in the delightful meadow
and allowed my horse to rest as I spent the night there.
730 Getting up towards dawn and mounting my horse,
I went up to the plain and stood there waiting.
As day was just beginning to gleam in the morning light
and the sun was shining on the mountain ridge,
look: Maximou appeared on the battle-field on her own.
735 She was seated on a black, most noble steed,
she wore a surcoat over her breastplate all of pure purple silk,
a green turban embroidered with gold,
a shield painted with eagle's wings,
an Arab spear and a sword slung from her belt.
740   I immediately moved off to meet her
and when we came near we both embraced,
greeting each other in a most friendly fashion, as was right,
and we began to do battle, encouraging our horses
and charging up and down for a little while;
745 we exchanged spear-thrusts, with neither being unseated.
So, quickly separating, we drew our swords
and began to strike persistently, attacking each other.
I avoided harming her, my good friend,
for it is a reproach to men not only to kill women
750 but even to start fighting with them.
But she was amongst those with a reputation for bravery at that time,
and because of that I was not at all ashamed of fighting;
I struck her right hand just above the fingers;
and the sword which she held fell to the ground;
755 she was seized by terror and very great fear.
    I shouted out: 'Maximou, don't be frightened;
I have pity on you since you are a woman and full of beauty.
And so that you may clearly know from my deeds who I am,
I shall use your horse to display my strength.'
760 And at once I drove my sword with a downward stroke
into the charger's loins and he was split down the middle,
half falling on one side with her
and the rest collapsing to the ground on the other side.
    She leapt up, very agitated,
765 and cried out in a choking voice: 'Have mercy on me,

---

736 καστόριν here does not mean 'beaver fur' (Haldon, 1990, 169); contrast E1494
where it probably does (Alexiou, 1979, 61).

'ἐλέησόν με, κύριε, τὴν κακῶς πλανηθεῖσαν·
μᾶλλον, εἰ οὐκ ἀπαξιοῖς, ποιήσωμεν φιλίαν,
ἔτι παρθένος γὰρ εἰμὶ ὑπ' οὐδενὸς φθαρεῖσα·
σὺ μόνος με ἐνίκησας, σύ με ἀποκερδίσεις·   E1566
770 ἕξεις δέ με καὶ συνεργὸν εἰς τοὺς ὑπεναντίους.'
       'Οὐκ ἀποθνήσκεις, Μαξιμοῦ,' πρὸς αὐτὴν ἄρτι ἔφην,
'τὸ δὲ ἔχειν σε γαμετὴν οὐ δυνατόν μοι ἔσται,
νόμιμον ἔχω γαμετὴν εὐγενῆ καὶ ὡραίαν,
ἧς ἀγάπην οὐδέποτε τολμήσω ἀθετῆσαι.
775 Λοιπὸν δεῦρο ὑπὸ σκιὰν ἀπέλθωμεν τοῦ δένδρου
καὶ διδάξω σε ἅπαντα τὰ κατ' ἐμὲ ὡς ἔχουν.'
       Ἐλθόντες δὲ πρὸς ποταμοῦ τὰ γειτνιῶντα δένδρα,
ἡ Μαξιμοῦ τὴν ἑαυτῆς ἀποπλύνασα χεῖρα
καὶ δόκιμον ἐν τῇ πληγῇ ἄλειμμα ἐπιθεῖσα,
780 ὅπερ φέρειν εἰώθαμεν ἀεὶ ἐν τοῖς πολέμοις,
ῥίπτει τὸ ἐπιλώρικον· πολὺς γὰρ ἦν ὁ καύσων.
Καὶ ὁ χιτὼν τῆς Μαξιμοῦς ὑπῆρχεν ἀραχνώδης·
πάντα καθάπερ ἔσοπτρον ἐνέφαινε τὰ μέλη
καὶ τοὺς μαστοὺς προκύπτοντας μικρὸν ἄρτι τῶν στέρνων.
785 Καὶ ἐτρώθη μου ἡ ψυχή, ὡραία γὰρ ὑπῆρχε

Καὶ ἐκ τοῦ ἵππου κατελθών, ἐφθέγγετο βοῶσα: Z3699
'Χαίροις, δεσπότης ὁ ἐμός,' ἐπάνω μου δραμοῦσα,   Z3700
'δούλη σου ὄντως γέγονα τῇ τοῦ πολέμου τύχῃ.'
Καὶ χεῖρά μου τὴν δεξιὰν ἡδέως κατεφίλει·
ὡς δὲ ἀνήφθη ὁ πυρσὸς ὁ τῆς ἐπιθυμίας,
οὐκ εἶχον, ὅστις γένωμαι, καθόλου ἐφλεγόμην.
Πάντα λοιπὸν ἐσπούδαζα φυγεῖν τὴν ἁμαρτίαν,   Z3705
καὶ ἐμαυτὸν κατηγορῶν ταῦτα ἐλογιζόμην:
'Ὢ δαίμων, διατὶ ἐρᾷς πάντων τῶν ἀλλοτρίων

---

772 ἔσται Legrand: ἔστι⁽ᵃⁱ⁾ G
783 ἐνέφαινε Legrand: ἐμφαίνοντο G
785 After this line a folio has been removed: the text provided in italics is Z3699–3741
(from Trapp's edition)

have mercy, lord, for I have erred greatly.
Or rather, if you do not think it beneath you, let us make a pact,
for I am still a virgin, not violated by any man.
You alone have defeated me, it is you who shall win me completely
770 and you shall have me as your comrade against your enemies.'
     'You are not going to die, Maximou,' I said to her then,
'but I cannot take you as my wife
for I have a lawful wife, high-born and beautiful,
whose love I shall never dare to deny.
775 Come then, let us go into the shade of the tree
and I shall tell you all about myself.'
     When we came to the trees that bordered the river
Maximou washed her hand
and put on the wound a tried ointment
780 which we are always accustomed to carry in battles;
she threw off her surcoat, for the heat was intense.
Maximou's shift was gossamer-thin,
and it revealed her limbs as in a mirror
and her breasts rising just a little above her chest.
785 And my soul was wounded, for she was beautiful

As I got down from the horse, she called out loudly,
'Greetings, my master,' as she ran towards me,   Z3700
'I have truly become your slave by the chance of war.'
And she kissed my right hand sweetly.
As the torch of my desire kindled,
I did not know who I was, I was all on fire.
Indeed I made every effort to escape the sin   Z3705
and, accusing myself, I argued thus,
'Demon, why do you love all that is not yours,

769–70 Maximou, having been defeated in her substitute masculine role, returns to the
feminine category and becomes seductive.
776 Maximou has just proposed marriage by placing herself in the role of reward for
valour. Digenis' continued contact with her seems at variance with his protestations that
he had no thought of the seduction which would occur.
785 After this line a folio has been lost from G, perhaps as a result of censorship (see
Introduction, pp. xviii–xix). The sense of the passage, and quite possibly much of the
wording too, can be found in Z3699–3739 (= T as corrected from A; reprinted here, in
italics, from Trapp's edition) which at this point has been following G rather than E. That
the wording is unlikely to be exactly that of G is indicated by presence of two lines in Z
after 3741 (= G6.786), which is common to Z and G, the fact that Z contains only 43
lines instead of the approximately 50 that the size of G's pages leads one to expect, and
the points noted at G6.786 below.

πηγὴν ἔχων ἀθόλωτον, ὅλην μεμυρισμένην·'
Ταῦτα διαλεγόμενος καθ' ἑαυτόν, ὦ φίλοι,
ἡ Μαξιμὼ τὸν ἔρωτα ἐξῆπτεν ἔτι μᾶλλον,   Z3710
τοξεύουσα τὰς ἀκοὰς λόγοις παγγλυκυτάτοις,
ἦτον γὰρ νέα καὶ καλή, ὡραία καὶ παρθένος·
ἡττήθη οὖν ὁ λογισμὸς βεβήλῳ ἐπιθυμίᾳ.
Αἰσχύνης γὰρ καὶ μίξεως ἁπάσης πληρωθείσης,
εἶτα αὐτὴν καταλιπών, προπέμψας τε ἐκεῖθεν,   Z3715
λόγον ἐξεῖπον πρὸς αὐτὴν παραμυθίας δῆθεν:
'"Υπαγε, κόρη μου, καλῶς καὶ μή μου ἐπιλάθου.'
Καὶ ἐν τῷ ἵππῳ ἐπιβὰς τὸν ποταμὸν διῆλθον·
ἡ δὲ πρὸς ὕδωρ λούσασα αὐτῆς τὴν παρθενίαν,
ἐμὴν τὴν ὑποχώρησιν ἠνάγκαζε βαρέως.   Z3720
Εἶτα παραγενόμενος πρὸς τὴν ἐμὴν φιλτάτην,
κατῆλθον ἐκ τοῦ ἵππου μου, ταύτην φιλῶ ἀπλήστως:
'Εἶδες, ψυχή μου,' ἔλεγον, 'ἐκδικητὴν ὃν ἔχεις,
καὶ οἵαν σοι ἀντίληψιν ὁ πλαστουργὸς παρέσχεν;'
Ἡ δέ τινα ἐν τῇ ψυχῇ ζηλοτυπίαν σχοῦσα,   Z3725
'"Εν ἅπασιν εὐχαριστῶ,' ἀντέφη, 'κύριέ μου,
δάκνει με δὲ τῆς Μαξιμοῦς ἡ πάντολμος βραδύτης·
τὸ τί ἐργάζου μετ' αὐτῆς ἐγὼ γὰρ οὐ γινώσκω.
Ἔστι καὶ τοίνυν ὁ Θεὸς ὁ τὰ κρυπτὰ γινώσκων
ὃς συγχωρήσει σοι, καλέ, ταύτην τὴν ἁμαρτίαν,   Z3730
ἀλλ' ὅρα μή, νεώτερε, πάλιν καὶ τοῦτο πράξῃς,
καὶ ἀποδώσῃ σοι Θεὸς ὁ κρίνων δικαιοσύνην·
ἐγὼ δὲ τὰς ἐλπίδας μου εἰς Θεὸν ἀνεθέμην,
ὅστις διαφυλάξῃ σε καὶ σώσῃ τὴν ψυχήν σου
καὶ χαίρειν ἀξιώσῃ με τὰ πάντερπνά σου κάλλη   Z3735
εἰς χρόνους πλείστους καὶ καλούς, πανεύμνοστέ μου κύρκα.'
Λόγοις δ' ὅμως πιθανικοῖς αὐτὴν παρεκρουόμην,
ἀγγέλλων τε τὸν πόλεμον τῆς Μαξιμοῦς ἀρχῆθεν,
τὴν χεῖρα πῶς ἐπλήγωσα τὴν δεξιὰν ἐκείνης   G6.786
προσέθηκα καὶ αἵματος ῥύσιν πολλὴν γενέσθαι,   Z3740
ἐξ οὗ θανεῖν τῇ Μαξιμῷ παρὰ μικρὸν συνέβη,

786 χεῖρα ὅπως ἐπλήγωσα τὴν δεξιὰν ἐκείνης 63r   Z3739

Z3708 μεμυρισμένην A: μεμερισμένην T
Z3711 τὰς ἀκοὰς A: ταῖς ἀκοαῖς T
Z3713 ἐπιθυμίᾳ Lambros: ἐπιθύμει T
Z3732 ἀποδώσῃ Sathas-Legrand: ἀποδούσει T

when you possess an undefiled spring full of perfume?'
  As I reasoned thus with myself, friends,
Maximou kindled my passion yet further,   Z3710
aiming most sweet words at my hearing,
for she was young and lovely, beautiful and a virgin.
So my reason was defeated by vile desire.
When the shame and the union were all completed,
then I left her, sending her away from there,   Z3715
and I addressed this speech of seeming comfort to her:
'Farewell, my girl, and do not forget me.'
And mounting my horse, I crossed the river
while she bathed her maidenhead in the water
and tried urgently to compel me to return.   Z3720
  Then returning to my dearest,
I dismounted from my horse and kissed her insatiably.
'Did you see, my soul,' I said, 'the avenger whom you have
and what sort of support the Creator has provided?'
  But she had some jealousy in her soul and replied: Z3725
'I thank you for everything, my lord;
but what irritates me is Maximou's most bold delay.
What you did with her I do not know.
But there is God, who knows all secrets,
and he will pardon you, my handsome one, for this sin.   Z3730
But see, young man, that you do not do this again
or God, who judges with justice, will punish you.
I have set my hopes on God:
may he preserve you and save your soul,
and allow me to enjoy all your delightful beauty   Z3735
for many fair years, my most handsome sweetheart.'
  Nevertheless I deceived her with my persuasive words,
as I told her of the battle with Maximou from the
beginning, how I wounded her right hand,
and I added that there was a great flow of blood
from which Maximou all but died

786 how I had wounded her right hand

Z3727 The adjective is appropriate to Maximou, since Digenis' wife seems here to be
adopting a conciliatory tone, but the delay (in the latter's terms at least) is in Digenis'
own return.
786 The lacuna seems to end at G6.786, which is almost identical to Z3739, but the
hypothesis of G6.787–8 appears to lack an apodosis like Z3741. Rather than propose a

καὶ εἰ μὴ θᾶττον ἐπέζευον καὶ ἐπέβρεχον ὕδωρ
ταύτην οἰκτείρας ὡς γυνὴν καὶ ἀσθενῆ τῇ φύσει·
'Τὴν μὲν χεῖρα ἀπέπλυνα τὴν πληγὴν καταδήσας,
790 διὰ τοῦτο ἐβράδυνα, φῶς μου μεμυρισμένον,
ἵν' ὅπως μὴ ὀνειδισθῶ ὡς γυναῖκα φονεύσας.'
Ταῦτα εἰπών, ἀναψυχὴν ἐλάμβανεν ἡ κόρη,
ἀληθεύειν νομίσασα ἐμὲ ἐν τοῖς ῥηθεῖσιν.
Εἶτα καὶ κατὰ νοῦν βαλὼν τὰ ῥήματα τῆς κόρης
795 καὶ ὅλως τῷ θυμῷ αὐτὸς εἰς ἄκρον ὑπερζέσας,
καβαλλικεύω παρευθύς, δῆθεν εἰς τὸ κυνῆγιν,
καὶ ταύτην δὲ καταλαβὼν ἀνηλεῶς ἀνεῖλον,
μοιχείαν, φόνον τότε γὰρ ἐκτελέσας ἀθλίως.
Καὶ οὕτως ὑποστρέψας γε ἔνθα ἦτον ἡ κόρη,
800 καὶ ἐκεῖσε τὴν ἅπασαν ποιήσαντες ἡμέραν
ἀμφότεροι κατήλθομεν τῇ ἐξῆς ἐν τῇ τένδᾳ
καὶ ἐπὶ τὴν ἀπόλαυσιν τῶν λειμώνων ἐκείνων·
καὶ μεθ' ἡμέρας σκέψεως καὶ βουλῆς παγκαλλίστης,
ἐν τῷ Εὐφράτῃ ἔκρινα τὴν οἴκησιν ποιῆσαι,
805 κατασκευάσαι τε λαμπρὸν καὶ ἐξαίσιον οἶκον.»

unless I had dismounted more quickly and splashed water,
having pity on her as a woman and weak by nature.
'I washed her hand thoroughly and bound up her wound,
790 and I am late for that reason, my perfumed light,
so that I should not be reproached for having killed a woman.'
    When I said this, the girl was comforted,
thinking that I had been truthful in what was said.
Then, turning the girl's remarks over in my mind
795 and working myself up in my anger,
I immediately rode off, as if to hunt,
and caught up with her and pitilessly slew her,
the promiscuous creature, committing a wretched murder.
    Then I returned to where the girl was;
800 we spent the whole day there
and both returned on the next day to the tent
and to the enjoyment of those meadows.
And after a time of reflection and fairest consideration,
I decided to build a dwelling by the Euphrates
805 and to construct a brilliant and magnificent house."

one-line lacuna after G6.788 to be filled with Z3741, the relevant lines are printed here
to allow the reader to decide.
791 This is presumably heroic shame for fighting an obvious inferior (cf. G6.749–52
above) rather than any motive connected with chivalry.
798 Literally Maximou is accused of being an adulteress, though the adultery is
committed by Digenis. No simple motivation has been found for the murder, which is not
present in E and is not taken up in Z. It is hard to be sure in what ethical framework to
place Maximou's fault and Digenis' retribution, on a continuum running from a
completely heroic morality to the narrowly religious ethos implied by G's moralising
passages. There is obvious contradiction between Digenis' willingness to be seduced and
his assumption of the right of condign punishment: legally he is guilty of seducing a
consenting virgin, which brings penalties for the man but not the woman (Laiou, 1993,
215–17), though in other respects Digenis' reaction is just an exaggerated version of
attitudes implicit in ecclesiastical texts (Laiou, 1993, 154–5). Only a little less blatant is
the inconsistency between the sympathetic portrayal of the warrior maiden, shown as
more heroic than the male guerrillas, and the brief narrative of her murder, motivated by
unheroic thoughts on Digenis' part. It seems that Maximou is a figure from heroic legend
suffering by incorporation into a poem whose governing morality is post-heroic.
Maximou in the poem represents a strong challenge to male supremacy, first in
masculine terms as a warrior, then in the more traditional female role of seductress. Like
the daughter of Aploravdis, she is guilty of cross-dressing, which probably added to the
fault. But Maximou is far more threatening than her predecessor. For this reason,
perhaps, she is punished by murder rather than the less final penalty of rape (cf.
Galatariotou, 1987, 59–66). Byzantine attitudes toward sexuality were ambivalent: on
the convergence of death and sexual behaviour of any sort see Galatariotou, 1989,
especially 104–7.
804–5 The link between Digenis' first-person narration and what follows is strengthened by these lines, which point forward more effectively than the backward link of
G7.5–6.

Λόγος ἕβδομος

Βασίλειος ὁ θαυμαστὸς καὶ Διγενὴς ᾿Ακρίτης,
τῶν Καππαδόκων ὁ τερπνὸς καὶ πανευθαλὴς ἔρνος,
ὁ τῆς ἀνδρείας στέφανος, ἡ κεφαλὴ τῆς τόλμης,
πάντων τῶν νέων ὁ τερπνὸς καὶ παγκάλλιστος κόσμος,
5 μετὰ τὸ πάσας ἀνδρικῶς τὰς ἄκρας ὑποτάξαι
πλείστας τε πόλεις κατασχὼν καὶ χώρας ἀπειθούντων 63v
οἰκῆσαι ἡρετίσατο πλησίον τοῦ Εὐφράτου.   *E1620*
Οὗτος δὲ πάντων ποταμὸς ὁ κάλλιστος ὑπῆρχεν,
τὴν κρήνην ἔχων ἐξ αὐτοῦ μεγάλου παραδείσου·
10 διὰ τοῦτο γλυκύτητα ἔχει εὐωδεστάτην,
ψυχρότητα χιόνος τε ἀρτίως λελυμένης.
     ᾿Εξ αὐτοῦ δὲ τοῦ ποταμοῦ ὕδωρ μετοχετεύσας,
ἄλλον τερπνὸν παράδεισον ἐφύτευσεν ἐκεῖθεν,
ἄλσος ξένον, εὐθέατον τοῖς ὀφθαλμοῖς τῷ ὄντι.
15 Περὶ τὸ ἄλσος τεῖχος ἦν αὔταρκες μὲν εἰς ὕψος,   *E1630*
πλευρὰς δὲ ἔχον τέσσαρας ὑπὸ ξυστῶν μαρμάρων.   *E1631*
     ῎Εσωθεν δὲ ἡ τῶν φυτῶν πανήγυρις ἐκόμα,
φαιδρῶς οἱ κλάδοι ἔβαλλον προσπίπτοντες ἀλλήλοις,
τοσαύτη τις ἐτύγχανε τῶν δένδρων ἁμιλλία·
20 ἄμπελοι ἑκατέρωθεν ἐξήρτηντο ὡραῖοι,
κάλαμοι ἐπεφύοντο εἰς ὕψος ἐπηρμένοι,
οἱ καρποὶ ἐξεκρέμαντο, ἀνθῶν τἆλλα ἐπ᾿ ἄλλων,

---

2 ὁ τερπνὸς καὶ πανευθαλὴς G: τὸ τερπνὸν καὶ πανευθαλὲς Legrand, cf. Z3768 (ῥόδον)
3 ἡ κεφαλὴ τῆς τόλμης Legrand: ἡ τῆς ἀνδρείας τόλμης G with κεφαλὴ τῆς in the margin
5 μετὰ ... ὑποτάξαι appears at the foot of 63r and top of 63v
7 οἰκῆσαι G: οἰκίσαι Eideneier, 1971, 316–18
8 ποταμὸς G: ποταμῶν Legrand, cf. Z3775
16 ἔχον Legrand: ἔχων G
19 ἁμιλλία G: ὁμιλία Ach.Tat. 1.15.2
22 ἀνθῶν τἆλλα Legrand: ἀνθ᾿ ὧν τ᾿ ἄλλα G

Seventh book

The marvellous Basil Digenis Akritis, the Frontiersman of Double
    Descent,
the delightful blossoming branch of the Cappadocians,
the crown of bravery, the summit of daring,
the joyous and fairest ornament of all young men,
5 after he had bravely subdued all the frontiers,
capturing very many cities and rebellious districts,
chose to settle close to the Euphrates.
This river was the loveliest of all,
with its source in the great Paradise itself;
10 because of this it has a most fragrant sweetness,
and a coldness from recently melted snow.
    Channelling water from this river,
he planted another delightful pleasure garden there,
a remarkable grove, truly a good sight for the eyes.
15 There was a wall around the grove, high enough,
with four sides of smoothed marble.
Within it waved a festival of plants;
branches bloomed brilliantly as they vied with each other
– such was the contest among the trees.
20 Beautiful vines were attached on either side,
reeds grew there reaching upwards,
fruits hung down while other plants bore flowers on flowers,

G7 is made up of a description of the house built by Digenis and his life in it with his wife,
and his mother until her death. These elements are present in E at E1606–59 (though
with only a hint of G's literary allusions) but are there combined with Digenis' other
building activity (of the bridge and tomb, at E1660–94). While the shortness of the book
may be due to some abbreviation in G (e.g. at G7.158) it seems more likely to be
attributable to the paucity of available material (and hence the amplifications derived
from Melitintiotis). *Digenis* will have contained passages on Digenis' building activities.
1 The attribution of the hero to the Cappadocians (reinforcing the poem's local
allegiances) and thus to the Byzantines overlooks his Arab father, and undermines the
epithet.
11–41 Cf. G6.18–28; these passages on the ideal garden reflect Achilles Tatius and
Melitiniotis (see Introduction, pp. xlv–xlvi).

ὁ λειμὼν φαιδρῶς ἔθαλλε τῶν δένδρων ὑποκάτω
ποικίλην ἔχων τὴν χροάν, τοῖς ἄνθεσιν ἀστράπτων,
25 τὰ μὲν εὐώδη νάρκισσα, ῥόδα τε καὶ μυρσίναι·
τὰ ῥόδα γῆς ἐτύγχανον πορφυρόβαφος κόσμος,
γάλακτος ἔστιλβον χροὰν οἱ νάρκισσοι ἐν μέρει,
τὰ ἴα ἀπαστράπτοντα χροὰν εἶχον θαλάσσης
ἐν γαλήνῃ ὑπὸ λεπτῆς σαλευομένης αὔρας·
30 ὕδωρ ἀφθόνως πάντοθεν ἔρρεε τῷ λειμῶνι.
Ὀρνίθων γένη ἱκανὰ ἐνέμοντο ἐκεῖσε, 64r
τὰ μὲν κολακευόμενα τροφὴν ἐν τοῖς ἀνθρώποις,
τὰ δὲ λοιπὰ ἐλεύθερον τὸ πτερὸν κεκτημένα
ἔπαιζον ἐποχούμενα πρὸς τῶν δένδρων τὰ ὕψη,
35 τὰ μὲν ᾄδοντα ᾄσμασι λιγυρῶς τὰ ὀρνίθια,
τὰ δὲ ἀγλαϊζόμενα τῇ στολῇ τῶν πτερύγων,
χειροήθεις ταῶνες μέν, ψιττακοὶ καὶ οἱ κύκνοι,
οἱ μὲν κύκνοι ἐν ὕδασι τὴν νομὴν ἐποιοῦντο,
ἐν τοῖς κλώνοις οἱ ψιττακοὶ ᾖδον περὶ τὰ δένδρα,   E1658
40 οἱ ταῶνες τὰς πτέρυγας κυκλοῦντες εἰς τὰ ἄνθη,
ἀντέλαμπεν ἡ τῶν ἀνθῶν ἐν ταῖς πτέρυξι θέα.
Μέσον αὐτοῦ τοῦ θαυμαστοῦ καὶ τερπνοῦ παραδείσου
οἶκον τερπνὸν ἀνήγειρεν ὁ γενναῖος Ἀκρίτης
εὐμεγέθη, τετράγωνον ἐκ λίθων πεπρισμένων,
45 ἄνωθεν δὲ μετὰ σεμνῶν κιόνων καὶ θυρίδων.
Τοὺς ὀρόφους ἐκόσμησε πάντας μετὰ μουσείου
ἐκ μαρμάρων πολυτελῶν τῇ αἴγλῃ ἀστραπτόντων·
τὸ ἔδαφος ἐφαίδρυνεν, ἐψήφωσεν ἐν λίθοις,
ἔσωθεν δὲ τριώροφα ποιήσας ὑπερῷα,
50 ἔχοντα ὕψος ἱκανόν, ὀρόφους παμποικίλους,
ἀνδρῶνας <τε> σταυροειδεῖς, πεντακούβουκλα ξένα
μετὰ μαρμάρων φαεινῶν λίαν ἀστραπηβόλων.
Τοσοῦτον δὲ ἐκάλλυνε τὸ ἔργον ὁ τεχνίτης,
ὥστε νομίζειν ὑφαντὰ τὰ ὁρώμενα εἶναι
55 ἔκ τε τῶν λίθων τῆς φαιδρᾶς καὶ πολυμόρφου θέας·
τὸ ἔδαφος κατέστρωσεν ἐκ λίθων ὀνυχίτων
ἠκονημένων ἰσχυρῶς, ὡς δοκεῖν τοὺς ὁρῶντας
ὕδωρ ὑπάρχειν πεπηγὸς εἰς κρυστάλλινον φύσιν. 64v
Ἀμφοτέρωθεν ἴδρυσε τῶν μερῶν ἐκ πλαγίου

37 ταῶνες μέν Legrand: μὲν ταῶνες G
45 σεμνῶν G: συχνῶν Papademetriou, 1957, 7, cf. VTh §3
51 ἀνδρῶνας Mavrogordato, cf. Mel. 829: ἀνδριάντας G τε added by Trapp, δὲ
suggested by Mavrogordato

the meadow bloomed brilliantly beneath the trees
with its many colours, gleaming with flowers,
25 sweet-scented narcissus, roses and myrtles.
The roses were a purple-tinted ornament to the earth,
the narcissus reflected in turn the colour of milk,
the glittering violets were the colour of the sea,
with its calm ruffled by a light breeze.
30 Water flowed abundantly everywhere in the meadow.
Several kinds of birds lived there;
some had been subdued and sought food among men,
but the rest, having won freedom for their wings,
played as they perched among the tree-tops;
35 some birds sang sweetly,
others were resplendent in the radiance of their wings,
tame peacocks, parrots and swans;
the swans browsed for food in the water,
the parrots sang in the branches among the trees,
40 the peacocks paraded their wings among the flowers
and reflected the flowers' colours in their wings.
    In the middle of this marvellous and delightful pleasure garden,
the noble Frontiersman built a delightful house,
of good size, four-square, of hewn stones,
45 with imposing columns and windows in the upper part.
He decorated all the ceilings with mosaics
from costly marbles, gleaming in their brilliance.
He made the floor bright and paved it with stone pieces.
Inside he made upper rooms with three floors,
50 fair in height, with ceilings of many shades
and cross-shaped halls, extraordinary five-domed chambers
with glittering marble that sparkled most radiantly.
The craftsman so beautified his work
that you might think that what you saw was woven
55 out of the precious stones' bright and multi-formed appearance.
He paved the floor with onyx
that had been so highly polished that onlookers thought
it was water frozen into ice.
At an angle on both sides he set up

42–101 The physical structures implied by this description are those of an eleventh- or
twelfth-century aristocratic house; see Xyngopoulos, 1948, 570, Hunt, 1984, 142–5
and Magdalino, 1984, 95–8.

60 χαμοτρικλίνους θαυμαστούς, εὐμήκεις, χρυσορόφους,
   ἐν οἷς πάντων τὰ τρόπαια τῶν πάλαι ἐν ἀνδρείᾳ
   λαμψάντων ἀνιστόρησε χρυσόμουσα, ὡραῖα,
   τὴν τοῦ Σαμψὼν ἀρχίσας τε πρὸς ἀλλοφύλους μάχην,
   λέοντα ὅπως ἔσχισε τῇ χειρὶ παραδόξως,
65 πύλας ὅπως μετὰ κλειθρῶν πόλεως ἀλλοφύλων
   ἐν τῷ λόφῳ ἠγάγετο, ὁπότε ἀπεκλείσθη,
   ἀλλοφύλων τοὺς ἐμπαιγμοὺς καὶ τὰς ἐξολοθρεύσεις,
   τελευταῖον τὴν τοῦ ναοῦ κατάλυσιν ἀθρόαν
   τὴν γεναμένην παρ' αὐτοῦ ἐν ταῖς πάλαι ἡμέραις
70 καὶ αὐτὸν ἀπολλύμενον μετὰ τῶν ἀλλοφύλων.
   Μέσον παράγει τὸν Δαβὶδ χωρὶς ὅπλων παντοίων,
   μόνην σφενδόνην τῇ χειρὶ κατέχων καὶ τὸν λίθον·
   ἐκεῖθεν δὲ τὸν Γολιὰθ μέγαν τῇ ἡλικίᾳ
   καὶ τῇ ἰδέᾳ φοβερὸν πολύν τε ἐν ἰσχύϊ,
75 πεφραγμένον ἐκ κεφαλῆς μέχρι ποδῶν σιδήρῳ
   καὶ τῇ χειρὶ ἀκόντιον φέροντα ὡς ἀττίον,
   ὁλοσίδηρον τῇ χροᾷ τῇ τοῦ ζωγράφου τέχνῃ
   ἔγραψε τοῦτον καὶ αὐτοῦ κινήματα πολέμου –
   λίθῳ εὐστόχως τε βληθεὶς ὁ Γολιὰθ εὐθέως
80 ἐπὶ τὴν γῆν κατέπεσε τρωμένος παραυτίκα –
   καὶ τὸν Δαβὶδ δραμόντα τε καὶ ἄραντα τὸ ξίφος
   καὶ τεμόντα τὴν κεφαλὴν καὶ λαβόντα τὸ νῖκος,
   εἶτα τὸν φθόνον τοῦ Σαούλ, φυγὴν τοῦ πραοτάτου,
   τὰς μυρίας ἐπιβουλάς, Θεοῦ τὰς ἐκδικήσεις. 65r
85 Ἀχιλλέως ἱστόρησε τοὺς μυθικοὺς πολέμους,
   τὸ κάλλος Ἀγαμέμνονος, σφαγὴν τὴν ὀλεθρίαν,
   Πηνελόπην τὴν σώφρονα, τοὺς κτανθέντας νυμφίους,
   Ὀδυσσέως τὴν θαυμαστὴν πρὸς τὸν Κύκλωπα τόλμην,
   Βελλεροφόντην κτείναντα Χίμαιραν τὴν πυρφόρον,
90 Ἀλεξάνδρου τὰ τρόπαια, τὴν τοῦ Δαρείου ἧτταν,
   Κανδάκης τὰ βασίλεια καὶ τὴν αὐτῆς σοφίαν,
   τὴν πρὸς Βραχμᾶνας ἄφιξιν, αὖθις πρὸς Ἀμαζόνας,
   λοιπά τε κατορθώματα τοῦ σοφοῦ Ἀλεξάνδρου,
   ἄλλα τε πλήθη θαυμαστά, πολυειδεῖς ἀνδρείας·

75 ἐκ κεφαλῆς Xyngopoulos. 1948. 554. cf. Mel. 1975: ἐν κεφαλῇ G
78 τοῦτον καὶ αὐτοῦ κινήματα πολέμου Xyngopoulos. 1948. 554: τούτου καὶ αὐτὰ
τὰ κινήματα πολέμου G
83 φθόνον Kalonaros. cf. Z3889: φόβον G
86 σφαγὴν Kalonaros. cf. Z3894: φυγὴν G
92 Βραχμᾶνας Legrand: βραγμᾶνας G

60　marvellous dining-chambers, of a good length, with golden ceilings,
　　on which he recorded the triumphs of all the illustrious men of valour
　　from the past in beautiful mosaics of gold,
　　beginning with Samson's battle against the Philistines,
　　how – unbelievably – he tore the lion apart with his hands,
65　how he carried off the aliens' gates, bolts and all,
　　to the hill when he had been imprisoned,
　　his mockery and overthrow of the aliens,
　　and finally the complete destruction of the temple,
　　that he achieved in days gone by,
70　when he destroyed himself together with the aliens.
　　In the middle he displayed David, without weapons of any kind,
　　holding only a sling in his hand and a stone.
　　And next Goliath, huge in stature,
　　terrifying in appearance and great in strength,
75　defended from head to foot with iron
　　and holding in his hand a javelin like a loom,
　　entirely iron in colour through the painter's art:
　　he depicted him and his activities in war –
　　Goliath, who had been swiftly struck by a well-aimed stone,
80　at once fell wounded to the ground –
　　and David, running up and raising his sword,
　　and cutting off Goliath's head and achieving victory;
　　then Saul's envy, the flight of that most gentle man,
　　the myriad plots and God's vengeance.
85　He recorded Achilles' legendary wars,
　　the beauty of Agamemnon, the deadly slaughter,
　　wise Penelope, the suitors who were slain,
　　Odysseus' marvellous daring against the Cyclops,
　　Bellerophon killing the fire-bearing Chimaira,
90　the triumphs of Alexander, the defeat of Dareios,
　　Kandake's palace and her wisdom,
　　the journey to the Brahmans and then to the Amazons,
　　and the rest of the wise Alexander's achievements
　　and a host of other marvellous feats, brave deeds of many kinds;

---

62 The fashion for decorating aristocratic houses in the twelfth century with scenes of past triumphs is discussed in Nelson-Magdalino, 1982. These scenes are drawn from the Old Testament, Greek mythology and the Alexander Romance.
75 Goliath is envisaged in the heavy *kataphrakt* armour that was revived in the tenth century (cf. Haldon, 1975, 30–4); cf. the emir's Arabs at E277.

95 τὰ τοῦ Μωσέως θαύματα, πληγὰς τῶν Αἰγυπτίων
Ἰουδαίων τὴν ἔξοδον, γογγυσμοὺς ἀγνωμόνων,
Θεοῦ τὴν ἀγανάκτησιν, θεράποντος δεήσεις
καὶ Ἰησοῦ τὰς τοῦ Ναυῆ ἐνδόξους ἀριστείας.
Ταῦτα καὶ ἄλλα πλείονα ἐν τοῖς δυσὶ τρικλίνοις
100 ὁ Διγενὴς ἱστόρησε χρυσόμουσα ποιήσας,
ἃ τοῖς ὁρῶσιν ἄπειρον τὴν ἡδονὴν παρεῖχον.
Ἐντὸς τοῦ οἴκου τῆς αὐλῆς ὑπῆρχε τὸ πεδίον
πολὺ ἔχον διάστημα εἴς τε μῆκος καὶ πλάτος·
τούτου ἐν μέσῳ ἵδρυσε ναόν, ἔνδοξον ἔργον,
105 ἁγίου ἐν ὀνόματι μάρτυρος Θεοδώρου
καὶ ἐν αὐτῷ τὸν ἴδιον πανέντιμον πατέρα
θάπτει κομίσας τὸν νεκρὸν ἀπὸ Καππαδοκίας
λίθοις τὸ μνῆμα φαεινοῖς, ὡς ἔπρεπε, κοσμήσας.
Τότε πεῖραν ὁ θαυμαστὸς πρῶτον θλίψεως ἔσχε·
110 μαθὼν γὰρ νόσον τῷ πατρὶ περιελθοῦσαν τότε 65v
καὶ ὅτι πέφυκε δεινὴ θανάτῳ γειτνιῶσα,
ἔσπευδε τοῦ καταλαβεῖν τὴν Καππαδόκων χώραν·
πλησίον δὲ τοῦ γονικοῦ ὡς ἐγένετο οἴκου,
ὀδυρομένους ἅπαντας ὁρᾷ τοὺς συναντῶντας
115 καὶ μαθὼν ὅτι ὁ πατὴρ ἀπέλιπε τὸν βίον,
τὴν ἐσθῆτα διέρρηξε καὶ τοῦ ἵππου κατῆλθεν·
ἔνδοθεν δὲ γενόμενος, περιπλακεὶς τὸ σῶμα,
θρηνῳδῶν ἀπεφθέγγετο μετὰ δακρύων τάδε:
«Ἀνάστα, πάτερ, θέασαι τὸ φίλτατόν σου τέκνον,
120 θέασαι τὸν μονογενῆ, λαλιὰν μικρὰν φθέγξον·
νουθέτησαι καὶ βούλευσαι, μή με σιγῶν παρέλθῃς.»
Εἶτα πάλιν αὐξήσας γε ἐπὶ πολὺ τὸν θρῆνον,
βοῶν ἐναπεφθέγγετο εἰς εὐήκοον πάντων:
«Οὐκ ἀποκρίνῃ μοι τῷ σῷ ποθεινοτάτῳ τέκνῳ;
125 Οὐκ ἀποφθέγγῃ μοι λαλῶν ὡς ἔθος εἶχες πάντα;
Οἴμοι σιγᾷ τὸ μαντικὸν καὶ θηγόρον στόμα,
οἴμοι ἐκλείσθη ἡ φωνὴ ἡ πᾶσιν ἡδυτάτη.
Ποῦ δὲ τὸ φῶς τῶν ὀφθαλμῶν, ποῦ τῆς μορφῆς τὸ κάλλος;
Τίς τὰς χεῖρας ἐδέσμευσε, τίς τὴν ἰσχὺν ἀφεῖλε;
130 Τίς τῶν ποδῶν ἐκώλυσε τὸν ἀνείκαστον δρόμον;
Τίς ἀγάπην τὴν ἄπειρον τὴν πρὸς ἐμέ σου, πάτερ,

95 Moses' miracles, the Egyptians' plagues,
the Exodus of the Jews, the complaints of the ungrateful,
God's wrath, the attendant's supplication,
the glorious exploits of Joshua son of Nun.
All these scenes and many more in the two dining-chambers
100 Digenis recorded in gold mosaic,
which provided boundless pleasure to those who saw them.
  Within the courtyard of the house was a flat area
of great size in both length and breadth.
In the middle of this Digenis set up a church, a glorious structure,
105 in the name of the martyr Saint Theodore;
and in it he buried his revered father,
bringing the body from Cappadocia
and adorning the tomb, as was fitting, with brilliant stones.
  Then it was that the marvellous young man first underwent the
    experience of grief;
110 for, learning that sickness had come upon his father at that time
and that it was severe and bordering on death,
he hastened to reach the land of the Cappadocians.
As he drew near his parents' house,
he saw that all who were coming to meet him were lamenting
115 and, learning that his father had departed this life,
he rent his garments and dismounted from his horse.
And when he had come inside and embraced the body,
he tearfully voiced these lamentations:
  "Arise, my father, look on your dearest child,
120 look on your only child, utter even one word;
give me counsel and advise me, do not slip away from me in silence."
  Then increasing his lamentation again to the highest degree,
he proclaimed at the top of his voice in the hearing of all:
  "Won't you reply to me your most beloved child?
125 Won't you respond to me with words as you always used to?
Alas, the prophetic and God-inspired mouth has fallen silent;
alas, the voice that was most sweet to all has been stilled.
Where is the light of my eyes, where is the beauty of his form?
Who has bound his hands, who has taken away his strength?
130 Who has hobbled the incomparable swiftness of his feet?
Who has dared to sever, father,

106–7 Though the move from Cappadocia to the Euphrates area is brought to our
attention we are not reminded that Digenis' father was the Arab emir.

χωρίσαι κατετόλμησεν; Ὢ τῆς παρανομίας,
ὢ τῆς ἀθρόας συμφορᾶς, ὢ τῆς πικρᾶς ὀδύνης.
Πῶς μετὰ πόνου τὴν ψυχὴν παρέδωκας καὶ λύπης
135 καλῶν με ἐξ ὀνόματος ἄχρι τέλους ζωῆς σου;
Ὢ εὐτυχέστατος ἐγὼ παρὰ βραχεῖαν ὥραν,
πάντως εἰ ἤκουσα φωνῆς, εὐχῆς τῆς τελευταίας,   66r
καὶ ταῖς ἀγκάλαις τὴν ψυχὴν ταῖς ἐμαῖς ἐπαφῆκες·
λοῦσαι τὸ σῶμα ταῖς χερσὶν εἶχον ἂν ταῖς ἰδίαις
140 καὶ καλύψαι τοὺς ὀφθαλμοὺς τοὺς σούς, ὦ καλὲ πάτερ·
νυνὶ δὲ ἀθλιώτερος εἰμὶ παντὸς ἀνθρώπου
καὶ τὰ σπλάγχνα τιτρώσκει μου ἡ ἄμετρος ὀδύνη·
εἴθε μοι μᾶλλον τοῦ θανεῖν ἢ κατιδεῖν τοιαῦτα.
Τί ἀγαθόν, ὦ θάνατε, ἐφθόνησας τοιοῦτον
145 λαβεῖν ἐμὲ ἀντὶ πατρὸς καὶ τοῦτον φθάσαι ζῶντα
καὶ ἀπεφάνθης ἄδικος παρὰ βραχεῖαν ὥραν;»
Ὡς ταῦτα καὶ τὰ ὅμοια ὁ Διγενὴς ἐθρήνει,
πεποίηκεν, ὡς λέγεται, καὶ τοὺς λίθους θρηνῆσαι
καὶ σὺν αὐτῷ ἡ θαυμαστὴ μήτηρ ἡ τοῦ Ἀκρίτου·
150 καὶ οὕτω συνετέλεσαν κηδεύσαντες ἐντίμως
τοῦ πατρός τε τὴν τελευτὴν οὐκ ὀλίγας ἡμέρας.
Εἶτα λαβὼν ὁ θαυμαστὸς τὸ σῶμα τοῦ πατρός του
καὶ τὴν μητέρα μετ᾽ αὐτοῦ ἦλθεν εἰς τὰ οἰκεῖα
καὶ οὕτω θάπτει δεύτερον ἐντίμως τὸν πατέρα
155 εἰς τὸν ναὸν ὅνπερ αὐτὸς ἀνήγειρεν ἐκ πόθου·
καὶ διῆγε μετὰ τοῦ υἱοῦ ἡ μήτηρ τοῦ Ἀκρίτου.
Τὰ δὲ μετέπειτα αὐτοῖς πολυέραστα ἔργα
μικρὸν ἐναποφήναντες ὑμῖν λέξομεν τάδε.
Οὕτω διῆγον χαίροντες καθ᾽ ἑκάστην ἡμέραν·
160 πολλάκις δὲ ἐλάμβανε κιθάραν πρὸ τοῦ τέλους
τοῦ ἀρίστου ὁ θαυμαστός, καὶ ἐπῆδεν ἡ κόρη
μέλος, ὁποῖον Σειρηνῶν ἢ πάντων ἀηδόνων
ὑπερέβαινεν ἡδονήν, τὰς ἀκοὰς ἐκπλῆττον·
τὸν ἦχον δὲ πρὸς ὀρχησμὸν ἐκτρέπων τῆς κιθάρας,   66v
165 εὐθὺς ἡ πολυώραια ἀνίστατο τῆς κλίνης,
βλαττὶν ἐξήπλωνεν ἐν γῇ, ἐπέβαινεν ἐν τούτῳ.

---

136 εὐτυχέστατος Legrand: ἀτυχέστατος G
162 Σειρηνῶν Legrand: σύριγγον G   πάντων Trapp: ποῖον G, cf. VTh §14, note 23
165 πολυώραια Legrand: πολυωραία G
166 ἐξήπλωνεν Legrand: ἐξήπλων G

your boundless love for me? O the lawlessness,
o the overwhelming misfortune, o the bitter agony!
Why did you surrender your soul in pain and grief,
135 calling me by name till the end of your life?
How most fortunate I would have been if for a brief instant
I could have heard your voice, your last prayer,
and you could have given up your soul in my arms;
I would have been able to wash your body with my own hands
140 and close your eyes, my good father.
Now I am more wretched than any man,
and agony without limit wounds my innermost being.
I would much rather have died than seen this.
Why, Death, have you begrudged me the happiness
145 of being taken in place of my father and of letting me see him still
    living?
Why have you shown yourself unjust for the sake of this brief instant?"
    As Digenis mourned in this and similar ways,
he made – so they say – even the rocks lament,
and with the Frontiersman, his marvellous mother.
150 And thus they performed with due honour the mourning rituals
for the passing of his father for several days.
Then the marvellous young man took his father's body
and his mother with him and came to his own dwelling place,
and thus he buried his father for a second time with due honour
155 in the church which he himself had raised out of his desire.
And the mother of Akritis the Frontiersman lived there with her son.
    As for his much-loved deeds after this,
we shall reveal a little about them and tell you this.
They spent their time happily each day in this way:
160 often the marvellous young man would take up his kithara before
    the end
of the evening meal and the girl would sing
a song that surpassed the sound of the Sirens
or all nightingales, astounding the hearing.
Then as he turned the kithara's tune to a dance,
165 the very beautiful girl would quickly arise from the couch
and spread a silken cloth on the ground and take her place on it.

---

158 This is either a sign of abbreviation in G or an indication that there was little more available on the hero. The rather pietistic account in Z3997–4063 draws on previous and subsequent passages on Digenis' home life.

Φράσαι δὲ ὅλως ἀπορῶ κινήματα τῆς κόρης,
τὰς τῶν χειρῶν μεταστροφάς, ποδῶν τὰς μεταβάσεις –
ῥάως ἐφέροντο συχνῶς ἐπόμεναι τῷ ἤχῳ –
170 λυγίσματα ἀκόλουθα κρούσμασι τῆς κιθάρας.
Οὐ γὰρ μέλιτος γλύκασμα τοῖς ἀγνοοῦσι πέλει
ἐφικτόν, οὕτω τὴν χαρὰν οὐκ ἔστιν ἀπαγγεῖλαι
καὶ τέρψιν τὴν ἐξαίσιον ἰδιωμάτων ταύτης.
Εἶθ' οὕτως ἀνιστάμενοι τῆς τραπέζης προσῆκον
175 τῶν ἡδέων ἐτρέφοντο, εἶτα πρὸς τὸν λειμῶνα
τὸν δηλωθέντα ἄνωθεν ὡραίου παραδείσου
σφόδρα ἀγαλλιώμενοι, Θεῷ εὐχαριστοῦντες
<οἱ> νέοι οἱ περίβλεπτοι καὶ εὐγενεῖς τῷ ὄντι.
Ἐν μόνον τούτων τὰς ψυχὰς ἐλύπει καθ' ἑκάστην,
180 ἀτεκνίας ἡ ἄσβεστος καὶ δεινοτάτη φλόγα,
ἧς μόνοι πεῖραν ἔλαβον οἱ τέκνων ἀποροῦντες,
μεγίστην τε τὴν συμφορὰν προξενεῖ τοῖς ἐν βίῳ.
Ὑπὲρ τούτου ἐδέοντο τοῦ Θεοῦ καθ' ἑκάστην
καὶ τῆς πρώτης τῶν ἀρετῶν ἐσεμνύνοντο σφόδρα,
185 τῆς εὐποιΐας λέγω δὴ καὶ τῆς ἐλεημοσύνης·
ὅμως θελήματι Θεοῦ ἥμαρτον τῆς ἐλπίδος,
ἀλλὰ λίαν ὡς σώφρονες τῷ Θεῷ ηὐχαρίστουν,
τοῖς οἰκείοις δὲ σφάλμασιν ἔγραφον τὴν αἰτίαν.
Ἐν τούτῳ νόσος τῇ μητρὶ ἐλθοῦσα τοῦ Ἀκρίτου,
190 διὰ τεσσάρων ἡμερῶν τὴν φωνὴν ἐπαφῆκε·
ἰσχυρῶς αὐτὴν ἔκλαυσε καὶ ἐπένθησε λίαν 67r
ὁ Διγενής, ἐν μνήματι σὺν τῷ πατρὶ κηδεύει.
Ζήσασα μετὰ τελευτὴν τοῦ ἀνδρὸς ἔτη πέντε
καὶ πᾶσιν ἐντρυφήσασα ἀγαθοῖς ἐν τῷ κόσμῳ,
195 ἡ ὄντως ἀξιέπαινος ἐν γυναιξὶ φανεῖσα,
ἡ ἐν τῷ κάλλει τρέψασα ποτὲ τοὺς πολεμίους,
πολλοὺς ἐλευθερώσασα δεινῆς αἰχμαλωσίας
καὶ εἰρήνην βραβεύσασα πόλεσί τε καὶ κώμαις·
καὶ γὰρ ἐκ ταύτης ἡ ἀρχὴ γέγονε τῶν κρειττόνων,
200 συνεργίᾳ τῇ θεϊκῇ τὴν ἔχθραν καθελοῦσα
καὶ χαρὰν ἀντεισάξασα πανταχοῦ καὶ εἰρήνην,

172 Οὐ Mavrogordato: ὡς G
178 οἱ¹ added by Legrand
179 Ἐν Legrand: ὂν G
190 φωνὴν G: ψυχὴν Mavrogordato
194 ἀγαθοῖς Legrand: ἀγαθοῖς τοῖς G

I am quite unable to describe the girl's movements,
the fluttering of her arms, the skipping of her feet
– which, following the tune, were often easily carried away with it –
170 the sinuous turns that matched the beat of the kithara.
Those who have not tasted honey cannot comprehend its sweetness,
and so it is impossible to describe the joy
and extraordinary delight of her expressions.
Thus, when they rose from the table, they had been appropriately
175 nourished with sweetness; and next, to the meadow
in the lovely pleasure garden already described,
rejoicing greatly and giving thanks to God,
these renowned and truly high-born young people would go.
One thing alone grieved their souls each day:
180 the unquenched and most dreadful flame of childlessness,
of which only those who lack children have experience,
and which ushers in the greatest misfortune to those in this life.
For this they prayed to God each day,
and they prided themselves on the first of the virtues especially,
185 I mean charity and alms-giving.
However, by God's will they were disappointed in their hope
but, in their prudence, they gave thanks to God
and ascribed the cause to their own wrong-doings.
In the meantime sickness came to the mother of Akritis the
Frontiersman;
190 within four days she ceased speaking.
Digenis wept for her vigorously and mourned deeply,
and laid her in a tomb with his father.
She had lived for five years after her husband's death,
and had delighted in all the good things of this world;
195 she had been truly praiseworthy among women,
she had once enchanted her enemies with her beauty,
she had set many free from dreadful captivity,
she had bestowed peace on cities and villages;
and through her there was a beginning of better things:
200 with divine assistance she destroyed enmity
and introduced joy and peace everywhere.

ῥίζαν καὶ κλάδον εὐγενῆ τεκοῦσα καὶ ὡραῖον·
ὃς πάντων τῶν Ἀγαρηνῶν φρυάγματα καθεῖλε
καὶ πόλεις προενόμευσε καὶ τῷ κράτει συνῆψε.

205 Πρὸ γὰρ τούτου τοῦ θαυμαστοῦ καὶ γενναίου Ἀκρίτου
ἀδεῶς ἐξερχόμενα γένη τῶν Αἰθιόπων
ἀφειδῶς ἐξηφάνιζον τὰς πόλεις τῶν Ῥωμαίων
καὶ οἱ τῶν δούλων ἔκγονοι παῖδας τῶν ἐλευθέρων
τοὺς τιμίους καὶ εὐγενεῖς ἐπὶ δουλείαν ἦγον.

210 Ἡνίκα δὲ ὁ δι' ἡμᾶς γεννηθεὶς ἐκ παρθένου
ὡς ἀγαθὸς ηὐδόκησε πάντας ἐλευθερῶσαι,
τὴν θαυμαστὴν καὶ ἔνδοξον ποιεῖ οἰκονομίαν
φίλον γενέσθαι τὸν ἐχθρὸν καὶ ἐξ αὐτοῦ τεχθῆναι
τὸν τῆς ἀνδρείας στέφανον, τὸν Διγενὴν Ἀκρίτην,

215 καὶ ἐγένετο ἀληθῶς ἐξ ἐχθρῶν σωτηρία,
τοσούτων γὰρ τῶν ἀγαθῶν παρ' αὐτοῦ ἐκαρποῦτο·
καὶ εἰς τέλος ἐπλήσθησαν οἱ αἰχμάλωτοι πάντες
ὡς δούλους κτῆσαι τοὺς αὐτῶν δεινοτάτους δεσπότας.
Ἆρα πόσης ἀπήλαυσαν οἱ συγγενεῖς ἐκείνων 67ᵛ

220 χαρμονῆς ὄντως τοὺς αὐτῶν δεξάμενοι γνωρίμους;
Πόλεμος δὲ τὸ σύνολον ἢ ἀκοὴ πολέμου
οὐδαμῶς ἐγνωρίζετο ἐν ταῖς αὐτοῦ ἡμέραις
ἀλλ' ἦν εἰρήνη πανταχοῦ, ἠρεμία μεγάλη,
καὶ πάντες ἄνθρωποι συχνῶς τῷ Θεῷ ηὐχαρίστουν

225 καὶ ἅπαντες τὸν Διγενὴν ἐκάλουν εὐεργέτην,
ἀντιλήπτορα μέγιστον καὶ σὺν Θεῷ προστάτην
καὶ πολλοὶ ἐπευφραίνοντο τῇ τούτου βασιλείᾳ
δοξάζοντες ἀσύγχυτον Τριάδα παναγίαν,
ᾗ πρέπει ἡ προσκύνησις εἰς ἅπαντας αἰῶνας.

202 G writes εἰρήνην with ὡραῖον in the margin
203 Ἀγαρηνῶν φρυάγματα Legrand: φρυάγματα ἀγαρηνῶν G
217 ἐπλήσθησαν G: ἐρρύσθησαν Tsopanakis, 1960, 81–2

bearing a root and a high-born and beautiful branch,
which destroyed all the insolence of the Agarenes
and plundered cities and joined them to the state.
205 For before Akritis the marvellous and noble Frontiersman,
the tribes of Ethiopians raided freely,
and ravaged the Romans' cities pitilessly;
the offspring of slaves carried off into slavery
the honourable and high-born children of free men.
210 When He who was born of a virgin for our sakes
consented out of his goodness to set all men free,
He granted the marvellous and glorious dispensation
that the enemy should become a friend, and from this enemy was born
the crown of bravery, Digenis Akritis, the Frontiersman of Double
Descent;
215 and he truly became a salvation from out of the enemy,
for so much good was reaped from him;
and finally all captives were fulfilled
when, though enslaved, they gained possession of their most dreadful
masters.
Indeed, how truly great was the delight of their kinsmen
220 when they received those known to them?
War or the rumour of war was in no way
whatsoever known in his days,
but there was peace everywhere, a great tranquillity;
everyone gave frequent thanks to God,
225 and everyone called Digenis their benefactor,
their greatest protector and defender with God.
And many rejoiced in his rule,
praising unceasingly the all-holy Trinity,
to whom is due worship throughout all ages.

203, 206 The Agarenes (i.e. sons of Hagar) and the Ethiopians are, as previously,
synonyms for Arabs.
208 A derogatory reference, of a sort not found in the earlier books, to the descent in
biblical terms of Arabs from Abraham's slave girl (Genesis 16). The oxymoron of the
descendants of slaves enslaving the children of the free is a recurrent theme in
Makremvolitis' novel.
229 An encomium of Digenis's mother in eirenic terms (hence presumably her name
Eirene in Z) moves to praise of Digenis himself, who has become a Christ-like symbol of
peace and unity. In the author's view the time of Digenis was a golden age; yet his
childlessness (the result of the moral lapses of G5 and 6?) ensures that not only is that age
past but that it is also irretrievable.

Τῆς αὐτοῦ τελευτῆς: λόγος ὄγδοος

Ἐπειδὴ πάντα τὰ τερπνὰ τοῦ πλάνου κόσμου τούτου   *E1695*
Ἅϊδης μαραίνει καὶ δεινὸς παραλαμβάνει Χάρων   *E1696, 1796*
καὶ ὡς ὄναρ παρέρχεται καὶ σκιὰ παρατρέχει,
καπνὸς ὥσπερ λυόμενος πᾶς πλοῦτος τοῦδε βίου,
5 κατέλαβε καὶ θάνατος τοῦ θαυμαστοῦ Ἀκρίτου,   *E1697*
γεναμένης τῆς ἀφορμῆς ἀπὸ τοῦ βαλανείου.
  Ποτὲ γὰρ φίλοι πρὸς αὐτὸν ἐλθόντες ἐκ τὸ Ἔμετ,
ὀρθόδοξοι ἀπὸ πατρὸς συγγενεῖς αὐτοῦ ὄντες
(οἱ γὰρ πλείονες συγγενεῖς ταῖς χρησταῖς νουθεσίαις
10 τοῦ πατρὸς ἐστηρίχθησαν πρὸς ὀρθόδοξον πίστιν),
εἶχον δὲ θέλημα πολύ, ἐπιθυμίαν πάντες
τοῦτον ὁμοῦ θεάσασθαι καὶ τὴν αὐτοῦ ἀνδρείαν·
τινὲς δὲ ὄντες ἀπ᾽ αὐτῶν τῆς πατρῴας θρησκείας
Χριστιανοὶ γεγόνασιν Ἀκρίτου νουθεσίᾳ.   68r
15 Ἐκείνων, ὡς δεδήλωται, πρὸς τοῦτον ἀφιγμένων,
ἀσμένως τούτους δέχεται ἡ φιλάγαθος γνώμη·
τούτων ὡς ὄντων εὐγενῶν κρειττόνων τε καὶ ἄλλων
δέδωκεν εἰς καταγωγὴν τερπνὸν ξενοδοχεῖον,
ὃ τῶν ἄλλων ἐτύγχανεν ἐγγύτερον τοῦ οἴκου·
20 καὶ μετ᾽ αὐτῶν ἐφ᾽ ἱκανὰς ἡμέρας διατρίψας,
πολλά τε καὶ ἐξαίσια ἀριστεύματα δράσας,
εἰς θήραν ἐξερχόμενος σὺν αὐτοῖς καθ᾽ ἑκάστην,
θάμβος μὲν εἶχεν ἅπαντας καὶ ἔκπληξις μεγίστη
κατανοοῦντας τὴν ἰσχὺν καὶ τὸν ἄπειρον δρόμον·
25 οὐδέπω γὰρ τὸ εὑρεθὲν εἶχε τοῦ ἀποδρᾶσαι
ἀλλ᾽ εἰς χεῖρας τὰς ἑαυτοῦ εἴ τι δ᾽ ἂν καὶ ὑπῆρχε,

---

7 Ἔμετ Mavrogordato: Ἔμελ G
24 κατανοοῦντας corr.: κατανοοῦντες G

The eighth book: his death

Since all the delights of this deceitful world
Hades shrivels and dread Charon takes them over,
and they slip by like a dream and run past like a shadow,
and all the wealth of this life is like dissolving smoke,
5 so death too caught up with Akritis the marvellous Frontiersman,
with its cause arising from the place he bathed in.
    On one occasion friends visited him from Amida;
they were orthodox kinsmen of his father
(for most of his kinsmen had been firmly established
10 in the orthodox faith by the sound counsel of his father);
all of them had a great wish, a desire,
to set eyes on him and his bravery.
Some of them who had adhered to their ancestral beliefs
became Christian under the Frontiersman's counsel.
15 So when these kinsmen reached him,
his benevolent disposition received them gladly.
Since they were high-born and greater than others,
he gave them for their lodging a delightful hospice
which was nearer his house than the rest.
20 He spent time with them for several days
and achieved many outstanding deeds of valour,
going out each day with them on the chase,
and wonderment seized them and the greatest amazement
when they perceived his strength and boundless speed;
25 for nothing had yet been found that could outstrip him,
but everything that existed fell into his hands,

G8 (cf. E1695–867) describes the sickness and death of Digenis, and of his wife (which
would have been part of *Digenis*), and the universal mourning that followed.
7 Apart from general statements about his campaigns and the encounters in G5, this is
almost the only occasion on which Digenis is shown interacting with Arabs.
16 A Byzantine circumlocution, meaning Digenis.
19 Digenis' large house with its walled garden (cf. G8.210) includes several detached
structures: the church (G7.104–5), and now the bath-house and the guest-quarters.

κἂν λέων, κἂν τε ἔλαφος, κἂν ἄλλο τι θηρίον·
οὐκ εἶχε κύνας μετ᾽ αὐτοῦ ἢ πάρδους πολυδρόμους,
οὐχ ἵππου ἐπεκάθητο, οὐ ξίφεσιν ἐχρᾶτο
30 ἀλλ᾽ ἦσαν ἅπαντα αὐτῷ χεῖρες μόνον καὶ πόδες.
Εἶτα προστάξας ἐν μιᾷ λουτρὸν εὐτρεπισθῆναι
κάλλιστον, ὃ πεποίηκε μέσον τοῦ παραδείσου,
τοῦ σὺν τοῖς φίλοις λούσασθαι, τὴν ἀφορμὴν ἐκεῖθεν
ἔσχεν ὁ πολυέραστος καὶ χρηστότατος οὗτος
35 νοσήματι περιπεσὼν λίαν χαλεπωτάτῳ,
ὃ παῖδες ὀπισθότονον τῶν ἰατρῶν καλοῦσιν.
Γνοὺς δὲ τοῦ πόνου τὸ σφοδρόν, καταλιπὼν τοὺς φίλους
ἐπὶ τὸν οἶκον ἔρχεται καὶ πεσὼν ἐπὶ κλίνης
τὴν ὀδύνην καθ᾽ ἑαυτὸν καὶ τὸν πόνον συνεῖχε
40 ἵνα μὴ θλίψῃ τὴν ψυχὴν τῆς πανεντίμου κόρης· 68v
ὡς δὲ μᾶλλον δεινότερος καὶ σφοδρότερος ἔτι
ὁ πόνος ἔθλιβεν αὐτόν, καὶ γνοῦσα τοῦτο ἡ κόρη,
ἀπὸ βάθους στενάξασα, «Ὦ κύριέ μου,» ἔφη,
«οὐκ ἐρεῖς μοι τί τὸ συμβὰν καὶ πιέζον σε ἄλγος;
45 Οὐ λέγεις, ὦ παμφίλτατε, τίς ἡ ἀδημονία;
Πλείονα γάρ μοι προξενεῖς σιωπῶν τὴν ὀδύνην,
καὶ τὴν ψυχὴν ἀναίρεις μοι, τὴν νόσον ἀποκρύπτων.»
Ὁ δὲ μᾶλλον τῷ στεναγμῷ ταύτην ἀλγήσας πλέον
(οὐ γὰρ ἐβούλετο ποτὲ κατιδεῖν τεθλιμμένην):
50 «Οὐδὲν ἄλλο, ἐμὴ ψυχή, πιέζει καὶ συντρίβει,
εἰ μὴ πόνος ἀφόρητος τὰ ὀστᾶ μου ἀπέσω·
ὀσφὺν γὰρ πᾶσαν καὶ νεφρούς, ῥάχιν, ὀστᾶ καὶ πάντας
τοὺς ἁρμούς μου διέλυσε, καὶ οὐ φέρω τοὺς πόνους.
Τὸν ἰατρὸν καλείτω τις τὸν τοῦ στρατοῦ ἐν τάχει.»

---

45 παμφίλτατε Legrand: πανφίλτατε G
54 Τὸν ἰατρὸν ... τὸν Krumbacher, 1904, 343, note 1: τῶν ἰατρῶν ... τῶν G

whether it was a lion or deer or any other wild beast.
He did not have dogs with him or fleet-footed leopards,
he did not sit upon a horse, he did not use swords
30 but his hands alone and feet were everything to him.
    Then one day he ordered the bath to be prepared,
the very splendid one which he had had made in the middle of the
    pleasure garden,
so that he could bathe with his friends. It was from this
that that well-beloved and most worthy man
35 succumbed to an extremely dangerous sickness,
which doctors call tetanus.
Recognising the severity of his pain and leaving his friends,
he went to the house and falling upon his couch
he kept the agony and the pain to himself,
40 so as not to distress the soul of the honourable girl.
But when, becoming yet more terrible and violent,
the pain distressed him, the girl realised this,
sighing deeply, and said to him: "My lord,
will you not tell me what is this grief that has come upon you and
    oppresses you?
45 Can you not explain, my dearest, what is this trouble?
For you cause me more anguish by keeping silent about your agony,
and you tear my soul from me by concealing your sickness."
    But he by his sighing upset her even more
(although he did not wish to see her troubled):
50 "Nothing else, my soul, oppresses me and wears me away
except the unendurable pain within my bones.
For my loins and kidneys, my back, bones and all
my sinews it has undone, and I cannot bear the pains.
Let someone summon the army doctor quickly."

30 Resuming Digenis' bare-handed exploits of G4.
31 On changing uses of bath-houses in urban Byzantine society from the social to the
merely hygienic, see Berger, 1982; little is known on rural bathing establishments such
as this. Baths come to play an important role in later romances; there is perhaps here a
hint of the Alexander legend, and his premature death from a chill caught while bathing.
36 'Doctors': literally 'sons of doctors', by analogy with the 'sons of Asklepios', a
conventional term for doctor. 'Tetanus': strictly speaking, tetanic recurvation in which
the spine curves back.
54 Roman army doctors were a repository of medical expertise (Davies, 1989, 209–36).
On Byzantine military medical specialists in battle, see the *Taktika* of Leo VI (12. 51–2; PG
107, col. 820) and cf. G6.780 for the ointment carried by Digenis in his duel with
Maximou. On the rising status of doctors between the tenth and twelfth centuries, see
Kazhdan, 1984.

55 Οὗ καὶ ἐλθόντος τῇ ἑξῆς καὶ σφυγμοῦ ἁψαμένου,
ἐκ τῆς πυρᾶς τὴν δύναμιν ἐπέγνω παρελθοῦσαν·
ἡ γὰρ νόσος κατὰ πολὺ νενίκηκε τὴν φύσιν.
Στενάξας οὖν ὁ ἰατρὸς καθ᾽ ἑαυτὸν καὶ κλαύσας,
ἐπέγνω ὁ θαυμάσιος φθάσαι τὸ τέλος ἤδη
60 καὶ μηδὲν εἰρηκὼς αὐτῷ τοῦ ἐξελθεῖν προστάττει,
τὴν δὲ κόρην εἰς τὸ ἐντὸς ὑπάρχουσαν ταμεῖον
εὐθὺς ἐκάλει πρὸς αὐτόν, ἡ δὲ παρῆν δραμοῦσα·
καὶ πνεῦμα συλλεξάμενος καὶ στενάξας ἐκ βάθους,
«Ὢ τῆς πικρᾶς,» ἐφθέγξατο, «φιλτάτης χωρισίας,
65 ὢ τῆς χαρᾶς καὶ τῶν τερπνῶν πάντων τοῦ κόσμου τούτου.
Ἀλλὰ κάθισον ἄντικρυς, χορτάσω σε τοῦ βλέπειν, 69r
ἄλλο γὰρ οὐ θεάσεις με τὸν σὲ πολλὰ ποθοῦντα·
καὶ ἐρῶ σοι τὰ ἀπ᾽ ἀρχῆς ἡμῖν συμβεβηκότα.
Μνήσκεσαι, ὦ ψυχὴ ἐμὴ καὶ φῶς τῶν ὀφθαλμῶν μου,
70 ὅπως μόνος τὴν ἁρπαγὴν ἐτόλμησα ποιῆσαι
τοὺς σοὺς γονεῖς μὴ πτοηθείς, μὴ δεδοικὼς τὰ πλήθη;
Τὸ τοῦ στρατοῦ ἀνείκαστον ἐπεχείρουν χωρίσαι
ἡμᾶς, ὦ περιπόθητε, ἐν τῷ ἀδήλῳ κάμπῳ,
οὓς μὴ πεισθέντας τοῦ στραφῆν παρέδωκα θανάτῳ·
75 καὶ ἀδελφοὺς ὅπως τοὺς σούς, σὸν πρόσταγμα φυλάξας,
ἐκ τῶν ἵππων κατέβαλον μηδ᾽ ὅλως τραυματίσας;
Μέμνησαι ὅπως μόνην σε λαβεῖν ἡρετισάμην
τῷ σῷ πατρὶ καταλιπὼν ἄχρι ζωῆς τὴν προῖκα;
Πάντως διὰ τὴν ἄπειρον ἀγάπην σου, φιλτάτη,
80 ταῦτα πάντα πεποίηκα ἵνα σε ἐκκερδήσω.   E1792
Μνημονεύεις, ψυχὴ <ἐμή>, εἰς τὸ Βλαττολιβάδιν,
ὅταν ὁ δράκων μόνην σε ἐν τῇ πηγῇ ὡς εὗρε
καὶ ἀναιδῶς πλανῆσαι σε ὁ δεινὸς ἐπεχείρει,
σὺ δὲ φωνὴν ἐξέπεμψας καλοῦσα βοηθόν με,
85 ἧς ἐπακούσας τάχιον ἐν τῇ πηγῇ εὑρέθην
καὶ τὰ αὐτοῦ φαντάσματα ἀντ᾽ οὐδενὸς νομίσας
τὰς κεφαλὰς ἀπέτεμον αὐτοῦ τὰς πυρφλεγούσας;
Ταῦτα δὲ κατετόλμησα διὰ τὴν σὴν ἀγάπην,
αἱρούμην γὰρ ἀποθανεῖν ἢ σὺ στενάξαι ὅλως.

66 κάθισον Legrand: καθίσον G
81 ἐμή added by Legrand

55 When the doctor came on the following day and took Digenis' pulse,
he realised from the fever that his strength had gone,
for the sickness had completely overcome his being.
    So as the doctor sighed within himself and wept,
the marvellous man realised that the end had already come
60 and, saying nothing to the doctor, ordered him to leave;
the girl who was in the inner store-room
he immediately summoned to him, and she came running.
He drew a breath and sighed deeply
and said: "Oh, the bitter separation from my dearest,
65 oh, the joy and all the delight of this world!
But sit before me, I shall take my fill of gazing on you,
for you will not see again me, I who desire you so much,
and I shall tell you from the beginning what befell us.
Do you remember, my soul and light of my eyes,
70 how I dared to abduct you on my own,
not fearing your parents, not being alarmed at the host?
The immense mass of the army tried to separate
us, my beloved, on the shadowy plain,
and those who would not retreat I handed over to death;
75 do you remember how, respecting your instructions, I threw your
        brothers
from their horses but did not wound them at all?
Do you remember how I chose to take you on your own,
abandoning your dowry to your father for his lifetime?
Yet it was out of my boundless love for you, my dearest,
80 that I did all this, so that I could win you.
Do you remember, my soul, at Vlattolivadin
when the serpent found you on your own by the spring,
and the dreadful creature tried shamelessly to seduce you
and you let out a shriek, calling for my help,
85 and I heard it and came quickly to the spring
and, thinking nothing of its transformations,
I cut off its fire-flaming heads?
I dared to do these things for love of you,
for I preferred death to your grieving in any way.

---

78 Normally the wife's dowry was in the husband's keeping but came under her control
if he predeceased her: the same principle seems to be functioning here though with the
father rather than the husband.
81 Vlattolivadin was in fact the place where the abductor of Aploravdis' daughter had
been attacked by the Arab Mousour (G5.165).

90 Μέμνησαι καὶ τοῦ λέοντος εἰς τὸ αὐτὸ λιβάδιν,
ὅπως ἐμοῦ καθεύδοντος, φῶς μου μεμυρισμένον,
ὥρμησε τοῦ σπαράξαι σε, σὺ δὲ φωνὴν ἀφῆκας,
ἧς ἐπακούσας πρὸς αὐτὸν κατεπήδησα θᾶττον 69v
καὶ θανατώσας ἀβλαβῆ ἐκ τῶν ὀνύχων τούτου
95 σὲ ἐρρυσάμην, πάντερπνε, ἐμπεπλησμένην φόβου;
Κιθάρας δὲ τῷ κρούσματι θέλων μεταβαλεῖν σε,
οἱ ἀπελάται τῷ αὐτῆς ἤχῳ ὁδηγηθέντες
πρὸς ἡμᾶς ἦλθον ἀναιδῶς οἱ τοῦ Ἰωαννακίου,
οἳ καὶ τόλμη ἐχρήσαντο ἡμᾶς ἀποχωρίσαι·
100 πάντως οἶδας, ψυχὴ ἐμή, τὰ εἰς αὐτοὺς πραχθέντα,
ἄνευ γὰρ ὅπλου ἅπαντας θανάτῳ παρεδόμην.
Ταῦτα δὲ ἕνεκα τῆς σῆς ἀγάπης ἐποιούμην,
ἧς οὐ τὸν κόσμον, οὐ τὸ ζῆν εἶχον προτιμητέον.
Μνήσκεσαι καὶ τῶν θαυμαστῶν ἀπελατῶν, ψυχή μου,
105 Φιλοπαππού τοῦ γέροντος, Κιννάμου καὶ Ἰωαννάκη,
τῶν ἐν ἀνδρείᾳ λαλητῶν, πάντη περιβοήτων,
ἄοπλον ἐν τῷ ποταμῷ ὅπως ἐνέτυχόν με
φαρίοις ἐποχούμενοι, οἱ τρεῖς καθωπλισμένοι;
Οἶδας ὅσα ἐσπούδασαν ἐμὲ τοῦ ἀποκτεῖναι,
110 ἡνίκα σε ἐσκέψαντο πρός με ἐπερχομένην;
Σὺ δὲ φωνήν μοι ἔπεμψας βοηθοῦσα τῷ λόγῳ·
"Ἀνδρίζου, ὦ παμφίλτατε, ἵνα μὴ χωρισθῶμεν.'
Παρ' ἧς πλέον δυναμωθεὶς τούτους ἐτροπωσάμην
καὶ κατὰ κράτος ἥττησα τῇ ῥάβδῳ τραυματίσας,
115 οἷς καὶ τὸ ζῆν ἐχάρισα δυσωπηθεὶς τοῖς λόγοις·
καὶ ταῦτα δι' ὑπερβολὴν ἐποιούμην ἀγάπης
τῆς σῆς, πανυπερπόθητε, ὅπως νά σε κερδήσω.
Τὴν Μαξιμοῦν ἐπέζευσα, τοὺς μετ' αὐτῆς ἀνεῖλον,
εἶτα πεισθεὶς τοῖς λόγοις σου, πάλιν ὀπίσω τρέχων
120 ἔσφαξα <τότε> καὶ αὐτὴν λάθρα σοῦ μὴ εἰδυίας. 70r
Καὶ ἄλλα πολλῷ πλείονα διὰ τὴν σὴν ἀγάπην,
ἐμὴ ψυχή, πεποίηκα ἵνα σε ἐκκερδήσω
καὶ τοῦ σκοποῦ ἀπέτυχον, ἥμαρτον τῆς ἐλπίδος·
καὶ γὰρ πληροφορήθητι βέβαιον ἀποθνήσκω,   E1793
125 ὁ Χάρων δέ με ἐκ παντὸς τὸν ἀήττητον τρέπει,   E1794

97 αὐτῆς Kalonaros: σαυτῆς G
101 ὅπλου Trapp, cf. 107 below: ὕπνου G
120 τότε added by Trapp
124 βέβαιον: G writes τέλειον with γράφε βέβαιον in the margin

90 Do you remember the lion in the same meadow,
   my perfumed light, how, while I slept,
   it charged up to tear you apart and you shouted out,
   and hearing you I rushed up to it in haste
   and slew it and rescued you from its claws,
95 my delightful girl, unharmed and full of fear?
   And while I wanted to distract you with the beat of the kithara,
   the guerrillas, guided by its sound,
   attacked us shamelessly, the followers of Ioannakis
   who tried to separate us by force.
100 You know, however, my soul, what was done to them,
   for without a weapon I handed them all over to death.
   These deeds I performed for the sake of your love,
   to which I preferred neither the world nor life.
   Do you remember, my soul, the marvellous guerrillas,
105 old Philopappous, Kinnamos and Ioannakis,
   renowned for their bravery, famous everywhere,
   how they came upon me unarmed in the river,
   while the three of them were riding their chargers and fully armed?
   You know how hard they tried to kill me
110 when they saw you coming towards me?
   You let out a shriek to help me with your words,
   'Be brave, my dearest, lest we be separated.'
   Strengthened the more by this, I routed them
   and defeated them completely and wounded them with my stick,
115 but granted them their lives after they had pleaded with me.
   And this deed I performed out of the excess of my love
   for you, my very dearly beloved girl, so that I could win you.
   I unhorsed Maximou, I destroyed those with her,
   then obeying your words I ran back
120 and slew her then secretly, without your knowledge.
   And many more other things for love of you, my soul,
   I achieved, so that I might win you,
   and I missed my aim, I failed in my expectations;
   for know for certain that I am dying,
125 Charon is totally defeating me who am unconquered,

121 Although other episodes are implied, this recapitulation of Digenis' career
summarises G's narrative quite accurately.
125 The theme of Digenis' death, and his struggle with the personified Charon, if not
traditional when *Digenis took shape, rapidly became so and spread widely (Saunier,
1972, 119–44).

Ἅδης χωρίζει τῆς πολλῆς ἀγάπης σου, φιλτάτη,   E1795
καὶ ὁ τάφος καλύπτει με πολὺν ἔχοντα πόνον   E1796
καὶ ὀδύνην ἀφόρητον διὰ τὴν σὴν χηρείαν.
Ἀλλ᾽, ὦ πανυπερπόθητε, ποίαν σου κλαύσω λύπην;
130 Πῶς σε παραμυθήσομαι; Ποῦ σε ἀφῶ τὴν ξένην;
Ποία μήτηρ συγκλαύσει σοι; Τίς πατὴρ ἐλεήσει
ἢ νουθετήσει ἀδελφός, τινὰ μὴ εὐποροῦσα;
Ἀλλὰ φύλαξον τοὺς ἐμούς, ὦ παμφιλτάτη, λόγους
καὶ τελευταίαν βούλησιν ἐμοῦ μὴ ἀθετήσῃς,
135 ἵνα βιώσῃ τοῦ λοιποῦ τινὰ μὴ φοβουμένη.
Οἶδ᾽ ὡς οὐχ ἕξεις δυνατὸν χηρείαν ὑπομεῖναι,   E1802
ἀλλ᾽ ἄνδρα μετὰ θάνατον ἐμὸν ἕτερον λάβῃς,
ἡ γὰρ νεότης ἐκ παντὸς βιάσει σε εἰς τοῦτο.
Καὶ βλέπεσαι μὴ πλανηθῇς εἰς πλοῦτον ἢ εἰς δόξαν,   E1607
140 ἀλλ᾽ εἰς ἀνδρεῖον ἄγουρον τολμηρὸν καὶ γενναῖον
καὶ βασιλεύσεις ἐπὶ γῆς ὡς πρότερον, ψυχή μου.»
    Ταῦτα σὺν δάκρυσιν εἰπὼν ἀπέπαυσε τὸν λόγον·
ἡ δὲ κόρη στενάξασα πικρῶς ἀπὸ καρδίας
καὶ δάκρυσι τὰς παρειὰς βρέξασα θερμοτέροις,
145 «Ὦ κύριέ μου,» ἔφησεν, «εἰς τὸν Θεὸν ἐλπίζω
καὶ εἰς τὴν ἄχραντον ἁγνὴν δέσποιναν Θεοτόκον·
οὐδεὶς ἄλλος γνωρίσει με, εἰ μὴ σύ, μέχρι τέλους 70v
καὶ τῆς δεινῆς λυτρώσει σε ἐν τάχει ἀρρωστίας.»
    Οὕτως εἰποῦσα ἔρχεται εἰς τὸ ἐντὸς ταμεῖον,
150 χεῖρας τε πρὸς ἀνατολὰς ἐκτείνασα καὶ ὄμμα,   E1806
δάκρυσί τε τὸ ἔδαφος καταβρέξασα ἅπαν
πρὸς τὸν Θεὸν τὸν ὕψιστον ἐπηύξατο τοιάδε·
    «Δέσποτα, δέσποτα Θεέ, ὁ κτίσας τοὺς αἰῶνας,   E902, 1808
ὁ στερεώσας οὐρανὸν καὶ γῆν θεμελιώσας   E1809
155 καὶ πάντα τὰ ὁρώμενα τῷ λόγῳ σου κοσμήσας,
ὁ ἐκ τῆς γῆς τὸν ἄνθρωπον σῇ χειρὶ πλαστουργήσας,   E1812
ὁ ἐκ μὴ ὄντων ἅπαντα παραγαγὼν εἰς εἶναι,
εἰσάκουσον δεήσεως ἐμοῦ τῆς ἀναξίας,   E1837
ἴδε μου τὴν ταπείνωσιν, ἴδε μου καὶ τὴν θλῖψιν·
160 καὶ ὥς ποτε παράλυτον ἐξήγειρας, οἰκτίρμον,
καὶ τὸ θυγάτριόν ποτε τὸ τοῦ ἑκατοντάρχου
καὶ νεκρὸν τετραήμερον Λάζαρον ἐκ τοῦ τάφου,   E1826

136 Οἶδ᾽ ὡς: G writes εἰδὼς with οἶδ᾽ ὡς in the margin
144 θερμοτέροις Legrand: θερμοτέρως G
161 Between θυγάτριόν and ποτε Trapp inserts σωτήρ, τῇ πίστει Χαναναίας, |
ὥσπερ τὸν παῖδα γάρ from Z4383–4, cf. Matthew 8.5–13, Luke 7.2–10

Hades is separating me from your great love, dearest,
and the grave covers me who am enduring great pain
and unbearable agony for your widowhood.
But, my most longed-for girl, what grief of yours shall I lament?
130 How shall I console you? Where am I to leave you, the foreigner?
What mother will weep with you? What father will pity you
or brother give you counsel when you lack for something?
But take note of my words, my dearest, do not set my last advice aside,
135 so that you may live hereafter fearing no one.
I know that you will not be able to endure widowhood,
but you are to take a second husband after my death,
for certainly your youth will compel you to do this.
And see that you are not led away towards wealth and reputation,
140 but towards a brave youngster who is daring and noble,
and you will reign over the earth as before, my soul."
　　Saying this tearfully, he ceased his speech.
The girl sighed bitterly from her heart
and wetted her cheeks with hot tears.
145 "My lord," she said, "I put my hope in God
and in the immaculate holy lady, the Mother of God;
no one else will know me until the end of time except you,
and He will redeem you quickly from this dreadful illness."
Saying this, she went to the inner store-room
150 and raising her hands and her gaze to the east
and drenching the whole floor with her tears,
she made this prayer to the most high God:
　　"Lord, Lord God, creator of the ages,
who fixed the heaven and established the earth
155 and ordered all visible things by your command,
who fashioned man from earth with your own hand,
who brought all things into being out of nothing,
hear the request made by me in my unworthiness,
look on my lowliness, look on my distress.
160 As you once raised the paralysed man, merciful one,
and once also the daughter of the centurion
and brought Lazarus from the tomb when he was four days dead,

130 Widows are traditionally vulnerable, though also capable in Byzantine society of
wielding considerable domestic and economic authority (Laiou, 1981). On ambivalent
attitudes to those outside the nuclear family, see Mullett, 1988.
138 Second marriages on the death of a spouse were legal and frequent but theoretically
not encouraged (Laiou, 1981, 235–6).

οὕτω καὶ νῦν ἀνάστησον νέον ἀπελπισμένον·   E1829
οἰκτείρησον ὡς ἀγαθὸς τὴν ἐμὴν εὐσπλαγχνίαν,
165 σπλαγχνίσθητι νεότητος, Χριστέ, τοῦ σοῦ οἰκέτου,
εἰ καὶ πολλὰ ἡμάρτομεν ἐνώπιόν σου, Λόγε,
καὶ παντελῶς ἀνάξιοι ἐσμὲν τοῦ σοῦ ἐλέους·
ἀλλ᾽ ὡς οἰκτίρμων δέησιν ἐκ ψυχῆς κατωδύνου
πρόσδεξαι καὶ ἀνάστησον νέον ἀπελπισμένον·   E1829
170 δάκρυα μὴ παρίδῃς μου, ἡ χαρὰ τῶν ἀγγέλων,
ἐλέησον, φιλάνθρωπε, τὴν ἐμὴν ξενιτείαν,
τὴν μοναξίαν οἴκτειρον, καὶ ἀνάστησον τοῦτον·
εἰ δ᾽ οὔ, κέλευσον, ὁ Θεὸς ὁ δυνάμενος πάντα,
πρὸ τούτου τελευτῆσαι με καὶ τὴν ψυχὴν ἀφεῖναι,
175 μὴ ἴδω τοῦτον ἄφωνον νεκρὸν ἐξηπλωμένον, 71r   E1853
μὴ ἴδω χεῖρας τὰς καλὰς ἀνδραγαθεῖν μαθούσας   E1855
δεδεμένας σταυροειδῶς, μενούσας ἀκινήτους,   E1856
κεκαλυμμένους ὀφθαλμούς, πόδας συνεσταλμένους·   E1854, 1856
μή με τοσαύτην κατιδεῖν παραχωρήσῃς θλῖψιν,   E1858
180 ὦ ποιητά μου καὶ Θεέ, ὡς δυνάμενος πάντα.»   E1860
    Ταῦτα ἡ κόρη σὺν πολλῇ συντριβῇ τῆς καρδίας
δεηθεῖσα, ὑπέστρεψε τοῦ ἰδεῖν τὸν Ἀκρίτην
καὶ ὁρᾷ τοῦτον ἄφωνον, οἴμοι, ψυχορραγοῦντα·   E1862
καὶ τὸν πόνον μὴ φέρουσα ὀδύνης τῆς ἀπείρου,   E1863
185 ἀπὸ ἀμέτρου καὶ πολλῆς πεσοῦσα ἀθυμίας
ἐπὶ τοῦ νέου συμπαθῶς ἐξέπνευσεν ἡ κόρη·
οὐδέπω γὰρ ἡ θαυμαστὴ θλίψεως πεῖραν ἔσχε,
διὰ τοῦτο ὑπενεγκεῖν ταύτην οὐκ ἠδυνήθη.
    Εἶτα ἰδὼν ὁ θαυμαστός, τῇ χειρὶ ψηλαφήσας
190 (καὶ γὰρ ἀκμὴν <αὐτὸς> ζῶν ἦν Θεοῦ τῇ εὐσπλαγχνίᾳ)
καὶ ταύτην θεασάμενος θανοῦσαν παραδόξως,
«Δόξα σοι,» ἔφη, «ὁ Θεὸς οἰκονομῶν τὰ πάντα,
τοῦ μὴ φέρειν ἀφόρητον πόνον ἐν τῇ ψυχῇ μου,
διὰ τὸ μόνην εἶναι τε καὶ ξένην ἐν τοῖς ὧδε.»
195   Καὶ τὰς χεῖρας σταυροειδῶς τελέσας ὁ γεννάδας
τὴν ψυχὴν μὲν παρέδωκεν ἀγγέλοις τοῦ Κυρίου
καὶ ἄμφω ἐτελεύτησαν οἱ περίβλεπτοι νέοι   E1867

190 αὐτὸς added by Legrand

even so raise up now this young man for whom there is no hope.
Since you are good, take pity on my compassion,
165 have compassion, Christ, on the youth of your servant,
even if we have sinned greatly in your sight, Word,
and are completely unworthy of your pity.
But as you are merciful accept this supplication from a soul in anguish
and raise up this young man for whom there is no hope.
170 Delight of the angels, do not despise my tears,
have pity, benevolent one, on my life of exile,
have mercy on my loneliness and raise him up.
If not, command, God, you who have power over all things,
that I die before he does and surrender my soul,
175 so that I do not see him stretched out as a speechless corpse,
so that I do not see his fair hands that were capable of brave deeds
clasped cross-wise and lying motionless,
his eyes covered, his feet drawn up.
Do not permit me to see such great grief,
180 my creator and God, who is capable of all things."
      When the girl with great affliction in her heart
had made this petition, she returned to look at Akritis the
      Frontiersman,
and she saw him speechless, alas, in his death throes.
And unable to bear the pain of her limitless agony,
185 in her immeasurable and great despondency she collapsed
on to the young man, and the girl expired in sympathy.
For the marvellous girl had not yet had experience of grief,
and so could not endure this anguish.
Then, looking at her and touching her with his hand, the marvellous
      young man
190 (for he had reached the fullness of his life by God's compassion)
saw that she had died unexpectedly
and said, "Thanks be to you, God who regulates all things,
that I do not have to bear unendurable pain in my soul
because she would be on her own and a foreigner amongst the people
      here."
195   And, folding his arms cross-wise, the noble youth
surrendered his soul to the angels of the Lord,
and both the renowned young people made an end

186 The expiry of the hero's wife (whether from sympathy or murder) on his death bed
is a motif not confined to this epic: Saunier, 1972, 129.

228   Διγενὴς Ἀκρίτης

ἐν μιᾷ ὥρᾳ τὰς ψυχὰς ἐκ συνθήματος ὥσπερ.   E1867
    Τούτων τὸν θάνατον ὁ παῖς οἰνοχόος ὡς εἶδε
200 τῷ δομεστίκῳ παρευθὺς δηλοῖ τῷ τραπεζίτῃ
    μετὰ κλαυθμοῦ καὶ ὀδυρμοῦ· οἱ δὲ πάλιν τοῖς ἔξω.
    Τῆς φήμης δὲ καὶ πόρρωθεν ἤδη διαδραμούσης, 71v
    ἄρχοντες τῆς ἀνατολῆς παρεγένοντο πλεῖστοι,
    Χαρζιανοί, Καππάδοκες, Κουκουλιθαριῶται,
205 Ποδανδῖται οἱ δόκιμοι, Ταρσῖται, Μαυρονῖται,
    Βαγδαῖται οἱ ἐκλεκτοὶ σὺν Βαθυρρυακίταις,
    Βαβυλώνιοι εὐγενεῖς καὶ πολλοὶ ἐκ τοῦ Ἔμετ
    ἔσπευσαν ὅπως εἰς ταφὴν φθάσωσι τοῦ Ἀκρίτου·
    καὶ τὸ πλῆθος ἀνείκαστον ἦτον συνηθροισμένον,
210 ὡς καὶ πάντα τὰ ἔξωθεν τοῦ οἴκου πεπληρῶσθαι.
    Τίς δὲ τοὺς θρήνους ἐξειπεῖν τοὺς τότε ἐξισχύσει,
    τὰ δάκρυα, τοὺς ὀδυρμούς, τῶν συμφορῶν τὸ πλῆθος;
    Ἅπαντες γὰρ παράφρονες τῇ λύπῃ γεγονότες,
    τὰς μὲν τρίχας ἀνέσπαον, ἔτιλλον γενειάδας,
215 ἐφώνουν: «Σείσθητι, ἡ γῆ· θρήνησον, πᾶς ὁ κόσμος·
    ὦ ἥλιε, ζοφώθητι, κρύψον σου τὰς ἀκτῖνας·
    σελήνη, μελανώθητι, μηκέτι δᾳδουχήσῃς·
    αἱ τῶν ἀστέρων ἅπασαι σβέσθητε φρυκτωρίαι·
    τὸ γὰρ ἄστρον τὸ φαεινὸν τὸ λάμψαν ἐν τῷ κόσμῳ,
220 ὁ Διγενὴς Βασίλειος, πάντων νέων ὁ κόσμος,
    καὶ ἡ τούτου ὁμόζυγος, τῶν γυναικῶν ἡ δόξα,
    ἐν μιᾷ ὥρᾳ ἔδυναν ἄφνω ἀπὸ τοῦ κόσμου.
    Δεῦτε πάντες οἱ ἐρασταὶ καὶ φίλοι τῆς ἀνδρείας,
    τὸν γενναῖον καὶ τολμηρὸν πενθήσατε Ἀκρίτην·
225 θρηνήσατε τὸν ἰσχυρὸν καὶ φοβερὸν τοῖς πᾶσι,
    τὸν πάντα ὑπενάντιον ἀφανίσαντα ἄνδρα
    καὶ γαλήνην βραβεύσαντα καὶ βαθεῖαν εἰρήνην.
    Γυναῖκες, δεῦτε κλαύσατε καλλονὴν ὑμετέραν,
    αἱ ἐν κάλλει καυχώμεναι, νεότητι θαρροῦσαι, 72r
230 τὴν ὡραίαν θρηνήσατε καὶ πανσώφρονα κόρην.

202 φήμης Legrand: φήμη G
205 Ποδανδῖται corr. from Πονδανδῖται Mavrogordato: Κονδανδίται G   Ταρσῖται
Kalonaros: Θαρσίται G
207 Ἔμετ Mavrogordato: Ἔμελ G

to their souls at the same instant, as if by agreement.
When the young cup-bearer saw their death
200 he at once told the household steward
with weeping and lamentation. And they in turn told those beyond
the family.
The news was already spreading far and wide,
and very many of the leading men of the East arrived,
men from Charziane, from Cappadocia, from Koukou Lithos,
205 the famed men of Podandos, men from Tarsos and the Black Mountain,
the picked men from Baghdad with those from Bathyrryax,
high-born Babylonians and many men from Amida
hastened to be present at the burial of Akritis the Frontiersman.
And a host of unimaginable size thronged together,
210 so much so that the entire outer courtyard of the house was full.
Who has the power to describe the laments on that occasion,
the tears, the wailings, the host of miseries?
For all were out of their minds with grief,
they tore their hair, they pulled out their beards,
215 they cried: "Be moved, earth; lament, all the world;
sun, be dimmed, hide your rays;
moon, be darkened, blaze forth no more.
Be quenched, all you beacon stars,
for the brilliant star that shone throughout the world,
220 Digenis Basil, Basil of Double Descent, the ornament of all young men,
and his wife, the glory of women,
have in the same instant slipped suddenly from the world.
Come here, all lovers and friends of bravery,
mourn for the noble and daring Frontiersman;
225 lament for one who was strong and fearsome to all,
who destroyed every opponent
and decreed tranquillity and deep peace.
Women, come here and weep for your own beauty,
you who boast of beauty and take pride in youth,
230 lament for the beautiful and most chaste girl.

198 E's version ends at this point. How much of G's final section existed in *Digenis*,
which would have included at some point a reference to Digenis' tomb (G8.240–4,
E1662–7), is not clear.
204–8 These place names (see Name Index and Map) span both sides of the frontier
region: the concept of the double descent of Digenis has now reappeared.
211 Elements of ritual lamentation can be discerned in this passage; on the traditional
formulation of the opening questions and the cumulative appeal to the heavenly
luminaries, see Alexiou, M., 1974, 162–3, 168–9.

Οἴμοι, τί τὸ ὁρώμενον; Ἄφνω δύο φωστῆρες
οἱ πάντα κόσμον λάμψαντες ἔδυναν πρὸ τῆς ὥρας.»
    Ταῦτα καὶ τούτοις ὅμοια ἔλεγον θρηνῳδοῦντες
οἱ παρόντες πρὸς τὴν ταφὴν τῶν εὐγενῶν σωμάτων.
235 Τῶν ὕμνων δὲ πρὸς τὴν ταφὴν καλῶς ἐκτελεσθέντων
καὶ ἅπαντα τοῖς πένησι δοθέντα τὰ ἐν οἴκῳ,
τὰ λείψανα ἐν μνήματι κηδεύσαντες πρεπόντως
τούτων τὸν τάφον ἔστησαν ἐπάνω εἰς κλεισοῦραν
παρέκει Τρώσεως τινὸς τόπου τοῦ καλουμένου.
240 Ἐπ᾽ ἀψίδος ἱστάμενος ὁ τάφος τοῦ Ἀκρίτου,
συντεθειμένος θαυμαστῶς ἐκ μαρμάρου πορφύρας,
243 τῆς ἀκρωρείας πόρρωθεν δυνάμενος ὀφθῆναι,
242 ἵν᾽ οἱ βλέποντες ἔξωθεν τοὺς νέους μακαρίζουν·
244 τὰ γὰρ εἰς ὕψος ὄντα τε μήκοθεν θεωροῦνται.
245 Εἶτ᾽ ἀναβάντες ἅπαντες οἱ τότε συνελθόντες,
οἱ μεγιστᾶνες, ἄρχοντες καὶ πάντες οἱ τῷ τότε
τὸν τάφον στεφανώσαντες καὶ κυκλώσαντες τοῦτον
τοιαῦτα λέγειν ἄρχονται δακρύοντες ἀσχέτως:
    «Ἴδετε ποῦ κατάκειται ἡ τόλμη τῆς ἀνδρείας,
250 ἴδετε ποῦ κατάκειται ὁ Διγενὴς Ἀκρίτης,
τῶν γονέων ὁ στέφανος, νέων πάντων ἡ δόξα,
ἴδετε ποῦ κατάκειται τὸ ἄνθος τῶν Ῥωμαίων,
βασιλέων τὸ καύχημα, εὐγενῶν ἡ λαμπρότης,
ὁ τοῖς λέουσι φοβερὸς καὶ πᾶσι τοῖς θηρίοις.
255 Οἴμοι, οἴμοι τί γέγονεν ἡ τοσαύτη ἀνδρεία;
Θεέ, καὶ ποῦ ἡ δύναμις καὶ ποῦ ἡ εὐτολμία, 72v
ποῦ φόβος ὁ ἀνείκαστος τοῦ ὀνόματος μόνου;
Εἰ γὰρ Ἀκρίτου ὄνομα τοῦ Διγενοῦς ἠκούσθη,
φρίκη πάντας ἐλάμβανεν καὶ δειλία μεγίστη,
260 τοσαύτην χάριν ἐκ Θεοῦ εἴληφεν ὁ γεννάδας

243. 242 put in this order by Eideneier. 1970. 319

Alas, what is it that we see? Two bright lights
that shone over the whole world have set before their time."
    These and similar things they said in their laments,
those who were present at the burial of the high-born bodies.
235   When the hymns at the burial had been duly performed
and everything in the house given to the poor,
they buried the remains fittingly in a monument
and built a tomb for them up in the pass
near a place called Trosis.
240 Akritis the Frontiersman's tomb was set on an arch,
it was constructed wondrously from purple marble
243 and it could be seen from a distance on the mountain ridge
242 so that strangers who saw it uttered blessings on the young people;
244 for what is raised high can be seen from far and wide.
245 Then they all climbed up, those who had gathered on that occasion,
the magnates, the leaders and all who at that time
had laid wreaths on the tomb; as they walked round it,
weeping uncontrollably, they began to speak:
    "See where the peak of bravery lies buried,
250 see where Digenis Akritis, the Frontiersman of Double Descent, lies
    buried,
the crown of his parents, the glory of all young men,
see where lies buried the flower of the Romans,
the boast of emperors, the illumination of the high-born,
who was fearsome to lions and all wild beasts.
255 Alas, alas, what has become of such bravery?
God, where is his might, where his courage
and where the incomparable fear brought from his name alone?
For if the name of the Frontiersman of Double Descent was heard,
panic and the greatest horror would seize every one,
260 such grace had the noble youth received from God

232 This phrase, which in Genesis is used of the sun and the moon, refers in twelfth-
century court symbolism to the emperor and empress (Hörandner, 1974, 102–7).
237 Various archaeological remains in the Euphrates area as well as a twelfth-century
development in tomb architecture have been associated with this description: see
Introduction, pp. xxxiii–xxxiv. G's reference to the tomb occurs on the hero's death, while
in E the tomb is listed amongst the hero's building achievements.
239 There is no recollection of any of the battles mentioned previously in connection
with this site (G6.117, 406).
240 Purple marble, i.e. porphyry, was used especially in imperial contexts.
249 Elements of the commemorative elegy, the second of the two types of lament
distinguished by M. Alexiou (1974, 108), can be discerned here.

ὡς μόνῳ τῷ ὀνόματι τρέπειν τοὺς ἐναντίους.
Εἰ γὰρ ποτὲ ὁ θαυμαστὸς ἐξῆλθε τοῦ θηρεῦσαι,
θηρία πάντα ἔτρεχον εἰς τὴν ἕλην ἀπέσω·
ἀρτίως δὲ ὑπὸ μικροῦ κατακρατεῖται τάφου,
265 ἄπρακτος, ἀνενέργητος ὁρώμενος τοῖς πᾶσιν.
Ἄρα τίς κατετόλμησε τὸν ἰσχυρὸν δεσμεῦσαι;
Ἄρα τίς τὸν ἀήττητον ἴσχυσεν ὑποτάξαι;
Θάνατος ὁ πικρότατος καὶ παραίτιος πᾶσι,
Χάρων ὁ τρισκατάρατος καὶ πάντας συναναίρων
270 καὶ Ἅδης ὁ ἀκόρεστος, οἱ τρεῖς ἀνθρωποκτόνοι,
οἱ τρεῖς ἀνελεήμονες, οἱ πᾶσαν ἡλικίαν
καὶ πᾶν κάλλος μαραίνοντες, φθείροντες πᾶσαν δόξαν·
οὐ γὰρ τῶν νέων φείδονται, οὐ γηραιοὺς αἰδοῦνται,
οὐ φοβοῦνται τοὺς ἰσχυρούς, οὐ τιμῶσι πλουσίους,
275 τὰ κάλλη οὐ σπλαγχνίζονται, ἀλλὰ κόνιν ποιοῦσιν,
πηλὸν καὶ τέφραν ἅπαντα ἐργάζονται δυσώδη.
Οὗτοι καὶ νῦν τὸν θαυμαστὸν Ἀκρίτην συλλαβόντες,
ὁ τάφος μὲν κατακρατεῖ, γῆ δὲ τοῦτον μαραίνει
καὶ σάρκας οἴμοι τὰς καλὰς σκώληκες δαπανῶσι,
280 Ἅδης μαραίνει τὰς καλὰς καὶ χιονώδεις σάρκας.
Καὶ διὰ ποίαν ἀφορμὴν ταῦτα ἡμῖν ἐπῆλθε;
Τῇ παραβάσει τοῦ Ἀδὰμ καὶ Θεοῦ ἀποφάσει.
Ἀλλ᾿, ὦ δέσποτα καὶ Θεέ, τοιοῦτον στρατιώτην 73v
οὕτω νέον, οὕτω καλὸν καὶ ἡδύτατον πᾶσι,
285 τί παρεχώρησας θανεῖν καὶ μὴ ζῆν παντὶ χρόνῳ;
''Ἀλλ᾿ οὐκ ἔστιν ὃς ζήσεται,' φησὶν ὁ Θεοπάτωρ,
'καὶ οὐκ ὄψεται θάνατον·' πρόσκαιρος γὰρ ὁ βίος,
πρόσκαιρα τὰ ὁρώμενα, ματαία πᾶσα δόξα.
Χριστέ, καὶ τίς ἀπέθανε τοιοῦτος ἐν τῷ κόσμῳ,
290 τὸ ἄνθος τῆς νεότητος, ἡ δόξα τῶν ἀνδρείων;
Χριστέ, καὶ ἃς ἀνέζησεν, ἃς ἔφερε τὸν νοῦν του,
ἃς τὸν ἐθεασάμεθα κρατοῦντα τὸ ῥαβδίν του,
ἃς ἀπεθάνομεν εὐθὺς καὶ μηδεὶς ὑπελείφθη.
Ὤμοι, φεῦ, φεῦ τῶν ἀγαθῶν πάντων τοῦ πλάνου κόσμου·
295 φεῦ τῆς τρυφῆς, φεῦ τῆς χαρᾶς, φεῦ νεότητος πάσης,
οὐαὶ τοῖς ἁμαρτάνουσι καὶ μὴ μετανοοῦσι,
τοῖς θαρροῦσι νεότητι, ἰσχύϊ καυχωμένοις.»
Ταῦτα καὶ τούτοις ὅμοια θρηνήσαντες ἐκ βάθους,

292 τὸ Legrand: τὸν G

that by his name alone he could rout his enemies.
For if ever the marvellous young man went out to hunt,
all the wild beasts ran for cover in the marsh.
But now he is held down by a small tomb,
265 seen by all to be incapable of movement, incapable of action.
Who then dared to bind this strong man?
Who had the strength to subdue him who had never been conquered?
It was Death, who is most bitter and destructive to all men,
Charon the thrice-accursed who gathers up everyone,
270 and insatiable Hades, the three who slay men,
the three who are without pity, who shrivel up every age
and all beauty, destroying every reputation.
For they do not spare young men, they do not respect the old,
they do not fear the strong, they do not honour the wealthy,
275 they have no compassion on beauty but bring it to dust,
they turn all things to evil-smelling clay and ash.
It is they who have now gathered up the marvellous Frontiersman,
the grave holds him down, earth shrivels him,
and worms, alas, consume his lovely flesh,
280 Hades shrivels his lovely snow-white flesh.
And what is the origin of these things that come upon us?
Adam's transgression and God's decision.
But, o Lord and God, why did you permit a soldier of this kind,
so young, so lovely and most sweet to all,
285 to die and not to live for all time?
But, says God's ancestor, there is no man who will live
and not see death; for life is transient,
and visible things are transient, and reputation is vain.
Christ, who is there like this who has died in the world,
290 the flower of youth, the glory of the brave?
Christ, let him live once more, let him bring his mind,
let us see him brandishing his stick,
let us die immediately and let no one be left.
Alas, woe, woe for all the good things of this deceitful world,
295 woe for delight, woe for joy, woe for all youth;
alas for those who sin and do not repent,
for those who trust in youth and boast in strength."
    Lamenting deeply these and similar things,

286 'God's ancestor': the psalmist David, and quoting Ps.88.49.
292 Digenis' 'traditional' weapon reappears for the last time.

οἴκαδε ἀνεχώρησαν οἱ ἐκεῖ ἀθροισθέντες
300 πρὸς τὴν ταφὴν τῶν εὐγενῶν καὶ εὐαγῶν σωμάτων.
   Ἀλλ᾽, ὦ Χριστὲ παμβασιλεῦ καὶ ποιητὰ τῶν ὅλων,
Βασίλειον τὸν εὐγενῆ, πολυέραστον κλάδον,
ὁμόζυγον τὴν εὐθαλῆ καὶ ὡραίαν σὺν τούτῳ
καὶ πάντας τερπομένους τε καὶ ζῶντας ὀρθοδόξως,
305 ὅταν καθίσῃς ἐπὶ γῆς κρῖναι ψυχὰς ἀνθρώπων,
τότε, Χριστέ μου, τήρησον καὶ φύλαξον ἀτρώτους,
τοῖς δεξιοῖς συντάττων τε μέρεσι τῶν προβάτων·
ἡμᾶς δὲ <πάντας> τοὺς τὸ ζῆν παρὰ σοῦ ἐσχηκότας
κράτυνον, σκέπασον φρουρῶν ἀπὸ τῶν ἐναντίων,
310 ἵν᾽ ὑμνῶμεν τὸ ἄχραντον καὶ μέγα ὄνομά σου
Πατρὸς ἅμα καὶ τοῦ Υἱοῦ καὶ Πνεύματος ἁγίου,
Τριάδος ἀσυγχύτου τε ὁμοφυοῦς καὶ θείας
εἰς ἀπεράντους καὶ μακροὺς αἰῶνας τῶν αἰώνων.

304 ὀρθοδόξως^ους G
308 πάντας added by Trapp
312 ὁμοφυοῦς Legrand: ὁμοφιοῦ G

they returned homewards, those who had gathered together there
300 for the burial of the high-born and holy bodies.
　　But, o Christ, emperor of all and creator of all things,
　– Basil, the high-born, the much loved branch,
　and with him his blossoming and lovely spouse,
　and all who rejoice and live in the orthodox faith –
305 when you come to earth to judge the souls of men,
　then, o my Christ, cherish and preserve them unharmed,
　setting them at your right hand with the sheep.
　And as for all of us who aspire to live with you,
　strengthen, protect and guard us from our enemies
310 so that we may sing the praises of your immaculate and great name,
　the Father with the Son and Holy Spirit,
　the Trinity, unmixed, of the same nature and divine,
　for long and unending ages upon ages.

E: Text and translation

«**Κ**ρότοι καὶ κτύποι καὶ ἀπειλαὶ μὴ σὲ καταπτοήσουν,   139r
                                                              G1.134, 135
μὴ φοβηθῇς τὸν θάνατον παρὰ μητρὸς κατάραν·   G1.138, 2.234
μητρὸς κατάραν φύλαττε καὶ μὴ πληγὰς καὶ πόνους.
4 Μέλη μέλη ἂν σὲ ποιήσουσιν, βλέπε ἐντροπὴν μὴ ποιήσῃς.
6 **Τ**οὺς πέντε ἃς μᾶς φονεύσουσιν καὶ τότε ἃς τὴν ἐπάρουν.
Μόνον προθύμως ἔξελθε εἰς τοῦ ἀμιρᾶ τὴν τόλμην.
Τὰ δύο σου χέρια φύλαττε καὶ ὁ Θεὸς νὰ μᾶς βοηθήσῃ.»
Καὶ ὁ ἀμιρᾶς 'καβαλίκευσεν, εἰς αὗτον ὑπαγαίνει.   G1.161
10 Φαρὶν ἐκαβαλίκευσεν φιτυλὸν καὶ ἀστεράτον·   G3.261
ὀμπρὸς εἰς τὸ μετώπιν του χρυσὸν ἀστέραν εἶχεν,
τὰ τέσσερά του ὀνύχια ἀργυροτσάπωτα ἦσαν,
καλιγοκάρφια ὀλάργυρα ἦτον καλιγωμένον,
ἡ οὐρά του σμυρνομένη <ἦτον>, μὲ τὸ μαργαριτάριν.|
15 Πρασινορόδινος ἀετὸς 'ς τὴν σέλαν ἐξοπίσω   139v
καὶ ἰσκιάζει τὰς κουτάλας του ἐκ τοῦ ἥλιου τὰς ἀκτίνας.
Κοντάριν ἐμαλάκιζε βένετον, χρυσωμένον.   G1.164
Καὶ τότε πάλιν ὁ ἀμιρᾶς τοῦτον τὸν λόγον λέγει:
«Ἀπὸ πολὺν <τὸν> πόλεμον καὶ ἀπὸ δοκιμασίας
20 καὶ πάλιν ἔχω ἀποδοχὴν νὰ ἐπάρω του τὸ νίκος.»
Σαρακηνὸς ἐλάλησεν τὸν ἀμιρὰν τῆς γλώσσης:
«Αὐτό, ἀμιρά, μὴ τὸ γελᾶς, μὴ τὸ κατονειδίζῃς·
ἐγὼ παιδὶν καλὸν θεωρῶ καὶ δυνατὸν πολέμου,
καὶ ἂν ἔχῃ καρδίαν ὁ ἄγουρος γλήγορα νὰ γυρίζῃ,
25 τὴν τόλμην του τὴν θεωρῶ
νὰ ἐπάρῃ καὶ τὸ ἀδέλφι του καὶ ὅλον μας τὸ κοῦρσος» –

4 Μέλη μέλη Karayanni, 1976, 79, cf. Spadaro, 1989, 174–5: μέλη καὶ μέλ Ε καὶ μέλη
Alexiou   After ποιήσῃς Ε has ἂν κατεβοῦμεν (=Ε5), deleted by Alexiou
9 'καβαλίκευσεν Trapp: ἐκαβαλήκευσεν Ε
14 σμυρνομένη Ε: σμυριδομένη Xanthoudidis, 1912, 544   ἦτον [ἦτον] added by
Alexiou
15 'ς Trapp, cf. Spadaro, 1989, 175: εἰς Ε
16 ἥλιου Trapp: ἡλίου Ε
17 βένετον Hesseling: βενέτου Ε
19 Ἀπὸ πολὺν τὸν Trapp: ἀπὸ πολὴν Ε Εἶμαι ἀπὸ πολὺν Alexiou   ἀπὸ πολὺν μου
Krumbacher, 1904, 316
20 του Alexiou : καὶ ἐτούτον Ε καὶ Krumbacher, 1904, 316
22 κατονειδίζῃς Krumbacher, 1904, 316: κᵀνιδίζης Ε
24 καρδίαν ὁ ἄγουρος Ε: ὁ ἄγουρος καρδίαν Alexiou γλήγορα νὰ γυρίζῃ Lambros,
1904, 383: ὅτι να γυρίζη ἐγλύγορα Ε
25 του τὴν Trapp: τούτην Ε
26–32 See the notes to the translation

"... Don't let noises and blows and threats shock you,
don't fear death rather than your mother's curse;
look out for your mother's curse and not for wounds and pain.
4 Even if they cut you to pieces, see that you don't disgrace yourself.
6 Let them kill the five of us and then let them take her.
Just set out eagerly against the emir's daring.
Take good care of your two hands and may God help us."
    The emir mounted and went towards him.
10 He had mounted a horse that was piebald and starred,
it had a golden star in front on its forehead,
its four hoofs were trimmed with silver,
it was shod with solid silver nails,
its tail was perfumed, set with pearls.
15 There was a green and rose eagle silk behind the saddle,
and this shaded its flanks from the rays of the sun.
The emir wielded a blue, gilded spear.
    Then in turn he uttered these words:
"After much fighting and great hardship
20 once again I expect to achieve victory over him."
    A Saracen addressed the emir in his own tongue:
"Do not mock him, emir, do not scoff at him;
I see a fine boy who is mighty in war,
and if the youngster has the spirit to turn quickly,
25 I can see he has the daring
to capture his sister and all our booty"

The text in E lacks its opening pages and up to around 100 lines, and begins on f. 139r
after a space left blank for illustration; see Introduction, pp. xix–xxii. The abducted girl's
brothers are encouraging the youngest in his challenge to the emir; the missing narrative
was probably similar to G1.1–133.
Lines 1–609 (cf. G1.134–3.343) are defined by Alexiou (cf. Ricks, 1990) as 'The Song of
the Emir'; there is no manuscript evidence for this division. The episode would have been
part of *Digenis: see Beaton, 1993b.
10–16 Compare the description of Maximou's horse at E1486–8.
15 Haldon, 1990, 221–2 refers to the multi-coloured eagle silks of Byzantine court
ceremonial in the tenth century, which were used for garments rather than saddlecloths.
21, 30, 46 Why is it surprising that the emir and his henchmen speak the same
language, whether Arabic or Syriac? Is there reference here to a dialect (Karayanni,
1976, 83)? At G1.218 an interpreter is needed between the Byzantine Greeks and the
Saracen peasant.

28 σπεύδει γὰρ καὶ ὁ φθόνος του μὴ καὶ εἰς δειλίαν τὸν φέρῃ.
27 Ταχέως ἐκαβαλίκευσαν, 'ς τὸν κάμπον κατεβαίνουν.
30 Σαρακηνὸς ἐλάλησεν τὸν ἀμιρὰν τῆς γλώσσης:
«Πίασε, μούλε, τὸν ἄγουρον, ταχέως νὰ τὸν νικήσῃς·
29 αὐτὸς σκυλὶ Ρωμαῖος ἔν', μὴ σὲ κακοδικήσῃ.»   G1.189
32 Εὐθὺς ἐκαβαλίκευσαν, 'ς τὸν κάμπον κατεβαίνουν.   G1.172
'Ως δράκοντες ἐσύριζαν καὶ ὡς λέοντες ἐβρυχοῦντα   G1.173-4
καὶ ὡς ἀετοὶ ἐπέτουντα, καὶ ἐσμίξασιν οἱ δύο·   G1.173
35 καὶ τότε νὰ ἰδῇς πόλεμον καλῶν παλληκαρίων.
Καὶ ἀπὸ τῆς μάχης τῆς πολλῆς κροῦσιν διλασυντόμως· 140r
καὶ ἀπὸ τὸν κτύπον τὸν πολὺν καὶ ἀπὸ τὸ δὸς καὶ λάβε
οἱ κάμποι φόβον εἴχασιν καὶ τὰ βουνιὰ ἀηδονοῦσαν,   G1.180
τὰ δένδρη ἐξεριζώνουντα καὶ ὁ ἥλιος ἐσκοτίσθη.
40 Τὸ αἷμαν ἐκατέρεεν εἰς τὰ σκαλόλουρά των   G1.181
καὶ ὁ ἴδρος τους ἐξέβαινεν ἀπάνω ἀπ' τὰ λουρίκια.
῏Ητον <καὶ> γὰρ τοῦ Κωνσταντῆ γοργότερος ὁ μαῦρος,
καὶ θαυμαστὸς νεώτερος ἦτον ὁ καβελάρης·
κατέβηκε εἰς τὸν ἀμιρὰν καὶ κρούει του ραβδέα
45 καὶ τότε ἐχέρισε ὁ ἀμιρὰς νὰ τρέμῃ καὶ νὰ φεύγῃ.
Σαρακηνὸς ἐλάλησεν τὸν ἀμιρὰν τῆς γλώσσης:
«Πίασε, μούλε, τὸν ἄγουρον, ταχέως νὰ τὸν νικήσῃς,
μὴ εἰς σύντομόν του γύρισμα πάρῃ τὴν κεφαλήν σου·
αὐτὸς καλὰ σ' ἐσέβηκεν, τώρα νὰ σὲ γκρεμνίσῃ.
50 Ἐγώ, μούλε, οὐ τὸ ἐγνοιάζομαι νὰ τὸν καταπονέσῃς,
ἀλλὰ μὴ τὸ καυχάσεται ὅτι ἔτρεψεν φουσάτα.»
Καὶ ὁ ἀμιρὰς ὡς τὸ ἤκουσεν, μακρέα τὸν ἀποξέβην,
ἔριψεν τὸ κοντάριν του καὶ δάκτυλον τοῦ δείχνει   G1.193-4
καὶ μετὰ τοῦ δακτύλου του τοιοῦτον λόγον λέγει:

28 σπεύδει Alexiou: σπουδὴ Ε (perhaps correctly: Prombonas, 1993, 74: μὴ καὶ = μὴ
'κε = μὴ οὐκ)   δειλίαν Alexiou: δηλεία Ε
27 'ς Alexiou: εἰς Ε
32 'ς Trapp: εἰς Ε
38 βουνιὰ Trapp: βουνία Ε   ἀηδονοῦσαν Politis, 1973, 344: ἠδονοῦσαν Ε
41 ἀπ' Trapp: ἀπὸ Ε
42 ῏Ητον καὶ Alexiou: ἦτον Ε ἤτονε Krumbacher, 1904, 317
43 θαυμαστὸς Alexiou, cf. Z340: καλώς Ε
44 κατέβηκε Alexiou: καὶ ἐκατέβηκεν Ε
45 ἐχέρισε Karayanni, 1976, 81–2, cf. Spadaro, 1989, 175: ἐχέρισεν Ε
47 Πίασε Alexiou, cf. 31: ὦ πίασε Ε
48 εἰς Alexiou: εἰς τὸ Ε
50 Ἐγώ, μούλε, οὐ τὸ Alexiou, note: ἐγὼ δὲ μοῦλε οὐδὲν τὸν Ε μούλε, ἐγὼ οὐδὲν τὸ
Spadaro, 1988, 145
51 φουσάτα Krumbacher, 1904, 317: φουσάτε Ε

28   – for his jealousy urged him on. hoping to make the emir show
    cowardice.
27   They mounted swiftly and they came to the battlefield.
30   A Saracen addressed the emir in his own tongue:
    "Seize the youngster, my lord, and grab a quick victory.
29   He is a Roman cur! Don't let him do you down!"
32   They mounted at once and they came to the battlefield.
    They hissed like serpents, they roared like lions,
    they soared like eagles, and the two clashed.
35   And then you could see a fight between fine brave youths.
    In the heat of the battle they struck continuously,
    and from the great clashing and the cut and thrust
    the plains grew fearful and the mountains re-echoed,
    trees were uprooted and the sun was darkened.
40   Blood flowed down over their horse-trappings
    and their sweat ran out over their breastplates.
    Constantine's black horse was speedier,
    and its rider was a marvellous young man.
    He charged at the emir and struck him a blow with his stick
45   and then the emir began to tremble and flee.
    A Saracen addressed the emir in his own tongue:
    "Seize the youngster, my lord, and grab a quick victory,
    so that he doesn't take your head off with his sudden turn.
    He has made a fine attack on you and now he might finish you off.
50   I don't think, my lord, you are going to do him much harm,
    but don't let him boast that he routed an army."
    When the emir heard this, he withdrew some way from the youth,
    he threw away his spear and showed him his finger,
    and with this gesture he said these words:

27–32 This passage, though defended by Prombonas (1993, 72–6), has given all editors
problems. Kalonaros and Trapp remove 27, 30 and 31, Alexiou obelises 27, Ricks
obelises 27, 28. With the lines rearranged thus (28, 27, 30, 31, 29, 32), E30–2 form a
narrative doublet to E21–7, opening with the Saracen's address and closing with the
speakers galloping off (cf. Fenik, 1991, 42–50).
31 The Arabic origin of μούλε (= lord) is discussed by Karayanni (1976, 83).
44 In G the stick is the weapon most characteristic of Digenis; we meet it early in E, in
the hands of the hero's future maternal uncle.
53–4 It has been suggested that this is a Muslim indication of submission, referring to
belief in the one God (Alexiou, 1979, 35 and 1985, note). At G1.194 the emir crosses his
fingers, apparently in defeat. Given the lack of clear medieval parallels, it is hard to decide
how either gesture is to be interpreted.

55 «Ζῆς, νὰ χαίρεσαι, νεώτερε, ἐδικόν σου ἔν᾽ τὸ νίκος.» G1.196
Τὸν λόγον οὐκ ἐπλήρωσεν, ἐστράφη ἐντροπιασμένος,
καὶ ὁ Κωνσταντίνος <ὁ μικρὸς> ὑπάει εἰς τοὺς ἐδικούς του.|

Καὶ οἱ πέντε ἐκαβαλίκευσαν, 'ς τὸν ἀμιρὰν ὑπάγουν: 140v
«Ὤ ἀμιρά, πρωταμιρὰ καὶ πρῶτε τῆς Συρίας, G1.100
60 ὤ ἀμιρά, δοῦλε Θεοῦ, πλήρωσον ὡς μᾶς εἶπες, G1.100
καὶ δεῖξε μας τὸ ἀδέλφιν μας νὰ χαροῦν οἱ ψυχές μας.» G1.206
Καὶ τότε πάλιν ὁ ἀμιρὰς μαινόμενος τοὺς λέγει:
«Ἐβγᾶτε εἰς τὰ φουσάτα μου, γυρεύσετε τὰς τέντας, G1.209
καὶ ἂν εὕρετε τὸ ἀδέλφι σας, εἰς μίαν νὰ σᾶς τὸ δώσω.»
65 Καὶ τότε οἱ πέντε ἀδελφοὶ τὰς τέντας ἐγυρεῦσαν,
ἐγύρευσαν καὶ οὐκ ηὖραν την, ἤρξαντο πάλιν κλαίειν. G1.214
Σαρακηνὸν ὑπάντησαν ἀπέξωθεν τὰς τέντας, G1.216
καὶ λόγια τοὺς ἐλάλησεν μετὰ πολλῆς ὀδύνης:
«Κἂν ψηλαφᾶτε, οἱ ἄρχοντες, ὡς δι᾽ ἄγαμον κοράσιον,
70 νὰ εἶν᾽ καὶ ἡ κόρη θαυμαστή, νὰ | ἔνι καὶ Ρωμαίισσα; 141r
Διέλθατε τὸ ἐπανώφορον, <εὑρήσετε> ῥυάκιν· G1.223
χθὲς ἐν αὐτῷ ἐσφάξαμεν ἡδονικὰ κοράσια, G1.224
διότι οὐδὲν ἠθέλασιν ὡσὰν τὰς ἐλαλοῦμαν.» G1.225
Καὶ ὡσὰν τὸ ἐκοῦσαν οἱ ἄρχοντες, ἐθλίβησαν μεγάλως
75 καὶ ὥραν πολλὴν ἐποίσασιν καὶ εἰς λογισμοὺς ἐμπῆκαν
καὶ μετὰ ὥρας περισσὰς ἐφέρασιν τὸν νοῦν τους·
τὰ δάκρυα τους σφουγγίζουσιν, τὰ ῥέτενα γυρίζουν,
καὶ ἦλθασιν καὶ ηὖρασιν τὸ ἑρμηνευθὲν τὸ ῥυάκιν.
Ἐκεῖ ηὖραν τὰ κοράσια εἰς τὸ αἷμαν κυλισμένα· G1.227

55 Ζῆς, νὰ χαίρεσαι, νεώτερε Spadaro, 1989, 176: ζῆς να χαῖρεσε καλὲ νεώτερε E νὰ
ζῆς, καλὲ νεώτερε Lambros, 1904, 383 ἔν᾽ Trapp: ἔνε E
56 ἐστράφη Karayanni, 1976, 85: ἐστράφην E
57 ὁ μικρὸς added by Alexiou
58 'ς Trapp: εἰς E
62 μαινόμενος E: ψευδόμενος Kalonaros τοὺς Kalonaros: τοῦ E
64 μίαν νὰ Alexiou: μίανα E
66 ἤρξαντο Krumbacher, 1904, 317: ἤρξατο E πάλιν κλαίειν Chatzis, 1930, 28:
πάλη να κλέουν E
67 τὰς E: τῆς Alexiou
68 τοὺς ἐλάλησεν Kalonaros: τοῦ ἐλαλήσασιν E
69 δι᾽ ἄγαμον Grégoire-Letocart, 1939, 211: διαγάμον E κοράσιον Karayanni, 1976,
85: κορασίου E
71 Διέλθατε Grégoire-Letocart, 1939, 212: μη ἔλθατε E ἐπανώφορον Alexiou:
ἐπάνμορφον E εὑρήσετε added by Grégoire-Letocart, cf. G1.223
75 ἐποίσασιν Xanthoudidis, 1912, 546, cf. Z394: ἐπιάσασιν E
77 σφουγγίζουσιν Alexiou: ἐσφουγκίζασιν E
78 ἑρμηνευθὲν τὸ E: ἑρμηνευθέντα Alexiou

55 "May you live and rejoice, young man, victory is yours."
He didn't finish what he was saying but he turned away in shame
and the young Constantine went off to his brothers.

The five mounted and they came to the emir:
"Emir, first of emirs and first man in Syria,
60 emir, servant of God, carry out what you promised us
and show us our sister, so that our souls may rejoice."
Then the emir in his fury said to them:
"Go out into my army, search the tents
and if you find your sister I'll give her to you at once."
65 So then the five brothers searched the tents,
they searched and did not find her, they began to weep once more.
They met a Saracen outside the tents
and he addressed them in great anguish:
"Perhaps you are looking, lords, for an unmarried girl,
70 a girl who is marvellous and also a Roman?
Go up to the high ground, you will find a ditch.
Yesterday we slaughtered some enchanting girls in it
because they didn't want to do what we told them."
When the lords heard this, they were greatly distressed;
75 they delayed for a long time, lost in thought,
and after very many hours they came to their senses.
They wiped their tears, they shook their reins
and went and found the ditch that had been spoken of.
There they found the girls dripping with blood,

55 The first words of this speech virtually mean "Congratulations!"
57 Note the patterning in this combat scene: the repeated interventions from the
Saracen (21, 30, 46), the piled-up animal similes (33–34) and those from empathising
nature (38–9); see Fenik, 1991, 57–66. The space left for an illustration and the large
capital marking line 58 indicates that the scribe perceived this as a significant stage in the
narrative.
69 At G1.128 the brothers are merely 'youngsters'.
73 There are probably sexual undertones here; cf. E123 and the brothers' relief that their
sister's virginity has been preserved.

80 τῶν μὲν αἱ χεῖρες ἔλειπον, ἄλλων οἱ κεφαλές των,   *G1.228*
    μαχαιροκοπημένες ἦν καὶ εἰς τὸ αἷμαν κυλισμένες.   *G1.227*
    Τὰς χεῖρας των ἐξήπλωσαν, τὰς κεφαλὰς κρατοῦσιν
    καὶ βλέπουν καὶ τὰ πρόσωπα, νὰ εὑροῦν τὴν ἀδελφήν τους
    καὶ ὅλας ἐγυρεύσασιν, στέκουν καὶ θεωροῦν τας
85 καὶ οὐδὲν ἐγνωρίσασιν ποσῶς τὴν ἀδελφήν τους,   *G1.230*
87 ὅτι συζουλισμένες ἦν καὶ εἰς τὸ αἷμαν κυλισμένες.   *G1.227*
88 Καὶ ὡς εἴδασιν παράνομα, τὰ ποῖα οὐδὲν ἐλπίζαν,
89 εἰς θλίψιν ἐσεβήκασιν καὶ κάθουνται καὶ κλαίουν·
86 χοῦμαν ἐπῆραν ἐκ τῆς γῆς, <'ς> τὰς κεφαλὰς τὸ βάνουν,   *G1.232*
90 τὸν ἥλιον ἐντρυχώνοντες με|τὰ πολλῶν δακρύων: 141v
    «Κὺρ Ἥλιε, τί νὰ ποιήσωμεν νὰ εὑροῦμεν τὸ ἀδέλφιν,
    καὶ πῶς νὰ τὴν γνωρίσωμεν, νὰ τὴν θέλωμεν θάψει;
    Ποῖον μαντάτο νὰ ὑπάγωμεν τὴν ταπεινήν μας μάνα;
    Κὺρ Ἥλιε, τί μᾶς ἔποικες καὶ ἐκακοδίκησές μας;
95 Καὶ ἀπὲ τοῦ νῦν οὐ πρέπει μας νὰ εἴμεσθε εἰς τὸν κόσμον·
    'ς τὸν κόσμον πολεμήσαμεν καὶ δικαιώνουν ἄλλους.
    Γῆ <ὅλη>, θρήνησον πικρῶς καὶ τὸ θέαμα κλαῦσον·
    εἶδες θαυμάσματα πολλά, νὰ σφάξουν ἀδελφήν μας.
    Ἢ πάλι ὅτι αἰχμαλώτευσαν τὴν ἡλιογεννημένην;
100 Κοράσια ἔσφαξαν πολλὰ καὶ ἐποῖκαν τὰ θυσίας
                 εἰς ναοὺς τῶν εἰδώλων,
    εἰς μασγίδια τουρκικὰ καὶ εἰς ναοὺς μεγάλους.
    Ἀφοῦ κατῆλθεν ὁ Χριστὸς ἐξ οὐρανοῦ εἰς τὸν κόσμον,
    ἐδίωξεν τὰς παρανόμας καὶ μυσαρὰς θυσίας,

80 τῶν μὲν Hesseling, cf. Z398: ἐμὲν (= αἱ μὲν) Ε
81 μαχαιροκοπημένες Alexiou: ὅλες μαχεροκοπιμένες Ε
82 κρατοῦσιν Alexiou, cf. Z403: των κροῦσιν Ε
83 εὑροῦν Alexiou: ἐγνωρίσουν Ε
85 ἐγνωρίσασιν corr., from ἐγνωρίσασι Alexiou: ὑμπορέσασιν, να ἐγνορίσουσιν Ε
86–89 This rearrangement (85, 87, 88, 89, 86) is proposed by Ricks
86 ἐπῆραν Hesseling: ἐπλήραν Ε 'ς added by Trapp κεφαλὰς Trapp: κεφαλάς των Ε
91 Κὺρ Ἥλιε Trapp: κυρίλιέ μου Ε νὰ εὑροῦμεν τὸ ἀδέλφιν Trapp: να ευροῦμεν τὴν ἀδελφήν μας Ε τὸ ἀδέλφιν μας νὰ εὑροῦμεν Alexiou
92 γνωρίσωμεν Trapp: ἐγνωρίσομεν Ε
93 νὰ Alexiou: να τὴν Ε
96 'ς corr. : ὅτι ἐμεῖς εἰς Ε ἐμεῖς 'ς Alexiou πολεμήσαμεν corr.: πολεμοῦμεν Ε
δικαιώνουν Alexiou: δικαιῶμεν Ε
97 ὅλη added
98 εἶδες Alexiou: ὅτι εἶδες Ε πολλά Alexiou: πολλὰ καὶ κακὰ Ε νὰ σφάξουν ἀδελφήν μας corr.: να σφάξουν τὴν ἀδελφήν μας Ε τὸ ἀδέλφιν μας νὰ σφάξουν Alexiou
99 πάλι Karayanni: πάλην Ε
100 Κοράσια Kyriakidis, 1951, 358: καὶ κοράσια Ε
101 omitted by Alexiou
102 τουρκικὰ Trapp: τούρκικα Ε

80 some lacked hands, others their heads,
they had been stabbed with daggers and were dripping with blood.
The brothers stretched out their hands, they picked up the heads,
and they looked at the faces too, to find their sister:
they examined all of them, they stood and looked at them
85 but in no way could they recognise their sister
87 because the girls had been crushed together and covered in blood.
88 When they saw these lawless deeds of a kind they had never expected,
89 they began to grieve, they sat and wept:
86 they took dust from the ground and sprinkled it on their heads,
90 beseeching the sun with many tears:
"Lord Sun, what shall we do to find our sister,
and how shall we recognise her to be able to bury her?
What message shall we bring to our miserable mother?
Lord Sun, why have you done this to us and wronged us?
95 From now on we should no longer live in the world:
we have fought in the world but vengeance is taken on others.
All the earth, lament bitterly and weep at this spectacle:
you have seen many incredible things, that they should have
    slaughtered our sister.
Or have they rather made the sun-born girl a prisoner?
100 They have slaughtered many girls and made sacrifices of them
                            in the temples of idols,
in Turkish mosques and in great temples.
When Christ came down to the world from heaven,
he rejected lawless and vile sacrifices,

86-9 The brothers sprinkle dust on their heads as a sign of mourning.
91 With its appeals to the sun and earth this speech has some of the marks of a ritual lament, a tradition of great antiquity (Alexiou, M., 1974, 55–78; Alexiou, note *ad loc.* on evidence from papyri). 'Sun-born' is reserved by E to describe the emir's mother (E99, 143, 218, 441) while in G it is used of Digenis' bride (4.350, 6.134) and Digenis himself (4.635, 4.807).
101-2 While idols are inappropriate in an aniconic Muslim place of worship and thus E101 is suspect (Kyriakidis, 1951, 358; Alexiou, note), the assumption of human sacrifice shows that strict accuracy about Muslim practices is not to be sought in the words of their Christian opponents.

105 ἔδειξεν καὶ τὸν θάνατον καλὸν 'ς τὸν κόσμον τοῦτον.
Καὶ μόνον δὲν τοὺς ἔσωζεν νὰ ἐβγάλουν τὴν ψυχήν σου,
ἀμὴ ἔκοψαν τὰ κάλλη σου καὶ οὐδὲν σὲ ἐγνωρίζουν.
Καὶ ἰδοὺ τὸ σῶμα φαίνεται, <ἀδέλφιν μας,> ὀμπρός μας,
τὴν δὲ μορφήν σου οὐ βλέπομεν, ἔδε ἀνομία μεγάλη.
110 Ἀμὴ ἡ ψυχὴ ὅταν ἐβγῆ, χάνεται καὶ ἡ | ὄψις. 142r
Ὀϊμέν, ἀδέλφι μας καλόν, οὐδὲν σὲ θεωροῦμεν·
ἐξέβηκέν σου καὶ ἡ ψυχή, ἐχάθη καὶ τὸ κάλλος.
Ὁ σκύλος σὲ ἐσκότωσεν καὶ ἐχάσεν σου τὰ κάλλη.
Ὦ πονηρίας, ὠμότητος, ὦ βία τῶν ἀλλοφύλων·
115 ὦ παναθλία, τί ἔπαθες ἐκ τῆς παραδικίας.
Καὶ οὐ βλέπει ὁ Θεὸς ἐξ οὐρανοῦ χυθέντα σου τὸ αἷμα;
Καὶ ὑπέμεινες, μακρόθυμε, τούτην τὴν ἀνομίαν;
Δέξου, καὶ λάβε, ἀδέλφι μας, θρήνους τῶν ἀδελφῶν σου·
ἄσπιλε, παμμακάριστε, δέξου πηγὰς δακρύων.
120 Μίαν μόνην σὲ εἴχαμεν, παραμυθίαν μεγάλην.
Ὡς προσδοκοῦμεν, ἔθανες καὶ δόξα σοι, ὁ Κύριος,
<δόξα σοι> ὅτι ἐφύλαξες τὴν παρθενίαν σου, κόρη.»
Τότε πολλὰ ἀναγκάσθησαν κλαίοντες τὴν ἀδελφήν τους,
καὶ ψηλαφῶντες ἀκριβῶς οὐκ ἡμποροῦν τὴν εὔρειν.| G1.255

125 **Κ**οινὸν τάφον ἐποίησαν καὶ ὅλες ἀπέσω ἐθάψαν 142v   G1.256
καὶ ἐστράφησαν 'ς τὸν ἀμιρὰν μετὰ κακῆς καρδίας.   G1.257
Ἔλυσαν τὰ φηκάρια τους καὶ οἱ πέντε ἐξεσπαθῶσαν
καὶ εἰς πρόσωπον τὸν ἀμιρὰν οὕτως τὸν συντυχαίνουν:
«Ὦ ἀμιρά, πρωτοαμιρὰ καὶ σκύλε τῆς Συρίας·   G1.100
130 τὸ ἀδέλφιν μας τὸ ἔρπαξες, μηδὲν μᾶς τὸ στερέψης.

---

105 καλὸν 'ς Alexiou: καλῶς εἰς Ε
107 ἔκοψαν Trapp: ἔκοψαν καὶ Ε
108 ἀδέλφιν μας added by Alexiou
110 Ἀμὴ Trapp: ἀμὴ ὅμως Ε   ἐβγῆ Trapp: εὔγη Ε
111 ἀδέλφι μας καλόν Trapp: ἀδελφή μας καλὸν ἐχάθης καὶ Ε
112 ἐχάθη Alexiou: ἐχάθηκεν Ε
116 οὐ βλέπει Alexiou: οὐκ ἐβλέπει Ε   χυθέντα Alexiou: χιθέντος Ε
118 ἀδέλφι Hesseling: ἀδελφή Ε
119 ἄσπιλε Alexiou: ἅπλωσε Ε
121 ἔθανες Chatzis, 1930, 28: ἐπόθανες Ε   Κύριος Alexiou: Θεός Ε
122 δόξα σοι added by Alexiou
123 Τότε Alexiou: καὶ τότε Ε
126 'ς Trapp: εἰς Ε
127 τους Hesseling: του Ε
128 εἰς πρόσωπον τὸν ἀμιρὰν Alexiou: κατὰ πρόσωπα τὸν ἀμυρὰν Ε καταπρόσωπα
αὐτὸν Trapp, cf. Ζ442

105 and showed that even death is good in this world.
And not only was it not enough for them to take your life
but they have put an end to your beauty, and you cannot be
recognised.
And look, your body is visible to us, sister of ours,
but we cannot distinguish which form is yours – oh, what great
lawlessness!
110 But when the soul departs, the countenance is lost too.
Alas, our lovely sister, we shall look on you no more;
your soul has departed and your beauty too has been lost.
The cur has killed you and destroyed your beauty.
Oh, the deceitfulness, the atrocity, the violence of foreigners!
115 Oh, most unhappy sister, what have you suffered from this travesty
of justice!
Does God not see from heaven your blood that has been spilt?
And have you endured this outrage, long-suffering one?
Accept and receive, sister of ours, your brothers' laments,
untainted and most blessed one, accept our streams of tears.
120 You were our one, our only sister, our great consolation.
You have died, or so we assume, but praise be to you, o Lord,
praise be to the Lord that you, girl, preserved your virginity."
Then they were very distressed as they wept for their sister
and in spite of searching around carefully they could not find her.

125 They made a common grave and buried them all in it
and returned to the emir in bitter spirits.
They undid their scabbards and the five drew their swords,
they addressed the emir thus to his face:
"Emir, first of emirs and cur of Syria,
130 you have abducted our sister, do not deprive us of her.

---

122 G1.234–54 does not explicitly make an issue of the girl's virginity; preservation of virginity tended to be a preoccupation of twelfth-century, rather than later, texts (Beck, 1984, 112–28).
130–1 The brothers' vacillation over acceptance of their sister's death may be defended on psychological grounds against accusations of textual inconsistency.

Ἦ δεῖξε μας τὸ ἀδέλφι μας ἤ κόπτομε καὶ ἐσέναν.»
Καὶ ὡς εἶδεν τούτους ὁ ἀμιράς, πολλὰ τοὺς ἐφοβήθην,
ἐστάθη καὶ ἀνερώταν τους: «Τίνες καὶ πόθεν εἶστε,   G1.263
καὶ ποίας γενεᾶς ὑπάρχετε ἀπὸ τῆς Ρωμανίας;»   G1.264
135   Καὶ τότε ὁ πρῶτος ἀδελφὸς οὕτως ἀπιλογᾶται:
«Ἡμεῖς γὰρ εὑρισκόμεθα ἀπὸ γενεᾶς μεγάλης·
† ὁ πατήρ μας ἦτον . . . τῶν Δουκάδων τὴν μερέαν· †   G1.266
† . . . † ἡ μήτηρ μας ἀπὸ τοὺς Κιρμαγάστρους·   G1.267
δώδεκα θείους εἴχαμεν καὶ ἔξι ἐξαδέλφους.   G1.268-9
140   Τὸν κύρην μας ἐξόρισαν διὰ μούρτη εἰς τὰ φουσάτα·   G1.270
ἐκεῖνοι ἂν σὲ εἶχαν εὑρεῖ, Συρίαν οὐκ ἐθεώρεις.
Πέντε ἀδελφοὺς ἐγέννησεν ἡ μάνα μας, τοὺς βλέπεις,
καὶ μίαν εἴχαμε ἀδελφήν, τὴν ἡλιογεννημένην,
144   καὶ οὕτως τὴν ἐχαιρόμασθε μὲ τὰς | ἀνδραγαθίας.»   143r
148   Καὶ τότε πάλιν ὁ ἀμιρὰς οὕτως ἀπιλογᾶται:
145   «Πατήρ μας ἦτον Ἀαρὼν καὶ θεῖος ὁ Καροήλης,   G1.285. 4.37
ὁ Μουσελὼμ ὁ ἐξάκουστος πατὴρ ἦν τοῦ πατρός μας
καὶ ἐκεῖ τοὺς ἐνταφίασαν 's τὸν τάφον τοῦ προφήτου.
149   Ἐμὲν ποτὲ οὐκ ἐπήντησεν στρατηγὸς ἤ τοπάρχης·   G1.297
150   φουσάτα πάλιν ἔντρεψα πέρσικα καὶ ρωμαίικα
καὶ κάστρα ἐπαράλαβα ἀμύθητα καὶ <πλεῖστα>,
ἡγεμόνας ἐπίασα Πέρσας καὶ στρατιώτας.
Τὸ θέαμα τὸ ἔπαθα εἰς ἐσᾶς ποτὲ οὐκ ἐλησμονῶ το·
ἀφῶν ἠρξάμην πολεμεῖν ἀνδραγαθίας μεγάλας,
155   οὐδὲν ηὑρέθηκεν κανεὶς ἵνα μὲ καταφθάση
καὶ πολεμήση, νεώτεροι, καὶ ἐπάρη μου τὸ κοῦρσος.
Καὶ ἐδάρτε τὸ ἔπαθα εἰς ἐσᾶς ποτὲ οὐκ ἐλησμονῶ το·

---

131 καὶ [κ'] ἐσέναν Alexiou: τὴν κεφαλήν σου Ε
136 εὑρισκόμεθα Hesseling: ἐβρισκόμ Ε (rest of word illegible)
137 . . . Ε (ink washed away): Hesseling supplied ἀπὸ   μερέαν Alexiou: μερέαν, καὶ γενέαν Ε
138 . . . : .δ. Ε ἡ δὲ Xanthoudidis, 1912. 547   μας corr.: μας εἶτον Ε
140 εἰς τὰ Alexiou: καὶ διὰ Ε
141 εὑρεῖ Trapp: εὕρη Ε   Συρίαν Alexiou: ποτὲ, Συρίαν Ε
143 εἴχαμε Alexiou: ἤχαμεν Ε
148 repositioned by Grégoire. 1940/1. 99
145 Πατήρ Trapp: ὁ πατήρ Ε   θεῖος Alexiou: ὁ θεῖός μας Ε
146 ἦν Chatzis, 1932. 286: εἶτον Ε
147 's Trapp: εἰς Ε
150 πέρσικα καὶ ρωμαίικα Alexiou: ρωμαϊκὰ καὶ πέρσικα Ε
152 πλεῖστα added by Trapp
156 πολεμήση Trapp: πολεμίσι με Ε   νεώτεροι Kalonaros: νεώτερε Ε

Either show us our sister or we cut you down too."
When the emir saw them, he was terrified of them;
he stood and asked them: "Who are you and where are you from?
And from what family are you in the Roman territory?"
135   Then the first brother replied like this:
"We happen to be from a great family.
Our father was . . . of the Doukas faction,
and our mother . . . from the Kirmagastroi;
we had twelve uncles and six cousins.
140 Our lord father was exiled for mutiny in the army;
if they had found you, you would never look on Syria again.
Our mother bore five brothers, whom you see,
and we had one sister, the sun-born girl.
144 And thus we have rejoiced in her, with our valiant deeds."
148   And then the emir replied in his turn:
145 "Our father was Aaron and our uncle Karoïlis,
and the famed Mouselom was our father's father,
and they buried them there at the Prophet's tomb.
149 No general or governor has ever stood in my way.
150 I have in turn routed armies both Persian and Roman,
and I have captured untold and innumerable fortresses.
I have seized Persian leaders and soldiers.
    The humiliation which I endured at your hands I shall never forget.
From the moment I began to achieve great deeds of valour in war,
155 no one could be found to get the better of me
and fight me, young men, and take my booty.
But now what I have suffered at your hands I shall never forget;

132 The emir in this version is not conspicuous for bravery.
134 At this point G1.264 refers to the brothers' 'theme', a term of territorial division of
diminished relevance by the twelfth century; cf. Galatariotou, 1993, 40.
137–8 On the genealogies and the clan names, see the Introduction, pp. xxxiv–xxxvi and
the Name Index.
148 The re-ordering of lines first proposed by Grégoire separates the two sets of
ancestors, and corresponds to the information given in G.
147 The prophet Mohammed's tomb is at Medina and prominent Muslims were formerly
buried within its precincts (EI under 'Baki ak Gharkad' and 'Medina'). E shows familiarity
with names and practices associated with Islam (e.g. at E164–5, 245–8, 285, 288–91,
537–8); see Alexiou, 1979, 33–5 and Galatariotou, 1993, 39.
150 'Persian' may refer to the early years of Islam but is not necessarily to be taken
literally: see Name Index. The places raided by the emir are listed at E732.

'ντρόπιασα τὰ φουσάτα μου καὶ ὅλην μου τὴν γενέαν.
Σήμερον νὰ ἀπόθανα καὶ οὐ θέλω τὴν ζωήν μου.
160 Ἀμὴ ἂς ἀφήσω τὰ πολλὰ καὶ τὸ φλυαροστομίζειν
καὶ ἐδὰ σᾶς λέγω φανερὰ ἅπασαν τὴν ἀλήθειαν,
ἂν ἕν' καὶ καταδέχεσθε νὰ μὲ ἔχετε γαμπρό σας·   G1.304
ἐγὼ ἔχω καὶ τὸ ἀδέλφι σας καὶ ὡς δι' αὐτὴν μὴ λυπᾶσθε.
Καὶ τοῦτο ὀμνύω καὶ λέγω σας μὰ τὸν <καλὸν> προφήτην,
165   τὸν μέγαν Μαχουμέτην:
οὔτε φίλημαν μὲ ἔδωκεν, οὔτε μιλίαν τῆς εἶπα. 143v   G1.308
Ἐσᾶς τοὺς πέντε ἐπάντεχεν ἡμέρας τε καὶ νύκτας
καὶ ἐγὼ ὡς δι' αὐτὸ τὴν ἤκρυβα καὶ ἀναγύριζά σας.
Καὶ ὑπᾶτε εἰς τὴν τέντα μου νὰ εὑρῆτε ἀδελφήν σας.   G1.309
170 Ἀραβίται οἱ ἄνομοι καὶ ἄλλας πολλὰς ἐπιάσαν
καὶ ἐπούλησαν καὶ ἐσφάξαν τας ἀνόμως καὶ ἀδίκως   G1.251
καὶ ἡ ἀδελφή σας ἔτυχεν ἐμένα εἰς τὸ κοῦρσος
καὶ αὐτὴν ἐπαραφύλαττα ὡς διὰ τὰ ὡραῖα της κάλλη.
Καὶ ὑπᾶτε, παραλάβετε ἀμόλυντον κοράσιον·
175 ἐγὼ δὲ διὰ τὰ κάλλη της καὶ τὴν πολλὴν εὐγένειαν   G1.305
ἀρνοῦμαι καὶ τὴν πίστι μου καὶ τὴν πολλὴν μου δόξαν
καὶ γίνομαι καὶ Χριστιανὸς καὶ μετὰ σᾶς νὰ ἔλθω.»   G1.306
        Καὶ τότε οἱ πέντε ἀδελφοὶ 'ς τὴν τένταν ὑπαγαίνουν
καὶ ηὗραν κλινάριν ἔμορφον, ξυλαλόην ἐφειασμένον,   G1.312
180 καὶ ἀπάνω πάπλωμα χρυσὸν καὶ ἀπάνω κεῖται κόρη   G1.312
καὶ ἐκάθετον ἡ λυγερὴ ὡς μῆλον μαραμένον
καὶ ἔκλαιεν καὶ ὀδύρετον, τὰ ἀδέλφια της ἐζήταν.
Αὐτὴ καὶ ἂν ἐμαραίνετον, ἔλαμπεν ὡς ὁ ἥλιος   G1.313
καὶ ὁμοίαζεν ἡ πανέμορφος ἀκτίναν τοῦ ἥλίου.   G1.313

---

158 'ντρόπιασα Trapp: ἐντροπίασα E
161 ἐδὰ Politis, 1973, 342: ἀποδὰ E
162–77 See notes to the translation for suggested rearrangements of these lines
162 γαμπρό σας Hesseling: γαμπρός σας E
164 καλὸν added by Alexiou
168 δι' αὐτὸ τὴν Alexiou: διατετούτην E
169 Καὶ corr.: καὶ τόρα E   ἀδελφήν corr.: τὴν ἀδελφήν E
170 Ἀραβίται οἱ ἄνομοι Trapp: οἱ ἄνομοι ἀραβεῖτε E   ἐπιάσαν Trapp: ἐπιάσασιν E
171 ἐσφάξαν τας Alexiou: ἐσφαξάν τας E
175 εὐγένειαν Trapp: εὐγενίαν E
176 πίστι Hesseling: πίσθη E
178 'ς Trapp: εἰς E
180 ἀπάνω² Alexiou: ἀπάνου E
182 τὰ Trapp: καὶ τὰ E

I have disgraced my army and my whole family.
If only I had died today – I no longer wish to live.
160 But let me stop this chattering and nonsense
and I shall now tell you the whole truth plainly,
in case you can accept me as your brother-in-law;
I have your sister, so do not be upset about her.
165 I swear this and I say to you by the good Prophet,
                              the great Mohammed,
she has not given me even a kiss, nor have I said one word to her.
She has been waiting day and night for you five
and because of that I hid her and deceived you.
So now come into my tent and find your sister.
170 The lawless Arabs captured many other girls
and sold them or slaughtered them lawlessly and unjustly,
but your sister fell to me in the booty,
and I took great care of her because of her delightful beauty.
Come, receive an unblemished girl.
175 For the sake of her beauty and her high nobility
I renounce my faith and my great reputation
and become a Christian and will go with you.''
     Then the five brothers entered the tent
and found a beautiful couch, constructed from aloe wood;
180 on it was a coverlet of gold and on it was lying their sister;
the slim girl was sitting there like a shrivelled apple,
and she was weeping and lamenting, asking for her brothers.
But even though she was shrivelled, she glowed like the sun,
the most beautiful girl was like a ray of sunshine.

162–77 A confused speech which it is hard to reorder convincingly either logically or
stylistically; Trapp suggests: 162, 175–7, 163–74, 178ff; Ricks: 170–3, 168–9, 167,
174ff, G1.301–9 and E agree that: the emir has not touched the girl, that she has asked
for her brothers, that the emir is willing to convert for her sake, that she is in the emir's
tent. E's connection of the emir's concealment of the girl with her need for her brothers
reflects the fear shown at E132.
177 The emir's decision to change faith would seem to be the climax of the speech.
180–5 A piling-up of contrasting images for the shrivelling yet radiant beauty.

185 Τὸ κάλλος ἐμαραίνετον τῆς θαυμαστῆς τῆς κόρης·
ὢ συμφορὰ καὶ θέαμα | καὶ ἀσωτίας ἔργον.   144r
Καὶ ὡς εἴδασιν τὰ ἀδέλφια της τὴν κόρην μαραμένην,
ἀντάμα οἱ πέντε ἐστέναξαν, τοιοῦτον λόγον εἶπαν:
«Ἐγείρου, ἡ βεργόλικος, γλυκύν μας τὸ ἀδέλφιν·
190 ἐμεῖς γὰρ ἐκρατοῦμαν σε ὡς γιὰ ἀποθαμένην   G1.324
καὶ ἐσὲν ὁ Θεὸς ἐφύλαξεν διὰ τὰ ὡραῖα σου κάλλη.
Τὸ ἄνθος τοῦ προσώπου σου ἐμάρανεν ἡ θλίψις.
Πολέμους οὐ φοβούμεθα διὰ τὴν σὴν ἀγάπην.»
Οἱ πέντε τὴν καταφιλοῦν καὶ ἐλιγοθυμῆσαν,
195 οἱ μὲν φιλοῦν τὰ χείλη της, οἱ ἄλλοι τοὺς ὀφθαλμούς της.   G1.204

Κάθουνται οἱ πέντε ἀδελφοὶ καὶ ὁ ἀμιρὰς ἐκεῖνος·
κοινὴν βουλὴν ἐδώκασιν νὰ πάρουν τον γαμπρόν τους,   G1.329
εἰς Ρωμανίαν νὰ ἔβγουν.   G1.329
Καὶ εἰς μίαν ὅρισε ὁ ἀμιράς· 144v
200 τοὺς ἀγούρους τοὺς θαυμαστοὺς τοὺς εἶχε εἰς τὴν βουλήν του,
200a   ἐκράτησεν μετ’ αὐτον·
τοὺς ἄλλους ἐπιλόγιασε καὶ ὑπᾶν εἰς τὴν Συρίαν.

Καὶ ὁ ἀμιρὰς ἐδιάγειρε <ἀντάμα> μὲ τὴν κόρην
203/4 καὶ μὲ τοὺς γυναικαδελφούς, ’ς τὴν Ρωμανίαν ὑπᾶσιν.
205 Ὀμπρὸς ὑπᾶν οἱ ἀγοῦροι του καὶ ὁ ἀμιρὰς ὀπίσω
καὶ τὸ κοράσιον εἰς κλουβίν, βαστοῦν την πέντε μοῦλες·
τριγύρου τὴν παρακρατοῦν τὰ πέντε της ἀδέλφια.
Καὶ βλέπει ὅλος ὁ λαὸς τὴν χαρὰν ταύτην ὅλην·
ὀπίσω τὴν ἀκολουθοῦν θαυμάζοντες τὴν κόρην·

185 θαυμαστῆς Hesseling: θαυμασθῆς E
188 ἐστέναξαν Trapp: ἐστενάξασιν E
190 γὰρ ἐκρατοῦμαν σε ὡς γιὰ ἀποθαμένην corr.: ἐμεῖς ὡς γιαποθαμένην σε
κρατοῦμαν E
193 οὐ φοβούμεθα Alexiou: ἐμεῖς οὐκ ἐφοβήθημαν E οὐ ’φοβήθημαν Trapp ’κ’
ἐφοβήθημαν Prombonas, 1993, 72
194 ἐλιγοθυμῆσαν Trapp: ἐλιγοθυμήσασιν E
197 τον Ricks: τὸν E
198 ἔβγουν Trapp: εὐγοῦν E
199 ὅρισε Politis, 1973, 344: ὅρισεν E   ἀμιράς Alexiou: ἀμυρὰς ἐκεῖνος E
200 ἀγούρους corr.: ἀγούρους του E   εἶχε Politis, 1973, 344: ἦχεν E
201 τοὺς Trapp: καὶ τοὺς E   ἐπιλόγιασε Trapp: ἐπιλογίασε E
202 ἀντάμα added by Alexiou
203/4 γυναικαδελφούς Alexiou: γυναικαδελφούς του E   ’ς Trapp: εἰς E
206 βαστοῦν Hesseling: βαστού E
209 ἀκολουθοῦν Hesseling: ἀκουλουθοῦν E

185 The marvellous girl's beauty had faded –
what a disaster, what humiliation and folly!
When her brothers saw that the girl's beauty had faded,
the five groaned together and said this:
    "Rise up, slender girl, our sweet sister;
190 we thought you were dead
but God has protected you because of your lovely beauty,
though grief has faded the flower of your face.
Because of our love for you, we have no fear of battles."
    The five kissed her and fainted away,
195 some kissed her lips, the others her eyes.

The five brothers sat down and so did the emir;
they made an agreement together to take him as their brother-in-law,
                            and to go to Roman territory.
And in an instant the emir gave instructions;
200 the marvellous youngsters whom he had under his command,
200a   he kept with him;
the others he dismissed and they went to Syria.

So the emir returned together with the girl
203/4 and his wife's brothers; they went to Roman territory.
205 His youngsters went in front and the emir behind,
and the girl came in a litter, carried by five mules;
her five brothers were around her in support.
Everyone observed the whole celebration,
they followed behind her, wondering at the girl.

190–3 A disjointed set of thoughts. Ricks moves 192 after 189.
198 The preservation of the girl's virginity makes the subsequent marriage less shameful, especially since the abduction had taken place under conditions of war (Laiou, 1993, 210).
203/4 A premature assumption of the relationship.

210 ἔβλεπαν τὴν αἰχμαλωσίαν
τὸ πῶς τὴν ἐλευθέρωσεν διὰ τὴν ἀγάπην κόρης.
Τὸ «Κύριε ἐλέησον» ἔκραξαν ὁποὺ τὴν ἐγλυτῶσαν
καὶ Ι ἐδάρτε ἦν ἐξακουστὸν εἰς ἅπασαν τὸν κόσμον 145r   G1.335
ὅτι κοράσιον πάντερπνον ἐνίκησεν φουσάτον   G1.336-7
215 κᾶν χιλιάδες ἑκατὸν ὡς γιὰ τὰ ὡραῖα της κάλλη
καὶ ἐδιάγειρεν τὸν ἀμιρὰν τὸν πρῶτον τῆς Συρίας.
Καὶ ἀφότις εὐλογήθησαν, ἐχαίρετον μετ' αὔτην.

Καὶ ἀφότις ἐκοιμήθηκεν τὴν ἡλιογεννημένην,
ἔτεκαν παῖδα θαυμαστόν, τὸν Διγενὴν Ἀκρίτην,   G2.48
220 φωστήραν τὸν αὐγερινόν, ἥλιον τὸν φωσφόρον,
καὶ περιέκλαμπρον τὸ φῶς εἰς ἅπασαν τὴν κτίσιν,
καὶ εἰς ἀπελάτας δυνατὸν καὶ εἰς τοὺς ἀνδρειωμένους.
Ἐγεννήθη, ἐμεγάλωσεν καὶ ἐγίνην τετραέτης,
ἐχέρισε καὶ ἐμάνθανε τὰς γονικάς του ἀνδρείας.
225   † Καὶ μὲ τοὺς χρόνους τοὺς πολλοὺς †
ἔπεψε Ι ἡ μάνα του χαρτὶν ἀπέσω ἀπὸ Συρίας, 145v   G2.50
<χαρτὶν τοὺς> θρήνους γέμοντα, ὀνειδισμοὺς καὶ θλίψεις: G2.51
«Τέκνον μου ποθεινότατον, ψυχή μου, ἀναπλοκή μου,   G2.53. 4.81
τί ἐσκότασες τὰ ὀμμάτια μου, τί ἔχασες τὸν ἑαυτόν σου;   G2.52
230 Τὸ γένος σου ἐντροπίασες εἰς τὴν Συρίαν ὅλην·   G2.55
χωριάτες ὀνειδίζουν μας τὰ ἔτη τῆς ζωῆς μας.
232/3 Δὲν εἶν' κοράσια εἰς τὸν Παδά, εἰς τοῦ Παστρᾶ τὸ κάστρον,
δὲν εἶν' κοράσια ἔμορφα κάτω εἰς τὴν Βαβυλώνα.

210 τὴν Politis, 1973, 345: ὅτι Ε αἰχμαλωσίαν Ε: αἰχμαλωσίαν καὶ ὅλον του τὸ
κοῦρσος Ricks, cf. E26
211 ἐλευθέρωσεν Politis, 1973, 345: ἐλευθέρωσεν ὁ ἀμυρὰς Ε ἀγάπην Alexiou:
ἀγάπην τῆς Ε
215 κᾶν Alexiou: καὶ Ε χιλιάδες ἑκατὸν Trapp: ἑκατὸν χιλιάδες Ε
218 τὴν Politis, 1973, 345: με τὴν Ε
221 περιέκλαμπρον Karayanni, 1976, 91: περιέλαμπρον Ε
222 εἰς¹ Alexiou: εἰς τοὺς Ε δυνατὸν Kalonaros: δυνατὸς Ε
223 Ἐγεννήθη Alexiou: ἐγενήθην καὶ Ε
225 μὲ τοὺς χρόνους τοὺς πολλοὺς Ε: μετὰ χρόνον οὐ πολὺν Alexiou (notes)
226 ἔπεψε ἡ μάνα του Alexiou: ἔπεψεν καὶ ἡ μάνα του τὸν ἀμυρὰν Ε
227 χαρτὶν τοὺς added by Alexiou ὀνειδισμοὺς Alexiou, cf. G2.51: ὀδυνηρὰς Ε
ὀδυνηροὺς Kalonaros
228 ἀναπλοκή Ε (Karayanni, 1976, 91; Spadaro, 1989, 177): ἀναπνοή Hesseling
229 ἑαυτόν Hesseling: ἐνιαυτόν Ε
230 ἐντροπίασες Trapp: ἐντροπίασες πολλὰ Ε
231 χωριάτες ὀνειδίζουν μας Alexiou: καὶ ὀνιδίζουν μας ἡ χωριάτες Ε
232/3 Δὲν εἶν' Alexiou: καὶ δὲν εἶναι Ε Παδά Alexiou: παδά, εἰς τοῦ παπαδὰ Ε
234 δὲν Trapp: καὶ οὐδὲν Ε εἶν' Politis, 1973, 345: εἶναι Ε κάτω Karayanni, 1976,
92: ἐκτ⁰ (= ἑκατὸν) Ε

210 They saw the emir's prisoners
and how he had released them out of love for a girl.
Those who had rescued her shouted out the "Lord, have mercy",
and from then on it was renowned throughout the whole world
that a quite delightful girl had defeated an army,
215 about a hundred thousand men, through her fair beauty,
and had won over the emir, the first man in Syria.
And when they were blessed in marriage, he had pleasure with her.

When he slept with the sun-born girl,
they bore a marvellous child, Digenis Akritis, the Frontiersman of
    Double Descent,
220 the morning star, the light-bearing sun,
and a brilliant light over all creation,
mighty amongst the guerrillas and men of bravery.
He was born, he grew up and reached the age of four,
and then he began to learn his father's bravery.
225   †And after a long time†
the emir's mother sent him a letter from Syria,
a letter full of laments, reproaches and grief:
    "My most beloved child, my soul, my comfort,
why have you dimmed my eyes, why have you destroyed yourself?
230 You have humiliated your family throughout all Syria;
peasants will be reproaching us all the years of our lives.
232/3 Are there no girls in Baghdad, in the fortress of Basra,
are there no beautiful girls down in Babylon

217 G1 ends at this point.
218–24 This passage, represented also in G at 2.47–9 (and hence also part of *Digenis),
interrupts the flow of the emir's story where loyalty to his mother is about to endanger
his new happiness. Alexiou considers that there is a lacuna before E225, Ricks that these
lines are an early interpolation. Here, as in G, the name Frontiersman and the term
'guerrillas' are introduced without explanation, with a presumption of familiarity. It is
uncertain whether Digenis Akritis is a name or a title, and so it has been translated here
(and elsewhere) as both.
228–91 Cf. G2.51–98. The two versions have many details in common but different
emphases: E foregrounds the attractions of the girls in Syria, G the breaking of faith.

235   τὸν ἥλιον <ν'> ἀντιτάσσουν;
Τὰ εὐγενικὰ τοῦ Χάλεπε κοράσια οὐκ ἐνθυμᾶσαι,
νὰ λάμπουν ὡς ὁ ἥλιος καὶ μυρίζουν ὡς μόσχος;
Καὶ δὲν θυμᾶσαι, τέκνον μου, κοράσια ὁποὺ ἀγάπας
καὶ δέρνουσιν τὰ στήθη των, παρηγορίαν οὐκ ἔχουν;
240 Οὐκ ἐνθυμᾶσαι, τέκνον μου, τοὺς θαυμαστούς σου παῖδας;
Ἐμὲν τὰ παραρίκτουσιν καὶ ὀνειδίζουσίν με
καὶ οἱ συγγενεῖς οἱ πρόλοιποι καὶ ὅλον τὸ φουσάτον,
ἐμὲν κατονειδίζουσιν ὡς διὰ σένα, τέκνον.
Ἤκουσα ἐγέννησας παιδίν, δράκοντα τῆς Συρίας,
245 καὶ ἀλὶ ἐμέν, <ἀλὶ ἐμέν,> ἂν μάθουν οἱ Κασίσοι,
ἂν τὸ μάθουν ἀπὸ τὸ Ἐμὲκ καὶ <τὸ> Ὀραζαβοῦρον,
μὴ ἀνοίξουν | τὸ μασγίδιν των τοῦ μέγα Μαχουμέτη,   146r
νὰ κλάψουν εἰς τὸ μνῆμαν του καὶ νὰ σοῦ καταρῶνται.
Καὶ οὐδὲν θυμᾶσαι, τέκνον μου, τί ἐποίκαμεν οἱ δύο μας;
. . .
250 Καὶ ἀπέκει ἐκατέβημαν 'ς τὸ μνῆμαν τοῦ προφήτου
καὶ ὑπέκλινες τὴν κεφαλήν, εὐχίσθηκά σου, τέκνον·
καὶ ὅταν ἤθελες δοξασθῆν καὶ ἐπαινεθῆν μεγάλως,   G2.81
ἐρνήθης καὶ τὸ γένος σου καὶ ὅλην σου τὴν Συρίαν.
Οὐδὲν θυμᾶσαι, τέκνον μου, τί ἔποικεν ὁ παππούς σου,   G2.60
255 πόσους Ρωμαίους ἔσφαξεν, πόσους δούλους ἐπῆρεν;   G2.61
Τὰς φυλακὰς ἐγέμισεν ἄρχοντας τῶν Ρωμαίων.   G2.62
Καὶ οὐδὲν θυμᾶσαι, τέκνον μου, τί ἔποικεν ὁ πατήρ σου;
Τὸ Κόνιον ἐκούρσευσεν μέχρι καὶ εἰς τὸ Ἀμόρι,
εἰς Νικομήδειαν ἔφθασεν καὶ εἰς Πραίνετον ἐπέβην,
260 καὶ ἂν οὐδὲν ἦτο ἡ θάλασσα, ἀκόμη εἶχε ὑπαγαίνει.

235 ν' added by Alexiou
238 δὲν θυμᾶσαι Ε, cf. E254, 264: οὐκ ἐνθυμᾶσαι Prombonas, 1993, 71, cf. E236, 240
241 Ἐμὲν Alexiou: ὅτι ἐμέναν Ε ἐμὲ Trapp
244 Ἤκουσα Alexiou: ἐγὼ ἤκουσα ὅτι Ε
245 ἀλὶ ἐμέν added by Alexiou   ἂν Alexiou: ἂν τὸ Ε
246 τὸ added by Trapp
247 μὴ Trapp: οὐ μὴ Ε
248 νὰ κλάψουν εἰς τὸ μνῆμαν του Trapp: καὶ εἰς τὸ μνῆμαν του να κλάψουν Ε
249 Alexiou suggests that one or two lines have been omitted at this point
250 'ς Trapp: εἰς Ε
255 πόσους¹ Trapp: τὸ πόσους Ε   πόσους² Alexiou: καὶ πόσους Ε
256 φυλακὰς Grégoire, 1929/30, 330: φάλαγγας Ε φάραγγας Hesseling
257 οὐδὲν Trapp: πάλην οὐδὲν Ε
258 τὸ Ἀμόρι Vogiatzidis, 1923/4, 62, cf. E 732: τὸν ἄμων Ε
259 Πραίνετον Pertusi, 1962, 44: πέρνετον Ε
260 ἦτο Alexiou (1990): εἶτον Ε   ἀκόμη εἶχε Alexiou: ἀκόμοι πάντα ἦχεν Ε πάντα εἶχεν Trapp

235   to rival the sun?
Do you not remember the noble girls of Aleppo,
that they shine like the sun and are perfumed like musk?
And do you not remember, my child, the girls whom you loved
and who beat their breasts and find no consolation?
240 Do you not remember, my child, your marvellous sons?
As for me, the rest of our kinsmen and all the army
accuse me of this and reproach me,
they reproach me severely because of you, my child.
I have heard that you have fathered a son, the dragon of Syria,
245 and woe is me, woe is me if the Kasisi learn of this,
if the people of Emek and Orazabouron learn of this,
in case they open their great mosque of Mohammed
to weep at his tomb and to curse you.
And do you not remember, my child, what the two of us did?
. . .
250 and from there we went to the Prophet's tomb
and you bowed your head, I gave you my blessing, my child;
but when you were about to be honoured and win great praise,
you renounced your family and the whole of your Syria.
Do you not remember, my child, what your grandfather did,
255 how many Romans he slew, how many slaves he captured?
He filled the prisons with Roman lords.
And do you not remember, my child, what your father did?
He raided Ikonion, as far even as Amorion,
he reached Nikomedia, and captured Prainetos
260 and if there had been no sea, he would have gone still further.

238–40 As in G2.86, the emir in his rapturous love for the girl had previously omitted to mention his family elsewhere.
245 On possible identifications for these and the following names, see Name Index.
249 At this point a line meaning 'When we went to Mecca' has probably fallen out of the text.
258 The emir's father and uncle sweep across Asia Minor in a route reminiscent of the Arab raids of the seventh and eighth centuries; cf. his uncle's route at G2.75–9.

Καὶ ὁ ἀδελφός μου, ὁ θεῖός σου, ὁ Μουρστασίτ, ἐπῆγεν,   G2.75
τὸν Ἕρμοναν ἀνέδραμεν καὶ τὸν Ζυγὸν ἐπιάσεν,
τὴν δὲ Ἀρμενίαν ἐξήλειψεν, πολὺν κακὸν ἐποίησεν.
Καὶ οὐδὲν θυμᾶσαι, τέκνον μου, τί ἐποῖκεν ὁ πατήρ σου;
265 Πόσα κοράσια ἤφερεν εἰς τῆς | Συρίας τὰ κάστρα,   146v
ρωμαϊκὰ καὶ περσικά;
Καὶ ἐσὺ ἐπαραξέβηκες ἀπὸ τοὺς συγγενούς σου,
τοὺς φίλους σου τοὺς εὐγενεῖς, διὰ Ρωμαίας ἀγάπην.
Καὶ πῶς σὲ παρεξέβαλεν ἡ χατζιροφαγούσα   G2.82
270 καὶ ἀρνήθης καὶ τὴν πίστιν σου καὶ ὅλην σου τὴν Συρίαν;
Τήν εἶχες εἰς τὸν στάβλον σου καὶ εἶχες την καὶ σκλάβαν,
                    ἐποῖκες την κυράν σου
καὶ γδύνεται καὶ θέτεις την σιμά σου, εἰς τὴν ἀγκάλην.
Ὅμως ἂν θέλης, τέκνον μου, νὰ ἔχης τὴν εὐχήν μου,
275 αὐτου φαρία σὲ ἔστειλα ἐπιλεκτά, δρομαῖα   G2.94
καὶ ἀγένεια παλληκάρια, εὐγενεῖς Ἀραβίτας,
πεντακοσίους ἄρχοντας χρυσοκλιβανιασμένους
καὶ τὸ λουρίκιν τὸ χρυσὸν τὸ ἐφόρει ὁ πατήρ σου.
279/80 Τὸν βάδεον καβαλίκευσε καὶ βάλε τὸ λουρίκιν   G2.95
καὶ οἱ φάρες ἂν σὲ ἀκολουθοῦν, ἐσὲν κανεὶς οὐ φθάνει.
Εἰ δὲ ἀγαπᾶς την περισσά, τέκνον, ὡσὰν μοῦ λέγουν,
                    ἔπαρε καὶ αὐτὴν μετὰ ἐσέναν.
Εἰ δὲ καὶ οὐκ ἔλθης τὸ γοργόν,
285 μὰ τὸν προφήτην τὸν καλόν, τὸν μέγαν Μαχουμέτην,
τὰ τέκνα σου νὰ σφάξουσιν καὶ ἐμέναν θέλουν πνίξει·   G2.85, 86
τὰ δὲ κοράσια | τὰ καλὰ ἄλλους νὰ περιλάβουν.   147r   G2.87, 108
Καὶ ἂν οὐδὲν ἔλθης τὸ γοργόν, κατέβην ἔχω εἰς Μάγγε
                    ’ς τὸ μνῆμαν τοῦ προφήτου,
290 καὶ κλίνειν ἔχω κεφαλὴν ὑπὲρ εὐχῆς μου πρώτης,

---

261 μου Trapp: μου καὶ E   σου Kalonaros: μου E   Μουρστασίτ Alexiou:
μουροτασίτης E
262 ἐπιάσεν Trapp: ἐπίασεν E
263 ἐξήλειψεν, πολὺν κακὸν Trapp: ἐξύληψέν την παντελῶς καὶ πολλὴν κακὸν τὴν E
268 τοὺς φίλους σου τοὺς εὐγενεῖς Politis, 1973, 343: ἀπὸ τοὺς εὐγενοῖς σου φίλους E
273 σιμά σου, εἰς τὴν ἀγκάλην Alexiou: σιμὰ εἰς τὴν ἀγκάλην σου E
275 ἐπιλεκτά Trapp: ἐπιλεκτὰ καὶ E
279/80 Τὸν βάδεον καβαλίκευσε καὶ βάλε Alexiou: καὶ τὸν βάδεον τὸν καβαλήκευ-
γεν, καὶ καβαλήκευσέ τον · καὶ ἔβαλε καὶ E
281 ἀκολουθοῦν Alexiou: ἀκουλουθοῦν E
282 δὲ Trapp: δὲ καὶ E
287 κοράσια Trapp: κοράσια σου E
288 εἰς Trapp: εἰς τὸ E
289 ’ς Trapp: εἰς E

And my brother, your uncle, Mourstasit, went out
and crossed over the Hermon and captured the Zygos mountain;
he wiped out Armenia, he did much damage.
And do you not remember, my child, what your father did?
265 How many girls did he bring to the fortresses of Syria,
Roman and Persian?
And you have broken away from your kinsmen
and your high-born friends, for the love of a Roman girl.
How did she, the pig-eater, so distract you
270 that you renounced your faith and the whole of your Syria?
The girl whom you kept in your stable and had as a slave
you have made your lady,
and she takes off her clothes and you hold her close to you in your
arms.
However, if you wish, my child, to have my blessing,
275 I have sent you there choice swift steeds
and brave beardless youths, high-born Arabs,
five hundred lords clad in gold cuirasses,
and the gold breastplate which your father wore.
279/80 Mount the chestnut horse and put on the breastplate,
and even if steeds pursue you, no one will overtake you.
If you love her very much, child, as they tell me,
bring her with you too.
But if you do not come quickly,
285 by the good Prophet, the great Mohammed,
they will slaughter your children and they will strangle me,
and the lovely girls will embrace other men.
If you do not come quickly, I shall be on my way to Mecca,
to the Prophet's tomb,
290 and I will bow my head over my first blessing.

277 The 'cuirasses' are part of the *kataphrakt* armour revived in the tenth century: cf.
Goliath at G7.75.
287 (cf. E238–9) The lovely girls are the emir's Syrian wives.

καὶ νὰ ἔχῃς τὴν κατάραν μου ὑπὲρ εὐχῆς γονέων.»   *G2.98*
Κ' ἐδῶκεν τους τὰ γράμματα καὶ εἰς Ρωμανίαν ἐβγῆκαν,   *G2.100*
καὶ ἤλθασιν καὶ ἀπλικεύσασιν <ἐκεῖ> εἰς τὸ Χαλκοπέτριν.   *G2.102*
Τὰ γράμματα ἔστειλαν κρυφὰ 'ς τὸν ἀμιρὰν ἐκεῖνον
295 καὶ οὕτως γὰρ ἐγράφασιν τὰ πιτάκια ἐκεῖνα:
«Ὁ ἀμιράς, ἀφέντης μας, τὸ φέγγος φέγγει ὅλον·
νύκτα ἂν περιπατήσωμεν, τὸ φέγγος φέγγει πάλε.»   *G2.104*

Ἀνέγνωσαν τὰ γράμματα καὶ οὕτως ἐδηλῶναν·
καὶ ὡς ἤκουσεν τὰ γράμματα, ἐθλίβην ἡ ψυχή του,
300 ἐκαύσθηκαν | τὰ σπλάγχνα του, ἐχάθην ἡ καρδία του,   147v
ἤκουσεν διὰ τὴν μάναν του, τὰ τέκνα του ἐνθυμήθη
καὶ τὰ κοράσια τὰ καλὰ τὰ πολυπόθητά του,
καὶ ἐνέγνωθεν τὰ γράμματα καὶ ἀπέκει ἐφίλησέν τα.
Ὡς λέων ἐβρυχίσθηκεν, σεβαίνει εἰς τὸ κουβούκλιν
305 καὶ τὴν καλήν του τὰ λαλεῖ καὶ τὴν βουλήν του λέγει
καὶ τέτοια συμβουλεύεται καὶ οὕτως τὴν συντυχαίνει:

«Ἡ μήτηρ μου μὲ ἀπέστειλεν γράμματα ἀπὸ Συρίας   *G2.127*
καὶ ἀγούρους μοῦ ἀπέστειλεν ἐνταῦθα νὰ μὲ πάρουν
καὶ νὰ μὲ πάρουσιν γοργόν, νὰ ὑπάγω μετ' ἐκείνους,
310 νὰ ἰδῶ καὶ τὴν μητέραν μου καὶ πάλι νὰ διαγείρω.»
Καὶ ταῦτα ἡ κόρη ὡς ἤκουσεν, βαρία ἀναστενάζει
καὶ ἐπήδησαν τὰ δάκρυα της καὶ ἐχάθηκεν ὁ νοῦς της·
καὶ ὁ νοῦς της συλλογίζεται ἵνα τὰ μαντατεύση
τὰ ἀ[δ]έλφιά της τὰ γλυκιά·   148r
315 καὶ πάλιν περικόπτεται διὰ ταραχὰς καὶ μάχας
καὶ πείθει την ὁ λογισμὸς <νὰ> μὴ τὸ ὁμολογήση,   *G4.518*
μὴ ἐκφανερώση τὰ κρυπτὰ μυστήρια τοῦ καλοῦ της.
Καὶ ὁ ὕστερός της ἀδελφὸς 'ς τὸν ὕπνον του <τὸ> εἶδεν·   *G2.136*
καὶ σκοτεινὰ σηκώνεται, λέγει τῶν ἀδελφῶν του:

292 Κ' ἐδῶκεν Hesseling: Καὶ δῶκεν E
293 ἀπλικεύσασιν Kalonaros: ἐπλεύσασιν E ἐκεῖ added by Alexiou
294 ἔστειλαν Alexiou: ἀπέστειλαν E 'ς Trapp: εἰς E
297 ἂν περιπατήσωμεν Alexiou, cf. Z652: καὶ ἂν περιπατοῦν E
310 νὰ¹ Trapp: καὶ να E
311 ὡς Alexiou: ὡς τὸ E
315 διὰ Trapp, cf. Z 681: ὡς δια E
316 καὶ Alexiou: ὅμως E την ὁ λογισμὸς νὰ Alexiou: τον τὸν λογισμὸν E
317 μὴ Trapp, cf. Z 682: να μὴ E
318 'ς Alexiou: εἰς E τὸ added by Alexiou
319 λέγει Trapp: λέγι το E

and you will have my curse in place of your parents' blessing."
She gave them the letter and they went off to Roman territory,
and they arrived and camped there at Chalkopetrin.
They sent the letter secretly to the emir,
295 and this is what they wrote in that message:
"Emir, our lord, the moon is shining at the full
and if we set off by night, the moon will be shining still."

They read out the letter and this is what it revealed.
When the emir heard the letter, his soul was grieved,
300 his affections were on fire, his heart was broken;
he heard about his mother, he remembered his children
and his lovely, most desirable girls;
he read the letter and then he kissed it.
He roared like a lion, he entered their chamber
305 and spoke to his beloved about this, and told her his plans;
he consulted her about them, and addressed her thus:

"My mother has sent me a letter from Syria
and she has sent me youngsters here to take me,
to take me quickly so that I go with them
310 and see my mother and return once more."
    When the girl heard this, she sighed deeply,
her tears sprang up and she went out of her mind.
And it came to mind that she should inform
her sweet brothers of this;
315 but once more she was alarmed about uproar and battles,
and her reason persuaded her not to confess the news
and not to reveal her beloved's hidden secrets.
    But her youngest brother saw this in his sleep
and got up in the dark and said to his brothers:

292 The emir's mother is repenting of her blessing mentioned at E251.
295 The letter was read aloud in the usual pre-modern manner (cf. E299) by unspecified persons and the contents are given proleptically.

262   Διγενὴς Ἀκρίτης

320 «Ἀπόψε εἶδα ὄνειρον καὶ οὕτως γὰρ δηλώνει·
     εἶδα εἰς τὸ Χαλκόπετρον γέρακας πετομένους   G2.140, 152
     καὶ ἀετὸς χρυσόπτερος ἐσέβη εἰς τὸ κουβούκλιν·   G2.143
     περιστερὰν ἐδίωκεν ἄσπρην ὡς εἶν' τὸ χιόνιν   G2.141
     καὶ ἥπλωσα τὰ χέρια μου κ' ἐπίασα καὶ τὰ δύο   G2.145
325 καὶ ἡ ψυχή μου ἐπόνεσε, καὶ ταχεῖα ἐσηκώθην.»   G2.146
     Καὶ τότε ὁ πρῶτος ἀδελφὸς οὕτως ἀπιλογᾶται: G2.147
     «Φαίνεταί μου ὅτι οἱ γέρακες ἄνδρες ἁρπάκτες ἔνι   G2.148
     καὶ ὁ ἀετὸς ὁ χρυσόπτερος, φαίνεται, ἔνι ὁ γαμπρός μας,   G2.149
     περιστερὰ τὸ ἀδέλφι μας· μὴ τὸ κακοδικήσῃ.   G2.150
330 Καὶ ἂς καβαλικεύσωμεν καὶ ἂς περιγυριστοῦμεν,
     ὅπου εἶδας τὸ ὄνειρον, ὅπου εἶδας τὰ γεράκια.»   G2.151
     Οἱ πέντε ἐκαβαλίκευσαν καὶ ὑπᾶν 'ς τὸ Χαλκοπέτριν.   G2.153
     Ἐκεῖ ηὗραν τοὺς Σαρακηνούς, εὐγενεῖς Ἀραβίτας·   G2.154
     γελῶντας τοὺς ἐλάλησαν, νὰ μὴ τοὺς ἐγνωρίσουν: |

335 «Καλῶς τὰ παλληκάρια μας, γεράκια τοῦ γαμπροῦ μας· 148ν
                                                                   G2.156
     τί ὧδε ἐπεζεύσατε καὶ οὐκ ἤλθετε εἰς τὸν οἶκον;»
     Σαρακηνὸς ἐλάλησεν, τὸν λέγασιν Μουσούφρην:
     «Χθὲς ἐπαραβραδιάστημαν καὶ ἐμείναμεν ἀπῶδε.»
     Καὶ τότε οἱ πέντε ἀδελφοὶ 'ς τὸν οἶκον ὑπαγαίνουν·
340 μὲ ταραχὰς ὑπήντησαν, τὸν ἀμιρὰν λαλοῦσιν:
     «Αὐτοῦ φαρία σὲ ἀπέστειλαν, ἐπίλεκτα, δρομαῖα
     καὶ ἀγένεια παλληκάρια ἀπὸ τοὺς Ἀραβίτας
     καὶ τὸ λουρίκιν τὸ χρυσόν, τὸ ἐφόρει ὁ πατήρ σου·

320 εἶδα Trapp: ἶδα ἀδέλφια μου Ε
321 εἶδα Trapp: ἐφάνη μου ὅτι εἶδα Ε   γέρακας πετομένους Alexiou: γεράκας
πετομένας Ε (Prombonas, 1985, 10)
322 ἐσέβη Alexiou: ἐσέβην Ε
325 ἡ ψυχή μου ἐπόνεσε Alexiou: πόνεσε ἡ ψυχή μου Ε   καὶ Trapp: καὶ διατοῦτο Ε
327 μου Politis, 1973, 345: μου ἀδέλφιά μου Ε
328 φαίνεται Alexiou, cf. Spadaro, 1989, 177: φένετε μου Ε
329 περιστερὰ Trapp: ἡ περιστέρα Ε
330 Καὶ Trapp: καὶ διασυντόμως Ε
331 εἶδας . . . εἶδας Trapp, cf. G2.151: ἴδαμεν . . . ἴδαμεν Ε
332 'ς Trapp: εἰς Ε
334 νὰ μὴ τοὺς ἐγνωρίσουν Alexiou: ἀμὴ οὐδὲν τοὺς ἐγνόρισαν Ε
336 οἶκον Trapp, cf. Z733: οἶκον τοῦ γαμπροῦ μας Ε
337 Σαρακηνὸς Trapp: καὶ τότε εἷς σαρακηνὸς Ε
338 Χθὲς Alexiou: ἐχθὲς Ε
339 'ς Trapp: εἰς Ε
340 μὲ ταραχὰς Hesseling: μεταχαρὰς Ε
343 καὶ Trapp: καὶ ἔστειλάν σου καὶ Ε

320 "I saw a dream tonight and this is what it reveals:
I saw hawks flying at Chalkopetron
and a gold-winged eagle entered the chamber,
it pursued a dove white as snow,
I held out my hands and caught both of them,
325 and my soul was troubled, so I got up quickly."
    And then the eldest brother replied thus:
"It seems to me that the hawks are abductors,
and the gold-winged eagle, it seems, is our brother-in-law,
the dove our sister; he must not harm her.
330 But let us mount our horses and search around
where you saw the dream and where you saw the hawks."
    The five mounted and went to Chalkopetrin.
There they found the Saracens, high-born Arabs.
They said to them laughingly, so that they should not understand
    their purpose:

335 "Welcome, our brave young men, hawks of our brother-in-law.
Why have you dismounted here and not come to the house?"
    A Saracen – his name was Mousoufris – said:
"We arrived rather late yesterday and stayed here."
    And then the five brothers went to the house;
340 in perturbation they confronted the emir and addressed him:
"They have sent choice swift steeds to you here,
and brave beardless youths from among the Arabs,
and the golden breastplate which your father wore.

321 Bird symbolism seems deeply embedded in *Digenis* and the whole romance tradition.
The dove regularly represents a young girl and the eagle a hero, while the hawk can be
both villain and hero (cf. E966).
337 No individual Arabs are named in G at this point.
343 The brothers should not be aware of these details since the contents of the emir's
mother's letter have not been revealed to them. Recapitulation of details is a feature of
oral story-telling; contrast G2.156–7 which avoids precision. Both versions include the
threat of not returning to Syria.

καὶ ἂν μισεύσειν βούλεσαι ἀπὸ τὴν Ρωμανίαν,
345 σήμερον ἔπαρε τὰ σὰ καὶ τὰ ἤφερες μὴ ἀφήσης.　　　　G2.169
Τὴν ἀδελφήν μας ἄφις την, τὸν παῖδα σου ἀπαρνήσου　　G2.168
καὶ ἡμεῖς νὰ τὸν ἐκθρέψωμεν καὶ ὁ Θεὸς νὰ τὸν δικαιώση.
Μὴ βουληθῆς, ὦ ἀμιρά, νὰ ἔβγης κρυφῶς | ἀπῶδε　　149r
καὶ ὅπου σὲ καταφθάσωμεν, ἄλλον Συρίαν οὐ βλέπεις.»　　G2.166

350 **Κ**αὶ ὡς τὸ ἤκουσεν ὁ ἀμιράς, πολλὰ τοὺς ἐφοβήθη,　　G2.170
ὁ νοῦς του ἐσυνετρόμαξεν καὶ οὐδὲν τοὺς ἀπεκρίθην.
Ὡς λέων ὠρυόμενος ἐσέβη εἰς τὸ κουβούκλιν,
τὴν κόρην ὀνειδίζοντα οὕτως τὴν συντυχαίνει:

«**Ο**ὕτως εἰσὶν οἱ Χριστιανοὶ καὶ οὕτως φυλάσσουν ὅρκους; |　149v
355 Καὶ οὐδὲν θυμᾶσαι ἀπὸ ἀρχῆς τὸ τί ἔπαθα δι᾿ ἐσέναν;
Δούλην σὲ ἐπῆρα ἀπὸ ἀρχῆς ἀπὸ τὰ γονικά σου
καὶ ἐσὺ ἔχεις . . . ἐμέναν τώρα δοῦλον　　　　　　　　G2.189
καὶ τὰ ὅριζες ἐγίνουντα, τὰ ἤθελες ἐποίουν.
Σκλάβαν σὲ ἐπῆρα <ἀπὸ ἀρχῆς> καὶ εἶχα σεν ὡς κυράν μου.　G2.188
360 Ἐμὲν ποτὲ οὐκ ἐπήντησεν στρατηγὸς ἢ τοπάρχης·
στανεό μου οὐδὲν μοῦ ἐμίλησαν, τινὰς μὴ τὸ καυχᾶται·
καὶ ὁ πόθος σου μὲ ἠνέγκασεν καὶ εἰς Ρωμανίαν ἐξέβην·　　G2.191
καὶ τὴν πίστιν μου ἀρνήθηκα, κυρά μου, ὡς διὰ ἐσέναν,　　G2.9
τοὺς θαυμαστοὺς ἀγούρους μου, καὶ μετὰ ἐσέναν ἦρθα.
365 Καὶ ἐδάρε μὲ κακοδικεῖς καὶ ἐπιβουλεύγεσαί με·
καὶ μὲ σκοτώσει θέλουσιν οἱ πέντε ἀδελφοί σου.
Πάντως ἂν σύρω τὸ σπαθὶν καὶ σφάξω τὸν ἑαυτόν μου,　　G2.196
αὔριον νὰ σὲ ὀνειδίζουσιν οἱ εὐγενεῖς Ρωμαῖοι,　　　　　G2.198

---

344 μισεύσειν βούλεσαι Alexiou: βούλεσε μισεύσιν κριφὸς E
347 ἐκθρέψωμεν Alexiou: ἀναθρέψομεν E
348 ἀπῶδε Kalonaros: ἐπόθεν E
352 ἐσέβη Alexiou: ἐσέβην E
353 ὀνειδίζοντα Trapp: κατόνιδίζοντα E
356 ἀπὸ ἀρχῆς Alexiou: ἀπαρχῆς E
359 ἀπὸ ἀρχῆς added by Alexiou ὡς Hesseling: οὐ E
360 στρατηγὸς Hesseling: στράτιος E, Alexiou (see Trapp, 1982, 351)
361 στανεό Kalonaros: καὶ στεανό E τινὰς Trapp: τινὸς· τινὰς E
362 ἠνέγκασεν E: ἠνάγκασεν Kalonaros
364 τοὺς θαυμαστοὺς ἀγούρους μου Alexiou: καὶ τοὺς ἀγούρους μου τοὺς θαυμαστούς E
366 καὶ μὲ σκοτώσει θέλουσιν Trapp: καὶ θέλουν με σκοτόσοι E
367 Πάντως Kalonaros: παντὸς E
368 αὔριον Alexiou: καὶ αὔριον E

So if you wish to leave Roman territory,
345 collect up your belongings today and don't leave behind anything that
    you brought.
Leave our sister behind, renounce your son
and we will bring him up and God will avenge him.
Don't expect, emir, to get away from here in secret,
and wherever we catch up with you, you will never see Syria again."

350 And when the emir heard this, he was very afraid of them,
his mind was terrified and he gave them no reply.
Bellowing like a lion, he entered their chamber,
and reproaching the girl he addressed her thus:

"Is this what Christians are like, and is this how they keep their oaths?
355 Do you not remember what I suffered because of you at the beginning?
I took you as a slave at the beginning from your father's estates,
and now you have me as your slave;
what you commanded has taken place and what you wanted I have
    done.
I took you as a slave in the beginning but I looked on you as my lady.
360 No general or governor has ever stood against me;
they have never spoken to me against my will – let no one boast of
    that.
Desire for you compelled me and I came to Roman territory,
and for your sake I renounced my faith, my lady,
and my marvellous youngsters, and I followed you.
365 But now you do me wrong and plot against me,
and your five brothers want to kill me.
Surely, if I draw my sword and kill myself,
tomorrow the high-born Romans will reproach you

351 Once again the emir is shown as a somewhat vulnerable figure.
357 The exemplification of the power of love through, e.g., the reversal of expected social
roles (as here) is fundamental to the poem.
364 Most of the 'youngsters' were sent back from the Roman-Syrian border when the
emir made his initial journey to the girl's home (E200).

ὅτι τὸν εἶχες εἰς βουλὴν καὶ ἐκεῖνος πάλι ἐσέναν

. . .

370 Τοὺς ἄνδρας κτείνει μάχαιρα, τὰ δὲ κοράσια ὁ Ἅδης.
Ἀλλά, ψυχή μου, ὀμμάτια μου, καρδιά μου, ἀναπνοή μου,
μὴ τὸ θλιβῆς γὰρ λέγω σε, μὴ τὸ καρδιοπονέσης.
Ἡ ἀγάπη γὰρ μὲ ἀνάγκασεν, πρὸς ὀλίγας ἡμέρας,
τῆς ταπεινῆς μου τῆς μητρὸς καὶ ὅλων τῶν συγγενῶν μου,
375 θέλω νὰ πάω νὰ τοὺς ἰδῶ καὶ πάλι νὰ ὑποστρέψω.
Εἶδα <καὶ> γάρ, ὀμμάτια μου, τὰ δάκρυα τῆς μητρός μου
καὶ | ὡς δι᾽ αὐτον ὑπαγαίνω· 150r
Μὰ τὸν κριτὴν τὸν φοβερόν, τὸν τρέμει πᾶσα ἡ κτίσις,
τὸν τρέμουν οἱ Σαρακηνοὶ καὶ οἱ Χριστιανοὶ <καὶ οἱ> πάντες,
380 δώδεκα νυκτοήμερα νὰ ποιήσω εἰς τὰ ἐδικά μου
καὶ ἄλλα εἰκοσιτέσσερα ὥστε νὰ πάγω νά ᾽ρθω.»
Καὶ τότε τὸ κοράσιον βαρέα ἀναστενάζει·
«Μάρτυρας νὰ εἶναι ὁ Ἥλιος ὁ φαίνων εἰς τὸν κόσμον·
ἀφ᾽ ἧς ἡμέρας μὲ ἔδειξες τὸ γράμμαν τῆς μητρός σου
385 καὶ ἀπότες ἐμολόγησες τὰ κρυφά σου μυστήρια,
ἂν τὰ εἶπα ἐγὼ τῶν ἀδελφῶν ἢ ἀνθρώπου γεννημένου,
νὰ τύχω εἰς θάνατον πικρόν, τὸν ποῖον οὐδὲν ὀλπίζω,
νὰ στερηθῶ σε καὶ τὸ φῶς τοῦ λάμποντος Ἡλίου.»
Καὶ τότε τὸ κοράσιον ἐστράφηκεν ὀπίσω,
390 τῶν ἀδελφῶν της ἔλεγεν μετὰ κακῆς καρδίας·

|

«Ἄρτι, ἀδέλφια μου καλά, διατί νὰ τὸν λυπᾶτε; 150v
Διατί τὸν ὀνειδίζετε καὶ ἦλθεν λυπημένος;
Κλαίοντα καὶ ὀδυρόμενος κεῖται εἰς τὸ κλινάριν
καὶ ἀποφυσᾶ ὡς ἡ θάλασσα καὶ βρουχᾶται ὡς λέων,

369 πάλι Alexiou: πάλην E
After 369 Alexiou suggests a line is omitted
370 ὁ Ἅδης E: ὀνείδη Grégoire-Letocart, 1939, 215
371 καρδιά Trapp: καρδία E
375 θέλω Trapp: καὶ θέλω E
376 Εἶδα καὶ γάρ corr.: εἶδα γάρ E Εἴδασι γὰρ τὰ Alexiou
377 αὐτον Alexiou: αὐτὸν E
378 Μὰ Trapp: καὶ μα E
379 καὶ οἱ added by Alexiou
380 νυκτοήμερα Alexiou: νυκτίμερα μόνον E
386 ἀδελφῶν ἢ Alexiou: ἀδελφῶν μου· ἢ ἂν τὰ ὁμολόγησα E
388 νὰ στερηθῶ σε corr.: καὶ νασε στεριθῶ E
390 τῶν ἀδελφῶν της Trapp: τὸν ἀδελφὸν της τὸν E
392 Διατί τὸν Trapp: διατί να τὸν E

because the man whom you had in your confidence as you were in his
. . .
370 Men are killed by the dagger, but girls by Hades.
But, my soul, my eyes, my heart, my breath,
don't grieve, I tell you, don't let your heart be pained.
It is love that has constrained me for a few days,
love for my unhappy mother and all my kinsmen.
375 I wish to go to see them, and to come back again.
For, my eyes, I have seen my mother's tears
                                and it is for that reason that I am going.
By the fearsome judge before whom all creation trembles,
before whom Saracens and all Christians tremble,
380 I shall spend twelve days and nights in my own country,
and a further twenty-four to go and to return."
        And then the girl sighed deeply:
"May the Sun which shines over the world be witness:
from the day you showed me the letter from your mother
385 and from the time you confessed your hidden secrets to me,
if I uttered them to my brothers or to any man alive,
may I suffer a bitter death of the sort I would never look for,
and may I be deprived of you and of the Sun's radiant light."
And then the girl went back
390 and said to her brothers with a bitter heart:

"Why, my fine brothers, do you upset him now?
Why do you reproach him, so that he has come in distressed?
He lies on the couch weeping and wailing
and rages like the sea and roars like a lion

---

369 It is very likely that a line on the girl's betrayal has dropped out of the E tradition,
and perhaps a threat of suicide by the emir (cf. E370); G2.199–200 is more reasonable.
Trapp's solution is to reposition E370 after 367.
383 Once more an appeal to the Sun; cf. E91 above.

395 καὶ θέλει ἀπὸ τῆς θλίψεως χαθῆ ἀπὸ τὸν κόσμον.
    Πάντως μετὰ θελήσεώς σας αὐτὸν ἐπῆρα ἄνδρα
                καὶ ἠξεύρετε καλὰ ὅτι δι' ἐμέναν
    ἐρνήθηκεν τὴν πίστιν του καὶ Χριστιανὸς ἐγίνη,
    εἰς Ρωμανίαν ἐξέβηκεν διὰ ἐμὲν καὶ σᾶς τοὺς πέντε·
400 καὶ ἐδὰ παραπονεῖτε τον καὶ ἐμέναν ὀνειδίζει.
    Καὶ <αὐτὸς> ἐμέναν ἔδειξεν τὸ γράμμαν τῆς μητρός του
    καὶ ἐμέναν κατεθάρρεψεν καὶ τὰς βουλάς του μοῦ εἶπεν·
    μητρὸς κατάραν θλίβεται καὶ θέλει νὰ ὑπάγη.   G2.228
    Καὶ ἐσεῖς πῶς ἐφυλάξατε κατάραν τῆς μητρός σας,   G2.231
405 ὅταν ἐκατεφθάσατε τὴν ἄκραν τῆς κλεισούρας;   G2.233
    Θάνατον οὐ 'φοβήθητε διὰ τὴν μητρὸς κατάραν.»   G2.234
        Τὰ ἀδέλφιά της λέγουσιν λόγους παρηγορίας:
    «Ἐμεῖς ἐσέναν ἔχομεν ζωὴν καὶ ἀναπνοήν μας   G2.240
    καὶ ὡς δι' αὐτὸν τὸ θλιβόμεθεν, μὴ πάγη καὶ ἀπομείνη·
410 ὅμως ἂν βούλεται ἀπελθεῖν,
    νὰ ἰδῆ καὶ τὴν μητέραν του καὶ πάλιν νὰ διαγείρη,
    ὅτι νὰ ἔρθη τὸ γοργὸν ἐμᾶς ἂς μᾶς ὁμόση,
    νὰ μὴν γενῆ Σαρακηνὸς καὶ ἐσὲν ἀλησμονήση.
    Καὶ νὰ τὸν ἀ‖ποβγάλωμεν καὶ ὁ Θεὸς νὰ τὸν βοηθήση.» 151r

415 **Ο**ἱ πέντε ἀντάμα ἐστάθησαν μετὰ τῆς ἀδελφῆς των
    καὶ εἰς τὸ κουβούκλιν ἤμπασιν, 'ς τὴν κλίνην τοῦ γαμπροῦ τους,
    καὶ ηὕρασιν τὸν νεώτερον κειτόμενον 'ς τὴν κλίνην·
    τὸν γρόθον του· εἰς τὸ μάγουλον εἶχεν ἀκουμπισμένον,
    τοὺς ὀφθαλμούς του ἠγρίωσεν ὡς λέων πειρασμένος·
420 τὰ δάκρυα του ἐκατέβαιναν ὡς ὄμβροι τοῦ Μαΐου.   G2.267
        Καὶ ὡς εἶδεν ὁ νεώτερος τοὺς γυναικαδελφούς του,
    γοργὸν ἐκατεπήδησεν καὶ προσυπήντησέ τους.

395 θέλει ἀπὸ τῆς θλίψεως Trapp: ἀπὸ τῆς θλίψεώσας θέλη Ε
396 Πάντως Trapp: παντὸς Ε   αὐτὸν corr. τὸν Ε
399 διὰ Trapp: ὡς δια Ε
400 ἐδὰ Trapp: ἐδάρε Ε
401 αὐτὸς added by Alexiou
406 Θάνατον οὐ 'φοβήθητε Trapp: θάνατον οὐκ ἐφοβήθητε Ε θανεῖν οὐκ ἐφοβήθητε
Alexiou   τὴν μητρὸς Alexiou: τῆς μητρός σας τὴν Ε
412 ὅτι νὰ ἔρθη τὸ γοργὸν ἐμᾶς ἂς μᾶς ὁμόση Trapp: ἐμὰς ἂς μας ὁμῶσι ὅτι να ἔρθη
τὸ γοργὸν Ε
413 γενῆ Trapp: γενῆ πάλην Ε
414 Καὶ Alexiou: καὶ ἡμεῖς Ε
416 'ς Trapp: εἰς Ε
417 'ς Trapp: εἰς Ε
418 εἰς τὸ μάγουλον εἶχεν Trapp: ἦχεν εἰς τὸ μάγουλόν του Ε

395 and is about to be lost to the world because of his grief.
Surely it was with your consent that I took him as my husband
                    and you well know that for my sake
he renounced his faith and became a Christian;
he set out for Roman territory because of me and you five,
400 and now you are upsetting him and he is reproaching me.
He showed me the letter from his mother
and he trusted me and told me his plans:
he is grieved over his mother's curse and wants to go.
But how did you watch out for your mother's curse
405 when you reached the top of the pass?
You did not fear death more than your mother's curse."
    Her brothers spoke words of comfort to her:
"We think of you as our life and breath,
and so we are concerned for him, in case he leaves and stays away;
410 but if he wants to go
to see his mother and to come back again,
let him swear to us that he will go quickly
and not become a Saracen and forget you.
Let us send him on his way and may God help him."

415 The five stood up together with their sister
and went into the chamber, to their brother-in-law's couch.
They found the young man lying on his couch;
he had leant his fist on his cheek,
his eyes were wild like a tormented lion's,
420 his tears rained down like showers in May.
    When the young man saw his wife's brothers,
he jumped up quickly and confronted them.

---

397 This line is necessary for sense; cf. G2.226.

Ἐκεῖνοι τὸν ἐλάλησαν λόγους ἡμερωμένους:
«Μὴ θλίβεσαι, νεώτερε, ἕνεκεν τῆς μητρός σου.
425 Χθὲς ἐκαβαλικεύσαμεν ἁμάδι καὶ οἱ πέντε
     καὶ ἐπήγαμεν <ἐκεῖ> εἰς τὸ Χαλκοπέτριν,
ὡς διὰ νὰ κυνηγήσωμεν τίποτε τῶν ἀγρίων·
καὶ εἴδαμεν | ἀπὸ μακρά, πέραν τοῦ ποταμίου, 151v
παλουκωσίες <καὶ> ἡστέκοντα δεμένα τὰ φαρία,
430 καὶ οἱ πέντε ἐπιλαλήσαμεν καὶ ἐπήγαμεν νὰ ἰδοῦμεν.
Καὶ ηὕραμεν τοὺς Σαρακηνούς, εὐγενεῖς Ἀραβίτας·
οἱ μὲν λουρικιασμένοι ἦσαν, ἄλλοι σουσανιασμένοι
καὶ ἐκρατοῦσαν 'ς τὰ χέρια των κοντάρια καὶ ραβδία,
πράσινα μακρυκόνταρα μετ' ἀσήμιν δεμένα.
435 Καὶ εἰς μίαν τοὺς ἐγνωρίσαμεν ὅτι ὡς διὰ ἐσέναν ἦλθαν,
διὰ ἐσέναν ἐκοπίασαν ἀπέσω ἀπὸ Συρίαν,
ἵνα σὲ ἐπάρουσιν κρυφῶς, καὶ νὰ ὑπᾶς μετὰ κείνους·
καὶ κατὰ τὴν ὑπόληψιν ἤλθαμεν εἰς ἐσέναν·
καὶ μὴ μᾶς μέφεσαι, γαμπρέ, διατὶ σὲ ἀγριομιλοῦμεν.
440 Καὶ ἂν θέλης πᾶν εἰς τὴν Συρίαν, θέλομεν νὰ ὀμόσης,
τῆς κόρης νὰ μὴν λησμονῇς, τῆς ἡλιογεννημένης,
καὶ τοῦ παγκάλου σου υἱοῦ, τοῦ Διγενῆ τ' Ἀκρίτη.
Καὶ μηδὲν σοῦ φανῇ κακὸν διατὶ ὀνειδίσαμέν σε,
ἀμὴ ἔβγαλέ την τὴν κακὴν καρδίαν ἀπὸ τὸν νοῦν σου
445 καὶ ἔχε ἡμερότηταν, μᾶλλον δὲ καὶ πραότην,
νὰ εἶσαι καὶ πανεύφημος 'ς ὅλην τὴν οἰκουμένην.
Καὶ ἐμεῖς νὰ σὲ ἀποβγάλωμεν καὶ ὁ Θεὸς νὰ σὲ βοηθήσῃ,
ὁποὺ τὸν κόσμον διακρατεῖ καὶ πάντας ἐπιβλέπει· |
καὶ πάλιν νὰ ὑποστραφῇς, νὰ ἔλθῃς διασυντόμως. 152r   G2.131
450 Εἰ δὲ καὶ βούλεσαι, γαμπρέ, ἄλλον <νὰ> μὴ ὑποστρέψῃς
καὶ νὰ ἀρνηθῇς τὸ ἀδέλφι μας

426 ἐκεῖ added by Alexiou
429 καὶ added by Kalonaros
432 λουρικιασμένοι ἦσαν [ἦσαν] Alexiou, cf. E945: λουρίκια ἐφορούσασιν Ε
σουσανιασμένοι Koukoules, 1913/4, 316, cf. E945: σουσινιασμένοι Ε
433 'ς Trapp: εἰς Ε
436 διὰ Alexiou: ὡς διὰ Ε
440 Καὶ Trapp: καὶ ἐσὺ Ε   νὰ Alexiou: να μας Ε
441 τῆς κόρης νὰ μὴν λησμονῇς Alexiou: να μὴν λησμονίσῃς τῆς κόρης Ε
443 κακὸν διατὶ ὀνειδίσαμέν σε Alexiou: νεότερε κακόν, διατί σε ὀνειδείσαμεν ὀψὲς Ε
444 ἔβγαλέ την τὴν κακὴν καρδίαν Alexiou: τὴν κακὴν καρδίαν ἔβγαλέ την Ε
445 ἔχε Hesseling: ἔχει Ε
446 'ς Trapp: εἰς Ε
448 ἐπιβλέπει Hesseling: ὑποβλέπει Ε
450 νὰ added by Alexiou

They spoke to him with peaceable words:
"Do not grieve, young man, for your mother's sake.
425 Yesterday we five mounted together
           and we went there to Chalkopetrin,
to hunt some wild animals.
And we saw from a long way off, beyond the river,
stakes with steeds tethered to them.
430 So we five spurred on and went to look.
And we found Saracens, high-born Arabs;
some were wearing breastplates, others mail,
and they held spears and sticks in their hands,
long green spears bound with silver.
435 And in an instant we realised that they had come for you,
it was for you that they had made the long journey from Syria,
to take you away secretly, and for you to go with them;
and in consequence we have come to see you.
Do not blame us, brother-in-law, for speaking to you harshly.
440 And if you want to go to Syria, we want you to swear
not to forget the sun-born girl
and your very handsome son, Digenis Akritis, the Frontiersman of
    Double Descent.
So do not think it wrong that we reproached you,
but think no more of your bitter attitude
445 and choose mildness, or rather meekness,
so that you become famous throughout the civilised world.
We will see you off from here and may God help you,
God who controls the world and watches over everyone.
May you return and come back rapidly.
450 But if you intend, brother-in-law, not to return again
and to renounce our sister

424-37 This recapitulation, once again perhaps showing patterning from oral story-
telling, contrasts with the succinct report of G2.245-8. The knowledge shown by the
brothers of the contents of the various messages is inconsistent but dramatic effect is the
over-riding consideration.
442 Again it is not clear whether these are names or titles, perhaps an indication that
this is a well-known story.

ἢ τὸ ἄνθος, τὸν αὐγερινόν, τὸν Διγενή σου παῖδαν,
ἐλπίζομεν εἰς τὸν Θεόν, ὁποὺ τοὺς πάντας βλέπει,
<ἄλλον> νὰ μὴ ἴδης τὴν Συρίαν, ἂν οὐδὲν ὑποστρέψης.»
455 Καὶ τότε ὁ νεώτερος βαρέως ἀναστενάζει
καὶ ἐπήδησαν τὰ δάκρυα του, τοιοῦτον λόγον λέγει·
«Κύριε, ἐὰν ἐγὼ ἐνθυμηθῶ ἐσᾶς νὰ λησμονήσω
ἢ τὸ ἄνθος τὸ ἐκλεκτόν, τὸν Διγενή μου παῖδα,   G3.54
καὶ ἂν οὐ διαγείρω ἐγλήγορα μετὰ καὶ τῆς μητρός μου,
460 νὰ ἐπάρω καὶ τὰ ἀδέλφια μου, νὰ ἔλθουν μετὰ ἐμέναν,
νὰ πάρω καὶ τὸ πλοῦτος μου καὶ τὰ φαρία μου ὅλα,
νὰ ἐβγάλω καὶ τὰ ἀμάλωτα ὁποὺ εἶναι εἰς τὴν Συρίαν,
μὴ ἰδῶ τὸν ἥλιον λάμποντα μηδὲ τὸ φῶς τοῦ κόσμου.»   G3.137
Καὶ πάραυτα ηὐτρέπισαν ἵνα τὸν ἀποβγάλουν
465 οἱ πέντε οἱ γυναικαδελφοὶ καὶ ὁ Διγενὴς Ἀκρίτης·
καὶ κονομᾶται ὁ νεώτερος ἵνα καβαλικεύση·
ἐσέβη εἰς τὸ κουβούκλιν του νὰ φιλήση τὴν κόρην·   G2.266
τὰ δάκρυα του ἐκατέβαιναν ὡς ὄμβροι τοῦ Μαΐου,   G2.267
οἱ στεναγμοί του ἔβγαιναν ὡσὰν βρονταὶ | καὶ κτύποι 152v G2.268
470 καὶ μὲ τὰ δάκρυα τὰ πολλά, τοὺς ἀναστεναγμούς του
ἐλάλησεν ὁ νεώτερος τὴν πολυποθητήν του·
«Δός μου, φῶς μου ἀνέσπερον, χρυσόμορφέ μου εἰκόνα,   G2.269
τὸ δακτυλίδιν τὸ φορεῖς εἰς τὸ μικρὸ δακτύλιν,   G2.269
νὰ τὸ ἔχω διὰ ἐνθύμησιν, κυρά, νὰ σοῦ θυμοῦμαι.»

475 Τὸ δακτυλίδιν ἤβγαλεν, γλήγορα τοῦ τὸ δίδει·
καὶ ὁ νεώτερος τὸ ἔβαλεν μετὰ πολλῶν δακρύων,
καὶ λόγια τὸν ἐλάλησεν ἐκ στεναγμοῦ καρδίας·
«Εὕρη σε ὁ Θεός, αὐθέντη μου, ἂ μὲ ἀπαλησμονήσης
ἢ <πάλιν> ἂν <ἐν>θυμηθῆς ἄλλην νὰ περιλάβης.»   G2.273

---

452 ἢ Alexiou: ἢ πάλιν E
453 ὁποὺ τοὺς πάντας βλέπει Alexiou: ὁ τοὺς πάντας ἐβλέπων E
454 ἄλλον added by Alexiou
459 οὐ Trapp: οὐδὲ E
460 νὰ¹ Trapp: καὶ νὰ E
462 νὰ Trapp: καὶ νὰ E
463 μὴ Trapp: νὰ μὴ E
467 ἐσέβη Alexiou: ἐσέβην E
470 τοὺς Alexiou: καὶ τοὺς E
475 Τὸ δακτυλίδιν ἤβγαλεν Trapp: Καὶ ἤβγαλεν τὸ δακτιλίδην της καὶ E
476 καὶ Alexiou: καὶ τότε E
479 πάλιν added by Trapp ἐνθυμηθῆς Trapp: θυμιθεὶς E

or the flower, the morning star, your son Digenis of Double Descent,
we trust in God, who watches over all mankind,
that you will not see Syria again, if you do not return."
455   And then the young man sighed deeply,
and his tears sprang up, and he said this:
"Lord, if ever I have in mind to forget you
or the choice flower, my son Digenis of Double Descent,
and if I do not return quickly with my mother
460 and get my brothers to come with me,
and fetch my wealth and all my steeds
and bring the prisoners who are in Syria,
may I not see the radiant sun nor the light of the world."
So immediately they made preparations to see him off,
465 his wife's five brothers and Digenis Akritis, the Frontiersman of
     Double Descent;
the young man got ready to mount.
He entered the chamber to kiss the girl,
his tears rained down like showers in May;
his sighs resounded like rolling thunder
470 and with many tears and groans
the young man spoke to his dearly longed-for girl :
     "Give me, my light without dusk, my golden icon,
the ring which you wear on your little finger,
to have as a remembrance, my lady, to remember you."

475 She took off her ring, she gave it to him quickly
and the young man put it on with many tears
as she addressed him from the misery of her heart:
     "May God find you out, my lord, if you forget me,
or indeed if you ever think of embracing another woman."

457 This passage is unusual in this poem in not alluding to the attractions of the beloved
woman. Perhaps the masculine values are here briefly redefined, or perhaps a line
referring to the girl has dropped out.
460 These brothers, only otherwise mentioned at E496, may be the kinsmen who were
trying to do away with the emir's mother.
465 Cf. E225; sufficient time has elapsed since his parents' marriage for Digenis to have
progressed beyond babyhood.

480 Καὶ τότε ἐπεριλάβασιν καὶ ἐθέκαν 'ς τὸ κουβούκλιν·
στρεφνά, γλυκιὰ ἐφιλήσασιν τῆς ἀποχωρισίας.　　　　G2.280
Καὶ εὐθὺς ἐκαβαλίκευσε, ἐκ τὸν οἶκον του ἀποβγαίνουν·
ὀμπρὸς ὑπᾶν τὰ ἀδέλφια της καὶ οἱ συγγενεῖς ὀπίσω·　153r
καὶ ὄνταν ἀποχαιρέτησεν τοὺς γυναικαδελφούς του,
485 ὀπίσω ἐστοχάζετον διὰ τὴν ποθητήν του
καὶ ἀναστέναζεν πικρῶς ὡς ὅσον ἐδυνέτον.

Καὶ τοὺς ἀγούρους του ἔλεγεν: «Ἀγοῦροι, ἐνδυναμοῦσθε·　G3.22
ποτὲ μηδὲν ὀκνήσετε, μὴ νύκταν μηδὲ ἡμέραν,
ὡς διὰ νὰ γείρω ἐγλήγορα ὡς διὰ τὴν ποθητήν μου.
490 Βροχάς, χειμώνας, παγετοὺς πάντες ἀγωνισθῆτε　　　G3.24
καὶ πάντα ἔχετε τὸν νοῦν εἰς τὰς στενὰς κλεισούρας,
μὴ ἀργήσω καὶ μὴ 'φιορκισθῶ καὶ λυπηθῇ ἡ ψυχή μου
καὶ ὁμοίως καὶ ἡ καλή μου.»
Καὶ ὁ ἀμιρὰς ἐκίνησεν, τὴν στράταν του ὑπαγαίνει.
495 Ἔρωταν εἶχεν περισσὸν ὡς διὰ τὴν ποθητήν του·
καὶ διὰ τὴν μητέραν του καὶ διὰ τοὺς ἀδελφούς του　153v
τρεῖς καβαλάρους ἔστειλεν, διὰ νὰ ὑπᾶν μαντάτον.
Καὶ τὰς ἀνδραγαθίας του ἐχέρισεν νὰ λέγη,
τοὺς ἀγούρους του ἔλεγεν, τὰ τέτοια τῶν ἐλάλει:
500 　　　　　　　　«Ἀγοῦροι μου, ἂν θυμᾶσθε,
τὸ πῶς σᾶς ὑπεξέβαλα ἀπὸ πολλῶν πολέμων
<καὶ> τὸ πῶς σᾶς ἐγλύτωσα διὰ τὰς ἀνδραγαθίας μου.
Πάντως, ἀγοῦροι μου, εἴδατε εἰς τὰ Μυλοκοπεῖα,　　　G3.67
ὅταν ἔφθασαν στρατηγοὶ καὶ ἐπῆραν σας δεμένους

480 ἐθέκαν 'ς Karayanni, 1976, 99: ἐθέκασιν εἰς E
481 στρεφνά, γλυκιὰ Alexiou: στρευνὰ γλυκία E
482 ἐκαβαλίκευσε Alexiou: ἐκαβαλήκευσεν E　ἐκ Xanthoudidis, 1912, 552: εἰς E
483 οἱ συγγενεῖς Trapp: τὸ συγγενικόν της E
484 ἀποχαιρέτησεν Kalonaros: ὑποχαιρέτησαν E
485 ὀπίσω Trapp: ὁ ἀμυρὰς ὀπίσω E
488 ὀκνήσετε Politis, 1973, 343–4: ὀκνίτε E
490 πάντες Kalonaros: πάντας E
491 νοῦν Trapp: νοῦν σας E
492 'φιορκισθῶ Morgan, 1960, 58: φιωρκίσω E
497 ἔστειλεν Alexiou: ἔστειλαν E
498 τὰς ἀνδραγαθίας του ἐχέρισεν νὰ λέγη Alexiou: τότε ἐχέρισεν να λέγει περὶ τὰς ἀνδραγαθίας του E
500 Ἀγοῦροι μου Alexiou: λέγω σας, ἀγούροι μου· ὅτι E
501 πῶς σᾶς Hesseling: πόσας E
502 καὶ added by Trapp　διὰ Trapp: ὡς διὰ E
503 Πάντως Trapp: καὶ πάντος E　ἀγοῦροι Alexiou: ἀγόρι E
504 ἔφθασαν Trapp: εὐφθάσασιν E

480   And then they embraced and lay down together in the chamber;
they kissed closely, sweetly because of their separation.
Immediately he mounted, and they left his house;
her brothers went in front and her kinsmen behind;
and when he had said farewell to his wife's brothers,
485 he gazed back at his beloved
and sighed bitterly with all his might.

And he said to his youngsters: "Youngsters, be strong,
don't be lazy either by night or by day,
so that I can return quickly to my beloved.
490 All of you, struggle against rain, storms and frosts,
and always be alert in the narrow passes
so that I am not late and break my oath and my soul is grieved
                        and also my beloved."
495   The emir set out, he went off on his journey.
He had an excessive passion for his beloved;
to his mother and his brothers
he sent three horsemen to bring the news.
And he began to tell of his valiant deeds,
he told them to his youngsters; this is what he said to them:
500   "My youngsters, you may remember
how I got you out of many wars,
how I rescued you through my valiant deeds.
Surely, my youngsters, you saw at Mylokopia,
when the generals arrived and captured and bound you

486 Although the role of love is as fundamental to the plot of E as of G, E has nothing to
match the musings on Eros at the beginning of G3; the first lexical equivalents of this
section are at G3.22 and E487.
497 Only one batch of messengers is sent by the emir, unlike the daily bulletins of G3.39.
503 On suggested identifications for this battle and its personalities, see the Introduction,
pp. xxxvii–xxxviii and the Name Index.

505 καὶ ἐγὼ ἐκυνήγουν, ἄγουροι, μὲ πέντε παλληκάρια,
μετὰ τοῦ Μουσῆ τὸν υἱὸν καὶ μὲ τὸν Ἀποχάλπην,
τὸν ἔγγοναν τοῦ Μαϊακῆ, καὶ ἄλλους τρεῖς στρατιῶτες·
καὶ ὡς τῶν ἠκούσαμεν φωνὴν καὶ κτύπον τῶν ἀρμάτων,
κατέβημεν χαρζανιστοὶ ἀνάμεσα τὸν κάμπον
510 καὶ τὰς τέντας εὑρήκαμεν σχοινοκομμένας ὅλας
καὶ ὁ κορνιακτὸς ἐστύλωνεν <'ς> τὸν οὐρανὸν ἀπάνω·
τὸ πῶς τοὺς ἐπροδράμαμεν καὶ ἐπιάσαμεν κλεισούρας.»
Καὶ μέσον ὁδοῦ ἐδιάβαιναν ἀδιάβατον καλάμιν·
λεοντάριν εἶδαν δυνατὸν τρώγοντα δαμαλίναν.   G3.92
515 Καὶ <τότε> ὡσὰν τὸ εἴδασιν οἱ ἀγοῦροι τοῦ νεωτέρου,   G3.93
ὀμπρὸς ὀπίσω ἐστράφησαν, κατεπίλασαν τὰ πλάγια.   154r
Καὶ ὡς εἶδεν τοῦτον ὁ ἀμιράς, ἄκο τὸ τίντα λέγει:
«Ἂν σὲ ἀφήσω, λέοντα, αὔριον νὰ τὸ καυχᾶσαι
καὶ νὰ μᾶς τ' ὀνειδίζουσιν οἱ θαυμαστοὶ ἀνδρειωμένοι.»

520 Καὶ σύρνει τὸ σπαθίτσιν του, κόπτει τὴν κεφαλήν του,
καὶ ἔσχισέν τον μέσα.
«Ἀλαλαῖ,» ἐφώναξεν τὸν πρωτοστράτοράν του·
«πέζευσε σύντομα, γοργόν, νὰ ἐπάρης τὸ δερμάτιν,
τὰ ὀδόντια καὶ τὰ ὀνύχια ὅλων τῶν ποδαρίων   G3.102-3
525 καὶ ἀπέκει ἄγωμέτε τα τὸν Διγενὴν Ἀκρίτην,   G3.106
<νὰ τὰ φορῆ,> νὰ τὰ θεωρῆ καὶ ἃ λάχη μᾶς θυμᾶται.»
Καὶ ὡσὰν ἀπεσώσασιν εἰς τοῦ Ραχὲ τὸ κάστρον,   G3.68, 111
<οἱ ἀγοῦροι του> ἐπλικεύσασιν ἀπέξωθεν τοῦ κάστρου·

---

505 ἄγουροι, μὲ Alexiou: ἀγούροι μου, μετὰ E
506 μετὰ Trapp: μὲ E
507 ἔγγοναν Trapp: ἔγγοναν τοῦ γέροντος E   ἄλλους Alexiou: ἄλλοι E
508 τῶν Xanthoudidis, 1912, 553: τὸ E   φωνὴν Trapp: τὴν φωνὴν E
509 κατέβημεν Chatzis, 1930, 28: ἐκατέβημεν E
510 σχοινοκομμένας Alexiou: σχηνοκοπιμένας E
511 'ς added by Alexiou
512 κλεισούρας Alexiou: τὰς κλησούρας E
513 μέσον ὁδοῦ E, cf. Mackridge, 1993b, 336, note 2: μέσον ὁποὺ Alexiou   ἐδιάβαιναν Xanthoudidis, 1912, 552: ἐδιάβενα E   ἀδιάβατον Hesseling: διάβατον E
514 εἶδαν Xanthoudidis, 1912, 552: ἴδα E
515 τότε added by Alexiou
522 Ἀλαλαῖ Alexiou, cf. Eideneier, 1982, 75: ἀλλὰ E
523 πέζευσε Hesseling: ἐπέζευσεν E
524 τὰ ὀδόντια Alexiou: καὶ τοὺς ὀδόντας του τοὺς μεγάλους E
525 ἄγωμέτε Xanthoudidis, 1912, 555: ἄγωμέ E
526 νὰ τὰ φορῆ added by Alexiou   νὰ² Alexiou: ἵνα E   μᾶς Trapp: να μας E
528 οἱ ἀγοῦροι του Alexiou: ἔξω E

505 while I was off hunting, youngsters, with five brave young men,
with the son of Mousis and with Apohalpis,
the grandson of Maiakis, and three other soldiers;
when we heard their cry and the clash of weapons,
we came down onto the battlefield, lashing our horses,
510 and found the tents all with their ropes cut
and the dust was spiralling up to heaven above
– how we caught up with them and captured the passes."
    While on their way they were passing through a trackless reed-bed;
they saw a mighty lion devouring a heifer.
515 And then when the young man's youngsters saw this,
they rushed backwards and forwards and took to the slopes.
But when the emir saw this, listen to what he said:
"If I leave you, lion, tomorrow you will boast of it
and the marvellous men of courage will reproach us for it."

520 And he drew his sword, he cut off its head
                                and split it down the middle.
"Hurrah!" he shouted to his protostrator,
"dismount immediately, quickly take its hide,
its teeth and the claws from all its paws,
525 and later let's bring them to Digenis Akritis, the Frontiersman of
        Double Descent,
for him to wear, to look at and, maybe, to remember us."
    And when they had made their way to the fortress of Raqqa,
his youngsters set up camp outside the fortress,

278 Διγενὴς Ἀκρίτης

καὶ ἔδραμεν ἡ μητέρα του ἀπέξω ἀπὸ τὸ κάστρον |
530 μετὰ τρεῖς ἅβρας †καὶ† μὲ τὸ συγγενικόν της. 154v
Καὶ ἑβδομήντα γέροντες ἐκ τοῦ Ραχὲ τὸ κάστρον
κανίσκια ὑπάγουσιν τοῦ νέου, ὁποὺ οὐκ ὀρπίζαν νὰ ἴδουν.
533 Καὶ τοῦ ἀμιρᾶ ἡ μάνα
533a οὕτως τὸν ἐπερίλαβεν, γλυκέα τὸν ἐφίλει
καὶ τέτοιον λόγον λέγει:
535 «Ἀλί, <ἀλί μου> τὴν ψυχὴν καὶ τὸ κακό μου γῆρας,
ἂν τὸ ἀκούσουν εἰς Αἴγυπτον, κάτω εἰς Βαβυλῶνα,
ἵνα <τὸ> ἀναγράψωσιν εἰς τοῦ Μακὲ τὸ μνῆμαν,
ἐσέναν καὶ τὸ γένος μας ἵνα μᾶς καταροῦνται.
Τέκνον μου πολυπόθητον, καρδία μου, ἀναπνοή μου,
540 τὸ φῶς τῶν ὀφθαλμῶν μου,
<οὐκ> εἶδες, τέκνον μου καλόν, τὸ μνῆμαν τοῦ προφήτου;» G3.139
Καὶ τότε πάλιν ὁ ἀμιρᾶς τῆς μητέρας του λέγει:
«Σώπασε, μῆτερ μου· καλὰ ’ν’ αὐτὰ τὰ συντυχαίνεις;
Ἐγὼ ἐγύρευσα Συρίαν, καὶ Ρωμανίαν ἀπόσω· | 155r

545 Ἐγὼ <τότε> ἐδιάβηκα χώρας τῶν Αἰθιόπων,
<καὶ> λόγους ἤκουσα ψευδεῖς καὶ γέλι’ ἦσαν καθόλου,
καὶ ποτὲ θεοὺς αὐτοὺς οὐδὲν τοὺς λέγω, ὅτι εἴδωλα εἶναι.
Ἀμ’ εἰς τὴν Ρωμανίαν
†εἶδαν οἱ ὀφθαλμοί μου τὴν† πανύμνητον Θεοτόκον·
550 ὢ καὶ <τὸ> τί τὴν ἀγαπῶ ἐξ ὅλης τῆς ψυχῆς μου.
Καὶ εἶδα, μάνα μου, νεκροὺς κ’ ἐτρέχαν τὸ ἅγιον μύρος·

529 ἀπέξω Trapp: ἀπέξω καὶ ἀπάνω E
530 μετὰ τρεῖς ἅβρας Alexiou: με τρεῖς ἀμερὰς E της corr.: της ὅλον E
531 ἑβδομήντα (originally written ο´) Alexiou: ὡς E
532 ὑπάγουσιν Alexiou: τοῦ ὑπαγένουσιν E οὐκ Alexiou: δὲν E ἴδουν Alexiou: ἰδοῦσιν E
535 ἀλί μου τὴν ψυχὴν Alexiou: τὴν ψυχήν μου E
536 ἀκούσουν Kalonaros: ἀκοῦσον E
537 τὸ ἀναγράψωσιν Alexiou: ἀντιγράψωσιν E
539 πολυπόθητον corr.: πολυπόθητον· ὀμάτιά μου E
541 οὐκ added by Alexiou
543 τὰ Alexiou: τὰ με E
544 ἀπόσω Trapp: ἀπόσω ἐκατέβηκα E
545 τότε added
546 καὶ added by Alexiou ψευδεῖς Alexiou: ψεματέρηνους E
548 Ἀμ’ εἰς Kalonaros: ἀμήναι εἰς E
549 εἶδαν οἱ ὀφθαλμοί μου τὴν E: perhaps εἴδασι τὰ ὀμμάτια μου
550 τὸ added by Alexiou
551 νεκροὺς κ’ ἐτρέχαν Alexiou: καὶ ἀνθρώπους νεκρούς, καὶ τρέχαν E τὸ Trapp: τὸν E

and his mother ran out from the fortress
530 with three attendants and her kinsfolk.
And seventy elders from the fortress of Raqqa
brought gifts to the young man whom they had not expected to see.
533   The emir's mother
533a embraced him thus, and kissed him sweetly
                        and spoke to him in this way:
535 "Alas, alas, my soul and my bitter old age,
if they hear of this in Egypt and down there in Cairo
so that they write it up on the tomb at Mecca
and curse you and our family!
540 My much loved child, my heart, my breath,
                        light of my eyes,
have you not seen, my dear child, the Prophet's tomb?"
    And then the emir said in reply to his mother:
"Hush, my mother; is what you are saying proper?
I have wandered over Syria and within Roman territory,

545 I ventured then across the lands of the Ethiopians,
and I have heard false stories and they were quite ridiculous,
and those I would never call gods because they are idols.
                    But in Roman territory
my eyes saw the much-hymned Theotokos
550 – oh, and how I love her with all my soul!
And I have seen, mother of mine, corpses from which flowed holy oil.

537 Alexiou's emendation reconstructs a Muslim practice of increasing a curse's effect by placing a document on a holy man's grave. Even so there is confusion since Mohammed's tomb was at Medina and not Mecca; see note at E147.
541 At this point G3.140–52 includes a list of miracles observed near the Prophet's tomb.
543 This style of censorious question recurs at E875, 957 and 1169. E and G have little in common in this speech, apart from the emir's mother's conversion; G3.171–98, for example, includes a paraphrase of the Nicene Creed.

καὶ ὁ Παράδεισος <αὐτὸς> εἰς Ρωμανίαν ἔναι.
Ἡ πίστις ἡ ἀληθινή, οἱ Χριστιανοὶ τὴν ἔχουν.
Καὶ ὁποὺ θέλει νὰ ἐλθῇ, μετὰ μέναν ἂς ἔλθη,
555   νὰ ἀκολουθήση σύντομα, <σύντομα> νὰ ὑπαγαίνω,
καὶ ὅσοι οὐδὲν θέλουν νὰ ἐλθοῦν, ἐδῶ ἂς ἀπομείνουν.
Σὺ δέ, μήτηρ γλυκεῖα μου, <ψυχῆς> παρηγορία,
ἔμπροσθέν μου ὑπάγαινε, νὰ ὑπάγω εἰς τὴν καλήν μου·
εἰ δέ, <μήτηρ,> καὶ οὐκ ἔρχεσαι, εὔχου μου ὅτι ὑπαγαίνω.»
560   Καὶ τότε ἡ μητέρα του, ἄκο καὶ τί τοῦ λέγει:
«Τέκνον μου ποθεινότατον, ἔρχομαι ὅπου θέλεις·
<ἔρχομαι> διὰ τὸ σπλάγχνον σου καὶ τὴν πολλήν σου ἀγάπην·
ἀρνοῦμαι καὶ τὸ γένος μου,
ἀρνοῦμαι καὶ τὸν Μαχουμέτ, τὸν μέγαν μας προφήτην.
565   Ἀλὶ καὶ τί μὲ ἐποίησες, ἀλὶ καὶ τί μὲ ἐποῖκες;»
Καὶ πάραυτα ὁ ἀμιρὰς πηδᾷ, καβαλικεύγει. |

Μὲ τὸν λαὸν καὶ ἀγούρους του πηδᾷ, καβαλικεύγει 155v
καὶ ἀπεσύναξεν αὐτὸς πᾶσαν αἰχμαλωσίαν
καὶ <ἐξαπ>έστειλεν αὐτὰ τὴν πολυπόθητήν του
570   καὶ μετὰ τὰ ἀμάλωτα ἄριφνους ἀνδρειωμένους.
571   Καὶ ἐχώρισεν καὶ ἐφόρτωσεν καμήλια κἂν διακόσια,
573   κἂν ἑκατὸν μουλάρια ἀσήμιν καὶ χρυσάφιν·
καὶ ἐφόρτωσεν ὁ ἀμιρὰς ὁλόχρυσα βλατία.
575   Καὶ <πάλιν> διεχώρισεν κἂν ἑκατὸν φαρία,
ὅλα καλὰ καὶ θαυμαστά, σελοχαλινωμένα,
καὶ <μετὰ ταῦτα> ἐκίνησεν εἰς Ρωμανίαν νὰ ὑπάγη.

552 αὐτὸς added by Trapp
554 ἐλθῇ Alexiou: ἔλθη E
555 ἀκολουθήση Kalonaros: ἀκολουθῇ E   σύντομα² added by Alexiou
557 ψυχῆς added by Trapp
559 μήτηρ added by Alexiou
562 ἔρχομαι added by Alexiou
564 Μαχουμέτ Trapp: μαχουμέτην E
567 Μὲ τὸν λαὸν καὶ ἀγούρους Alexiou: καὶ με τὸν λαόν του καὶ με τοὺς ἀγούρους E
568 Before καὶ Ricks deletes εἰς τοῦ παγδά ειπαγένει
569 ἐξαπέστειλεν Alexiou: ἔστειλεν E
570 μετὰ Trapp: με E   ἀμάλωτα Kalonaros: ὁμάλωτα E
571 ἐφόρτωσεν Alexiou: ἐφόρτωσεν καὶ ἔστειλεν E   διακόσια Alexiou: διακόσια· καὶ ἐχώρισεν καὶ ἐφόρτωσεν (=572) E
574 καὶ Kalonaros: καὶ ὅλα E   ὁλόχρυσα Hesseling: ὅλων χρυσὰ E
575 πάλιν added by Alexiou   ἑκατὸν Alexiou: ἑκατὸν, διακόσια E
576 σελοχαλινωμένα Hesseling: σεληνοχαληνομένα E
577 μετὰ ταῦτα added by Trapp. cf. Z1151

And Paradise itself is in Roman territory!
As for the true faith, the Christians have it.
So whoever wants to come, let him come with me
555 and follow soon for I am leaving soon;
and all those who don't want to come, let them stay here.
But you, my sweet mother, my soul's comfort,
come with me so that I can go to my beloved.
But if you do not come, mother, give me your blessing when I go."
560   And then his mother, listen to what she said to him:
"My much loved child, I will go wherever you wish,
I go out of compassion for you and out of my great love for you.
I renounce my family,
I renounce Mohammed, our great Prophet.
565 Alas, what have you done to me, alas what did you do to me?"
     And straight away the emir sprang into the saddle.

With his company and his youngsters he sprang into the saddle.
568 He collected together all his prisoners
and sent them off to his dearly loved girl,
570 and with the captives he sent innumerable brave men.
571 He selected and loaded about two hundred camels,
573 and about a hundred mules with silver and gold
and the emir loaded them with silken fabrics all of gold.
575 Once again he selected about a hundred steeds,
all handsome and marvellous, with saddles and bridles;
and the emir set off for Roman territory.

552–3 Ricks inverts these lines, to enhance the reference to Paradise, taken by him as a
symbol of earthly love; gardens enclosing a young girl have erotic overtones in medieval
Greek as well as Western medieval vernacular literature (Littlewood, 1979). But this
passage deals on the surface with the advantages of Orthodox Christianity.
568 The deleted reference to Baghdad is logically suspect since the distances involved are
great and no reason has been given for the emir to have captives there.
569 At this point G3.246 makes only a general reference to the treasure the emir brings
back with him.

Καὶ <πάλιν> διεχώρισεν χιλίους Ἀραβίτας,
ὁλολουρίκους καὶ καλούς, χρυσοκλιβανιασμένους,
580 νὰ περπατοῦσιν ἔμπροσθεν τοῦ <θαυμαστοῦ> ἀγούρου
καὶ ἄλλες κᾶν χιλιάδες δύο τὸν ἀμιρὰν ἀντάμα. |
. . .
583 |Καὶ ἡ κόρη μὲ τὸν ἄγουρον μόνοι των ᾽ς τὸ κουβούκλιν 157r G2.266
φιλοῦν, καὶ οἱ βάγιες ραίνουν τους μετὰ ροδοσταμάτων
585 καὶ ἐδρόσιζαν τὰ χείλη των ἐκ τὸν γλυκὺν τὸν πόθον.
586 Καὶ τότε ὡς τὸ ἤκουσαν οἱ γυναικαδελφοί του,
588 ἐξαίφνης ἐσεβήκασιν ἀπέσω εἰς τὸ κουβούκλιν
καὶ τὸν γαμπρόν τους ηὕρηκαν μετὰ τῆς ἀδελφῆς των
590 καὶ ἐκάμνασιν τὸ ἡξεύρετε, τὸ κάμνουν οἱ ἀγαποῦντες,
καὶ ἐντράπησαν τὰ ἀδέλφια της καὶ ἐστάθησαν ἀπέξω
καὶ εἶχαν χαρὰν ἐξαίρετην, χαρὰν ἀλλὰ μεγάλην.
Τὸν Διγενὴν ἐπῆραν τον οἱ βάγιες καὶ ἤφεράν τον·
τὸ νὰ τὸν ἰδῆ ὁ ἀμιράς, ἐπίασε, ἐφίλησέν τον
595 καὶ ἐθεώρει τον λοιπὸν καὶ ἀποκαμαρωνέ τον
καὶ ἐχαίρετο ὅτι εἶν᾽ ἔμορφος μετὰ τῆς ποθητῆς του,
ἀμάδιν καὶ ἡ μητέρα του καὶ οἱ γυναικαδελφοί του
καὶ ὅλη ἡ συντροφία του καὶ ὅλον τὸ φουσάτον.
599/600 Καὶ τὰ γομάρια ἐφθάσασιν ἐκεῖ ὅπου ἐπιθυμοῦσαν,
601/2 καὶ τὰ ἔβαλαν ᾽ς τὸ σπίτιν του καὶ τὰ φαρία | εἰς τὸν στάβλον· 157v
τοὺς δὲ ἀγούρους του τοὺς καλούς, Πέρσας καὶ Ἀραβίτας,
φιλοτιμίας ἔδωσεν ἐκ τὰ πεθερικά του

578 πάλιν added by Alexiou
580 περπατοῦσιν corr., cf. E821: περιπατοῦσιν E θαυμαστοῦ added
581 χιλιάδες δύο Alexiou: δύο χιλιάδες E
583 Before this line E includes a line of obscure sense (=582), first deleted by Kalonaros:
ὅτι να τὸν ἴδω ἤτους· καὶ να με γλυκοφιλήσει
583 μόνοι των ᾽ς Alexiou: μοναχί τον εἰς E
584 φιλοῦν Alexiou: ἐφιλοῦσαν E ραίνουν τους Alexiou: τοὺς ἔρεναν E
588 ἐξαίφνης Alexiou: με τήν μάναν τους ἀντάμα (=587)· ἐξέφνης E ἐσεβήκασιν corr.:
ἐξεπίδησαν, καὶ ἐσέβηκαν E
590 ἀγαποῦντες Hesseling: ἀγαποῦντε E
592 χαρὰν Alexiou: γὰρ E ἀλλὰ E (Spadaro, 1989, 173): πολλὰ Kalonaros
594 τὸ Alexiou: καὶ τὸ E ἐπίασε, ἐφίλησέν corr.: ἐπίασεν καὶ κατεφίλησέν E
595 ἐθεώρει Alexiou: ἐθόρι E
596 ἐχαίρετο ὅτι εἶν᾽ ἔμορφος Alexiou: ἐθόρι τον ὅτι εἶτον αἵμορφον, καὶ ἐχαίρετον E
597 ἀμάδιν [ἀμάδι] Alexiou: ἀμάδιν με τὸ τέκνον του E
599/600 ἐφθάσασιν Alexiou: ἐυθάσσιν, φορτωμένα τοῦ ἀμυρᾶ E
601/2 τὰ ἔβαλαν ᾽ς corr.: ἔβαλαν τὸ πρᾶγμα εἰς E φαρία Alexiou: φαρία ἔβαλαν E
604 φιλοτιμίας ἔδωσεν corr.: ὅλους ἔδωσεν φιλοτιμίας μεγάλας, καὶ χαρίσματα E
Alexiou proposes ἔδωσεν ὅλους <ὁ ἀμιρὰς> φιλοτιμίας μεγάλας | <καὶ ἐπῆραν> καὶ
χαρίσματα

Once again he selected out a thousand Arabs,
all with breastplates and handsome, with gold cuirasses,
580 to proceed in front of the marvellous youngster
and another two thousand or so to go with the emir.
      . . .
583 The girl and the youngster, on their own in their chamber,
kissed and the maid-servants sprinkled them with rose-water,
585 while they refreshed their lips with their sweet desire.
586   Then, when his wife's brothers heard of this,
588 they burst into the chamber unexpectedly
and found their brother-in-law with their sister
590 and they were doing what you know lovers do;
her brothers were abashed and stood outside,
but they felt matchless joy, great joy indeed.
      The maid-servants took Digenis and brought him in;
when the emir saw him, he picked him up, he kissed him
585 and gazed at him then and admired him
and rejoiced in his beauty with his wife,
together with his mother and his wife's brothers
and all their companions and the whole army.
599/600   The baggage arrived where they had been waiting for it;
601/602 they placed it in the house and the steeds in the stable.
And as for his handsome youngsters, Persians and Arabs,
the emir bestowed rewards on them from his parents-in-law

580 Who is this 'youngster'? Is it the young Digenis, for whom these men are to be an
elite bodyguard on the emir's return?
581–2 The final stages of the emir's return (cf. G3.248–80) would have been covered by
f.156, now missing in E. E582 (which has been omitted, see apparatus) is garbled;
Alexiou (cf. Spadaro, 1989, 177–8) suggests it represents the last line of the emir's
speech of greeting.
584 Cf. G3.282–3. Splashing lovers with water has a parallel in Heliodoros; see
Introduction, pp. xlvi–xlvii.

605 καὶ <ἐξ>απέστειλεν αὐτοὺς πάλιν εἰς τὴν Συρίαν.
Κἂν Ἀραβίτας ἑκατὸν ἐκράτησεν καὶ μόνον,
καὶ ἐκράτησεν τὴν μάναν του μετὰ τοὺς ἀδελφούς του
καὶ ἐβάπτισεν <ὁ ἀμιρὰς> ἅπαντα τὸν λαόν του   G3.330
καὶ τόπον τοὺς ἐχάρισε καὶ ἐκάθετο ὁ λαός του.
610   Καὶ τότε <πάλιν> τὸ παιδὶν ὁ Διγενὴς Ἀκρίτης   G3.339
<γλυκέα> ἀναθρέφετον, ὡς πρέπει καὶ ὡς ἀξιάζει,
καὶ ὡς <ὁ> ἥλιος ἔλαμπεν <λαμπρὰ> τὸ πρόσωπόν του
καὶ ὡς κυπαρίσσι ἐτρέφετον τὴν ἅπασαν ἡμέραν·
χέρι ἔβανε καὶ δύνεται ὥσπερ καὶ ἀνδρειωμένος.
615   Τὸ χαλινάρι ὅνταν κρατεῖ, ἐπῆρεν καὶ κοντάριν
νὰ ὑπάγη μὲ τοὺς κυνηγοὺς διὰ νὰ περιδιαβάση.
Κ' ἐθώρει τὸ παιδόπουλον τὸ πλῆθος τῶν θηρίων
καὶ ἐκατέβηκεν τὸ παιδὶν 'ς τὴν μέσην τῶν θηρίων.
Ἐδὰ ἂς σᾶς ἀφηγήσωμαι περὶ τὰς ἀμωρίας του.
620   Ὁ Θεὸς τοῦ ἔδωσε εὐτυχίαν εἰς τὴν πολλήν του ἀνδρείαν
καὶ ὅπου καὶ ἂν τύχη †... † ποιεῖ ἀνδραγαθίας.
622/623   Ὁ θαυμαστὸς Βασίλειος, τὸ φῶς τῶν | ἀνδρειωμένων 158r
περὶ ἀπελάτων ἤκουσε εὐγενικῶν καὶ ἀνδρείων,
625   ὅτι κρατοῦν στενώματα καὶ ποιοῦν ἀντραγαθίας
καὶ ζῆλος ἦλθεν εἰς αὐτὸν νὰ ἰδῆ τοὺς ἀπελάτας.
Καὶ ἔκατσεν καὶ εὐθείασεν ὡραῖον, τερπνὸν λαβοῦτον·

605 ἐξαπέστειλεν Trapp: ἀπέστειλεν Ε
606 Κἂν Ἀραβίτας ἑκατὸν Alexiou: κἂν ἑκατὸν ἀραβήτας after καὶ ἐκράτησεν μόνον
Ε   ἐκράτησεν καὶ μόνον corr.: καὶ ἐκράτησεν μόνον Ε
607 μάναν Alexiou: μράν (= μητέραν) Ε
608 ὁ ἀμιρὰς added by Alexiou
609 τόπον τους ἐχάρισε Trapp: ἐχάρισέ τους τόπον Ε   ἐκάθετο Trapp: ἐκάθετον Ε
610 πάλιν added by Karayanni, 1976, 103
611 γλυκέα added   ἀναθρέφετον Hesseling: ἀναθρεφέτων Ε
612 ὁ added   λαμπρὰ added
613 κυπαρίσσι ἐτρέφετον corr.: κυπαρίσην ἀνατρέφετον Ε
614 χέρι ἔβανε καὶ corr.: καὶ ἔβανεν χαίριν καὶ να Ε
615 Τὸ χαλινάρι ὅνταν κρατεῖ, ἐπῆρεν καὶ κοντάριν corr.: ὅτι ἐδύνετον κρατὴν τὸ
χαληνάριν· ἐπῆρεν κοντάριν καὶ ραβδίν Ε
616 διὰ Trapp: ὡς διὰ Ε
617 Κ' ἐθώρει Trapp: καὶ θόρι Ε
618 'ς Trapp: εἰς Ε
619 ἀφηγήσωμαι Karayanni, 1976, 103: ἀφηγήσωμεν Ε
620 ἔδωσε corr.: ἔδωσεν Ε
622/623 ἀνδρειωμένων Alexiou: ἀπελάτων, ἡ δόϊξα τῶν ἀνδριομένων (=623) Ε
625 ἀντραγαθίας Trapp: ἀντραγαθίας μεγάλας Ε

605 and sent them back to Syria.
   He kept about a hundred Arabs only with him,
   and he kept his mother and his brothers;
   the emir baptised all his company
   and granted them land, and his company settled there.
610   Then the child, Digenis Akritis, the Frontiersman of Double Descent,
   was brought up sweetly as is proper and fit,
   and his face glowed brightly like the sun
   and he continued to thrive every day like a cypress;
   he began to have strength like a brave man.
615 As soon as he could grasp the reins, he took a spear
   to go with the hunters and roam around.
   And the little child saw a host of wild beasts
   and the child went in amongst the wild beasts.
   Now let me tell you about his infancy.
620 God gave him good fortune in his acts of great bravery
   and wherever he went he achieved feats of valour.
622/623   The marvellous Vasilis, the light of the brave,
   heard about the noble and brave guerrillas,
625 that they held the passes and performed valiant deeds,
   and enthusiasm came over him to see the guerrillas.
   So he sat down and prepared a beautiful, delightful lute;

610–792 At this point questions of the structure of E and its relationship to G and
Digenis become acute. Kalonaros, largely followed by Trapp, suggests that the order of
lines and episodes (cf. the sequence in G) should be: 609 (cf. G3.338–9), 702–41 (cf.
G4.4–51: role of Eros and summary of the emir's story), 610–19 (cf. G4.52–71: growth
of Digenis), 742–91 (cf. G4.72–163: Digenis's first hunt, with text missing after 791, see
below), 620–701 (Digenis' first visit to the guerrillas), 792 ff. (cf. G4.373: return from
hunt). Note that E620–701, placed by Z1028–92 between G4.253–4 during Digenis'
return from the hunt, are not now represented in G at all and probably never were
(MacAlister, 1984). E's order of lines has been retained here.
610–21 Relegated by Alexiou to an appendix on the grounds that they are a late
attempt to impose a narrative flow on an episodic text, and repositioned by Kalonaros and
Trapp, these lines are problematic and need even more intervention than elsewhere to
heal the metre; they form a bridging passage from the emir's tale to the story of Digenis,
though not marked off in any way in the manuscript. For similar bridging passages see
G3.339–43 and 4.52–71.
622–701 This section forms Alexiou's 'Digenis and the Guerrillas'.
622/623 'Vasilis', the more modern equivalent in English of the hero's first name 'Basil',
has been chosen to point the contrast between the linguistic usages of E and G.
624 Digenis' connection with the guerrillas is emphasised before he encounters them, an
indication that the material on Digenis had its own traditions.
627 A stringed instrument is an unusual implement to take on a dangerous expedition;
that it was part of Digenis' traditional accoutrements is suggested by its presence in the
so-called Akritic plates (Notopoulos, 1964; Frantz, 1940/1).

ἐπῆρεν το καὶ ἐξέβηκεν ἀπὸ τὰ γονικά του
καὶ εἰς μίαν ἐκατέλαβεν καὶ τὰς στενὰς κλεισούρας.
630 Καὶ ὡς ὑπῆγεν μοναχός,
εὖρεν καλάμιν καὶ νερὸν καὶ ἦτον ἀπέσω λέων –
καὶ τρίτον τὸν ἐγύρισεν καὶ ἐμπασίαν οὐκ ηὖρεν –
καὶ εἶχεν γροθέαν ἐξηστρεπτὴν ἀπὸ Γιαννάκη χέρια.
Καὶ ὡς εἶδεν τὸν λέοντα ὁ Διγενὴς Ἀκρίτης,
635 ἀπὸ καρδίας ἐστέναξεν, ἐκ βάθους τῆς ψυχῆς του:
«Πότε νὰ ἰδοῦν τὰ μάτια μου τὸ φῶς τῶν ἀπελάτων,

Νὰ γομωστοῦν τὰ ὀμμάτια μου τὸ φῶς τῶν ἀπελάτων;»   158v
Τὸν νεροφόρον ηὖρηκεν, τὸν εἶχαν οἱ ἀπελάτες,
καὶ αὐτὸν τὸν ἐρώτησεν ὁ Διγενὴς Ἀκρίτης:
640 «Τὸν Θεόν, καλὲ νεώτερε, ποῦ μένουν οἱ ἀπελάτες;»
Καὶ ὁ νεροφόρος <παρευθὺς> τὸν Διγενὴν ἐλάλει:
«Τὸν Θεόν, καλὲ νεώτερε, τί τοὺς καταγυρεύεις;»
«Γυρεύγω καὶ κατερωτῶ νὰ εἶμαι καὶ ἐγὼ ἀπελάτης,
ἵνα ρογεύωμαι καὶ ἐγὼ μετὰ τῶν ἀπελάτων.»
645 Ὁ νεροφόρος παίρνει τον, 'ς τὸ λησταρχεῖον ὑπάγει.

Ἐκεῖ ηὖρεν τὸν Φιλοπαππούν καὶ ἐκείτετο εἰς κλινάριν·
πολλῶν θηρίων δέρματα εἶχεν ἀπάνω κάτω,
τὸν λέοντα καὶ τὸν σύαγρον εἶχεν προσκεφαλάδιν.
Καὶ ὑπόκυψεν ὁ | νεώτερος καὶ χαμηλὰ ἐπροσκύναν.   159r   G4.674
650 <Καὶ ὁ γέρων> ὁ Φιλοπαππούς οὕτως τὸν ἀπεκρίθην:

628 του Kyriakidis, 1926, 60: του ἀπέσω E
629 ἐκατέλαβεν corr.: ἐκατέμαθεν E
630 ὑπῆγεν μοναχός corr.: ὑπῆγενεν μοναχός του E
631 εὖρεν Kalonaros: εὖρεν καὶ E
633 καὶ Alexiou: καὶ ὁ λέων E   Γιαννάκη Alexiou: τοῦ γιανάκι τὰ E
636 μάτια E: ὀμμάτια Alexiou
639 αὐτὸν Kalonaros: αὐτὸς E εὐθὺς Alexiou
641 παρευθὺς added by Trapp, cf. Z1566
642 Θεόν Hesseling: θν᾿ σου E
645 Ὁ νεροφόρος παίρνει τον corr.: ἀπῆρε τον ὁ νεροφόρος (νεροφός Prombonas,
1985, 10–11) E   'ς Alexiou: καὶ εἰς E   ὑπάγει corr.: ὑπαγένει E
646 Ἐκεῖ Alexiou: κεῖ E (capital omitted) ἐκείτετο Krumbacher, 1904, 329: ἐκίτετον
E   εἰς Trapp: εἰς τὸ E
647 κάτω Krumbacher, 1904, 329: ἀποκάτω E
648 τὸν λέοντα καὶ τὸν σύαγρον Krumbacher, 1904, 329: τῶν λεόντων· κὶ τῶν
σιαγρὸν E
649 νεώτερος Trapp: νεότερος τὴν κεφαλὴν E
650 Καὶ ὁ γέρων added by Trapp, cf. E656

he took it and left his parents' estates
and in an instant he reached the narrow passes.
630 And as he went forward on his own,
he found a reed-bed and water and there was a lion within
– and he searched around three times and could not find an entrance –
a lion that had received a back-handed blow from Giannakis.
When Digenis Akritis, the Frontiersman of Double Descent, saw the
    lion,
635 he sighed from the bottom of his heart, from the depth of his soul:
"When will my eyes see the light of the guerrillas,

so that my eyes may be filled with the light of the guerrillas?"
He found the water-carrier employed by the guerrillas
and Digenis Akritis asked him:
640 "By God, fine young man, where do the guerrillas live?"
And the water-carrier said immediately to Digenis:
"By God, fine young man, why are you seeking them out?"
"I am seeking them out and asking about them so as to become a
    guerrilla myself,
so that I too can be enrolled among the guerrillas."
645 The water-carrier took him and brought him to the robbers'
    headquarters.

There he found Philopappous reclining on his couch,
with many animal skins all around him;
he had a lion and a boar for his pillow.
The young man bowed and made deep obeisance.
650 And old Philopappous answered him like this:

630 The first mention in E of Digenis' characteristic preference for acting alone.
632 The opening lines of this episode are condensed and confused. The abrupt reference
to Giannakis also implies that this was material familar to the poet and his audience.
637 The repeated phrases frame a picture space in the manuscript.
640, 642 There is probably some irony in the water-carrier's direct reflection of Digenis'
oath – though there is so much repetition in this poem that such judgements remain
uncertain.
644 The technical term 'enrolled' implies that the guerrillas have a military function.
648 Philopappous is shown to place emphasis on wild animal skins (cf. E664), which
contribute to his characterisation.

«Καλῶς ἦλθες, νεώτερε, ἂν οὐκ εἶσαι προδότης.»
Καὶ τότε ὁ νεώτερος οὕτως ἀπιλογᾶται·
«῍Ω μὰ τὸν Θεόν, Φιλοπαππού, οὐκ εἶμαι ἐγὼ προδότης·
γυρεύγω καὶ κατερωτῶ νὰ εἶμαι καὶ ἐγὼ ἀπελάτης,
655   ἵνα ρογεύγωμαι καὶ ἐγὼ μετὰ τῶν ἀπελάτων.»
Καὶ ὁ γέρων ὁ Φιλοπαππούς οὕτως τὸν ἀπεκρίθην·
«Θεωρῶ σε, κύρκα, ὑπόλιγνον καὶ ὡς ἀχαμνὰ ζωσμένον
καὶ χαμηλὰ ἡ ποδέα σου καὶ οὐ ποιεῖς ἐσὺ ἀπελάτης.
Ἐὰν καυχᾶσαι, νεώτερε, νὰ εἶσαι ἀπελάτης,
660   δύνασαι ἐπάρειν τὸ ραβδίν, νὰ κατεβῆς 'ς τὴν βίγλαν
καὶ νὰ νηστεύσης, νεώτερε, κᾶν δεκαπέντε ἡμέρας,
νὰ μῆδε φᾶς, νὰ μῆδεν πιῆς, νὰ μῆδε ὕπνον χορτάσης,
καὶ ἀπέκει ὡς λέων νὰ βρουχισθῆς, νὰ ἔβγουν τὰ λεοντάρια,
νὰ ἐπάρης τὰ δερμάτια των καὶ ἐδῶ νὰ <μὲ> τὰ φέρης;
665   Καὶ δύνασαι, νεώτερε, νὰ κατεβῆς 'ς τὴν βίγλαν
καὶ νὰ διαβοῦν οἱ ἄρχοντες, μὲ τὸν γαμπρόν, τὴν νύμφην,
καὶ μὲ ὅλον τὸ φουσάτον τους καὶ ἐσὺ νὰ ἔμπης 'ς τὴν μέσην,
νὰ ἐπάρης τὴν νεόνυμφον καὶ ἐδῶ νὰ μὲ τὴν φέρης;»
Καὶ τότε δὲ καὶ ὁ Διγενὴς οὕτως τὸν συντυχαίνει·   159v
670   «Ἄλλα μὲ εἶπέ, Φιλοπαππού, τὰ οὐ δύναμαι νὰ ποίσω·
αὐτά, γέρον, τὰ μὲ λαλεῖς, πέντε χρονῶν τὰ ἐποῖκα.
Ἀμὴ ἄκουσόν μου, γέροντα· μίλιν ἂν ἦτον ἕναν
ὀρυάκιν εἰς τὸ πλάτος,
<καὶ> διπλοπόδης πάραυτα εἰς μίαν νὰ τὸ πηδήσω,
675   καὶ τὸν λαγὸν 'ς τ' ἀνήφορον τρίτο νὰ τὸν γυρίσω,
πέρδικα ὄντα χαμοπετᾶ, ν' ἀπλώσω νὰ τὴν πάρω.»
Καὶ τότε καὶ ὁ Φιλοπαππούς τοιοῦτον λόγον λέγει·

653 οὐκ Alexiou (note), Garandoudis, 1993, 206: οὐδὲν E
655 ρογεύγωμαι Alexiou: ρογεύγομεν E
657 σε Hesseling: τε E   ζωσμένον Xanthoudidis, 1912, 556: ζοσμένος E
660 νὰ corr.: καὶ E   'ς Trapp: εἰς E
662 πιῆς Hesseling: πὶς E
663 ὡς λέων νὰ βρουχισθῆς Alexiou: να βρουχισθεὶς ὡς λέων E
664 μὲ added by Hesseling, cf. E668
665 Καὶ Alexiou: καὶ πάλιν E   'ς Trapp: εἰς E
666 τὸν γαμπρόν, τὴν νύμφην Alexiou: τὴν νύμφην καὶ με τὸν γαμπρόν E
667 τὸ φουσάτον τους Alexiou: του τὸ φουσάτον E   'ς corr.: εἰς E
669 Διγενὴς Kalonaros: εὐγενὴς E
670 τὰ οὐ Alexiou: ὁπού οὐδὲν E
671 γέρον, τὰ Karayanni, 1976, 105–6: γέροντα E
674 καὶ added by Alexiou
675 'ς Trapp: εἰς E
676 πέρδικα corr.: τὴν πέρδικαν E

"Welcome, young man, providing you are not a traitor."
And the young man replied like this:
"By God, Philopappous, I am no traitor.
I am seeking and demanding to become a guerrilla myself,
655 so that I too can be enrolled among the guerrillas."
And old Philopappous answered him like this:
"I can see, my sweetheart, that you are rather slender and delicately
dressed
and your kilt is long: you would never make a guerrilla.
If you boast, young man, of becoming a guerrilla,
660 can you take your stick to go out on guard,
go without food, young man, for about fifteen days,
and eat nothing, drink nothing, go without your sleep,
and then roar like a lion to bring out the lions
and get their hides and bring them back to me here?
655 And can you, young man, go out on guard
and when the lords go by with the bride-groom and the bride
and all their army, can you burst into their midst
and seize the newly-wedded bride and bring her back to me here?"
And then Digenis addressed him thus:
670 "Tell me, Philopappous, about something I can't do!
What you are talking about, old man, I did when I was five.
But listen to me, old man. If there were a stream
one mile wide,
even with my two feet together I would leap across it in an instant,
675 and I would run down the hare on a slope three times
and I would stretch out and catch the partridge as it flies low."
And then Philopappous uttered these words:

657 κύρκα (of debatable etymology; see Kriaras, 1969– under this word) is usually
taken as a diminutive of κύρ; it is most frequently found as an endearment used by a girl
of her lover. Here, where it is applied by a seasoned warrior to a youth, the implication
must be that Digenis looks more like a ladies' man than a fighter.
658 This in the only reference in E to Digenis' ποδέα, where it seems effeminate rather
than heroic; see Introduction, p. xl.
665 For Philopappous bride-snatching is a major and admirable part of the guerrillas'
activities, the ultimate hunt; see Mackridge, 1993a and contrast Laiou, 1993, 205–6.

«Σύρετε ἀργυρὸν σελίν, νὰ κάτση ὁ κὺρ Βασίλης.»
Τραπέζιν ἧστεσαν ὀμπρός, νὰ φάγουν καὶ νὰ πίουν.
680 Καλὰ ἔφαγαν, καλὰ ἔπιαν, καλὰ ἐκαλοψυχῆσαν·
<καὶ τότε> ἄλλος ἔλεγεν: «Ἐγὼ ἀπαντῶ πενήντα»·
<καὶ πάλιν> ἄλλος ἔλεγεν: «Ἐγὼ ἀπαντῶ ἑβδομήντα»·
<καὶ πάλιν> ἄλλος ἔλεγεν: «Ἐγὼ ἀπαντῶ διακόσιους.»

Ὁ νεώτερος ἐκάθετον, ποτέ του οὐκ ἐλάλει. 160r
685 <Καὶ ὁ γέρων> ὁ Φιλοπαππούς τὸν νεώτερον ἐλάλει:
«Ἐσὺ <δὲ> πόσους δύνασαι, Βασίλη, ἀπαντῆσαι;»
Ὁ δὲ νεώτερος <εὐθὺς> τὸν γέρονταν ἐλάλει:
«<Ἕναν,> ἐὰν ἔναι ὡσὰν ἐμέν, δύναμαι ἀπαντῆσαι·
εἰ δὲ ἔναι δυνατώτερος, νὰ δώση καὶ τὸν δώσω.
690 Καὶ δεῦτε, ἀγοῦροι, ἂς λάβωμεν ὑπόκοντα ραβδία
καὶ ἂς κατάβωμεν <ἅπαντες> κάτω εἰς τὴν ὁμαλίαν,
ἵνα <ἀλλήλους> δώσωμεν χωριατικὰς ραβδέας.»
Καὶ πάραυτα ἐπήρασιν ὑπόκοντα ραβδία
καὶ <ὅλοι> ἐκατέβησαν κάτω εἰς τὴν ὁμαλίαν,
695 ὅπως <ἀλλήλους> δώσουσιν χωριατικὰς ραβδέας.

<Καὶ> τότε <δὲ> ὁ Διγενὴς ἔριξεν τὸ ραβδίν του·
τοὺς μὲν γροθέας ἔκρουεν, τοὺς ἄλλους σφοντυλέας
ἀλλὰ ἐ|πέσασι ὁλονῶν ραβδία τῶν ἀπελάτων 160v
καὶ ἐφορτώθην τα ὁ Διγενής, τὸν γέρον τὰ ὑπαγαίνει:
700 «Παράλαβε, Φιλοπαππού, ραβδιὰ τῶν ἀπελάτων

678 κὺρ Trapp: κήριος E
680 Καλὰ¹ and 2 Alexiou: καὶ καλὰ E   καλὰ³ Alexiou: καὶ E
681 καὶ τότε added by Alexiou
682 καὶ πάλιν added by Alexiou
683 καὶ πάλιν added by Alexiou   διακόσιους Alexiou: διακοσίους E
684 Ὁ Trapp: Ὁ δὲ E
685 Καὶ ὁ γέρων ὁ Alexiou, cf. E650, 656: ὁ δὲ E Ὁ δὲ γέρων Trapp
686 δὲ added by Trapp, cf. Z1605
687 εὐθὺς added by Trapp, cf. Z1606
688 Ἕναν added by Hesseling
689 νὰ corr.: να με E μὲ Alexiou   τὸν Alexiou: να τὸν E
691 ἅπαντες added by Trapp
692 ἀλλήλους added by Alexiou
693 Καὶ πάραυτα corr.: ἀλλὰ E
694 ὅλοι added by Trapp, cf. Z1614
695 ἀλλήλους added by Alexiou   χωριατικὰς Alexiou: χωριάτικας E
696 Καὶ τότε δὲ Alexiou: Τότε E
698 ἐπέσασι corr.: ἐπέσασιν E   ραβδία Trapp, cf. E700: τὰ ραβδία E

"Draw up a silver stool for Sir Vasilis to sit down."
They put a table in front of them so they could eat and drink.
680 They ate well, they drank well, they were well away with their high
        spirits.
And then one of them said: "I can fight against fifty."
And another said in turn: "I can fight against seventy."
And another said in turn: "I can fight against two hundred."

685 But the young man sat and never said a word.
And old Philopappous said to the young man:
"And you, Vasilis, how many can you fight against?"
        And at once the young man said to the old man:
"Only one, if he is like me, can I fight against;
if he is stronger, let him strike me and I will strike him.
But come, lads, let's take our short sticks
690 and let's all go down to the level ground
so that we can have a stick fight with each other in country style."
        And at once they took their short sticks
and all went down to the level ground
695 to have a stick fight with each other in country style.

But then Digenis threw down his stick.
Some he struck with his fist, others with the flat of his hand on the
        neck
and all the guerrillas dropped their sticks.
Digenis bundled them up and carried them off to the old man.
700 "Accept, Philopappous, the guerrillas' sticks,

678 'κύρ', verging on the modern 'κύριος', implies a provisional social acceptance of the
young hero; one is tempted to translate the phrase as 'Mr Vasilis'.
681 For a similar triple boast see Sachlikis, Ἀφήγησις παράξενος (Papadimitriou,
1896), lines 817–23 (MacAlister, 1984, 561), and in other literary contexts the *gabs*
(boasts) in the *Chanson de Roland* (laisses 70–9) or the twelfth-century *Pèlerinage de
Charlemagne* (laisses 24–37). This whole passage is full of the patterning of oral story-
telling.

καὶ ἂν οὐ σοῦ ἀρέσῃ, γέροντα, καὶ ἐσὲ νὰ τὸ ποιήσω.»
Ὁ ἔρως τίκτει τὸ φιλὶν καὶ τὸ φιλὶ τὸν πόθον,   G4.6
ὁ πόθος δίδει μέριμνας, ἔννοιάς τε καὶ φροντίδας,   G4.8
κατατολμᾶ καὶ κίνδυνον καὶ χωρισμὸν γονέων,   G4.9, 11
705 θάλασσαν ἀντιμάχεται, τὸ πῦρ οὐ διαλογίζει   G4.12
καὶ τίποτε οὐ λογίζεται ὁ ποθῶν διὰ τὴν ἀγάπην·   G4.14
ἐγκρεμνοὺς οὐ λογίζεται, τοὺς ποταμοὺς οὐδόλως,
τὰς ἀγρυπνίας ἀνάπαυσιν καὶ τὰς κλεισούρας κάμπους.   G4.16–17
Καὶ ὅσοι βασανίζεσθε δι’ ἀγάπην κορασίου,
710 ἀκούσατε διὰ γραφῆς <ἐκείνων> τῶν Ἑλλήνων
πόσα καὶ αὐτοὶ ὑπομείνασιν βάσανα διὰ τὸν πόθον.
Βλέπετε, οἱ ἀναγινώσκοντες, τοὺς ἀριστεῖς ἐκείνους,
τοὺς Ἕλληνας, τοὺς θαυμαστοὺς καὶ ὀνομαστοὺς στρατιώτας,
<καὶ> ὅλα ὅσα ἐγίνουντα διὰ ἐκείνην τὴν Ἑλένην,
715 ὅτε ἐκατεπολέμησαν ἅπασαν τὴν Ἀσίαν,
καὶ πάντες ἐδοξάσθησαν διὰ περισσὴν ἀνδρείαν,
καὶ πάλιν εἰς ἐρωτικὰ ἄλλος τις οὐχ ὑπέστη.
Καὶ οὐ λέγομεν καυχίσματα ἢ πλάσματα καὶ μύθους   G4.27
ἃ Ὅμηρος ἐψεύσατο καὶ | ἄλλοι τῶν Ἑλλήνων. 161r
720 Ταῦτα γὰρ μῦθοι <οὐ> λέγονται, καυχίσματα οὐ λαλοῦνται,
ἀλλ’ ἀληθεύουν ἐκ παντός· μηδεὶς οὖν ἀπιστήσῃ   G4.36
ὡς λέγω τὴν ἀλήθειαν τοῦ θαυμαστοῦ Ἀκρίτη.
Πατήρ του ἦτον ὁ ἀμιράς, ὁ Μούσουρος ἐκεῖνος,

701 οὐ Alexiou: ουδέν E
702 ἔρως Alexiou: ἔρων E
703 μέριμνας Hesseling: μέρεμνας E
704 κατατολμᾶ Chatzis, 1930, 19, cf. G4.11: κατὰ πολλήν E καὶ ἀπειλήν Alexiou, note
705 θάλασσαν Alexiou: ἡ θάλασσα E
706 ὁ ποθῶν Alexiou: πόθων ἡ ὡς E πόθος Garandoudis, 1993, 207
707 ἐγκρεμνοὺς Trapp: καὶ τοὺς ἐγκρεμνοὺς E
708 τὰς ἀγρυπνίας ἀνάπαυσιν καὶ τὰς κλεισούρας κάμπους Politis, 1973, 344: καὶ τὰς κλησούρας κάμπους· τὰς ἀγριπνίας ἀνάπαυσις E
710 ἐκείνων added by Kyriakidis, 1946, 422
711 διὰ Alexiou: ὡς δια E
712 ἀριστεῖς Alexiou: ἀστέρας E
713 τοὺς¹ Kalonaros: τὰς E
714 καὶ ὅλα Alexiou: ἀλλὰ E   διὰ Trapp: ὡς διὰ E
715 ὅτε ἐκατεπολέμησαν Kalonaros: ὅτι ἐκατεπολέμισεν E   Ἀσίαν Alexiou: Συρίαν E
716 διὰ περισσὴν Alexiou: ὡς διὰ τὴν περισὴν του E
718 μύθους Hesseling: θύμους E
719 ἃ Alexiou: ὁ E   Ὅμηρος Chatzis, 1930a, 235: ἀμυρὰς E
720 οὐ added by Karayanni, 1976, 106, 125
723 Πατήρ Alexiou: ὁ πατήρ E

and if this is not to your liking, old man, I shall do the same to you."
   Love begets the kiss and the kiss desire,
desire gives rise to anxieties, worries and concerns;
it ventures on danger and separation from parents,
705 it fights against the sea, it reckons fire as nothing
and, because of love, he who desires pays no heed to anything;
he pays no heed to cliffs, none at all to rivers,
he counts sleeplessness as rest and mountain passes as plains.
   And all you who are tormented by love of a girl,
710 you have heard in the writings of the famous Hellenes
how many torments they too endured for the sake of desire.
Look, readers, at those valiant men,
the Hellenes, marvellous and renowned soldiers,
and all that happened for the sake of the famous Helen,
715 when they waged war throughout Asia
and all were praised for prodigious bravery,
and yet not even one of them could withstand the force of passion.
And we are not repeating the boasts or fictions and stories
which Homer and other Hellenes falsely invented.
720 For these events are not stories that are told nor boasting that is
     repeated
but they are all completely true: let no one disbelieve
that I am telling the truth about Akritis, the marvellous Frontiersman.
   His father was the emir, the famous Mousouros

701–1088 These lines form Alexiou's 'The Youth and Wedding of Akritis'; cf.
G4.1–952. Digenis' hunting and courtship would have been part of *Digenis.
702–38 Cf. G4.4–64. This passage on love, present in G as well as E, was clearly part of
*Digenis; it marks the beginning of G4 and the opening of the third section that can be
distinguished in E. The emphasis on the hazards implicit in love (fire, shipwreck and in
particular the separation from parents) seems to place the original version of these lines
in the context of the novel-writing experiment of the mid-twelfth century. G and E share
the same sequence of material: reflection on love and recapitulation of the emir's tale
followed by the young Digenis' wish to go hunting.
719 The characterisation of the Homeric stories as false is a theme current in the twelfth
century; see note on G4.25–36.
723 The emir's genealogy has been given previously at E145; here we are told his name.

ὁποὺ ἀνατράφην εἰς Συρίαν, ἀπέσω εἰς Βαβυλῶνα,
725 καὶ ὡς διὰ ἀνδρείαν του τὴν πολλήν, τὴν περισσήν του φρόνα,
συμβουλὴν ἐποιήσασιν οἱ γέροντες Συρίας
καὶ τὸν σουλτάνον τὸ εἴπασιν καὶ ἀμιρὰν τὸν ἐποῖκαν.
Καὶ τρισχιλίους τὸν ἔδωσαν Τούρκους καὶ Ἀραβίτας   G4.38
καὶ ἐποίησαν τον ἐξακουστὸν εἰς πᾶσαν τὴν Συρίαν·
730 καὶ εἶχεν καὶ τοὺς ἀγούρους του ἄλλους πεντακοσίους.
Ἐπῆρεν τους καὶ ἐξέβηκεν ἔξω εἰς Ρωμανίαν·   G4.40
τὸ Ἡρακλέως ἐκούρσευσεν, τὸ Κόνιον καὶ Ἀμόρι.   G4.41
Κοράσιον ἀπήρπαξεν, τοῦ Ἀκρίτη τὴν μητέραν,   G4.43
καὶ ἀπὸ τὰ κάλλη τὰ πολλά, τὰ ἐβάσταζεν ἡ κόρη,   G4.44
735 ἐγίνετον Χριστιανὸς καὶ αὐτὴν εὐλογήθη.   G4.46
Καὶ ὁ εἷς τῆς κόρης ἀδελφὸς ἦτον ὁ Κωνσταντίνος,
αὐτὸς γὰρ ἐπολέμησεν ἀμιράν, τὸν γαμπρόν του,
τὸν θαυμαστὸν νεώτερον, τοῦ Ἀκρίτη τὸν πατέρα.
Καὶ τότε | ὁ Ἀκρίτης <Διγενῆς>, ὁ θαυμαστὸς ἐκεῖνος, 161v
740 μόνος του ὑπεθαύμαζεν διὰ τὰς ἀνδραγαθίας του
καὶ ἀπὸ μικρόθεν ἤρξατο τὸν ἑαυτόν του δοξάζει.
Καὶ <τότε> ὡσὰν ἐγένετο δώδεκα ἐτῶν καὶ μόνον,   G4.85
ἦλθεν πρὸς τὸν πατέραν του, τοιαῦτα τὸν συντυχαίνει·
«Ὡς πότε θέλω κυνηγᾶν λαγούδια καὶ περδίκια;
745 Αὐτὰ τῶν χωριατῶν εἰσίν, τοῦ κυνηγᾶν περδίκια,
ἄρχοντες δὲ νεώτεροι καὶ εὐγενῶν παιδία
λέοντας καὶ ἄρκους κυνηγοῦν καὶ ἄλλα δεινὰ θηρία.
Καὶ οὐ θέλω δοξασθῆναι ἐγὼ ὡς ἀπὸ τοῦ πατρός μου,
ἀλλὰ δοξάσειν <θέλω> ἐγὼ πατέραν καὶ μητέραν·
750 νὰ δοξασθῆς, ἀφέντα μου, ἐκ τὲς ἀνδραγαθίες μου.

724 εἰς¹ Alexiou: εἰς τὴν E εἰς² Trapp: εἰς τὴν E
725 ἀνδρείαν Alexiou: τὴν ἀνδρίαν E του² corr.: τὴν E φρόνα Alexiou. note:
φρόνεσιν E
726 γέροντες Trapp: γέροντες ἁπάσης τῆς E
728 τρισχιλίους Kalonaros: τρεῖς χιλίους E
729 πᾶσαν Alexiou: ἅπασαν E
732 Ἡρακλέως Alexiou: ἡράκλεος E
736 τῆς κόρης ἀδελφὸς Trapp: ἀδελφὸς τῆς κόρης E
739 Διγενῆς added by Alexiou
740 ὑπεθαύμαζεν E: ἐθαυμάζετο Trapp
741 ἑαυτόν Hesseling: ἐνιαυτόν E
742 τότε added by Alexiou
743 ἦλθεν corr.: προσῆλθεν E
745 χωριατῶν Hesseling: χωριάτων E
748 οὐ Trapp: ὡς E δοξασθῆναι ἐγὼ ὡς Alexiou: καὶ ἐγὼ δοξασθῆνε, ὁσὰν E
749 θέλω added by Hesseling

who grew up in Syria, in Babylon,
725 and because of his great bravery and his prodigious good sense
the elders of Syria held a council
and spoke of it to the sultan and made him emir.
They gave him three thousand Turks and Arabs
and made him renowned through all Syria.
730 And he also had his own youngsters, another five hundred.
He took them and went off into Roman territory.
He ravaged Herakleion, Ikonion and Amorion.
He abducted a girl, the mother of Akritis the Frontiersman,
and because of the great beauty which the girl showed,
735 he became a Christian and married her.
One of the girl's brothers was Constantine,
and he fought the emir, his brother-in-law,
that marvellous young man, the father of Akritis the Frontiersman.
      And then that marvellous Digenis Akritis,
740 through his own efforts, was admired for his valiant deeds
and from childhood began to win glory for himself.
Then just as he was turning twelve,
he went up to his father and this is what he said to him:
      "How long shall I be hunting hares and partridges?
745 Hunting partridges is what peasants do,
but young lords and the sons of the high-born
hunt lions and bears and other fierce beasts.
I don't want to be famous because of my father
but I want to bring fame to my father and mother,
750 and I want you to be famous, my lord father, because of my valiant
      deeds.

732 This series of towns corresponds to the raids mentioned at G1.292–5 and repeated
at G4.41–3, details not previously given in E.

Δεῦτε ἂς καβαλικεύσωμεν καὶ ὑπᾶμεν 'ς τὸ κυνήγιν.»
Καὶ αὐτὸς ἐκαβαλίκευσεν ὁ Διγενὴς Ἀκρίτης
καὶ ὁ πατήρ του ὁ ἀμιρὰς καὶ ὁ θεῖός του ὁ Κωνσταντίνος,   G4.103
καὶ ἐβάσταζαν γεράκια ἄσπρα ἐκ τοὺς μουτάτους.
755 Ἀλλὰ ὄνταν ἀπεσώσασιν εἰς τὰ ὄρη τὰ μεγάλα,
δύο ἀρκούδια ἐπήδησαν ἀπόσω ἀπὸ τὸ δάσος,
ἀρσενικὸν καὶ θηλυκόν, εἶχαν καὶ δύο κουλούκια.   G4.108
Καὶ εὐθὺς τὸ ἰδεῖν τα ὁ Διγενής, τὸν θεῖον του οὕτως λέγει:
«Τί 'ναι ἐκεῖνα, ὁ θεῖός μου, ὁποὺ ἀlπηδοῦν καὶ φεύγουν;»   162r
760   Καὶ ὁ θεῖός του λέγει:
«Αὐτὰ εἶναι, <ὦ> Διγενή, τὰ λέγουσιν ἀρκούδια
καὶ ὁποὺ εὑρεθῇ νὰ πιάσῃ τα, ἔναι πολλὰ ἀνδρειωμένος.»
Καὶ ὁ Διγενὴς ὡς τὸ ἤκουσεν, <πεζὸς> μὲ τὸ καλίκιν
                        εἰς αὐτα κατεβαίνει
765 καὶ τὸ ραβδίν του ἐσήκωσεν καὶ ἐπρόλαβεν τὰ <ἀρκούδια>.

Τὸ θηλυκὸν εἰς πόλεμον διὰ τὰ κουλούκια ἐστάθην,   G4.122
καὶ ἐκεῖνος ἦτο ἐγλήγορος καὶ ἀπάνω του ἐκατέβην·
καὶ οὐκ ἐσυνέφθασεν γοργόν, ἵνα ραβδέα τοῦ δώσῃ,   G4.125
ἀλλὰ ὡσὰν τοῦ ἐσίμωσεν, κλειδώνει το εἰς τὰς χεῖρας
770 καὶ ἔσφιξεν τοὺς βραχίονάς του καὶ εὐθὺς ἀπέπνιξέν το.   G4.127
Καὶ ὡς εἶδεν τὸ ἑταίριν του, ἐστράφην ἐξοπίσω
καὶ μίλιν τοῦ <ἀπεξέβηκεν> | φευγόμενον ἐξ αὐτον.   162v
Καὶ ὁ <θαυμαστὸς> νεώτερος εἶχεν γοργὸν τὸ στρέμμαν,
ἦτον καὶ <γὰρ> ὑπόστεγνος καὶ ἐγνώθουντα οἱ νεφροί του,
775 καὶ εἰς τέσσαρα πηδήματα τὸν ἄρκον καταφθάνει
καὶ ἀπὸ τὸ κατωμάγουλον γοργὸν πιάνει, κρατεῖ τον   G4.135
καὶ εἰς δύο μέρη τὸν ἔσχισεν, στέκει καὶ θεωρεῖ τον.

751 ὑπᾶμεν Alexiou: ἂς ὑπάγομεν E   'ς Trapp: εἰς E
752 αὐτὸς E: εὐθὺς Alexiou
754 ἐβάσταζαν Alexiou, cf. Z1384: ἐβάσταζεν E
761 ὦ added
762 ὁποὺ Alexiou, 1988, 194: ὁπίος E   πιάσῃ τα corr., cf. Alexiou, note: τὰ σκοτόσει διγενῆ E
763 πεζὸς μὲ τὸ καλίκιν Ricks, cf. E1323: με τα καλίτζηά του E
765 ἐπρόλαβεν Alexiou: ἐμπρόλαβεν E   ἀρκούδια added by Alexiou, cf. G4.121
766 διὰ τὰ κουλούκια ἐστάθην Alexiou: ἐστάθην ὡς δια τὰ κουλούκια E
767 ἐκεῖνος ἦτο ἐγλήγορος Alexiou: ἐκήνον εἶτον ἐγλύγορον E
769 χεῖρας Trapp: χείρας του E
772 ἀπεξέβηκεν Xanthoudidis, 1912, 557, cf. E1316, 1411: ἀ . . . . . E (page trimmed)
φευγόμενον Kalonaros: φευγόμενος E
773 θαυμαστὸς added, cf. E43, 738: Διγενὴς ὁ Alexiou
774 γὰρ added by Alexiou
776 κατωμάγουλον Kalonaros: κατὰ μάγουλον E

Come, let us mount and go off hunting."
    So Digenis Akritis, the Frontiersman of Double Descent, mounted,
    as did his father the emir and his uncle Constantine;
    they were carrying white hawks that had moulted.
755 But when they reached the high mountains,
    two bears rushed out of the wood,
    a male and a female, and they had two cubs.
    As soon as Digenis saw them, he addressed his uncle thus:
    "What are these, my uncle, which rush out and run away?"
760   His uncle said to him:
    "These, Digenis, are what are called bears
    and anyone who is able to catch them is very brave."
    When Digenis, on foot and in his boots, heard this
                                                he went after them
765 and raised his stick and overtook the bears.

    The female stood her ground and did battle for her cubs,
    but he was quick and went for her
    yet did not close up quickly to strike her with his stick,
    but as he got near, he locked her in his arms
770 and tightened his grasp and promptly throttled her.
    When her mate saw this, he turned round
    and ran a mile away in flight from Digenis.
    But the marvellous young man could spin round swiftly,
    for he had little fat on him and his ribs stood out,
775 and with four bounds he caught up with the bear.
    He seized it quickly by the lower jaw, held it
    and tore it in two; he stood and gazed at it.

---

763 Digenis fights the bears with minimal weapons and finally his bare hands (cf.
G4.111, where he is motivated by instructions from his uncle).

Ὁ θεῖος του καὶ ὁ πατὴρ οἱ δύο ὁμάδι ὑπᾶσιν,
στέκονται καὶ θαυμάζονται τὰς τάξεις τοῦ νεωτέρου·
780 ὦμον πρὸς ὦμον ἔθηκαν καὶ πρὸς ἀλλήλους λέγουν: G4.156
«Κυρά μου, μήτηρ τοῦ Θεοῦ, καὶ Θεὲ πανοικτίρμων,   G4.157
πράγματα βλέπομεν φρικτὰ 'ς τὸν νεώτερον ἐτοῦτον·   G4.157
τοῦτον ὁ Θεὸς τὸν ἔστειλεν ὡς διὰ τοὺς ἀνδρειωμένους   G4.159
καὶ οἱ ἀπελάτες νὰ τρέμουσιν τὰ ἔτη τῆς ζωῆς τους.»
785   Καὶ <οὕτως> συντυχαίνοντα ὁ θεῖος του καὶ ὁ πατήρ του,   G4.161
λέοντα δεινὸν εἴδασιν ἀπέσω εἰς τὸ καλάμιν·   G4.162
βούβαλον ἐπεκάθετο ἀπὸ τὰ ὠτία ὡς τὸ οὐράδιν
καὶ ἐβύζανεν τὸ αἷμαν του, στανέου του τὸν ἐκράτει·
καὶ ὡς τὸ εἶδεν ὁ κύρης του καὶ ὁ θεῖος του ὁ Κωνσταντίνος,
790 τὸν λέοντα τοῦ ἐδείξασιν διὰ νὰ τὸν δοκιμάσουν·
γυρίζουν καὶ θεωροῦσιν τον ὅτι ἔβγαινε ἀπ᾽ τὸ δάσος.
. . .
«<ὡς διὰ νὰ τὸ ἔχω συνο>δείαν 'ς τὴν στράταν ὁποὺ ὑπάγω· |
ὅτι καὶ μοναχὸς εἶμαι καὶ μόνος θέλω ὁδεύειν.»   163r
Σ τὰ γονικά του ἀπέσωσεν ἀφρόντιστος καὶ σῶος,
795 ἐπῆγεν καὶ ἐπέζευσεν
καὶ ἀνέσια ἐσύντυχεν τὸν πρωτοστράτορά του: G4.375
«Στράτορα, πρωτοστράτορα καὶ πρῶτε τῶν στρατόρων,
ἀπόστρωσε τὸν γρίβαν μου καὶ στρῶσε μου τὸν μαῦρον,   G4.376
τὸν εἶχεν πάντα ὁ θεῖος μου εἰς τὰς ἀνδραγαθίας του.

778 πατὴρ Trapp: πατήρ του E   ὁμάδι Alexiou: ὁμάδιν E
779 τάξεις E: πράξεις Alexiou
782 'ς Trapp: εἰς E
784 νὰ Alexiou, note: να τὸν E
785 οὕτως added by Alexiou   συντυχαίνοντα Kalonaros: συντυχένουν τα E
787 βούβαλον Hesseling: βούβολον E   ὠτία ὡς Kyriakidis, 1946, 426: ὁτία του ἕως E
788 αἷμαν Kyriakidis, 1946, 427: γάλαν E
789 του¹ Xanthoudidis, 1912, 557: τῆς E
790 τὸν λέοντα Kalonaros: καὶ τὸν λέοντα E   διὰ Trapp: ὡς δια E   δοκιμάσουν Trapp: ἀποδοκιμάσουν E
791 γυρίζουν Alexiou: καὶ γυρίζουν E   θεωροῦσιν Alexiou: θεοροῦν E   ἔβγαινε ἀπ᾽ Alexiou: εὔγενεν ἀπὸ E
792 ὡς διὰ νὰ τὸ ἔχω added by Alexiou   συνοδείαν Kyriakidis, 1926, 81: δίαν E   'ς Alexiou: εἰς E   ὑπάγω corr.: εἰπιέννω E
794 'Σ Trapp: εἰς E
795 ἐπέζευσεν Trapp: ἐπέζευσεν κάτω E
796 πρωτοστράτορά Politis, 1973, 346: προτοστάτορά E
798 γρίβαν Alexiou, note: μαῦρον E   μαῦρον Alexiou, cf. E844, G4.376: γρίβαν E

His uncle and his father both came up together
and stood amazed at the young man's performance.
780 They put shoulder to shoulder and said to each other:
"My lady, Mother of God, and all merciful God,
we behold terrifying achievements in this young man.
God has sent him for men of bravery
and the guerrillas will be terrified all the years of their lives."
785   And while his uncle and his father talked in this way,
they saw an awesome lion inside the reed-bed;
it was crouched over a buffalo from its ears to its tail
and was sucking its blood, holding it down against its will.
When his lord father and his uncle Constantine saw it,
790 they showed him the lion, to test him.
They turned and watched it as it came out of the wood.
. . .
"so that I can have it as an escort on the journey which I am making,
because I am on my own and wish to travel alone."
He reached his parents' estates without difficulties and in safety,
795 he went and dismounted
and quietly addressed his protostrator:
"Groom, chief groom and chief of grooms,
unsaddle my grey horse and saddle for me the black
which my uncle always used in his valiant deeds.

780 The deer episode of G4.140–54 is not represented in E, though E has a lacuna
shortly in which something of this may have appeared.
791 After 791 there is a lacuna, but the original error occurred in E's exemplar and not
in E itself since the text resumes in mid-word in 792, the last line of f. 162v; that is, the
loss of text is not due to damage in E. Passages are missing equivalent to G4.163–253
(the end of the hunt and Digenis' triumphal return home; at this point the Z text
incorporates E622–70, Digenis' first meeting with the guerrillas) and G4.254–373
(Digenis' encounter with the girl on the route home and his songs to her); E resumes at
the end of the last song. It is impossible to estimate how many lines have been lost.
792 We must assume that the song Digenis is singing ends with an appeal to the moon
(cf. G4.372) to escort him in the abduction.
793 See Laiou, 1993, 201–11, especially 205–6, for arguments that in pursuing what
was technically a consensual elopement rather than an abduction Digenis was acting
within ecclesiastical norms. The elopement was capable of leading to marriage, whereas
the seduction was subject to severe penalties.
797 On the triple patterning of this line (reminiscent of the phrases used of the emir at
E59, 129), see Fenik, 1991, 89, 125; the whole passage is patterned with balanced
repetitions many of which are also visible in G4.376–8. This speech would seem to have
been a memorable moment in the Digenis story. The protostrator's function as controller
of horses seems to outweigh any of the ceremonial functions this title carried with it in
late Byzantine society (cf. Introduction, pp. xxxviii–xxxix).
799 The uncle's black horse has appeared at E42.

800 Τρεῖς ἴγκλες μοῦ τὸν ἴγκλωσε καὶ τρεῖς ὀμπροστελίνες   G4.377
καὶ τὸν βαρὺν χαλίναρον διὰ νὰ γοργογυρίζη,   G4.379
καὶ κρέμασε εἰς τὴν σέλαν μου καὶ τὸ βαρὺν σπαθί μου,   G4.378
ὅτι εἰς ἀνάγκην φοβερὰν καὶ εἰς ἁρπαγὴν ὑπάγω.»
Τὸν λόγον οὐκ ἐπλήρωσεν οὐδὲ τὴν συντυχίαν,
805 καὶ εὐθὺς ἐκατεπήδησεν, 's τὴν σκάλαν ἀναβαίνει.
Καὶ ἐξέβην ἡ μητέρα του, κρατεῖ, καταφιλεῖ τον·
«Καλῶς ἦρθες, τὸ τέκνον μου, ἂν μοῦ ἦφερες κυνήγιν.»
Καὶ τότε πάλε ὁ Διγενὴς οὕτως ἀπιλογᾶται·
«Τὰ <θαυμαστὰ> κυνήγια μου νὰ ἔλθουν καὶ νὰ τὰ ἴδης.»
810 Καὶ τότε ἡ μητέρα του ἤρξατο εὔχεσθαίν του·
«Δέσποινά μου πανύμνητε, κυρὰ εὐλογημένη,
δοξάζω, μεγαλύνω σε καὶ υἱὸν τὸν Θεόν σου,
ὅτι ἔδωκές με νεώτερον τὸν ὁ κόσμος οὐκ ἔχει
καὶ χάρισέ μου τον νὰ ζῆ εἰς χρόνους ἀμετρήτους,
815 νὰ τὸν θωρῶ, νὰ χαίρωμαι τὰ ἔτη τῆς ζωῆς μου.» |
Καὶ εὐθὺς κρατεῖ, καταφιλεῖ τὰ ὀμμάτια τοῦ νεωτέρου   163v
καὶ ἐσήκωσεν τὰς χεῖρας της 's τὸν οὐρανὸν ἀπάνω·
«Δέσποινά μου πανύμνητε, κυρία μου εὐλογημένη,
τὸν νεώτερον τὸν μὲ ἔδωκες τὸν θαυμαστὸν Ἀκρίτην,
820 δός τον μακροημέρευσιν τὰ ἔτη τῆς ζωῆς του,
νὰ περπατῆ ἀφρόντιστος, νὰ χαίρεται τὸν κόσμον,
τὸν βίον του ἀδιάλειπτον τὰ ἔτη τῆς ζωῆς του,
νὰ τὸν φοβοῦνται πάντοτε ἔθνη τῆς οἰκουμένης.»
Καὶ τότε ὁ νεώτερος γοργὸν ἐξυπολύθη,
825 τὰ καλίτσια του ἔβγαλεν καὶ ἐκάτσεν εἰς τὸ δεῖπνον.
Καὶ ἀφότου ἀποδείπνησεν, ἐμπαίνει εἰς τὸ κουβούκλιν   G4.396
καὶ ἐπῆρεν τὸ θαμπούριν του καὶ ἀποκατάστησέν το.

801 τὸν Kalonaros: τὸ E
802 κρέμασε Alexiou: κρέμησε καὶ E
805 's Trapp: εἰς E ἀναβαίνει Alexiou: ἀνηβένη E
808 πάλε Politis, 1973, 342: πάλεν E
809 θαυμαστὰ added ἴδης Hesseling: ἰδῆς E
817 's Trapp: εἰς E
820 'τον Trapp: τον ζωὴν καὶ E
823 νὰ Trapp: καὶ να E

800 Gird on for me three saddle girths and three martingales
and the heavy bit so that he can turn quickly,
and hang my heavy sword by my saddle
because I am setting out on a fearsome adventure and on an
    abduction."
He completed neither his speech nor the conversation,
805 but immediately dismounted and climbed the stairs.
His mother came out, she embraced him, she kissed him:
"Welcome, my child, if you have brought me game from hunting."
And then Digenis replied to her thus in turn:
"My marvellous game will come and you will see it."
810   And then his mother began to pray for him:
"My Mistress ever-hymned, blessed Lady,
I glorify, I magnify you and God, your son,
because you have given me a young man like no other in the world,
and grant me that he live for years without number,
815 so that I can see him and rejoice all the years of my life."
And immediately she embraced him, she kissed the young man's
    eyes
and raised her hands to heaven above:
"My Mistress ever-hymned, my blessed Lady,
the young man you have given me, Akritis, the marvellous
    Frontiersman,
820 give him length of days for all the years of his life
so that he may journey without care, may rejoice in this world,
in unbroken existence for all the years of his life,
so that the peoples of the world may fear him always."
And then the young man quickly untied his shoes,
825 he took off his boots and sat down to dinner.
When he had finished his meal, he entered his chamber
and picked up his tamboura and tuned it.

803 Abductions (of young women, that is, potential brides) seem to be the highest form
of hunting known to this society (Ricks, 1989b); cf. the guerrillas' comments at E668.
But compare this with Laiou's emphasis on a consensual elopement (see note on E793).
810–15 Religious overtones, very conspicuous in G, are not absent from E. To judge
from fluency of expression and accuracy of orthography here and at E1805 ff., the scribe
of E seems more comfortable with such passages than with secular material.
823 A forward hint to Digenis' universal role that is implied at his death (cf. E1701–4).
825 Perhaps an indication of Arab etiquette (see Alexiou, 1985, note), though also a
universal act of good house-keeping in a hot and dusty environment.
827 θαμπούριν (E) and κιθάρα (G4.390) seem to refer to the same instrument, the
ancestor of the modern baglama (Anoyianakis, 1962 on a tenth- to eleventh-century
example from Corinth, and also Anoyianakis, 1972, 175).

Ὄφιων δερμάτια ἔσχισεν καὶ ἐποίησεν του τὰς κόρδας,
<ἐποίησε> καὶ τὰ δόντια των πανέμνοστα τριπάρια.
830 Γοργὸν γὰρ ὑποδέθηκεν, 'ς τὸν στάβλον κατεβαίνει,
πηδᾶ καὶ ἐκαβαλίκευσεν καὶ ἐπῆρεν τὸ σπαθίν του
καὶ ἐπῆρεν τὸ θαμπούριν του καὶ ἀποκατάστησέν το
καὶ ἔκρουεν τὸ λαβοῦτον του καὶ ἀηδόνει καὶ ἐτραγούδει,
ἀηδονικὰ ἐτραγούδησεν καὶ χαμηλὰ τὸ κρούει
835 καὶ ἐκίνησεν τὴν στράταν του καὶ ὑπάγει εἰς τὸ κοράσιον.
Καὶ ὅταν γὰρ ἀπέσωσεν 'ς τοῦ στρατηγοῦ τοὺς οἴκους,
σφικτὰ τὰς κόρδας ἔδησεν καὶ ἐλάλησεν μεγάλως 164r
καὶ ἐκεῖνος χαμηλότερα καὶ ἐβγαίνει τῆς φωνῆς του·
«Εἴτις ἐφίλησεν μακράν, γοργὸν οὐκ ὑπαγαίνει,   G4.401-2
840 τὰς νύκτας οὐ περιπατεῖ, τὸν ὕπνον οὐ στερεῖται,   G4.401-2
οὐ θέλει τὸν Παράδεισον μὲ τὰ μυρίσματά του·
ἐγὼ μακρὰ ἐφίλησα, ἀλλὰ γοργὸν ὑπάγω   G4.403
καὶ ἐγὼ ὡς διὰ τὴν πανεύνοστην ὕπνον οὐδὲν κοιμοῦμαι.»
Ἦτον λαμπρὸς ὁ μαῦρος του, καὶ ἔφεγγεν τὸ φεγγάρι,   G4.407
845 καὶ ὡς δι' αὐτον ἀπεσώθηκεν 'ς τοῦ στρατηγοῦ τοὺς οἴκους.
Καὶ ὅταν ἀπέσωσεν ἐκεῖ, τὴν κόρην οὕτως λέγει·
«Σύ, κόρη, ἀπεμερίμνησες καὶ ἀμέριμνα κοιμᾶσαι
καὶ ἐβγαίνεις ἐκ τὸν ὅρκον σου, πανθαύμαστον κοράσιον.
Πιστεύω, ἀπολησμόνησες τὰ χθεσινά σου λόγια,
850 καλή, τὰ ἐσυντυχαίναμεν οἱ δύο μοναχοί μας,
καὶ ὅρκους τοὺς ἐμόσαμεν, νὰ μὴ ἀποχωριστοῦμεν.»
Καὶ ἐκείνη τὸν ἐγνώρισεν ἀπὸ τοῦ τραγουδίου·
ἐφύρθη καὶ ἐσηκώθηκεν καὶ ἐπῆρε τὸ λουρίν της,
γοργὸν ἐκατεπήδησεν καὶ ἐβγαίνει εἰς παραθύριν.

855 **Κ**αὶ τότε τὸ κοράσιον τὸν νέον κατονειδίζει· 164v

829 ἐποίησε added by Kyriakidis, 1926, 22
830 γὰρ ὑποδέθηκεν corr.: γὰρ ἐποδέθηκεν E καθυποδέθηκεν Alexiou   'ς Trapp: εἰς E
836 'ς Trapp: εἰς E
842 μακρὰ E: μακρὰν Alexiou, cf. E839
843 πανεύνοστην Alexiou: πανεύγνωστην E
844 τὸ corr., cf. Kyriakidis, 1926, 79: ὡς τὸ E
845 αὐτον Alexiou: αὐτὸν E   'ς Trapp: εἰς E
847 Σύ Alexiou: ἐσύ E   ἀμέριμνα Kalonaros: ἀμέρεμνα E
848 καὶ Kyriakidis, 1926, 23: καὶ βέβεον E
851 ἀποχωριστοῦμεν Kalonaros: ἀπεχωριστοῦμεν E
854 εἰς Trapp: εἰς τὸ E
855 νέον Trapp: νεότερον E

He slit snakes' skins and made the instrument's strings,
and used their teeth as delightful pegs.
830 He quickly put on his shoes again, he went down to the stable,
he sprang into the saddle and took his sword;
he took his tamboura and tuned it
and plucked his lute and lifted up his voice and sang,
sweetly he sang and softly he played it
835 as he set out on his journey and went off to the girl.
    And when he reached the general's house,
he tightened the strings firmly and the lute sounded loudly
while he sang out yet more softly:
"Any one who has his love at a distance and cannot make swift
    journeys to her,
840 does not travel by night, does not lose his sleep
and does not long for Paradise with its sweet odours.
I have my love at a distance but I make a swift journey
and I cannot sleep at all because of the most beautiful girl."
    His black horse gleamed, the moon shone bright,
845 and thus he reached the general's house.
    When he got there he addressed the girl thus:
"You, girl, have forgotten your worries and sleep without a care,
you have broken your oath, marvellous girl.
You have forgotten, I believe, your words of yesterday,
850 my beloved, which the two of us exchanged on our own,
and the oaths that we swore not to be parted."
    And she recognised him from the song;
she was dismayed, got up and took her belt,
she jumped down quickly and came to the window.

855 And then the girl reproached the young man:

828–9 A difficult passage, not present in G. Kyriakidis, 1926, 71 cites a folk song
parallel for Digenis' lyre with strings of snake skin. Building on ὄϊων of Z1805, itself a
reaction to this line of E, Alexiou adds προβάτων ἔκλωσε ἔντερα, 'he twisted sheep guts',
arguing that snake skin was used to cover the sound box, sheep guts for the strings and
sheep teeth for tuning pegs, where snakes' fangs are certainly a bizarre concept. Alexiou's
suggestion, however, seems to assume that Z is using a manuscript from the E tradition,
rather than E itself.
839 While it is tempting to emend μακράν to ἐγγύς, 'near' (cf. G4.401), the text as it
stands contrasts a lackadaisical lover at a distance with the special urgency of Digenis'
love that defeats distance.
845 Further narrative reduplication (cf. E836).

«Ἐγώ, κύρκα, ὀνειδίζω σε, διατὶ ἐπαραβραδιάστης G4.439
καὶ ὡς ὀκνηρὸν καὶ ράθυμον πάντα νὰ σὲ ὀνειδίζω. G4.440
Καὶ τὸ λαβοῦτο σου, τὸ κρούεις, ἔβλεπε ποῦ τὸ κρούεις. G4.441
Δὲν ἠξεύρεις, ὀμμάτια μου, τὸ φῶς τῶν ὀφθαλμῶν μου,
860 ὅτι ἂν γροικήση ὁ κύρης μου καὶ ὅλη μου ἡ γενέα, G4.442
νὰ στερηθῆς τὴν νεότην σου τὴν ὡραίαν ὡς διὰ ἐμέναν·
Ὅτι πολλοὶ ἐδοκίμασαν ἀγνώστως νὰ μὲ πάρουν
καὶ ἐγροίκησέν το ὁ κύρης μου καὶ ἐκακοδίκησέν τους; G4.442
Οὕτως καὶ ἐσὺ τὴν νεότη σου ἔβλεπε τὴν ὡραίαν.
865 Καὶ ἐγὼ ἠξεύρω, ὀμμάτια μου, τὸ φῶς τῶν ὀμματίων μου,
ὅτι πόθος σὲ ἐπόνεσεν, ἡ ἀγάπη ἐφλόγισέν σε, G4.450
τὸν νοῦν σου ἐπαρεσάλευσεν, τὸν λογισμόν σου ἐπῆρεν G4.451
καὶ εἰς θάνατον σὲ ἔριψεν ὡς δι᾽ ἐμὲ ν᾽ ἀποθάνης· G4.451
καὶ θεωρῶ σε μοναχὸν καὶ οὐκ ἔχω τί ποιήσει.
870 Αὐθέντα μου, ἂν κατεβῶ καὶ ἐπάρης με μεδ᾽ ἔσου
καὶ φθάσουν σε τ᾽ ἀδέλφια μου καὶ τὸ συγγενικόν μου, G4.453
ἐσέναν νὰ σκοτώσουσιν καὶ ἐμένα νὰ διαγείρουν
νὰ στερηθῆς τὴν νεότην σου τὴν ὡραίαν ὡς δι᾽ ἐμέναν.»
Καὶ τότε ὁ νεώτερος οὕτως ἀπιλογᾶται·
875 «Καλὰ λέγεις, κοράσιον; Οὕτως μοῦ συντυχαίνεις;
Ἐγὼ μόνος μου μοναχὸς φουλσάτα πολεμίζω 165r
καὶ ὅλα νὰ νικήσω G4.465
καὶ κάστρα νὰ ἀντιμαχιστῶ, θηρία νὰ φονεύσω,
καὶ ἐσὺ ἀδελφούς σου μοῦ λαλεῖς, πατέραν καὶ γενέαν;
880 Κουροῦνες πόσες ἠμποροῦν ἀετοῦ βρῶμα νὰ πάρουν;
Καλή μου, ἂν ἐμετάγνωσες καὶ ἔχεις ἀλλοῦ τὸν πόθον, G4.475
εἰπέ μου τὴν ἀλήθειαν, κυρά, νὰ ὑπαγαίνω.
Εἰδὲ ἂν θέλης ὁλόψυχα, καλή, ὅτι νὰ φιλοῦμε,
ὡς ὅτι ἕν᾽ τὸ κατάψυχον, μικρὸν μὴ ἀναπαγοῦμεν,

856 ὀνειδίζω Alexiou: κατνίζο E
857 ὀκνηρὸν Kyriakidis, 1926, 24: κνιρὸν E
859 ὀμμάτια Alexiou: μάτιά E
860 ὅτι ἂν Alexiou: ὅτι ἄνσε E
863 το Trapp: τους E
864 τὴν νεότη σου ἔβλεπε Alexiou: ὁμάτιά μου ἔβλεπε τὴν νεότη σου E
866 ἐπόνεσεν corr.: ἐκατεπόνεσεν E
868 ἐμὲ Kyriakidis, 1926, 24: ἐμοῦ E
870 κατεβῶ Trapp, cf. Z1863: παρακατεβῶ E
873 νὰ Kyriakidis, 1926, 24: καὶ να E
876 μου E: καὶ Alexiou, cf. E1523
877 ὅλα νὰ E: μοναχός μου δύναμαι ὅλα νὰ τὰ Alexiou
884 ἕν᾽ Alexiou: ἕνε E μὴ Alexiou: ἀς E

"It is I who am reproaching you, sweetheart, for having delayed so
    long;
and I shall always reproach you for being hesitant and lethargic.
And as for the lute you are playing, watch where you are playing it.
Don't you know, my eyes, light of my eyes,
860 that if my lord father and all my family become aware of you,
you will be deprived of your lovely youthfulness because of me?
Don't you know that many have tried to seize me by stealth
and my lord father became aware of them and did dreadful things
    to them?
And so you should watch out for your lovely youthfulness.
865 And I know, my eyes, light of my eyes,
that desire has tormented you, love has enflamed you,
it has unhinged your mind, taken away your reason
and hurled you towards death, to die because of me,
and I see that you are on your own and there is nothing I can do.
870 My lord, if I come down and you take me with you
and my brothers and my kinsmen catch up with you,
they will slaughter you and take me back,
and you will be deprived of your lovely youthfulness because of me."
    And then the young man replied thus:
875 "Are you right, girl? Do you talk to me like this?
I alone, on my own, I fight armies,
                                I shall defeat them all
and do battle against fortresses, slay wild beasts
yet you speak to me of your brothers, your father and your family?
880 How many crows are needed to seize an eagle's prey?
My beloved, if you have changed your mind and your desire is for
    another,
tell me the truth, my lady, and I will leave.
But if you want us with all your soul, my beloved, to love each other,
so long as it is cool let us not rest for even a little,

862–3 The vigour with which the girl's suitors have been repulsed by her father is
described in G at 4.292–9, a passage that falls in the lacuna following E791.
873 = 861 This line should be retained, although deleted by Trapp, as the punch-line to
a speech composed of duplicated elements.

885 μὴ καρτερεύσωμεν ἐδῶ καὶ καύση μας τὸ κάμα
καὶ στέκη καὶ φλογίζη μας ἡ καῦσις τοῦ ἡλίου
καὶ καύση καὶ μαράνη μας τούτην τὴν στράταν ὅλην.
Καὶ ἔλα γοργόν, κοράσιον, μὴ μᾶς νοήση ὁ κόσμος.
Καὶ μὴ δοκῇς, βεργόλικε, ἡ πάντερπνος ἡ κόρη,
890 ὡς διὰ φόβον τοῦ λαοῦ λέγω σου νὰ ὑπᾶμεν –
μὰ τὸν ἅγιον μου Θεόδωρον, τὸν μέγαν ἀπελάτην –   G4.477
ὅτι μηδὲ μᾶς νοήσουσιν καὶ ἀποκλείσουν μας ὧδε·
ἀμὴ εἰς τὸν κάμπο, λέγω σοι, ὅσοι θέλουν ἂς ἔρθουν,
καὶ νὰ ἴδης κύρκαν τὸν φιλεῖς καὶ πλέον νὰ μὲ ἀγαπήσης
895 καὶ τότε νὰ ἴδης ἄγουρον τὸν ὁ κόσμος οὐκ ἔχει.»
Καὶ τότε τὸ κοράσιον τὸν νεώτερον ἐλάλει:
«Ἐδὰ διὰ σέν, αὐθέντη μου, ἀρνοῦμαι τοὺς γονεῖς μου   G4.512
καὶ τὰ καλά μου ἀδέλφια | καὶ τὸν πολύν μου πλοῦτον 165v G4.513
καὶ ἐσέναν ἐξακολουθῶ διὰ τὸν πολύν σου πόθον
900 καὶ εὕρη σε ὁ Θεός, αὐθέντη μου, ἂν μὲ παραπονέσης.»   G4.515–6
Καὶ ἐδάκρυσεν ὁ νεώτερος καὶ μὲ ὅρκον τὴν ὁμνέει:
«Κύριε Θεὲ φιλάνθρωπε, ὁ κτίσας τοὺς αἰῶνας,   G8.153
ἐὰν ἐγὼ ἐνθυμηθῶ νὰ σὲ παραπονέσω,
θηρία νὰ μὲ διαμοιραστοῦν
905 καὶ οὐ μὴ χαρῶ τὴν νεότην μου, τὴν περισσήν μου ἀνδρείαν
καὶ οὐ μὴ ταφῶ ὡς Χριστιανὸς καὶ οὐ μὴ κατευοδοῦμαι,   G4.560
νὰ μηδὲ τῆς μητέρας μου εὐχὴν κληρονομήσω   G4.561
καὶ οὐ μὴ χαρῶ τὴν περισσὴν ἀγάπην ἐδική σου,
ἐὰν ποτὲ ἐνθυμηθῶ νὰ σὲ παραπονέσω·
910 ἀμὲ καὶ ἐσύ, μαυρόμματε, βλέπε τὸ ἀσκάνδαλόν σου.
Καὶ ἐγείρου, κοράσιον μου, ἔλα ἂς περιπατοῦμεν.»
Καὶ εὐθὺς ἐκατεπήδησεν τὴν χαμηλὴν θυρίδαν,   G4.585
εἰς αὐτὸν δὲ ἐπήδησεν καὶ ἐκρέμασεν εἰς αὐτον.
Ἐκεῖνος τὴν ἐδέξατο ὀμπρὸς 'ς τὸ μπροστοκούρβιν,   G4.586

886 φλογίζη μας Xanthoudidis, 1912, 559: φλογίζομε E
893 κάμπο Hesseling: κάμπτω E
894 καὶ¹ Alexiou: καὶ τότε E
895 ἴδης Spadaro, 1988, 232: ἵδῆς E
899 διὰ Trapp: ὡς δια E
909 ἐὰν Kyriakidis, 1926, 26: ἐὰν ἐγὼ E
910 μαυρόμματε Xanthoudidis, 1912, 559, cf. G4.541: βλερώματα E ὀμμάτια μου
Karayanni, 1976, 107 ἱλαρόμματε Alexiou βλέπε Kalonaros: βλέπο E ἀσκάνδαλόν
Alexiou: ἀσκανδάλιστόν E
911 κοράσιον Trapp: κοράσιόν E ἂς Alexiou: νὰ E
914 'ς Trapp: εἰς E μπροστοκούρβιν Kyriakidis, 1926, 26, cf. E941: μπιστωκούρβην
E

885 let us not linger here for the heat to burn us
and the heat from the sun continue to scorch us
and burn us and shrivel us up over the whole journey.
But come quickly, girl, so that people don't notice us.
And don't think, slender one, my most charming girl,
890 that it is out of fear of the people that I say we should go
– by my saint Theodore, the great guerrilla –
so that they won't notice us and trap us here.
But on the battlefield, I tell you, let all come who want to
and then you will see the sweetheart whom you adore and you will
love me even more,
895 and then you will see a youngster such as the world does not possess."
And then the girl said to the young man:
"From now on, my lord, for your sake I renounce my parents
and my fine brothers and my great wealth
and I follow you out of my great desire for you,
900 and may God find you out, my lord, if you cause me pain."
And the young man wept and swore to her with an oath:
"Benevolent Lord God, creator of the ages,
if I think of causing you pain,
may wild beasts tear me apart
905 and may I not take pleasure in my youthfulness, my prodigious
bravery,
and may I not be buried as a Christian and may I never prosper,
may I never inherit my mother's blessing
and may I never take pleasure in your prodigious love,
if ever I think of causing you pain.
910 But you, dark-eyed one, see that you give no offence.
So rise up, my girl, come, let us be on our way."
And immediately she jumped down from the low window
and jumped on him and clung to him.
He put her up in front of his saddle,

897 The strength of the family unit in the society depicted in G and E is underlined by
the fear with which the younger generation views the breaking of parental ties.

308   Διγενὴς Ἀκρίτης

915 στρεφνά, γλυκιὰ ἐφιλήσασιν ὡς καὶ τὸ δίκαιον εἶχαν   G4.588
καὶ ἐπίασαν τὴν στράταν τους, χαιράμενοι ὑπαγαίνουν.
Καὶ ἐστράφην ὁ νεώτερος, φωνὴν μεγάλην σύρ|νει· 166r
«Εὔχου με, κύρη στρατηγέ, μετὰ τῆς θυγατρός σου.»   G4.594

Καὶ ἐκεῖνος ὡς τὸ ἤκουσεν καὶ τὸν ἠχὸν τοῦ μαύρου,
920 φωνὴν μεγάλην ἔσυρεν· «Ἐχάσα τὸ παιδίν μου.
Ἀγοῦροι ἀπὸ τοῦ Λύκαντος, ἀγοῦροι ἀπὸ τὴν βίγλαν,
βοηθεῖτε εἰς τὸν παγκόπελον, ἐπῆρεν τὸ παιδίν μου.»
Καὶ ὅσα ἄστρα ἔν' 'ς τὸν οὐρανὸν καὶ φύλλα ἔναι εἰς τὰ δένδρα,
καὶ ὅσα πουλίτσια πίνουσιν εἰς τὴν Ἰκέαν τὴν λίμνην,
925 οὕτως ἐκαταπέτουντα οἱ σέλες εἰς τοὺς μαύρους.
Καὶ ὅσοι τὸν ἐγνωρίζασιν ἔστρωναν καὶ ἀποστρῶναν,
καὶ ὅσοι οὐ|δὲν τὸν ἐγνώριζαν πηδοῦν, καβαλικεύουν. 166v
Σουδάλης ὁ Σαρακηνὸς ἀπὸ τὴν πέραν βίγλαν
ὀκτὼ τέντας ἐπήδησεν καὶ δεκαοκτὼ κουρτίνες,
930 φαρία τεσσαράκοντα νὰ κάτση εἰς τὸ ἐδικόν του·
ἐβάστα καὶ εἰς τὴν χέραν του ραβδὶν κασιδολίτσιν·
ὅλον τὸ βλέμμαν καὶ τὸν νοῦν ἔριψεν εἰς Ἀκρίτην
κ' ἐπτέρνισεν τὸν μαῦρον του, ἀπάνου του ὑπαγαίνει.
Καὶ εὐθὺς τὸ ἰδεῖν ὁ Διγενής, τὴν κόρην συντυχαίνει:
935 «Βλέπεις, καλή, Σαρακηνὸν πῶς μᾶς καταδιώκει;
Ἄρτι, κυρά μου, πρόσεξε τὸ τί τὸν θέλω ποίσει.»
Καὶ ἐπέζευσε τὴν λυγερήν, κάτω τὴν ἀποθέτει
καὶ αὐτὸς ἐκαβαλίκευσεν, εἰς αὐτὸν κατεβαίνει
καὶ ἐπῆρεν τὸ κοντάριν του καὶ προσυπήντησέν του
940 καὶ ὀμπρός του τὸν ἐλάλησεν: «Σαρακηνέ, μὲ δέχου.»
Καὶ κονταρέαν τὸν ἔδωκεν ὀμπρὸς 'ς τὸ μπροστοκούρβιν
καὶ εὐθὺς τὸν ἐθανάτωσεν, αὐτὸν καὶ τὸ φαρίν του.

915 γλυκιὰ Hesseling: γλυκία Ε
919 καὶ Alexiou: ἐκ Ε   τὸν ἠχὸν Hesseling: τῶν ηχῶν Ε
922 βοηθεῖτε Alexiou: βοηθήσατε Ε
923 ἔν' 'ς Alexiou: ἐνε εἰς Ε
926 ἐγνωρίζασιν Kalonaros: ἐγνωρίζουσιν Ε
930 τὸ Alexiou: τὸν Ε
933 κ' ἐπτέρνισεν Hesseling: καὶ πτέρνησεν Ε
934 τὸ Politis, 1973, 344: τὸν Ε
935 Σαρακηνὸν Trapp, cf. Z1994: τὸν σαρακηνὸν Ε
937 ἀποθέτει Xanthoudidis, 1912, 559: ἀποθέτην Ε
940 ὀμπρός του corr.: ὀμπρὸς Ε πρῶτον Alexiou, cf. Z1999
941 'ς Trapp: εἰς Ε

915 they embraced tightly, sweetly as was right,
and they set off on their journey, making their way joyfully.
And the young man turned, he let out a great shout:
"Give me your blessing, lord general, together with your daughter."

And when the general heard this and the sound of the horse,
920 he let out a great shout: "I have lost my child!
Youngsters from Lykandos, youngsters from the guard,
come to my help against this misbegotten wretch, he has run off with
    my child!"
As many stars as are in heaven and leaves on trees
and as many birds as drink from lake Ikea,
925 so many were the saddles flung on the black horses.
And all those who knew him saddled up and then took their saddles off,
but all those who did not know of him sprang into the saddle.
    Soudalis the Saracen from the outer guard
jumped over eight tents and eighteen screens
930 and forty horses to land on his own.
In his hand he wielded an iron-tipped stick.
All his gaze and his attention he directed to Akritis the Frontiersman
and he spurred on his horse, he bore down on him.
As soon as Digenis saw this, he said to the girl:
935 "Do you see, beloved, how the Saracen pursues us?
Now, my lady, pay attention to what I shall do to him."
He took the slender girl from the horse, he set her down
and mounted himself; he went for him
and seized his spear and confronted him
940 and said to his face: "Saracen, take this from me."
And he gave him a spear-thrust right in front of the saddle,
and killed him at once, him and his steed.

924 A passage which combines geographical names of apparent antiquity (Lykandos
E922, Ikea E924) and a three-fold pattern reminiscent of folk song (cf. especially the *Song
of Armouris* 77–9, 144–6).
927 There are similar reactions from the guerrillas in the Maximou episode (E1442–3,
etc); the terror inspired by Digenis must be a traditional characteristic of the hero.
928 Another fossilised name; see Name Index.

|

Καὶ εὐθὺς ἐκατεπήδησεν καὶ ἐπῆρεν τὸ κοράσιον. 167r
Γοργὸν ἐκαβαλίκευσαν ἄλλοι τριακόσιοι ἀγοῦροι,
945 οἱ μὲν σουσανιασμένοι ἦσαν, ἄλλοι λουρικιασμένοι,
εἶχεν καὶ καβαλάριους ἀπέσω ἀπὲ τὸ Ἡράκλιν·
φωνιάζουν καὶ ἀνταρεύγονται καὶ ταραχὰς σηκώνουν
καὶ ἐκεῖ τὸν ἐκατέφθασαν εἰς τόπον λιβαδήσον.
Καὶ ἐστράφη ὁ νεώτερος, τὴν κόρην οὕτως λέγει:
950 «Βλέπεις, κοράσιον μου καλόν, τὸ τί λαὸς μᾶς διώκει;»
Ὡς τὸ ἤκουσεν, ἐφάνη της διὰ φόβον τῆς τὸ λέγει
καὶ κλαίουσα τὸν ἔλεγεν ἐκ στεναγμοῦ καρδίας:
«Ἄφις με, ἀφέντη μου καλέ, ἄφις με ἃς ἀποθάνω·
μόνη μου ἔποικα τὸ κακόν, μόνη μου ἃς ἀπολάβω·
955 καὶ ἐσὺ ἔχεις μαῦρον καλὸν καὶ σῶσε τὸν ἑαυτόν σου.»
Καὶ τότε ὁ νεώτερος τοιαῦτα τὴν ἐλάλει:
«Καλὰ λέγεις, κοράσιον μου, γλυκέα μου συνοδεία;
Ἐγὼ εἶπα το νὰ τοὺς ἰδῆς τὸ τί λαὸς μᾶς διώκει,
μὴ μὲ ὀνειδίζῃς αὔριον ὅτι κλεψίαν σ᾽ ἐπῆρα,
960 καὶ νὰ ἰδῆς κύρκαν τὸν φιλεῖς καὶ πλέον νὰ μὲ ἀγαπήσης.»
Καὶ ἐπῆρεν την καὶ ἐκάτσε την ἀπάνω εἰς τὸ λιθάριν·
τὸ ρέτενον ἐγύρισεν καὶ εἰς αὔτους κατεβαίνει
καὶ ἕνα ἐξ αὔτους ἐχώρισεν καὶ ἐδῶκεν του σπαθέαν 167v
καὶ μέσα τὸν ἐχώρισεν αὐτὸν καὶ τὸ φαρίν του
965 καὶ ὡς εἶδαν οἱ ἀπομένοντες ἐστράφησαν ὀπίσω.
Καὶ ὁ νεώτερος ὁμοίαζεν ἄσπρον καλὸν γεράκιν,
ὅταν ζυγώνη πέρδικα καὶ ἔμπη ἀπέσω εἰς δάσος·
οὕτως τοὺς ἐπεσκόρπισεν ὁ νεώτερος ἐκείνους.
Πέντε ἐξ αὐτῶν ἐχώρισαν καὶ ἦσαν οἱ ἀδελφοί της
970 καὶ ἐπιλάλησαν τὰ φαρία καὶ ὑπᾶν εἰς τὸ κοράσιον

---

945 ἄλλοι Alexiou, cf. E432: ἠμὲν (= οἱ μὲν) E
946 καβαλάριους Alexiou: καβαλάρους E
947 φωνιάζουν καὶ ἀνταρεύγονται Alexiou: καὶ ἐφωνίαζαν καὶ ἀνταρεύγοντα E
948 λιβαδήσον Xanthoudidis, 1912, 559: λιβαδίζει E λιβαδίων Hesseling λιβαδίου Karayanni, 1976, 108
951 Ὡς Alexiou: ἐκήνη ὡς E της Alexiou: της ὅτι E
955 ἔχεις μαῦρον καλὸν Trapp: μαῦρον καλὸν ἔχεις [ἔχεις Alexiou] E, Alexiou
959 μὴ Trapp: να μί E
960 καὶ[1] Alexiou: καὶ τότε E πλέον Alexiou: πλέο E ἀγαπήσης Hesseling: ἠγαπήσης E
963 ἕνα Alexiou: ἔναν E
967 ὅταν Trapp: ὀσὰν ὅταν E
970 φαρία Politis, 1973, 344: φαρία των E

And he at once jumped down and seized the girl.
Another three hundred youngsters mounted quickly,
945 some were in mail, others had breastplates,
and there were also cavalry from Herakleion.
They shouted and whooped and raised an uproar,
and they caught up with him there in a grassy spot.
      The young man turned, he spoke thus to the girl:
950 "Do you see, my lovely girl, what a crowd is pursuing us?"
When she heard this, it seemed to her that he told her this out of fear
and, weeping, she said to him with a heart-felt sigh:
"Leave me, my fair lord, leave me to die;
I alone did wrong, and let me alone bear the consequences.
955 You have a fine black horse, save yourself."
      But then the young man said this to her:
"Are you right, my girl, my sweet companion?
I told you to see what a crowd is pursuing us
so that you won't reproach me tomorrow for having stolen you away.
960 and so that you can see the sweetheart whom you love and love me
      even more."
      And he took her and set her down on a rock.
He pulled the reins round and went for them
and separated out one of them and struck him a blow with his sword,
and split him and his horse down the middle;
965 when the survivors saw this, they turned back.
And the young man was like a handsome white hawk
when it chases a partridge and goes into a wood;
just so did the young man scatter them.
      Five of them separated off, and they were her brothers;
970 they urged their steeds on and came up to the girl.

---

969 Once again the family consists of five brothers and a sister. This probably represents
the society's ideal gender mix – and perhaps also a structural element in the development
of the story.

καὶ ὁ νέος 'ς τὸν νοῦν τοὺς ἔβαλεν, μὴ ἁρπάξουσιν τὴν κόρην·
πλησίον τους ἐπήδησεν καὶ ἐπισταπόδησέν τους
καὶ ἐκεῖνοι πάλι ἐστράφησαν καὶ ὑπᾶν εἰς τὸ κοράσιον.
973a <Καὶ τότε πάλι ὁ Διγενὴς> τὸ ἰδεῖν τοὺς νεωτέρους,
γοργὸν ἐπῆρεν τὸ ραβδὶν καὶ προσυπήντησέν τους·
975 ἕναν χωρίζει ἐξ αὐτῶν καὶ ἐδῶκεν του ραβδέαν·
τὸ ἰδεῖν οἱ ἀπομένοντες, ἐκεῖ τὸν προσκυνοῦσιν.
Καὶ ὁ κύρης τους ὁ στρατηγὸς ἀπέσωσεν ἐκεῖσε
κλαίων καὶ ὀδυρόμενος·
τὸ νὰ τὸν ἴδη ὁ Διγενής, ἔδεσε τὰ χέριά του   G4.674
980 καὶ χαμηλὰ ἐπροσκύνα τον, κύρην καὶ πενθερόν του,   G4.674
καὶ μετὰ τὸ προσκύνημαν ἄκο τὰ τί τοῦ λέγει:
«Εὔχου μου, κύρη στρατηγέ, μετὰ τῆς θυγατρός σου   G4.594
καὶ βλέπε μηδὲν λυπηθῆς, | καλὸν γαμπρὸν ἐπῆρες· 168r
τὸν κόσμον καὶ ἂν ἐγύρευες, κάλλιον οὐκ εἶχες εὕρειν.
985 Καὶ ἂν θέλης, κύρη στρατηγέ, δουλείαν νὰ σὲ ποιήσω·
καὶ τότε, <ἀφέντη μου>, νὰ ἰδῆς τὸ τί γαμπρὸν ἐπῆρες.»   G4.681
Καὶ τότε καὶ ὁ στρατηγὸς τοιοῦτον λόγον λέγει:
«Εὐχαριστῶ σε, Θεὲ καλέ, τὴν ἄφραστον προνοίαν
καὶ τὴν φιλανθρωπίαν σου τὴν εἰς ἐμὲν δειχθεῖσαν,
990 ὅτι ἐπῆρα γαμπρὸν καλόν, τὸν ὁ κόσμος οὐκ ἔχει.   G4.690
Στράφου, καλὲ νεώτερε, εἰς τὰ πενθερικά σου,
νὰ ἐπάρης καὶ τὴν προίκαν σου, τριακόσια κιντηνάρια,   G4.705-6
ὅτι καὶ χωρισμένα εἶν' ἀπὸ τοὺς ἀδελφούς της·
πάλιν δὲ διὰ τὰ κάλλη της, τὰ βλέπομεν εἰς αὔτην,
995 δίδω σου τὸ λογάρι μου, τρεῖς λίτρες κιντηνάρια   G4.709
καὶ ἐγκόλφια ὁλόχρυσα, τὰ ἔχει ἐκ τῆς μητρός της,   G4.713
καὶ νὰ σὲ ἰδῆ ἡ στρατήγισσα καὶ νὰ χαρῆ ἡ ψυχή της   G4.730
καὶ νὰ σᾶς εὐλογήσωμεν καὶ τότε νὰ στραφοῦμε.»
Καὶ πάλιν ὁ νεώτερος οὕτως τὸν ἀπεκρίθη:

971 νέος Alexiou: νεότερος Ε   'ς τὸν νοῦν τοὺς corr.: εἰς τὸν νοῦν του τοὺς Ε
973a Καὶ τότε πάλι ὁ Διγενὴς added by Alexiou
977 ἀπέσωσεν ἐκεῖσε Trapp: ἐκεῖ ἀπέσωσεν Ε
979 ἴδη Trapp: ἰδῆ Ε   ὁ Alexiou: καὶ ὁ Ε
983 βλέπε Trapp: βλέπε αὐφέντι Ε
985 δουλείαν νὰ σὲ ποιήσω Alexiou: τοῦ να σε ποιήσω δουλείαν Ε
986 ἀφέντη μου added by Alexiou. from E983
989 δειχθεῖσαν Kalonaros: διχθήσα Ε
998 στραφοῦμε Ε: στραφῆτε Ricks

And the young man watched them carefully so that they should not
   abduct the girl.
He rushed up to them and forced them back
but they turned once again and came up to the girl.
973a Then as Digenis saw the young men once again,
   he quickly took his stick and confronted them.
975 He separated out one of them and struck him a blow with his stick.
On seeing this, the survivors made obeisance to him on the spot.
   And their lord father the general reached there,
weeping and wailing.
On seeing him, Digenis clasped his hands together
980 and made deep obeisance to him as his lord and his father-in-law,
and after the obeisance, listen to what he said to him:
"Give me your blessing, lord general, together with your daughter:
and see that you are not distressed – you have acquired a fine
   son-in-law.
If you were to search the world, you would find no finer.
985 And if you wish, lord general, I shall do you service:
and then, my lord, you will see what sort of son-in-law you have
   acquired."
   And then the general said this:
"I thank you, good God, for your inexpressible providence
and the benevolence which you have shown me,
990 because I have acquired a fine son-in-law such as the world does not
   possess.
Come back, fine young man, to your father-in-law's estates
to receive your dowry, three hundred *centenaria*
which are separated off from her brothers' due:
further, because of the beauty which we see in her,
995 I give you my treasure, three pounds of *centenaria*
and amulets of solid gold which she has from her mother:
and may the general's lady see you and her soul rejoice,
and may we bless you both in marriage and then return."
   But the young man made this reply in his turn:

976 Note the parallels between this fight and that at E964–5: cf. Fenik, 1991, 57–66 on
combat structures in oral-derived poetry.
992 The terms *centenaria* and pounds (*litrai*) seem embedded in descriptions of Digenis'
dowry. E's usage does not have the consistency of G4.706–9: *centenaria* should be used of
numbers of coins, *litrai* of weights (Kriaras, 1969–, under κεντηνάριον: Magdalino,
1993b, 4, note 4). Digenis' refusal of the dowry at E1007, cf. G4.746, has to do with the
power games inherent in a marriage alliance (Angold, 1989, 111–12).

1000 «Ἂν ἕν' καὶ θέλεις, πενθερέ, νὰ ποίσωμεν τοὺς γάμους,
ἐλᾶτε ἐσεῖς 'ς τὸν οἶκον μου μετὰ τῆς πενθερᾶς μου
καὶ νὰ μᾶς εὐλογήσουσιν καὶ πάλιν νὰ στραφοῦμεν
καὶ νὰ ἔλθωμεν 'ς τὸν οἶκον σου,
νὰ μᾶς ἰδῇ ἡ στρατήγισσα καὶ νὰ χαρῇ | ἡ ψυχή της.   168v
1005 Εἰ δὲ καὶ οὐ θέλεις νὰ ἐλθῇς, ἰδοὺ ἐγὼ <ὑπαγαίνω,>
παίρνω τὴν θυγατέρα σου καὶ ὑπάω 'ς τὰ γονικά μου·
τὴν δὲ προίκα ἂς τὴν ἔχουσιν οἱ γυναικαδελφοί μου·   G4.746
καὶ μόνην κόρην ἔλαβα καὶ τίποτε οὐ χρήζω.»
Καὶ τότε ὁ νεώτερος πηδᾷ, καβαλικεύει,
1010 καὶ ἀφότου ἐκαβαλίκευσεν, ὑπάγει εἰς τὸ κοράσιον.
Καὶ τότε <πάλι> ὁ στρατηγὸς
κλαίει γὰρ καὶ ὀδύρεται, οὐκ ἠμπορεῖ ὑπομένει,
κάθεται καὶ μοιρολογᾷ τὴν ἁρπαγὴν τῆς κόρης·
τὰ ρέτενα γυρίζουσιν, 'ς τὰ σπίτια των ὑπᾶσιν.
015/16 Καὶ τότε ἡ στρατήγισσα οὐκ ἠμπορεῖ ὑπομένει·
κλαίουσα καὶ ὀδυρόμενη τὸν στρατηγὸν ἐλάλει·
«Πῶς ἐσυνέβην εἰς ἐμᾶς καὶ ἐπῆρεν τὸ παιδί μας;
Πάντως ἂς τὸ ἠξεύραμεν καὶ ἂς ἦτον μὲ βουλήν μας,
1020 καὶ νὰ τὴν ἀπεβγάλαμεν ὡς πρέπει καὶ ὡς ἀξίζει
καὶ ἐδάρτε μὴ μᾶς ἔφλεγεν ἡ ἁρπαγὴ τῆς κόρης
καὶ πόνον νὰ τὸ ἔχωμεν τὰ ἔτη τῆς ζωῆς μας,
023/24 νὰ μᾶς φλογίζη ὁ πόνος της τὸ πῶς μόνη ὑπαγαίνει.»
1025 Ἀκρίτης δὲ χαιρόμενος μετὰ τῆς ποθητῆς του
ἐκεῖ τὴν ἐπερίλαβε 'ς τὰς κατακρύας βρύσας

1001 'ς Trapp: εἰς E
1003 'ς Trapp: εἰς E
1004 νὰ¹ Trapp: καὶ να E
1005 ὑπαγαίνω added by Karayanni, 1976, 109
1006 ὑπάω 'ς Karayanni, 1976, 109: ὑπάγω εἰς E
1007 προίκα Alexiou: πρίκα μου τὴν πολλὴν E   ἔχουσιν Karayanni, 1976, 125:
ἔχουν E
1008 καὶ¹ Alexiou, cf. E1300: καὶ ἐγὼ E
1011 πάλι added by Karayanni, 1976, 109
1012 ὑπομένει corr.: πομένη E
1014 'ς Trapp: εἰς E
1015/16 στρατήγισσα Trapp: στρατίγησα κλέϊ καὶ ὀδύρετε (=1016, 1st half) E
ὑπομένει corr.: πομένι E
1019 Πάντως Trapp: παντὸς E   μὲ Alexiou: με τὴν E
1020 ἀπεβγάλαμεν Alexiou: ἤχαμεν ἀπευγάλην E
1022 μας Kalonaros: μου E
1023/24 της Alexiou: της, τὰ ἔτη τῆς ζωῆς μας E   ὑπαγαίνει Kalonaros: ὑπαγένης E
1026 'ς Karayanni, 1976, 109: εἰς E

1000 "If it is your wish, father-in-law, that we hold the marriage,
come to my house with my mother-in-law
and let them bless us in marriage and after that let us return
and come to your house
so that the general's lady may see us and her soul rejoice.
1005 But if you don't want to come, see, I am setting off;
I am taking your daughter and going to my parents' estates.
As for the dowry, let my wife's brothers have it;
I have taken only the girl and want nothing else."
    Then the young man sprang into the saddle
1010 and when he had mounted, he went up to the girl.
    And then once more the general
wept and wailed, he could not bear it,
he sat down and uttered a lament for his daughter's abduction.
They pulled the reins around, they went to their homes.
1015/16   But then the general's lady could not bear it;
weeping and wailing, she said to the general:
"How has this happened to us, that he has seized our child?
If only we had known about this and it had happened with our
    consent,
1020 we could have sent her off in the right and proper way,
and our daughter's abduction would not now enflame us;
but we shall have anguish for all the years of our lives,
1023/24 and anguish for her will torment us because she goes off unescorted."
1025   Akritis the Frontiersman, rejoicing with his beloved,
embraced her there by the ice-cold springs

1001–4 The mother-in-law and the general's lady are in fact the same person. Perhaps
the point is that she wishes to see the new familial relationship sanctioned within her
own establishment.

316   Διγενὴς Ἀκρίτης

καὶ | ἐπῆρεν τὸ κοράσιον καὶ ὑπᾶ εἰς τὰ γονικά του.   169r
　　Πρὶν φθάση εἰς τὸν οἶκον του, ἐνόησεν ὁ πατήρ του
καὶ βίγλας ἔστησεν πολλὰς καὶ ἀναμένασίν τον·
1030 καὶ ὡς εἴδασιν ὅτι ἔρχεται ὁ θαυμαστὸς Ἀκρίτης,
γοργὸν ἐκαβαλίκευσαν <ὁ> θεῖος καὶ ὁ πατήρ του
καὶ ὅλη του ἡ γενεὰ καὶ τριακόσιοι ἀγοῦροι.
Οἱ μὲν τσουκάνας ἔπαιζαν, οἱ ἄλλοι τραγουδοῦσιν
καὶ πᾶν εἰς τὸ κοράσιον.
1035 Καὶ ἡ κόρη, ὡς εἶδε τὸν λαὸν καὶ ὡς εἶδεν τόσον πλῆθος,
　　　　　　　πολλὰ τοὺς ἐφοβήθην
καὶ ἀνατρομάζουσα ἔλεγεν τὸν πολυπόθητόν της:
«Ἂν εἶναι ξένοι, αὐθέντη μου, πάντως νὰ μᾶς χωρίσουν.»   G4. 804
Καὶ τότε ὁ νεώτερος τὴν κόρην οὕτως λέγει:
1040 «Αὐτὸς ὁ πενθερός σου ἐστὶν καὶ δι’ ἐμᾶς ἐξῆλθε.»   G4.806
Καὶ τότε καὶ ἡ λυγερὴ μεγάλως τὸ ἐχάρη
καὶ ἀγάλια ἀγάλια ἔλεγεν τὸν πολυπόθητόν της:
«Τί οὐκ ἤκουσες τὸν κύρην μου διὰ νὰ στραφῆς ὀπίσω;   G4.809
Καὶ νὰ εἶχα τὰς βαγίας μου καὶ τὴν ἐξόπλισίν μου   G4.810
1045 καὶ ὅλον μου τὸ συγγενικὸν μετὰ τῆς πενθερᾶς σου
καὶ νὰ ἔγνωκεν καὶ ὁ κύρης σου καὶ τὴν ἐμὴν τὴν δόξαν.»   G4.811
Καὶ τότε ὁ νεώτερος τέτοια τὴν κόρην λέγει:
«Ὁ κύρης μου τὸν κύρην σου καλὰ τὸν ἐγνωρίζει
καὶ εἰς τοῦτο οὐ μὴ τὸν μέψεται, ὡς διὰ τὴν μοναξίαν.»   G4.813
1050 Ἕξι συρτὰ | ἐπαρέσυρναν ’ς τὴν ἁρπαγὴν τῆς κόρης   169v
καὶ ἦσαν γυναίκεια, πάντερπνα, τὰ σελοχάλινά των.
Καὶ ἐπέζευσεν ὁ κύρης των καὶ ἐφίλει καὶ τοὺς δύο   G4.818
καὶ στέφανα ὁλόχρυσα τὰς κεφαλάς των θέτει
καὶ τὸν Θεὸν παρακαλεῖ καὶ εὐχὰς τὸν ἀποπέμπει:

1027 καὶ¹ Trapp: καὶ ἀπέκι E
1028 ἐνόησεν Alexiou: ἐνόησέν τους E
1031 ὁ added by Alexiou
1032 ὅλη Hesseling: ὅλος E
1036 Alexiou (note) suggests καὶ πρὸς αὐτοὺς ὑπήγαιναν before πολλὰ
1038 πάντως Trapp: παντὸς E
1040 ἐξῆλθε corr.: ἔρχετε E ἔρχεται Prombonas, 1985, 10 κοπιάζει Alexiou. cf. G4.806
1043 Τί Alexiou: διατί E
1044 εἶχα Alexiou: ἦχα καὶ E
1048 κύρην σου Alexiou: κύριοσου E
1049 τὸν Alexiou: τὸ E
1050 ’ς Trapp: εἰς E
1051 πάντερπνα Hesseling: πάντρεπνα E
1054 τὸν² Alexiou: τῶν E ἀποπέμπει E: ἀναπέμπει Alexiou

and took the girl and went to his parents' estates.
　　Before he reached his house his father had thought of him
　　and set many guards, and they watched for him.
1030　When they saw that Akritis the marvellous Frontiersman was coming,
　　his uncle and his father mounted quickly,
　　as did all his family and three hundred youngsters.
　　Some were playing drums, others were singing,
　　and they went towards the girl.
1035　And when the girl saw the crowd and when she saw such a throng,
　　　　　　　　she was very frightened of them
　　and trembling all over she said to her beloved:
　　"If they are strangers, my lord, they will certainly separate us."
　　And then the young man addressed the girl thus:
1040　"This is your father-in-law and he is coming out to meet us."
　　Then the slender girl rejoiced greatly
　　　　and she said gently to her beloved:
　　"Why didn't you listen to my lord father and go back?
　　I would have had my serving girls and my retinue
1045　and all my kinsmen together with your mother-in-law,
　　and your lord father would have been aware of my rank."
　　　　And then the young man said this to the girl:
　　"My lord father is well aware of your lord father
　　and will not hold him at fault because you are unescorted."
1050　　They brought up six led horses at the girl's abduction,
　　and their bridles and saddles were made for women and very pretty.
　　Their lord father dismounted and kissed the two of them;
　　he placed crowns of solid gold on their heads
　　and called upon God and sent prayers up to him:

1050 While the use of ἁρπαγή, 'abduction', here for the girl's arrival for her marriage
may owe something to the poet's use of formulaic phrases (Ricks, note), it is more
probably a reflection of the bride-snatching elements of marriage rituals: Angold, 1989
and Mackridge, 1993a.

1055 «Κύριος <ὁ> πάντων δυνατὸς ἐσᾶς νὰ εὐλογήσῃ,   G4.819
ὁ κτίσας γῆν καὶ οὐρανὸν καὶ θάλασσαν πεδήσας
καὶ στήσας στῦλον τοῦ πυρὸς ἀνάμεσα πελάγου,
ἀξιώσῃ σας νὰ χαίρεσθε τὰ ἔτη τῆς ζωῆς σας.»   G4.758
Σ τὴν σέλαν τὴν ἐκάθισεν τὴν μαργαριταρένιαν   G4.822
1060 καὶ ὁ λαὸς ἐκαβαλίκευσεν μετὰ πολυχρονίων.
Τὰ βότανα ἐλαλούδιζαν καὶ τὰ βουνία ἐψηλῶναν   G4.838
καὶ τὰ ἄστρη παρασκύπτουσιν εἰς τὴν χαρὰν ἐκείνην.   G4.840
Καὶ μετὰ πάσης ταραχῆς, μετὰ ὀψικίου μεγάλου,
εἰς τὸν οἶκον του ἀπέσωσεν, μεσὰ εἰς τὰ γονικά του,
1065 καὶ τῶν δύο τῶν εὐχήθηκεν ἡ μήτηρ καὶ ὁ πατήρ του.
Καὶ ὁ ἔρως ἐξεπλέρωσε πάσας των τὰς ἐλπίδας·
καὶ πάντα τὰ θελήματα καὶ τὰ ἐξαρέσκιά του,
τοῦ ἔρωτος τοῦ ἡδονικοῦ, χαρμονικῶς τελοῦσιν.
Ὁ δὲ τοῦ Ἀκρίτη ὁ πενθερός, ὁ θαυμαστὸς ἐκεῖνος, |
1070 ἀφότου ἀπεχαιρέτισεν Ἀκρίτην τὸν γαμπρόν του, 170r

Ἀπῆλθεν εἰς τὸν οἶκον του καὶ ἐθρήνησε μεγάλως·
χαρίσματα οἰκονόμησεν ὅτι νὰ τοῦ ἀποστείλῃ·
δώδεκα πάρδους διαλεκτοὺς ἀπὸ Συρίαν ἀπέσω,   G4.904
μουλάρια δώδεκα βλατίν, σελοχαλινωμένα,   G4.901
1075 καὶ χυμευτάρια ὁλόχρυσα, ὡς καὶ βαγίτσες δέκα
καὶ ἀτσουπάδας δώδεκα ὡς διὰ ὑποταγήν του   G4.903
(καὶ ἀνήβαινεν ἡ προίκα του κἂν τριακοσίες χιλιάδες)
καὶ εἰκόνες ὁλοχυμευτὲς τοὺς τρεῖς ἀρχιστρατήγους   G4.907
– καὶ εἶχαν λιθάρια ἀτίμητα, λυχνίτας καὶ ὑακίνθους –
1080 καὶ τοῦ Σχοδρόη τὸ σπαθίν, | τὸ θαυμαστὸν ἐκεῖνον· 170v   G4.912
ἐδῶκαν του καὶ λέοντα, θηρίον ἡμερωμένον,
καὶ ἡ κόρη τὸν ἐχαίρετον καὶ ὁ νεώτερος Ἀκρίτης.

1055 ὁ added by Alexiou. cf. E1114   νὰ Trapp: να σας E
1059 Σ Trapp: εἰς E
1063 μετὰ² Alexiou: καὶ μετὰ E   Trapp places 1063 after 1060. cf. Z2196–7
1064 εἰς ['ς] Alexiou: καὶ εἰς E
1065 ἡ μήτηρ καὶ ὁ πατήρ Trapp: ὁ πατήρ καὶ ἡ μήτηρ E
1066 ἔρως Chatzis. 1930. 29: ἔρωτας E   των Kalonaros: του E
1067 πάντα Kalonaros: πάντων E   του Alexiou: των E
1070 ἀπεχαιρέτισεν Kalonaros: ἐπεχερέτισεν E
1072 χαρίσματα Trapp: καὶ χαρίσματα E   ἀποστείλη Alexiou: ἀπεστείλη E
1074 μουλάρια δώδεκα βλατίν Alexiou: καὶ δώδεκα μουλάρια βλατὴν E καὶ δώδεκα
μουλάρια Trapp
1079 λυχνίτας Xanthoudidis. 1912. 560: λυχνίας E
1080 Σχοδρόη E: Χοσρόη Kalonaros. cf. G4.912

1055 "May the Lord who has power over all things bless you;
he who has created earth and heaven and put limits on the sea
and set a pillar of fire in the midst of the deep,
may he grant you happiness all the years of your lives."
He placed her on the saddle set with pearls
1060 and the crowd rode off amid acclamations.
The plants bloomed and the mountains grew tall
and the stars bent down to see that celebration.
With a mighty commotion and a great procession
he reached his house on his parents' estates,
1065 and his father and mother gave their blessing to the two of them.
Eros fulfilled all their expectations,
and all the wishes and delights of
Eros the voluptuary they accomplished joyfully.
Akritis the Frontiersman's father-in-law, that marvellous man,
1070 when he said farewell to Akritis, his son-in-law,

he returned to his house and lamented greatly;
he prepared gifts that he could send him:
twelve choice leopards from Syria,
twelve mule-loads of silks, saddled and bridled,
1075 and enamelled jewels set in gold, and also ten maid-servants
and twelve African body-guards at his command
(the value of the dowry was up to three hundred thousand)
and icons, all enamelled, of the three archgenerals
– these were set with stones beyond price, rubies and aquamarines –
1080 and Chosroes' sword, that marvellous weapon;
and they gave him also a lion, a wild beast that had been tamed,
and the girl and Akritis the young Frontiersman found him quite
delightful.

1072 The evidence of the material common to G and E suggests that *Digenis* included
the father-in-law's offer of a dowry (E992), Digenis' rejection of it (E1007), the father-in-
law's despatch of lavish gifts nonetheless and the three-month wedding. E's treatment is
more elliptical than that of G.
1074 Proposed emendations omit the silks (Trapp) or leave the problem of pack animals
which are also saddled and bridled (Alexiou).
1077 Presumably coins; cf. the three pounds of *centenaria* of E995.

Καὶ ἐκράτησεν ὁ γάμος τους τρεῖς μῆνας ἀκεραίους·   G4.931
καὶ μετὰ τὴν συμπλήρωσιν τῶν τριῶν μηνῶν ἐκείνων   G4.933
1085 ὁ στρατηγὸς χαιρόμενος ὑπᾶ εἰς τὰ γονικά του.
Καὶ ὁ νεώτερος ἐχαίρετον μετὰ καὶ τῆς καλῆς του
εἰς τόπους ὑπολίβαδους καὶ ὅπου κατάσκια δένδρη
καὶ ὕδατα ψυχρότατα, μόνος μὲ τὴν καλήν του.

1092 Ὁ θαυμαστὸς Καππάδοκας Βασίλειος Ἀκρίτης,
ἀφῶν τὴν κόρην ἥρπαξεν ἀπὸ τὰ γονικά της,
ἀπῆλθεν εἰς τὸν οἶκον του καὶ ἐφίλησαν τὰ δύο.
1095 Κατέλαβεν ὁ θάνατος καὶ ἔθαναν οἱ γονεῖς του
καὶ μοναχὸς ἀπέμεινεν | μετὰ τῆς ποθητῆς του.   171r
1097   Ἐξέβηκεν ὁ Διγενὴς νὰ παραδιαβάση.
1089 **Ἀ**νάμεσα γὰρ τῆς ὁδοῦ, καθὼς ἐπερπατοῦσαν   (170v)
φωνὴ παρὰ τοῦ δράκοντος εἰς τὸν Ἀκρίτην ἦλθεν,
1091 καὶ ὁ Θεὸς οὐκ ἤθελεν ἵνα αὐτὸν ἀπολέση.
1098 Καὶ ὑπάντησέν του ὁ δράκοντας καὶ ἀπάνου του ὑπαγαίνει·   (171r)
καὶ τότε δὲ καὶ ὁ Διγενὴς τὸν δράκοντα οὕτως λέγει:
1100 «Ἄ θέλης, ἂς παλεύσωμεν ἢ ἂς δώσωμεν ραβδέας·
ἕτοιμος εἶμαι πανταχοῦ, καὶ ὅπου κελεύεις, ἔλα.»   G2.133
. . .
Καὶ πάλιν μὲ ἀνέδειξεν ὀρέαν τὴν δρακοντέαν
καὶ τέτοια λόγια μὲ λαλεῖ, ὡς διὰ νὰ μ' ἐντραλίση:
«Τίποτε, Ἀκρίτη, οὐ θέλω σε δοκιμαστῶ μετ' ἔσου·
1105 οὐ θέλω νὰ παλεύσωμεν – εἰς ἁρπαγὴν νὰ πᾶμε·

1083 τους Alexiou: του E
1088 ψυχρότατα Hesseling: ψυχρόματα E
1095 ἔθαναν Trapp: ἀπόθαναν E ἔθανον Chatzis, 1930, 28
1096 ἀπέμεινεν Alexiou: ὑπέμεινεν E
1097 παραδιαβάσ Alexiou: παραδιαβάσι, μετὰ τῆς ποθητής του E
1089 ἐπερπατοῦσαν corr.: ἐπεριπατοῦσαν E
1101 Alexiou suggests there is a brief lacuna at this point, cf. πάλιν 1102
1104 σε E: νὰ Hesseling
1105 παλεύσωμεν Hesseling: σαλεύσωμεν E   νὰ πᾶμε E: ὑπάγω Ricks

Their wedding lasted for three whole months
and after the completion of these three months
1085 the general went rejoicing to his ancestral estates.
And the young man rejoiced with his beloved
in verdant meadows, and where the trees were shady
and the streams very cold, on his own with his beloved.

1092 When the marvellous Cappadocian, Vasilis Akritis the Frontiersman,
abducted the girl from her parents' estates,
he went to his house and the two of them kissed.
1095 Death intervened and his parents died
and he remained on his own together with his beloved.
1097   Digenis went out to amuse himself.
1089 While they were making their way along the road,
a cry came to the Frontiersman from the serpent,
1091 but God did not wish to destroy him.
1098 The serpent confronted him and set on him,
and then Digenis spoke thus to the serpent:
1100 "If you wish, let us wrestle or let us fight with sticks;
I am ready in every way and so, come on wherever you like"
. . .
And once more he showed me his serpent's tail
and addressed these words to me, to confuse me:
"I don't in the least want, Akritis the Frontiersman, to come to grips
   with you;
1105 I don't want us to wrestle – let's go off on an abduction;

1085 Presumably the general had accompanied the dowry.
1088 Note that Digenis is now 'on his own', but with the girl.
1089–98 A confused sequence of lines (cf. G4.953–70), marking a transition from the
youthful exploits and wedding of Digenis to adventures that are narrated in the first
person (see note at G4.1091). All editors resort to drastic rearrangement here: Kalonaros:
1086, 1092–7, 1087–91, 1098 ff.; Trapp: 1086, 1092–4, 1606–7, 1097, 1087–91,
1098ff.; Alexiou: 1088, 1092–7, 1091, 1089–90, 1098 ff.: Ricks follows Alexiou but
relegates the rearranged sequence 1092–8 to a note. This edition prefers to keep
1089–91 together after 1097. Note that 1089 is marked in the manuscript by an initial
capital and comes after a space left blank for a picture (not indicated here because of the
rearrangement of lines); 1089–91 could represent the remains of a caption (cf. the
repeated lines at E636–7). E does not include two episodes found in G: the visit from the
emperor (G4.971–1093) and the encounter with Aploravdis' daughter (G5).
1089–605 This section makes up Alexiou's fourth song, 'The Serpent, the Lion, the
Guerrillas and Maximou' (cf. G6.1–798).
1095 The death of Digenis' parents occurs much later in G's narrative, at G7.189.
1102 πάλιν suggests that there had been a previous display, and hence there must be a
brief lacuna.

ἀνάμενε ὥραν, ἄγουρε, νὰ πάρω τὴν καλήν σου,
εἰδέ, πλανᾶται ἡ νεότης σου, νὰ χάσης τὴν ζωήν σου.»
Καθὼς εἶπεν τὸν λόγον του καὶ ἐλάλει μετὰ μένα,
ταῦτα μεταμορφώνεται, τρεῖς κεφαλὰς μὲ δείχνει· G6.65
1110 ἡ μία ἦτον γέροντος, ἡ ἄλλη νεωτέρου,
ἡ δὲ μεσαία ὄφεως, δράκοντος τῆς γεέννης.
Καὶ ὡς ἤκουσα τὴν ἀπειλὴν καὶ τὸν λόγον τὸν εἶπεν,
καὶ ἡ ψυχή μου ἐτρόμαξεν καὶ ὡσὰν <ν΄> ἀκροφοβήθην.
Καὶ Θεὸς ὁ πάντων δυνατὸς οὐ θέλει νὰ μὲ χάση·
1115 ἐβάστουν τὸ σπαθίτσιν μου 'ς τὸ ἀριστερόν μου μέρος·
τὴν ποθητήν μου ἐπέζευσα, κάτω τὴν ἀποθέτω
καὶ τὸ σπαθίν μου ἐξέσυρα,
καὶ εἰς μίαν σπαθίαν πάραυτα τὲς τρεῖς ἀντάμα ἐπαίρνω·
καὶ ὁ κορνιακτὸς τοῦ δράκοντος ἐστύλωσεν μεγάλως. |

171v

1120 **Κ**αὶ τὸ κοράσιο ἐγέλασεν, μεγάλως τὸ ἀποδέχθην G6.86
καὶ σὺν ἐκείνης τῆς χαρᾶς πάλιν γελᾶ ἡ κόρη.
Καὶ ὁ συρισμὸς τοῦ δράκοντος, τὸ γέλιον τῆς καλῆς μου
λέοντας μέγας τὸ ἤκουσεν ἀπέσω ἀπὲ καλάμιν· G4.162. 6.91
καὶ κτύπον ἤκουσα οὐρᾶς καὶ τὰ πλευρά του δέρνει,
1125 καὶ ἐκ τὸ καλάμι ἐξέβηκεν ὡς θάλασσα ἀγριωμένη.
Καὶ <γὰρ> ὡς εἶδεν τὸ θηρίον ἐμὲν καὶ τὴν καλήν μου,
ἐσήκωσεν τὸ οὐράδιν του καὶ τὰ πλευρά του δέρνει,
τοὺς ὀφθαλμούς του ἐθόλωσεν, βούλεται νὰ μᾶς φάη.

1106 ὥραν Alexiou: μίαν ὥραν E
1107 ζωήν σου Hesseling: καλήν σου ζωὴν E
1111 μεσαία Trapp: μεσέα εἶτον E γεέννης Karayanni. 1976. 230: γενέας E
1112 ἤκουσα Kalonaros: ἤκουσεν E
1113 μου Kalonaros: του E ν΄ added by Alexiou ἀκροφοβήθην Kalonaros: ἀκροφοβήθη E
1115 σπαθίτσιν Garandoudis. 1993. 213. cf. E520, 1245: ραβδίν E σπαθίν Alexiou 'ς corr.: εἰς E
1116 ποθητήν Trapp: πολυποθητήν E ἀποθέτω Xanthoudidis, 1912. 559: ἀποδέρνω E
1117 ἐξέσυρα Kalonaros: ἐξέσυρα, κάτω τὴν ἀποσήρνω E
1118 τὲς τρεῖς ἀντάμα Alexiou: ἀντάμα ταῖς τρεῖς E
1119 μεγάλως Trapp: μεγ΄ E (page trimmed)
1120 κοράσιο Karayanni. 1976. 112: κοράσιον E
1123 ἀπὲ Alexiou: ἀπὲ τὸ E
1124 καὶ[2] Alexiou, cf. E1127: εἰς E
1125 καλάμι Karayanni. 1976. 112: καλάμην E
1126 γὰρ added

wait a while, youngster, for me to seize your beloved;
if not, your youthfulness may be deceived into losing you your life."
   As he was making this speech and speaking with me,
he immediately transformed himself, he showed me three heads
1110   – one was that of an old man, the second that of a young man
and the one in the middle was a snake's, the serpent of Gehenna.
When I heard the threat and the speech which he made,
my soul trembled and it was as though I was almost afraid.
   But God who has power over all things did not wish to lose me.
1115 I was carrying my sword by my left side;
I made my beloved dismount, I set her down
and I unsheathed my sword;
with one blow of the sword I promptly struck off the three heads
   together.
And the dust from the serpent spiralled high in the air.

1120 The girl laughed, she enjoyed it greatly
and at this delight once more the girl laughed.
The hissing of the serpent, my beloved's laughter
– a huge lion heard this from within a reed-bed;
I heard the swishing of its tail as it lashed its flanks
1125 and it came out of the reed-bed like a tempestuous sea.
When the wild beast saw me and my beloved,
it raised its tail and lashed its flanks,
its eyes glazed over, it wanted to devour us.

1109 On the serpent, see G6.47, note. A three-headed allegorical figure, of Eros, also
appears at *Livistros* E416–27; such figures have a long classical pedigree (e.g. Panofsky,
1970, 184–6).

Καὶ τότε τὸ κοράσιον ἀπήλπισεν τελείως
1130 καὶ ἐμὲν τὰ τέτοια ἐλάλησεν βλέποντα τὸ θηρίον:
«Βλέπε, ἀφέντη μου καλέ, τὸ θηρίον μὴ μᾶς φάγη.»
Καὶ ἀναπηδῶ ἐκ τὴν κλίνην μου, πηδῶ ἔξω τῆς τέντας,
γοργὸν ἐπῆρα τὸ σπαθὶν καὶ προσυπήντησά του·
καὶ ἐγὼ πάντοτε ἐσπούδαζα ἵνα τόνε προλάβω,
1135 καὶ ἐλκεῖνος εἶχεν τὴν βουλὴν ἵνα μὲ ἀποπέση· 172r
καὶ ἀνέκλασεν τὸ οὐράδιν του καὶ ἀπάνου μου κατέβη.
Καὶ μίαν σπαθέαν τοῦ ἔδωσα 'ς τὰς δισσουμέας ἀπάνω
καὶ ἡ κεφαλή του ἐχώθηκεν ἀπέσωθεν τῆς βάλτης.

Καὶ ἀπῆρα τὸ κοράσιον, εἰς τὴν τέντα μου ὑπάγω
1140 καὶ ἡ κόρη οὕτως λέγει με, οὕτω παρακαλεῖ με:
«Νὰ ἐπιχαρῆς τὰ κάλλη μου, τὴν περισσήν σου ἀνδρείαν,
ἔπαρε τὸ λαβοῦτο σου καὶ παῖξε το ὀλίγον,   G6.101
ὅτι ἐραθύμησα, <καλέ,> ἐκ τῶν θηρίων τὸν φόβον   G6.102
καὶ ἡγρίωσεν ἡ καρδία μου ἐκ τῶν θηρίων τὸ αἷμα.»
1145   Καὶ ἐπῆρα τὸ λαβοῦτο μου καὶ θέλω νὰ ἀκροπαίξω
καὶ εὐθέως δὲ καὶ ἡ λυγερὴ τραγούδημαν ἐλάλει:
«Εὐχαριστῶ τοὺς ἔρωτας, καλὸν ἄνδρα μ' ἐδῶκαν,   G6.105
νὰ τὸν θωρῶ, νὰ χαίρωμαι τὰ ἔτη τῆς ζωῆς μου.»
Καὶ ἐκ τὸν ἦχον τοῦ θαμπουρίου καὶ ἐκ τὸν ἦχον τῆς κόρης
1150 κτύπος ἐβγῆκε ἐκ τὰ βουνά, τὰ ὄρη ἐκιλαδοῦσαν.
Οἱ ἀπελάτες θαυμάζουσιν τὴν ἡδονὴν τῆς κόρης· |
ζῆλος ἐνέπεσε εἰς αὐτοὺς ἵνα τὴν ἀφαρπάξουν 172v
καὶ ἀπὸ μακρέας φωνάζουσιν ἀναίσχυντα λαλίας:
«Ἄφες, καλέ, τὴν λυγερὴν καὶ σῶσε τὸν ἑαυτόν σου·   G6.131
1155 σώνουν τὰ τὴν ἐφίλησες καὶ τὴν περιεπλάκης
καὶ μὴ πλανᾶται ἡ νεότης σου νὰ χάσης τὴν ζωήν σου.»
Καὶ ἡ κόρη ὡς εἶδεν τὸν λαὸν καὶ ὡς εἶδε τόσον πλῆθος,
ὅτι ἦσαν †... † τρακόσοι ἀπελάτες

1129 ἀπήλπισεν Alexiou, cf. note: ἀπήρπισέν με Ε
1134 τόνε [τονὲ] προλάβω Alexiou: τὸν ἐπρολάβω Ε
1136 ἀνέκλασεν Alexiou: ἄνκλασεν Ε ἀπάνου μου κατέβη Trapp: σύντομα ἀπάνου μου καταβένει Ε
1137 'ς Trapp: εἰς Ε
1139 ἀπῆρα Trapp: ἀπῆρεν Ε μου ὑπάγω Trapp: του ὑπάη Ε
1143 καλέ added by Alexiou
1149 τὸν ἦχον (twice) Hesseling: τῶν ἠχῶν Ε
1150 ἐβγῆκε Karayanni, 1976, 112: εὐγῆκεν Ε ἐκ Ε: εἰς Alexiou
1152 ἐνέπεσε Alexiou: ἐνέπεσεν Ε
1155 τὰ Alexiou: σε Ε
1156 νεότης Alexiou: νεότη Ε

Then the girl despaired completely
1130 and said this to me as she looked at the beast:
"My handsome lord, see that the beast does not devour us."
So I leaped up from my couch, I rushed out of the tent;
I seized my sword quickly and confronted the beast.
I put every effort into getting the better of it
1135 but it was intent on attacking me.
It arched its tail and charged at me.
I gave it one blow with the sword between its shoulder blades
and its head disappeared into the marsh.

Then I took the girl and went into my tent,
1140 and the girl spoke to me thus, this is the plea she made to me:
"To celebrate my beauty and your prodigious bravery,
take your lute and play it a little,
because I am despondent, my beloved, from fear of the beasts,
and my heart has been disturbed by the beasts' blood."
1145 So I took my lute and I was about to play it
when the slender girl at once began a song:
"I thank the Erotes who have given me a fine husband
– may I behold him, may I rejoice in him all the years of my life."
And from the sound of the tamboura and the sound of the girl
1150 a noise resounded from the hills, the mountains rang.
The guerrillas were amazed at the girl's charm;
eagerness to abduct her came over them
as they yelled offensive comments from a distance:
"Leave the slender girl, my friend, and save yourself.
1155 The kisses and embraces you have given her are quite enough,
and don't let your youthfulness be deceived into losing you your life."
When the girl saw the throng and when she saw such a crowd,
that there were three hundred guerrillas

1132 That Digenis was lying on his couch when the lion attacked is an element present in both G and E, though more neatly integrated at G6.94 than here where we last saw him on horseback.
1151 The guerrillas, alerted by the girl's singing (cf. G6.124 ff.), appear abruptly in this version.

καὶ εἶχαν ἄρματα καλά, ἱππάρια ἀφιρωμένα,
1160 καὶ ἐξοπλισμένοι δυνατὰ καὶ ἦσαν λουρικιασμένοι,
τὰ λόγια ταῦτα ἐπίστευσεν καὶ ἐμὲν τοιαῦτα ἐλάλει:
«Ὀϊμέν, ἀφέντη μου καλέ, βέβαιον νὰ μᾶς χωρίσουν
σήμερον ἀπ’ ἀλλήλων.»
Σφικτὰ σφικτὰ μὲ ἐφίλησεν καὶ οὕτως μὲ συντυχαίνει:
1165 «Αὐθέντη μου, ἂς φιλήσωμεν τῆς ἀποχωρισίας.»
Κλαίουσα γὰρ μὲ ἔλεγεν ἐκ στεναγμοῦ καρδίας:
«Σήμερον χωριζόμεθα, τίς νὰ τὸ ὑπομένη;»
Ἐγὼ δὲ <τότε> ἐγέλασα καὶ τὸ κοράσιον λέγω:
«Καλὰ λέγεις, κοράσιον; Οὕτως μὲ συντυχαίνεις;
1170 Ἐμᾶς ὁ Θεὸς <μᾶς> ἔσμιξεν, ἄνθρωποι οὐ χωρίζουν.   G6.143
Δός μου, ξανθή, ὑπολούρικον, δός μοι καὶ τὸ ραβδίν μου
καὶ βλέπε, αὐθέντρια καὶ κυρά, τὸ τί τοὺς θέλω ποίσει.»
Γοργὸν ἐπῆρα τὸ ραβδὶν καὶ προσυπήντησά τους
καὶ ἐκεῖνοι ἐμὲν ἐκρούγασιν καὶ ἐξέβαιναν οἱ κτύποι·
1175 καὶ ἐγὼ ὅσον <τοὺς> ἤκρουγα, ἐγίνονταν οἱ φόνοι·
καὶ ἡ | γῆ τοὺς ἐδαπάνησεν ψυχῇ τιμωρουμένους.   173r
Καὶ ἦτον κορνιακτὸς πολὺς καὶ ἦτον καὶ ἀνεμοζάλη.
Καὶ <τότε> ὅσοι ἔφευγαν <καὶ> οὐδὲν τοὺς ἐθεώρουν,
δι’ αὐτοὺς μὲ κόπτει ὁ πόνος
1180 καὶ ἡ λύπη νὰ μὲ συνταφῇ καὶ θλίψιν νὰ τὸ ἔχω,
ὅτι ὄνταν ἐθερμάθηκα, οὐκ ηὕρισκα νὰ κόπτω.
Καὶ τότε ἀπομερίμνησα τὸ κρούειν καὶ τὸ λαμβάνειν.

Στρέφομαι, περιβλέπομαι <ὡς> διὰ τὴν ποθητήν μου·
βλέπω την ὅτι ἐκάθητον ἀπάνω εἰς τὸ κλινάριν

1159 ἱππάρια ἀφιρωμένα Trapp: ὑπάριαφυρομένα Ε
1162 βέβαιον Trapp: καὶ βέβαιον Ε
1165 ἀποχωρισίας Alexiou: ἀπὸ χωρισίας μας Ε
1168 τότε added by Alexiou
1170 μᾶς added by Alexiou
1171 ξανθή Kalonaros: ξαθή Ε   μοι Ε: μου Alexiou
1172 βλέπε Alexiou: τότε Ε   αὐθέντρια Kalonaros: αὐθέτρια Ε   τὸ Alexiou: βλέπε τὸ
Ε
1175 τοὺς added by Alexiou
1176 ψυχῇ τιμωρουμένους Trapp: ψυχῇ τιμωρουμένη Ε
1178 τότε added by Alexiou   καὶ added by Alexiou
1179 δι’ αὐτοὺς Alexiou: καὶ δι’ αὐτοὺς Ε
1180 θλίψιν Hesseling: θλίψη Ε
1182 λαμβάνειν Alexiou: λαμβάνη Ε
1183 ὡς added by Alexiou   ποθητήν Trapp: πολιποθυτήν Ε
1184 βλέπω corr.: καὶ βλέπω Ε

and they had fine weapons and armoured horses
1160 and were strongly equipped and were wearing breastplates,
she promptly believed their words and said this to me:
"Alas, my beloved lord, they will certainly separate us
                from each other today."
She hugged and kissed me tightly and addressed me thus:
1165 "My lord, let us kiss each other farewell."
Weeping she said to me with a heart-felt sigh:
"Today we are separated – who can bear it?"
    But then I laughed and said to the girl:
"Are you right, girl? Are you talking to me like this?
1170 It is God who has joined us: men will not separate us.
Give me my surcoat, my blonde beauty, give me my stick as well
and see, my mistress and my lady, what I shall do to them."
    Quickly I took my stick and confronted them
as they struck at me and their blows rang out;
1175 but as often as I struck at them, deaths followed,
and the earth consumed those who had paid with their souls.
And there was much dust and a huge gale.
Then for all those who had fled and I could no longer see,
                distress tormented me;
1180 grief will never leave me and I shall be sorrowful,
because now that I was aroused I could find no one to strike.
Then I lost interest in giving and taking blows.

I turned and looked round for my beloved,
I saw her seated on her couch

1170 On the significance of this phrase from Matthew 19.6 (cf. G6.143; E1305) for the literary context of *Digenis*, see the Introduction, p. xliv.

1185 καὶ ἔχυσα τὰ μανίκια μου καὶ πρὸς αὐτὴν ὑπάγω.   G6.158
Καὶ ἐκείνη ἐκατεπήδησεν καὶ πρὸς ἐμένα ἦλθεν·
κρύον νερὸν μὲ ἔφερεν δοκοῦσα ὅτι ἐκουράσθην,
ἐγὼ δὲ τὴν ἐλάλησα καὶ οὕτως μὲ συντυχαίνει:
«Πίνε νερόν, αὐθέντη μου, ὅτι πολλὰ ἐκουράσθης.»
1190   Καὶ ἐγὼ πάλιν τὴν λέγω:
«Καλή, ὡς οὐχ ηὕρηκα τινὰν νὰ μὲ παραποινέση 173v
καὶ νὰ σταθῆ εἰς τὸ πλάγι μου καὶ ἐμπλήση με ραβδέας,
πῶς ἤθελα νὰ κουρασθῶ δίχως καμίας ἀνάγκης;
Ἀλλ᾽ ὕπαγε εἰς τὴν τέντα μου καὶ φέρε μου ν᾽ ἀλλάξω
1195 καὶ τὰ φορῶ ὑπερύψα τα εἰς τὸ αἷμα τῶν ἀνθρώπων.»
Καὶ ἡ κόρη ὑπᾶ εἰς τὴν κλίνην μου νὰ <μοῦ> φέρη νὰ ἀλλάξω
καὶ ἐγὼ ηὕρηκα σκιὸν δενδροῦ καὶ ἐκούμπισα εἰς τὴν ρίζαν.
    Καὶ ὅσον νὰ ὑπάη ἡ λυγερὴ νὰ μοῦ φέρη ν᾽ ἀλλάξω,
τρεῖς καβελάροι ἀνέβαιναν τὴν παρεποταμίαν.   G6.176
1200 Ὁ εἷς ἦτον νεώτερος, ἀγένειον παλληκάριν,
καὶ ὁ ἄλλος ἦτον κουρευτός, γέρων ἐξοπλισμένος,
καὶ ὁ ἀπεκεῖ τὸ γένειον εἶχε νὰ στεφανώνη.
Καὶ οἱ τρεῖς ἀντάμα ἐστάθησαν καὶ οὕτως μὲ συντυχαίνουν:
«Μήνα ἐδιάβησαν ἀπεδῶ, νεώτερε, ἀπελάτες;»
1205   Ἐγὼ δὲ οὐκ ἐφοβήθην τους ἵνα τοὺς προσεγέρθω
καὶ ἵνα τοὺς κρύψω τίποτες ἐκ τὴν ἐμὴν ἀνδρείαν·
κάθομαι, διηγοῦμαι τους περὶ τοὺς ἀπελάτας:
«Ἄρχοντες, ἦρθαν εἰς ἐμὲν νὰ ἐπάρουν τὴν καλήν μου
καὶ ἐγώ, ὡς μὲ ἐλέγασιν ἵνα τὴν ἐξαφήσω
1210 ὅτι εἶχαν πόθον εἰς αὐτὴν ἄπειρόν τε καὶ μέγαν,   G4.696
καὶ ἄρματα οὐκ εἶχα μετ᾽ ἐμέν, ἄλογον οὐδὲ ἕνα,
μὲ τῆς μητρός μου τὴν εὐχὴν πεζὸς ὑπῆγα εἰς αὗτους·

1185 ὑπάγω Trapp: ὑπαγένω Ε
1186 ἐμένα Kalonaros: ἐμὲν Ε
1189 Πίνε Ε: Πίε Alexiou
1191 ὡς οὐχ Trapp: ὥσον Ε νὰ Trapp: ὅτι να Ε
1193 νὰ κουρασθῶ Trapp: κουρασθῆ Ε
1194 Ἀλλ᾽ Trapp: μᾶλον Ε
1195 ὑπερύψα τα Xanthoudidis, 1912, 562: ὑπερίψετα Ε ἐρύπησα Trapp τὰ ἐρύπησα Alexiou
1196 ὑπᾶ Alexiou, cf. E1085: ὑπάγι Ε μοῦ added by Mackridge, 1993b, 336, cf. E1198
1202 ἀπεκεῖ Alexiou: ἄλλος Ε εἶχε Alexiou: ἐπέκι Ε
1204 Μήνα (= μήπως) Spadaro, 1989, 180: μῆνα Ε
1206 καὶ ἵνα Ε: ἦ να Alexiou
1208 ἦρθαν Trapp: ἐδῶ ἦρθαν Ε
1210 εἶχαν Alexiou: ηχα ἐγὼ Ε εἶχα Trapp
1211 καὶ Trapp: καὶ ἐγὼ Ε

1185 so I shook off my sleeve-guards and went towards her.
She leaped down and came towards me.
She brought me cold water, thinking that I was weary,
and I spoke to her and she addressed me thus:
"Drink some water, my lord, for you are very weary."
1190   I in turn said to her:
"Beloved, since I have not found anyone to trouble me
and stand beside me and beat me with his stick,
how could I be weary without any need?
But come to my tent and fetch me clothes to change into,
1195 for I have soiled what I am wearing with men's blood."
So the girl went to my bed to fetch clothes for me to change into
while I found shade from a tree and sat at its foot.
    While the slender girl had gone to fetch me clothes to change into,
three horsemen came along the river bank.
1200 One was a young man, a beardless young warrior,
the next had cropped hair, an old man in full armour,
and the other one had a beard that stood out all round.
The three stopped together and addressed me thus:
"Perhaps some guerrillas passed by here, young man?"
1205   I was not so afraid of them as to rise courteously before them
or to conceal any of my bravery from them.
I sat and told them all about the guerrillas:
"My lords, they came at me to seize my beloved,
and as for me, when they told me to let her go
1210 because they had a great and boundless desire for her,
as I had no weapons with me, not even one horse,
I went at them on foot supported only by my mother's blessing;

1199–315 E and G6.176–307 agree over the salient points of Digenis' encounter with
the guerrillas but the details vary with the different narrative styles.
1202 The three ages of man; cf. the transformation of the serpent at E1109–11.

καὶ τὸ κακὸν τὸ ἐπάθασιν οὐ μὴ σᾶς ἔχει λάθειν.»

Καὶ εὐθὺς οἱ τρεῖς ὡς | τὸ ἤκουσαν, παράξενον ἐφάνη,   174r
1215 ἀλλήλως ἐβλεμμάτισαν καὶ πρὸς ἀλλήλους λέγουν:
«Μὴ τοῦτος εἶν' τὸν λέγουσιν ὁ Διγενὴς Ἀκρίτης;   G6.190
Ἀλλὰ ἂς τὸν δοκιμάσωμεν κᾶν εἷς ἀπὸ τοὺς τρεῖς μας
καὶ εἰς μίαν ν' ἀπεικάσωμεν ὅτι ἀληθῶς μᾶς λέγει.»

Καὶ εἷς ἐξ αὐτῶν μὲ ἐλάλησεν, δοκῶ, τὸν εἶχαν πρῶτον:
1220 «Ἐκείνους, τοὺς γυρεύγομεν καὶ τοὺς καταρωτοῦμεν,
τριακόσιοι εἶναι ἐξωλούρικοι μετὰ καὶ τῶν ἀρμάτων·
καὶ ἐσὲν θεωροῦμεν μοναχόν, <πεζὸν μὲ τὸ καλίκιν,>
καὶ μὲ τὸ μοναπλούτσικον, καὶ πῶς τοὺς εἶχες τρέψειν;
Ἀμὲ ἂν λαλῇς ἀλήθειαν, ὡς λέγεις καὶ ὡς καυχᾶσαι,
1225 ἕναν ἐκλέξου ἀφ' ἡμῶν, ὃν θέλεις καὶ κελεύεις,   G6.197, 213
καὶ αὐτὸς νὰ ἔλθη πρὸς ἐσὲν καὶ δότε οἱ δύο ραβδέας
καὶ τότε νὰ νοήσωμεν ὅτι ἀληθῶς μᾶς λέγεις.»

Γοργὸν ἐκατεπήδησα καὶ ἐστάθην ἔμπροσθέν των
καὶ λόγους τοὺς ἐλάλησα οὐχὶ πρὸς καυχησίαν:
1230 «Μὰ τὸν ἐξουσιαστὴν Χριστόν, ὃν τρέμει πᾶσα ἡ κτίσις,
ἀφῶν ἠρξάμην πολεμεῖν εἰς ἕναν οὐκ ἐβγῆκα·
εἰς χιλίους ἐκατέβηκα καὶ εἰς τετρακισχιλίους
καὶ ἦσαν ὁλοσίδεροι καὶ τετραλυγισμένοι
καὶ εἶχαν ἄρματα καλά, ἱππάρια ἀφιρωμένα,
1235 καὶ ἐδὰ ἄρτε εἰς ἕναν μοναχὸν θέλω νὰ πολεμήσω;
Ὑπᾶτε καὶ πεζεύσετε καὶ ἐλᾶτε οἱ τρεῖς εἰς ἕναν·   G6.200
εἰ δὲ οὐ καταδέχεσθε, ἐλᾶτε καβαλάροι.»   174v   G6.201

Καὶ εἷς ἐξ αὐτῶν μὲ ἐλάλησεν, δοκῶ, τὸν εἶχαν πρῶτον,
ὁ γέρων ὁ Φιλοπαππποὺς ὁ πρῶτος ἀπελάτης:
1240 «Αὐτὰ εἰς ἐμὲν μηδὲν τὰ εἰπῇς, νὰ ἔχωμεν καταδίκην
καὶ αὔριον νὰ τὸ καυχᾶσαι,
ὅτι ἀπελάτες θαυμαστοὶ ἐσέναν πολεμοῦσιν·
ἐγὼ εἶμαι ὁ Φιλοπαππποὺς, Κίνναμος καὶ Γιαννάκης.»   G6.211-2, 548

Καὶ ἐγλήγορα ἐπήδησεν ἀπὸ <τὸ> ἄλογόν του

1214 παράξενον Alexiou: παράξενον τὸν E
1216 λέγουσιν Trapp: λέγουν E
1217 κᾶν εἷς Alexiou: κανὶς E
1222 πεζὸν μὲ τὸ καλίκιν added by Trapp. cf. E1323
1223 τρέψειν Hesseling: τέρψιν E
1235 ἐδὰ ἄρτε E: ἐδάρτε Trapp
1236 Ὑπᾶτε Trapp: ἀμὴ ὑπάτε E
1237 οὐ E: καὶ Xanthoudidis. 1912, 563   ἐλᾶτε Kalonaros: ἐλάτε καὶ E
1240 τὰ Alexiou: τὸ E   νὰ Alexiou: να τὸ E
1244 ἐπήδησεν Alexiou: ἐπίδυσεν, ὁ φιλοπαπποὺς E   τὸ added by Trapp

And you cannot have failed to notice the disaster they suffered."
Immediately the three heard this, it seemed strange to them.
1215 They eyed one another and said to each other:
"Can this be the one they call Digenis Akritis, the Frontiersman of
Double Descent?
But let us test him, one of the three of us
and in an instant we shall be able to work out if he is telling us the
truth."
And one of them said to me – I think he was their leader:
1220 "Those men we are looking for and asking about,
there are three hundred of them in breastplates and with weapons,
but we can see that you are on your own, on foot and in boots
and a simple tunic, how could you have routed them?
But if you are telling the truth, as you say and as you boast,
1225 choose any one of us you would like to pick,
and let him attack you and the two of you can fight with sticks,
and then we shall know if you are telling us the truth."
I jumped up quickly and stood in front of them;
I said to them, with no intention of boasting:
1230 "By Christ the omnipotent, before whom all creation trembles,
from the time I began to fight I have not set out against one man.
I have gone out against a thousand and against four thousand,
all clad in iron but very nimble,
and they had good weapons and armoured horses,
1235 and now indeed am I to fight against one man on his own?
Come along and dismount and attack three against one;
and if you don't accept this, attack me on horseback."
And one of them said to me – I think he was their leader –
old Philopappous, the chief guerrilla:
1240 "Don't say such things to me to disgrace us
so that tomorrow you can boast
that the marvellous guerrillas fought against you.
I am Philopappous, these are Kinnamos and Giannakis."
He leaped swiftly down from his horse

1245 καὶ σύρνει τὸ σπαθίτσιν του καὶ σύντομα ἐκατέβην
ἵνα σπαθέαν μὲ δώση·
καὶ ὥστε νὰ πάρω τὸ σπαθὶν ἐκ τοῦ δένδρου τὴν ῥίζαν,
σπαθέαν μίαν μὲ ἔδωκεν εἰς τὸ χεροσκουτάριν.   G6.219
Καὶ ἦτον ὁ γέρων δυνατὸς καὶ τὸ ἅρμαν του καινούριον
1250 καὶ μοναχὸν τὸ κράτημαν <μ'> ἀπόμεινε εἰς τὸ χέριν·   G6.220
τοῦ σκουταρίου τσακίσματα ἔπεσαν ἔμπροσθέν μου.
Καὶ τότε τὸν ἐλάλησαν: «Φιλοπαππού, ἄλλην μίαν.»   G6.222
Καὶ ἐγὼ οὐκ ἐκατεδέχθην το ἵνα μοῦ δευτερώση·
δαμὶν ἐπιστοπόδησα καὶ δίδω του ῥαβδέαν,
1255 καὶ εἰς μίαν ἔπεσαν τὰ ἅρματα καὶ ἀπὸ τὰς δύο του χεῖρας
καὶ ἐστέναξεν, ἐδάκρυσεν ὁ γέρων καὶ ὑπηγαίνει.
Καὶ οἱ ἄλλοι συνεσπούδαζαν καὶ ἐπέπεσάν με οἱ δύο
καὶ τότε ἐνόησα πόλεμον καλῶν παλληκαρίων· 175r
εἰς τὸ κρούειν καὶ εἰς τὸ δέχεσθαι ηὗρηκα τὸν Γιαννάκην
1260 καὶ εἰς τὰ πυκνογυρίσματα τὸν Κίνναμον τὸν Λέον.
Εἰς αὗτον τὸν νοῦν μου ἔβαλα, κρυφῶς νὰ μὴ μὲ δώση,
καὶ τὴν καλήν μου ἐλάλησα φωνὴν ἀπὸ μακρόθεν:
«Ἄρτε, καλή μου, πέρασε τὰ κρύα καὶ τὰ χιονάτα
καὶ φέρε μου ὑπολούρικον, διὰ νὰ κρατῶ εἰς τὸ χέριν,
1265 ἵνα τοὺς ποίσω τὸ γοργὸν νὰ φύγουν ἔμπροσθέν μου.»
Καὶ ἐκείνη ἐπιβουλεύτη με καὶ φέρνει μου ἱματίτσιν·
καὶ ἐγὼ ἐκ τὴν βίαν μου τὴν πολλὴν τυλίγω το εἰς τὸ χέριν
καὶ εἰς αὗτους κατεβαίνω.
Τὸν Γιαννάκην ἐχώρισα, διὰ νὰ τὸν δοκιμάσω,
1270 καὶ ἐκεῖνος μὲ ἐπέβλεπεν, ἵνα σπαθέαν μὲ δώση,
καὶ ἐξηστρεφτὴν τοῦ ἔδωσα ἀπάνω εἰς τὸν βραχίοναν   G6.251
καὶ τὸ σπαθίν του ἐξέπεσεν καὶ ἡ χείρα του ἐκρεμάστην   G6.252
καὶ ἀνάσκελα ἐξήπλωσεν ὁ θαυμαστὸς Γιαννάκης.

Καὶ ὡς εἶδεν τοῦτο ὁ Κίνναμος πηδᾶ, καβαλικεύει 175v
1275 καὶ ἀπάνω μου ἐπιλάλησεν, ἵνα σπαθέαν μὲ δώση·
καλὴν ῥαβδέαν ἔδωκα τὴν φάραν 'ς τὸ κεφάλιν

1246 σπαθέαν corr.: ῥαβδέαν F.
1250 μ' added by Alexiou ἀπόμεινε Alexiou: ἀπόμηνεν E
1251 σκουταρίου Trapp: σκουταρίου μου E ἔπεσαν Hesseling: ἔπεσεν E
1252 ἐλάλησαν Kalonaros, cf. G6.221: ἐλάλησα E ἄλλην Trapp: ἄλη E
1269 διὰ Trapp: ὡς διὰ E δοκιμάσω Trapp: ἀποδοκιμάσω E
1272 καὶ ἡ χείρα του Alexiou: εἰς τὴν χείραν E
1275 σπαθέαν Alexiou, cf. Z3111: παρέαν E
1276 φάραν Kalonaros: φαρέαν E 'ς Trapp: εἰς E

1245 and drew his sword and quickly set on me
                              to give me a blow;
      and before I could pick up my sword from the root of the tree
      he gave me a blow with his sword on my hand-shield.
      The old man was powerful and his weapon was new
1250 so only the handle was left in my hand:
      pieces of the shield were scattered in front of me.
      Then they called out to him: "Philopappous, hit him again!"
          But I did not allow him a second attempt;
      I jumped back a little and gave him a blow with my stick
1255 and in an instant his weapons fell from both his hands;
      the old man groaned, he wept and went away.
      The others increased their efforts and the two of them fell on me,
      and then I appreciated a battle with fine warriors:
      I found Giannakis expert in giving and taking blows
1260 and Leo Kinnamos in making swift turns.
          I turned my attention to him so that he should not strike me
              unexpectedly
      and I let out a shout from a distance to my beloved:
      "Come on, my love, cross the cold and snowy waters
      and bring me my surcoat to hold in my hand,
1265 so that I can make them run away from me quickly."
          But she had some scheme against me and brought me my tunic;
      and I in my great haste wrapped it round my arm
                              and charged at them.
          I separated off Giannakis to try him out;
1270 he was watching me, to give me a blow with his sword,
      but I struck him a back-handed blow on the arm
      and his sword fell and his arm hung down,
      and the marvellous Giannakis collapsed with his legs in the air.

      When Kinnamos saw this, he sprang into the saddle
1275 and galloped at me to give me a blow with his sword;
      but I gave his steed a good blow on the head with my stick

---

1267 Digenis has asked for his surcoat, presumably made of padded leather (Kolias,
1988, 59), to replace his shield but is brought only his tunic, a lighter garment which
offers no real protection: the girl's action is taken as hostile (contrast G6.244–8).

καὶ μὲ τὸν καβαλάρην της ἔπεσεν ἔμπροσθέν μου.
Καὶ ἐγὼ πάλι τὸν ἔλεγα ἂς σηκωθῇ, μὴ κεῖται:
«Ἐγείρου ἀπ' αὖτου, Κίνναμε· κειτόμενον οὐ κρῶ σε·   G6.266
1280 ἄμε, περισωρεύθητι καί, ἂν θέλης, πάλιν ἔλα.»

Γοργὸν πάλιν σηκώνεται, πηδᾶ, καβαλικεύει
καὶ ἐπῆρεν τὸ κοντάριν του, τρανὰ ἐπεγυρίστην
καὶ σύντομα ἐπιλάλησεν τὴν κονταρέαν μὲ δώσει·
καὶ τὸ κοντάριν του ἔριψα ἀπὸ τὴν φάραν κάτω
1285 καὶ τὸν ἀγκώναν του ἥπλωσεν 'ς τὸν κάμπον ὡς σκουτέλιν.
Καὶ ἐγὼ ταῦτα τὸν ἔλεγα ἂς σηκωθῇ, μὴ κεῖται:
«Ἐγείρου ἀπ' αὖτου, Κίνναμε, κειⁱτόμενον οὐ κρῶ σε.»   176r   G6.266
Καὶ ὡς εἶδεν ὁ Φιλοπαπποὺς, κειτόμενος θαυμάζει·
«Εὐλόγησεν σου ὁ Θεός, νεώτερε, τὴν ἀνδρείαν,
1290 ν' ἀξιωθῇς νὰ χαίρεσαι τὰ ἔτη τῆς ζωῆς σου·   G4.758
καὶ ἂν οὐκ ἔναι εἰς λύπην σου καὶ οὐκ ἔναι πρὸς χολήν σου,
ὅρισε <μας> νὰ ἔλθωμεν νὰ στέκωμεν μεδ' ἔσου
καὶ κεφαλὴν νὰ σὲ ἔχωμεν εἰς ὅλα τὰ φουσάτα
καὶ εἰς τοὺς ἀπελάτας,
1295 νὰ κάμωμεν ταξίδια ὅπου καὶ ἂν μᾶς ὁρίσης
καὶ σὺ νὰ μεταβάλλεσαι μετὰ τῆς ποθητῆς σου.»
Καὶ τότε τὸν ἐλάλησα κενοδοξούμενός τον:
«Ἐγείρου ἀπ' αὖτου, Φ'λοπαπποῦ, καὶ ὄνειρα μὴ βλέπης·   G6.283
ἐγὼ μονογενὴς εἶμαι καὶ μόνος θέλω ὁδεύειν   G6.288-9
1300 καὶ μόνος κόρην ἔλαβα καὶ τίποτα οὐ χρήζω.
Ποτέ μου οὐκ ἐσυνήθισα ἀνδραγαθεῖν μὲ ἄλλους.
Ἔπαρε τὰ φουσάτα σου καὶ τοὺς καλούς σου ἀγούρους
καὶ ὑπᾶτε, κυνηγήσετε ὅπου εἶστε μαθημένοι
καὶ ἐγὼ καὶ τὸ κοράσιον μου νὰ εἴμεθεν ἀντάμα,

1277 ἔπεσεν Alexiou, note, cf. Z3113: ἔπεσαν E
1279 σε Hesseling: σου E
1280 περισωρεύθητι corr., cf. Z3116: περισορεύτητε E   ἂν θέλης, πάλιν Trapp: πάλιν ἂν θέλης E
1283 τὴν Alexiou: καὶ E
1285 'ς Trapp: εἰς E
1289 νεώτερε Alexiou: νεότερε τὴν περισήν σου E
1292 μας added by Trapp
1293 κεφαλὴν νὰ σε ἔχωμεν Alexiou: να σε ἔχωμεν κεφαλὴν, ἀπάνου E
1297 κενοδοξούμενός Alexiou: καὶ νοδοξούμενόν E
1298 Φ'λοπαπποῦ Alexiou: φιλοπαποῦ E
1299 ἐγὼ Alexiou: ἀμὴ ἐγὼ E
1300 μόνος Alexiou, note: μόνην E

and it fell with its rider in front of me.
Then I told him to get up, not to lie down:
"Rise up from there, Kinnamos; I won't hit you when you're down.
1280 Come on, pull yourself together and if you want to, have another go."

He got up again quickly, he sprang into the saddle
and seized his spear; he turned around neatly
and briskly galloped up to give me a blow with the spear.
But I knocked his spear down under his steed
1285 and his elbow was shattered on the ground like a broken pot.
I told him at once to get up, not to lie down:
"Rise up from there, Kinnamos; I won't hit you when you're down."
    When Philopappous saw this as he lay there, he was amazed:
"God has blessed your bravery, young man;
1290 may you be granted happiness all the years of your life.
But if it does not distress you and does not enrage you,
tell us to come and join with you
so that we have you as our head over the whole army
                            and the guerrillas,
1295 so that we can make expeditions wherever you tell us
and you may move around with your beloved."
    So then I said to him, treating him with contempt:
"Rise up from there, Philopappous, and stop dreaming.
I am an only child and I wish to travel on my own;
1300 on my own I won my girl and I need nothing else.
I have never been in the habit of performing valiant deeds with others.
Take your armies and your fine youngsters
and go and hunt where you know what you are doing;
I and my girl will be together

1305 ὅτι οὓς ἔσμιξεν ὁ Θεὸς ἄνθρωποι οὐ χωρίζουν·　　　　G6.143
　　　ὥστε ἔναι ὁ Θεὸς 'ς τοὺς οὐρανοὺς καὶ διακρατεῖ τὸν κόσμον,
　　　ἄνθρωπος οὐ χωρίζει με ἀπὸ τῆς ποθητῆς μου.
　　　Ἐδά, ἂν πάλι θέλετε †νὰ μὲ δοκιμάσετε,†
　　　ὑπᾶτε καὶ σωρεύσετε ἀπείρους ἀπελάτες, | 176v
1310 ὅπου οὐκ οἶδαν τὴν πεῖραν <μου> καὶ ἐμὲν οὐκ ἐγνωρίζουν,　　G6.294
　　　καὶ ἐγὼ ὧδε νὰ σᾶς καρτερῶ καὶ νὰ σᾶς περιμένω
　　　<καὶ νὰ> ἔχω καὶ τὰ ἄλογα καὶ τὰ ἅρματά μου ὅλα
　　　καὶ τότε νὰ νοήσετε πῶς κρῶ καὶ καβαλάρης.»
　　　Καὶ ἐπῆρεν ὁ Φιλοπαππούς τὰ δύο παλληκάρια
1315 καὶ ἐκεῖθεν ἐπηγαίνασιν ὅθεν καὶ ὅπου ἦλθαν.

　　　Καὶ τότε ἀπεξέβηκαν ὡς ἀπὸ μίλιν ἕνα
　　　καὶ οἱ τρεῖς ἀπομαζώχθησαν καὶ εἰς ἕναν τόπον στέκουν·　　G6.311
　　　στέκουν καὶ διαλογίζουνται καὶ πρὸς ἀλλήλους λέγουν:
　　　«Πῶς ἐσυνέβην εἰς ἐμᾶς καὶ ἀτιμώθη ἡ ἀνδρεία μας;
1320 Εἰς τὸν Ἀφράτην ποταμόν, κάτω εἰς τὸ Σαμουσάτο,
　　　πέντε χιλιάδες ηὗραν μας καὶ οὐ κατεχώρισάν μας
　　　καὶ πάλιν ἐκρατοῦμαν τους, κανεὶς οὐκ ἐντραλίσθην·
　　　καὶ αὐτὸς ὡς ἦτον μοναχός, πεζὸς μὲ τὸ καλίκιν
　　　καὶ μὲ τὸ μονα|πλούτσικον, καὶ πῶς μᾶς εἶχεν τρέψειν;»　177r
1325 Καὶ τότε †ὁ γέροντας†, ἄκο τὸ τί τοὺς λέγει:
　　　«Οὗτος οὐκ ἔστιν ἄνθρωπος ἀπὸ τὸν κόσμον τοῦτον·　　G4.158
　　　νὰ μὴ φοβᾶται τὰς πληγάς, νὰ μὴ φοβᾶται ξίφη.
　　　Αὐτὸς <καὶ> γὰρ θηρίον ἔνι καὶ τὸν τόπον του βλέπει.»
　　　Καὶ ὁ γέρων ὁ Φιλοπαππούς πάλιν τὰ <τέ>τοια λέγει:
1330 «Αὐτὰ ὅλα τὰ λέγετε παρηγορίες μας εἶναι·
　　　ἀμὴ εἶδα καλὸν νεώτερον τὸν ὁ κόσμος οὐκ ἔχει,

1306 'ς Trapp: εἰς E
1308 πάλι θέλετε Alexiou: θέλετε πάλι E　δοκιμάσετε Hesseling: κιμάσετε E. cf.
Mackridge, 1993b, 336
1310 μου added by Kalonaros
1312 καὶ νὰ added by Alexiou　ἄλογα Alexiou: ἀλογά μου E
1315 ὅπου Trapp: ὁποὺ E
1319 ἀτιμώθη ἡ ἀνδρεία Alexiou: ἀτίμοσε τὴν ἀνδρίαν E
1321 ηὗραν μας Alexiou: μας ἥβρικαν E
1324 μοναπλούτσικον Kalonaros: μουναπλούτζηκων E　τρέψειν Hesseling: τέρψιν E
1325 γέροντας E: a name may be concealed here
1326 τοῦτον Alexiou: τοῦτο E
1328 καὶ added by Alexiou
1329 τὰ τέτοια Karayanni, 1976, 116: τάτια E

1305 because those whom God has joined men will not separate.
　　　As long as God is in the heavens and controls the world,
　　　no man will separate me from my beloved.
　　　Now, if you want to test me again,
　　　come and collect up inexperienced guerrillas
1310 who have no experience of me and don't know me,
　　　and I'll expect you here and wait for you;
　　　I'll have my horses and all my weapons,
　　　and then you will understand what blows I can also strike from
　　　　　horseback."
　　　So Philopappous took the two brave youths
1315 and they went back where they had come from.

　　　And then they went about a mile away
　　　and the three huddled together and stood in the one place;
　　　they stood and held a discussion, and said to each other:
　　　"How can this have happened to us, that our bravery has been
　　　　　dishonoured?
1320 By the river Euphrates, down at Samosata,
　　　five thousand men encountered us and could not divide us,
　　　while we in turn defeated them; not one of us was thrown into
　　　　　confusion.
　　　Yet this man, on his own, on foot and in boots,
　　　and in a simple tunic, how could he have routed us?"
1325 And then listen to what the old man said to them:
　　　"This is not a man from this world
　　　– not to be afraid of wounds, not to be afraid of swords!
　　　This is a wild beast and he is watching over his territory."
　　　And old Philopappous in his turn said this:
1330 "Everything you say is just to console us.
　　　But what I saw was a fine young man, such as the world does not
　　　　　possess,

1305 The repetition of Matthew 19.6 further reinforces the motif of the indissolubility of
marriage.
1313 Previously he had only been on foot, but was victorious nonetheless.
1325 Logically, in view of the speech at 1331 ff., these lines must be spoken by one or
more of the other guerrillas, not by 'the old man' (Philopappous).

νὰ μὴν τοῦ λείπη τίποτες, ἔν' περιγυρισμένος.
Τοῦτα ὁ Θεὸς τοῦ τὰ ἔδωκεν, ἔχει μέγιστον κάλλος
                 καὶ ἀνδρείαν περισσοτέραν
1335 καὶ τόλμην ὑπὲρ ἅπασαν καὶ γνώμην θηριώδην.
Καλόν μας τοῦτο ἐγίνετον
ὅτι οὐκ ἔτυχαν ἄνθρωποι, νὰ στέκουν νὰ γελοῦσιν.
Καὶ τὸ ὄνομαν τὸ ἐλάβαμεν ἀπὸ τοὺς ἀπελάτας   G6.341
σήμερον τὸ ἐχάσαμεν καὶ οὐ χρήζουν μας πλέον.
1340 Ἀμὴ ἂν ἀκοῦτε λόγους μου καὶ ἐμπῆτε εἰς τὴν βουλήν μου,
μὴ τὸ καταφρονέσωμεν καὶ ἐπάρη το συνήθειον
καὶ οὐ μὴ μᾶς ἀφῆ ἀπὸ τοῦ νῦν ποιεῖν ἀνδραγαθίας.
Ἀμὴ ἂς ποίσωμεν καπνὸν νὰ ἔλθουν οἱ ἀπελάτες,
καπνὸν πολὺν ἂς ποίσωμεν καὶ ἂν ζοῦσι, νὰ ἐπανέλθουν·
1345 ἴσως καὶ ἂν ἐκαυχήσατο, ἐκείνους οὐ μὴ ἐδεῖρεν.»   G6.346
Καὶ εἰς τὸ βουνὶν ὑπήγασιν καὶ ἐποῖκαν τὸ σημάδιν,
καὶ τρία μερόνυκτα ἧπτασιν, κανεὶς οὐδὲν | ἐφάνη·   177v
καὶ τότε <οἱ> ἀπελάται οἱ δύο, Κίνναμος καὶ Γιαννάκης,
Φιλοπαππποῦν τὸν γέροντα οὕτως τὸν συντυχαίνουν:
1350 «Πολλὰ μᾶς ἐδοκίμασες καὶ ἐπιλέκτους μᾶς ηὗρες·
ἐφ' ὅσον ἔδειρεν ἐμᾶς, τοὺς ἄλλους τί γυρεύεις;
Ἀμὴ ἄγωμε εἰς τὴν Μαξιμοῦ καὶ παρακάλεσέ την,
καὶ ἄμποτε νὰ παρακληθῆ καὶ νὰ μᾶς ἐπακούση·
καὶ ἐκείνη ἔχει λαὸν πολὺν καὶ νὰ μᾶς ἐπακούση.   G6.377
1355 Καὶ νὰ τὸν παραπέσωμεν ἄγνωστα καὶ τὴν νύκταν
καὶ νὰ τόνε παιδεύσωμεν καὶ οὐ μὴ μᾶς κόπτη ὁ πόνος.»
Καὶ τότε καὶ ὁ Φιλοπαπποὺς πηδᾶ, καβαλικεύει,
μόνος τὴν στράταν ἔπιασεν, 'ς τὴν Μαξιμοὺν ὑπάγει.   G6.385
Καὶ ὡς τὸν εἶδεν ἡ Μαξιμού, πλειστάκις ἐταράχθη·
1360 τὸν Μιλιμίτην ἔστειλεν καὶ προσυπήντησέ του:

1332 νὰ μὴν τοῦ λείπη τίποτες, ἔν' περιγυρισμένος Alexiou: ἔνε περιγυρισμένος· να μὴν τοῦ λύπη τίποτες E
1333 μέγιστον κάλλος Hesseling: γὰρ μεγίστην καλὴν E μεγίστην κάλλην Alexiou
1337 οὐκ corr.: οὐδὲν E   νὰ² Alexiou: να μας E
1339 πλέον Trapp: ἄλλον πλέον E
1345 ἐδεῖρεν Alexiou: τοὺς δήρι E
1348 οἱ ἀπελάται οἱ δύο Alexiou: οἱ δύο ἀπελάτες E
1350 ἐδοκίμασες . . . ηὗρες Xanthoudidis, 1912, 564: ἐδοκίμασεν . . . ἤβρεν E
1352 παρακάλεσέ Hesseling: παρεκάλεσέ E
1354 ἐκείνη Hesseling: ἐκήνην E   ἔχει λαὸν πολὺν Trapp: λαὸν πολλὴν ἔχει E
1356 τόνε παιδεύσωμεν Kalonaros: τὸ ἐπαιδεύσωμεν E
1358 ἔπιασεν, 'ς Trapp: ἐπίασεν· εἰς E
1359 πλειστάκις E: πολλὰ τὸ Alexiou, cf. E1363
1360 ἔστειλεν Kalonaros: ἔστειλαν E

who lacks nothing – he is well turned out.
God has granted him all this: he has the greatest good looks
                 and prodigious bravery
1335 and surpassing daring and a savage intelligence.
It was a good thing for us
that there was no one around to stand and laugh.
As for the reputation we had achieved among the guerrillas,
today we lost it and they don't need us any more.
1340 But if you listen to my words and join in my plan,
let us not belittle the matter and allow him to make a habit
from now on of preventing us performing valiant deeds.
But let's make smoke to bring the guerrillas in;
let's make a lot of smoke and if they are still alive, they will come back.
1345 Perhaps, if he was boasting, he hasn't thrashed them after all."
    So they went to the mountain and set off the beacon;
for three days and nights they kept it burning, but no one appeared.
Then the two guerrillas, Kinnamos and Giannakis,
addressed old Philopappous thus:
1350 "You have tested us on many occasions and found us excellent;
since he thrashed us, why are you looking for the others?
But let's go to Maximou and you ask her,
and perhaps she will be persuaded and will listen to us.
She has many troops and she will listen to us.
1355 Let's make a secret attack on him unexpectedly by night,
and let's teach him a lesson so that our grief won't break our hearts."
    Then Philopappous sprang into the saddle,
he set off on his journey on his own, he went to Maximou.
When Maximou saw him, she was extremely disturbed.
1360 She sent Milimitsis and he met him:

«Καλῶς ἦλθες, Φιλοπαππού, γεράκιν μου μουτάτον.
Τὰ παλληκάρια ποῦ ἄφηκες, Γιαννάκην καὶ τὸν Λέον,
καὶ ἐσὺ πῶς ἦλθες μοναχός; Πολλὰ τὸ ἐταράχθην·
ἔθλιψες τὴν καρδίαν μου καὶ ἐπαραπόνεσές με.»
1365   Καὶ ὁ γέρων ὁ Φιλοπαππούς ψευδεῖς λόγους τῆς εἶπεν:
«Εἰς τὰ βουνὰ ἐπερίτρεχα καὶ κορυφὰς ὀρέων,
ἐθεώρουν <τότε> τὰ κλαδία καὶ τὰς στενὰς κλεισούρας,
ἐθεώρουν καὶ τοὺς λέοντας ἀπέσω εἰς | τὸ καλάμιν 178r
καὶ τοὺς ἐλάφους ἔβλεπα ἀπέσω εἰς τὸ ἄλσος
1370   καὶ ὀρδινιαζόμουν νὰ ἐμπῶ <καὶ> νὰ τὰ πολεμήσω
καὶ ἐσὺ ἐγνωρίζεις με καλὰ ὅτι ὀκνηρὸς οὐκ εἶμαι·
ἔφθασαν οἱ ἀπελάτες μου, μηνύματα μὲ φέρνουν:
τὴν κόρην τὴν ἐφύλαγα λόγου τοῦ Γιαννακίου,   G6.415
ὁ Ἀκρίτης τὴν ἀφήρπαξεν καὶ χαίρεται μετ' αὔτην
1375   καὶ ηὗρε λιβάδια ἔνδροσα, ὡραῖα κατάσκια δένδρη
καὶ τὰ κυνήγια ὑπέρπλουτα ὡς ἤθελεν καὶ ἐπόθειν,
ἐλάφους τε καὶ συαγροὺς καὶ πέρδικας ὡραίας·
καταφιλεῖ τὴν λυγερὴν καὶ χαίρεται μετ' αὔτης.
Καὶ ἂν θέλης, θεραπεύσωμεν Γιαννάκην καὶ τὸν Λέον,
1380   τὸν Κίνναμον τὸν θαυμαστόν, κ' ἐμὲν τὸν σὸν ἱκέτην.
Κόπιασε, αὐθέντρια καὶ κυρά, καὶ ἂς ποίσωμεν δουλείαν
καὶ ἂς θαραπευθοῦμεν καὶ ἡμεῖς διὰ τὴν σὴν ἀγάπην,
ὅτι οὐκ ἐπερηφάνευσες κοπιάσειν εἰς δουλείαν.»
Καὶ ὡς τὸ ἤκουσεν ἡ Μαξιμού, φωνὴν μεγάλην σύρνει:
1385   «Φιλοπαππού, γνωρίζεις με παρὰ τοὺς ἄλλους πλέον
καὶ ἐν ἀκριβείᾳ νὰ τὸ εἰπῆς τὸ πῶς μὲ ἐγνωρίζεις,
ὅτι ὅπου καὶ ἂν εὑρέθημαν, ἐμέναν προσκαλοῦνται·
πολέμους γὰρ καὶ ἀπειλὰς καὶ θορυβὰς μεγάλας
ἡ Μαξιμοὺ οὐ φοβεῖται τους, πάντες ἂς τὸ γιλνώσκουν· 178v
1390   καὶ ἐδάρτε, Φιλοπαππού, θέλεις μὲ κοπιάσει;

1362 Τὰ παλληκάρια ποῦ ἄφηκες Alexiou: ποῦ ἄφικες τὰς παληκαρία σου E
1363 τὸ ἐταράχθην Xanthoudidis, 1912, 565: τὸν ἐταράχθη E
1366 ὀρέων Krumbacher, 1904, 331: τῶν ὀρέων E
1367 τότε added
1370 ἐμπῶ Alexiou: ἔμπω E καὶ added
1374 τὴν Hesseling: τῆς E
1378 μετ' αὔτης E: μετ' αὔτην Alexiou, cf. E1374
1379 θεραπεύσωμεν Alexiou: κηρὰν αθεραπεύσωμεν E
1381 Κόπιασε Alexiou: κοπίασε E
1383 ἐπερηφάνευσες Politis, 1973, 347: ἐπεριφάνευσεν E
1388 θορυβὰς Alexiou: θόριβας E
1389 πάντες Hesseling: πάντας E
1390 ἐδάρτε E: ἐδάρτε ἐσύ Alexiou

"Welcome, Philopappous, my moulting hawk!
Where have you left your brave warriors, Giannakis and Leos,
and why have you come on your own? I have been very disturbed by
    this.
You have grieved my heart and caused me pain."
1365   Old Philopappous spoke lying words to her:
"I was roaming the hills and the mountain peaks,
I was gazing then at the branches and the narrow passes,
I was gazing also at the lions in the reed-bed,
I saw deer in the grove,
1370 and I was getting myself ready to go off to do battle with them,
for you are well aware that I am not lazy;
my guerrillas turned up, bringing me messages:
the girl I was keeping for Giannakis,
Akritis the Frontiersman had abducted her and was taking his
    pleasure with her;
1375 he has found well watered meadows, beautiful shady trees
and hunting as abundant as he could wish or desire,
deer and wild boar and beautiful partridges;
he is kissing the slender girl and taking his pleasure with her.
But if you are willing, let's give assistance to Giannakis and Leos,
1380 to the marvellous Kinnamos, and to me, your suppliant.
Come on, my mistress and lady, and let's get some work done
and let's all find assistance through your love,
since you have not been too proud to come to do some work."
    When Maximou heard this, she raised a great shout:
1385 "Philopappous, you know me better than anyone else,
and you really can say that you know me,
that wherever I may be they can call on me;
for wars and threats and great uproars
– everyone should know that Maximou is not afraid of them;
1390 and now, Philopappous, are you going to tire me out?

1361 Even if 'moulting' is to be construed as a reference to baldness the epithet does not
seem very complimentary: moulting hawks were at a disadvantage.
1374 Philopappous reveals the identity of the prospective opponent, whose reputation
seems unknown to Maximou.
1383 The implication (cf. E809 and G6.408) is that the girl represents the ultimate prey
(Ricks, 1989b).

Ἀπέλθει θέλω καὶ ἐγὼ καὶ νὰ τὸν δοκιμάσω
καὶ νὰ τὸν κοπανίσωμεν, νὰ πάρωμεν τὴν κόρην.
Νὰ κοπιάσω καὶ ἐγὼ καὶ ὅλα μου τὰ φουσάτα
καὶ ἂν οὐ τὸν εὔρωμεν ἐκεῖ, ἔδε ἀνομία μεγάλη.
1395 Νὰ σοῦ ὑπακούσω, γέροντα, καὶ νὰ ἔλθω μετὰ σένα·
μὰ τὴν ἀνδρείαν τὴν περισσήν, τὴν ὁ Θεὸς μοῦ ἐδῶκεν,
'ς τὸν οὐρανὸν καὶ ἂν ἀνεβῆ, εἰς τὰ νέφη καὶ ἂν δράμη,
'ς τὴν θάλασσαν καὶ ἂν περπατῆ, ἡ κόρη οὐκ ἐξεγλεῖ μου.»
Τὸν Μιλιμίτσην ἔκραξεν, βουλεύεται μετ᾽ αὖτον:
1400 «Ὁ γέρων ὁ Φιλοπαππούς πάλιν κυνήγια ἔχει   G6.430-1
καὶ κράζει μας νὰ ἀπέλθωμεν καὶ ἐμεῖς <ὁμοῦ> μετ᾽ αὖτον·
καὶ ὑπάγετε, σωρεύσετε χιλίους ἀπελάτας
καὶ ἀπ᾽ τοὺς χιλίους μοῦ χώρισε κἂν ἑκατὸν ἀγούρους   G6.435
καὶ ἂς ἔχουν ἄρματα καλά, ἱππάρια ἀφιρωμένα,   G6.436
1405 καὶ ἂς εἶναι περιγυριστοί, νὰ κροῦν καλὰς ραβδέας
καὶ κονταρέας ἔμνοστας, σπαθέας αἱματωμένας
καὶ αὐτὸν νὰ καταλάχωμεν, τὸν ἄγουρον τὸν λέγουν,
νὰ τόνε κοπανίσωμεν, νὰ ἐπάρωμεν τὴν κόρην.»
Καὶ ὁ Μιλιμίτσης ἔποικεν ὡς ἐπαρακειλεύθη,   179r
1410 καὶ ἐπῆρε τους ἡ Μαξιμοῦ καὶ ἔρχεται εἰς ἐμέναν.
Καὶ ἀπέτις ἐξέβηκαν κανένα μίλι, δύο,
εὐθὺς οἱ ἀπελάτες της, Κίνναμος καὶ Γιαννάκης,
ἐπῆραν τὸ στρατὶν στρατὶν καὶ προσυπήντησάν της:
«Καλῶς ἦρθες, κυρία μου, αὐθέντρια εὐγενεστάτη,
1415 ὁ Θεός ἐσέναν ἔπεψεν, ἀνδρεία τῶν ἀπελάτων.»
Τότε στραφοῦσα ἡ Μαξιμοῦ τοὺς ἀπελάτας λέγει:
«Καλῶς τὰ παλληκάρια μου, Γιαννάκην καὶ τὸν Λέον·
διατί ἐπαροκνήσατε καὶ οὐκ ἤλθατε εἰς ἐμέναν;

1391 Ἀπέλθει corr.: ἔλθη E
1392 κοπανίσωμεν Trapp, cf. E1408: κοπανίσω E
1393 ἐγὼ Spadaro, 1989, 180–1: τοὺς καβαλάρους μου E
1394 οὐ Alexiou: ουδὲν E
1396 μὰ Alexiou, note: μὲ E
1397 'ς Trapp: εἰς E
1398 'ς Trapp: εἰς E   περπατῆ Trapp: περιπατῆ E
1399 βουλεύεται Hesseling: καὶ βούλετε E
1401 ὁμοῦ added by Alexiou   αὖτον Alexiou, note: ἀυτοῦνον E
1403 ἀπ᾽ Alexiou: ἀπὸ E
1405 ἂς εἶναι περιγυριστοί Xanthoudidis, 1912, 566: ἀσύνεπεριγύριστὴ E
1408 τόνε κοπανίσωμεν Kalonaros: τὸν ἐκοπανίσομεν E
1409 ἔποικεν ὡς Alexiou: ἐποίησεν· καθὼς E
1411 ἐξέβηκαν E: ἀπεξέβηκαν Alexiou
1416 στραφοῦσα Hesseling, cf. E1502: στραφοῦ E στραφεῖσα Alexiou
1418 ἐπαροκνήσατε Hesseling: οὐκ επαρεκνίσατε E   εἰς Trapp: πρὸς E

I too want to set off and test him
and for us to batter him and take the girl.
I shall come myself and all my armies too
and if we don't find him there, that's a great injustice.
1395 I shall listen to you, old man, and I'll come with you:
by the prodigious bravery which God has given me,
even if she rises up to the heavens, even if she runs through the clouds,
even if she walks on the sea, the girl won't slip past me."
   She called out to Milimitsis, she consulted him:
1400 "Old Philopappous has some prey once again,
and is calling on us to go with him as well.
So go and collect a thousand guerrillas,
and from the thousand select for me about a hundred youngsters;
they should have fine weapons and armoured horses,
1405 and they should be well turned out, able to give good blows with sticks
and splendid spear-thrusts and bloody cuts with the sword;
then let's catch up with him, the youngster they are talking about,
and batter him and take the girl."
   Milimitsis did as he was asked,
1410 and Maximou took them and set off against me.
When they had travelled about a mile or two,
immediately her guerrillas Kinnamos and Giannakis
came along the route and met her:
"Welcome, my lady, most high-born mistress;
1415 it is God who has sent you, the bravery of the guerrillas."
   Then Maximou, turning round, said to the guerrillas:
"Greetings, my brave youths, Giannakis and Leos;
why were you lazy and didn't come to me?

1397-8 Cf. *Livistros* E522 ff. A good example of triple patterning in folk-song style, here with biblical overtones.
1403-4 See the note at G6.438-45.
1412 Why Kinnamos Leos and Giannakis have a special relationship to Maximou is not clear; cf. G6.393 where they are Philopappous' sons.

†Ἐγὼ ὡς γυναῖκα εἶμαι ἀλλὰ† οὐκ ὤκνησα τοῦ νὰ ἔλθω·
1420 ἀπέλθω ἔχω καὶ ἐγὼ καὶ νὰ σᾶς θαραπεύσω.»
Καὶ ἐγὼ πάντα εἶχα τὸν σκοπὸν καὶ πάντα ἀπάντεχά τους·
ὁρίζω τοὺς ἀγούρους μου καὶ φέρνουν μου φαρία,
τέσσερα <φέρνουν> φοβερὰ πουλάρια ἐκ τῶν φαρίων
καὶ ἦσαν καὶ τὰ τέσσερα ρωμαϊκὰ κουρεμένα.
1425 Καὶ τὰ τέσσερα ὑπόστρωσα καὶ ὑποχαλίνωσά τα
καὶ ἔμπροσθεν εἰς τὴν τέντα μου βόσκουν εἰς τὸ λιβάδιν.
Καὶ ἐστάθην καὶ ἐβλέπω τους τὸ πότε θέλουν ἔλθει·
καὶ κτύπον ἤκουσα πολύν, μέγαν τῶν σκουταρίων
καὶ εἰς τὴν ψυχήν μου ἔλεγα: «Αὐτοί 'ναι καὶ ἀποσώνουν.»
1430 Καὶ βλέπω τὸν | Φιλοπαππού μετὰ τὸν Μιλιμίτσην 179v G6.479
καὶ ἀκούω καὶ λέγουν ὡς δι' ἐμὲν ἀπρεπεστάτους λόγους:
«Ἐδῶ ἂς τὸν γυρεύσωμεν, ὁποὺ τὴν κόρην ἔχει, G6.484
καὶ ἂς τὸν περιπέσωμεν, 'ς τὴν μέσην του νὰ ὑπᾶμεν,
πρὶν νοήση ὁ νεώτερος καὶ ἐπάρη τ' ἄρματά του.»
1435 Στραφεὶς τότε ὁ πρωτοληστὴς τὸν γέροντα ὑβρίζει:
«Εἰς ἑκατὸν ἐπιλεκτοὺς ποτὲ οὐκ ἐφοβήθην
καὶ ἐδάρτε εἰς ἕναν μοναχὸν θέλω στέκει νὰ ἐβλέπω; G6.493
Καὶ μετὰ ποῖον πρόσωπον τὴν Μαξιμοὺ νὰ ἰδοῦμεν;»
Καὶ ἀγνώστως εἶδα γαληνὰ καὶ ἔρχουνταν πρὸς ἐμέναν.
1440 Πηδῶ κ' ἐκαβαλίκευσα τὴν θαυμαστὴν τὴν φάραν
καὶ ὀλίγον ἀπεξέβηκα καὶ ἐστάθην νὰ μὲ δοῦσιν·
καὶ τὸ ἰδεῖν με ὁ Φ'λοπαππούς παραμερέαν ἐστάθην,
ὅτι καλὰ ἐγνώριζεν τὸ πῶς τὸν θαραπεύω·
καὶ ὁ Μιλιμίτσης ὁ ληστὴς ἀπάνω μου ἐκατέβην·
1445 κοντάριν ἐμαλάκιζεν τὴν κονταρέαν μὲ δώσει, G6.504
καὶ τὸ κοντάριν του ἔριψα καὶ ἐδῶσα του ραβδέαν·

1421 πάντα¹ Kalonaros: πάντοτε E
1422 φέρνουν Hesseling: φέρνη E
1423 φέρνουν added by Alexiou
1425 Καὶ Alexiou: καὶ τότε καὶ E
1427 ἐστάθην Trapp: ἐστάθη ἐγὼ E καὶ ἐβλέπω E: κ' ἔβλεπα Alexiou
1431 λέγουν corr.: λέγουσιν E λέγουσι Karayanni, 1976, 117
1433 'ς Trapp: εἰς E
1435 Στραφεὶς τότε Spadaro, 1989, 181: τότε στραφῆς E
1437 στέκει E: στέκειν Alexiou
1439 ἀγνώστως Xanthoudidis, 1912, 566: ἀναγνῶστος E
1440 κ' ἐκαβαλίκευσα Hesseling: καὶ καβαλήκευσα E
1441 ἀπεξέβηκα Alexiou: ἐπεξέβηκα E ἐστάθην Hesseling: ἐστάθη E
1442 Φ'λοπαππούς Politis, 1973, 347: φιλοπαπούς E

I am a woman but I wasn't too lazy to come.
1420 I shall come out to assist you."
        I was always keeping watch and always expecting them.
        I gave orders to my youngsters and they brought me chargers,
        they brought four fearsome colts from among the chargers,
        and all four were trimmed in the Roman manner.
1425 I saddled the four of them and put bridles on them,
        and they grazed in the meadow in front of my tent.
        I stood and watched for when the guerrillas would come.
        Then I heard a loud noise, a great clattering of shields
        and I said in my heart: "Here they are and they are getting near."
1430   I saw Philopappous with Milimitsis,
        and I heard them saying most unbecoming things about me:
        "Let's search here for him, the one who's got the girl,
        and let's attack him and get to close quarters
        before the young man realises and picks up his weapons."
1435   Then the brigand chief turned and abused the old man:
        "I have never been frightened in front of a hundred picked men
        and now am I about to stand on my guard in front of one man on
            his own?
        However should we have the face to look at Maximou?"
        Without them realising, I quietly watched them coming towards
            me.
1440 I sprang into the saddle on my marvellous steed
        and I went out for a short distance and stood still for them to see me:
        on seeing me Philopappous stood to one side
        because he well knew how I would treat him,
        but the brigand Milimitsis charged at me.
1445 He was wielding a spear to strike me with it,
        but I flung his spear aside and struck him with my stick;

1422 This is the first time that 'youngsters' have appeared with Digenis, rather than
with the emir.
1429 Trapp moves the arming-scene of E1461–72 to this point (presumably justified by
Z3556–7 and Z's omission of this scene later), but note that the guerrillas' comments at
1434 are predicated on Digenis being unarmed. Repeated arming scenes are
characteristic of heroic poetry (Fenik, 1991, 52–4).
1435 There seems to be a distinction between the guerrillas, led by Philopappous, and
the brigands, led by Milimitsis though presumably under Maximou's command and
called guerrillas elsewhere.

μάθε καὶ πῶς τὸν ἔδωσα 'ς τὰς δισσουμέας ἀπάνω
καὶ σύσσελον τὸν ἔριψα ἀπὸ τὴν φάραν κάτω. |

180r

Καὶ ἐγὼ ἤλπιζα νὰ σηκωθῆ, νὰ ἔλθη πρὸς ἐμέναν·
1450   εἶχα τὸν νοῦν μου εἰς αὖτον.
Καὶ ὁ γέρων ὁ Φιλοπαππούς ἀπὸ πλαγίου μου ἦλθεν   G6.509
καὶ κονταρέαν μὲ ἔδωκεν τὴν φάραν 'ς τὰ μηρία   G6.510
καὶ ἐπεσφίκτηκεν πολλὰ καὶ ἐλάκτισεν μεγάλως·
καὶ εὐθὺς ἐκοντογύρισα καὶ βλέπω τον καὶ φεύγει
1455 καὶ τότε τὸν ἐλάλησα φωνὴν ἀπὸ μακρόθεν:
«Ἀνάμενέ με, Φ'λοπαππού, οὐδ' ἐντρέπεσαι νὰ φεύγης;
Ἀνάμενε καὶ ἅς δώσωμεν, χαρῆς καὶ ἅς δευτερώσης,
ὅτι ἔβλεπά σε ταπεινὸν καὶ ὡσὰν ὑποθλιμμένον·
καὶ ἐδὰ βλέπω ἐπλανέθηκα, Φιλοπαππού μου, γέρον,
1460 καὶ ἐδὰ βλέπω ἐλυσσίασες καὶ ἐκρυφοδάκησές με.»   G6.516
Καὶ ἐγὼ γοργὸν ἐγύρισα καὶ ἐφόρεσα λουρίκιν,
βιατάριν ἔβαλα τερπνόν, καθάριον βαγδαΐτην,
πράσινον ἀραβίτικον ἀπάνω εἰς τὸ λουρίκιν·
οἱ ρίζες ἦσαν πιθαμή, ὁλόχρυσα λεοντάρια,
1465 καὶ τὰ κολμπία ὁλοχύμευτα, μὲ τὸ μαργαριτάριν. 180v G4.222, 240, 792
Καὶ ἐστράφηκα καὶ εἶδα τους ὅλους ἀπὸ μακρόθεν
καὶ ἔρχουντα καὶ ἤβλεπαν, ὡς καὶ τὸ δίκαιον εἶχαν,
καὶ τὰ κοντάρια ἐχύνασιν καὶ ἤρχοντα πρὸς ἐμέναν.
Καὶ ἐγὼ γοργὸν ἐπήδησα καὶ ἐπῆρα μίαν σέλαν·
1470 στρώνω πουλάριν θαυμαστόν, πουλάριν κουρεμένον,
ρωμαϊκόν, πανώραιον, ἦτον καὶ τετραέτης
καὶ ἔστρωσα καὶ ἐχαλίνωσα καὶ ἐκαβαλίκευσά το

1447 'ς Trapp: εἰς E
1450 αὖτον Ricks: αὖτους E
1452 'ς Trapp: εἰς E
1453 ἐπεσφίκτηκεν Xanthoudidis, 1912, 567: ἐπεσφίκτισεν E
1456 Φ'λοπαππού Politis, 1973, 347: φιλοπαπού E   οὐδ' ἐντρέπεσαι E: perhaps δὲν
ντρέπεσαι
1459 βλέπω Politis, 1973, 344: βλέπω ὅτι E   ἐπλανέθηκα Alexiou: ἐπλανέθηκες E
1460 βλέπω Alexiou: βλέπω ὅτι E
1462 βαγδαΐτην Kalonaros: μαγδαΐτην E
1464 πιθαμή Alexiou: πιθαμήν E
1465 κομπία Trapp: κομπία ἦσαν E
1470 στρώνω Alexiou: καὶ ἔστροσα E
1472 καὶ ἐκαβαλίκευσά το Politis, 1973, 344: το καὶ ἐκαβαλήκευσα E

let me tell you how I struck him between the shoulder-blades
and I flung him down from his charger, saddle and all.

I expected him to get up, to attack me;
1450   my attention was on him.
But old Philopappous came up beside me
and gave me a spear thrust in my charger's haunches
and it pulled up in pain and kicked hard.
Immediately I turned around abruptly and saw him running away;
1455 then I let out a shout to him from a distance:
"Wait for me, Philopappous; aren't you ashamed to be running away?
Wait, let's fight; perhaps you should try again,
because I thought that you were feeble and somewhat distressed
but now I see that I had made a mistake, Philopappous, my old man,
1460 now I see that you have turned rabid and snapped at me
        unexpectedly."
        I turned round quickly and put on a breastplate,
I wore a delightful garment of pure Baghdad fabric,
of Arab green, over the breastplate;
the hem was some nine inches wide, with lions embroidered in gold,
1465 and the enamelled buttons were inlaid with pearls.
I turned and saw them all at a distance,
and they were coming up watchfully, as was right;
they brandished their spears and came at me.
But I quickly jumped up and seized a saddle;
1470 I saddled a marvellous colt, a trimmed colt,
Roman, very beautiful, and four years old;
I put a saddle and bridle on it and I mounted

1461 The climactic encounter demands the hero's most spectacular accoutrements, and
an opponent to match.

καὶ τὴν καλήν μου ἐλάλησα παραγγελίαν τοιαύτην:
τὸν τόπον νὰ παρεδιαβῆ, νὰ κατεβῆ ὀλίγον,
1475 νὰ βλέπη, νὰ στοχάζεται τὸ τί τοὺς θέλω κάμει·
καὶ λόγον τὴν ἐλάλησα, παραγγελίαν τοιαύτην:
«Καλή μου καὶ πανθαύμαστη, τὸ ἄνθος τῶν ἐρώτων,
κἂν ὅσοι μὲ ἀποπέφτουσι, βλέπε <νὰ> μὴ φωνιάξης
καὶ ἀκούσω τὴν φωνίτσα σου καὶ σκοτιστῶ εἰς ἐσέναν
1480 καὶ λάθη με καὶ δώσουν με σπαθέαν ἢ ραβδέαν
καὶ πάρη τους ἡ ὄρεξι καὶ ἔλθουν πρὸς ἐσέναν.»
Καὶ ἐγὼ . . . ἐστάθην εἰς λιθάριν
καὶ ἔμπηξα τὸ κοντάριν μου καὶ ἐστάθηκα καὶ ἐθεώρουν
τὸ πότε νὰ ἔλθουν εἰς ἐμὲν <Κίνναμος> καὶ Γιαννάκης
1485 καὶ σὺν <αὐτοῖς> καὶ <ἡ> Μαξιμοῦ καὶ ἦτον καὶ γαυριασμένη.
Φαρὶν ἐκαβαλίκευσε, πολλὰ ἦτον ὡραῖον· |
ἡ χύτη καὶ τὸ οὐράδιν του μὲ τὴν χινέαν βαμμένα, 181r   G6.553
τὰ τέσσερά του ὀνύχια ἀσήμιν τσαπωμένα,   G6.554
τὸ χαλινάριν της πλεκτὸν μὲ τὰ χρυσὰ λιλούδια.   G4.239
1490 Καὶ ἡ φορεσία της θαυμαστὴ ἦτον, παραλλαγμένη·
λουρίκιν ἀργυρὸν φορεῖ διὰ λίθων πολυτίμων,   G6.556
καὶ τὸ κασίδι χυμευτὸν ἦτον, παραλλαγμένον,
μὲ τὰ χρυσὰ μετώπια, μὲ τοὺς χρυσοὺς τοὺς κόμπους·
τουβία ὀξυκάστορα μὲ τὸ μαργαριτάριν   G4.226
1495 καὶ τὰ ποδηματίτσια της χρυσὰ διακεντισμένα,
τὰ καύκαλα ἦσαν χυμευτὰ καὶ οἱ πτέρνες μὲ τοὺς λίθους.
Πέντε τὴν ἐπαρέτρεχον ἀπόθεν καὶ ἀπεκεῖθεν
καὶ ἐκ τὰ ἱππάρια ἐγνώρισα καὶ ἐκ τῆς φορεσίας
<ὅτι> ἦτον ὁ Φιλοπαππούς, Κίνναμος καὶ Γιαννάκης   G6.211–2, 548

1473 ἐλάλησα Alexiou, cf. E1476: ἐλάλουν E   παραγγελίαν Hesseling: παραγγελία E
1477 ἐρώτων Hesseling: ὁρώτων E
1478 ἀποπέφτουσι Karayanni, 1976, 117–18: ἀπὸπέυθουσι E   νὰ added by Alexiou
1483 μου Hesseling: του E
1484 ἐμὲν Politis, 1973, 348: ἐμέναν E   Κίνναμος added by Alexiou, cf. G6.548
Γιαννάκης Alexiou: γιανάκι E
1485 σὺν αὐτοῖς (perhaps αὐτῶν, cf. E1121) καὶ ἡ Alexiou, cf. G6.547: σὺ καὶ E
1486 ἐκαβαλίκευσε Hesseling: ἐκαβαλήκευγε E   πολλὰ Kalonaros: οὐδὲ πολλὰ E
1487 χύτη Trapp: χύτη του E   χινέαν βαμμένα Hesseling: χυνέαναασμένα E
1492 παραλλαγμένον Xanthoudidis, 1912, 568: παραλαγμένη E
1494 τουβία ὀξυκάστορα Grégoire-Letocart, 1939, 222: τοῦ βίου ὀξικάτορα E
1496 καύκαλα Xanthoudidis, 1912, 568: καύχαλα E
1497 Πέντε Hesseling: πεζῆ E
1498 ἐγνώρισα Trapp: τοὺς ἐγνώρισα E
1499 ὅτι ἦτον corr.: ἦτον γὰρ E

and I called out this advice to my beloved
– she was to move from the place and go down a little,
1475 to watch and observe what I would do to them;
and I called out a message to her, this advice:
"My beloved and marvellous girl, the flower of the Erotes,
however many are attacking me, see that you don't cry out
and don't let me hear a shriek from you so I get myself killed for
   your sake
1480 through not noticing them striking at me with sword or stick,
and don't let them get the idea of attacking you."
I stood on a rock
and planted my spear and stood and watched
for when Kinnamos and Giannakis would attack me,
1485 and with them Maximou who was flushed with pride.
She was mounted on a charger which was very beautiful.
Its mane and tail were dyed with henna,
its four hoofs were shod with silver,
its bridle was plaited with golden flowers.
1490 Her garments were marvellous, magnificent;
she wore a silver breast-plate with precious stones,
and her helmet was inlaid and magnificent,
with golden visor and golden clasps;
her leggings were of mauve beaver-fur set with pearls
1495 and her little shoes were embroidered with gold,
the uppers and the heels were enamelled and inlaid with gems.
   Five men escorted her on one side and the other
and I recognised from their horses and their garments
that they were Philopappous, Kinnamos and Giannakis,

1500 καὶ ὁ θαυμαστὸς ὁ Λίανδρος μετὰ τὸν Μιλιμίτσην.   G6.549
Καὶ ὅταν <ὅλοι> ἐσίμωσαν τοῦ ποταμοῦ τὸ χεῖλος,   G6.550
τότε στραφοῦσα ἡ Μαξιμοῦ τὸν γέρονταν ἐλάλει: G6.557
«Ποῦ εἶναι τὰ φουσάτα του τὰ θέλω πολεμήσει
καὶ ποῦ εἶναι οἱ καβαλάροι του, ποῦ 'ναι οἱ ἀνδρειωμένοι
1505   τοὺς θέλω πολεμήσει;»
Καὶ ὁ γέρων ὁ Φιλοπαππούς τὴν Μαξιμοὺν ἐλάλει:
«Θωρεῖς αὐτὸν τὸν ἄγουρον ποὺ στέκει εἰς τὸ λιθάριν
καὶ ἔστησεν τὸ κοντάριν του καὶ ἀπάνου του ἀκουμπίζει;
Ἐκδέχεται νὰ ὑπάγωμεν ὅλοι ἀπάνου εἰς αὐτον,
1510 κἂν τάχα μοναχὸς ἐστίν, ἐμᾶς οὐδὲν φοβᾶται. |
Ἂν εὕρη τόπον νὰ ἐμπῆ εἰς τὸν λαόν μας μέσα, 181v
ὥσπερ πετρίτης ἄχρωμος, ὅταν ἐμπῆ εἰς κυνήγιν,
καὶ χύση τὸ πτερούγιν του καὶ τὰ ὄρνεα ἀποκτείνη,
οὕτως ἐμᾶς ἂν γυριστῆ, τινὰς νὰ μὴν τὸν δώση.
1515 Ἀλλὰ ἂς προκαρτερέψωμεν καὶ τότε ἂς τὸν ἰδοῦμε
καὶ νὰ τὸν περιφέρωμε, καὶ οὐ μὴ καβαλικεύση·
εἰ δὲ καθίση εἰς ἄλογον, ἀπιλογίαν μᾶς κάμνει.»
Καὶ τότε ἡ κούρβα ἡ Μαξιμοῦ τὸν γέροντα ἀτιμάζει:
«Ἔβγα ἀπ' ἐδῶ, λυσσόγερε, υἱὲ τῆς ἀπωλείας·
1520 ὡς καὶ ἀπ' τὰ γέρα τὰ πολλὰ ὁ κῶλος σου ἐτσιγκρίασε.
Ἐγὼ ἔλεγα φουσάτα ἔχει καὶ ἀγούρους ἀνδρειωμένους,
καὶ ἐπῆρα τὰ φουσάτα μου καὶ ἦλθα νὰ πολεμήσω.
Ἐγὼ μόνη καὶ μοναχὴ νὰ κατεβῶ εἰς αὐτον,
νὰ κόψω τὸ κεφάλιν του καὶ ἐδῶ νὰ σᾶς τὸ φέρω,   G6.567
1525 νὰ ἐπάρω τὸ κοράσιον καὶ ἐδῶ νὰ σᾶς τὸ φέρω,
νὰ ἐπάρω τὴν πεθύμιαν σας καὶ ἐδῶ νὰ σᾶς τὴν φέρω
                            καὶ ἐσεῖς μὴ κουρασθῆτε.»
Καὶ σύντομα ἐπιλάλησεν τὸν ποταμὸν περάσει   G6.568
καὶ ἐγὼ δὲ τὴν ἐλάλησα φωνὴν ἀπὸ μακρόθεν: G6.569

1501 ὅλοι added by Alexiou:
1502 στραφοῦσα E, cf. E1416: στραφεῖσα Kyriakidis, 1926, 31
1503 του Hesseling: σου E
1505 τοὺς Trapp: ποῦ τοὺς E
1512 εἰς Kalonaros: εἰς τὸ E
1515 ἂς² Alexiou: να E
1516 μὴ Kyriakidis, 1926, 30: μίμας E
1518 γέροντα Hesseling: γέρονταν E
1520 ἀπ' τὰ γέρα Alexiou: ἀπὸ τὰ γέρα σου E   ἐτσιγκρίασε Andriotis, 1941, 16: ἐτζηκρίασε E
1521 Ἐγὼ Alexiou: ἐγὼ γὰρ E
1526 πεθύμιαν Alexiou: πεθυμίαν E

1500 and the marvellous Liandros with Milimitsis.
When they had all come near to the edge of the river,
then Maximou turned and said to the old man:
"Where are his armies which I am to fight
and where are his horsemen, where are the brave men
1505   whom I am to fight?"
      The old Philopappous said to Maximou:
"Do you see that youngster standing on the rock,
who has planted his spear and is leaning on it?
He is waiting for all of us to attack him,
1510 and even though he is on his own, he is not afraid of us.
If he finds a spot where he can get in amongst our followers,
just like a light-coloured falcon when it goes on the chase
and spreads out its wings and kills birds,
even so if he makes preparations against us, no one will be able to
      strike him.
1515 But let's wait for him and then let's have a look at him
and we'll surround him and stop him mounting.
If he gets on his horse, he'll send us on our way."
      Then that slut Maximou insulted the old man:
"Get out of here, mad old man, son of perdition;
1520 extreme old age has withered your cock.
I reckoned he had armies and brave youngsters;
so I brought my armies and I came to make war.
Alone and on my own I'll attack him,
I'll cut off his head and bring it to you here,
1525 I'll get the girl and bring her to you here,
I'll get what you desire and bring it to you here,
                        and you needn't put yourselves out."
      Immediately she urged her horse on to cross the river.
But I yelled to her from a distance:

1518 Despite the quasi-heroic description of her appearance on horse-back, E's
vocabulary for Maximou (cf. E1567-8) betrays a total lack of sympathy for a woman
who has moved beyond the conventional female role.
1524-8 An unusual and repetitious example of triple patterning leading to an ironic
climax.

1530 «Αὐτόθε στέκου, Μαξιμού, ὅθεν μηδὲν περάσῃς.   G6.569
Τοὺς ἄνδρας πρέπει νὰ περνοῦν, ἀμὴ ὄχι τὰς γυναίκας.   G6.570
Περάσειν ἔχω, Μαξιμού, ὡς διὰ σὲν τὸ ποτάμιν
καὶ νὰ σοῦ ἀντιμέψωμεν, ὡς καὶ τὸ δίκαιον ἔχεις.»   G6.571
      Τὸν γρίβα μου ἐπιλάλησα τὸν | ποταμὸν περάσει,   182r
1535 καὶ εἶχεν νερὸν ὁ ποταμὸς πολὺν καὶ βουρκωμένον
καὶ ἐξέπεσεν ὁ γρίβας μου καὶ ἐχώθην ἕως τραχήλου·
καὶ δένδρον ἔπεψεν ὁ Θεὸς ἀπέσω εἰς τὸ ποτάμιν,
καὶ ἂν εἶχεν λείπειν τὸ δενδρόν, ἐπνίγετον ὁ Ἀκρίτης.
      Καὶ ὡς εἶδεν τοῦτο ἡ Μαξιμού, ἀπάνω μου ἐκατέβη·
1540 κοντάριν ἐμαλάκιζεν τὴν κονταρέαν μὲ δώσει
καὶ ταῦτα τὸ κοντάριν τῆς ἔριψα παρὰ μία
καὶ σύντομα ἔριψα ραβδίν, τὴν Μαξιμοὺν ἐλάλουν:
«Ἐλεῶ τὰ κάλλη σου, κυρά, βλέπε μὴ κινδυνεύσῃς·   G6.757
ἀλλὰ ἂς δώσω, <Μαξιμού,> τὴν φάραν σου ραβδέαν
1545 καὶ ἐκ τὴν ραβδέαν, Μαξιμού, νόησε μὲ τίναν ἔχεις.»
      Καὶ ἐγὼ ραβδέαν ἔδωσα τὴν φάραν ’ς τὰς κουτάλας
καὶ ἀνάσκελα ἐξήπλωσεν ἡ θαυμαστὴ ἡ φάρα.

      Καὶ τότε πάλι ἡ Μαξιμοὺ οὕτως μὲ παρεκάλει:
«Κύρκα, φοβήσου τὸν Θεὸν καὶ ἀπὲ συμπάθησέ μου
1550 καὶ ἂς φέρουν πάλιν ἄλογον, διὰ νὰ κάτσω ἀπάνω
καὶ νὰ νοήσῃς, ἄγουρε, | καὶ τὴν ἐμὴν ἀνδρείαν.»   182v   G6.677
      Καὶ ἐγὼ αὐτὴν παραχωρῶ ἵνα καβαλικεύσῃ·
καὶ ἂν ἔνι ἡ γεῦσις ἔμνοστος, πάλιν ἂς δευτερώσῃ.
      Τὸν Λίανδρον ἐφώνιαζεν καὶ φέρνει τῆς ἱππάριν,
1555 πηδᾶ κ’ ἐκαβαλίκευσε καὶ παίρνει καὶ κοντάριν
καὶ ἀπὸ μακρέα μ’ ἐφώναζε: «Ἐδὰ σὲ βλέπω, Ἀκρίτη.»
      Καὶ τὸ κοντάρι ἐμάκρυνε τὴν κονταρίαν μὲ δώσει.
Σπαθέαν τῆς φάρας ἔδωκα ἀπάνω εἰς τὸ κεφάλιν·
τὰ δύο μέρη ἐσχίσθησαν καὶ ἔπεσαν παρὰ μίαν·

1531 πρέπει Hesseling: πέρπει E
1534 τὸν Kyriakidis, 1926, 31: τὸν | τὸν E (over page-break)
1537 καὶ Hesseling: καὶ εἰς E
1538 ὁ Kyriakidis, 1926, 31: ὁ θαυμαστὸς E
1543 κυρά Alexiou: μαξιμού E
1544 Μαξιμού added by Alexiou
1545 Μαξιμού Alexiou: ἡ μαξιμού E
1546 φάραν Kyriakidis, 1926, 32: φάραν τῆς E   ’ς Trapp: εἰς E
1548 πάλι Politis, 1973, 342: πάλην E
1549 ἀπὲ Alexiou: ἀπέκι E
1555 κ’ ἐκαβαλίκευσε Kalonaros: καὶ καβαλήκευσε E
1557 κοντάρι Kyriakidis, 1926, 32: κοντάριν τῆς E

1530 "Stay there, Maximou, don't cross over from there;
it's proper for men to cross over but not women.
I shall cross the river, Maximou, for you
and we'll give you the recompense which is your right."
I urged on my grey horse to cross the river
1535 but the river was high and murky
and my grey horse slipped and fell in up to his neck;
but God had sent a tree down into the river
and if the tree had not been there, Akritis the Frontiersman would
    have drowned.
When Maximou saw this, she charged at me;
1540 she wielded her spear to give me a thrust
but then I instantly knocked her spear away
and promptly knocked away her stick; I said to Maximou:
"I have compassion on your beauty, lady, be careful that you don't
    run into danger;
but let me give your charger, Maximou, a blow with my stick
1545 and from the blow, Maximou, understand with whom you are
    dealing."
I gave the charger a blow on its flanks with my stick
and the marvellous charger collapsed with its legs in the air.

Then in turn Maximou pleaded with me thus:
"Sweetheart, fear God and from now on pardon me;
1550 let them bring another horse for me to sit on
and you will understand, youngster, my bravery also."
I allowed her to remount
and, if the experience were to her taste, she could make another
    attempt.
She shouted out to Liandros and he brought her a horse;
1555 she sprang into the saddle and took a spear as well
and shouted to me from a distance: "Now I'm ready for you, Akritis
    the Frontiersman!"
She thrust her spear forward, to strike me with it.
I struck a blow with my sword on her charger's head;
the two halves were split apart and fell in an instant.

1542–63 These lines are unnecessarily rearranged by Trapp to correspond to G thus:
1541, 1558–62, 1549–57, 1542–8, 1563ff.

1560 ἦτον καὶ <ἡ> σέλα πάντερπνος, ὅλη κατεζουλίστην,
καὶ ἀπέμεινεν ἡ Μαξιμού, πεζή, ἐλεεινή εἰς τὸν κάμπον.
Τὸ ὑπόδημά μου ἐφίλησεν καὶ οὕτως μὲ παρεκάλει:
«Κύρκα, φοβήσου τὸν Θεόν, πάλιν συμπάθησέ με
εἰς τὴν μωρίαν τούτην·
1565 παρὰ σαλῶν καὶ ἄτακτων ἀνθρώπων ἐδιδάχθην·
καὶ ἐσὺ μόνος μὲ κέρδισε καὶ ἄλλος μὴ μὲ κερδίση.»   G6.769
Καὶ <τότε> ἐγὼ τὴν Μαξιμοῦ οὕτως ἀπιλογήθην:
«Μὰ τὸν Θεόν, ἡ Μαξιμού, οὐκ ἔν’ τὸ ἐνθύμημά σου·
τὴν κόρην τὴν ἐγὼ φιλῶ τῶν εὐγενῶν ὑπάρχει·
1570 ἔχει γὰρ πλοῦτος ἄπειρον καὶ συγγενοὺς ἐνδόξους
καὶ ἀδέλφια πολυορεκτικὰ καὶ ἀδελφοὺς πλουσίους,
καὶ πάντας ἐξηρνήσατο καὶ μετὰ μέναν ἦλθεν·
καὶ ὁ Θεὸς ὁ πάντων δυνατὸς αὐτὸς νὰ μᾶς χωρίση.
Εἰ δὲ ἂν ὁρμῆς νὰ πορνευθῆς, ἐγὼ νὰ σοῦ τὸ ποίσω.»
1575   Καὶ ἐπέζευlσα τὸν μαῦρον μου καὶ λύω τ’ ἄρματά μου,   183r
καὶ τὸ ἐπεθύμα ἡ Μαξιμού γοργὸν τῆς τὸ ἐποῖκα·
καὶ ἀπείτις τῆς τὸ ἔκαμα τῆς Μαξιμοῦς τῆς κούρβας,
εὐθὺς ἐκαβαλίκευσα καὶ ἐπῆγα εἰς τὸ κοράσιον.
Καὶ τότε τῆς βεργόλικος ἄκο τὸ τί τῆς λέγω:
1580 «Εἶδες, ὀμμάτια μου καλά, τί ἀνδραγαθίας ἐποῖκα;»
Καὶ τότε τὸ κοράσιον ἄκου τὸ τί μοῦ λέγει:
«Εἶδα σε, ὀμμάτια μου καλά, τὸ φῶς τῶν ὀφθαλμῶν μου,
τὸ πῶς ἐμονομάχησες ὅλους τοὺς ἀπελάτας,
καὶ ὅταν ἐμονομάχησες τὴν Μαξιμοὺν τὴν κόρην·
1585 καὶ εἰς τὸ στενὸν τὸ πέραμαν, εἰς τὸ βαθὺν τὸ ρυάκιν,
πολλὰ πολλὰ μοῦ ἄργησες· πιστεύω νὰ τὴν εἶχες.»
Καὶ τότε τὴν βεργόλικον οὕτως τὴν συντυχαίνω:
«Ὡς ἔδωσα τὸ ἱππάριν της τὴν ὕστεραν ραβδέαν,
ἐξέπεσεν ἡ Μαξιμού ἀπὸ τὸ ἱππάριν κάτω·

1560 ἡ added by Kalonaros
1565 παρὰ Ricks: ὅτι παρα E
1566 κέρδισε E: ἐκέρδισες Ricks, cf. G6.769
1567 τότε added by Alexiou
1569 τὴν κόρην E: ἡ κόρη Alexiou
1574 πορνευθῆς Grégoire-Letocart, 1939, 223: πορευθὴς E
1577 ἔκαμα corr.: ἔκαμα ἐγὼ E
1579 λέγω Kalonaros: λέγει E
1580 τί ἀνδραγαθίας Alexiou: ἀνδραγαθίας τὰς E
1581 μοῦ Hesseling: τοῦ E
1588 Ὡς ἔδωσα Trapp: ὁσὰν ἐδῶσα E
1589 ἐξέπεσεν Alexiou: καὶ ἐξέπεσεν E

1560 The saddle was very pretty but it was completely crushed
and Maximou was left there on foot, pitiable on the battlefield.
    She kissed my shoe and pleaded with me thus:
"Sweetheart, fear God and once again pardon me
                for this stupidity;
1565 I have been instructed by mad and unruly men;
take me, you alone – no one else may."
    And then I replied thus to Maximou:
"By God, Maximou, what you want is impossible.
The girl whom I love comes from a high-born family;
1570 she has boundless wealth and glorious kinsmen
and highly desirable sisters and rich brothers,
but she has renounced all these and come with me,
and it is God who has power over all things who will separate us.
But if you are starting to prostitute yourself, let me do the job for
you."
1575   So I dismounted from my black steed and undid my armour
and quickly did to Maximou what she desired.
And after I had done this to Maximou, the slut,
I immediately mounted and went to the girl.
    Listen to what I said then to the slender girl:
1580 "Did you see, my lovely eyes, what brave deeds I did?"
    Listen to what the girl then said to me:
"I saw you, my dear eyes, light of my eyes,
how you fought all the guerrillas on your own
and when you fought the girl Maximou on your own.
1585 And by the narrow crossing, by the deep stream
you lingered a long, long time: I believe you had her."
    Then I responded thus to the slim girl:
"When I gave her horse the final blow with my stick,
Maximou fell down from her horse;

1574 The dynamics of this situation are expressed less crudely in G, probably because a censor has intervened.
1575 The horse was grey last time it was mentioned (1534), though μαῦρον verges on being a generic word for 'horse'.
1586 In contrast to G6.793 the girl is cynically aware of Digenis' treatment of Maximou.

1590 ἦτον καὶ <ἡ> σέλα πάντερπνος, ὅλη κατεζουλίστην,
καὶ πίστευσέ με, λυγερή, ὅτι ἀλήθειαν σὲ λέγω,
ὅτι πολλὰ ἐλυπήθηκα τὰ δύο τῆς τὰ φαρία.»
Καὶ τότε τὸ κοράσιον ἐγέλασε μεγάλως,
στρεφνά, γλυκέα μ᾿ ἐφίλησε καὶ ἐμὲν ἐσυχνοφίλει.
1595 Καὶ τότε τὸ κοράσιον οὕτως τὸ συντυχαίνω·
«Μετὰ τὸ φθείρειν Μαξιμοὺν τρία κακὰ τὴν ἐποῖκα·
πρῶτον μὲν ὅτι εἶχα την, δεύτερον ὅτι ἐντράπη, Ι
τρίτον καὶ περισσότερον ἐχάσε τὴν ἀνδρείαν της 183v
καὶ πομπεμένη ἀπόφευγεν ἀπὸ τὸν Μιλιμίτσην.»
1600 Καὶ ὁ Λίανδρος ὁ ταπεινός, πλήρης κατησχυμένος,
καὶ οἱ ἑκατὸν οἱ πρόλοιποι τῆς Μαξιμοῦς οἱ ἀγοῦροι
καὶ ὁ θαυμαστὸς ὁ Κίνναμος, ἀλλὰ καὶ ὁ κὺρ Γιαννάκης
καὶ ἄλλοι ἀπελάτες ἑκατόν, καὶ ὁ Φ᾿λοπαππούς ὁ γέρων
πάντες ἐξεσκορπίσθησαν ἐκ τοῦ Ἀκρίτη τὸν φόβον,
1605 νὰ μὴ τοὺς καταφθάση ἐκεῖ καὶ ὅλους κακοδικήση.
    Ὡς ἔχει ἡ νεότης πάντοτε τὴν ἡδονὴν εἰς κόρον   G5.1-2
καὶ συνεπαίρνεται πολλὰ εἰς πλοῦτον καὶ εἰς δόξαν,   G8.139
πάντα ἐσυνετέλεσεν ὁ Διγενὴς Ἀκρίτης.
Ἦτον πάντοτε ἐξάκουστος εἰς ἀριστείας μεγάλας·
1610 ἀπὸ γὰρ τὴν ἀνατολὴν μέχρι τοῦ ἡλίου τὴν δύσιν
τὸ ὄνομάν του ἐξήγουν το εἰς ὅλον γὰρ τὸν κόσμον.
Καὶ ἀφῶν τὸν ἐφοβήθηκεν ἡ Οἰκουμένη ὅλη
καὶ ἀμιράδας ὑπέταξεν, ἀλλὰ καὶ Ἀραβίτας
καὶ ἀρχιληστὰς ἐφόνευσεν καὶ ὅλους τοὺς ἀπελάτας,
1615 καὶ ἀπότι ἀπομερίμνησεν τὸ κρούειν καὶ τὸ λαμβάνειν,
καὶ μέριμναν οὐδὲν εἶχεν περὶ ἄλλας ἐμνοστίας,
ἔδοξεν τὸν νεώτερον εἰς κάμπον κατοικῆσαι.
    Πᾶσαν κατεψηλάφησεν τὴν παραποταμίαν

1590 ἡ σέλα Kalonaros: σέλαν E
1594 ἐφίλησε Ricks, cf. E915: ἐπερίλαβε E
1595 τὸ Alexiou: τὴν E   συντυχαίνω Kalonaros: συντυχένη E
1596 Μαξιμοὺν Alexiou: τὴν μαξιμοῦν E
1602 κὺρ Trapp: κύριος E
1603 ἄλλοι Alexiou: οἱ ἄλλοι E   Φ᾿λοπαππούς Alexiou: Φιλοπαπούς E
1606 εἰς κόρον Alexiou: τῆς κόρης E
1610 μέχρι Trapp: καὶ μέχρι E
1611 του Trapp: του πολλὰ E   ἐξήγουν Alexiou: ἐξιγοῦν E
1612 ἀφῶν Alexiou: ἀφ᾿ ὅτου E
1613 ὑπέταξεν Kalonaros, cf. G7.5: ἐπόταξεν E
1614 ἀρχιληστὰς Kalonaros: ἀρχιλίστας E
1615 ἀπότι Trapp: ἀπότης E
1618 παραποταμίαν Hesseling: παραμίαν E

1590 the saddle was very pretty but it was completely crushed;
and believe me, slender one, that I am telling you the truth,
that I was very upset about her two chargers."
      And then the girl laughed loudly,
she embraced me tightly and sweetly and covered me with kisses.
1595   Then I responded thus to the girl:
"When I violated Maximou, I wronged her in three ways:
first, because I had her, second, because she was disgraced,
and third and worst of all, she lost her valour
and she was humiliated and fled from Milimitsis."
1600   The miserable Liandros, completely ashamed,
and Maximou's hundred remaining youngsters
and the marvellous Kinnamos and also Sir Giannakis
and a hundred other guerrillas and old Philopappous
all scattered because of their fear of Akritis the Frontiersman,
1605 in case he caught up with them and did them some harm.
      Since youthfulness always carries pleasure to excess
and is excited by wealth and reputation,
Digenis Akritis, the Frontiersman of Double Descent, accomplished
      everything.
He was forever renowned for great deeds of valour;
1610 from the east as far as the setting sun
they told stories of his name throughout the whole world.
And when all the inhabited world was in fear of him
and he had subdued emirs and Arabs too
and killed brigand chiefs and all the guerrillas,
1615 and when he grew weary of giving and taking blows
and had no interest in other delights,
the young man decided to settle on the plain.
      He had explored the whole area around the river,

1595 Maximou has not only transgressed the norms of acceptable female behaviour, she
has also failed according to the male warrior code: her punishment in this version,
however, stops short of death (contrast G6.797–8). The final sexual act is at one level the
imposition of male physical superiority, no less brutal because Maximou has been
brought to request it. At another level it might be seen as her return to a more
conventional female role in the male-dominated values of the poem (see Ekdawi et al.,
1993). Nevertheless in legal terms it was probably Digenis and not Maximou who was
liable for punishment (Laiou, 1993, 215–17).
1606–94 A new episode, Alexiou's fifth song 'The dwelling-place, the garden and the
tomb', corresponding to G7: it will have been represented in *Digenis.
1606–7 These lines loosely reflect G5.1–2.

καὶ οὐκ ηὗρεν τόπον ἀρεστὸν νὰ | κατοικήση Ἀκρίτης   184r
1620 καὶ εἰς τὸν Ἀφράτην ποταμὸν τοῦ ἄρεσε κατοικῆσαι   G7.7
καὶ ὡς ἤθελεν καὶ ἐπόθει <το> ἐποῖκεν καὶ τὰ κάστρη·
καὶ ἀνέδραμεν τοῦ ποταμοῦ πᾶσαν τοποθεσίαν.
  Καὶ εἰς τόπον ὑπολίβαδον ἦτον πολὺς δενδριώνας
καὶ γύρωθεν ἐστέκασιν ὡραῖα κατάσκια δένδρη
1625 καὶ ὕδατα πανώραια ἐκ τὰ ὄρη κατεβαίνουν
καὶ ἐφαίνετο ἡ τοποθεσία πανώραια ὡς παραδείσιν.
  Καὶ ἐδίωξε τὸν ποταμὸν ἐξ αὗτον τὸ λιβάδιν
καὶ ἐποίησεν τόπον πάντερπνον καὶ ὡραῖον παραδείσιν
καὶ ἐποίησεν περίχωρον, καὶ ὡραῖον ἦν χωρίον.
1630 Τείχια τοῦ ἔκτισε λαμπρὰ μετὰ τοὺς προμαχιώνας,   G7.15
καὶ ἀπέξω ὀρθομαρμάρωσις φαίνεται ἀπὸ μακρόθεν,   G7.16
πάντερπνος, ξενοχάραγος, ἐξέχωρος ἐκ πάντων.
Καὶ κατὰ ρίζα τοῦ δενδροῦ πηγάδιν ἀναβλύζει.
  Καὶ ἀπέκλεισεν τὰ τέσσερα τοῦ ποταμοῦ κλωνάρια
1635 καὶ ἀρδεύει τὸ παράβουνον καὶ ὅλον τὸ ἀνατρέχει.
Φισκίνας ἔστησε πολλὰς ἀπὸ χυτοῦ ἐκτισμένας,
διὰ τὸ ποτίζειν ἐξ αὐτὰς τόπους ἀποκλεισθέντας·
ἐποίησεν βιβάρια πανθαύμαστα ἰχθύων.
        . . . εἰς τοῦ ἀμιρᾶ τοὺς οἴκους.
1640 Καὶ ἐφέρασιν τὸν βάρσαμον ἐκ τῆς Αἰγύπτου χώρας· |
1642 τὰ φύλλα του εἶναι πράσινα καὶ κόκκινον τὸ ἄνθος   184v
καὶ ἡ ρίζα του εἶναι πιθαμὴ καὶ ὅλη ξυλαλόη
        καὶ ὁ καρπός του ἔναι μόσχος
1645 καὶ οἱ κλῶνοι του εἶναι κόκκινοι καὶ φιλωτὰ κλωσμένοι
καὶ ἐξέρχεται ἐκ τὴν ρίζαν του ὕδωρ καὶ ἔναι χιονάτο,
1647 μυρίζει δὲ ὡς ροδόσταμον καὶ ἀπολιγώνει ἀνθρώπους·

1620 τοῦ ἄρεσε corr.: ἐκεῖ ἄρεσε Ε   κατοικῆσαι Alexiou, cf. Z3774: τοῦ νεοτέρου
κατοικία Ε
1621 το added by Alexiou
1624 γύρωθεν Alexiou: ἐγύρωθεν Ε
1626 ἐφαίνετο Hesseling: φένε Ε
1628 παραδείσιν Hesseling: παρεδείσιν Ε
1629 ἦν corr.: γὰρ Ε
1630 προμαχιώνας Hesseling: τρομαχιῶνας Ε
1631 ἀπέξω Hesseling: ἀπέσω Ε
1634 ἀπέκλεισεν Alexiou: ὑπέκλησεν Ε
1635 ἀρδεύει Xanthoudidis, 1912, 569: ἀρδεύιν Ε
1636 ἐκτισμένας Alexiou, 1979, 108: οἰκονισμένας Ε οἰκονομημένας Alexiou οἰκονο-
μισμένας Hesseling
1637 ἐξ αὐτὰς Vogiatzidis, 1923/4, 78: εἰς αὐτοὺς Ε   τόπους Xanthoudidis, 1912,
569: τόπος Ε   ἀποκλεισθέντας Kalonaros: ἀπεκλισθέντας Ε
1645 κόκκινοι Hesseling: κόκκινος Ε   κλωσμένοι Hesseling: κλωσμένα Ε

but Akritis the Frontiersman had found no agreeable place to live,
1620 yet he liked to live by the river Euphrates:
and so he built his fortress as he wanted and desired,
and he roamed around every site by the river.
In a spot with verdant meadows there was a large grove
and all round stood beautiful shady trees:
1625 very beautiful streams flowed down from the mountains,
and the site seemed very beautiful, like a pleasure garden.
He diverted the river away from this meadow
and created a delightful spot and a lovely pleasure garden:
he made a country estate which was a lovely place.
1630 He built there resplendent walls with battlements
and the marble cladding on the outside could be seen from a distance,
quite delightful, incomparable, distinct from any other.
And at the foot of the tree a spring bubbled up.
He dammed the four branches of the river
1635 and irrigated the mountain-side so that the water ran all over it.
He set up many pools, made of forged metal,
so that enclosed areas could be watered by them:
he also made the most marvellous ponds for fish.
. . . to the emir's houses.
1640 They brought the balsam tree from the land of Egypt:
1642 its leaves are green and its flower red;
its root is some nine inches thick and smelling all of aloes,
and its fruit is perfumed;
1645 its branches are red and amorously intertwined
while water comes out of its root, icy cold
1647 and perfumed like rosewater; it makes men faint.

1624–59 The literary background in Achilles Tatius and Makremvolitis to this description of an ideal garden is discussed in the Introduction, p. xlv–xlvi.
1633 A forward reference to the tree described in E1642–7, perhaps to be omitted here as a doublet of 1646.
1636–47 A confused passage: at 1639 either a phrase has fallen out or the scribe is harking back to previous references to building activities; 1641 breaks into the description of the balsam tree and could be repositioned either before 1640 (as does Alexiou) or after 1647 (as here).
1636 A difficult half-line, where no emendation yet proposed gives both satisfactory sense and metre.

1641 καὶ ἐφύτευσαν φοινίκια 'ς αὐτὸν τὸ παραδείσιν·
1648   Καὶ αὐλὴν ἐποῖκεν θαυμαστήν, πανώραιαν φισκίναν,
καὶ τὰ 'μπροσθεν †τοῦ μηστοῦ† μεμυρισμένα δένδρη.
1650 Ἐποίησεν καὶ ἀνώγαιον, αὐλὴν δὲ ὑπερῶον
καὶ τὴν ἐπερικύκλωσεν ὅλην τριγύρου γύρου
καὶ ἐπέστησεν ὁλόχρυσα καὶ ὁλάργυρα ζωδία,
λέοντας, πάρδους καὶ ἀετούς, πέρδικας καὶ νεράδας
καὶ χύνουν ἐκ τοῦ στόματος καὶ ἐκ τῶν πτερουγίων
1655 νερὸν καθάριον, κρούσταλλον, ὕδωρ μεμυρισμένον·
ταῦτα δὲ †ἐμπαίνουσιν† εἰς πανωραίας φισκίνας.
Καὶ ἐκρέμασεν χρυσόκλημαν εἰς τοῦ δενδροῦ τοὺς κλώνους   G6.28
καὶ ἔχουν ὡραίους ψιττακοὺς καὶ κιλαδοῦν καὶ λέγουν: G7.39
«Χαίρου, Ἀκρίτη, χαίρου <ἐσὺ> μετὰ τῆς ποθητῆς σου.»
1660   Ἐποίησεν γέφυραν τερπνὴν ἀπάνω εἰς τὸν Εὐφράτην·
βαστᾶ την μονοκέρατον ἀπὸ πέρα ἕως πέρα.
Καὶ ἔκτισεν τετρακάμαρον 'ς τὴν γέφυραν ἀπάνω,
ὑπόθολον, πανθαύμαστον, μετὰ λευκῶν μαρμάρων·
βαστοῦν το κιόνια πάντερπνα, πράσινα, πανωραῖα.   185r
1665 Καὶ κάτωθεν ὑπέστησεν κιβούριν τοῦ θανάτου,
εὐθὺς ἵνα ἀποτεθῆ τὸ σῶμα τοῦ νεωτέρου.
Ἀκούσατε, θαυμάσατε τὸν τάφον τοῦ νεωτέρου,
ὅτι ἦτον θαυμαστὸς πολλά, παρὰ τοὺς ἄλλους πλέον,
παρὰ τοῦ βασιλεύσαντος ἐκ τῆς Περσίας χώρας·
. . .
1670 ἐποίησεν πολυμήχανον καὶ πανωραῖον τάφον
καὶ ἐτέθην ἡ βασίλισσα τοῦ πρὸς Παρασογάρδου.

1641 'ς Trapp: εἰς E
1648 θαυμαστήν Hesseling: θαυμασθὴν E
1649 τοῦ μηστοῦ E: τοῦ ξυστοῦ Xanthoudidis, 1912. 570 μυριστικὰ Hesseling
ἐκόσμησε Kalonaros
1651 τὴν Alexiou: ὅλην τὴν E   ὅλην Alexiou: αὐτὴν E
1652 ἐπέστησεν Alexiou: ἀπέστησεν E   ζωδία Alexiou: ζώδια E
1657 χρυσόκλημαν E: χρυσόκλωβα Alexiou
1659 ἐσὺ added by Spadaro, 1989, 182
1660 γέφυραν Kalonaros: γεφύριαν E
1661 την Grégoire, 1942, 94: το E
1662 'ς Trapp: εἰς E
1664 βαστοῦν το Kriaras, 1953, 384: βαστοῦντα E
1665 κάτωθεν Xyngopoulos, 1967, 24: ἀπάνωθεν E
1669 ἐκ τῆς Περσίας χώρας E: εἰς τὴν Περσίαν χώραν Alexiou   After 1669 Alexiou
proposes a short lacuna containing a relative pronoun
1671 ἐτέθην Grégoire, 1931a, 508: ἐτέχθην E

1641 They planted palm trees in this garden.
He built a marvellous courtyard and a very beautiful pool
and in front . . . perfumed trees.
1650 He built also an upper storey, a courtyard on a higher level
and encircled the whole of it on all sides
and set up figures of animals, made of solid gold and silver,
lions, leopards and eagles, partridges and neraïdes;
these poured out from their mouths and their wings
1655 pure water, crystal clear, water that was perfumed;
then they entered very lovely pools.
And he hung a golden vine from the tree's branches,
which had beautiful parrots which sang and said:
"Greetings, Akritis, Frontiersman, greetings to you with your beloved."
1660　He constructed a delightful bridge over the Euphrates;
he carried a single arch from one side to the other.
And he built a four-vaulted chamber on the bridge,
domed, very marvellous, made of white marble.
It was supported by most delightful columns, green and very beautiful,
1665 and under the dome he placed a monumental sarcophagus
so that the young man's body could be placed there without delay.
　Listen, marvel at the young man's tomb,
because it was very marvellous, more than all others,
more than that of the emperor from the land of Persia;
. . .
1670 for he had constructed a very intricate and very beautiful tomb
in which was interred the empress near Pasargadai.

1649 A phrase referring to some part of the building has fallen out of the text.
1653 'Neraïdes' are descendants of the ancient water nymphs who are well on their way
to becoming seductive modern fairies.
1656 Presumably the unexpressed subject of 'entered' referred to water.
1660 In this part of the manuscript, though sections of the text are signalled by capital
letters, there are no spaces for illustrations.
1661 Digenis' tomb is referred to in G in the context of his funeral (G8.230–44), which
is not mentioned in E. At this stage G (7.107. 192) refers to the burial in Digenis' palace
of his parents. *Digenis would thus have mentioned tombs of some sort in the account of
the palace. On sites suggested for the tomb, see the Introduction, p. xxxiv.
1666 Logically the construction of the tomb to prevent delay in burial after death does
not imply that Digenis is ill. Structurally this is an anticipation of the coming death-bed
scene.
1669 Alexiou proposes a short lacuna at this point containing a relative pronoun.

Οὗτος γὰρ ὁ παγκάλλιστος καὶ πανωραῖος τάφος,
μὴ τὸν δοκῆτε, οἱ ἄρχοντες, ὅτι ψευδὴς ὑπάρχει,
ἀλλ᾽ ἐκ παντὸς πιστεύετε ὅτι ἀληθὴς ὑπάρχει,
1675   ὅτι βεβαίως εἴρηται εἰς πάντα ἀληθεύων.
Οὐ μόνον εἰς τὸν θάνατον,
ἀπάνω εἰς τὸν τάφον του ἐν ἀληθείᾳ τὸ λέγω.
   Εἰς τὸ κουβούκλιν δὲ σιμά, ἔμπροσθεν τῆς φισκίνας,
εἰς τὸ ἀπεσκίασμα τοῦ δενδροῦ ὡραῖον κρεβάτιν στέκει·
1680   οἱ ῥίζες ἦσαν σμάραγδοι καὶ τὰ κανόνια κρύα
καὶ τὰ ποδάρια ὁλόχρυσα, διὰ λίθων πολυτίμων·
ἡ μέση δὲ τοῦ κράβατου θεμένη ὀξὺν μετάξιν
καὶ κεῖται σαρακήνικον μεταξωτὸν τὸ πεύχιν
καὶ ἀπάνω κεῖται πιλωτόν, ὀξὺν πρασινοβούλιν,
1685   καὶ ὑφάπλωμα σωληνωτὸν μὲ τὰς χρυσᾶς νεράδας·
καὶ κεῖται ἀπάλνω ὁ Διγενὴς πλάγιον ἀκουμπισμένος.   185v
Καὶ ἔμπροσθεν τῶν γονάτων του κάθεται ἡ ποθητή του
καὶ τριγύρου του στέκουσιν τριακόσια παλληκάρια
καὶ οἱ τριακόσιοι εἶναι ἔμορφοι καὶ κόκκινα φοροῦσιν·
1690   βαστοῦν σπαθία ὁλοψήφωτα καὶ στέκουν ἔμπροσθέν του,
τοὺς εἶχεν πάντας φύλακας εἰς τὰς στενὰς κλεισούρας
καὶ ἐφύλαττον τὴν Ῥωμανίαν ἀπὸ βάρβαρα ἔθνη·
καὶ ὡσὰν πουλίτσια πάντερπνα, ὅταν ἀποπετάσουν,
καὶ φέρνουν κτύπον πάντερπνον τὸν θαυμαστὸν Ἀκρίτην.
1695   Ἐπειδὴ πάντα τὰ τερπνὰ τοῦ πλάνου κόσμου τούτου   G8.1
θάνατος τὰ ὑποκρατεῖ καὶ Ἅδης τὰ κερδαίνει,   G8.2
κατέφθασεν καὶ σήμερον τοῦ Διγενῆ Ἀκρίτη.   G8.5
Κατανοῶντες κλαύσατε τὸν Διγενὴν Ἀκρίτην
καὶ βλέποντες θρηνήσατε ἀπὸ βαθέων καρδίας
1700   τὴν συμφορὰν τὴν γίνεται, θέαμαν καὶ ὀδύνην.

1672 πανωραῖος Krumbacher, 1904, 333: πανσῖος E
1673 μὴ Kyriakidis, 1946, 422: ὡς E   ὑπάρχει Krumbacher, 1904, 333: ὑπάρχεις E
1674 ἀληθὴς Trapp: ἀληθὲς E
1675 βεβαίως Krumbacher, 1904, 333: βαίβεος E   πάντα ἀληθεύων Alexiou: πάντας
ἀληθεΰϊν E
1680 σμάραγδοι Alexiou: σμαραγδὴ E
1682 κράβατου Kyriakidis, 1948, 484: κραβάτου E   θεμένη Alexiou: δεμένη E
1685 σωληνωτὸν Xanthoudidis, 1912, 571: σεληνοτὸν E
1689 εἶναι [εἶν'] Alexiou: ἦσαν E
1694 καὶ φέρνουν E: ἐκφέρουν Alexiou

As for this very magnificent and very beautiful tomb,
do not think, lords, that it is a lie
but believe fully that it really exists,
1675 that certainly it has been described with complete truth.
Not only by death
but also by his tomb, what I am telling you is the truth.
   Close by the chamber, in front of the pool,
in the shade of the tree stood a beautiful couch.
1680 Its feet were of emeralds, its stretchers of crystal,
its legs all of gold with precious stones.
The centre of the couch was covered with mauve silk
and a silken Saracen rug lay there;
on that there was a mauve woollen cloth with green spots,
1685 and a quilted coverlet with golden neraïdes;
on this lay Digenis, reclining on his side.
His beloved sat by his knees
and round him stood three hundred brave young men;
the three hundred were handsome and robed in red.
1690 They carried swords inlaid with stones and they stood in front of him;
he used them all as guards in the narrow passes
and they protected Roman territory against barbarian peoples.
Like delightful birds when they fly back to roost,
they too made a most delightful sound before Akritis, the marvellous
   Frontiersman.
1695   Since all the delightful things of this deceitful world
death subdues and Hades takes into his possession,
on this day death has caught up also with the Frontiersman of
   Double Descent.
Understand this and weep for Digenis Akritis;
behold him, and lament from the depths of your heart
1700 the misfortune that is taking place, the spectacle and the pain.

1676–7 These lines are probably an oath attesting the veracity of claims about the tomb.
Kalonaros and Trapp removed E1676 and attached 1677 to the following sentence, thus
setting Digenis' couch on his tomb. The implausibility of the latter scenario makes the
weak syntax of the former more acceptable.
1694 The comparison between the armed warriors (chattering and perhaps clattering
their weapons) and the roosting flock of birds is intended to underline the essentially
peaceable nature of Digenis' way of life.
1695–793 Alexiou's sixth song, 'The Death of the Frontiersman'; cf. G8.1–198; much
of this would have been present in *Digenis.
1700 The appeal to the wider world is an element in the ritual lament; Alexiou. M.,
1974, 171–7.

Ἀπότε ἐκτίστην ὁ παρὼν καὶ δόλιος κόσμος οὗτος,
εἰς τὰς γενέας ἅπασας τοιοῦτος οὐκ ἐφάνη,
οἷος τοῦτος ὁ νεώτερος ὁ θαυμαστὸς Ἀκρίτης
εἰς ἀνδρείαν, εἰς ἔπαινον, εἰς δόξαν, εἰς λογάριν.
1705 Καὶ σήμερον πλερώνεται καὶ χάνεται ἐκ τὸν κόσμον,
εἰς νόσον γὰρ θανάσιμον ἔπεσεν καὶ ἀποθνήσκει.
Καὶ ἔμπηξε τοὺς ἀγκώνους του | εἰς τὸ προσκέφαλόν του 198r
καὶ τοὺς ἀγούρους του ἔλεγεν, οὕτως τοὺς παραγγέλλει:
«Θυμᾶσθε, παλληκάρια μου, τῆς Ἀραβίας τοὺς κάμπους,
1710 ὅτι ἦσαν κάμποι ἄνυδροι καὶ καύματα μεγάλα,
ὅντε μᾶς ἐγυρίσασιν ἔνοπλοι Ἀραβίτες
καὶ ἐγλήγορα οὐκ εὑρέθητε ὅλοι ἀρματωμένοι
καὶ οἱ τριακόσιοι ἐκύκλωσαν καὶ ἔβαλάν με εἰς τὴν μέσην
καὶ ἕως νὰ καβαλικεύσετε, ἐσκόρπισά τους ὅλους.
1715 Πάλιν, ἀγοῦροι μου, εἴδετε καὶ ἄλλον θαῦμαν μέγαν·
εἰς τὸ στενὸν τὸ πέραμαν τοῦ ποταμοῦ τοῦ Ἀφράτου
ἦτον ὁ κάλαμος δασὸς καὶ ὑπόδροσος ὁ τόπος·
ἐκεῖ ἔστησα τὴν τέντα μου νὰ περιαναπαυθοῦμεν,
καὶ ἀπότι ἀναπαύθημαν, ἔδοξε μας μετριάζειν
1720 καὶ ὅλοι σας ἀνατρέχετε ἀπέσω εἰς <τὸ> ποτάμιν.
Καὶ ἐξέβησαν δύο λέοντες <ὁμοῦ> μὲ τὰς λεαίνας
καὶ ἔσυρναν τὰ λεοντόπουλα ὅλα παρακρουσμένα·
καὶ ὡσὰν τὰ εἴδετε, ἀγοῦροι μου, <εὐθὺς> ἐφύγετε ὅλοι
καὶ ἐμὲν μόνον ἀφήσετε ἀπέσω εἰς τὰ θηρία,
1725 καὶ εἴδετε ὅτι ἐπέζευσα, μὲ τὸ ραβδὶν τὰ ἐσέβην.
Καὶ οἱ λέοντες ἀποπίσω μου ἤρχουντα νὰ μὲ φᾶσιν,
καὶ ὡς ἔδωκα τὴν λέαιναν ἀπάνω εἰς τὸ κεφάλιν,
οἱ λέοντες ἐμπήκασιν ἀπέσω εἰς τὸ καλάμιν.

1701 Ἀπότε Trapp: ὅτι ἀπὸ ταῖς E
1703 οἷος τοῦτος ὁ νεώτερος ὁ θαυμαστὸς Ἀκρίτης Kalonaros: οἷον τοῦτον τὸν νεότερον τὸν θαυμαστὸν Ἀκρίτην E
1704 εἰς ἀνδρείαν Trapp: οὗται εἰς ἀνδρίαν, οὗται E
1713 ἐκύκλωσαν καὶ ἔβαλάν Alexiou: ἔβαλαν, καὶ ἐκύκλωσαν E
1714 ἕως Alexiou: ὅσω ποῦ E
1717 κάλαμος Alexiou: καλάμιος E καλαμιὸς Politis, N.G., 1920, 242 δασὸς Politis, ibid.: δάσος E
1720 τὸ added by Alexiou
1721 δύο Alexiou, cf. E1726, 1728: εἴκοσι E ὁμοῦ μὲ τὰς λεαίνας Alexiou: με τὰς λένας E
1723 εὐθὺς ἐφύγετε ὅλοι Alexiou: ὅλοι ἐφύγεται E
1726 οἱ Alexiou: δύο E ἤρχουντα Alexiou: ἤρχουντε E
1727 λέαιναν Krumbacher, 1904, 334: ἔλεναν E
1728 οἱ Alexiou: οἱ δύο E

From the time when this present deceptive world was created
no one has appeared amongst all generations
to compare with this young man, Akritis the marvellous Frontiersman,
in bravery, in praise, in reputation, in wealth.
1705 Yet today he has reached his end and is being lost to the world,
for he has succumbed to a fatal disease and is dying.
 He rested his elbows on his pillow
and spoke to his youngsters: he addressed them thus:
"Remember, my brave young men, the plains of Arabia,
1710 that the plains were waterless and the heat great
when armed Arabs surrounded us;
at first you were not all fully armed
when the three hundred of them attacked and had me encircled in
 their midst,
but by the time you had mounted I had scattered them all.
1715 At another time, my youngsters, you saw a further great marvel.
At the narrow crossing over the river Euphrates
there was a thick reed-bed and the place was rather cool.
I put up my tent there so that we could take some rest,
and when we had rested we decided to have some fun;
1720 all of you ran off into the river.
Two lions appeared, with their lionesses,
and they were bringing their cubs, in high spirits.
When you saw them, my youngsters, you all promptly ran away
and left me on my own among the wild beasts;
1725 you saw how I dismounted, how I laid into them with my stick.
The lions came up behind me to devour me
but when I struck the lioness on the head
the lions went back into the reed-bed.

1708 'Youngsters' appear in E in the service of the emir. Digenis' father-in-law, the guerrillas and Maximou, but the only reference to any activity of theirs with Digenis comes incidentally at E1422.
1709–14 Not an episode recorded previously in E; the closest parallel comes at E500–12 though there the reference is to the emir's deeds at the battle of Mylokopia.
1721 The only wild beasts with cubs dealt with by Digenis are bears at E755–77; there were no youngsters present.

Μὰ | τὸν Θεόν, <ἀγοῦροι μου,> ἀλήθειαν σᾶς <τὸ> λέγω·   198v
1730 μὰ τὸ μυστήριον τὸ φρικτὸν ὁποὺ μὲ παραστέκει,
οὐκ ἐσυνέκρινα ποτὲ θάνατον ἐδικόν σας·
διὰ τοῦτο σᾶς ἐνθύμισα, ὡς διὰ νὰ μοῦ θυμᾶσθε.
Καὶ εἰς τὰ ἄλλα οὐδὲν ἐφθάσετε, τὰ μόνος μου ἐπολέμουν,
καὶ ἐγὼ μόνος σᾶς ἔβλεπα ἐσᾶς καὶ τὴν καλήν μου.
1735 Καὶ πάλιν εἰς τὴν τέντα μου πόσοι ἀπελάτες ἦλθαν,
ποίας τρικυμίας ὑπέμεινα εἰς τὰς βαρέας ἀνάγκας
καὶ πόσοι ἐβουλήθησαν νὰ μὲ τὴν ἀφαρπάξουν,
τὴν πάγκαλον, τὴν πάμνοστον, ὡραίαν ποθητήν μου,
ἀρχὴν ὄνταν ἐξέβηκεν ἀπὸ τὰ γονικά της.
1740 Ἐγὼ καὶ τούτη μοναχοὶ ὁδεύαμεν ἀντάμα
καὶ δράκος μᾶς ἐλάλησεν μέσ᾽ ἀπὸ τὸ καλάμιν
καὶ παλληκάρι ἐγίνετον ἡδονικὸν καὶ ὡραῖον·
ἱστίαν καὶ φλόγαν ἤβγαλεν ἀπὸ τοῦ στόματός του
καὶ ἄγρια μοῦ ἐλάλησεν, ἵνα μοῦ τὴν ἐπάρη
1745   καὶ ἐμένα νὰ φάγη.
Καὶ ὁ Θεὸς ὁ πάντων δυνατὸς καὶ πάντων κυριεύων
αὐτὸς μᾶς ἐβοήθησεν· καὶ οὐδὲν κακόν μ᾽ ἐποῖκεν.
Καὶ εἴδετε, παλληκάρια μου, μόνος πῶς ἐπειράσθην
καὶ ἐσεῖς ἀλλοῦ ηὑρίσκεσθε καὶ μετ᾽ ἐμὲν οὐκ ἦσθε.
1750   Τοιοῦτον πάλιν λέγω σας ὀρθῶς καὶ νουθετῶ σας·
ἔχετε πάντοτε εἰς νοῦν μελέτη τοῦ θανάτου,
ἔχετε ἀγάπην ἄπειρον ἀμφότεροι εἰς τὸν κόσμον 199r
καὶ ὁ Θεὸς ὁ πάντων δυνατός, ὁ συνέχων τὴν κτίσιν,
αὐτὸς νὰ σᾶς κατευοδοῖ εἰς ἀριστείαν μεγάλην·
1755 καὶ πάντες μέλλομεν σταθῆν τὴν φοβερὰν ἡμέραν
                          ἐλέγχουσαν τὰς πράξεις

1729 ἀγοῦροι μου added by Trapp τὸ added by Alexiou
1732 ἐνθύμισα Alexiou: ἐνεθύμησα E
1733 μόνος μου ἐπολέμουν Alexiou: ἐπολέμουν μοναξός μου E
1734 σᾶς Alexiou: να σας E
1736 ποίας Alexiou: καὶ πόσας E
1737 νὰ Trapp: ἵνα E
1738 πάμνοστον Krumbacher, 1904, 335: πάνμνοστον E ποθητήν Kalonaros: ποθητί E
1742 παλληκάρι ἐγίνετον Alexiou: ἐγίνετον παλικάριν E
1747 κακόν μ᾽ ἐποῖκεν Spadaro, 1989, 182–3: μας ἐπίκεν κακὸν E
1748 πῶς Trapp: τὸ πῶς E ἐπειράσθην Kalonaros: ἐπειράσθη E
1749 ἀλλοῦ Kalonaros: ἄλλου ἀλλοῦ E ἦσθε Alexiou: ἦσθεν E
1752 ἔχετε Trapp: ἀλλ᾽ ἔχετε E
1755 σταθῆν Alexiou: παρασταθῆν E τὴν φοβερὰν ἡμέραν Kalonaros: τῆς φοβερὰς ἡμέρας E

By God, my youngsters, I am telling you the truth;
1730 by the dread mystery which is approaching me,
I have never assented to your death;
I have reminded you of this, so that you remember me.
You were not up to any of the other contests which I fought on my
own,
when I on my own looked out for you and my lovely girl.
1735 And once again, remember how many guerrillas came to my tent,
how many tempests I endured at a time of deep crisis,
and how many plotted to abduct her from me,
my very lovely, quite enchanting and beautiful beloved,
when at the beginning she left her father's estates.
1740 She and I were travelling together on our own,
when a serpent addressed me from the reed-bed
and turned himself into a pleasant and handsome youth.
He spewed fire and flame from his jaws
1745 and addressed me savagely, so as to seize her from me
and devour me.
But God, who has power over all things and is lord over all,
it was he who helped us; and the serpent did me no harm.
And you have seen, my brave young men, what trials I underwent
on my own
when you were off elsewhere and were not with me.
1750   I am saying this to you once more correctly and I advise you:
always keep in mind your preparation for death,
maintain all of you a boundless love for all people,
and may God, who has power over all things and who maintains his
creation,
himself guide you to great achievements.
1755 We shall all stand on that fearsome day
which will see our deeds judged,

καὶ ἕκαστος λάβῃ ἀνταμοιβὴν ἐκ τοῦ ἰδίου ἔργου
καὶ ὁ Θεὸς ὁ πολυεύσπλαγχνος νὰ μὴ σᾶς διαχωρίσῃ.
Τοὺς τριακοσίους ἀφήνω σας ἀπὸ ἑνὸς φαρίου,
1760 καὶ ἀπὸ λουρικίων τριῶν καὶ ἀπὸ ἑνὸς σπαθίου,
τοὺς τριακοσίους ἀφήνω σας ἀπὸ ἑνὸς ραβδίου.
Καὶ πάλιν τοῦτο λέγω σας, πάλιν νὰ μοῦ θυμᾶσθε,
μὴ εἰσέλθετε, ἀγοῦροι μου, εἰς ἕτερον αὐθέντην,
ὅτι Ἀκρίτην ἕτερον εἰς κόσμον οὐ θεωρεῖτε.»
1765 Καὶ ἀφότου ἀπεπλήρωσεν ὅλην τὴν χάριν τούτην,
ἐσκέφθην ἄγγελον πυρὸς ἀπ᾽ οὐρανοῦ ἐπελθόντα·
καὶ ὡς τὸν εἶδε ὁ Διγενής, ἐτρόμαξεν μεγάλως
καὶ τὴν καλήν του ἐφώνιαξεν νὰ ἰδῇ τὴν φαντασίαν:
«Βλέπεις, καλή, τὸν ἄγγελον, ὁποὺ μὲ θέλει πάρει;
1770 Ἐλύθησαν τὰ χέρια μου ἐκ τὴν ἰδέαν τοῦ ἀγγέλου
καὶ ἐλύθησαν οἱ ὦμοι μου ἐκ τὴν ἰδέαν τοῦ ἀγγέλου.»
Τὸν ἄγγελον δικολογᾶ καὶ τὴν καλήν του λέγει:
1773 «Καλή, ὡς εἶδες ἀπ᾽ ἀρχῆς, ὅτε εἴχαμεν τὸν πόθον,
1787 θυμᾶσαι, ἠξεύρεις, λυγερή, τὰ πρωτινὰ ἐκεῖνα,   (199v)
ὅτι πολλοὶ ἐβουλεύθησαν τοῦ νὰ μὲ θανατώσουν,
καὶ πάντας τοὺς ἐζύγωνα καὶ ἄλλα πλέα ἔκαμά τους·
1790 <τοὺς> λῃστάδας ἐπάταξα καὶ ὅλην τὴν Συρίαν,
τὰς ἐρήμους κατέστησα πόλεις κατοικημένας·
ταῦτα ἐποίησα, καλή, ἐσένα νὰ κερδέσω·   G8.80
ἀλλὰ πληροφορέσου το ὅτι ἐγὼ ἀποθνήσκω.   G8.124
Ὁ Χάρος τρέπει ἐκ παντὸς τὸν μήποτε τραπέντα,   G8.125
1795 ὁ Χάροντας χωρίζει με ἀπὸ σοῦ τῆς φιλτάτης,   G8.126
ὁ Ἅδης παραλαμβάνει με· πολὺν ἔχω τὸν πόνον   G8.2. 127
1797 | σοῦ τῆς ἀθλίας ἕνεκεν τῆς ταπεινῆς τῆς χήρας.   200r
1774 Σή|μερον χωριζόμεθα καὶ ἀπέρχομαι εἰς τὸν κόσμον   (199r/v)

1760 ἀπὸ λουρικίων τριῶν καὶ ἀπὸ ἑνὸς σπαθίου Alexiou: ἀπὸ ἑνὸς σπαθίου, καὶ ἀπὸ τριῶν λουρικίων Ε
1762 πάλιν² Hesseling: πάλι Ε
1764 Ἀκρίτην ἕτερον Alexiou: ἄλλον Ἀκρίτην Ε
1766 ἐπελθόντα Alexiou: ἀπελθόντος Ε
1767 εἶδε Alexiou: εἶδεν Ε
1768 ἐφώνιαξεν Krumbacher. 1904. 336: ἐφονίαζεν Ε
1773 ὅτε Alexiou: ὅτι Ε
1787 θυμᾶσαι Alexiou: θυμάσε καὶ Ε
1788 πολλοὶ Alexiou: πολλὰ Ε
1789 πάντας τοὺς ἐζύγωνα Alexiou: ἐγὼ πάντα ἐζήγωνα τους Ε   πλέα Krumbacher. 1904. 336: πλέα παρα τοῦτα Ε
1790 τοὺς added by Trapp
1791 κατέστησα Kalonaros: κατοίκησα Ε

and each will receive recompense for his own deeds,
and may God the all-compassionate not divide you.
  I leave the three hundred of you each one charger,
1760 and three breastplates each and one sword,
and I leave the three hundred of you each one stick.
And I say to you again, again so that you remember me,
do not enter, my youngsters, the service of another lord
because you will never see another Akritis, another Frontiersman in
  this world."
1765   And when he had completed all this gift-giving,
he saw an angel of fire descending from heaven.
When Digenis saw this, he trembled greatly
and called to his beloved to see the vision:
"Do you see, my dearest, the angel who will take me away?
1770 My arms grow weak at the sight of the angel,
and my shoulders grow weak at the sight of the angel."
  He defended himself before the angel and said to his beloved:
1773 "Dearest, as you saw at the beginning, when we had such passion,
1787 you remember, you know, my slender one, in those first days
that many plotted to kill me
but I chased them all away and did many other things to them;
1790 I subdued the brigands and all Syria;
I turned the deserts into inhabited cities;
I did all this, my beloved, to win you.
But you should know that I am dying.
Charos is totally defeating one who has never been defeated,
1795 Charos is separating me from you, my dearest,
Hades has hold of me; great is the pain I have
1797 for you, the pitiable widow, in your affliction.
1774 Today we are being separated and I leave for the dark world

1772 The angel is not part of G's version of this scene.
1773ff. There is a disjunction in sense between 1773/74. Various solutions present
themselves: that adopted here (1773, 1787-97, 1774-86, 1798-); Trapp 1773,
1787-97, 1774-8, 1798-804, 1779-86, 1805- ; Alexiou 1773, 1787-93, 1774-86,
1794- . None is especially convincing.
1792 Digenis' encounter with Charos dominates his appearance in later folk-song
(Saunier, 1972).
1794-1867 (cf. G8.125-98) Alexiou considers E's text from this point an 'epilogue' and
relegates it to an appendix; however, the elements in common with G (common lines and
most conspicuously the simultaneous death of Digenis and his wife) indicate that this
section must have been part of *Digenis (Introduction, p. xxviii). With the limited evidence
at our disposal, any other conclusion has elements of special pleading.

1775 τὸν μαῦρον, σκοτεινότατον, καὶ πάγω κάτω εἰς Ἅδην·
σήμερον <γὰρ> πληρώνει με ὁ θάνατος καὶ ὑπάγω.
Καλή μου, μὴ μὲ δικαστῆς εἰς τὸν ἐκεῖσε κόσμον,
μὴ σταθῶμεν ἀμφότεροι εἰς τὸ δεινὸν κριτήριον.
Οἶδα φαγεῖν καὶ πιεῖν ἔχεις καὶ <νὰ> λουσθῆς καὶ ἀλλάξης
1780 καὶ ἐσὲν ἀφήνω σε πλουσίαν πολλὰ ἀπὸ παντόθεν·
λογάριν ἔχεις περισσόν, ἀσήμιν καὶ χρυσάφιν,
οἱ τρίκλινοί μου γέμουσιν βλατία ὑφασμένα.
Μηδέν, <καλή μου,> ἐνθυμηθῆς ἄλλον νὰ περιλάβης·
Καὶ ἂν θυμηθῆς, ἃς θυμηθῆς καλοῦ νεωτέρου ἀγάπην,
1785 νὰ μὴ φοβᾶται κίνδυνον εἰς τοὺς βαρέους πολέμους·
1786 καὶ πάντα φέρνε κατὰ νοῦν καὶ ἐμὲν μὴ λησμονήσῃς.
1798 Λοιπὸν δυσώπει τὸν Θεὸν ἐκ βάθους τῆς καρδίας,   (200r)
ἱκέτευε τὸν συμπαθῆ καὶ φιλάνθρωπον μόνον,
1800 ὅπως νὰ μεταμεληθῆ καὶ ἀφήση τὴν ψυχήν μου.
Εἰ δὲ οὐ παρακληθῆ ὁ Θεὸς καὶ θέλη νὰ ἀποθάνω,
τὸν τῆς χηρείας καύσωνα οὐ δύνασαι ὑπομένειν,   G8.136
ὡς διατὶ οὐδὲν ἔχεις τινὰν εἰς ἐτοῦτον τὸν κόσμον,
οὐ κύρην, οὐδὲ ἀδέλφια, οὐδὲ προστάτην ἄλλον.»
1805   Ἐκείνη δὲ ὡς ἤκουσεν τὰ λόγια τοῦ καλοῦ της,
εὐθέως πρὸς ἀνατολὰς τὰς χεῖρας ἐκπετάσας   G2.250. 8.150
καὶ πρὸς Θεὸν ἐλάλησεν φωνὴν πολλὰ θλιμμένην:
«Κύριε Θεέ, παμβασιλεῦ, ὁ κτίσας τοὺς αἰώνας,   G8.153
ὁ στερεώσας οὐρανὸν καὶ γῆν θεμελιώσας,   G8.154
1810 ὁ θάλασσαν τὴν ἄπειρον ψάμμῳ περιτειχίσας
καὶ τοὺς ἰχθύας πρὸς αὐτῆς προστάξας ζωογονᾶσθαι,
ὁ πλάσας δὲ καὶ τὸν Ἀδὰμ ἀπὸ γῆς καὶ τὴν Εὔαν,   G8.156
ὁ τὸν τερπνὸν παράδεισον χειρὶ καταφυτεύσας,
ὁ λόγῳ συστησάμενος ὄρη τε καὶ τὰς νάπας,

1776 γὰρ added by Trapp
1778 σταθῶμεν Alexiou: ἰσταθώμεν E
1779 Οἶδα Alexiou: ἐγὼ ἴδα E   νὰ added by Alexiou
1783 Μηδέν, καλή μου Alexiou: καὶ μὴ δὲν ἄλλον E
1784 Καὶ Kalonaros: ἀλλὰ E   ἃς θυμηθῆς Alexiou: θυμίσου E   καλοῦ Hesseling: ἀλοῦ E
1785 κίνδυνον Kalonaros: πόλεμον E
1786 πάντα Alexiou: πάντας E   καὶ ἐμὲν Alexiou: καὶ μὲν E
1798 βάθους Hesseling: βάθου E
1799 ἱκέτευε τὸν συμπαθῆ καὶ φιλάνθρωπον μόνον Trapp, cf. Z4339: κατὰ τὸ
συμπαθὲς καὶ φιλάνθρωπος μόνος E
1802 χηρείας Hesseling: χωρίας E   δύνασαι Hesseling: δύναμε E
1804 οὐ Alexiou: οὐδὲ E   προστάτην Krumbacher, 1904. 337: προτοστάτην E
1811 ζωογονᾶσθαι Hesseling: ζωογονάστε E

1775 of deep shadow, I go below to Hades;
      today death brings me to my end and I depart.
      My beloved, do not judge me in the world beyond
      lest we both stand before the dread judgement seat.
      I know that you have enough to eat and drink and to wash and
         change your clothes,
1780 and I leave you a wealthy woman on every account;
      you have an abundant fortune of silver and gold,
      my chambers are full of woven silks.
      Do not, my beloved, consider embracing another;
      but if you think of it, think of the love of a handsome young man
1785 who will not be afraid of danger in fierce fighting.
1786 And always keep me in your mind, do not forget me.
1798 So beseech God from the depth of your heart,
      plead with him who alone is kind and benevolent,
1800 to repent and relinquish my soul.
      But if God rejects your plea and intends me to die,
      you will not be able to endure the torment of widowhood
      since you have no one in this world,
      no lord father nor brothers nor any other protector."
1805   When she heard her beloved's words
      she immediately stretched out her hands to the east
      and addressed a voice of great grief to God:
      "Lord God, ruler of all, creator of the ages,
      who fixed the heaven and established the earth,
1810 who walled the boundless sea around with sand
      and instructed the fish to reproduce within it;
      who created Adam from earth, and Eve;
      who planted the delightful Paradise with his hand;
      who with his word set up the mountains and valleys,

1786 There is ambivalence here: E seems to make Digenis forbid the girl ever to marry
again whilst including his advice about her choice should she do so. *Digenis* (cf.
G8.137–8) presumably advised remarriage for the girl's protection.
1803–4 The girl's parents and five brothers appeared to have been reconciled to her
marriage with Digenis. It is not clear why they are excluded from any role in her future.
1806, 1822 Masculine participles referring to the girl in a passage at the most learned
language register of the poem undermine its credibility.

1815 φῶς καὶ ἀέραν δι' ἐμὲ δείξας τὴν τρισαθλίαν,
ὁ κατελθὼν ἐξ οὐρανοῦ, ὡς ἠθέλησας, Λόγε,
καὶ σαρκοφόρος δι' ἐμὲ γεγονώς, πλαστουργέ μου,
καὶ μητέραν τὴν ἄχραντον παρθένον ἀπειργάσω
καὶ γεννηθεὶς ἀρρεύστως
0/21 καὶ παθών, ὡς ηὐδόκησας σταυρωθῆναι, Χριστέ μου,
ἀνάστασιν δωρούμενος κἀμοὶ τῷ πεπτωκότι,
ἀνάστησον, φιλάνθρωπε, καὶ τὸν | ἐμὸν αὐθέντην   200v
καὶ δός του ὑγείαν ἀπὸ ἀρχῆς ὡς ἐλεήμων, Λόγε,
1825 καὶ μὴ ἰδῶ <τὸν> θάνατον ποτὲ τοῦ ποθητοῦ μου.
Ἀλλ' ὡς ποτὲ τὸν Λάζαρον ἀνέστησας, Χριστέ μου,   G8.162
καὶ εἶδας γάρ, φιλάνθρωπε, Μάρθαν καὶ τὴν Μαρίαν
θερμῶς κινούσας δάκρυα,
οὕτως καὶ νῦν ἀνάστησον νέον ἀπελπισμένον   G8.163. 169
1830 ἀπὸ πάντων <τῶν> ἰατρῶν, γνωρίμων τε καὶ φίλων
καὶ ἐν σοὶ ἀναθέμενον τὰς ἐλπίδας ἁπάσας
καὶ εἰς τὴν σὴν βοήθειαν ἀεὶ ἐπιθαρροῦντα.
Ναί, δέσποτα φιλάνθρωπε, μόνε καρδιογνῶστα,
ὁ δι' ἐμὲ . . . ἑκουσίως πτωχεύσας,
1835 ὁ τὴν ἐμὴν ἀσθένειαν ἐθελοντὶ φορέσας,
<ὁ> διαθρέψας ἄπειρον πλῆθος ἐκ πέντε ἄρτων,
μὴ παρίδης τὴν δέησιν ἐμοῦ τῆς ἀναξίας,   G8.158
ἀλλ' ἐξαπόστειλον ταχὺ ἔλεος ἐξ ἁγίου,
κλῖνον τὸ οὖς σου, δέσποτα, εἰσάκουσον εὐχῆς μου,   G4.371
1840 πρόφθασον ἐν ἀνάγκαις νῦν, πρόφθασον ἐν τῇ θλίψει,
ἐλθὲ εἰς τὴν βοήθειαν ἡμῶν τῶν δεομένων
1842 καὶ τὰ ἐλέη σου ἡμῖν θαυμάστωσον, οἰκτίρμων.
1844 Ἐκ θανάτου ἀνάστησον, εὔσπλαγχνε, σὸν ἱκέτην,
1845 ἐκ θανάτου ἐξάρπασον νέον μὴ μεταγνόντα·
αὐτὸς γὰρ ἔφης, δέσποτα, κἂν ὅλως μὴ θελῆσαι

1815 τὴν τρισαθλίαν Alexiou: τη συ αθλία E perhaps τὴν σὴν ἀθλίαν
1818 παρθένον Grégoire-Letocart. 1939. 224. cf. Z4373: οὐρανὸν E
1820/21 ὡς Alexiou: ὡς αὐτὸς ἴδας καὶ ὡς E
1825 τὸν added by Krumbacher. 1904. 337
1827 Μάρθαν καὶ τὴν Μαρίαν Trapp: μάρθας καὶ τῆς μαρίας E
1828 κινούσας Kalonaros: κινοῦσα E
1830 πάντων Hesseling: παντῶν E   τῶν added by Krumbacher. 1904. 338
1831 ἐν σοὶ Kalonaros: ἐσὺ E
1832 ἐπιθαρροῦντα Papadimitriou (Karayanni. 1976. 121): εὐφοροῦνται E
1835 ἐθελοντὶ Kalonaros: ἐθέλοντι E
1836 ὁ added by Kalonaros
1842 ἡμῖν Alexiou: ἡμῶν E   After οἰκτίρμων E adds ἐκ θανάτου ἀνάστησον ἱκέτην
(=1843). removed by Krumbacher. 1904. 338

1815 revealing light and air, for the sake of me the thrice afflicted;
Word, who came down from heaven as you wished;
who put on flesh, my Creator, for my sake;
and you made an immaculate virgin your mother
                              and were born unchanged
1820/21 and suffered, as you consented to be crucified, my Christ,
bestowing resurrection even on me the sinner;
benevolent God, raise up my lord too
and grant him health once again, since you are merciful, Word,
1825 and let me never see my beloved's death.
But as you once raised up Lazarus, my Christ
– for, benevolent one, you saw Martha and Mary
passionately shedding tears –
so now raise up this young man for whom there is no hope,
1830 from all doctors, acquaintances and friends,
and who places all his hopes in you
and always trusts in your aid.
Yes, benevolent Lord, who alone knows hearts,
who for me willingly endured poverty,
1835 who of your own volition have borne my weakness,
who nourished a boundless multitude with five loaves,
do not despise this plea from me in my unworthiness
but send down quickly pity out of your holy store;
incline your ear, Lord, hear my prayer;
1840 make haste now in my distress, make haste in my grief,
come to the aid of us who beseech you
1842 and in your pity display your mercy before us.
1844 Raise your suppliant from death, compassionate one,
1845 take back from death a young man who has not repented;
for you yourself have said, Lord, that you in no way desire

ἁμαρτωλοῦ τὸν θάνατον ὅπως νὰ ἐπιστρέψῃ.
Καὶ νῦν, φιλάνθρωπε Θεέ, βοήθει τῷ κειμένῳ
<καὶ> ἔκτεινον | τὴν κραταιὰν χεῖραν ὡς εὐεργέτης   201r
1850 καὶ ὡς τὸν Πέτρον ἔσωσας θαλασσίου κινδύνου,
οὕτω καὶ νῦν ἐλέησον ἱκέτην σου ἀχρεῖον·
εἰ δ' οὔ, κέλευσον, δέσποτα, πρῶτον ἐμὲ τεθνάναι·
μὴ ἴδω τοῦτον ἄφωνον, κατακείμενον ἄπνουν,   G8.175
κεκαλυμμένους ὀφθαλμοὺς ἔχοντα τοὺς ὡραίους·   G8.178
1855 μὴ ἰδῶ χεῖρας τὰς καλάς, ἀνδραγαθεῖν μαθούσας,   G8.176
δεδεμένας σταυροειδῶς, νεκρικὰ συσταλμένας.   G8.177-8
Μή μου τὰ δάκρυα, Χριστέ, παρίδῃς δεομένης,
μή με τοσαύτην κατιδεῖν παραχωρήσῃς θλίψιν,   G8.179
ἀλλ' ἔπαρόν μου τὴν ψυχὴν πρὸ τοῦ γενέσθαι ταῦτα·
1860 πάντα γὰρ λόγῳ δύνασαι, οὐδὲν ἀδυνατεῖ σοι.»   G2.16, 8.180
Ὡς δὲ καὶ ταῦτα ἔλεγε μετὰ πολλῶν δακρύων,
στραφεῖσα τοῦτον αἰφνιδίως ὁρᾷ ψυχορραγοῦντα.   G8.183
Καὶ τὸν πόνον τὸν ἄπειρον φέρειν μὴ δυναμένη   G8.184
πάνυ ἐλιγοθύμησε βαπτισθεῖσα τὴν θλίψιν
1865 καὶ πεσοῦσα ἐπὶ τῆς γῆς παρέδωκεν τὸ πνεῦμα,
οὐ γὰρ ἐγίνωσκε ποτὲ ὑπάρχουσαν τὴν θλίψιν,
καὶ ἐν μιᾷ ἀμφότεροι τῇ ὥρᾳ τελευτῶσιν.   G8.197-8

1849 καὶ added by Kalonaros   κραταιὰν Krumbacher, 1904, 338: κραιτεὰν E
1850 Πέτρον Krumbacher, 1904, 338: παρὸν E   θαλασσίου Alexiou: θαλάτισου E
1853 ἴδω Krumbacher, 1904, 338: ἰδῶ E   ἄφωνον Krumbacher, ibid.: ἄμφονον E
κατακείμενον Hesseling: κατικειμένον E
1854 κεκαλυμμένους Xanthoudidis, 1912, 572: καὶ καλημένους E
1855 ἀνδραγαθεῖν Hesseling: ἀδραγαθην E
1856 δεδεμένας Krumbacher, 1904, 338: δεδεμένα E   νεκρικὰ Krumbacher, 1904, 338:
νεκρῆκα E
1858 παραχωρήσῃς Krumbacher, 1904, 338: παράχωρίσας E
1861 ταῦτα Krumbacher, 1904, 338: τὰ E
1862 στραφεῖσα Krumbacher, 1904, 338: στραφῆ E   αἰφνιδίως Alexiou: ἐφνιδος E
ὁρᾷ Kalonaros: ὥρα E
1863 δυναμένη Krumbacher, 1904, 338: δυνάμη E
1864 ἐλιγοθύμησε Hesseling: ἐλιγόθυμησε E
1866 ὑπάρχουσαν τὴν Kalonaros: τὴν ὑπηρμένην E
1867 ἐν μιᾷ Krumbacher, 1904, 339: ἐμιᾶ E   τῇ ὥρᾳ Trapp: τὴν ὥραν E   τελευτῶσιν
Kalonaros: τελευτόσα E

the death of a sinner, so that he may mend his ways.
So now, benevolent God, help him who is lying here
and stretch out your mighty hand as a benefactor,
1850 and as you saved Peter from danger at sea,
even so pity now your wretched suppliant;
if not, command me, Lord, to die first.
May I not see him speechless, lying without breath,
with his beautiful eyes covered.
1855 May I not see his dear hands, skilled at performing great deeds,
clasped cross-wise, contracted in death.
Do not despise my tears, as I beseech you, Christ;
do not permit me to see such great grief
but take my soul before this happens,
1860 for you are capable of all things with a word; there is nothing you
cannot do.''
As she said this with many tears,
she turned and suddenly saw him in his death throes.
Not being able to endure the limitless pain,
she fainted quite away, baptised into grief;
1865 falling to the ground she gave up her spirit,
for she had never known before that grief existed;
and at the same instant both expired.

1867 G continues with an account of the hero's funeral, his tomb and the universal
mourning that his death generated.

Bibliography

Abbreviations

BMGS	*Byzantine and Modern Greek Studies*
BZ	*Byzantinische Zeitschrift*
DOP	*Dumbarton Oaks Papers*
EI	*Encyclopaedia of Islam* (2nd edn) 1960–
GRBS	*Greek, Roman and Byzantine Studies*
JÖB	*Jahrbuch der Österreichischen Byzantinistik*
LSJ	Liddell, H. G., Scott, R. and Jones, H. S. 1940. *A Greek-English Lexicon* (9th edn) Oxford
ODB	*Oxford Dictionary of Byzantium*. A. Kazhdan (ed.) 1990, Oxford and New York
PG	*Patrologia Graeca*
PW	*Paulys Real-Encyclopädie der classischen Altertumwissenschaft.* G. Wissowa (ed.) 1893–

Achilleis N:. *L'Achilléïde byzantine, avec une introduction, des observations et un index*. D. C. Hesseling (ed. and trans.) 1919. Amsterdam.

Achilles Tatius. *Achilles Tatius*. S. Gaselee (ed. and trans.) 1917. Harvard and London.

Adontz, N. 1929/30. 'Les fonds historiques de l'épopée byzantine Digénis Akritas.' *BZ* 29: 198–227.

Agapitos, P. A. and Smith, O. L. 1994. 'Scribes and manuscripts of Byzantine vernacular romances: palaeographical facts and editorial implications.' Ἑλληνικά 44: 61–80.

Alexiou, M. 1974. *The Ritual Lament in Greek Tradition*. Cambridge.

Alexiou, S. 1979. Ἀκριτικά. Iraklio.

　　1985. Βασίλειος Διγενὴς Ἀκρίτης καὶ τὸ Ἄσμα τοῦ Ἀρμούρη. Athens.

　　1988. Review of Prombonas, 1985. Ἑλληνικά 39: 189–95.

　　1990. Βασίλειος Διγενὴς Ἀκρίτης. Athens.

　　1995. 'Βυζαντινοὶ "Δεκαενπτασύλλαβοι"'. Παλίμψηστον 14/15: 11–20.

Anderson, J. C. and Jeffreys, M. J. 1994. 'The decoration of the sevastokratorissa's tent.' *Byzantion* 64: 8–18.

Andriotis, N. P. 1941. 'Μεσαιωνικὰ καὶ νέα Ἑλληνικά.' Ἀθηνᾶ 51 [pub. 1946]: 15–54.

376

Angold, M. (ed.) 1984. *The Byzantine Aristocracy IX to XIII centuries*. BAR International Series 221. Oxford.

Angold, M. 1989. 'The wedding of Digenes Akrites: love and marriage in Byzantium in the eleventh and twelfth centuries', in Ἡ καθημερινὴ ζωὴ στὸ Βυζάντιο: 201–15. Athens.

Anoyianakis, Ph. (Ἀνωγειανάκης) 1962. ' Ἕνα βυζαντινὸ μουσικὸ ὄργανο.' Χριστιανικὴ Ἀρχαιολογικὴ Ἑταιρεία, Δελτίον ser. 4, no. 3: 115–23.

1972. ' Ἑλληνικὰ λαϊκὰ μουσικὰ ὄργανα.' Λαογραφία 28: 175–329.

Bakker, W. F. and van Gemert, A. F. (eds.) 1988. Ἱστορία τοῦ Βελισαρίου. Athens.

Bartikian, H. 1966. 'Notes sur l'épopée byzantine Digenis Akritas.' *Revue des Etudes Arméniennes* 3: 147–76.

1968. 'Sur quelques questions relatives à l'épopée byzantine de Digenis Akritas.' *Revue des Etudes Arméniennes* 5: 295–305.

1993. 'Armenia and Armenians in Byzantine epic', in Beaton and Ricks, 1993: 86–92.

Beaton, R. 1980. *Folk Poetry of Modern Greece*. Cambridge.

1989. *The Medieval Greek Romance*. Cambridge.

1993a. '*Digenes Akrites* on the computer: a comparative study of the E and G versions', in Panayotakis 1993, vol. 2: 42–68.

1993b. 'An epic in the making? The early versions of Digenes Akrites', in Beaton and Ricks, 1993: 55–72.

1996. 'Cappadocians at court: Digenes and Timarion', in Mullett and Smythe, 1996: 329–38.

Beaton, R. and Ricks, D. 1993. *Digenes Akrites: New Approaches to Byzantine Heroic Poetry*. London.

Beck, H.-G. 1971. *Geschichte der byzantinischen Volksliteratur*. Munich.

1984. *Byzantinisches Erotikon*. Bayerische Akademie der Wissenschaften, Phil-Hist. Klasse, Sitzungsberichte: Jahrg. 1984, Hft. 5. Munich.

Belting, H. 1990. *Bild und Kult: eine Geschichte des Bildes vor dem Zeitalter der Kunst*. Munich.

Berger, A. 1982. *Das Bad in der byzantinischen Zeit*. Munich.

Bouvier, B. 1960. Δημοτικὰ τραγούδια ἀπὸ χειρόγραφο τῆς Μονῆς Ἰβήρων. Athens.

Browning, R. 1983. *Medieval and Modern Greek* (2nd edn). Cambridge.

Bryer, A. A. M. 1993. 'The historian's Digenes Akrites', in Beaton and Ricks, 1993: 93–102.

Cameron, A. 1980. 'The sceptic and the shroud: inaugural lecture at King's College, London.' Reprinted in *Continuity and Change in Sixth-Century Byzantium*, no. V. 1981. London.

Cameron, A. and Herrin, J. 1984. *Constantinople in the Early Eighth Century: The Parastaseis Syntomoi Chronikai*. Leiden.

Chatzis, A. Ch. (Χατζῆς) 1930. Προλεγόμενα εἰς τὴν τοῦ Εὐσταθίου Μακρεμβολίτου Ἀκριτηΐδα (Ὁμηρικαὶ ἔρευναι 1). Athens.

1930a. 'Εὐστάθιος Μακρεμβολίτης καὶ "Ομηρος.' Ἐπετηρὶς Ἑταιρείας Βυζαντινῶν Σπουδῶν 7: 234–5.

1932. 'Εὐστάθιος Μακρεμβολίτης καὶ Ἀκριτηΐς.' Byzantinische-Neugriechicher Jahrbuch 9: 256–92.

1951. 'Εὐστάθιος Μακρεμβολίτης καὶ Ἀκριτηΐς.' Ἀθηνᾶ 55: 205–7.

Chatziyakoumis, M. K. (Χατζηγιακουμής) 1977. Τὰ μεσαιωνικὰ δημώδη κείμενα: συμβολὴ στὴ μελέτη καὶ στὴν ἔκδοσή τους. Athens.

Conca, F. (ed.) 1994. Il romanzo bizantino del XII secolo. Turin.

Constantine Porphyrogenitus. Constantini Porphyrogeniti de caerimoniis. J. Reiske (ed.) 1829. Bonn.

Curtius, E. R. 1953. European Literature in the Latin Middle Ages (transl. W. R. Trask). London.

Danezis, G. 1987. Spaneas: Vorlage, Quellen, Versionen. Miscellanea Byzantina Monacensia 31. Munich.

Dangitsis, K. (Δαγκίτσης) 1958/9. 'Παρατηρήσεις σὲ μία νέα ἔκδοση ἑνὸς Ἀκριτικοῦ κειμένου.' Ἑλληνικά 16: 226–30.

Davies, R. 1989. Service in the Roman Army. Edinburgh.

De Andrés, G. 1967. Catálogo de los Códices Griegos de la Real Biblioteca de El Escorial, vol. 3. Madrid.

Delehaye, H. and Peeters, P. 1925. Acta Sanctorum Novembris, vol. 4. Brussels.

Dennis, G. T. 1981. Das Strategikon des Maurikios (with German translation by E. Gamillscheg). Vienna.

1984. Maurice's Strategikon. Philadelphia.

1985. Three Byzantine Military Treatises: Text, Translation and Notes. Washington, DC.

Dörrie, H. 1964. Die Königskult des Antiochos von Kommagene im Licht neuer Inschriften-Funde. Göttingen.

DuCange, C. 1688. Glossarium ad scriptores mediae et infimae graecitatis. Lyons.

Dyck, A. R. 1983. 'On Digenis Akritas Grottaferrata version, Book 5.' GRBS 24: 185–92.

1986. Michael Psellus, The Essays on Euripides and George of Pisidia and on Heliodorus and Achilles Tatius. Vienna.

1987. 'On Digenes Akrites, Grottaferrata version, Book 6.' GRBS 28: 349–69.

Eideneier, H. 1989. 'Ptochoprodromologica.' BZ 82: 73–86.

1991. Ptochoprodromos: Einführung, kritische Ausgabe, deutsche Übersetzung, Glossar. Cologne.

Eideneier, N. 1970. 'Διορθωτικὰ στὸ κείμενο τοῦ Διγενῆ τῆς Κρυπτοφέρρης.' Ἑλληνικά 23: 299–319.

Ekdawi, S., Fann, P. and Philokyprou, E. 1993. 'Fair maids and affronts to their sex: the characterization and structural roles of men and women in the Escorial Διγενὴς Ἀκρίτης.' BMGS 17: 25–42.

Fenik, B. 1991. Digenis: epic and popular style in the Escorial version. Iraklio.

Frantz, A. 1940/1. 'A Byzantine epic and its illustrators.' Byzantion 15: 87–91.

Galatariotou, C. 1987. 'Structural oppositions in the Grottaferrata *Digenes Akrites.' BMGS* 11: 29–68.

　　1989. '*Eros* and *Thanatos*: a Byzantine hermit's conception of sexuality.' *BMGS* 13: 95–138.

　　1993. 'The primacy of the Escorial *Digenis*: an open and shut case?', in Beaton and Ricks, 1993: 38–54.

　　1996. 'Open space / closed space: the perceived worlds of Kekaumenos and Digenes Akrites', in Mullet and Smythe, 1996: 303–28.

Garandoudis, E. (Γαραντούδης) 1993. 'Προβλήματα περιγραφῆς καὶ ἀνάλυσης τῶν πρωτονεοελληνικῶν δεκαπεντασυλλάβων: – μετρικὴ ἀποκατάσταση τῶν δημωδῶν κειμένων', in Panayotakis, 1993, vol. 1: 188–22.

Garsoian, N. G. 1967. *The Paulician Heresy.* The Hague/Paris.

Gärtner, H. 1969. 'Charikleia in Byzanz.' *Antike und Abendland* 15: 47–69.

Genesios. *Iosephi Genesii Regum Libri Quattuor.* Lesmüller-Werner, A. and Thurn, I. 1978. Berlin.

Gleixner, H. J. 1961. *Das Alexanderbild der Byzantiner.* Munich.

Goar, J. 1730. *Euchologium sive rituale graecorum* (2nd edn). Venice.

Goody, J. and Watt, I. 1968. 'The consequences of literacy', in J. Goody (ed.), *Literacy in Traditional Societies*: 27–84. Cambridge.

Graham, H. F. 1968. 'The Tale of Devgenij.' *Byzantinoslavica* 29: 51–91.

Grégoire, H. 1929/30. 'Michel III et Basile le Macédonien dans les inscriptions d'Ancyre.' *Byzantion* 5: 327–40.

　　1931a. 'Le tombeau et la date de Digénis Akritas.' *Byzantion* 6: 481–508.

　　1931b. 'L'épopée byzantine et ses rapports avec l'épopée turque et l'épopée romane.' *Académie Royale de Belgique, Bulletin de la Classe des Lettres et Sciences Morales et Politiques,* 5e série, t. xvii, n. 12: 463–93.

　　1932a. 'Autour de Digénis Akritas; 1. Les cantilènes et la date de la recension d'Andros Trébizonde; 2. Notes complementaires.' *Byzantion* 7: 287–302, 317–20.

　　1932b. 'Les recherches récentes sur l'épopée byzantine', in *L'Antiquité Classique*: 419–39. Louvain.

　　1933. 'Etudes sur l'épopée byzantine.' *Revue des Etudes Grecques* 46: 26–69.

　　1936. 'L'Amazone Maximô?' *Annuaire de l'Institut de Philologie et d'Histoire orientales et slaves* 4 = *Mélanges Franz Cumont*: 723–30.

　　1940/1. 'Notes on the Byzantine epic.' *Byzantion* 15: 92–103.

　　1942. *Ὁ Διγενὴς Ἀκρίτας.* New York.

Grégoire, H. and Letocart, M. 1939. 'Trente-cinq corrections au texte de Digénis selon l'Escorialensis.' *Byzantion* 14: 211–25.

Haldon, J. F. 1975. 'Some aspects of Byzantine military technology from the sixth to the tenth centuries.' *BMGS* 1: 11–48.

　　1990. *Constantine Porphyrogenitus: Three Treatises on Imperial Military Expeditions.* Vienna.

Hatto, A. T. (ed.) 1965. *Eos: An Enquiry into the Theme of Lovers' Meetings and Partings at Dawn*. London.

Heliodoros. *Héliodore. Les Ethiopiques*, 3 vols. R. M. Rattenbury and T. W. Lumb (ed. and trans.) 1935–43. Paris.

Hendy, M. F. 1969. *Coinage and Money in the Byzantine Empire, 1081–1261*. Washington, DC.

1985. *Studies in the Byzantine Monetary Economy*. Cambridge.

Hild, F. 1977. *Das byzantinische Strassensystem in Kappadokien*. Vienna.

Hillberg, I. 1876. Εὐσταθίου Πρωτονωβελισίμου τοῦ Μακρεμβολίτου τῶν καθ᾽ Ὑσμίνην καὶ Ὑσμινίαν λόγοι ια΄. Vienna.

Hoepfner, W. 1983. *Arsameia am Nymphaios*, vol. 2. Istanbuler Forschungen 33. Tübingen.

Holton, D. 1993. 'The formation of the future in Modern Greek literary texts up to the 17th century', in Panayotakis, 1993, vol. 1: 118–28.

Honigmann, E. 1935. *Die Ostgrenze des byzantinisches Reiches von 363 bis 1071* = A. Vasiliev, *Byzance et les Arabes*, vol. 3. Brussels.

Hörandner, W. 1974. *Theodoros Prodromos: Historische Gedichte*. Vienna.

Hunt, L.-A. 1984. 'Comnenian aristocratic palace decorations: descriptions and Islamic connections', in Angold, 1984: 138–57.

Huxley, G. 1974. 'Antecedents and context of Digenes Akrites.' *GRBS* 15: 317–38.

1975. 'The emperor Michael II and the battle of Bishop's Meadow (AD 863).' *GRBS* 16: 443–50.

Ioannidis S. ('Ιωαννίδης) 1870. Ἱστορία καὶ στατιστικὴ Τραπεζοῦντος καὶ τῆς περὶ ταύτην χώρας. Constantinople.

1887. Ἔπος μεσαιωνικὸν ἐκ τοῦ χειρογράφου Τραπεζοῦντος, Βασίλειος Διγενῆς Ἀκρίτης ὁ Καππαδόκης. Constantinople.

Jacob, A. 1977. 'Les écritures de Terre d'Otrante', in *La paléographie grecque et byzantine*: 269–81. Paris.

Jeffreys, E. M. 1978. 'The Judgement of Paris in later Byzantine literature.' *Byzantion* 48: 112–31.

1980. 'The Comnenian background to the *romans d'antiquité*.' *Byzantion* 50: 455–86 = Jeffreys, E. M. and M. J., 1983, no. X.

1993. 'The Grottaferrata version of Digenes: a reassessment', in Beaton and Ricks, 1993: 26–37.

1995. 'Maximou and Digenis.' *Byzantinoslavica* 56: 367–76.

1996. 'Digenis and Charos: G and E reconsidered', in C. N. Constantinides, N. M. Panagiotakes, E. M. Jeffreys and A. D. Angelou (eds.), Venice, Φιλέλλην, *Studies in honour of Robert Browning*: 117–31.

forthcoming b. 'Byzantium's epic past: a twelfth-century perspective', in T. Hillard, R. Kearsley, C. E. V. Nixon and A. Nobbs (eds.), *Festschrift for Edwin Judge*. Sydney.

Jeffreys, E. M. and M. J. 1979. 'The traditional style of early demotic verse.' *BMGS* 5: 115–39 = Jeffreys, E. M. and M. J., 1983, no. III.

1983. *Popular Literature in Late Byzantium*. London.

Jeffreys, M. J. 1973. 'Formulas in the *Chronicle of the Morea.' DOP* 27: 163–95 = Jeffreys, E. M. and M. J., 1983, no. II.

1974. 'The nature and origins of the political verse.' *DOP* 28: 142–95 = Jeffreys, E. M. and M. J., 1983, no. IV.

1975. 'Digenis Akritas Manuscript Z.' *Dodone* (Ioannina) 4: 163–201 = Jeffreys, E. M. and M. J., 1983, no. V.

1976. 'The astrological prologue of *Digenis Akritas.' Byzantion* 46: 375–97 = Jeffreys, E. M. and M. J., 1983, no. VI.

1978. 'Digenis Akritas and Commagene.' *Svenska Forskningsinstitutet i Istanbul Meddelanden* 3: 5–28 = Jeffreys, E. M. and M. J., 1983, no. VII.

1993. 'Early Modern Greek verse: parallels and frameworks.' *Modern Greek Studies (Australia and New Zealand)* 1: 31–48.

1997. 'The use of later manuscripts to reconstruct the Escorial version of Digenis Akritis.' *Byzantion* 67: 60–9.

Joseph, B. 1990. *Morphology and Universals in Syntactic Change.* New York and London.

Justinian, *Novellae*. R. Schöll and W. Kroll (eds.) 1928. Berlin.

Kalonaros, P. (Καλονάρος) 1941. *Βασίλειος Διγενῆς Ἀκρίτας.* 2 vols. Reprinted 1970. Athens (cited as Kalonaros in textual apparatus and elsewhere as Kalonaros, 1941.1 or 2, with page number).

Kambylis, A. 1995. 'Textkritik und Metrik: Überlegungen zu ihren Verhältnis zueinander.' *BZ* 88: 38–67.

Karayanni, I. (Καραγιάννη) 1976. *Ὁ Διγενῆς Ἀκρίτας τοῦ Ἐσκοριάλ: συμβολὴ στὴ μελέτη τοῦ κειμένου.* Ioannina.

Karolidis, P. (Καρολίδης) 1905/6. 'Σημειώσεις κριτικαί, ἱστορικαὶ καὶ τοπογραφικαὶ εἰς τὸ μεσαιωνικὸν ἔπος «Ἀκρίτας».' *Ἐπιστημονικὴ Ἐπετηρὶς Πανεπιστημίου Ἀθηνῶν* 2: 188–246.

1926. 'Τὸ ἔπος τοῦ Διγενῆ Ἀκρίτη.' *Ἐπετηρὶς Ἑταιρείας Βυζαντινῶν Σπουδῶν* 3: 329–32.

Kazhdan, A. 1967. 'Bemerkungen zu Niketas Eugenianos.' *JÖB* 16: 101–17.

1984. 'The image of the medical doctor in Byzantine literature of the tenth to twelfth centuries.' *DOP* 38: 44–51.

Kechaioglou, G. (Κεχαγίογλου) 1993. 'Digenes Akrites in prose: the Andros version in the context of Modern Greek literature', in Beaton and Ricks, 1993: 116–30.

Kekavmenos. *Cecaumeni Strategicon.* B. Wassiliewsky and V. Jernstedt (eds.) 1896. St Petersburg.

Kolias, T. G. 1988. *Byzantinische Waffen: ein Beitrag zur byzantinische Waffenkunde von den Anfängen bis zur lateinischen Eroberung.* Byzantina Vindobonensia 17. Vienna.

Koukoules, Ph. (Κουκουλές) 1913/14. 'Σημειώματα.' *Λαογραφία* 4: 316.

Kriaras, E. (Κριαράς) 1953. 'Ἀκριτικά', in *Προσφορὰ εἰς Στίλπωνα Π. Κυριακίδην.* 383–8. *Ἑλληνικά:* Παράρτημα 4. Thessaloniki.

1969–. *Λεξικὸ τῆς μεσαιωνικῆς ἑλληνικῆς δημώδους γραμματείας 1100–1669.* Thessaloniki.

Krumbacher, K. 1904. 'Eine neue Handschrift des Digenis Akritas.' *Sitzungs-berichte der philos.-philol. und hist. Kl., Kgl. Bay. Akad. der Wiss.*, Hft. 2: 309–53.

Kuz'mina, B. D. 1962. *Devgenievo dejanie.* Moscow.

Kyriakidis, S. (Κυριακίδης) 1926. Ὁ Διγενὴς Ἀκρίτας. Athens.

 1932. Review of Grégoire, 1931a etc. Λαογραφία 10: 623–62.

 1946. 'Ἀκριτικαὶ μελέται', in *Miscellanea Giovanni Mercati*, vol. 3 = Studi e Testi 123: 399–430. Vatican.

 1948. 'Ἡ δημώδης ἑλληνικὴ ποίησις καὶ ἡ ἱστορία τοῦ ἑλληνικοῦ ἔθνους.' Λαογραφία 12: 465–502.

 1951. 'Σημειώματα.' *BZ* 44: 358–61.

 1956. Review of Mavrogordato, 1956. Ἑλληνικά 14: 550.

 1958. 'Forschungsbericht zum Akritas-Epos.' *Berichte zum XI. Internationalen Byzantinisten-Kongress Munich, 1958*, Hft. 2.2.

Laiou, A. 1981. 'The role of women in Byzantine society.' *JÖB* 31.1: 233–60.

 1992. *Mariage, amour et parenté à Byzance aux XIe–XIIIe siècles.* Paris.

 1993. 'Sex, consent and coercion in Byzantium', in A. Laiou (ed.), *Consent and Coercion to Sex and Marriage in Ancient and Medieval Societies*: 109–221. Washington, DC.

Lambros, S. (Λάμπρος) (ed.) 1880. *Collection de romans grecs.* Paris.

 1904. Review of Krumbacher, 1904. Νέος Ἑλληνομνήμων 1: 380–3.

Legrand, E. 1902. *Les exploits de Digenis Akritas d'après le manuscrit de Grotta-Ferrata* (2nd edn). Paris.

Lemerle, P. 1973. 'L'histoire des Pauliciens d'Asie Mineure d'après les sources grecques.' *Travaux et Mémoires* 5: 1–145.

 1977. *Cinq études sur le XIe siècle byzantin.* Paris.

Leo Diaconus. *Leonis Diaconi historiae libri X.* K. B. Hase (ed.) 1828. Bonn.

Littlewood, A. R. 1979. 'Romantic paradises: the role of the garden in the Byzantine romance.' *BMGS* 5: 95–114.

Lord, A. B. 1960. *The Singer of Tales.* Cambridge, Mass.

MacAlister, S. 1984. 'Digenis Akritas: the first scene with the apelatai.' *Byzantion* 54: 551–74.

Mackridge, P. 1990. 'The metrical structure of the oral decapentasyllable.' *BMGS* 14: 200–12.

 1993a. '"None but the brave deserve the fair": abduction, elopement, seduction and marriage in the Escorial *Digenes Akrites* and Modern Greek heroic songs', in Beaton and Ricks, 1993: 150–60.

 1993b. 'An editorial problem in medieval Greek texts: the position of the object clitic pronoun in the Escorial *Digenes Akrites*', in Panayotakis, 1993, vol. 1: 325–42.

Magdalino, P. 1984. 'The Byzantine aristocratic *oikos*', in Angold, 1984: 92–111.

 1989. 'Honour among the Romaioi: the framework of social values in the world of Digenes Akrites and Kekaumenos.' *BMGS* 13: 183–218.

1992. 'Eros the King and the King of *Amours*: some observations on *Hysmine and Hysminias.'* *DOP* 46: 197–204.

1993a. *The Empire of Manuel Komnenos 1143–1180*. Cambridge.

1993b. '*Digenes Akrites* and Byzantine literature: the twelfth-century background to the Grottaferrata version', in Beaton and Ricks, 1993: 1–14.

Magie, D. 1950. *Roman Rule in Asia Minor*, 2 vols. Princeton.

Mango, C. 1981. 'Discontinuity with the classical past', in M. Mullett and R. Scott (eds.), *Byzantium and the Classical Tradition*: 48–57. Birmingham.

Markopoulos, A. (Μαρκόπουλος) 1989. ''Ο Διγενὴς 'Ακρίτης καὶ ἡ βυζαντινὴ χρονογραφία -- μία πρώτη προσέγγιση.' 'Αριάδνη 5: 165–71.

Mavrogordato, J. 1956. *Digenes Akrites*. Oxford (cited as Mavrogordato in textual apparatus and Mavrogordato, 1956 elsewhere).

Mel. Theodoros Melitiniotis, Εἰς τὴν Σωφροσύνην. E. Miller (ed.) 1858. 'Poème allégorique de Meliténiote.' *Notices et extraits des manuscrits de la Bibliothèque nationale* 19.2: 1–138.

Miliarakis, A. (Μηλιαράκης) 1881. *Βασίλειος Διγενὴς 'Ακρίτας κατὰ τὸ ἐν 'Ανδρῳ χειρόγραφον.* Athens.

Mitsakis, K. (Μητσάκης) 1963. *Προβλήματα σχετικὰ μὲ τὸ κείμενο, τὶς πηγὲς καὶ τὴ χρονολόγηση τῆς 'Αχιλληΐδας.* Thessaloniki.

Moennig, U. 1987. *Zur Überlieferungsgeschichte des mittel- und neugriechischen Alexanderromans*. Cologne.

1993. 'Digenes = Alexander? The relationships between *Digenes Akrites* and the Byzantine *Alexander Romance* in its Modern Greek versions', in Beaton and Ricks, 1993: 103–15.

Morgan, G. 1960. 'Cretan poetry: sources and inspiration.' *Κρητικὰ Χρονικά* 14: 7–68, 203–70, 394–404.

Mullett, M. 1988. 'Byzantium: a friendly society?' *Past and Present* 118: 3–24.

Mullett, M. and Smythe, D. (eds). 1996. *Alexios I Komnenos. I. Papers*. Belfast.

Muralt, E. de 1855. *Essai de chronographie byzantine*. St Petersburg.

Nelson, R. and Magdalino, P. 1982. 'The emperor in Byzantine art of the twelfth century.' *Byzantinische Forschungen* 8: 123–83.

Notopoulos, J. A. 1964. 'Akritan iconography on Byzantine pottery.' *Hesperia* 33: 108–33.

Odorico, P. 1986. *Il prato e l'ape: il sapere sentenzioso del monaco Giovanni*. Vienna.

1989. 'La sapienza del Digenis: materiali per lo studio dei *loci similes* nella recenzione di Grottaferrata.' *Byzantion* 59: 137–63.

Oikonomidès, N. 1979. 'L'épopée de Digénis et la frontière orientale de Byzance aux Xe et XIe siècles.' *Travaux et Mémoires* 7: 375–97.

Ong, W. J. 1982. *Orality and Literacy: The Technologizing of the Word*. London.

Panayotakis, N. (ed.) 1993. *'Αρχὲς τῆς Νεοελληνικῆς Λογοτεχνίας*. Proceedings of the Second International Conference 'Neograeca medii aevi', 2 vols. Istituto Ellenico di Studi Bizantini e Postbizantini de Venezia.

Panofsky, E. 1970. 'Titian's Allegory of prudence: a postscript', in *Meaning in the Visual Arts* (1st edn 1955): 181–205. Harmondsworth.

Papadimitriou, S. D. 1896. 'Stefan Sachlikis i ego stichotvorenie "Aphegesis Paraxenos".' *Letopis* 3 (Odessa): 1–256.

Papadimitriou, G. (Παπαδημητρίου) 1947. ''Ακριτικά.' *La Croix* 1 (Athens, 1948): 120–46.

1957. 'Αἱ πηγαὶ τῆς 'Ακριτηΐδος.' *Ὁ Βιβλιόφιλος* 11: 3–8.

Papadopoulos-Kerameus, A. (Παπαδόπουλος-Κεραμεύς) 1912. ''Ελληνικοὶ κώδικες Τραπεζοῦντος.' *Vizantijskij Vremennik* 19: 224–81.

Paschalis, D. (Πασχάλης) 1926. 'Οἱ δέκα λόγοι τοῦ Διγενοῦς 'Ακρίτου.' *Λαογραφία* 9: 305–440.

Pattenden, P. 1983. 'The Byzantine early warning system.' *Byzantion* 53: 258–99.

Pertusi, A. 1962. 'Alcune note sull' epica bizantina.' *Aevum* 36: 14–45.

1970. 'La poesia epica bizantina e la sua formazione: problemi sul fondo storico e la struttura letteraria del "Digenis Akritas"', in *La poesia epica e la sua formazione*: 481–594. Rome.

1971. 'Tra storia e leggenda: akritai e ghazi sulla frontiera orientale di Bisanzio', in *Actes du XIVe Congrès International d'Etudes Byzantines, Rapports II*: 27–71. Bucharest.

Petta, M. 1972. 'Codici greci della Puglia trasferiti in biblioteche italiane ed estere.' *Bollettini della Badia Greca di Grottaferrata* 26: 83–129.

Polemis, D. I. 1968. *The Doukai: A Contribution to Byzantine Prosopography*. London.

Politis, L. (Πολίτης) 1966. 'Φιλολογικὰ σὲ παλαιότερα κείμενα.' *Ἑλληνικά* 19: 351–61.

1967. *Ποιητικὴ 'Ανθολογία* Α': 15–38 (extracts from G). Athens.

1970. 'L'épopée byzantine de Digénis Akritas. Problèmes de la tradition du texte et des rapports avec les chansons akritiques', in *La poesia epica e la sua formazione*: 541–81. Rome = *Paléographie et littérature byzantine et néo-grecque*, no. XX, 1975. London.

1973. 'Digénis Akritas: à propos de la nouvelle édition de l'épopée byzantine.' *Scriptorium* 27: 327–51.

1991. *Κατάλογος χειρογράφων τοῦ Πανεπιστημίου Θεσσαλονίκης.* P. Sotiroudis and A. Sakellaridis-Sotiridis (eds.). Thessaloniki.

Politis, N. G. (Πολίτης) 1909. ''Ακριτικὰ ἄσματα. 'Ο θάνατος τοῦ Διγενῆ.' *Λαογραφία* 1: 169–275.

1920. 'Περὶ τοῦ ἐθνικοῦ ἔπους τῶν νεωτέρων 'Ελλήνων', in *Λαογραφικὰ Σύμμεικτα, τόμος* Α': 237–60. Athens.

Pring, J. 1965. 'Modern Greek (chapter on 'dawn poetry')', in Hatto, 1965: 264–70.

Prombonas, I. K. (Προμπονάς) 1985. *'Ακριτικά* Α'. Athens.

1989. 'Τὰ ρ. ἐπαραβραδιάστης καὶ καυχάσεται στὸν Διγενὴ Esc.' *'Αριάδνη* 5: 149–52.

1993. Ἐνδείξεις γιὰ ποντιακὴ καταγωγὴ τοῦ «Διγενὴ Ἀκρίτη»', in Panayotakis, 1993, vol. 2: 69–76.

Psellos. *Michele Psello: Imperatori di Bisanzio*, 2 vols. S. Impellizzeri (ed.) 1984. Fondazione Lorenzo Vallo.

Ricks, D. 1989a. 'Is the Escorial *Akrites* a unitary poem?' *Byzantion* 59: 184–207.

1989b. 'The pleasures of the chase: a motif in *Digenes Akrites*.' *BMGS* 13: 290–5.

1990. *Byzantine Heroic Poetry*. Bristol and New Rochelle.

Rocchi, A. 1884. *Codices Cryptenses seu Abbatiae Cryptae Ferratae in Tusculano*. Rome.

Roueché, C. 1988. 'Byzantine writers and readers: storytelling in the eleventh century', in R. Beaton (ed.), *The Greek Novel AD1–1985*: 123–32. London.

Sandys, J. E. 1908. A *History of Classical Scholarship*, 2 vols. Cambridge.

Sathas, C. and Legrand, E. 1875. *Les exploits de Digénis Akritas*. Paris.

Saunier, G. 1972. 'Le combat avec Charos dans les chansons populaires grecques.' Ἑλληνικά 25: 119–53, 335–70.

Setton, K. M. (ed.) 1969. *A History of the Crusades*. Vol. 1: M. W. Baldwin (ed.) *The First Hundred Years*. Madison and London.

Sifakis, G. M. (Σηφάκης) 1989. 'Ζητήματα ποιητικῆς τοῦ Διγενῆ E καὶ τῶν ἀκριτκῶν τραγουδιῶν.' Ἀριάδνη 5: 125–40.

Spadaro, G. 1988. 'Su tre luoghi controversi del Digenis Akritis escorialiense.' *Studi di Filologia Bizantina* 4 = *Quaderni del Siculorum Gymnasium* 16: 143–9.

1989. 'Nota di critica testuale al "Digenis Akritis" dell' Escorial.' Ἀριάδνη 5: 173–83.

Synesius. *Synesius, Epistulae*. R. Hercher (ed.) 1873. *Epistolographi Graeci*. Paris.

Syrkin, A. J. 1960. *Digenis Akrit*. Moscow.

Talbot, A.-M. 1996. *Holy Women of Byzantium*. Washington, DC.

Theophanes. *Theophanis Chronographia*, 2 vols. C. de Boor (ed.) 1883–5. Leipzig.

Theophanes Continuatus. *Theophanes Continuatus*. I. Bekker (ed.) 1838. Bonn.

Thompson, S. 1946. *The Folktale*. Berkeley.

TIB 2: Hild, F. and Restle, M. 1981. *Kappadokien. Tabula Imperii Byzantini 2*. Vienna.

TIB 4: Belke, K. and Restle, M. 1984. *Galatien und Lykaonien. Tabula Imperii Byzantini 4*. Vienna.

TIB 5: Hild, F. and Hellenkemper, H. 1990. *Kilikien und Isaurien. Tabula Imperii Byzantini 5*. Vienna.

Tiftixoglu, V. 1974. 'Digenes, das "Sophrosyne"-Gedicht des Meliteniotes und der byzantinischen Fünfzehnsilber.' *BZ* 67: 1–63.

Thraede, K. 1970. *Grundzüge griechisch-römischer Brieftopik*. Munich.

Trapp, E. 1971a. *Digenes Akrites, synoptische Ausgabe der ältesten Versionen*. Vienna.

1971b. 'Pontische Elemente im Wortschatz des Digenesepos.' *Revue des Etudes Sud-Est Européennes* 9: 603.

1972. 'Digenis Akrites: Epos oder Roman?' *Studi classici in onore di Quintino Cataudella*, vol. 2: 637–43. Catania.

1976. 'Hagiographische Elemente im Digenes-Epos.' *Analecta Bollandiana* 94: 175–87.

1976–. *Prosopographisches Lexikon der Palaiologenzeit*. Vienna.

1982. Review of Alexiou 1985. *BZ* 75: 350–3.

Treitinger, O. 1938. *Die oströmische Kaiser- und Reichsidee nach ihrer Gestaltung im höfischen Zeremoniell*. Jena.

Tsopanakis, A. (Τσοπανάκης) 1960. ''Ερμηνευτικὰ καὶ διορθωτικὰ στὸ κείμενο τοῦ Διγενῆ 'Ακρίτα.' *Ελληνικά* 17: 75–94.

Vasiliev, A. A. 1935. *Byzance et les Arabes*, vol. 1. Brussels.

Veloudis, G. 1965. *Der neugriechschen Alexander. Tradition in Wandel und Bewahrung*. Munich.

Vogiatzidis, I. K. (Βογιατζίδης) 1923/4. ''Ακριτικαὶ Μελέται.' *BZ* 24: 61–78.

Vogt, A. 1935. *Le Livre des Cérémonies: Commentaire*, vol. 1. Paris.

VTh. *Vitae Theoctistae*, in Delehaye and Peeters 1925: 221–33.

Wassiliewsky-Jernstedt 1896: see Kekavmenos.

Wood, D. 1958. 'The Koukoulithariotai in Digenis Akritas.' *Byzantion* 28: 91–3.

Xanthoudidis, S. (Ξανθουδίδης) 1912. 'Διγενῆς 'Ακρίτας κατὰ τὸ χειρόγραφον 'Εσκωριάλ.' *Χριστιανικὴ Κρήτη* 1: 523–71.

Xyngopoulos, A. (Ξυγγόπουλος) 1948. 'Τὸ ἀνάκτορον τοῦ Διγενῆ 'Ακρίτα.' *Λαογραφία* 12: 560.

1967. ''Ο τάφος τοῦ Διγενῆ.' *Ελληνικά* 20: 24–8.

Name index

Aaron	E145; father of the emir, grandfather of Digenis (see Table 2); perhaps the caliph Harun-al-Rashid (789–809), whose chief residence was at Raqqa on the Euphrates: Alexiou, 1979, 25–7; cf. Ambron
Abasgia	G4.905; on the eastern coast of the Black Sea
Abydos	G2.77; city on the Hellespont
Achilles	G4.27 G7.85; legendary hero of the Trojan War
Adam	G8.282 E1812; the first man
Agamemnon	G7.86; Greek leader in Trojan War, slain by his wife on his return from Troy
Agarenes	G1.28 G7.203; Arabs, referring to descent from Hagar, Abraham's bond-woman in the Old Testament (Genesis 16)
Akritis	G2.48 G3.106 G3.339 G4.1 G4.53 G4.104 G4.323 G4.844 G4.916 G4.963 G4.1011 G5.11 G5.169 G6.2 G6.190 G7.1 G7.156 G7.189 G7.205 G7.214 G8.5 G8.182 G8.208 G8.240 G8.251 E219 E442 E465 E525 E610 E634 E639 E722 E733 E738 E739 E752 E819 E932 E1025 E1030 E1069 E1070 E1082 E1092 E1104 E1216 E1374 E1538 E1556 E1604 E1608 E1619 E1659 E1694 E1698 E1703 E1764; see also Basil, Digenis, Double Descent, Frontiersman and Vasilis
Aleppo	E236, in Syria
Alexander	G4.29 G6.387 G7.90 G7.93; Alexander of Macedon (356–323 BC)
Amazons	G6.386 G7.92; legendary female warriors and ancestors of Maximou
Ambron	G1.285 G4.37; grandfather of the emir, great-grandfather of Digenis (see Table 2); perhaps 'Umar, emir of Melitene, intermittent supporter of the Paulician heretics, killed at the battle of Porson in 863; Vasiliev, 1935, 249–56; Grégoire, 1929/30, 335–7; Huxley, 1975; cf. Aaron
Amorion	G1.8 G1.295 E258 E732; city in Asia Minor, often attacked during Arab raids of seventh and eighth centuries and dramatically sacked in 838; TIB 4, 122–5
Anatolikon	G1.265; one of the original Byzantine themes; its eastern

Ankyra	districts were separated off in the early ninth century to form the theme of Cappadocia; TIB 2, 75, TIB 4, 63–6 G1.11 G2.77; mod. Ankara, captured by Arabs in 838, the Paulicians in 871, the Turks in 1080 and briefly Byzantine once more after 1101; TIB 2, 78–81; TIB 4, 126–30
Antakinos	G4.54; Digenis' maternal grandfather, exiled by the emperor Basil; named Andronikos at Z1317. Suggested identifications: the Doux who persecuted the Paulicians ca. 855 or his son Andronikos who was forcibly converted to Islam and died ca. 908: Kyriakidis, 1932, 636–50; Polemis, 1968, 16–21; Karolidis (1905/6, 224, note 3) notes a Byzantine general 'Antaki kafir' ('the faithless man from Antioch') in the Turkish epic of Said-Battal
Antiochos	G5.259; Byzantine general, killed in the Anti-Tauros mountains by the Persians (probably Turks), father of the abductor of Aploravdis' daughter; possibly a general from Antioch, or possibly Antiochos of Kommagene (Grégoire, 1936, 725)
Aphrike	G2.78; Tephrike (in the Byzantine sources; al-Abruq or al-Abriq in the Arabic), mod. Divrigi, in east Cappadocia, possibly a reference to the main centre of the ninth-century heretical Paulician rebels whose names lurk in the emir's ancestry (cf. Chrysovergis); TIB 2, 294–5
Aploravdis	G5.67; emir of Meferke; suggested identifications: Ἀβδουρραχίμ (Karolidis, 1905/6, 242), Ἀποτάγλε / Abu Taglib, emir of Meferke in 976 (Mavrogordato, 1956, 146), Ἀπελβάρτ / Abu-l-ward, one of two emirs of that name in Manzikert in the ninth and tenth centuries (Bartikian, 1966, 147–52)
Apohalpis	E506; suggested identifications: Abu-Hafs / Ἀπόχαψ Arab emir in Crete in 824 (Theophanes Continuatus, 2.24; Xanthoudidis, 1912, 552); Abu-Hafs / Ἀπόχαψ who made peace with the Byzantines in 928 (Theophanes Continuatus, 6.24; Kalonaros, 1941: 2, 149); Abuharp whose son was defeated by Basil II in 1003 (Muralt, 1855, 580); Χαλέ/Χαλέβ, Arab admiral in 672/3 (Theophanes, A.M. 6164 [353.17]; Alexiou, 1979, 28); Apu'kap, duke of Edessa, 1032–4 (Bartikian, 1968, 303–5)
Arab, Arabs	G1.46 G1.287 G2.99 G2.154 G5.161 G5.178 G5.201 E170 E276 E333 E342 E431 E578 E603 E606 E728 E1613 E1711
Arabia	G5.25 G5.163 E1709
Armenia	G1.7 E263; areas in eastern Asia Minor between the Black and Caspian Seas, intermittently within Byzantine or Arab

jurisdiction, or independent

Asia	E715; Asia Minor
Assyrians	G3.151; ruled by Naaman (see below)
Babylon	G1.6 G4.968 E234 E724, Babylonians G8.207; fabled city of Mesopotamia, largely in ruins by the Byzantine period
Baghdad	G1.278 G4.969 G8.206 E232 E568; capital of the Abbasid caliphate from 750 to 1258
Basil	G1.2 G1.26 G2.48 G4.49 G4.66 G4.75 G4.109 G4.323 G4.974 G4.1088 G6.190 G7.1 G8.220 G8.302; first name of the Frontiersman of Double Descent; see also Akritis, Digenis, Double Descent, Frontiersman and Vasilis
Basil	G4.56 G4.973; emperor; suggested identifications: Basil I, ruled 867–86 (Kalonaros, 1941:2, 67–8, associating the phrase from *Vita Theoctistae* §2 with Basil rather than his son Leo; Grégoire, 1931a, 488–9); Basil II Bulgaroktonos, ruled 976–1025 (Mavrogordato, 1956, lxxxii), whose death may be seen as marking the end of Byzantine glory (G4.974)
Basra	E233; city near the Persian Gulf; identified as such by Karolidis, 1926, 330 and Alexiou, 1979, 18
Bathyrryax	G8.206; the mustering point (or *aplikton*) for the army from the Armeniakon theme; TIB 2, 157–8
Bellerophon	G7.89; mythological hero, who overcame the monstrous Chimaira with the aid of his winged horse, Pegasos
Black Mountain, men of	G8.205; men of the Black Snow G4.969; inhabitants of the Amanus, the Black Mountain behind Antioch; TIB 5, 174–6
Brahmans	G6.387 G7.92; Indian sages whom Alexander of Macedon had visited on his expeditions
Cairo	E536, in Egypt
Cappadocia	G1.7 G1.56 G3.248 G4.42 G7.107 G8.204; Byzantine theme, formed from the eastern districts of Armenia (TIB 2, 75); the family of the emir's wife, the Frontiersman's mother, was connected with this area (G1.56, 3.248, 4.42)
Cappadocian(s)	G5.18 G7.112; with special reference to the Frontiersman: G3.106 G7.2 E1092
Chalkopetrin	E293 E321 E332 E426; 'Bronze Rock' (Alexiou, 1979, 23: a more convincing form than Lakkopetra: see below); unidentifiable and not the same place as Chalkourgia
Chalkourgia	G5.238 G5.257; 'Bronze Working', possibly a mining area; not Chalkis (a mine near Ariaratheia; TIB 2, 162–3) since Chalkourgia is near the border with Syria; see Alexiou, 1979, 23 on possible etymologies
Charon, Charos	Charon G8.2 G8.125 G8.269, Charos E1794 E1795; personification of Death

Charziane   G1.6 G1.56 G4.42 G8.204; Armenian administrative
                 district of Xorjean (Bartikian, 1968, 295–9; TIB 2, 164);
                 Trapp, 1971a emends to Χαρσιανή, the Byzantine theme
                 of Charsianon
Chimaira   G7.89: mythical beast slain by Bellerophon
Chosroes   G4.912 E1080; possibly Chosroes II of Persia (590–627);
                 his sword was part of the Frontiersman's bride's dowry
Chrysovergis   G1.284: the emir's father; suggested identification: the
                 Paulician Chrysocheir, died ca. 878/9 (Karolidis, 1905/6,
                 225; Mavrogordato, 1956, lxiii–iv; Huxley, 1974,
                 319–23; for a sceptical view: Lemerle, 1973, 110–13)
Constantine   G1.131 G4.103 E42 E57 E736 E753 E789: the youngest
                 of the five brothers of the emir's bride, the Frontiersman's
                 mother (a name which reappears in later ballads)
Constantine   G1.267 Constantine Doukas, from whom is descended the
                 mother of the emir's bride; on heroic deeds associated in
                 literary texts with the Doukas family and the name
                 Constantine, see Polemis, 1968, 14–15
Cyclops   G7.88: mythical giant slain by Odysseus
Dareios   G7.90: the Persian emperor (Darius III, c. 380–330 BC)
                 defeated by Alexander of Macedon
David   G7.71 G7.81: the youthful Old Testament hero, king and
                 psalmist; also 'God's ancestor' G8.286
Delilah   G2.200: Old Testament woman who caused the death of
                 the strong man Samson
Difficult   G1.90: a mountain pass called Difficult, identified as the
                 Cilician Gates in the Taurus by Kalonaros, 1941:2, 6; cf.
                 Podandos, below
Digenis   G2.48 G3.106 G3.339 G4.49 G4.53 G4.187 G4.301
                 G4.323 G4.914 G4.951 G4.1012 G6.2 G7.1 G7.100
                 G7.147 G7.192 G7.214 G7.225 G8.56 G8.220 G8.259
                 E219 E442 E452 E457 E465 E525 E593 E610 E634
                 E639 E641 E669 E696 E699 E739 E752 E758 E760
                 E763 E752 E772 E808 E934 E979 E1097 E1099 E1216
                 E1608 E1686 E1698 E1767; epithet ('of Double Des-
                 cent') used as a proper name for the hero of the poem:
                 see also Akritis, Basil, Double Descent, Frontiersman and
                 Vasilis
Dilemite, Dilemites G1.45 G1.155: Dilemitai/Daylamites, an Arab emirate in
                 Armenia which in the early eleventh century was
                 expanding into the frontier region; EI, under 'Daylam'
Dimitrios   G1.25 G6.701: St Dimitrios, associated with Thessaloniki
                 from the sixth century, often appearing on icons together
                 with St George
Double Descent, of G2.48 G2.291 G3.106 G3.339 G4.50 G4.323 G4.1011

G6.2 G7.1 G7.214 G8.220 G8.251 G8.259 E219 E442 E452 E458 E465 E525 E610 E634 E752 E1216 E1608; epithet used of the hero of the poem; see also Akritis, Basil, Digenis, Frontiersman and Vasilis

Doukas family, house of Doukas   G1.267 G4.43 G4.59 G4.325 family from which came the mother of the emir's bride, that is, the Frontiersman's maternal grandmother; E137 family from which came the father of the emir's bride, that is, the Frontiersman's maternal grandfather (cf. the suggested identification of Antakinos, this grandfather, so named in G only, as Andronikos Doux); on the Doukas family in the background to the poem see Kyriakidis, 1932, 636–50 with Polemis, 1968, 16–21

Doukas   G6.14 G6.414: the general, father of the Frontiersman's bride, and hence at G4.325 the girl is related to Digenis through the Doukas family

Egypt   G3.155 E536 E1640

Egyptians   G7.95

Emek   E246: identified as Homs (Arabic: Hims; Greek: Ἔμεσα, Ἔμετζα) in Syria, base of the Assassin sect, by Alexiou, 1979, 19; and as Mecca by Kalonaros, 1941:2, 149

Emet   G8.7 G8.207: identified as Amida (Greek: Ἔμετ) by Karolidis, 1905/6, 243

Ethiopians   G1.32 G4.970 G5.223 G7.206 E545

Euphrates   G4.994 G4.1006 G6.727 G6.804 G7.7 E1320 E1620 E1660 E1716; river

Eve   E1812, the first woman

Frontiersman   G1.2 G2.48 G3.106 G3.339 G4.1 G4.53 G4.66 G4.104 G4.844 G4.916 G4.963 G4.1008 G4.1011 G4.1089 G5.11 G5.169 G5.187 G5.199 G6.1 G6.190 G7.1 G7.43 G7.149 G7.156 G7.189 G7.205 G7.214 G8.5 G8.14 G8.182 G8.208 G8.224 G8.240 G8.251 G8.259 G8.277 E219 E442 E465 E525 E610 E634 E639 E722 E733 E738 E752 E819 E932 E1025 E1030 E1069 E1082 E1092 E1104 E1216 E1374 E1538 E1556 E1604 E1608 E1619 E1659 E1694 E1697 E1703 E1764: see also Akritis, Basil, Digenis, Double Descent and Vasilis

Gehenna   G3.197 E1111; Jewish concept of Hell

George   G1.23 G6.701: St George, a military saint of obscure origins but the focus of a flourishing cult, often appearing on icons with St Dimitrios

Giannakis   E633 E1243 E1259 E1269 E1273 E1348 E1362 E1373 E1379 E1412 E1417 E1484 E1499 E1602; the youngest of the guerrillas; cf. Ioannakis

Goliath   G7.73 G7.79; the Old Testament Philistine giant

Hades	G2.90 G2.278 G3.74 G4.678 G8.2 G8.126 G8.270 G8.280 E370 E1696 E1775 E1796; Death, the Underworld
Hektor	G4.28; legendary hero of the Trojan War
Helen	E714; legendary heroine of the Trojan War
Hellenes	E710 E713 E719; fought in the Trojan War as recounted by Homer
Herakleia	G1.294; town of Herakles G1.50 G4.41; Herakleion E732 E946; Herakleia in Cappadocia, held by the Arabs on several occasions in the ninth century; TIB 2, 188–9; mod. Eregli
Hermon	E262; river in Anatolia; TIB 2, 190
Hexakomia	G2.78; briefly the seat of a Byzantine *strategos* in the late tenth century; Oikonomidès 1979, 391; TIB 2, 190–1
Homer	G4.27 E719; author of false legends about the Hellenes
Ikea	E924, a lake; suggested identifications: Nikaia (Kyriakidis, 1946, 428); a lake near Herakleia with an island Ikis-Anta (Kalonaros, 1941:2, 167); Achaia (Pertusi, 1962, 45); otherwise unidentified local toponym perhaps linked with the lake near Herakleia (Alexiou, 1985, 113)
Ikonion	G1.8 G1.295 G4.1043 E258 E732; frequently attacked by Arab raiders in eighth to tenth centuries and capital of Seljuk Turks from 1084; TIB 4, 176–8; mod. Konya
Ioannakis	G4.33 G6.121 G6.211 G6.236 G6.249 G6.351 G6.396 G6.415 G6.450 G6.548 G6.620 G8.98 G8.105; the youngest of the guerrillas; at G6.393 he is Philopappous' son; cf. Giannakis
Ishmaelites	G1.28; Arabs, referring to descent from the son of Hagar, Abraham's bond-woman in the Old Testament (Genesis 16)
Jews, Exodus of	G7.96
Joshua, son of Nun	G7.98; Old Testament leader
Kandake	G7.91; legendary queen who seduced Alexander of Macedon
Karoïlis	E145 (cf. Mourtasit); Karoïs G1.285 G4.37; Moursis Karoïs G2.75 – Arab uncle(s) of the emir (see Table 2); suggested identification: Karbeas, the Paulician leader, allied to the emir of Melitene and possibly killed at the battle of Porson, 863 (Karolidis, 1905/6, 224; Grégoire, 1929/30, 329–30; Alexiou, 1979, 27–28; Lemerle, 1973, 113–15 is sceptical)
Karoïs	see Karoïlis
Kasisi	E245; suggested identification: the Assassins, a sect of fanatic and murderous Muslims (Karolidis, 1926, 330; Kalonaros, 1941:2, 140; Alexiou, 1979, 30–31, 117); Muslim pilgrims, priests or functionaries (Galatariotou,

Kinnamades	1993, 47–9) G1.266 G4.54: family from which is descended Antakinos, the father of the emir's bride, the Frontiersman's mother (see Table 2): not a prominent Anatolian family, though known in the eleventh century (Beck, 1971, 86) and subsequently in the twelfth (e.g. the historian John Kinnamos); the name is otherwise recorded as that of an Arsacid Parthian ruler (Josephos, *Antiquitates Judaicae* 20. 3.2: Karolidis, 1905/6, 223; Kalonaros, 1941:1, 36); Alexiou, 1979, 22, speculates (unconvincingly: Galatariotou, 1993, 42) that this may be a corruption of the even rarer Kirmagastroi (E138): there is no suggestion of kinship with the guerrilla Kinnamos
Kinnamos	G4.33 G6.122 G6.211 G6.235 G6.255 G6.396 G6.473 G6.489 G6.548 G6.620 G6.622 G6.262 G6.630 G6.265 G6.518 G8.105 E1243 E1260 E1274 E1279 E1287 E1348 E1380 E1412 E1484 E1499 E1602; Leos Kinnamos E1260; Leos E1362 E1379 E1417; one of the guerrillas; at G6.393 he is Philopappous' son: see comments under Kinnamades
Kirmagastroi	E138: family of the emir's bride, the Frontiersman's mother: an otherwise unknown name (Galatariotou, 1993, 42); suggested derivations: from a title 'magistros' with prefix 'kir' ('lord'; Karolidis, 1905/6, 224); derived from a place name, e.g. Magarsa in Cilicia (Pertusi, 1970, 492; Alexiou, 1979, 21–2)
Koukou Lithos	G 8.204: the men from Koukou Lithos: perhaps a reference to a mountain pass on the route between Caesarea and Melitene (Hild, 1977, 98; TIB 2, 46, 92); alternatively a reference to the hood-like rock formations near Göreme in Cappadocia (κουκούλα, hood; λίθος, rock; Wood, 1958): Mavrogordato's emendation (1956) to 'men of the Boukellariot theme' is unnecessary
Kufah	G1.292 G4.39: in southern Mesopotamia (Grégoire, 1931b, 492; *EI.* under 'al-Kufa': founded 638 AD and in ruins by the twelfth century): or Kafar/Kafartab, supposed birthplace of Helena, mother of Constantine the Great (Karolidis, 1905/6, 226, supported by Trapp: for location see Setton, 1969, 645 and map 5)
Lakkopetra	G2.101 G2.140: 'Hollow Rock', cf. Chalkopetrin ('Bronze Rock'). Unidentifiable but not the same place as Chalkourgia. Kalonaros, 1941:1, 47 (reporting Ioannidis, 1887, 5): a 'White Rock' between the Antitauros mountains and Parnadros which is locally considered to be a dwelling place for the Frontiersman

Lazarus   G8.162 E1826; brother of Martha and Mary, raised from the dead by Christ

Leander   G6.549 G6.620 G6.622 G6.628 E1500 E1554 E1600; one of the guerrillas

Leos   see Kinnamos

Lykandos   E921; a strategically sited fortress in the Antitauros mountains important in the tenth century; TIB 2.224–6

Macedon   see Alexander

Maiakis   E507; suggested identifications: an Armenian named Hmayeak, putative grandfather of Apuk'ap, duke of Edessa, 1032–1034 (Bartikian, 1968, 303–5); Maniakis, general, died 1043: Trapp, 1971a, 383

Martha   E1827; sister of Lazarus and Mary

Mary   E1827; sister of Lazarus and Martha

Mary   G3.177: Mother of Christ; cf. Theotokos

Maximou   G6.375 G6.385 G6.424 G6.452 G6.454 G6.469 G6.546 G6.551 G6.569 G6.578 G6.583 G6.609 G6.644 G6.678 G6.711 G6.734 G6.756 G6.771 G6.778 G6.782 G8.118 E1352 E1358 E1359 E1384 E1389 E1410 E1416 E1438 E1485 E1502 E1506 E1518 E1530 E1532 E1539 E1542 E1544 E1545 E1548 E1561 E1567 E1568 E1576 E1577 E1584 E1589 E1596 E1601; female guerrilla leader, kinswoman of Philopappous; in G a descendant of the Amazons brought from India by Alexander

Mecca   E288 E537; Mecca (cf. G1.101)

Meferke   G5.66; base of the emir Aploravdis; to be identified as Martyropolis / Mayyafariqin, modern Silvan, captured by the Arabs in 640 and finally retaken by John Kourkouas in 942; ca. 976 the emir of Mayyafariqin acknowledged dependence on Byzantium (ODB, under Martyropolis)

Melanthia   G5.68: wife of Aploravdis (a name typical of the ancient and medieval Greek romances; Kalonaros, 1941:1, 142)

Melimitzis, Milimitsis   G6.427 G6.472 G6.479 G6.490 G6.503 E1360 E1399 E1409 E1430 E1444 E1500 E1599; suggested identification: Melias/Mleh, d. 934 (ODB under Melias), Armenian prince, sometime controller of Lykandos (Adontz, 1929/30, 216; Grégoire, 1933, 64, 66–9)

Mellokopia   G3.67: Mylokopia E503; suggested identification: Malakopea not far from Nazianzus, where rock formations resemble mill stones and may account for the Arabic form of the place name, possibly reflected in E (TIB 2.227; Grégoire, 1929/30, 338; Alexiou, 1979, 23); also identified as site of the battle of Porson (863), whose location is set relative to Amnisos (Genesios 4.15,

Theophanes Continuatus 4.25) and far from Malokopea;
Huxley, 1975 postulates two battles

Milimitsis   see Melimitzis

Mohammed   G 1.288 E165 E247 E285 E564; the Prophet of Islam

Moses   G7.95; the Old Testament prophet

Mouroufris   E337; one of the Arabs who came to fetch the emir

Moursis   see Karoïs; Arab uncle(s) of the emir (two figures treated as one at G2.75)

Mourstasit   E261; one of the emir's two uncles (cf. Karoïlis), combined as Moursis Karoïs in G2.75 and Mousour from Tarsus at Z619; Alexiou, 1979, 29 finds an analogy for the form in Mustarshid, the name of a twelfth-century caliph

Mouselom   E146; father of Aaron, grandfather of the emir and great-grandfather of the Frontiersman (see Table 2); Grégoire, 1940/41, 99 points to a similarity in form with the name of Maslamah, who laid siege to Constantinople in 717, cf. Alexiou, 1979, 27

Mousis   E506; the son of Mousis was one of the emir's comrades in arms at the battle of Mylokopia

Mousour   G5.168 G5.203 G5.215 G5.261; the Arab highwayman, killed by Digenis; he had captured the seducer of Aploravdis' daughter

Mousouros   E723; the emir, the Frontiersman's father (unnamed in G)

Mylokopia   see Mellokopia

Naaman   G3.150; an unidentified Muslim holy man; the identification of the *mandylin*, the towel of Naaman, as the *mandylion*, the kerchief of Naaman brought to Constantinople in 944 by John Korkouas (Grégoire, 1931a, 486–90; Cameron, 1980), has been rebutted by, e.g., Huxley, 1974, 324 on the grounds that a Muslim would be unlikely to venerate a Christian relic; not mentioned in E (Alexiou, 1979, 53)

Nikomedia   E259; furthest point of the emir's father's raids

Nun   see Joshua

Odysseus   G4.260 G7.88; the wandering and wily Homeric hero

Orazabouron   E246; suggested identifications: an Armenian form of the name Orthaga or Orgatha found in Ptolemy 5.18.12 (Karolidis, 1926, 331); Dayr ar Zawr, north east of Hims (Alexiou, 1985, νθ′, 88); neither very convincing

Panormos   G1.101; the ancient name for Jeddah (Diodorus Siculus 3.38.33), the port for pilgrims approaching the Holy Cities of Mecca and Medina (Karolidis, 1905/6, 222)

Panthia   G1.284; the emir's mother (a name typical of ancient and medieval romance heroines)

Pasargadai   E1671; site of Persian royal tombs (*PW*, Suppl. 9, col. 777;